PROLIFERATION OF INTERNATIONAL ORGANIZATIONS

LEGAL ASPECTS OF
INTERNATIONAL ORGANIZATION

VOLUME 37

Proliferation of International Organizations

Legal Issues

edited by

Niels M. Blokker & Henry G. Schermers

KLUWER LAW INTERNATIONAL
THE HAGUE / LONDON / BOSTON

A C.I.P. Catalogue record for this book is available from the Library of Congress.

ISBN 90-411-1535-8

Published by Kluwer Law International,
P.O. Box 85889, 2508 CN The Hague, The Netherlands.

Sold and distributed in North, Central and South America
by Kluwer Law International,
675 Massachusetts Avenue, Cambridge, MA 02139, U.S.A.

In all other countries, sold and distributed
by Kluwer Law International, Distribution Centre,
P.O. Box 322, 3300 AH Dordrecht, The Netherlands.

Printed on acid-free paper

All Rights Reserved
© 2001 Kluwer Law International
Kluwer Law International incorporates the publishing programmes of
Graham & Trotman Ltd, Kluwer Law and Taxation Publishers,
and Martinus Nijhoff Publishers.

No part of the material protected by this copyright notice may be reproduced or
utilized in any form or by any means, electronic or mechanical,
including photocopying, recording or by any information storage and
retrieval system, without written permission from the copyright owner.

Printed in the Netherlands.

PREFACE

The proliferation of international organizations is presently a hot issue. New international organizations have been created over the last few years such as the Organization for the Prohibition of Chemical Weapons and the World Trade Organization. At the same time a certain reluctance may be observed – often dictated by the fear for new costly bureaucracies – to creating new organizations. This is perhaps to be expected in a neo-liberal era of privatization, of more market and less government. It is often concluded that the costs of the creation of a new international organization outweigh the benefits. In addition, questions often emerge concerning the co-ordination of activities of international organizations. Overlapping activities and conflicting competences frequently occur and the need for co-ordination is evident. The events in former Yugoslavia are an example. Both during the armed conflicts in Bosnia and Kosovo and afterwards in the era of reconstruction, the need to co-ordinate the work of organizations such as the UN, NATO, the EU, the World Bank, OSCE, and the Council of Europe was vital.

Against this background, a number of legal issues which have not yet been researched extensively have become more important, perhaps the only exception being the proliferation of international tribunals. Questions include the following: Why were new organizations created while others already existed in the same or a related field? What specific legal problems arose that were related to the coexistence of different organizations working (partly) in the same area? What mechanisms or instruments have been developed to co-ordinate the activities and to solve legal problems?

These and other questions were discussed during a conference that took place from 18 to 20 November 1999 in the Academy Building of Leiden University, the Netherlands. The conference was organized under the auspices of the Europa Institute and the E.M. Meijers Institute of the Leiden Law Faculty. A large number of experts, both academics and practitioners, participated. Presentations were given, and the participants exchanged their views and experiences.

The purpose of this book is to present the issues discussed during the Leiden conference to a larger audience. This book is more than a collection of papers prepared for the conference. The papers were adapted where authors considered this appropriate. In some cases, papers have been substantially expanded. Furthermore, the conference has stimulated some participants who did not present a paper to contribute to this book.

Therefore, we feel safe in concluding that both the idea – launched some three years ago – as well as the *travaux préparatoires* in preparing this conference and subsequently this book has catered to a need.

This book follows the structure of the conference. In the first part a number of topics will be discussed that explore the general theme from various angles, both academic and practical. First, there is a general introduction to the theme of the book, followed by a contribution concentrating on the attitude of states towards the proliferation of international organizations. Two further contributions will focus on possible ways to demarcate the working areas of international organizations: geographic demarcation (co-ordination between universal and regional organizations) and functional demarcation (between the UN and its specialized agencies, with reference to the 1996 WHO Advisory Opinion of the International Court of Justice). Some case studies of very different areas of international co-operation will be presented. The World Bank experience is discussed, as well as the proliferation of disarmament organizations and the case of multilateral environmental conventions.

Within the general proliferation theme one may distinguish, more specifically, the proliferation of law-making and judicial organs of international organizations. One contribution will examine the role of the International Law Commission (ILC). Among the questions addressed is the question of whether the ILC should concentrate on more general areas of international law, such as state responsibility, or should also be involved in law-making in more specialized areas such as telecommunications or human rights law. Further contributions will discuss the proliferation of judicial organs. Following a general analysis of the proliferation of international tribunals, presidents, members and officials of the International Court of Justice, the Law of the Sea Tribunal, the WTO's Appellate Body and the European Court of Human Rights will offer their comments.

The remainder of the book is devoted to two selected issues with which many organizations are increasingly confronted nowadays. First is the proliferation of standards. The more variety there is amongst the members of an organization, the more relevant the question becomes of whether the organization should maintain lower but at least uniform standards, or whether it is preferable to have different standards. This has long been a familiar issue within the International Labour

Organization. More recently, the issue has presented itself within the Council of Europe and the European Union, in view of their accomplished or forthcoming expansion of membership. The second issue is that of accountability, a prominent topic nowadays on the agenda of international organizations. As many organizations have developed or are developing their own accountability regimes, the question of the extent to which there is a need for general rules on accountability of international organizations will be examined. Additionally, one case study will analyze the question of whether the World Bank Inspection Panel will present an example of an 'accountability instrument' that could also be useful for other international organizations. The final contribution will offer some reflections inspired by the discussions during the conference.

We would like to express our deep appreciation to a large number of people and organizations without whose help it would not have been possible to organize the conference and prepare this book. First of all we express our gratitude to the sponsors of the conference: the Ministry of Foreign Affairs and the Ministry of the Interior, the Royal Dutch Academy of Sciences, the Cornelis van Vollenhoven Foundation, the Legatum Visserianum, the Europa Institute, the Leiden Law Faculty and Leiden University. We also warm-heartedly thank our colleagues whose assistance in the preparations has been indispensable. Without mentioning each of them individually, we would like to make an exception for our conference manager, Ms. Ine Houweling. The idea of organizing a conference is one thing, managing such a venture is something different. We are indebted to her for the smooth running of the conference. Last but not least, we greatly appreciate the support given by Kluwer Law International, not only by fully taking care of the work involved in this publication, but also by offering suggestions for participants to the conference and contributors to this book.

We greatly enjoyed this project in all its stages and hope that this book will contribute to further discussions both in the academic world and in practice.

Niels M. Blokker & Henry G. Schermers
Leiden, July 2000

TABLE OF CONTENTS

Preface	v
Proliferation of International Organizations: an Exploratory Introduction *Niels M. Blokker*	1
The Attitude of States towards the Proliferation of International Organizations *Ignaz Seidl-Hohenveldern*	51
Co-ordination between Universal and Regional Organizations *Christian Dominicé*	65
The World Court, the WHO, and the UN System *Nigel D. White*	85
Techniques to Avoid Proliferation of International Organizations – The Experience of the World Bank *Ibrahim F.I. Shihata*	111
The Proliferation of Arms Control Organizations *Paul C. Szasz*	135
The Proliferation of International Institutions Dealing with International Environmental Matters *Gerhard Loibl*	151
Organizational Proliferation and Centralization under the Treaty on European Union *Armin von Bogdandy*	177

The Proliferation of Law-Making Organs: A New Role
for the International Law Commission?
 Rosanne van Alebeek   219

The Proliferation of Administrative Tribunals
 Paul C. Szasz   241

The International Court of Justice and other
International Courts
 Hugh Thirlway   251

The Proliferation of International Judicial Organs:
the Role of the International Court of Justice
 Dietmar W. Prager   279

The Dispute Settlement System of the World Trade
Organization: Institutions, Process and Practice
 Florentino Feliciano and
 Peter L.H. Van den Bossche   297

Comments
 Thomas A. Mensah   351

Comments
 Christos Rozakis   361

Flexibility and the International Labour Organization
 Dominick Devlin   365

The European Union and the Concept of Flexibility:
Proliferation of Legal Systems within International
Organizations
 Ige F. Dekker and
 Ramses A. Wessel   381

Extending the European Family of Nations: The
Response of the Council of Europe to Growing
Membership
 Rick Lawson   415

The Primary Model Rules of Accountability of
    International Organizations: The Principles and
    Rules Governing their Conduct or the Yardsticks
    for their Accountability
        Karel Wellens   433

Views from Practice
        Larry D. Johnson   471

The World Bank Inspection Panel: A Model for other
    International Organizations?
        Sabine Schlemmer-Schulte   483

Final Remarks
        Henry G. Schermers   549

Index   563

PROLIFERATION OF INTERNATIONAL ORGANIZATIONS: AN EXPLORATORY INTRODUCTION

*Niels Blokker**

INTRODUCTION

In the year 1900 only a few international organizations existed, such as the Rhine and Danube Commissions and communication organizations like the Universal Postal Union and the International Telegraphic Union. Notwithstanding visionary studies such as Lorimer's detailed *Scheme for the Organisation of an International Government* (1884), it was only in exceptional cases that States would structure their co-operation within the framework of a new legal entity.

This reluctance to create international organizations came to an end during and immediately after the Second World War. There was a true *hausse* at the time in the creation of new organizations, governing international co-operation in all kinds of areas, both at the global and the regional level. Gradually "a kind of superstructure over and above the society of States" emerged.[1] However, whereas for the society of States a substantial body of rules of international law has been developed, such a body of rules is largely absent for this "superstructure".

Today the existence of so many international organizations often leads to questions to which there are no easy answers. Overlapping activities and conflicting competences occur frequently and the need for co-ordination is evident. The events in former Yugoslavia are an example. Both during the armed conflicts in Bosnia and Kosovo and afterwards in the era of reconstruction, the need to coordinate the work of

---

[*] Ministry of Foreign Affairs, the Netherlands, and senior lecturer in the law of international organizations, *Europa Instituut*, Law Faculty, Leiden University. The views expressed are my own. I thank Dr. Rick Lawson for his comments on a draft of this contribution and Ms. Nini Visscher for her research assistance.

[1] H. Mosler, *The International Society as a Legal Community*, 140 RdC (1974 IV), at 189.

organizations such as the UN, NATO, the EU, the World Bank, OSCE, and the Council of Europe was vital.

The creation of international organizations, their development and proliferation is a fundamental development that requires our attention. However fundamental, the legal issues resulting from the proliferation of international organizations have not been researched extensively yet. What has been examined, in particular during the last few years, are elements of this larger subject, such as the proliferation of international tribunals. The main aim of this introduction is to introduce the wider issue of the proliferation of international organizations and to explore some general legal issues.

Although it is generally assumed that there is a proliferation of international organizations, there are good reasons to examine first of all if this is indeed true (Section 2). Subsequently Section 3 will briefly analyze how this proliferation can be explained. The largest part of this introduction (Section 4) is devoted to some general legal issues related to the proliferation of international organizations. A core issue is the delimitation of competences. Three case studies are presented to further illustrate this. Some general observations are made, and the case for an "inter-organization principle of good neighbourliness" is examined. Finally two frameworks for the delimitation of competences are briefly analyzed, the decentralized framework of the UN family and the centralized framework of the European Union.

PROLIFERATION OF INTERNATIONAL ORGANIZATIONS: IS THE TRUISM TRUE?

If there is one question concerning the theme of this book that seems to be superfluous, it is the question of proliferation itself. It is difficult to find a publication about international organizations in which it is not mentioned or denied that there is a proliferation of international organizations. However, there are three good reasons for nevertheless examining if this truism is true.

Mushrooming of International Organizations? A Brief Quantitative Analysis

First of all, there is the apparently easy question if there are more international organizations today than five, ten, or fifty years ago.

The most authoritative and up to date source of information for answering this question is the Yearbook of International Organizations. Most authors use this source when examining the number of international organizations and refer to a figure indicating the number of "intergovernmental organizations".[2] Until the mid-1980s literature could safely conclude on this basis that there was a true mushrooming of international organizations.[3]

Perhaps somewhat unexpected, the Yearbooks after 1985 show a significant decrease of this number. The latest issue of this Yearbook reports that, following an initial rise from 37 in 1909 to 118 in 1954 and to 365 in 1984, this number went down considerably since the second half of the 1980s: 309 in 1988, 286 in 1992, 260 in 1996, and 241 in 2000.[4] Therefore, if this classification would cover all public international organizations the conclusion would be that the number of organizations has decreased significantly over the last fifteen years. Scholars seem to be in serious difficulties now if they want to give a scientific

---

[2] See e.g. P. Reuter, Institutions internationales (7[t] ed. 1972), at 198; A. Cassese, International Law in a Divided World (1986), at 85; D. Dormoy, Droit des organisations internationales (1995), at 4. In the latest edition of the Yearbook (1999-2000, Vol. 1B, at 2356), it is explained that the table presented "suggests different answers to the question 'How many international organizations are there?'". The first answer is of special relevance here: "conventional intergovernmental organizations, when attaching importance to the non-existence of international non-governmental organizations in terms of international law". Although this wrongly indicates that NGO's do not exist under international law, it rightly distinguishes between these two types of international organizations. It is assumed in this Yearbook that "an organization is intergovernmental if it is established by signature of an agreement engendering obligations between governments, whether or not that agreement is eventually published" (id., at 2354). From a legal perspective it is indeed the origin and public function that distinguish intergovernmental organizations from NGO's.

[3] See e.g. W.J. Feld and R.S. Jordan, with L. Hurwitz, International Organizations – A Comparative Approach (1983), at 9: using the Yearbook of International Organizations, it is observed that "[t]he number of IGOs and INGO's has grown tremendously since World War II. The total of IGO's operating in 1977 was about 308; their number may reach 380 by 1985".

[4] Yearbook of International Organizations (2000-2001), Vol. 1B, at 2407. If this is examined in more detail, looking at the four subcategories distinguished in the Yearbook (types A (federations of international organizations), B (universal membership organizations), C (intercontinental membership organizations), and D (regionally oriented membership organizations), this decrease is to a limited extent explained by the declining number of intercontinental membership organizations (from 51 in 1984 to 33 in 2000), but mainly by the reduction of regionally oriented membership organizations (from 283 in 1984 to 230 in 1988, and further down to 172 in 2000). See Yearbook 2000-2001, Vol. 1B, at 2407 (Appendix 3: table 2).

underpinning for the observation that there is a proliferation of international organizations.

However – as is often overlooked – public international organizations can also be found in other subdivisions of this Yearbook classification, such as "organizations emanating from places or persons or other bodies",[5] "organizations of special form",[6] or "multilateral treaties and intergovernmental agreements". The figures for these subdivisions reveal a true explosion of international organizations.

It appears therefore that the above mentioned decrease does not relate to a sudden dissolution of so many organizations but to a transfer to one of the other subdivisions, as was confirmed by one of the editors of the Yearbook.[7] Although it seems true that there is a proliferation of international organizations, certainly if the present situation is compared to that of 25 or 50 years ago, it is difficult to give precise figures. Much also depends on the definition of public international organizations. A careful analysis of the Yearbook figures has been made by Amerasinghe. He concludes that "it may be possible [...] to conjecture that the figure for public international organizations as such is certainly over 500 and probably under 700".[8] A similar estimate was made earlier by Virally.[9]

Less Public International Organizations in an Era of Privatization? International Organizations as Chameleons

In an era that is characterized by privatization, by more market and less government, it may be expected that there is not much interest in

---

[5] For example, organizations created by other international organizations such as the Joint Vienna Institute are classified in this category (*id.* at 1690).

[6] For example the Inter-American Development Bank (*id.* at 1122), Mercosur (Southern Common Market; *id.*, at 2104), the European Communities (*id.* Vol. 1A, at 711-714) and the European Union (*id.* Vol. 1A, at 876).

[7] One of the editors of the Yearbook wrote to the present author that this question is not one of a decreasing number of organizations but "increasing selectivity on our part". The parameters were changed during this period and some of the organizations previously included were "transferred" to other categories.

[8] C.F. Amerasinghe, Principles of the Institutional Law of International Organizations (1996), at 6 (footnote 10).

[9] M. Virally, *Panorama du droit international contemporain*, 183 RdC (1983 V), at 252 (footnote 86).

international governance through international organizations.[10] This is true to a certain degree. For example, whereas it was fashionable in the 1970s to create intergovernmental commodity agreements that in some cases had market intervention mechanisms, since the 1980s such agreements lost favour in particular of developed countries. The death-knell was rung over the more interventionist commodity agreements with the collapse of the 6th Tin Agreement, until then generally considered to be the most successful example in the long history of intergovernmental co-operation between commodity importing and exporting countries. Today little is heard of international commodity organizations.

However, at the same time this turning tide also reveals the chameleonic nature of international organizations that may change colours when the spirit of the age is deviating from the one prevailing when they were created. A good example is an organization that is virtually unknown, the International Center for Public Enterprises. It was created in 1974 to improve the performance of public enterprises in developing countries. When the concept of public enterprises lost most of the sympathy it once enjoyed among the member States, the organization was restructured. Since 1996 it is known under the name of International Center for the *Promotion* of Enterprises and its objective is now to promote enterprise development in the developing and transitional economies.[11]

In addition, not only do existing organizations change colours, but also new organizations are created to serve new needs. Examples are the European Bank for Reconstruction and Development and the Joint Vienna Institute, whose creation followed the collapse of the Soviet Union.

Although it is difficult again to draw detailed conclusions, the net result seems to be positive in quantitative terms. While international organizations are occasionally dissolved, others are restructured and new ones are created. The era of privatization did not stop the proliferation of international organizations.

---

[10] Cf. M. Bettati, Le droit des organisations internationales (1987), at 121: "Au 'moins d'Etat' de l'ordre interne corresponds un 'moins d'inter-Etat' de l'ordre international".

[11] Emphasis added. See Yearbook of International Organizations 2000-2001, Vol. 1B, at 1261-1262.

More Flexible Frameworks for a Zap Society? Instant International Organizations and International Organizations as Stabilizers

A third reason for questioning the truism that there is a proliferation of international organizations is that they are sometimes considered too bureaucratic, too lethargic as instruments for the dynamic co-operation that is sought. States often prefer more flexible and ad hoc forms of co-operation. Since 1975 the G-7 (now G-8) meetings have developed into a powerful forum for policy co-ordination, in economic affairs, and increasingly also in many other areas. For example a G-8 consensus was crucial in the spring of 1999 to "solve" the Kosovo crisis.

And there are many more examples. Ad hoc frameworks are often created to deal with a short- or medium term need for co-operation. For example, in May 1999 a high-level steering group for the Balkans was created, chaired jointly by the EU and the World Bank. This group was established by signing a statement by the European Commission and the World Bank.[12] This statement set out the objectives, modalities and procedures according to which they will coordinate "the response of the international community to the crisis in Kosovo".[13] One of the four basic principles agreed upon for this operation is to "keep structures light and efficient, and where possible build on existing structures". A joint office was set up in Brussels and a small Task Force was created composed of officials from the Commission and the World Bank. The Task Force started its work immediately.[14]

Furthermore, there is an increasing number of joint programmes of international organizations to deal with issues that "belong" to the fields of operation of different organizations. Take UNAIDS as an example. Its current official name is Joint United Nations Programme on HIV/AIDS.[15] Its mission is to "lead, strengthen and support an expanded response aimed at preventing the transmission of HIV, providing care and support, reducing the vulnerability of individuals and communities to HIV/AIDS, and alleviating the impact of the epi-

---

[12] On 27 April 1999, a special high-level meeting of governments and international agencies was held in Washington, and the World Bank and the Commission were called upon to coordinate needs assessment and modalities for assistance. The statement mentioned above is the answer to this call.

[13] Europe, 15 May 1999, at 10.

[14] *Id.*

[15] Its original name was Joint and Co-sponsored United Nations Programme on HIV/AIDS. ECOSOC "took note" of the change of name in its Res. 1999/36.

demic".[16] The legal basis for the programme stems from two sources. The programme was established in 1993 by six UN organs and organizations: UNICEF, UNDP, UNFPA, UNESCO, WHO and the World Bank. The establishment of this programme was subsequently endorsed by ECOSOC.[17] At the request of ECOSOC, a Memorandum of Understanding (MoU) was concluded in 1995 between the six co-sponsoring organs and organizations,[18] who were joined in April 1999 by the UN International Drug Control Programme (UNDCP). In a final provision, this MoU stipulates that "the co-sponsoring organizations assume no liability for the acts or omissions of the Executive Director or his/her staff".[19]

In these documents the objectives, substance and structure of the programme are laid down. The structure is relatively simple. A (Geneva based) Secretariat is headed by an Executive Director who is appointed by the UN Secretary-General. There is a staff of some 130 professionals. Apart from the Secretariat, there are two organs that are related to the two sources that were involved in the creation of UNAIDS. The supreme organ, the "governing body" of UNAIDS, is the Programme Coordinating Board. This Board is composed of representatives of 22 States, elected by ECOSOC. The most important donor countries are usually represented, but not always; for example, in 1999 the US was not a member, while it is the largest donor, providing for 25% of the budget (the size of the UNAIDS budget for 1999 was US$ 60 million).

---

[16] UN Doc. E/1997/63, at 6 (para. 11).
[17] Res. E/1994/24.
[18] Reproduced as Appendix to UN Doc. E/1996/92. From 1986 the WHO had the lead responsibility on AIDS in the UN system. In 1993, the World Health Assembly requested the WHO Director-General to study the feasibility and practicability of establishing a joint and co-sponsored UN programme on HIV and AIDS (Res. WHA46.37). This was supported by ECOSOC in its Resolution 1993/51. The programme was established by the six sponsoring organizations, and this was subsequently endorsed by ECOSOC in Res. 1994/24. In this resolution, ECOSOC called for the full implementation of the programme by January 1996, and requested the six sponsoring organizations to produce by January 1995 a more detailed proposal, "and to attach to this proposal an annex containing the proposed legal document that the six co-sponsors will sign to establish the programme formally". It took more time to prepare this proposal, and in its Resolution 1995/2 ECOSOC called upon the six organizations "to finalize and sign a legal document in the form of a memorandum of understanding". This MoU was concluded in 1995. Subsequently it took several months before it was signed by the participating organs and organizations. The programme started functioning in January 1996.
[19] Para. 12.4.

An interesting element of the functioning of this organ is the substantial involvement of non-governmental organizations.[20] NGO's have no right of vote, but in practice take part in the deliberations on an equal basis.[21] A third body is the Committee of co-sponsoring organizations, composed of the heads of these organizations or their representatives. Their task is to "serve as the forum in which the co-sponsoring organizations may meet on a regular basis to consider matters concerning the programme", and to "provide the input of the co-sponsoring organizations into the policies and strategies of the programme".[22]

Why was UNAIDS created in this special way? Essentially because governments wanted a quick and flexible response to the AIDS problem. There was the fear that it would take years to set up a full-fledged international organization in view of the necessary ratifications and the need to build up a new structure for co-operation in this area. Essentially it was also created in this way in view of the urgent need to coordinate the AIDS activities of the sponsoring organizations. According to the ECOSOC, UNAIDS "constitutes an important example of effective system-wide co-ordination in the context of the United Nations reform efforts".[23] There was a very strong wish to immediately concentrate on the substance and not to loose time in institutional tomfoolery.

Nevertheless, there was a need for some "tomfoolery", and this was borrowed from a full-fledged international organization, the World Health Organization, which from 1986 had the lead responsibility on AIDS in the UN system. The 1995 MoU stipulates that "WHO shall provide administration of the Programme".[24] WHO has established a Trust Fund for the receipt and disbursement of financial contributions to the programme, and the appointment, promotion and termination of Secretariat staff is implemented by the WHO. Where agreements are concluded this is done by WHO, although recently a co-operation agreement with the Organization of African Unity was concluded by the Executive Director of UNAIDS on behalf of UNAIDS.[25]

---

[20] The arrangements for NGO participation in the work of the Board are laid down in an Annex to ECOSOC Res. 1995/2.
[21] This also appears from the fact that NGO's are not put at the end of the speaking order as often is the case in the UN. Furthermore there is a special arrangement for financial support of the participating NGO's.
[22] MoU on UNAIDS, *op. cit.* note 18, para. 6.
[23] ECOSOC Res. 1999/36, Preamble.
[24] Para. 11.
[25] Agreement of 17 September 1999 (text obtained from UNAIDS).

Here one can also find the main reason why it is unclear if UNAIDS should or should not be considered as an international organization. One of the elements in the definition of an international organization is usually the requirement that the established body has a will of its own, a *volonté distincte*. It is not clear if this requirement is fulfilled in the case of UNAIDS. For many of its activities UNAIDS seems to borrow the *volonté distincte* of WHO. Interestingly, the requirement of a *volonté distincte* traditionally means *distincte* from the member States, but in this case the issue is whether or not UNAIDS is *distincte* from its seven co-sponsoring organizations, in particular WHO. Related to this, it is understandable that these co-sponsors took into account the possibility that third parties would pierce the rather thin veil of UNAIDS and claim that the co-sponsors are liable for certain acts or omissions of the Executive Director or his/her staff. Hence the provision in the MoU that no such liability is assumed. But it leaves third parties with a question to which there is no easy answer: who is liable?

There are more of such joint programmes and similar forms of cooperation, often in this twilight zone in between organizations having a separate legal status and looser frameworks. Examples are the Global Environmental Facility, originally established in 1991 by the World Bank, the Intergovernmental Panel on Climate Change (set up by the World Meteorological Organization and the UN Environmental Programme in 1988), and the Joint WHO/FAO/UNEP/UNHCS Panel of Experts on Environmental Management for Vector Control, originally created between WHO and FAO in 1978.[26] Another example is the Arctic Council established in 1996. Canada originally proposed to create this body as a "regular" international organization, but this was rejected by the US. Finally a Declaration was adopted, establishing the Council as a "high level forum".[27] It has been suggested that the Council lacks legal personality;[28] the Declaration is silent on this issue.

Similar developments take place within the European Union. Curtin has identified the existence of a number of "unidentified or disguised international organizations".[29] A number of frameworks for

---

[26] See H.G. Schermers and N.M. Blokker, International Institutional Law (3rd ed. 1995), at 27 and 1076-1077. See also H.G. Schermers, Integratie van internationale organisaties, Inaugural lecture Leiden (1978).

[27] 35 ILM 1382 (1996).

[28] E.T. Bloom, *Establishment of the Arctic Council*, 93 AJIL 712-722 (1999).

[29] D.M. Curtin, *Criminal Justice, Unidentified International Organizations and Human Rights Protection in Europe*, in C.H. Brants, C. Kelk, M. Moerings (eds.), Er is

co-operation have been created by the EU member States that are not widely recognized as international organizations even though they are. Moreover, "they are also considered "unidentified" because of the facile assumption often made that the co-operation in question takes place under the auspices of the EC/EU as such (or closely related to it as with regard to Schengen)".[30] Curtin concludes that both Europol and the Schengen Implementation Agreement are in fact international organizations, legally separate from the EU. She refers to the view of the Dutch government that the Executive Committee of the Schengen Implementation Agreement is a "light" international organization and observes that "international organizations it seems have also been caught up in the fad for slim line production and profile".[31]

So it is true that the tide has turned. Whereas once an organization was established almost automatically as soon as an international problem and the need to cooperate were identified, the opposite is often true today. At present, States almost instinctively express their wish *not* to create a new organization if a new international problem and the need to cooperate present themselves. Or they do not want to explicitly give legal personality to something that is generally seen as an international organization: the case of the European Union.

Nevertheless, in some of these cases the conclusion cannot be avoided that an international organization and a new legal person have in fact been established. Sometimes immediately, as a kind of instant international organization, and sometimes gradually, through a process of institutionalization. Of course, this partly depends on the definition used.

The point here is that, first of all, the quest for flexibility has resulted in the establishment of instant "flex-organizations" whether or not they are identified or disguised. Secondly, it is not enough in our zap world to have such flexible and ad hoc frameworks only, whether or not they are international organizations. These frameworks may also be somewhat volatile and can only function because there is a strong and stable network of (semi-) permanent organizations. There is complementarity. The G-8 consensus on Kosovo was essential but not sufficient for the establishment of a peace building framework. This framework was provided by Security Council Resolution 1244. Like-

---

meer. Opstellen over mensenrechten in internationaal en nationaal perspectief 63-76 (1996), at 66-70.

[30] *Id.*, at 66.
[31] *Id.*, at 67.

wise, UNAIDS usually borrows the *volonté distincte* of the WHO. Furthermore, it may happen that flexible and ad hoc frameworks themselves may develop into true international organizations, even if they have not been created as such.

International organizations may sometimes be sluggish, they are also instruments for stability. The *accelerando* of world affairs does not lead to a decreasing number of international organizations.

Conclusion

It should be concluded that, although it is difficult to present a solid quantitative underpinning and although "privatization" and "zap" arguments militate against it, there apparently are stronger factors that bring about the past and present proliferation of international organizations. The focus will now shift to these factors.

EXPLANATIONS

Before examining problems and legal issues related to the proliferation of international organizations it is first necessary to find explanations for this phenomenon. Of course, like human beings, each international organization has its own *raison d'être* and is unique. Nevertheless, behind these individual explanations it seems possible to find general reasons why so many organizations have been created.

It is generally recognized that there is one fundamental, overarching explanation that is usually summarized in catchwords such as globalization and interdependence. An increasing number of State functions can no longer be performed in splendid isolation. World trade, sustainable development, human rights, not to forget the maintenance of peace and security, have all outgrown the national legal order and have become the subject of international regulation. Not within one single supranational global legal order but within a dispersed, large number of individual and specialized legal frameworks, often international organizations. The internationalization of these issues requires the internationalization of national regulation. International co-operation is a must in many areas, and often it has been considered necessary to structure such co-operation within existing or newly created international organizations. If a new problem such as aids occurs, existing organizations are often keen on occupying such a newly emerging functional *terra nullius*. But it also happens that a new organization is created to administer the new territory. In short, as it was put by UN Secretary-General Kofi Annan in his address to the UN General Assembly in September, 1999: "[s]tate sovereignty, in its most basic sense, is being redefined by the forces of globalization and international co-operation".[32]

This is often recognized in constitutions of international organizations. According to Article 11.1 of the League of Nations Covenant, "[a]ny war, or threat of war, whether immediately affecting any of the Members of the League or not, is hereby declared a matter of concern to the whole League [...]". Article 1.1 of the Constitution of the Universal Postal Union provides: "[t]he countries adopting this Constitution shall comprise, under the title of the Universal Postal Union, a single postal territory for the reciprocal exchange of letter-post items".[33] It is stated in the Preamble of the 1997 EUROCONTROL Revised Convention, which has not yet entered into force, that this revision is necessary "in order to provide for the establishment of a uniform European air traffic management system"; strengthened co-operation between the member States must be "based upon the fundamental principle that the airspace should from the perspective of the airspace users, be considered as a seamless system". Much shorter, since 1997 EUROCONTROL's new slogan is: "One Sky for Europe".[34] A final example is the euro area or euro zone (*euroland* in Dutch), a reference to the eleven EU members that participate in the Economic and Monetary Union. In these and other cases, a fictitious functional territory (or: sky) is created as it were, in which the organization has jurisdiction.

The fundamental nature of globalization makes international co-operation inevitable. The costs of non-co-operation have increased. Formally States may decide not to cooperate, but increasingly this sovereign freedom of decision is eroded by the facts and forces of interdependence. In the case of East Timor, Indonesia's consent was considered a prerequisite for a Security Council authorization to send the multinational force Interfet,[35] but the existing economic and financial

---

[32] UN Press Release SG/SM/7136 and GA/9596, 20 September 1999.
[33] This phrase was already included in the original UPU Treaty of 1874.
[34] See Skyway (The EUROCONTROL Magazine), Vol. 2, No. 6 (Summer 1997), at 33.
[35] Security Council Res. 1264. This resolution condemned the acts of violence following the ballot of 30 August 1999, in which a majority of the people of East Timor voted to start a process leading towards independence, authorized the establishment of Interfet "pursuant to the request of the Government of Indonesia",

ties of States and international organizations (IMF, World Bank) with Indonesia were used to enforce such consent.

One of the legal implications of the inevitability or, more positively, the obviousness of international co-operation is a provision governing the entry into force of some more recent constitutions of international organizations. In the case of the 1994 Marrakesh Agreement establishing the WTO, it was determined that this treaty would in principle enter into force on a predetermined date, 1 January 1995, and not after a certain number of ratifications would have been made.[36] In a way, such provisions "codify" what has been well established practice in some areas. For example, even before World War II amendments to the UPU Convention had to be ratified, but this was nothing more than a formality. Refusal to ratify would involve leaving the UPU and no State could afford to do this.[37]

Behind this grand explanation for the proliferation of international organizations one may find various more specific explanations. The significant rise of regional organizations since the 1950s is related to the coming into being of a large number of new States in the era of decolonization and following the collapse of the Soviet Union.[38] The creation of organizations such as the Organization of African Unity and, more recently, the Baltic Council, the organization called Black Sea Economic Co-operation and the Commonwealth of Independent States should be seen in this context. In Africa in particular the proliferation of regional economic organizations has reached proportions that are difficult to grasp although the last few years attempts have been made to structure these organizations within the pan-African framework of the OAU Treaty Establishing the African Economic Community.[39]

The tension between State sovereignty and the need to cooperate, between independence and interdependence, is perceptible within any international organization but is of course most acute in the case of these organizations of new-born States. Both elements can be found, side by side, in Article II of the OAU Constitution. According to this

---

and authorized the States participating in this multinational force "to take all necessary measures".

[36] Final Act embodying the results of the Uruguay Round of Multilateral Trade Negotiations, paragraph 3.
[37] See J.L. Brierly, The Law of Nations (4th ed. 1949), at 94.
[38] Cf. M. Shaw, International Law (1997), at 893-894.
[39] 30 ILM 1241 (1991). See T. Mulat, *Multilateralism and Africa's Regional Economic Communities*, 32 JWT 115-138 (1998). Mulat reports (at 120-121) that in West Africa alone "there were 40 or so intergovernmental organizations".

article, the purposes of the OAU are, *inter alia*, "to promote the unity and solidarity of the African States" as well as "to defend their sovereignty, their territorial integrity and independence". Likewise, the constitution of the Commonwealth of Independent States mentions as "principles" on which relations between the member States are built *inter alia* "development of mutually advantageous economic, scientific, and technical co-operation, and expansion of the processes of integration" and also "spiritual unity of their peoples" (Article 3). It is also full of references to the principle of State sovereignty and related principles (e.g. territorial integrity, non-interference) and, seemingly to avoid any misunderstandings, provides as part of Article 1: "[t]he Commonwealth is not a State and does not possess supranational powers".[40]

SOME LEGAL ISSUES

INTRODUCTION

Now it has been established that there is not only a steadily growing number of international organizations but also a firm undercurrent of developments explaining such growth, further questions may be asked. There are practical questions such as, first of all: is proliferation a problem? Different answers may be given to this question. In 1974 Secretary-General Waldheim of the UN observed with regard to the UN family that, although the resulting institutional complexity

> may be regarded as a by-product of the vitality of the idea of international co-operation and of the shifting needs of the world community, it inevitably tends to magnify the problems of co-ordination and to increase the difficulties of attaining an integrated approach to the complex problems of international development and co-operation.[41]

Most other observers also tend to emphasize the disadvantages of proliferation. In 1960, Hammerskjöld spoke about the risk of disintegration of the international framework through a proliferation of organs, and stated that

> we may come to face a situation where the very growth of the framework for international co-operation tends to lead to an ultimate

---

[40] The text of this constitution is reproduced in Z. Brzezinsky and P. Sullivan, Russia and the Commonwealth of Independent States – Documents, Data, and Analysis (1997), at 506 ff.
[41] UN Doc. E/5524/Add.1, at 2. In a slightly different wording: E/5524/Add.3, at 38.

weakening ... [i]t is as if we were to permit the growth of a tree to be weakened by the development of too many branches, finally sapping its strength so that it breaks down under its own weight.[42]

Bindschedler concludes his description of general aspects of international organizations for the Encyclopedia of Public International Law with the following observation: "[t]here is also a tendency to extend the already excessive growth of organizations even further, which very often leads to duplication, rivalries and inefficiency".[43]

Whatever is true of these observations, there are also various legal questions stemming from the proliferation of international organizations. For example already in 1951 Jenks argued that "the practice of international organizations has become an important element in the growth of international law itself".[44] If such practice would be varied and inconsistent it might "destroy the authority of existing principles and usage, or [...] make it difficult for new principles or usage to secure general acceptance". It is therefore, according to Jenks, "of primary importance for the whole future of international law that the practice of the different international organizations in regard to matters of international law should be sufficiently uniform to operate as a constructive influence in the development of the customary law of nations".[45]

In this Section a few general legal issues will be discussed. Others, and also a number of more specific legal aspects will be covered by the other contributions to this book. A first and most general legal issue is the delimitation of competences between international organizations. It is generally recognized that the proliferation of international organizations creates problems of co-ordination,[46] and different frameworks have been created for dealing with these problems. The UN Charter offers a decentralized framework for social and economic co-operation. Practice in this area has shown how unmanageable the co-ordination problem is at the global level. A centralized framework exists within the European Union. With its expanding powers and membership, the Union is increasingly facing co-ordination problems, but both its re-

---

[42] United Nations Review, vol.6, no. 12 (June 1960), at 29.
[43] R.L. Bindschedler, *International Organizations, General Aspects*, in: Encyclopedia of Public International Law, Vol. II (1995), at 1308.
[44] C. Wilfred Jenks, *Co-ordination in International Organization: an Introductory Survey*, 28 BYbIL 1951, at 33.
[45] Id.
[46] A. El Erian, *The Legal Organization of International Society*, in M. Sørensen (ed.), Manual of Public International Law 55-115 (1968), at 67 and 102-106.

gional and more coherent nature as well as its supranational foundation seem to offer better prospects for solving these problems.

Delimitation of Competences

Introduction

It may be helpful to start by presenting three cases taken from recent practice. Stories are telling. A first story is that of the relationship between the United Nations Development Programme (UNDP) and the World Bank. The other two cases concern the European Union and involve the relations with Eurocontrol and the Western European Union. Next, some general observations will be made concerning the delimitation of competences of international organizations and the case for an "inter-organization principle of good neighbourliness" is examined.

Three cases

Co-ordination of the co-ordination: the case of UNDP and the World Bank[47]

There is a long list of differences between the World Bank and UNDP. The World Bank is an international organization and a specialized agency within the UN family, while UNDP is an organ of the General Assembly. The World Bank borrows money on the capital markets and was originally created for the long term financing of projects related to postwar reconstruction and development. UNDP was established in 1965 by the General Assembly and was in fact a merger of the Extended Programme of Technical Assistance and the Special Fund, in order to create one unified, central financing and coordinating body within the field of technical assistance.[48] UNDP's money comes from voluntary contributions by UN member States.[49]

Since their creation both the World Bank and UNDP underwent a considerable development. The World Bank is now with its affiliate

---

[47] I would like to thank J. Berteling (The Netherlands Ministry of Foreign Affairs) and J.W. Swietering (UNDP) for giving me most of the documents on the basis of which this case study was written.

[48] H. Sahlmann and B. Blank, *UNDP*, in R. Wolfrum (ed.), United Nations: Law, Policies and Practice, Vol. 2, at 1284.

[49] Ten countries provide around 80% of the contributions to UNDP (as reported in Our Global Neighbourhood by the Commission on Global Governance (1995), at 273).

organizations the World Bank Group, and is nowadays seen as the most authoritative institution for the financing of projects in developing countries. Because of its expertise, it is widely considered as the leading international development co-operation agency.[50] UNDP has been qualified as a bureaucratic institution having country offices of divergent quality; its value has been proved in particular in "post conflict countries" where its neutral role is often preferred over that of bilateral donors and international financial institutions.[51]

In 1977 the General Assembly created the new post of Resident Co-ordinator who has to represent not only UNDP (as is the case for Resident Representatives) but the UN system as a whole.[52] Today one of UNDP's main tasks is to coordinate the activities of all parts of the UN family within developing countries. In 1997 its UN Development Assistance Framework (UNDAF) was introduced, defined as "the planning and programming mechanism that coordinates the United Nations response to the [challenges of development]",[53] a "strategic planning and collaborative programming framework that helps to identify priorities for United Nations action".[54]

But increasingly the World Bank also claims a role in this traditional UNDP niche. Early 1999 World Bank President Wolfensohn launched the idea to formulate for each developing country a Comprehensive Development Framework (CDF) that is now tried out in 13 countries and areas including the West Bank and the Gaza. According to the Bank, the CDF is "owned" by the receiving country that determines and directs its own development agenda, "with the Bank and the country's other partners each defining their support in their respective

---

[50] Cf. H.O. Ruding, *The Development and Future Role of the International Monetary Fund and the World Bank*, in J. Harrod and N. Schrijver, The UN Under Attack (1988), at 62: "It is the combination of substantial financial resources with the technical know-how of the highly professional World Bank staff which uniquely qualifies the bank as a development agency".

[51] De kwaliteit van de VN als kanaal voor ontwikkelingssamenwerking, policy paper prepared by the Dutch Minister of Development Co-operation (September 1999), Second Chamber 1998-1999, Doc. number 26714, nr.1, at 19-20.

[52] In 1989 and 1992 the General Assembly recommended that the contribution of the UN system to the "country strategy note" (formulated by developing countries to better integrate UN assistance into the national development process) should be formulated under the leadership of the Resident Co-ordinator.

[53] Report of the Secretary-General on the work of the Organization (1999), UN Doc. A/54/1, at 17 (para. 128).

[54] UNDP paper on UNDAF (on file with the author).

business plans". The CDF is a process, not a blueprint.[55] It was difficult not to consider this a frontal attack on UNDP's role in the area of co-ordination of UN assistance to developing countries. The resemblances between UNDAF and CDF are striking. Both have been described by their creators as instruments that are characterized by their "holistic" approach.[56] Both aim to bring more coherence into development assistance provided by UN organs and organizations. Both have claimed to start from the receiving country's priorities, even using the same expression: "the country is in the driver's seat".[57] The question becomes urgent who co-ordinates the co-ordinators, or: who is the Ultimate Co-ordinator?

While in recent years successful attempts have been made to intensify co-operation between the UN and the Bretton Woods organizations, there is still much to be done. One problem, or "challenge" as it is usually called, is that this relationship is somewhat unbalanced: stronger Bretton Woods involvement in the work of the UN is a long standing wish of the UN[58] that is now coming true. But this love seems to be largely one-sided and therefore a poor basis for a sustainable relationship. Little is heard of Bretton Woods dreams of closer UN involvement in its activities.[59] Against this background the World Bank appears to be in a stronger position when attempts are made to harmonize UNDP's Development Assistance Framework and the Bank's Comprehensive Development Framework. And the "challenges" for the relationship between the Bretton Woods organizations and the UN concern in particular the relationship between these two co-ordination mechanisms.[60]

---

[55] Website www.worldbank.org/cdf/overview.htm (on file with the author).
[56] UNDP: see UNDAF paper obtained from UNDP (on file with the author); World Bank: website www.worldbank.org/cdf/overview.htm (on file with the author); speech by World Bank President Wolfensohn to the Annual Meetings of the World Bank Group and the IMF, 28 September 1999.
[57] World Bank: website www.worldbank.org/cdf/overview.htm (on file with the author); speech by World Bank President Wolfensohn to the Annual Meetings of the World Bank Group and the IMF, 28 September 1999. UNDP: Doc. DP/1999/15 (Annual report of the Administrator for 1998), at 17.
[58] See e.g. Agenda for Development: recommendations, UN Doc. A/49/665 (presented in 1994 by Secretary-General Boutros Ghali), paras. 49-56.
[59] Or, as it is put in UN Doc. E/1999/56, at 8: "Challenges [...] also concern making the efforts towards increased interaction between the United Nations and the Bretton Woods institutions more reciprocal".
[60] Id.

Moreover, the competition between these mechanisms and their operators has a financial dimension. While in the 1970s a substantial number of Bank activities were financed by UNDP, the last number of years such activities are increasingly financed by the Bank itself. And this is also true for other specialized agencies.[61] In addition, UNDP's income – voluntary contributions – has declined from $1.2 billion in 1992 to $718 million in 1999.[62] In financial terms, the importance of UNDP as a financing institution has significantly decreased and this obviously has implications for its role as co-ordinator.[63] As is usually the case: he who pays the piper calls the tune.

The legal basis for the relationship between the World Bank and UNDP is provided by the 1947 relationship agreement between the UN and the World Bank. However, this agreement offers surprisingly little guidance to solve today's problems.[64] It stresses that the Bank is "an independent international organization" (Article I.2), that representatives of both parties are entitled to attend each other's meetings (Article II). The two organizations may propose the inclusion of items in each other's agendas, but there is only an obligation to "give due consideration" to such proposals (Article III). Both parties "shall consult together and exchange views on matters of mutual interest" (Article IV). And there are more of such provisions, which essentially create a modest procedural framework for co-operation should parties wish to cooperate. There is no substantial provision that could serve as a point of departure for the delimitation of competences between the two organizations. In addition, the agreement reveals a certain reluctance to approach the issue of the delimitation of competences from a legal angle. According to Article VIII the Bank is authorized to request advisory opinions of the ICJ "on any legal question arising within the scope of the Bank's activities *other than questions relating to the relationship between the Bank and the United Nations or any specialized agency*".[65]

---

[61] Relatie Wereldbank – VN-organisaties (unpublished report by J. Berteling for the Dutch Minister of Development Co-operation, February 2000), at 17 (on file with the author).

[62] As mentioned in the Statement of Administrator Malloch Brown before the Executive Board of UNDP and UNFPA, 13 September 1999 (website www.undp.org/dpa/statements/administ/1999/sep/13sep99.htm (on file with the author).

[63] Relatie Wereldbank – VN-organisaties (*op. cit.* note 61), at 17.

[64] The text of this agreement is reproduced in YUN 1947-48, at 872-874.

[65] Italics added.

A pragmatic approach seems to offer better prospects. The Administrator of UNDP is appointed by the UN Secretary-General, and in spring 1999 Mark Malloch Brown – whose previous post happened to be that of Vice President of the World Bank – was appointed to this post. In his first official address to UNDP's Executive Board Malloch Brown openly discussed UNDP's difficult position and his determination to improve this.[66] It remains to be seen how this will affect the delimitation of competences in the area of the co-ordination of development assistance.

The European Union and Eurocontrol

A second case is that of the European Community and Eurocontrol. The original delimitation of competences between the two organizations was far from clear. Against the background of its larger integration objectives the EC Treaty has a number of specific provisions on transport. According to Article 70 (ex 74) the EC objectives shall in transport matters be pursued by member States within the framework of a common transport policy. It is explicitly provided that this applies to transport by rail, road and inland waterway; the Council may decide "whether, to what extent and by what procedure appropriate provisions may be laid down for sea and air transport".[67]

Thus a common air transport policy was not established in 1957 and the competence was given to the Council to subsequently develop such a policy. This was done by the Council only gradually, in particular since the mid-1970s.[68] Since 1 April 1997 there is an internal Community air transport market.[69] Within the Community's air transport policy, the field of air safety and air traffic management is of special importance here, as this is the core business of another international

---

[66] *Op cit.* note 62. One of his observations was: "We are quite simply failing our constituency, the world's poorest. Our actions are in direct opposition to the words we exchange across this floor. Here we talk of co-operation, reform and growth. Outside this room the reality is falling resources, and not reform – but the hollowing out of UNDP's capacity to reduce poverty. This week I hope we can begin to connect the world of this room with the world outside. UNDP's problem is that too many of its friends are in this room, not enough in the world outside".

[67] Art. 80 (ex 84) EC.

[68] See for a further analysis P.J.G. Kapteyn and P. VerLoren van Themaat, Introduction to the Law of the European Communities (3rd ed. 1998), at 1172-1207; J. Erdmenger in H. von der Groeben, J. Thiesing, C.-D. Ehlermann (Hrsg.), Kommentar zum EU-/EG-Vertrag (5e neubearbeitete Auflage), at 1/1766-1776.

[69] Council Regulation 2408/92 on access for Community air carriers to intra-Community air routes (OJ 1992, L 240/8).

organization, Eurocontrol. The EC is engaged in air traffic management, namely through research and development, implementation of certain Eurocontrol rules,[70] and the Trans European Networks programme, which includes the setting up of a Global Navigation Satellite System.

Eurocontrol's official name is European Organization for the Safety of Air Navigation. Created in 1960, membership grew from 6 in 1960 to 29 in 2000. All EU members except Finland are Eurocontrol members. The EC has applied to become a member of Eurocontrol. Eurocontrol was originally established to "strengthen [...] co-operation in matters of air navigation and in particular to provide for the common organization of the air traffic services in the upper airspace".[71]

However, increased traffic delays strongly urged member States to intensify co-operation and work towards air traffic management at a pan-European level. In 1997 a Revised Convention was signed that has not yet entered into force. According to Article 1.1 of the Revised Convention, member States aim to "achieve harmonization and integration with the aim of establishing a uniform European air traffic management system".

The Revised Convention explicitly provides that it is for Eurocontrol to carry out the objectives agreed to. In the Preamble, member States consider "that Eurocontrol constitutes for the Contracting Parties the body for co-operation in the field of air traffic management". At the same time member States desire "to extend and to strengthen co-operation with the European or international institutions which have an interest in the execution of the tasks entrusted to Eurocontrol in order to increase its efficiency" (Preamble).

Since 1980 the relationship between the EC and Eurocontrol is governed by an exchange of letters.[72] The future relationship between the EU and Eurocontrol is uncertain. On the one hand, it is sometimes thought that in a distant future Eurocontrol will have found its place within the structure of the European Union, more specifically within the European Community. The advantage would be that the elaboration and application of a European air traffic management system

---

[70] E.g. Council Directive 93/65/EEC of 19 July 1993, on the definition and use of compatible technical specifications for the procurement of air traffic management equipment and systems, as amended by Commission Directive 97/15/EC of 27 March 1997 (drawn up to make Eurocontrol standards mandatory under EC law).
[71] Art. 1, paragraph 1 of the 1960 Eurocontrol Convention.
[72] Not published. See Erdmenger, *op. cit.* note 68, at 1/1669.

would be embedded within a strong supranational context. Directly applicable decisions could be taken and a structure would be available that would provide answers to questions of interpretation and enforcement. On the other hand, mainly in view of its significantly larger membership, there are voices against such a development and in favour of a continued separate status for Eurocontrol. It remains to be seen how the December 1999 decision of the European Council to conduct accession negotiations with 12 applicants and the real perspective of a Union having 27 members in 2004 will influence this debate.[73]

The European Union and the Western European Union

Similar questions emerge in the relations of the EC with other organizations. The Western European Union (WEU), for example, was created before the establishment of the EEC in 1957. The WEU underwent a number of changes in the course of its existence. Originally it was created as a restructured version of the 1948 Brussels Treaty Organization, essentially as a mechanism to supervise Western Germany's rearmament. NATO had decided in favour of such rearmament and the European Defence Community was stillborn. Gradually the WEU fell into a dormant existence and was mainly used as a framework within which the possible admission of the United Kingdom to the EC was discussed. A new stage in the life of the WEU arrived when the organization became the forum for defence co-operation among Western European countries, as a result both of the US policy to decrease its role in defence co-operation in Western Europe and of the ambition of European States to strengthen their own contribution to such co-operation. These substantial changes of colours of the organization did not take place through amendment of the constitution, but by a number of official declarations.[74]

The WEU was encapsulated within the EU structure by the 1992 Maastricht Treaty on European Union (TEU):

> [t]he Union requests the Western European Union (WEU), *which is an integral part of the development of the Union*, to elaborate and implement decisions and actions of the Union which have defence implications. The Council shall, in agreement with the institutions of the WEU, adopt the necessary practical arrangements.[75]

---

[73] See Europe No. 7612, 11 December 1999, at 3-4.
[74] In particular the 1984 Rome Declaration.
[75] Art. J.4, paragraph 2 (italics added).

The 1997 Treaty of Amsterdam moreover provides that "[t]he Union shall ... foster closer institutional relations with the WEU with a view to the possibility of the integration of the WEU into the Union, should the European Council so decide".[76] However, in June 1999 on the occasion of the Cologne Summit the European Council adopted a declaration in which it agreed on the aim to develop EU policies in the area of security itself rather than using the WEU for this purpose. The Council is asked to prepare definite decisions in this area that are scheduled to be taken by the end of the year 2000.[77] The Declaration explicitly provided that "[i]n that event, the WEU as an organization would have completed its purpose".[78] The WEU Parliamentary Assembly expressed its concern about these developments and criticized this bypassing of the WEU.[79] The Assembly is

> [c]onvinced [...] that transferring certain functions from an organization bringing together 28 countries including ten with powers of decision to an organization with fifteen will not resolve the fundamental difficulties Europe has with taking joint decisions, if there is no change to the rule on consensus.[80]

The 1954 Modified Brussels Treaty provides that it shall remain in force for fifty years.[81] At present it seems that the distribution of its property has already started, perhaps triggered by the Kosovo crisis. As far as institutional aspects are concerned, in November 1999 the EU's "Mr. CFSP" Solana was also appointed as Secretary-General of the WEU.[82] With regard to substance, the European Council (following the Amsterdam Treaty) has taken from the WEU property the so-called Petersberg tasks: humanitarian and rescue tasks, peace-keeping tasks and tasks of combat forces in crisis management, including peace-

---

[76] TEU Art. 17 (ex J.7). The following procedure for such integration is laid down in this article: the European Council shall "recommend to the member States the adoption of such a decision in accordance with their respective constitutional requirements". See on the post-Amsterdam discussions concerning the possible integration of WEU within the EU M. Jopp and H. Ojanen (eds.), European Security Integration: Implications for Non-alignment and Alliances (1999).

[77] Europe Documents No. 2142, at 2 (para. 5).

[78] Id.

[79] See Recommendation 653 of the Assembly (on security and defence: the challenge for Europe after Cologne), adopted 19 October 1999 (www.weu.int/assembly, on file with the author).

[80] Id., para. (ix).

[81] Art. XII.

[82] Europe No. 7597, 20 November 1999, at 3.

making.[83] It is not clear what will happen to other WEU functions, in particular to the Article V obligation for all 10 members to afford, in case of an armed attack on one of them in Europe, "the party so attacked all the military and other aid and assistance in their power". The fear has been expressed that these other tasks will mostly be left to NATO, and that the ideal of a common EU defence will be given a rather minimal interpretation. Moreover, according to the North Atlantic Treaty there is a right but no *obligation* for member States to afford an attacked member State all the military and other aid and assistance in their power. Hence, this obligation would disappear with the WEU.

Against this background there is a problem of diverging membership, and in this case the problem is more serious than in the case of Eurocontrol. The WEU has a mixed bag of participants, with a concomitant mix of rights and obligations. There are ten full members, all EU members.[84] It has six associate members, all non-EU NATO members.[85] A third group of participants ("observers") is composed of the five non-NATO EU members.[86] And finally, the WEU has seven Central European associate partners.[87] Only the ten full members have full decision-making rights in the WEU. When the WEU will terminate, this will have different implications for these four groups of members. The non-EU participants in WEU will only have NATO as a forum. Within the EU, it remains to be seen how the five current non-NATO EU members will be associated with future European defence discussions.

Here also, the future enlargement of the Union will add new dimensions. The issue of non-EU participants is likely to evaporate almost completely, as most non-EU members of WEU will join the Union. But the second issue will become more complex. In a Union of 27 members not all members may want to participate in the Union's common defence policy. It seems that the number of participants will be directly related to the scope of this policy: the more comprehensive

---

[83] European Council, Cologne Summit, Presidency Conclusions, para. 56 (reproduced in Europe No. 7480); in addition, the Presidency Report on strengthening of the common European policy on security and defence, Europe Documents No. 2142, at 3 (para. 2).

[84] Belgium, France, Germany, Greece, Italy, Luxembourg, Netherlands, Portugal, Spain, United Kingdom.

[85] Czech Republic, Hungary, Iceland, Norway, Poland, Turkey.

[86] Austria, Denmark, Finland, Ireland, Sweden.

[87] Bulgaria, Estonia, Latvia, Lithuania, Romania, Slovakia, Slovenia.

this policy, the fewer the number of participants. Essentially, the issue of "deepening vs. enlarging" is likely to emerge here as well. On the short term, it appears that the WEU will disappear and that some of its competences will be transferred to the EU. In the long run, it may be that within the Union some members may agree *inter se* to form a core group whose relation to the Union is uncertain and may vary from limited "enhanced co-operation" to a small descendant of the WEU.

Some general observations – the need for a principle of good neighbourliness

Many more examples could be given, each of them having its own particularities. There are examples concerning the relationship of the European Communities with other international organizations such as the European Space Agency[88] and the Council of Europe.[89] There are also many examples concerning the relationships between other organizations.[90] However, the three cases described above suffice as an introduction to the following observations of a more general nature concerning the delimitation of competences between international organizations.

A distinction can be made between such delimitation at the creation of an organization and subsequently, during its operation in practice. At the creation of an organization its founders agree upon the objectives and competences of their offspring. It is entirely in their

---

[88] See the European Commission Working Document "Towards a Coherent European Approach for Space" (Doc. SEC(1999)789, final, 7 June 1999); Annex 1 to this document contains "preliminary conclusions of the joint report on synergy between the Community and ESA"; see also Council Resolution 1999/C 375/01 (on developing a coherent European space strategy), OJ 1999, C 375/1.

[89] In this context reference can be made to the EU decision – taken at the June 1999 meeting of the European Council – to draw up an EU Charter of Fundamental Rights. During the 14th quadripartite meeting between the EU and the Council of Europe on 6 October 1999, the EU representatives indicated that this Charter "had not to be seen as creating a rival system to that of the [European Convention on Human Rights]" (see Europe No. 7569, 9 October 1999, at 6). Nevertheless, it is clear that the relationship between the future Charter and the European Convention would need further clarification.

[90] For example the relationship of the World Trade Organization with other organizations and international agreements. This was the subject of European Commissioner Pascal Lamy's address to a Jean Monnet colloquium on 21 October 1999, in which he observed that increasingly the WTO's dispute settlement provisions are used to enforce fundamental rules developed elsewhere (e.g. in the areas of international labour law and international environmental law). See Europe No. 7592, 13 November 1999, at 3-4.

hands whether or not the new organization will have competences that overlap with existing organizations. In some cases it is specifically provided in what areas the organization will not be competent. The Statute of the Council of Europe provides that "matters relating to national defence do not fall within the scope of the Council of Europe".[91] And it is usually true that technical organizations have specifically delimited competences. The International Office of Epizootics studies animal diseases and their prevention; there is little risk that its activities will overlap with those of the World Meteorological Organization.

Possibilities of overlapping competences at the creation of a new organization are generally likely to exist in the cases of organizations having more general objectives and related competences. This is inevitable. Moreover, it is often not wrong at all. The UN General Assembly does of course have the power to engage itself in almost anything, but the same is true for a number of general regional organizations such as the Organization of African Unity. In such cases overlap does not appear to be harmful if both organizations are aware of each others competences and can complement their activities taking into account their global and regional orientation.

But also within regions a new organization may be created having competences that overlap considerably with existing organizations. In 1948 the Brussels Treaty Organization was created that in 1954 was transformed into the WEU. The Brussels Treaty covers an area of co-operation of considerable latitude, including human rights, culture, economic and social affairs as well as collective self-defence. One year after the creation of the Brussels Treaty Organization the Statute of the Council of Europe was signed by ten countries including the five member States of the Brussels Treaty Organization. The aims and competences of the Council of Europe are very broad as well. According to Article 1 of the Statute, the Council's aim is to achieve a "greater unity between its members for the purposes of safeguarding and realizing the ideals and principles which are their common heritage and facilitating their economic and social progress". The Council's organs have to pursue this aim "by discussion of questions of common concern and by agreements and common action in economic, social, cultural, scientific, legal and administrative matters and in the maintenance and further education of human rights and fundamental freedoms".[92] And when six

---

[91] Art. 1(d).
[92] Art. 1.

Council of Europe members sought closer co-operation they created the Coal and Steel Community, whose objectives and competences clearly overlapped to some extent with those of the Brussels Treaty Organization and the Council of Europe.

These overlaps were not simply taken for granted. Article 1 of the Brussels Treaty, left unchanged in the 1954 amendment establishing the WEU, provided that co-operation between the parties "shall not involve any duplication of, or prejudice to, the work of other economic organizations in which the High Contracting Parties are or may be represented but shall on the contrary assist the work of those organizations".[93] Also, it was foreseen that integration between the six members of the Coal and Steel Community could be very successful and leave behind the other members of the Council of Europe. The Eden plan of 1952 "proposed that the Council should be remodelled so that its organs could serve as the institutions of the ECSC, the proposed EDC and any future, similar organizations; naturally, the organs would in such case be limited to the Six".[94] However, the final ECSC Protocol on Relations with the Council of Europe was far less ambitious than the Eden plan.[95] It has six articles, according to which the ECSC would send information to the Council. In addition, governments of the six founding member States were invited to recommend to their parliaments that the members of the ECSC Assembly should preferably be chosen from among the representatives in the Consultative Assembly of the Council of Europe.

Overlaps with existing organizations were of course impossible to avoid when the EEC was created and the six founding States were "determined to lay the foundation of an ever closer union among the peoples of Europe", were "resolved [...] to preserve and strengthen peace and liberty",[96] and provided the Community with a very large arsenal of powers to pursue these aims. Aware of such overlaps, the founding States also included a number of provisions laying down the framework rules for relations with other organizations. In Article 302 EC (229 old) the power to ensure the maintenance of all appropriate relations with the UN and other organizations is attributed to the Commission. Articles 303-304 EC (230 and 231 old) govern relations

---

[93] The Brussels Treaty is reproduced in UNTS No. 304.
[94] D.W. Bowett, The Law of International Institutions (4th ed. 1982), at 180.
[95] As embodied in the Protocol to the Treaty on Relations with the Council of Europe, reproduced in 1 European Yearbook (1955), at 451.
[96] EC Treaty, Preamble.

with the Council of Europe and the OECD; it is simply stated that "the Community shall establish" co-operation with these organizations. According to Article 306 EC (233 old), the EC Treaty provisions shall not preclude the existence or completion of regional unions between Belgium and Luxembourg, or between these countries and the Netherlands. Finally, Article 307 EC (234 old) provides that rights and obligations arising from agreements concluded before 1958 between one or more members on the one hand, and one or more third countries on the other "shall not be affected" by the provisions of the EC Treaty; in addition it has a number of rules to deal with such incompatibilities.

These examples demonstrate that – at least in these important cases – there is an awareness amongst the founders of a new "general" international organization of possible overlaps and of the need to lay down rules governing the relationship with "neighbour" organizations. This is not to say that such awareness always results in adequate delimitation provisions. Such rules will usually provide not much more than a framework or at least a legal basis for further, more detailed rules. And often it is simply provided that the constitution of the newly established organization does not affect pre-existing obligations of the parties.

While such provisions may not always be adequate, it is also obvious that it is difficult to do more. A frozen delimitation of competences is difficult to reconcile with the usual dynamics that a "general" international organization is expected to display. Thus a future delimitation of competences is not fixed. Instead it may be provided that the newly established organization shall cooperate with its neighbours, but even without procedural provisions like these such co-operation should be permitted as an implied power of international organizations.

The delimitation of competences between international organizations becomes a more complex affair during the life of the organization. While such delimitation may be agreed among the founders of an organization, it is also inherent in the creation of an international organization that the original objectives and competences will further develop, possibly through amendment of the constitution but always and more often by interpretation, in response to developments in practice.[97] Often there is also fear for such developments and member States voice concern over what is sometimes referred to as "mission creep" or,

---

[97] See further T. Sato, Evolving Constitutions of International Organizations (1996) and M.M. Martin Martinez, National Sovereignty and International Organizations (1996). See also the contribution by Shihata to this book, in particular paragraph III, where four examples of expansion of World Bank function through interpretation are discussed.

within the European context, "creeping integration". The fascinating related legal concepts are "constitutional change" or "constitutional development", an area full of dynamic and sometimes controversial notions such as implied and inherent powers, teleologic interpretation etc. In such future developments the debate of the original delimitations of competences may be re-opened, with the organizations involved as weaker or stronger participants in the discussion.[98] This is also reflected in "practice of the organization" as a relatively new and increasingly accepted means of interpretation of the law of the organization.[99]

Against this background of the delimitation of competences when international organizations are created, the more complex subsequent adjustments of such delimitations in practice, and the still continuing process of proliferation of international organizations the question may be raised if there is a need for rules or principles to offer some guidance for this process of delimitation of competences. At present this process is largely dependent upon ad hoc initiatives, mostly by States (backed by power) but sometimes also by international organizations (backed by their "independent" and "functional" orientation). For this reason, since the nature and intensity of the problem of delimitation of competences of international organizations have outgrown the level of individual and ad hoc solutions, it is sometimes suggested to find solutions of a more structural nature. In 1960, Dupuy concluded his study for the Hague Academy with the observation that in the relations between international organizations there is "une norme fondamentale qui leur impose de coopérer et de coordonner leurs activités au bénéfice d'un intérêt plus vaste que celui assigné à chacune d'elles: l'intérêt de la communauté universelle des Nations".[100] Morgenstern wrote in 1986:

---

[98] For example, the EC institutions are involved in the procedure for amending the EU Treaty.

[99] E. Lauterpacht, *The Development of the Law of International Organization by the Decisions of International Tribunals*, 152 RdC (1976 IV), in particular at 447-465. Concerning the legal basis for recourse to and acceptance of the practice of an organization as an element in the interpretation of constitutions of international organizations, Lauterpacht concludes: "[i]t is probably necessary to recognize that recourse to the practice of international organizations now stands on an independent legal basis; that is to say, that there exists a specific rule of the law of international organization to the effect that recourse to such practice is admissible and that States, on joining international organizations, impliedly accept the permissibility of constitutional development in this manner" (*id.*, at 460).

[100] R.J. Dupuy, *Le droit des relations entre les organisations internationales*, 100 RdC 457-587 (1960 II), at 584. Cf. also, with regard to the UN family, the dissenting opinion by Judge Weeramantry to the Advisory Opinion of the ICJ of 8 July 1996 re-

"[i]nter-State relations are based on the principle of respect for the independence and sovereignty of each State. Some comparable principle may be needed in inter-organization relations".[101] There is much to be said for the suggestion to have such a principle that could be named the inter-organization principle of good neighbourliness.

International organizations usually have been given a degree of independence by their members. Such independence is fundamentally different from that of States as it is related to the specific function of the organization. International organizations have no territory. The basis of their independence is the function for which they have been created and which they have to carry out. This is reflected in large parts of the law of international organizations, such as those parts dealing with the powers of organizations, their privileges and immunities and the means of interpretation of their law. Whereas the principle of good neighbourliness of States is territory-based, its inter-organization equivalent is function-based. As for States, it is often no longer possible for organizations to carry out their functions independently. In carrying out their tasks, international organizations should be aware of, and take into account, the tasks of organizations that are competent in a neighbouring field.

It does not often occur that international tribunals are called upon to apply this principle (as far as it exists), or the ideas behind it. A recent example is a decision of the International Criminal Tribunal for the Former Yugoslavia (ICTY) in the Simic case, in which it dealt with the issue of whether an employee of the International Committee of the Red Cross (ICRC) may be called as a witness.[102] The ICTY extensively considered and took into account the ICRC's mandate under conventional and customary international law and the fundamental principles on which the ICRC relies in the performance of its mandate, in particular the principles of neutrality, impartiality and independence.[103] The ICTY concluded "that the ICRC has a right under customary

---

quested by the WHO (*Legality of the Use by a State of Nuclear Weapons in Armed Conflict*), ICJ Rep. 1996, at 170: "The family of United Nations agencies, in working harmoniously for the common welfare of the global community, will need to work as a team, each helping the other with the special expertise that lies within its province".

[101] F. Morgenstern, Legal problems of international organizations (1986), at 26.
[102] Case No. IT-95-9-PT (Simic), Trial Chamber Decision on the Prosecution Motion under Rule 73 for a Ruling Concerning the Testimony of a Witness, 27 July 1999.
[103] *Id.*, paras.45-74.

international law to non-disclosure of the Information".[104] In its findings, the Tribunal stated that the ICRC's role is unique, mentioning in a footnote that "[f]or this reason, the finding by the Trial Chamber that the ICRC has a right to non-disclosure does not "open the floodgates" in respect of other organizations".[105] The Trial Chamber also deemed it important to

> touch on the issue of the relationship between the International Tribunal and the ICRC. They are two independent international institutions, each with a unique mandate conferred upon them by the international community. Both mandates are based on international humanitarian law and ultimately geared towards the better implementation thereof. Although both share common goals, their functions and tasks are different. The ICRC's activities have been described as "preventive", while the International Tribunal is empowered to prosecute breaches of international humanitarian law once they have occurred.[106]

Another recent example taken from the case-law of the ICTY is the judgment of 15 July 1999 in the Tadic case.[107] In this judgment the ICTY dealt with the question when armed forces may be regarded as acting on behalf of a foreign power. As was observed by the ICTY, "a high degree of control has been authoritatively suggested by the International Court of Justice in *Nicaragua*", the so-called effective control test.[108] The ICTY Appeals Chamber carefully examined this test and finally concluded that "with respect, it does not hold the *Nicaragua* test to be persuasive".[109] On the one hand, the ICTY clearly departed from the ICJ case-law on this point. However, on the other hand, it did so only after an extensive analysis of this case-law, of case-law of other courts, and of the differences and similarities between the relevant cases. This example is somewhat different from the previous one in the Simic case, as it does not concern respect for the mandate of another

---

[104] *Id.*, para. 74.

[105] *Id.*, para. 72. In this way, the Trial Chamber distinguishes this case from cases concerning staff members of other international organizations (e.g. UN forces such as UNPROFOR or "coalition forces" such as IFOR, SFOR and KFOR) as possible witnesses. See further on this issue D. Sarooshi, *The Powers of the United Nations International Criminal Tribunals*, 2 Max Planck Yearbook of United Nations Law 141-167 (1998).

[106] *Id.*, para.79.

[107] Appeals Chamber judgement, Prosecutor v. Dusko Tadic (Tadic IT-94-1).

[108] *Id.*, para. 99.

[109] *Id.*, paras. 115-145.

organization, but respect for the case-law of the "senior" international court, the ICJ.[110]

An inter-organization principle of good-neighbourliness would have both negative and positive dimensions. The negative dimension amounts to a hands-off principle: international organizations should not without very good reasons interfere in each others domain, and this should enable them to live in "peaceful coexistence". But good-neighbourliness between international organizations would also need a positive dimension. Sometimes, and increasingly, it is necessary for organizations to cooperate actively. As for States, it is often no longer possible to carry out functions independently, in isolation, no matter if it concerns man-made or non man-made disasters. The reconstruction and development of Kosovo cannot and is not a task of one organization. Aids cannot and is not fought by the World Health Organization alone. And, more specifically, it is useful for the European Court of Human Rights, when confronted with the problem of the applicability of Article 6, paragraph 1, of the European Convention on Human Rights (right to a fair trial) to disputes raised by servants of the State over their conditions of service, to have regard to the practice of the European Communities, in particular the case-law of the EC Court, on the definition of "public servants" excluded from the scope of Article 6, paragraph 1.[111]

To some extent, this principle of good-neighbourliness would resemble the European Community's notion of institutional balance. According to this notion Community institutions have to take into account each other's powers. As the Court of Justice considered:[112]

> [t]he treaties set up a system for distributing powers among the different Community institutions, assigning to each institution its own rôle in the institutional structure of the Community and the accomplishment of the tasks entrusted to the Community. Observance of the institutional balance means that each of the institutions must exercise its powers with due regard for the powers for the other institutions. It also requires that it should be possible to penalize any breach

---

[110] Cf. the observations by Mensah in his contribution to this book.

[111] As it did in its judgment in the case of *Pellegrin v. France* (Application No. 28541/95), 8 December 1999 (see in particular paragraphs 37-41 and 66 of this judgment).

[112] Case C-70/88 *Parliament v. Council*, [1990] ECR I-2041. See for an analysis S. Prechal, *Institutional Balance: a Fragile Principle with Uncertain Contents*, in T. Heukels, N. Blokker, M. Brus (eds.), The European Union after Amsterdam – A Legal Analysis 273-294 (1998).

of that rule which may occur. The Court, which under the Treaties has the task of ensuring that in the interpretation and application of the treaties the law is observed, must therefore be able to maintain the institutional balance [...]

However, while within the EC respect for the institutional balance is supervised by the Court of Justice, such judicial supervision is generally absent in the international legal order. Moreover, as will be discussed in the next section, there are indications that States are reluctant to submit these delimitation problems to judicial review.

FRAMEWORKS FOR THE DELIMITATION OF COMPETENCES

Introduction

Several frameworks have been set up in practice in an attempt to remedy difficulties involved in the delimitation of competences between international organizations. A decentralized and a centralized framework will be examined. First a brief overview is given of the UN family with more than 50 years of experience in this area. Secondly the more recent case of the European Union will be analyzed.

The decentralized approach – The United Nations: the family as a cornerstone in the web of international organizations?

Families or systems of international organizations

In some cases the delimitation of competences is structured through a framework for co-ordination between a limited number of international organizations. When the UN was created such a framework was set up for its relations with the specialized agencies, to be discussed in this section. This framework is usually called the UN system or the UN family.[113] There are more examples, such as the World Bank Group, consisting of the World Bank itself and a number of affiliate organizations with functions related to those of the World Bank but nevertheless to be carried out in a separate organization: the International Finance Corporation (IFC), the International Development Association (IDA), the International Centre for Settlement of Investment Disputes (ICSID), and the Multilateral Investment Guarantee Agency (MIGA).

---

[113] As Bastid has rightly observed, the notion of UN family "peut évoquer suivant les circonstances le noeud de vipères ou la chaleur confiante du foyer"; S. Bastid, *Sur quelques problèmes juridiques de co-ordination dans la famille des Nations Unies*, in Mélanges Reuter (1981), at 75.

IFC and IDA use the organs and staff of the Bank and their members must be members of the Bank. MIGA has a separate Board of Directors, but most of the members of this Board are also Executive Directors of the World Bank. The President of the World Bank is *ex officio* President of the boards of each affiliate organization, and the Bank's General Counsel has traditionally been elected ICSID's Secretary-General.[114] Another example is the League of Arab States that has close links with 17 "League of Arab States Specialized Agencies".[115] Such families are all created to facilitate co-ordination between the different parts of the system. The UN system, the mother of all families, will now be examined in some more detail after a brief overview of the relevant experience of the League of Nations.

The League experience

As in other areas, the drafters of the UN Charter benefited from the League experience. The drafters of the League were confronted with the same question of linking the new general world organization to existing specialized organizations, but could of course not build upon previous experience. When the League was created, some 20 specialized organizations existed, ranging from the Universal Postal Union to the Nansen International Office for Refugees. Moreover, together with the League, the International Labour Organisation (ILO) was created. In institutional respects, the ILO was dependent on the League: members of the League became automatically members of the ILO, and the International Labour Office had the right to be assisted by the League Secretariat. For the other specialized organizations already existing when the League was established, linkage to the League was made subject to the consent of all members of these organizations. No such consent was required for organizations postdating the creation of the League; it was simply provided that such organizations "shall be placed under the direction of the League".[116]

In practice only six specialized organizations were linked to the League on the basis of this provision.[117] The pre-existing organizations

---

[114] See more in detail the contribution by Shihata to this book.
[115] Yearbook of International Organizations 2000-2001, at 1735.
[116] Covenant, Art. 24.1.
[117] And not even always the most prominent ones: the International Bureau for Information and Enquiries regarding Relief to Foreigners (linked in 1921), the International Hydrographic Organizations (1921), the International Commission for Air Navigation (1922), the International Central Office for the Control of

in most cases preferred to remain independent and members that were not members of the League were unwilling to become directed by it.[118] On the other hand, during the existence of the League a large number of committees were created for international co-operation in areas such as communications and economics and finances, transit, health, opium, traffic in women and children. These committees were placed under the authority of the Council and the Assembly. Co-operation in these areas was thus "centralized" within the framework of the League. These committees were generally considered very successful.[119]

The League experience in the field of social and economic co-operation was reviewed in 1939 by the Bruce Committee. The Committee's report (usually referred to as the Bruce report) was published 22 August 1939, a few days before Germany invaded Poland. The report described the League's work in economic and social affairs and concluded that "the scope of [... that] work is vast and the contribution which it is making, and has already made, towards improving the health and welfare of the ordinary man in every continent of the world is an impressive one".[120] In view of the growth and the envisaged expansion of this work of the League, the Committee proposed the creation of a "Central Committee for Economic and Social Questions", for which it prepared a brief "draft constitution".[121] The Committee had to be "superimposed" on the existing League Committees; its task would be "the direction and supervision of the work of the committees dealing with economic and social questions".[122] In making this proposal, the Committee's first aim was

---

Liquor Traffic in Africa (1922), the Nansen International Office for Refugees (1931) and the International Exhibitions Bureau (1931).

[118] Bowett, *op. cit.* note 94, at 9.

[119] According to F.P. Walters, A History of the League of Nations (1952) at 175-176: "In nothing did the historical development of the League differ more widely from the League as it was foreseen in Paris than in the creation and growth of its social and economic institutions. [...] ... an immense contribution to human welfare and a necessary element in the complex life of the modern world". M. Virally, L'Organisation Mondiale (1972), refers to this League system of functional committees as "un système très centralisé. [...] Leur prolifération et l'importance qu'ils avaient acquise dans la vie internationale en vingt ans font contraste avec l'affaiblissement progressif et le dépérissement des organes politiques de la Société. C'est pourtant un aspect du bilan de la S.d.N. qui est presque toujours oublié aujourd'hui" (at 45).

[120] League of Nations Doc. A.23.1939, at 11. See on this report V.-Y. Ghebali, La Société des Nations et la Réforme Bruce, 1939-1940 (1970).

[121] Bruce report, at 21-22.

[122] *Id.*, at 21.

to increase the efficiency of the work as a whole, and in particular:

(a) To bring all this part of the work of the League under the supervision of an agency which should be both effective and representative;

(b) To meet the fact that the development in the nature of the work results in a growing inter-connection between the activities of the different organizations, and that therefore a coordinating direction is more and more required.[123]

The UN Charter

While it came too late for the League, the Bruce report was an essential source of inspiration when the Charter provisions on social and economic co-operation were drafted.[124] Provisions on economic and social co-operation are more prominent in the Charter than in the League Covenant, as can be seen from the Preamble, the purposes of the UN laid down in Article 1, Chapter IX of the Charter, and the creation of ECOSOC as one of the six principal organs of the UN. Co-operation in these areas is both a goal of the UN in itself (Article 1, paragraph 3) and an instrument for "the creation of conditions of stability and well-being which are necessary for peaceful and friendly relations among nations" (Article 55). One could therefore expect that a strong system would be established (similar to the proposal made by the Bruce Committee) in which the UN could control the activities of the organizations concerned.

However, the Charter provides for a somewhat loose framework of "functional decentralization", in contradistinction to the more centralized League system and the Bruce proposals.[125] It was decided that co-operation in these areas could best be carried out by specialized organizations that were to be associated with the UN through relationship agreements.[126] One important reason why this model was preferred was the wish to put the specialized agencies at sufficient distance from the political "mother" organization. If certain States would not become a member of the UN – as the US had never been a member of the League – they could still be members of the specialized agencies. If the

---

[123] *Id.*, at 19.
[124] See in greater detail UN Doc. E/5524/Add.1.
[125] See Dupuy, *op. cit.* note 100, at 571 ff. On the advantages of functional decentralization see D. Mitrany, A Working Peace System (1943).
[126] See in particular Arts. 57 and 63 of the Charter.

UN would fail, the specialized agencies would not necessarily fail with it.

Inherent in this choice was the need to bring these independent organizations into some relationship with the UN to achieve a coordination of policies and activities. The UN Charter attributes this coordination task to ECOSOC under the final responsibility of the General Assembly.[127] The Charter contains hardly any further details regarding the relationship between the UN and the specialized agencies. The drafters of the Charter did clearly not want to straitjacket the agencies. The agreements to be concluded had to define "the terms on which the agency concerned shall be brought into relationship with the United Nations".[128]

Relationship agreements and the WHO Advisory Opinion

On this basis 16 agreements have been concluded.[129] These agreements have a similar structure but their contents are widely diverging. They certainly do not *ex post* establish the uniformity that was avoided by the Charter. Their diversity extends from a rather intimate relationship of the UN with UNESCO to a much more distant one with the Bretton Woods organizations. If one day one of the few non-members of the UN such as Vatican City (Holy See), East Timor, Palestine or any future newly created State apply to become a member of UNESCO, the UNESCO Secretariat has to transmit this application "immediately" to ECOSOC; "[t]he Council may recommend the rejection of such applications and any such recommendation shall be accepted by [UNESCO]".[130] Close relations always have financial dimensions. In this regard the UN-UNESCO agreement provides that both organizations "shall consult together concerning appropriate arrangements for the inclusion of the budget of [UNESCO] within a general budget of the United Nations".[131] One will look in vain for provisions such as these in the agreements of the UN with the Bretton Woods organizations, the provisions of which come close to saying that there is no sincere interest in mutual relations.

---

[127] UN Charter, Arts. 60, 63, 64.
[128] UN Charter, Art. 63(1).
[129] See for a brief history of the agreements UN Doc. E/5524/Add.2.
[130] Agreement between the UN and UNESCO, Art. II (reproduced in YUN 1946-47, at 717).
[131] *Id.*, Art. XVI.2. A similar provision is included in a number of other agreements, such as those with the ILO and the FAO.

Despite the differences between these agreements, there are similarities as well, and one of them is of significance here. There is remarkable uniformity where the agreements authorize the specialized agencies to request advisory opinions from the ICJ, which is of course a principal organ of one of the parties of the relationship agreement. In these authorizations questions relating to the relationship between the agency concerned and the United Nations or any specialized agency are excluded. It is not clear why such questions were precluded from judicial review by the Court. Nevertheless, somewhat surprisingly against this background, the existence of such a provision in the UN-WHO relationship agreement did not prevent the Court in its 1996 WHO Nuclear Weapons Advisory Opinion to take into account in its considerations the relationship between the two organizations. It took the view that the responsibilities of the WHO "are necessarily restricted to the sphere of public "health" and cannot encroach on the responsibilities of other parts of the United Nations system. And there is no doubt that questions concerning the use of force, the regulation of armaments and disarmament are within the competence of the United Nations and lie outside that of the specialized agencies".[132]

The UN system in practice

The general lack of coherence in the relationship between the UN and the specialized agencies has been deepened in practice.[133] At the risk of overworking the metaphor, the UN family is of an anarchic nature. Its members educate themselves; there is little parental authority. At most there are loose and informal ties. It is usually not the formal structures but good personal relationships that make the difference and stimulate family building. The emphasis is on the independence of the constituent parts, not on the unity of the whole. A few general observations can be made on the development of the UN system in practice.

A usual starting point is the role of ECOSOC that is commonly criticized.[134] To a certain extent this is the wrong target as already since

---

[132] *Legality of the Use by a State of Nuclear Weapons in Armed Conflict*, Advisory Opinion requested by the WHO, 8 July 1996, General List No. 93, para. 26. On this Opinion, see the contribution by White in this book.

[133] Dupuy observed in 1960: "les institutions spécialisées sont autour et non au-dessous des Nations Unies" (*op. cit.* note 100, at 579). Virally wrote in 1972: "[c]ette autonomie [of the spags] est si totale qu'on peut la qualifier, sans forcer les mots, de souveraine" (L'Organisation Mondiale, at 65).

[134] Cf. K. Hüfner, UN-system, in Wolfrum, *op. cit.* note 48, at 1366: "with regard to the necessary system co-ordination, ECOSOC is the crucial weak spot".

the 1950s it is increasingly the General Assembly that has assumed its responsibility in the area of co-ordination. Nevertheless, it is primarily about ECOSOC's role that a semi-permanent discussion is taking place, under different headings such as "rationalization" and, more recently, "revitalization". Since long and on many occasions it has been proposed that ECOSOC should be restructured into an "Economic Security Council".[135] One of these proposals was made by Maurice Bertrand in 1985 and drew heavily upon the institutional structure of the European Communities.[136] It is clear why such proposals are made regularly. With the ever increasing number of bodies, programmes etc. goes the need for more co-ordination and the wish to "upgrade" ECOSOC. Only most recently these proposals seem to have some impact in practice. Not only did the UN Secretary-General suggest a fundamental rethinking of the role of the Council,[137] in practice some changes in the functioning of ECOSOC have been implemented. For example, since 1998 annual one-day meetings have taken place between representatives of ECOSOC on the one hand, and of the IMF and World Bank on the other, in an attempt to improve ECOSOC's working relations with the Bretton Woods organizations.

However well-intended, these attempts do not seem to be capable of dealing more fundamentally with the co-ordination problem. There is a deeply-felt and long-standing disinterest in establishing closer bonds between parts of the UN family. Some examples may be given to illustrate this. First of all, as mentioned above, a number of agreements between the UN and the specialized agencies refer to the idea of including the budget of the agencies concerned in a general budget of the UN. However, consultations during the first years of the UN on the

---

[135] For example by M. Bertrand, The Third Generation World Organization (1989), at 87 ("... so as to give it a prestige at least equal to that of the Security Council"), and by the Commission on Global Governance (*op. cit.* note 49, at 153-162). Earlier, in 1973, UN Secretary-General Waldheim stated that "[t]he reassertion of the constitutional authority of the Economic and Social Council within the system and its fulfilment of the function of providing the conceptual framework for the entire system of United Nations organizations would certainly be an important step in balancing the tendency to fragmentation" (UN Doc. GAOR, Suppl. no. 1A (A/9001/Add.1), at 7).

[136] M. Bertrand, Some Reflections on Reform of the United Nations, UN Doc. JIU/REP/85/9 (also published as an annex to UN Doc. A/40/988), at 52-53 and 61-62.

[137] UN Doc. A/51/950, at 43 (para. 130). According to the Secretary-General, "if the objectives of the United Nations are to be fully realized, a much greater degree of concerted will and coordinated action is required throughout the system as a whole" (*id.*, at 27 (para. 86)).

implementation of this idea resulted in the conclusion that the difficulties in merging the budgets were insuperable at the time.[138] The budgetary powers of the agencies had to be transferred to the UN General Assembly, and national delegations to the UN General Assembly had to be expanded due to the required expertise for taking decisions not only on the more general UN issues, but also on the much more technical issues of the agencies. On the one hand, the outcome of these discussions may be disappointing; the result is almost complete financial independence of the agencies, and this is indeed a first condition for their general autonomy.[139] On the other hand it illustrates the strong disinterest in creating closer ties within the UN family, thus reconfirming the original choice in favour of functional decentralization.

A second example is the debate that took place in the early 1970s to review the relationship agreements. In 1973 ECOSOC decided to carry out such a review "with a view to strengthening the coherence of the system and its capacity to fulfil, in particular, the objectives of the International Development Strategy in an effective and coordinated manner".[140] Nevertheless, in the end the agreements were left unamended.[141] One may speculate of course what the outcome of this debate would have been. On the one hand practice of the 1950s and 1960s justifies the speculation that UN ties would have been made looser. On the other hand, the last concluded agreements with specialized agencies, those with WIPO, IFAD en UNIDO, do not seem to support this view.

However, and this is a third example, a more recent potential candidate for the conclusion of a relationship agreement, the World Trade Organization, lacks even a constitutional provision on this. As is also often the case in the UN's relations with the Bretton Woods organizations, there is a stark contrast between WTO's silence on the issue and the enthusiasm on the part of the UN. On the one hand, the former UN Secretary-General Boutros-Ghali stated that "[m]aintaining the integrity and comprehensive nature of the United Nations system should be a major, constant concern of the international community. In this context, the desirability of bringing new organizations such as the

---

[138] C. Wilfred Jenks, *Co-ordination: a new problem of International Organization*, 77 RdC 157-303 (1950 II), at 228-238 (para. 108). See UN Docs. A/394/Rev.1; A/404; A/449; A/497; E/5524/Add.3, at 2-5.
[139] M. Virally, L'Organisation Mondiale (1972), at 65.
[140] Res. 1768 (LIV).
[141] See UN Doc. E/5524 with addenda.

World Trade Organization, endowed with wide international responsibilities in fields of international economic and social co-operation, into relationship with the United Nations, deserves priority attention".[142] The WTO, on the other hand, "saw no grounds for formal institutional links between the WTO and the United Nations".[143] The relationship between the two organizations is governed by an exchange of letters, in which it is agreed to exchange information and in which provision is made for reciprocal representation, participation of the WTO in the ACC, co-operation between secretariats, etc.[144]

The web of relationship agreements within the UN family was not, and has not been developed into a substitute for centralization à la the League of Nations. Moreover, even if the UN Charter would have laid down such a centralized system, it is uncertain if it would have removed the co-ordination problem – that to an important degree is a national problem – and it is certain that other problems would have emerged. For example, the US withdrew for a period of three years from the ILO and has ceased to be a member of UNESCO from 1984 till date. US dissatisfaction with these organizations would have to be expressed in other ways in case the ILO and UNESCO would have been UN organs.

The UN co-ordination problem and the semi-permanent search for solutions to it seem to be inherent in the existing structure of socio-economic co-operation, the basis for which was laid down in the Charter. In 1945 there must have been a strong belief in "autonomous" co-ordination through functional decentralization. But at the time the UN had 50 members and there were only a few specialized agencies. Now there are 188 members and 16 specialized agencies. This does certainly not suggest that a more centralized mechanism would have been established should the UN have been created yesterday. But it does have implications for the co-ordination problem and for solutions that are proposed.

---

[142] Agenda for Development: recommendations, UN Doc. A/49/665, para. 60.
[143] WTO Doc. WT/GC/W/10, at 1.
[144] *Id.*, Annex.

The search for solutions to the co-ordination problem

Any attempts to deal with the co-ordination problem must depart from the generally held view that it is first of all a national problem.[145] This has been recognized from the outset.[146] "Co-ordination begins at home", as has rightly been emphasized in a Dutch policy paper.[147] Likewise, the Council of Europe's Committee of Wise Persons in 1998 recommended: "[w]e stress the importance of co-ordination and co-operation in national capitals, between those responsible for allocating tasks to the different European organizations, in order to ensure complementarity and to avoid unnecessary duplication and overlap".[148] And the UN Secretary-General, in discussing the "challenges" for the relationship between the UN and the Bretton Woods organizations, stated: "Member States can contribute to this process [of collaboration and co-operation] immeasurably by better co-ordination of their individual positions at the United Nations and Bretton Woods institutions".[149] To the extent that the co-ordination problem originates at the national level, it seems difficult for solutions at the international level to be effective. In addition, this also demonstrates that a centralized structure existing at the national level is by no means a panacea for solving the co-ordination problem.

At the same time however, the UN co-ordination problem is more than a national problem only. Powers have been transferred to an increasing number of international organizations that have a will of their own. The development of their policies and activities is by no means under the full control of the member States. UNAIDS was established by six UN organs and organizations. The way in which UNDP and the World Bank use their competences is not fully decided by the member States. To the extent that problems of co-ordination arise in such cases, measures are also required at the international level.

It has been observed that many of the solutions proposed amount to *procedural* solutions that usually give more authority to the global

---

[145] See in particular G. Cohen Jonathan, *L'État face à la prolifération des organisations internationales*, in Les organisations internationales contemporaines (Société Française pour le Droit International, Colloque de Strasbourg, 1988), at 177-203.

[146] See e.g. UN General Assembly Resolution 125 (II) adopted 20 November 1947, para. 1. See also UN Doc. E/5524/Add.5, at 34.

[147] De kwaliteit van de VN als kanaal voor ontwikkelingssamenwerking, *op cit.* note 51, at 4.

[148] Final report to the Committee of Ministers, Doc. CM(98)178, 20 October 1998, para. 28.

[149] E/1999/56, at 8.

level, by creating new organs or new positions within the Secretariat.[150] Such procedural solutions are criticized by French authors in particular, who have articulate views on this. According to Bertrand, the central problem is *substance*: the definition of the objectives that member States want to give to a system of global organizations; real consensus in fact only exists in a few technical areas such as post, telecommunication and meteorology.[151] According to Virally, more in general, there is a tendency to cling the study of the UN system to that of the State.[152] As a result, it is simply suggested to strengthen the organization and to give it powers and organs similar to those existing at the level of the State. This suggestion is rejected by Virally as it ignores the fundamentally different nature of the UN system; "[c]e qui est bon pour une nation n'est pas nécessairement bon pour la communauté des peuples de la terre".[153]

This may be convincing, but it is also question-begging. If it is agreed that the UN system lacks coherence and must be made more unified, what other remedies exist than those that give more authority to the central level? And one of the French authors mentioned above has even made suggestions in this direction: Bertrand was among the advocates of the creation of an Economic Security Council.[154] However, as discussed above, in practice there is a deeply-felt and long-standing disinterest in strengthening the ties between parts of the UN family. This seems to be a time-honoured paradox of the UN system: the wish to combine the autonomy of the parts of the system with greater coherence.

The experience of the UN family demonstrates that the decentralized solution to the problem of delimiting the competences of international organizations has its limitations. Although it may facilitate cooperation among the different organizations, the system has no in-built mechanism to arrive at border demarcations where necessary. This is essentially left to the market mechanism called functionalism, in which each organization is allowed to pursue its own aims and in which de-

---

[150] M. Bertrand in J.-P. Cot and A. Pellet, La Charte des Nations Unies (1985), at 919-920.
[151] Id.
[152] M. Virally, L'Organisation Mondiale (1972), at 19. According to Virally, "cette vue est entièrement erronée, qu'elle traduit une méconnaisance complète de la réalité et conduit à un diagnostic désastreux".
[153] Id., at 24.
[154] See his report "Some reflections on reform of the United Nations", *op. cit.* note 136.

marcation decisions are taken on an ad hoc basis. The next paragraph will examine if the centralized approach of the European Union offers better prospects.

The centralized approach – The European Union: a true union or pillar proliferation?

As opposed to the UN and to regional co-operation such as that within the framework of the League of Arab States, nothing like an EC family was founded in the EEC treaty. A few provisions deal with the relationship between the three Communities. Although the EC treaties are separate – there are still three Communities[155] – they are also firmly interlinked through the merger of the institutions, and of course also because the Communities have always had the same member States.

Outside the interrelationship between the three Communities, no strong and fixed ties with other organizations were foreseen in 1957. Although the Communities have always had wider political objectives, the emphasis in the activities of the EC during the transitional period was on the creation of a common market. This in itself did not bring the need to structure co-operation with other Western European organizations within a system such as that of the UN. What was necessary was a formal basis for the establishment of relations with some specific organizations such as the OECD and Benelux, and such a basis is provided in Articles 302 (ex 229) and following of the EC Treaty.

However, the dynamic development of European integration has put higher on the agenda the relationship of the Communities with other organizations and the need of co-ordination. The integration efforts gradually expanded into many areas not previously covered by the Treaties. Co-operation started and developed between member States in areas such as foreign policy and security, combating terrorism, drug addiction and fraud, asylum policies and employment. Few parts of European societies were left untouched by the process of integration. In a number of areas such co-operation between the member States originally started outside the framework of the EC Treaty, sometimes through rather secretive frameworks such as TREVI.[156]

---

[155] This is the generally held view. Other opinions have also been expressed, for example by Von Bogdandy and Nettesheim. See their *Ex Pluribus Unum: Fusion of the European Communities into the European Union*, 2 European Law Journal (1996), at 267. See most recently A. von Bogdandy in this book.

[156] TREVI is the French abbreviation for *Terrorisme, Radicalisme, Extrémisme et Violence Internationale*. Cf. Curtin, *op. cit.* note 29.

A major effort to encapsulate these "bottom-up established" regimes into one overall framework was the establishment of the European Union in 1992. Using the three Communities as its foundation, two supplementary pillars were built containing a common foreign and security policy and provisions on co-operation in the fields of justice and home affairs. However, co-operation in these two new pillars was essentially organized not along supranational lines, but through intergovernmental structures: as a rule unanimity decision-making in the Council and only very limited involvement of the other Community institutions. This was the price to be paid for including these new and traditionally sensitive areas of co-operation within one Union. It is one of the paradoxes of the Union: on the one hand these fields of co-operation have now been brought within the Union, on the other hand this has been responsible for the genesis of a Union of "bits and pieces" as was forcefully argued in 1992 by Curtin.[157]

The true nature of the new creature has puzzled both practitioners and scholars. The easiest answer has been couched in Latin and is of a charming simplicity: the Union's structure is *sui generis*. This is of course a nice example of legal escapism, although the complexities involved in trying to characterize the Union may finally end in a reappraisal of such a way out. The Union puzzle has so many pieces of diverging sizes that are moreover subject to permanent change that it is difficult not to use metaphors of different nationality such as a Greek temple, a French gothic cathedral and a Russian doll.

Legal scholars, at first mainly in Germany but soon also elsewhere, came to widely diverging conclusions in their analyses of the Union. According to Koenig and Pechstein, the Union does not have legal personality and is not an international organization, but only a mixture of the three Communities and intergovernmental co-operation in the second and third pillar.[158] At the other end of the spectrum one finds views such as those by Von Bogdandy and Nettesheim, claiming that the Union is a new legal person that has absorbed the Communities.[159]

In practice the Union's member States refused to explicitly give the Union the status of a legal person, first in Maastricht without much discussion and subsequently in Amsterdam. The road between Maastricht and Amsterdam was full of debate on the issue of legal personality

---

[157] D.M. Curtin, The Constitutional Structure of the Union: A Europe of Bits and Pieces, 30 CMLRev. 17-69 (1993).
[158] C. Koenig and M. Pechstein, Die Europäische Union (1995).
[159] *Op. cit.* note 155.

that regained an amount of political attention that is precedented only by the early UN years, between San Francisco in 1945 and the Hague in 1949. In both cases these political discussions are full of references to the fear of a super State. However, only in the case of the European Union the discussion has reached extreme dimensions. First of all conceptually, where it has sometimes been claimed that the Union cannot be a legal person as long as it houses co-operation of an intergovernmental nature. If this would be true, most international organizations whose legal personality is undisputed today would not be legal persons as they are as intergovernmental as the second and third pillar of the Union, or even more. But it is most of all in practice that the debate is reaching extreme dimensions, and this is likely to become the decisive reason why sooner or later the Union will be a full-fledged legal person. In real life the Union exists, well-alive and fully recognized, by its own citizens (who are formally Union citizens), by third countries and by other international organizations, to such an extent that it comes close to a legal fiction to consider the Union as a kind of legal *persona non grata*.

If the Union is now considered more in general, it is of particular interest for the present study to see what the effects have been of bringing under one Union both the three supranational Communities and the mostly intergovernmental co-operation in the other pillars. Some observers initially feared that this merger would make the first pillar less supranational and would jeopardize the integration process. However, both practice and the 1997 Amsterdam Treaty point in a different direction.

The Amsterdam Treaty has fortified the robustness of the first pillar and, at the same time, essentially maintained the three pillar structure of the Union. At the same time, practice and the Amsterdam Treaty have decreased the rather marked distinction between the supranational vs. intergovernmental nature of co-operation in the three pillars; in this sense there is more unity now.[160] In Amsterdam, the second and third pillar have been "infected" "with an extra dose of *méthode communautaire*"; it has thus been "recognized that successful and effective co-operation between States is sometimes better served by the severe regime of institutional constraints and limitations of sover-

---

[160] See more extensively B. de Witte, *The Pillar Structure and the Nature of the European Union: Greek Temple or French Gothic Cathedral?*, in Heukels, Blokker, Brus (eds.), *op. cit.* note 112, at 51-68; D.M. Curtin and I.F. Dekker, *The European Union as a "Layered" International Organization: Institutional Unity in Disguise*, in P. Craig and G. de Búrca (eds.), The Evolution of EU Law 83-136 (1999).

eignty practiced within the European Community than by the lax *entre nous* atmosphere of the second and third pillars".[161] However at the same time, the other way around, more intergovernmentalism has been given to the first pillar under the Amsterdam Treaty.[162]

Research by Curtin and Dekker has convincingly demonstrated that the Union can now best be seen as "a highly sophisticated "layered" international organization, harbouring beneath its outer shell various autonomous and interlinked entities with their own specific roles and legal systems".[163] It is difficult to identify more specific factors to which the increase in unity can be attributed. Curtin and Dekker's analysis however underlines the importance of the single institutional structure of the Union, as prescribed by Article 3 of the Union Treaty. There is an evolving symmetry in the day-to-day operation of the institutions under the three pillars, notwithstanding often considerable differences in formal competences.[164] Within the second and third pillar, the institutions "have been influenced to a considerable extent by their functions, roles and practices in the context of the EC Treaties".[165]

The scope of the "appeal *communautaire*" is not limited to the member States when they negotiated and concluded the Amsterdam Treaty and to the applicant countries, but also extends to international organizations. The examples of EUROCONTROL and the WEU have been discussed, but the same is true for a number of other organizations, such as the European Space Agency and the European Conference of Postal and Telecommunications Administrations (43 members) for which the EC works as a magnet.[166]

If these trends continue in the near future, and the Union will have some 27 members as presently agreed, it seems likely that the Union will incorporate a number of international organizations, or the remains of them. It remains to be seen however, to what extent this increase in unity will have to be paid by an emerging patchwork of frameworks,

---

[161] De Witte, *op. cit.* note 160, at 56.
[162] In particular in the new Title 4 of the EC Treaty (visas, asylum, immigration and other policies related to free movement of persons).
[163] *Op. cit.* note 160, at 132.
[164] *Id.*, at 104, 112-126.
[165] *Id.*, at 131-132.
[166] The comparison is made by K.-U. Schrogl, *Die Europäische Gemeinschaft als Magnet*, Europa-Archiv, Folge 18/1993, at 525-532.

pillars or even organizations *inside* the Union. It has been suggested, for example, to create a fourth pillar for defence co-operation.[167]

The few years of experience since the conclusion of the Maastricht Treaty have demonstrated the *influence bienfaisante du milieu*, the beneficial influence of the supranational Communities over the other parts of the Union. It also demonstrates that there may be some truth in the view that an adequate and semi-permanent delimitation of competences as well as effective co-ordination need "vertical" solutions, not as a substitute for consensus on substance, but as a better mechanism than the UN's market mechanism of functional decentralization.

Nevertheless, at the same time it is necessary to be careful not to generalize too easily this recent EU practice. What is true now for the Union may not be true in some future. Perhaps within ten years from now intergovernmentalism will be more dominant in the Union. Perhaps there will be a very large Union housing a much smaller core group and a number of largely autonomous organizations or other frameworks for co-operation. But also, and even more, what is true now for the Union may not be true for other international organizations. Like human beings, each international organization is unique, not to say *sui generis*.

SUMMARY

In other contributions to this book the focus will turn to some specific functions of international organizations. These issues covered by the other contributions are part of the larger phenomenon of the proliferation of international organizations that has so far not been studied extensively. In this introduction an attempt has been made to explore briefly some of the general and legal issues involved.

It has been demonstrated that there is a proliferation of organizations despite the existence of some factors that discourage this trend. There is a proliferation of organizations because of the proliferation of

---

[167] *Inter alia* by C. Grant, Can Britain Lead in Europe? (Centre for European Reform, London 1998), as mentioned in Jopp and Ojanen (eds.), *op. cit.* note 76, at 33 ff. However, this suggestion was rejected in the report prepared by a three "wise men" group chaired by Jean-Luc Dehaene (at the request of European Commission President Prodi) and presented on 18 October 1999. It paid attention to the issue of European defence policy and stated that "[n]ew institutional arrangements will be needed; they should fit in the single institutional framework of the Union and not lead to the creation of a fourth pillar" (at 14).

States since 1945, but most fundamentally it is the process of globalization that explains why new organizations continue to be created.

A core legal issue is the delimitation of competences between international organizations, first of all when an organization is created, but in particular during its further life. Three cases have been briefly discussed to illustrate this. In practice the delimitation of competences is generally taking place in an ad hoc manner, and it seems useful to promote the development of a "principle of good neighbourliness" for international organizations, although it will be difficult to implement such a principle in areas where strong judicial organs are absent. Apart from this, at present there are two mechanisms to deal with the delimitation problem: the decentralized approach and the centralized approach. The cases of the UN family and of the European Union show how these approaches may or may not work in practice. There are many differences, for example between the "top down" way in which the UN family was created and the "bottom up" way in which the EU has developed and is developing. But both cases reveal the complexities involved in delimitating competences and, more generally, coordinating policies and activities of different organizations with often different members. One of the paradoxes of the proliferation of international organizations is that both attempts to deal with this proliferation involve the creation of new organizations.

THE ATTITUDE OF STATES TOWARDS THE PROLIFERATION OF INTERNATIONAL ORGANIZATIONS

Prof. Emeritus Dr. Dr. h.c. Ignaz Seidl-Hohenveldern[*]

THE NOTION OF INTERNATIONAL ORGANIZATIONS

The proliferation of International organizations has been criticized by the public in general as well as within the scientific community. Not only does the number of organizations increase, inter-State co-operation has led also to the forming of types of organs other than classical International organizations.[1] In the last resort, however, International organizations are established by States. The member-States of an organization are rightly held to be the masters of the Treaty[2] establishing the Organization[3]. Thus, this criticism should be directed to the States having established a plethora of organizations covering the same or closely connected fields (e.g. environment, human rights) in a global and/or in a regional context. When establishing an organization, States will not always aim to obtain the solution which would be the best according to the rules of administrative science. They will approach the problem in a much more pragmatic spirit, paying all too much regard to political considerations.

This attitude of States led to cases where the very existence of a new organization remained open to doubt. In order to make it evident that the member-states or the CSCE, in the Final Act of the Helsinki Conference of 1975[4] did assume only commitments which were

---

[*] Professor emeritus of International Law, Vienna University, Doctor honoris causa University Paris V, Member of the Institut de Droit International.
[1] Cf infra notes 4-13, notes 22-25 and 33-34.
[2] But see notes 4-5 *infra*.
[3] I. Seidl-Hohenveldern, *Corporations in and under International Law* Cambridge UK, Grotius Publications, 1987, pp. 75ss.
[4] 70 *AJIL* (1976) pp. 417 ss.

politically, but not legally binding[5], they refrained from incorporating these commitments into a treaty. Yet, they felt compelled to control the observance of their not legally binding[5] commitments. Such a follow-up is all the more necessary where commitments are assumed only in the form of soft law or else non-complying States would gain unjust advantages[6] The CSCE commitments are based merely on the Final Act of the Helsinki Conference and not on a Treaty. By this fact. they had become only soft law The follow-up was ensured by holding periodic follow-up conferences and by the establishment of a secretariat, this arrangement, thus, could have qualified as an organization[7] Yet, only as a result of its Budapest Conference of 1994 did the CSCE change its name to Organization on Security and Co-operation in Europe (OSCE)[8] – and, even so, some doubts remain, as to whether the OSCE is indeed an international organization[9] In the domestic law of the m ember States such doubts were due to the fact that thew CSE/OSCE was established by a not legally binding expression of the will of the member-states, whereas legal persons can be established only by legally binding acts. Art. H point 11 of the Supplementary Document to give effect to certain provisions contained in the Charter of Paris for a New Europe[10] invites the host countries to grant to the CSCE institutions legal personality under domestic law and the appropriate diplomatic immunities – yet, this document, in its turn , is only soft law. Anyhow, as the member-states have complied with this demand,[11] the legal personality of the

---

[5] On this notion M. Virally, "La distinction entre textes internationaux de portée juridique et textes internationaux dépourvus de portée juridique (à l'exception des textes émanant des organisations internationales)" *60 Annuaire de l'institut de droit international* (1983) (Paris, Pedone 1984) pp. 166-371 and Ch Ahlström, *The Status of Multilateral Export Control Regimes – An Examination of Legal and Non-Legal Agreements in International Co-operation* (Uppsala, Iustus Förlag 1999) pp. 269-275.

[6] I. Seidl-Hohenveldern, "International Economic Soft Law", 163 *Coll. Courses* (1979, III) pp. 207-209.

[7] I. Seidl-Hohenveldern, (note 3 *supra*) p. 72.

[8] I. Seidl-Hohenveldern/G. Loibl, *Das Recht der Internationalen Organisationen einschliesslich der Supranationalen Gemeinschaften* (Cologne, Heymanns, 6th ed. 1996) p. 320.

[9] I. Seidl-Hohenveldern, "Internationale Organisationen aufgrund von soft law" in U. Beyerlin et al. (eds), *Festschrft für Rudolf Bernhardt* (Heidelberg Springer 1995) pp.230-233.

[10] 21 November 1990, A Bloed/P. van Dijk, *The Human Dimension of the Helsinki Process* (Dordrecht Nijhoff 1991) p. 189.

OSCE/CSCXE is ensured at least by the operation of the appropriate domestic conflict of law rules. The latter determine the existence of the legal personality of an entity on the basis of its national law. The legal personality granted to CSCE/OSCE in Austria, one of its seat countries, thus would be respected also outside Austria.[12]

On the international law level the legal personality of OSCE can be implied from the part it plays in the OSCE Procedure for Peaceful Settlement of Disputes.[13] Any subsisting doubts concerning this personality[14] have been dispelled by subsequent practice.

Doubts have been cast also on the existence of the European Union (EU) as a legal person. Is the EU itself the only subject of International law exercising the competences contained in the Amsterdam Treaty,[15] does it enjoy a legal personality of its own side by side with the EC, ECSC and EAC or does it lack legal personality? The dominant view in the EC adheres to this last alternative.[16] Actually, in Amsterdam, the member-states rejected a proposal to grant legal personality to the EU as such. They thus wanted to demonstrate that their control of the two new columns of European activities added by the Maastricht Treaty (CFSP and CJHAJ, now PJCC) would remain tighter than in the supranational EC, ECSC and EAC. Yet, according to Art. 34 of the EU Treaty the EU can establish agreements in its own name. This and the power allotted to the European Council in Art 4 of the EU Treaty to act as organ of the EU appear sufficient proof for the existence of a legal personality of the EU.[17]

---

[11] Austrian Bundesgesetzblatt No. 339/1991, *Cf* I. Seidl-Hohenveldern, (note 9 *supra*) p. 139.
[12] *Cf. Arab Monetary Fund v. Hashim and Others* (No. 3) 1 *All ER* 685 (1991), 85 ILR p.1 and I. Seidl-Hohenveldern, *Ibid*, pp. 236 and 239.
[13] A. Bloed/P. Van Dijk (note 10 *supra*) p. 307 ss.
[14] Th. Schweisfurth, "Die juristische Mutation der KSZE" in U. Beyerlin *et al.* (eds.) note 9 *supra*) p. 228.
[15] See the contribution by Von Bogdandy to this book, p. 177 ss.
[16] R. Streinz, *Europarecht* (Heidelberg, C. F. Müller, 4th ed. 1999) p. 45-46.
[17] I. Seidl-Hohenveldern/T. Stein, *Völkerrecht* (10th ed., Cologne, Heymanns, 2000), p. 161, Marginal Note 802a.

PROLIFERATION WITHIN THE UN SYSTEM

When the UN were established a choice had to be made concerning its powers. Should all subject-matters requiring international co-operation be concentrated in a single monster organization or should the different matters be dealt with by Specialized Agencies, the founding member-states of the UN thus contributing to the proliferation of international organizations? The latter view prevailed – and rightly so, even from the point of view of administrative science. Whoever has worked in one of the larger national ministries, e.g. of the Interior or for Culture and Education knows that frictions and duplicate work between the several departments of such a ministry will be just as frequent as between several ministries. On the international level the concentration of all powers in a single organization would have produced the same effects. These effects would hardly have been counter-balanced by the fact that co-ordination *prima facie* appears easier to obtain within a single organization.

Thus, Special Agencies were set up under the umbrella of the United Nations. Recently, in its Advisory Opinion requested by WHO on the legality of the Use by a State of Nuclear Weapons in Armed Conflict the ICJ held that Specialized Agencies have "sectorial powers" in the field attributed to them by their member-States, whereas, by contrast, the UN itself is invested with powers of a general scope.[18] It follows therefrom that WHO is not entitled to ask an advisory opinion on this matter, as the latter does not fall within the "scope of the activities" of WHO.[19] There exists a need for better co-operation between the UN and its Specialized Agencies. It is regrettable that an important means to achieve such co-operation between the UN and its Specialized Agencies was abandoned long ago. Originally, the Specialized Agencies had to submit to the Economic and Social Council their draft budgets before they were adopted.[20] The Council thus could detect duplications and warn the Agencies to avoid them. However, nowadays, the Agencies assume that their duty to report pursuant to Art. 64 of the Charter has been

---

[18] ICJ Advisory Opinion of 8 July 1996 on the Legality of the Use by a State of Nuclear Weapons in Armed Conflict, ICJ Reports 1996, p. 80 para. 26.

[19] *Ibid.* p. 83 para. 29.

[20] H. Schermers/N.M. Blokker, *International Institutional Law* (The Hague, Nijhoff, 3rd ed. 1995) p. 1081, para 1723.

complied with, if they report on their budget after adoption, thus, when the harm has already been done.[21]

In the United Nations several functions are exercised in a semiautonomous way by entities which might just as well have been allocated to international organizations of their own, possible linked with the UN as Specialized Agencies.[22] There are several reasons behind the decision to let these entities act within the UN as such. This may have been done for reasons of economy and co-operation. UNICEF may have been too small to justify establishing it as a Specialized Agency. However it was the political will of the member-States which justified the dissolution of the International Refugee Organization and the allotment of its tasks to the UN High Commissioner for Refugees as an organ of the UN itself.[23] On the other hand, UNIDO had originally been established in 1966 as a subsidiary organ of the UN's General Assembly pursuant to Art. 22 of the Charter. In a long drawn-out process between 1975 and 1966 UNIDO was transformed into a Specialized Agency.[24] From the point of view of the Third World the creation e.g. of UNCTAD[25] as such a subsidiary organ by a simple vote in the General Assembly offered the advantage to avoid the loss of momentum which the length of the ratification process would entail and – indirectly – a guarantee of its continued existence and financing. The Western States had to support and finance this subsidiary organ out of the general UN budget. They would have been able to terminate such support only by terminating their support of the UN as such.

FLEXIBILITY

States try to avoid the creation of new organizations by incorporating more than one set of commitments in the Statutes of a single

---

[21] *Ibid.*

[22] On this topic P. Szasz, "The Complexification of the United Nations System", 3 *Max Planck Yearbook of United Nations Law* (1999) p. 5.

[23] P. Szasz, *ibid.*,p. 5.

[24] M. Hentz, "UNIDO: Umwandlung in eine Sonderorganisation der Vereinten Nationen", 34 UN (1986) pp. 106-108, K.H. Köppinger, *Der Weg der UNIDO in die Selbständigkeit*, (Thesis Cologne University 1981), I. Seidl-Hohenveldern, "Article 104" in B. Simma, *The Charter of the United Nations. A Commentary* (Oxford University Press 1995) pp. 1130-1131, Marginal Notes 24-27.

[25] M.K. Ruge, *Der Beitrag von Unctad zur Herausbildung des Entwicklungsvölkerrechts* p. 202-207.

organization. Thus, the European Patent Union (EPU) provides for an inner circle within EPU. This circle is formed by the European States who are members of the EC. The latter thereby assume obligations which are stricter than those accepted by the other member-states. In the EC, similar inner circles exist for the "Schengen regime and for the EURO Zone. The other EC member-states do not have to assume the obligations established therein. It might have been conceivable to establish these regimes as separate organizations, all the more so, since, in 1999, Iceland and Norway associated themselves with the Schengen regime. However, not only the cost factor led to the establishment of such inner circles, the lines of information, too, will be shorter and co- operation more efficient than should otherwise be the case.

States also try to increase the acceptance of international organizations by offering other flexible solutions, without establishing such an inner circle. They accept the adherence of States, although the latter do not fully comply with the rules laid down or by authorizing them to accept sterner rules, e.g. for the protection of the this treaty's aim to establish uniform conditions, e.g. for the free circulation of goods. Such flexibility, if pushed to extremes, might lead to secessions and to the establishment of rival organizations.

Human Rights may serve as an example. Here, conflicts over the values to be protected led to the establishment of different protection systems by the Council of Europe, the United Nations and several regional organizations, each of them having its own judiciary organ. Only in the very long run, there may be hope that these systems could be joined in a single one. This would pre-suppose *inter alia* that the ideological differences could be overcome which lead powerful States to reject the very idea of social human rights and even more so the guarantee of such rights by international organizations.

A warning may be sounded against the recent practice of the European Court of Human Rights to enlarge the material scope of acceptance of the Convention by simply holding reservations made by States at the moment of their adherence to the Convention no longer applicable,[26] – or, at least, by interpreting such reservations in so

---

[26] *Belilos case*, Judgment of 29 April 1988, *Publications of the European Court of Human Rights, Serie A, Judgments and Decisions*, Vol. 132 (1988), 25-2, paras 52-55 as quoted by L. Sucharipa-Behrman, "The Legal Effects of Reservations to Multilateral Conventions". 1 *Austrian Review of International and European Law* (ARIEL) (1996) p. 83.

restrictive a way that they no longer correspond to the intentions of the State having made them, – yet, binding this State to the entire text of the Convention. When this State made its reservation, adherence thereunder did enlarge the geographical scope of the protection of human rights. It seems unfair, that the other member-states had admitted the State concerned on these terms and then let the organs established by the member-states start to interpret them away. It is not surprising that the Belilos judgment led the Swiss government almost to denounce the Convention,[27] yet, it appears by now to be generally accepted.[28]

SPECIALIZATION AS A CAUSE OF PROLIFERATION

Recently it has become the fashion that States having participated in one of the world-wide conferences dealing with world-wide problems like the protection of the environment feel compelled to crown their meeting by the establishment of one or several organs to further promote the efforts achieved and to settle disputes concerning the interpretation of the commitments assumed. The States thus contribute to the proliferation of organizations. It is true that the conventions adopted by such conferences are vaguely worded. They therefore need dispute settlement organs, all the more so if they contain soft law. Soft law depends on the voluntary acceptance by the States having accepted it. The latter only will continue to obey such soft law, if there exists a formal or informal means of redress to prevent that a non-complying State does not gain an unjust advantage. There thus exists a need for follow-up entities and for dispute settlement organs, but do these tasks really have to be entrusted to new organizations? Could not follow-up measures be entrusted to the organization having, in the first place, convened the conference concerned? Could not dispute settlement be left to the ICJ, the principal judicial organ of the UN? It is unconvincing to allege that the matters concerned are so special that they should better be dealt with by a special court to be established. The subject-matters before domestic courts are wider apart than those which might arise in

---

[27] *Ibid.*
[28] B. Simma, "Reservations to Human Rights Treaties – Some Recent Developments" in G. Hafner et al. (eds.) *Liber Amicorum Ignaz Seidl-Hohenveldern* (The Hague, Kluwer, 1998) p. 671.

international relations, yet domestic law is far away from establishing a special court for every such subject-matter. Problems of venue, especially of NGO and private persons, hitherto excluded from the ICJ's jurisdiction, might be overcome just as well by modifying the venue rules of the ICJ. Seen in this light, the establishing of the Seabed Tribunal could well have been dispensed with and ILOAT and UNAT should never have been set up as separate courts.[29] The most convincing reason for the creation of new dispute-settlement instances appears to be the intention to reduce the all too heavy workload of the ICJ.

Could the temptation to create new follow-up and dispute settlement organs be reduced if we were to follow suggestions to leave the codification and progressive development of international law to the ILC? As the law stands, the latter would not be a principal law-giver of the UN as the final adoption of the texts elaborated by the ILC is left to the General Assembly. With all due respect to the efforts of the ILC we fail to notice any sizeable difference in quality between texts adopted on the basis of a report by the ILC or without such a report. In spite of a long list of topics whose codification, in theory, would appear desirable the ILC tends to hold most of them to be too politicized to reach agreement on a text even within the ILC itself, let alone in the General Assembly. The ILC therefore envisages no longer to produce draft conventions but rather guidelines in the style of the US Restatement of International Law.[30] The latter certainly would be of great scientific interest, but could hardly serve as basis for a codification conference. Having presided such a conference myself I know how much give-and-take is required to come to a text satisfactory at least to the quorum required by the conference for its adoption. As the votes of delegates to such a conference mainly will be influenced by political considerations, frankly divergent political proposals may serve as a better basis for give-and-take than the report of the independent experts of the ICJ, which, due to the very absence

---

[29] M. Lachs, "The Judiciary and the International Civil Service. Some Suggestions" in K.H. Böckstiegel *et al.* (eds.), *Festschrift für Ignaz Seidl-Hohenveldern* (Cologne, Heymanns 1988) pp. 313.

[30] G. Hafner, "Kodifikation und Weiterentwicklung des Völkerrechts" in F. Cede/L. Sucharipa-Behrmann (eds.) *Die Vereinten Nationen* (Vienna, Manz, 1999) p. 142.

of government instructions, practically may lean so much to one side as to render give-and-take extremely difficult.[31]

CO-ORDINATION

The proliferation of International Organizations has led to the necessity at least to co-ordinate their activities. A relatively simple way to do so could make use of the fact that membership in a large number of organizations, especially on the wold-wide level, is more or less identical. The member-States of these various organizations thus could co-ordinate the activities of the latter by giving to their delegates in the main organs thereof instructions to this effect. However, the States, as masters of the Treaty, may speak with different voices in organizations whose composition is more or less identical. Thus when the General Assembly of the United Nations decided to break off relations with South Africa on account of the latter's apartheid regime, some Specialized Agencies refused to follow its example. Thus, the World Meteorological Organization maintained its relations with South Africa. The representatives of the member-states in WMO were more interested in obtaining weather information from the Cape than to sanction a racist regime. Prior to World War II it would have been less likely that a State thus would have spoken with two tongues in different organizations. At that rime, relations with foreign States and international organizations had to pass through the Ministry of Foreign Affairs. The latter would let its own views and the over-all interest of the State in its foreign relations prevail over those of the Ministry competent in the special matter concerned. However, at least since Art. 33 of the Constitution of the World Health Organization (WHO)[32] authorized the WHO Secretariat to communicate directly with the Ministries of Health of the member-states, the monopoly of the Ministry of Foreign Affairs began to crumble.

---

[31] I. Seidl-Hohenveldern, "Das Wiener Übereinkommen über Staatennachfolge in Vermögen, Archive und Schulden von Staaten", 34 *Österr Zeitschrift f. öff. Recht* (1983) pp 183-190, id., "Impressions d'un President d'une Conférence de Codification des Nations Unies", in M. Medina et al. (eds). *Estudios en honor del profesor D. Antonio Truyol Serre* (Madrid, Centro de Estudios Constitucionales Universidad Complutense, 1986) pp. 1135-1137.

[32] P. J.G. Kapteyn et al. (eds.) *International Organization and Integration* (The Hague, Nijhoff 1982) Volume I B 5. A.

The need to co-ordinate the activities of the UN as such and its Specialized Agencies has led to the establishment of "Programmes" in various fields, e.g. UNEP. These Programmes co-ordinate the activities of the organizations concerned in a given field, e.g. the protection of the environment. They are established not by the member-states of the several organizations concerned but by these organizations themselves. According to the widely accepted definition of an international organization these Programmes would qualify as such organizations[33] – although, generally, they are considered as units (quasi-autonomous bodies) within the UN family.[34]

Recently, it has been suggested that organizations should co-operate and co-ordinate their activities even without any formal links, out of a spirit of "good neighbourliness".[35] Reality, helas, is far away from this ideal. Organizations try to defend their turf with utmost energy – and sometimes by strange means, according to my personal experience. When I was drafting staff rules for OEEC in 1948 I asked a colleague from UNESCO how his organization had solved a certain problem and mentioned his assistance in my draft. As state delegates to OEEC and to UNESCO frequently were the same persons this fact became known to UNESCO, who dismissed the agent concerned for having communicated this information to an outside person. In quite another context the Court of Justice of the European Communities (CJEC) rejected the plea that the courts of one organization should not sit in judgment on the acts of another organization,[36] when a Belgian Court asked for a preliminary ruling that the establishment of uniform route charges by EUROCONTROL amounted to an abuse of a dominant position. The CJEC justified this by the argument that it would be the Belgian court having asked for the preliminary ruling which thus would sit in judgment on the acts of EUROCONTROL.[37] However, as this court is bound to comply with the preliminary ruling

---

[33] I. Seidl-Hohenveldern/G. Loibl, *Das Recht der Internationalen Organisationen einschliesslich der Supranationalen Gemeinschaften* (6th ed., Cologne, Heymanns 1996) p. 4.

[34] H. Sahlmann/Blanck, "UNDP", in R. Wolfrum/C.H. Philipp (eds.) 2 *United Nations Law, Policies and Practice* (Munich, Beck 1995) p. 1289 and M. Kilian, "UNEP", *ibid.* p. 1296.

[35] See the contribution of Blokker to this book, in particular pp. 29-33.

[36] I had sustained this view in an Opinion given to EUROCONTROL.

[37] *SAT Fluggesellschaft mbH v. EUROCONTROL*; CJEC 19 January 1994) *ECR* I-43, 101 *ILR* 20, 25 and the conclusions of Advocate General G. Tesauro, *ibid.* p. 14-15.

this reasoning is just as specious as that of the inquisition handing over a heretic to the secular authorities as "the Church does not thirst for blood". It is true that after thus having assumed jurisdiction the CJEC found that the establishment of uniform route charges for air safety control was justified by this public purpose and hence did not amount to the abuse of a dominant position. We hesitate, however, to see in this finding a manifestation of the spirit of good neighbourliness. The result appeared to be inescapable given the facts of the case.

TERMINATION

By Privatization

Let us signal a development which is likely to reduce in the near future the volume of activities and possibly even the number of inter-State international organizations – the phenomenon of privatization. The existence of organizations is affected by the current trend to privatization, spreading over from the field of the domestic law of the member-states, to that of organizations. Recently, some organizations have begun to detach their commercial activities from the organizational framework, limiting the latter to main decisions of policy, Thus, INTELSAT and EMBL have established corporations under domestic or international law to pursue these commercial activities, e.g., to sell licences to pharmaceutical products discovered by the researchers of EMBL. This development is to be welcomed. It will reduce the likelihood of conflicts concerning the immunities of such organizations. These corporations, even if established under international law, will not enjoy immunity.[38] Moreover, should they go bankrupt, the member-states of the mother-organization will not be responsible for their debts.[39]

Last, but not least, the privatization of domestic public services may lead to a privatization of international organizations. Already

---

[38] I. Seidl-Hohenveldern, "Le droit applicable aux entreprises internationales communes, étatiques ou para-étatiques, 60 I *Ann IDI* (1983) p. 34ss.

[39] R. Higgins, "The legal consequences for member-states of the non-fulfilment by international organizations of their obligations towards third parties", 66 I *Ann IDI* (1995) p. 462 and the ensuing resolution of the Institute of International Law, 66 II *Ann IDI* (1995) p. 449.

now, the members of the World Tourism Organization[40] are the State Tourist Services and – as affiliate members – national and international associations working in this field. In Austria, this has created difficulties. The law authorizing the Government to grant by decree privileges and immunities to international organizations originally had defined organizations as "inter-State organizations".[41] As the World Tourism Organization was no longer properly speaking an "inter-State" organization, the law had to be amended so as to grant it privileges and immunities.[42]

Of course, participation by NGOs even in decision-making organs is no longer a novelty. It dates back to the tripartism introduced by the ILO. Let us record in this context the misgivings of States to allow NGOs a wider than the consultative status they enjoy in the UN, the Council of Europe and EC. NGOs have gained considerable political influence, mainly thanks to the internet.[43] They lobby and pressure inter-State conferences by holding meetings. Public opinion, in general, welcomes their activities. Yet, States rightly distrust the single-mindedness of the several NGOs, putting their limited interest absolute, while States have to take into account all aspects affected by the NGOs' proposals, some of which may be contrary to the public weal. Moreover, in the pursuit of their purposes, NGOs occasionally resort to questionable means. Thus the campaign against Shell on account of its intention to sink the Brent Star oil-drilling platform was based on false information.

Last, but not least, NGOs lack democratic approval. One might object that inter-State organizations also do not enjoy direct democratic approval for their decisions, although the delegates of most member-states will be responsible to a democratically elected parliament, which, thus can exercise an indirect control of the organization. Especially, the World Bank group is accused of acting undemocratically, as voting there is based on the weight of the financial participation of the several member-states. However, in a bank, it appears logical that the weight as the vote of the partners

---

[40] Austrian Bundesgesetzblatt No. 343/1976.
[41] Austrian Bundesgesetzblatt No. 56/1957.
[42] Austrian Bundesgesetzblatt No. 677/1977 in the version of Law No. 2/1997.
[43] K. Girsberger, "Entstaatlichung der friedlichen Konfliktregelung zwischen nichtstaatlichen Wirkungseinheiten: Umfang and Grenzen" and K. Boele-Woelki "internet und IPR: Wo geht jemand ins Netz?" 39 *Berichte der Deutchen Gesellschaft für Völkerrecht* (Heidelberg, C.F. Müller, 2000) pp. 231-265 and pp. 307-346 respectively.

thereof, when adopting policy decisions, will correspond to the individual risk incurred by each of them. The Third World asks for the "democratization" of this procedure, meaning thereby a vote on the basis of "one State, one vote". However, how democratic is a system, where the vote of Nauru has the same weight as the vote of India?[44]

Within a foreseeable future, privatization may lead to the disappearance of the State, at least in the field of the activities of some international organizations, whose activities on the domestic level have been privatized. We think especially of the Universal Postal Union (UPU), but the first steps in this direction have already been made in the field of the international organizations for telecommunication by satellites.[45] At present, it is still an inter-State organization, the member-States being represented by delegates chosen and instructed by the Ministry which, on the domestic level, acts as the supreme supervisory authority of the now privatized postal service. However, do these State authorities have adequate powers to co-ordinate the activities of the several private firms, acting moreover in the territory of more than one State? Yet, the very purpose of the UPU is to co-ordinate postal activities across national borders. Each of the multinational firms running or scheduled to run postal services in more than one country will co-ordinate its own services according to its own ends. But who is to co-ordinate the activities of the several multi-national postal firms – a co-ordination required to ensure international uniform postal services of the same quality as at the time, when States did establish the UPU. As likely as not, these firms will enter into a cartel agreement and the several States would be ill-advised were they to attempt to break it up. Thus, at least in part, the history of international organizations has come to a full circle, as the predecessors of the several commodity agreements had been international cartels[46] and the predecessor of the World Tourism Organization was an NGO.[47]

---

[44] Seidl-Hohenveldern, *International Economic Law* (The Hague, Kluwer, 3rd ed. 1999) p. 82.

[45] L. Ravillon, "Les organisations internationales de télécommunications par satellites: Vers une privatisation?", 44 Ann. Fr. Dr. Int. (1998), p. 544 ss.

[46] I. Seidl-Hohenveldern, *ibid.* p. 4 e.g., The International Tin Cartel and the Tin Producers' Association, A. Weber, *Geschichte der Internationalen Wirtschaftsorganisationen*, (Stuttgart, Franz Steiner, 1983) p. 54-55 and 94.

[47] J. Castaneda, "Une nouvelle méthode pour la création d'organismes internationaux-le cas récent de l'UIOOT" *AFDI* 1970, p.p. 625 ss.

Dissolution by the Member States

Once established, international organizations try to continue their existence at almost any price. Thus, OEEC changed its object and name and increased the geographic scope of its membership to a considerable extent. UNIDO and EAC appear to have outlived their utility. If WTO really succeeds in finding satisfactory solutions to all the problems falling in its competence, the utility of OECD and of UNCTAD likewise may become questionable. There certainly exists a certain interest for free-trade economy States and for Third World States respectively to co-ordinate the attitude of the respective group of States in WTO – but do they need to maintain international organizations for this purpose? Yet, it will prove very difficult to overcome the inertia opposing all changes and the vested interest of the secretarial of organizations threatened with dissolution.

It is evident, that member-states if they really want to put an end to some instances of proliferation, have the power to do so. As the member-States are the masters of the Treaty, no remedy would be open to an international organization, if its member-states should decide to dissolve it or to merge it with another organization It has often been suggested to dissolve the EAC and to attribute its competences to the EEC. Art. 17 of the European Union Treaty appears to envisage in the long run not only to avail itself of the WEU, but to merge the WEU with the EU.

An outright dissolution of an organization will be rare. Member-States rather will use the power of the purse to dry out an organization in whose existence they are no longer interested. At present, especially the United States insist on strict economies in the field of international co-operation by means of international organizations. It will remain to be seen, whether the misgivings about the proliferation of organizations mentioned in the present text, especially the apprehension of waste of scarce resources by overlapping, will win the day or whether a better co-ordination of the activities of the several organizations will prove sufficient. A need for further specialization may lead even in future to the creation of new organization, although such specialization may not always justify such a step. The creation of quasi-autonomous bodies within an organization or a flexibility of the structures of an organization may prove sufficient. Be that as it may be, the decision always will be up to the member-States.

CO-ORDINATION BETWEEN UNIVERSAL AND REGIONAL ORGANIZATIONS

Christian Dominicé *

INTRODUCTION

The proliferation, or, if this word sounds pejorative, the multiplication of international governmental organizations is, to a large extent, the result of a tension between, on the one hand, the basic principle of State sovereignty as main feature of the international society, and, on the other hand, the evident awareness that many fundamental problems facing governments today cannot be dealt with within the border of each single State acting alone.[1]

As a consequence, the principles of speciality and voluntarism are predominant. They certainly contribute to amplify the phenomenon of multiplication.

As to the first, it is obvious that there are very few "general" organizations, with a broad field of activities. Most international organizations are "sectorial", with a narrow field of activity. Due to the evolution and development of various social, economic, scientific factors, the need to create new organizations, in new fields, does not cease to exist, but there is now a certain sense of restraint.

Regarding the principle of voluntarism, which means that each State is free to become a member of an organization or not, we can see that there is, as far as membership is concerned, a great variety of organizations, created according to the specific interest of States.

Those trends are not likely to show significant modifications in the near future because the international society will not undergo spectacular changes. In some parts of the world regional groupings may take up an increasing role through integration processes involving several States, but those States will not disappear as such.

---

*   Honorary Professor at the University of Geneva.
[1] *Cf.* H.G Schermers and N. M. Blokker, *International Institutional Law* (3rd ed. 1995), p. 4 (para. 8).

It is probably accurate to say that we will continue to face, in the years to come, a great number and a vast diversity of international organizations.

It is within this context that the question of co-ordination between universal and regional organizations will be considered.[2]

The very notion of co-ordination is to be understood broadly. We must address first the question of the relationship in general between those two types of organizations, and then we may consider whether co-ordination could mean rationalization through a sensible division of tasks, for example.

It is evident that each single universal or regional organization could have much to say about all kinds of relationships and co-ordination procedures in the perspective which is here considered.

The purpose of this short paper is however to focus on the main characteristics of the universal-regional dimension.

GENERAL ASPECTS OF THE UNIVERSAL-REGIONAL DIMENSION

Main Categories of Organizations

In every classification of international organizations, the distinction between universal and regional organizations is presented as particularly important.[3]

In fact, most organizations belong to one of those categories, even if there is a variety of partial, sectorial, non regional organizations. Therefore, the question of the relationship between them is of great interest.

First question, is there any kind of subordination? In a federal State, the composing units are subordinated to the federal (central) authorities. This is a consequence of the fact that a federal structure is a particular way of dealing with internal territorial sovereignty and

---

[2] Cf. M. Virally, Les relations entre organisations régionales et organisations universelles, in *Régionalisme et universalisme dans le droit international contemporain*, Société française pour le droit international (Colloque de Bordeaux, 1976), Pedone, 1977, p. 147.

[3] Cf. M. Virally, Définition et classification des organisations internationales : approche juridique, in *Le concept d'organisation internationale* (G. Abi-Saab, ed.), 1980, p. 51 ; H.G. Schermers and N.M. Blokker, *op.cit.* (n. 1), p. 33.

competences. The "public power" (puissance publique), which does exist as inherent attribute and characteristic of a State, is structured and organized in a specific way, according to the principle of federalism.

On the international sphere, there is no such exclusive public power with territorial sovereignty.

The various organizations, both universal and regional, are created by autonomous international treaties, independently of each other. There only exists a legal link of subordination – in a true "vertical" dimension – when there is a specific treaty provision to that effect, but otherwise the distinction universal - regional has merely a geographical meaning indicating that the universal organization is dealing with the whole world, whereas the regional one has merely a geographically limited field of action. Both are, in international law, on the same footing as autonomous entities without territorial sovereignty.

However, there are questions which deserve consideration: Is there a point in suggesting a kind of a horizontal division of tasks and fields of action ("universal matters" versus "regional matters")?

Would it be advisable that regional organizations, in certain fields, would accept by convention obligations towards universal organizations?

These questions are among those which may be kept in mind when the actual practice is under scrutiny. Both categories of organizations must be first shortly identified.

Universal Organizations

Universal organizations are those which do not necessarily have all States as their members, but which may be open to all States. They can be said to have "vocation" to attract all States, and this indicates that they have a field of action which makes it necessary, or at least desirable, that all States should be bound by the same obligations and invited to cooperate within the same framework.

There are of course differences between those organizations.

For example, not all of them, although described as universal, are easy to adhere to. A State which is a Member of the United Nations can become a Member of the International Labour Organizations very easily, by unilateral declaration[4], but on the other hand to become a member of the World Bank, the International Monetary Fund or the World Trade Organization requires negotiations which may be very

---

[4] Constitution of the International Labour Organization, art. 1,3.

hard, and acceptance by other Members. For years, China has been behind the door of WTO and there are still problems to be solved before that country can be admitted as full Member.

The main difference, however, is between *general or global*, on the one hand, and on the other hand, *sectorial* organizations.[5]

There is only one general organization, the Organization of the United Nations, which can deal with a very broad field of matters, including the highly political question of peace and security, or social and economic matters. To have a broad field of activities does not mean to have much power, but the qualification general or global is justified by the competence *ratione materiae*.[6] It can be stressed nevertheless that the notion is not merely quantitative. The main feature is the political role in the field of peace and security.

The other universal organizations are *sectorial*, each of them having a limited, specialized field of action.

It is estimated that there are 35-50 universal governmental organizations,[7] depending on how they are counted. For example, the World Bank may be counted for several organizations, because of its subsidiaries with independent legal personality.

The whole of governmental organizations is estimated at approximately 350 ; this indicates that the universal organizations constitute a relatively small part of them.[8]

Among the universal organizations, the striking feature is however the great variety of sectorial organizations. Of course, some of them are particularly important: the specialized agencies of the UN system, WTO, and some others. There are also less important organizations. The fact is that we can observe a vertical division of matters.

In federal States the vertical division corresponds, on the central level, to the general division according to the functions (legislative, executive, judiciary) of a Public Power. On the universal level of international organizations, the division however is according to fields of action, or competences *ratione materiae*.

---

[5] H. G. Schermers and N. M. Blokker, *op.cit.*(n. 1), p. 43.

[6] *A contrario* there is the limited competence *ratione materiae* of a sectorial organization, such as WHO, *cf. Legality of the Use by a State of Nuclear Weapons in Armed Conflict*, Advisory Opinion, ICJ Reports, p. 66, ad para. 25.

[7] *Yearbook of International Organizations*, vol. 3, 1999-2000, p. 1636.

[8] *Eod. loc.*

Since membership may vary – not all universal organizations being universal in their membership – the general picture of institutionalized co-operation at world level is very heterogenous.

REGIONAL ORGANIZATIONS

Governmental organizations are in large majority organizations with limited membership. They may be called either "closed" organizations (as proposed by *Professor Schermers*)[9] or otherwise (*Virally* says "organisations partielles").[10]

The geographical factor is present in many of them, although some specific organizations are based on another criterion (the Organization of Petroleum Exporting Countries - OPEC). The geographical factor is predominant in such organizations as the Organization of American States (OAS), the Organization of African Unity (OAU), the Council of Europe, or the European Union (EU), or even the League of Arab States. Besides those rather general, or partially general, organizations, sectorial regional organizations exist, which facilitate co-operation between States of the same region.

On this aspect, it can be observed that on the regional level there are few really general organizations. Apart from OAS and OAU, none of them has general competences, the EU being a special case.

There are important organizations of course, but with sectorial objectives: ESA, the various free trade areas, etc.

It can be observed simultaneously that the only general and partial organizations are regional ones.

However, there are organizations which appear to be regional, because they are composed mainly of States of the same region, but which are not exclusively regional. The Organization for Security and Co-operation in Europe (OSCE) has Members which are not European.

The case of NATO is a special one[11], because that organization has claimed for long not to be a regional organization but a collective self-defence organization based upon article 51 of the UN Charter, in order to avoid the application of Chapter VIII. Recently, however, NATO

---

[9] H. G. Schermers and N. M. Blokker, *op.cit.* (n. 1), p. 37.
[10] M. Virally, *loc.cit.* (n. 3), p. 61.
[11] *Cf.* R. Higgins, Some thoughts on the evolving relationship between the Security Council and NATO, Boutros Boutros-Ghali *Amicorum Discipulorumque Liber*, Bruxelles, 1998, p. 511.

has been considered, for functional purposes, to be a regional organization, although it is not exclusively regional.

It must be observed that those atypical organizations are mainly active in the fields of peace and security, and that Chapter VIII, which deals precisely with maintenance of peace and security, refers to "regional arrangements or agencies", which is broader than "regional organization".

The *Agenda for peace* presents also a particularly broad notion of regional organizations.[12]

Therefore, for several reasons, in the discussion of the relations between universal and regional organizations, it is appropriate to make a distinction between "ordinary relations" and the special field of maintenance of peace and security.

PERMANENT RELATIONS

Preliminary Observations

By "permanent relations" we mean merely that we are dealing here with ordinary or day-to-day work of international organizations (the question of the maintenance of peace and security being discussed later).

In the analysis of relations between universal and regional organizations, co-ordination must be understood here in a rather broad meaning. There may be conflicts, possibly subordination, co-ordination under various forms.[13]

Three main structures will be considered: hierarchy, participation, and co-ordination procedures.

This vast and complex field of relations must be understood within the context of present day international law based upon State sovereignty.

As already indicated, there is no analogy with federal structures and principles in constitutional law. It might be that in a distant future, an harmonious and appropriate construction of the international

---

[12] *An Agenda for Peace*, 1992 (A/47/277-S 2 4111) stresses in Chapter VII the importance of the co-operation with regional arrangements and organizations and includes even in that category the "Friends of the Secretary General", 31 ILM (1992) 970.

[13] See M. Virally, *loc. cit.* (n. 2), p. 154.

community, or world society, could be based upon a kind of a confederation of regions, continents or sub-continents. At present, regional organizations, which are functional and based on the free participation of sovereign States, cannot be compared with composing units of confederations.

In general terms, it cannot be observed that a legal subordination is actually established between universal and regional organizations.

It is clear that when the Member States of a regional organization are also Members of a universal organization, they are bound by the obligations resulting from that latter membership, and consequently the regional organization is also bound. Depending on the constitution or Charter of the universal organization, primacy may be given to its law (as stipulated in article 103 of the UN Charter), but the power to give orders or impose new obligations is very limited, when it does exist, and it is directed towards Member States.

HIERARCHY

At least in theory, it could be possible to think of a hierarchy between universal and regional organizations. For reasons already indicated, this is not the case.

Naturally, but this is something different, inside one organization, a hierarchy of organs may be instituted. When decentralization is desirable, regional commissions or offices can be created. Within the UN, for example, the regional economic commissions have been very useful, but they are organs of the UN. The same can be said of the regional offices of ILO.

In the case of WHO, there are regional organizations, with independent legal personality. They are integral parts of WHO (art. 45 of the Constitution).[14]

The World Bank also has subordinated entities (IFC, IDA, MIGA) with autonomous international personality.

An interesting example is that of the International Telecommunication Union. Here, we have an institution dealing with a matter which is of evident concern to each single country and where co-operation is needed. Closer co-operation between countries of the same

---

[14] *Cf.* Y. Beigbeder, L'Organisation mondiale de la Santé, PUF "Que Sais-je ?", 1997 ; for an example of a Regional Office, see the Advisory Opinion of the ICJ : *Interpretation of the Agreement of 25 March 1951 between the WHO and Egypt*, Advisory Opinion, I.C.J. Reports 1980, p. 73.

region seems also to be self-evident. One could think of a hierarchy of institutions.

Actually, the Constitution of ITU refers several times to regional organizations.[15]

But there are no changes to the general features we have already met: the members of ITU are States, the regional organizations are bound by the rules of the organization only through their Member States, and between universal and regional level there is mutual information and co-operation.

As a brief conclusion, it can be observed that unless a universal organization creates its own regional entities, there is no hierarchical power between universal and regional organizations, with the exception of the powers of the Security Council according to Chapter VII and VIII of the UN Charter.

PARTICIPATION

A particular type of "vertical" relation exists when a regional organization is accepted as full member of a universal organization.

Sometimes, the term "participation" is used to cover also the situation where observer status is granted to a regional organization.[16] That situation is considered later. Here, the notion of participation is limited to membership.

According to art. XI of the Constitution of the World Trade Organization of 1994, the European Communities are recognized among the original Members of the Organization. This can be understood because most of the competences which are relevant to the rules and activities of GATT/WTO are now competences of the Communities. Therefore the European Commission is entitled to speak and negotiate on behalf of the Communities and the Member States.

It is of interest to note that the Member States (today fifteen) are still members of WTO. There is here a case of parallel membership of a regional organization and its members. When there is a vote (the

---

[15] See art. 21,2 c) "enhance the growth of telecommunications through co-operation with regional telecommunications organizations ..." ; art. 43 : "Members reserve the right to convene regional conferences, to make regional arrangements and to form regional organizations, for the purpose of settling telecommunication questions which are susceptible of being treated on a regional basis". There are various other references in other acts.

[16] *Cf.* For example J.P. Jacqué, *La participation de la CEE aux organisations internationales universelles*, AFDI, 1975, p. 924.

consensus being the rule at WTO), each member of the WTO shall have one vote: "where the European Communities exercise their right to vote, they shall have a number of votes equal to the number of their member States which are Members of the WTO" (art. IX, 1 of the WTO Constitution).[17]

Such a parallel participation as a Member exists also with FAO.[18]

In some other cases, the Communities alone are Members of the Organisation, for example in the Sugar Council.[19]

The nature of the participation of the regional organization as a Member of a universal organization will vary depending on the role and activities of the latter.

In the case of WTO, the organization is administering a set of rules, a code on commercial relations, and constitutes simultaneously a framework for permanent negotiations and settlement of disputes. The participation of a Member to the work within the Organization is different from what it is within an organization the activities of which are more operational and imply co-operation for the execution of projects.

The interesting thing to note here is the substitution which occurs when a regional organization takes the place of its member States.

In WTO, customs unions according to art. XXIV of GATT, if based upon a treaty giving supranational competence to common institutions, may lead to such a substitution.

OTHER TYPES OF RELATIONS

As a preliminary remark, it can be said that co-ordination is better established and easier to observe in horizontal relations: For example within the UN system, on the universal level, or on the regional level. It

---

[17] A note to art. IX reads : "The number of votes of the European Communities and their member States shall in no case exceed the number of the member States of the European Communities".

[18] *Cf.* J. Sack, The European Community's Membership of International Organizations, 32 *Common Market Law Review* (1995), p. 1227 : *Cf.* R. Frid, The Relations between the EC and International Organizations (1995). The Constitution of FAO was amended in 1991 for that purpose. There is also a parallel membership in some closed organizations such as EBRD.

[19] Also : Olive Oil Agreement, Coffee Agreement as well as Fisheries Organizations (*cf.* R. Frid, *op.cit.*, n. 18, Chap. 7).

is evident that overlaps must be avoided, that joint projects need close co-operation, etc.[20]

In the vertical dimension, the problem is different.[21]

In specialized or technical fields, such as those administered by the specialized agencies of the UN system, the universal organization has very often a normative function, which is not the only one but which is important. The organization is used to deal with its Member States, both at the preliminary phase of consultations and negotiation, and at the phase of implementation of rules, standards, or even conventions adopted within the organization (ILO). Regional organizations do not take the place of Member States.[22] They want to be associated, if not to the implementation, which generally rests with the States, at least to the elaboration of norms and standards. Thus, the main form of co-ordination or co-operation is participation short of membership, with observer status in various organs. The ITU, for example, has extensive contacts with many regional organizations associated informally to the work of subsidiary organs.

Apart from that type of marginal participation with observer status, which is frequent, the agreement is the instrument which can be used. It is difficult to get a comprehensive picture of the various agreements, protocols, memoranda of understanding, concluded by regional organizations. The European Communities, certainly constitute a special case, due to their competences in external relations. In general terms, it is for the purpose of achieving joint operations that agreements are resorted to. As an example, on 24 August 1999, a Memorandum of Understanding was concluded between the International Labour Organization and the Pan-American Health Organization "so support Latin America and Caribbean countries in the extension of social protection in health to excluded populations".[23]

---

[20] For the "UN family", see particularly H. G. Schermers and Niels M. Blokker, *op.cit.* (n. 1) at 1057 : S. Bastid, *Sur quelques problèmes juridiques de coordination dans la famille des Nations Unies*, Mélanges Reuter, Paris, 1981, p. 75.

[21] *Cf.* J.P. Cot, La Communauté européenne, l'Union européenne et l'organisation des Nations Unies, Boutros Boutros-Ghali *Amicorum Discipulorumque Liber*, Bruxelles, 1998, p. 327 ; see also the articles by R. Frid (n. 18) and J.P. Jacqué (n. 16).

[22] In spite of the introduction of the European common currency, Members of the IMF remain the States, *cf.* J.P. Cot, *loc.cit.* (n. 21), p. 344.

[23] This Memorandum entered into force upon tis signature. Kindly communicated by the ILO in Geneva.

Summary

The basic structure is still the relations between the universal organization and its Member States. They have the power and they are the contributors.

Regional organizations, although their role may be very useful for their Member States, are marginal actors.

Things change, and there is an evolution, when a regional organization has supra-national competences and can become a member of a universal organization.

The EU/EC is a major actor in WTO.

When and where this is going to occur in other regions of the world is still to be seen.

MAINTENANCE OF PEACE AND SECURITY

Peaceful Settlement of Local Disputes

General remarks
In their broadest meaning, peaceful actions include measures aiming at preventing disputes, suggestions and help for a settlement, as well as co-operation in the process of reconstruction after a crisis and fighting. Peacekeeping with troops, if based on the consent of the States concerned, is also included within this notion.

At first sight, it may seem evident that every action or measure which can contribute to preventing or appeasing a conflict involving States belonging to the same region should be dealt with at the regional level. Proximity, common cultural values, are factors which should facilitate peaceful procedures. Reality is different. As shown by practice, regional organizations have often been unable to handle local disputes.[24] Furthermore there is not always a regional organization available. The global regional organizations are really very few.

In a field where flexibility is certainly needed, the final aim being the settlement of a dispute, it is not possible to find very firm guidance in practice. The interpretation of article 52 of the Charter of the UN is not settled on some points, for example the meaning of "regional

---

[24] *Cf.* R. Higgins, *loc.cit.*(note 11), p. 520-521.

arrangements" or "local disputes".²⁵ But is it true that the problem is not primarily legal.

Some general aspects of the question may be pointed out, but before that, it can be observed that, for various reasons, including legal ones, there is a difference between two situations: first, when the States involved in a conflict are members of the regional organization concerned ; second when there is a conflict concerning one or several States outside the organization. The former situation is first considered here, and some observations will be presented on the latter.

Priority of regional mechanisms

Article 52 must be read as indicating that regional mechanisms, when available, are to be used first. It is the role of regional organizations and arrangements competent to deal with a conflict to take the initiative and to offer a framework for prevention and settlement.

This would be in line with article 33 of the Charter as well as with several statements and resolutions, including chap. VII of the *Agenda for peace* presented by Secretary General Boutros-Ghali in 1992.

It is also to be hoped that in the long run conflicts can be solved at the regional level in a kind of an institutionalization of the world based upon regional structures.

For the time being, we must observe that, in spite of some improvements, much is still to be done to develop the presence and the efficiency of regional arrangements and agencies.²⁶

Therefore the role of the Security Council under Chapter VI of the Charter remains important, both because of the failure of the regional agencies, and as an expression of the system of the Charter.

---

[25] *Cf.* J. Cardona Llorens. La coopération entre les Nations Unies et les accords et organismes régionaux pour le règlement pacifique des affaires relatives au maintien de la paix et de la sécurité internationales, in Boutros Boutros-Ghali *Amicorum Discipulorumque Liber*, Bruxelles, 1998, p. 251, at 253 ; U. Beyerlin, *Regional Arrangements*, in R. Wolfrum, *UN Laws, Politics, Practices*, 2 vol, Nijhoff, 1995, vol. 2, p. 1040 ; J.P. Cot et H. Pellet, La Charte des Nations Unies, 1991, art. 52 (E. Kodjo), p. 795 ; B. Simma ed., *The Charter of the United Nations. A Commentary*, 1994, art. 52 (M. Schweizer), p. 679.

[26] See particularly C. Gray, *Regional Arrangements and the United Nations Collective Security System*, in H. Fox ed., *The Changing Constitution of the United Nations*, 1997, p. 91 ; B. Rivlin, *Regional Arrangements and the UN System for Collective Security*, in *International Relations*, 1992, p. 96 ; R. Wolfrum, *Der Beitrag regionaler Abmachungen zur Friedenssicherung ; Möglichkeiten und Grenzen*, 53 ZaöRVR (1993), 603.

Security Council

The Security Council is not only a substitute when a regional agency is unable to handle a dispute. It can be requested to consider a dispute which has been referred to a regional agency.

Article 52, par. 4 is explicit concerning the application of articles 34 and 35 of the Charter.

However, a distinction must be made between these procedural aspects and the question as to whether or not the Security Council should deal with the merit of the dispute. In certain cases, the Security Council, after considering the dispute, may leave it to the regional organization for settlement, or even recommend such a course of action. It has been done in several instances, particularly in Latin-American cases.[27] This is in accordance with par. 3 of article 52 of the Charter.

Apart from those legal aspects, and setting aside the disputes in respect of which it is appropriate for the Security Council to leave the matter to be settled by a regional organization, it must be stressed that co-operation and co-ordination are much to be preferred to competition about competences.

As pointed out by Secretary General Boutros-Ghali in his *Agenda for Peace* several examples can be shown of such common efforts.[28]

Such common action may take place at any stage of a conflict, from the very first stage of prevention until the ultimate phase of reconstruction.

Disputes involving non-member States of a regional organization

Article 52 of the Charter deals with the situation where the parties to a dispute are members of the same organization. This is particularly clear in par. 2 which requests the States concerned "to make every effort to achieve pacific settlement".

The question may be asked of the role of regional organizations in other situations.

---

[27] *Cf.* M. Schweizer, *loc.cit.* (n. 25), p. 699 : A. Le Roy Bennet, *International Organizations*, 5th ed 1991, p. 219.

[28] See 31 ILM 970 (1992) : Somalia, Cambodia, El Salvador, Nicaragua, the Balkans. See also P.M. Dupuy, Le maintien de la paix, in René-Jean Dupuy éd., *Manuel sur les organisations internationales*, 2ème éd., 1998, p. 563, particulièrement Par. 4. L'action des organisations régionales en faveur du maintien de la paix, p. 598, which gives examples of co-operation between the UN and regional organizations.

Theoretically, it is possible to think of a dispute between one member of a regional organization and a third State, between outside States (the ex-Yugoslav States after the secession of some of them), or even of an internal conflict within a third State, such as the Kosovo crisis.

Such situations do not fall under the provisions of Article 52, but it is evident that they may be of great concern for a regional organization with geographical proximity. The European Community, then European Union, has been and still is an active participant in the search for a settlement of the crisis in the Balkans. The example of the Arbitration Commission (Commission Badinter), illustrates this type of action.[29]

Every kind of diplomatic or other type of action which is available for the member States of the organization can be resorted to by the latter. Because of the political weight which an important regional organization may have, the impact of its action is likely to be stronger.

The forms of co-ordination with UN actions depend on the circumstances.

This is also and particularly true when a peace-keeping operation is decided: in the case of Yugoslavia and the ex-Yugoslavia it has been seen that the UN and regional organizations acted simultaneously and in co-ordination even before the use of force was decided.[30]

ENFORCEMENT ACTIONS

Article 53 of the UN Charter

The first two sentences of Article 53 are relevant here. They read as follows: "The Security Council shall, where appropriate, utilize such regional arrangements or agencies for enforcement action under its authority. But no enforcement action shall be taken under regional arrangements or by regional agencies without the authorization of the Security Council".

---

[29] The Arbitration Commission (Commission Badinter) was created in 1991 on the initiative of the European Communities, see A. Pellet, Note sur la Commission d'arbitrage de la Conférence européenne pour la paix en Yougoslavie, *AFDI* 1991, p. 329. The Commission delivered important opinions on legal aspects of the Yugoslav conflict. They are analyzed in Pellet's article.

[30] See for example. Res. 713(1991) and 743 (1992) of the Security Council.

That provision is in accordance with the philosophy underlying the system of the Charter, which is to centralize the power to take coercive measures.

However, article 53 is to be understood and applied within the context of present day international society, the main features of which being that economic measures can only be implemented by States, even when acting collectively within a regional organization, and that the UN has no autonomous military forces available for the Security Council to take action under article 42 of the Charter.

The main aspects to be considered are (i) the right of the Security Council to "utilize" regional arrangements or agencies, and (ii) the meaning of the "authorization" which the regional organizations must obtain from the Security Council in order to act legally when taking the initiative of enforcement actions.

Action by the Security Council.

The Security Council shall "utilize" regional arrangements or agencies. What does it mean? The answer to that question may be summarized in a few basic principles:

(i) It is clear that art. 53,1 does not confer additional authority on the Security Council. It can only act within the competences given to it by Chapter VII.[31]

(ii) When the Security Council has the power to impose duties upon States, this applies also to organizations – including regional organizations – when their members are members of the United Nations. Whatever the distribution of power within an organization, the measures ordered by the Security Council must be given effect. Thus, if non military measures are to be included within the meaning of enforcement action in article 53, the Security Council can involve regional organizations when ordering measures in accordance with article 41 of the Charter.[32]

(iii) The main problem is with military measures. The Security Council has the power to take action on the basis of article 42, but provided military means are made available, which is not the case. On the other hand, it cannot impose on Member States to take military action.

---

[31] *Cf.* G. Ress, Commentary of art. 53, B. Simma ed., *op.cit.* (n. 25), p. 730.
[32] *Cf.* for example Res. 757 (1992), art. 10-11.

However, according to a substantial practice, the Security Council can authorize States to take military action. The purpose of such an action must be clearly stated, and the control of the Security Council must be maintained.[33]

Such an authorization can also be given to a regional arrangement or agency, as illustrated by Resolution 836 in the Bosnian crisis, but the Member States remain at the heart of the authorization. Par. 10 of Res. 836 (1993) reads:

...

"10. *Decides* that, ..., Member States, acting nationally or through regional organizations or arrangements, can take, under the authority of the Security Council and subject to close co-ordination with the Secretary-General and the United Nations Protection Force (UNPROFOR) all necessary measures, through the use of air power, in and around the safe areas in the Republic of Bosnia and Herzegovina, to support the Force in the performance of its mandate set out in paragraphs 5 and 9 above ; "

This can be considered as a case of implementation of Chapter VIII. It should be recalled that such an authorization is permissive but not mandatory. On the other hand, the "dual key" approach used in the case of Bosnia and Herzegovina shows that control, or even co-decision, can remain in the hand of the UN.

This problem of control is a major one when the authorization to use force, often qualified as "delegation", is given to a regional organization.[34] Depending on the circumstances, the focus and modalities of co-operation or co-ordination with the Security Council, through the Secretary General, may be organized in various ways. It is important that clear procedures should be instituted.

Action taken by a regional organization

It might well be that when the Charter was drafted, more was expected to be achieved by regional arrangements or agencies to maintain peace and security in particular areas. But it was clear from the outset that any

---

[33] Res. 678 (1990) in the Gulf crisis is the first of a series of resolutions, in various conflicts and situations, authorizing the use of force.

[34] *Cf.* D. Sarooshi, The United Nations and the development of collective security, Oxford, 1999, particularly p. 83 f. : D. Momtaz, La délégation par le Conseil de Sécurité de l'exécution de ses actions coercitives aux organisations régionales, *AFDI* 1997, p. 105.

enforcement action should be under the control of the Security Council as stated in article 53, second sentence.

a. As far as military enforcement is concerned, the question is: what type of military action is subject to article 53, and are there exceptions? Briefly summarized, three observations may be presented:
   (i) First, there are military actions which are not "enforcement actions", because they are not taken against the will of a State.[35] For example, in the conflict in Liberia, the military intervention decided by ECOWAS (Economic Community of West African States) was officially made on the basis of an invitation by the legal authorities. Although not any kind of invitation can be accepted as appropriate basis for intervention, in that particular case it seems that it was accepted.[36]
   (ii) Enforcement actions must be authorized by the Security Council. Apparently, this applies also to auxiliary military measures. When the embargo against Yugoslavia was ordered (Res. 713 (1991) and 757 (1992)), NATO and WEU ordered their navy to watch commercial shipping in the Adriatic sea, but it was not until an authorization had been given by the Security Council that they were able to inspect and verify cargoes and destinations of maritime shipping (Res. 787 (1992)).[37]
   (iii) The third observation concerns a question which is particularly acute after the military intervention of NATO in the Kosovo crisis during last spring. Is there an exception to article 53 in case of humanitarian emergency of large amplitude with respect to which, however, the Security Council refuses to act?

By its action, the Security Council has shown in several occasions that situations characterized by grave and large scale violations of human rights, or substantial violations of humanitarian law in internal conflicts, must be considered as a threat to the peace, therefore

---

[35] *Certain expenses of the United Nations*, Advisory Opinion of 20 July 1962, ICJ Reports 1962, p. 151 at 177.

[36] *Cf.* G. Nolte, *International Legal Aspects of the Liberian Conflict*, 53 ZaöRVR (1993), p. 603 ; U. Beyerlin, *loc.cit.* (n. 25), p. 1047 ; C. Gray, *loc.cit.* (n. 26), p. 101.

[37] Res. 787 (1992), par. 12 : "Acting under Chapters VII and VIII of the Charter of the United Nations, [the Security Council] calls upon States, acting nationally or through regional agencies or arrangements, to use such measures commensurate with the specific circumstances as may be necessary under the authority of the Security Council to halt all inward and outward maritime shipping in order to inspect and verify their cargoes and destinations and to ensure strict implementation of the provisions of resolutions 713 (1991) and 757 (1992)".

justifying various measures including enforcement actions. Then, when in a clear situation of humanitarian emergency, the Security Council refuses to act, there is an argument for allowing an action by a regional arrangement. On the other hand, that doctrine could open the door to abuses. The question is controversial.[38]

b. Turning now to non-military enforcement action, we make two short observations.

(i) There is a controversy on the question whether "enforcement action" in the meaning of article 53 includes non-military measures. The answer appears to be in the affirmative if the text is read in its context, taking into account Chapter VII of the Charter.

On the other hand, it has been contended in the cases of the Dominican Republic and Grenada that Article 53 does not apply to non military measures. The Security Council did not react.[39]

It seems reasonable to consider that when a regional organization is able to restore peace and security within its own field of operation by taking non-military action directed at one of its members, there is no reason for the Security Council's intervention. But, of course, certain types of measures can only have effect if also applied by third States, and this makes necessary a request to the Security Council to act under article 41 of the Charter (ex.: the case of Liberia, Res. 788 (1992)).

(ii) On the other hand, if a regional organization wishes to take action against third States, an authorization by the Security Council, in accordance with article 53 of the Charter, is needed.

Here again, the question may be raised if a unilateral action – *i.e.* without prior authorization of the Security Council – can be taken when a State is seriously violating obligations *erga omnes* or rules of *ius cogens*. According to present day customary international law, the States are allowed to take unilateral action in such cases. *A fortiori* that right can be invoked by States acting collectively through a regional organization.

---

[38] *Cf.* J. A. Frowein, Legal Consequences for International Law Enforcement in Case of Security Council Inaction, in J. Delbrück ed., *The Future of International Law Enforcement*, Berlin 1993, p. 111.

[39] *Cf.* G. Ress, Commentary of Art. 53, in Simma ed (n. 25), p. 732.

Summary

With the question of maintenance of peace and security, we are considering a field of particular political importance where pragmatism is the main characteristic.

Regional organizations which have the competence and the political strength to deal with the prevention and settlement of conflicts are few, and they are not present everywhere.

The role they have played so far is not very encouraging, but it is possible to observe a trend, for example in Africa and in Latin America, towards a more positive action and influence of regional organizations.

Perhaps the more striking recent phenomenon is the common action or combination of efforts between the UN and regional organizations to deal with a crisis. This type of co-ordination between universal and regional level is to be fostered.[40]

CONCLUSIONS

The distinction between permanent relations and the specific problem of maintenance of peace and security seems to correspond to two very different sets of relations.

Universal organizations are working – but for the UN – in specialized fields. They aim generally – but not all of them – at developing uniform rules and standards. This is in line with international law, which is a legal order composed of rules of universal validity, very few of them being local or regional.

The main actors of the normative process, even within international organizations, are States. They contribute to the creation of new rules, and they are responsible for implementing them.

In such a framework, the role of regional organizations remains modest. It can be important on the regional level, as illustrated by the substantial work of the Council of Europe to foster co-operation in the legal field, but this does not imply that the regional organizations are important actors within universal organizations.

The normative process is an interaction between States and the Organizations (ILO, ITU, WMO, WHO, WTO, etc.), with the

---

[40] *Cf.* Resolution 49/57 (9 December 1994) of the UN General Assembly: "Declaration on the Enhancement of Co-operation between the United Nations and Regional Arrangements or Agencies in the Maintenance of International Peace and Security".

specific exception that when a supranational organization is given legislative authority in a particular field (EC with respect to trade regulation) it can become a member of a universal organization, taking the place of its member States or parallel to them.

Whether that phenomenon is likely to develop and to simplify the membership in certain organizations is still to be seen.

When operational activities, and not normative action, are at stake, co-operation between universal and regional organizations can be achieved, when desirable, through agreements, but there is no link of subordination.

If maintenance of peace and security is considered, there is no clear guidance. Chapter VIII of the Charter is of course relevant, but it depends much on the circumstances and the region concerned whether or not regional organizations can have a useful role, particularly with respect to prevention and diplomatic settlement. In certain regions of the world there seems to be a growing awareness of the potentiality of regional mechanisms.

Enforcement action needs anyhow a reappraisal. Co-ordination between Security Council, regional organizations – and also non governmental organizations – may be a good way of dealing with a crisis, but adjustment to the particular circumstances of the case must be sought.

It is too early to think of the institutionalization of the world society on the basis of regional institutions. Nevertheless, when political conditions make it possible, consolidation of regional organizations could open constructive perspectives.

THE WORLD COURT, THE WHO, AND THE UN SYSTEM

*Nigel D. White**

INTRODUCTION

The UN family or system of organizations has undoubted problems of lack of co-ordination, bureaucracy and inefficiency.[1] Furthermore there is a perception of endemic politicization throughout the system, caused, in part, by the linkage of technical functional organizations with the political organs of the UN. In its 1996 advisory opinion on *Legality of the Use by a State of Nuclear Weapons in Armed Conflict*,[2] the World Court took the opportunity raised by the WHO's request on the matter to comment on the nature of the UN system and the organizations that make it up.

The main issue examined in this piece is whether the *WHO Opinion* is based on an accurate perception of the UN system. It also considers the closely related issue of whether the opinion is a beneficial one by laying down a clear legal framework for the operation of the system, a framework that may remedy some of the defects mentioned above. Current or future universal organizations,[3] particularly technical or functional ones, operating outside the system may be deterred from becoming part of the UN system because of its deficiencies. The clearer delimitations within the system offered by the Court's opinion may, if

---

[*] Professor of International Organisations Law, Law School, the University of Nottingham, UK.
[1] P. Taylor, *International Organizations in the Modern World* (London: Pinter, 1993) 115; R. Righter, *Utopia Lost: The United Nations and World Order* (New York: The Twentieth Century Fund Press, 1995) 280-89. See generally, D. Williams, *The Specialized Agencies and the United Nations: The System in Crisis* (London: Hurst, 1987). But see J. Harrod, "United Nations Specialized Agencies: From Functionalist Intervention to International Co-Operation?", in J. Harrod and N. Schrijver (eds.), *The UN Under Attack* (Aldershot: Avebury, 1988) 130-44.
[2] Hereinafter the *WHO Opinion*, I.C.J. Reports, 1996, 66.
[3] See generally H.G. Schermers and N.M. Blokker, *International Institutional Law* (The Hague: Martinus Nijhoff, 3rd ed., 1995) 35-6.

acted upon, make the system more attractive to such universal organizations. The benefit of drawing into the UN system these organizations will be the possibility of achieving greater unity. Given the likelihood of greater proliferation in technical organizations and bodies, the premise underlying this paper is that greater consistency, particularly in law-making and application, would be achieved if such entities were part of the UN system.

THE UN 'SYSTEM'?

In the *WHO Opinion*, the Court expressed its view about the UN, in particular its relationship to the specialized agencies. After examining the provisions of Chapter IX of the UN Charter, it stated that these provisions demonstrated that the UN Charter "laid down the basis of a 'system' designed to organize international co-operation in a coherent fashion by bringing the United Nations, invested with *powers of a general scope*, into relationship with various autonomous and complementary organizations, invested with *sectorial powers*".[4] Thus the competence of the WHO was not only conditioned by "the general principle of speciality", identified by the Court as applicable to all international organizations and returned to later in this paper, but also by "the logic of the overall system contemplated by the Charter".[5] The concept of "sectorial powers" is fascinating,[6] and it deserves greater consideration in the light not simply of the opinion itself, but more so in the light of a consideration of the UN system.

In what sense is there a UN system and in what sense is the Court referring to it? Is the Court's opinion based on an accurate analysis of the system, or is it based on flawed assumptions, or is it based on a vision of the system which does not exist but may be posited as some sort of ideal?

Of course the Court was aware that the UN family or system does not simply consist of the UN and its specialized agencies, although it must be said the distinction drawn by the Court between general and sectorial does *seem* only to embrace these aspects of the system. The Court was concerned with international organizations properly so

---

[4] *Ibid.*, at 80.
[5] *Ibid.*
[6] But see M. Bothe, "The WHO Request", in L.B. De Chazournes and P. Sands, *International Law, the International Court of Justice and Nuclear Weapons* (Cambridge: Cambridge University Press, 1998) 103 at 107.

called as reflected in its discussion of speciality as a governing principle. It was after all concerned with the competence of the WHO, an organization having international legal personality. However, when widening its discussion to the UN system, it could, perhaps should, have considered the many subsidiary bodies and organs established by the principal organs of the UN to deal with sectorial, as opposed to general, matters. Of course these subsidiary bodies do not have powers *per se* in the sense of an IGO, but they do exercise powers delegated to them by the main organs,[7] and they do have a considerable impact in the different areas in which the UN operates. Mention need only be made of subsidiary bodies established by the General Assembly – the UN Development Programme (UNDP); the United Nations Children's Fund (UNICEF); the UN High Commissioner for Refugees (UNHCR); the UN Conference on Trade and Development (UNCTAD); the World Food Programme (WFP); the United Nations Environment Programme (UNEP); and the United Nations High Commissioner for Human Rights. ECOSOC and the Security Council have also created a significant number of important bodies, mention can be made of the regional economic commissions, the Human Rights Commission, the UN Compensation Commission, and the international criminal tribunals.

The existence of a plethora of organizations and organs with overlapping functions is immediately apparent. In addition, it may be possible to include in the UN system bodies established under treaties sponsored by the UN – examples would include the Human Rights Committee, the Law of the Sea Tribunal and the Permanent International Criminal Court.

The Court's legal framework for the UN system seems to consist of the UN as one unit including the subsidiary bodies established by the UN's main organs, and the specialized agencies as separate units, the division being made on functional grounds. However, it can be seen that in terms of functions the system is much more complex. Indeed, in the UN system the problem is not so much that of proliferation of organizations but of the multiplication of subsidiary bodies established by organizations.

Furthermore, the Court's vision of the system is very much framed in the immediate post-war period. The proliferation of additional Funds, Programmes and Commissions within the UN system, was as a

---

[7] On the distinction between the delegation of powers to subsidiary bodies and the delegation of functions see D. Sarooshi, *The United Nations and the Development of Collective Security* (Oxford: Clarendon Press, 1999) 4-16.

result of "new tasks appearing which had simply not been anticipated when the specialized agencies were established". "Hence the Funds and Programmes were set up ... to cover, however imperfectly, some of the functional gaps between the specialized agencies."[8]

By looking beyond the hard shell of the organizations operating in the UN system and examining instead the entities – organizations, organs, committees, and individuals – operating under the aegis of the UN umbrella, it might be possible to obtain a more accurate picture of the UN system. From this perspective there are many possible ways in which the UN might operate as a system. Three will be expounded here: first the UN as an umbrella covering a collection of groupings of states, each grouping having its own agenda; second, the UN as an organization enabling those entities operating under it to form systems which deal with different goals; and finally the UN as a complete functioning system.

UN Umbrella

In this conception, the United Nations is simply a label under which all the bodies act in an unco-ordinated, almost anarchic way. These bodies are simply convenient fora for states to meet on various issues. There is no sense that they are acting within the context of a wider system with integrated and co-ordinated functions and goals. The portrayal of the self-interested state as the dominant actor results in a "pessimistic analysis of the prospects for international co-operation and the capabilities of international institutions".[9] Although there appears to be some co-operation by states, coming together in varying combinations in the various entities acting under the UN umbrella, the lack of co-ordinated direction to these bodies gives them the appearance of convenient conference venues for states to meet and formalise the balance of power between them in different contexts.[10] The derivative nature of these bodies signifies that they do not have any controlling effect on the states themselves through the enactment and enforcement of rules and principles. States "function in a ... environment that is defined by their own interests, power, and interaction. These orientations are resistant

---

[8] Taylor, *op.cit.*, 16.
[9] J.M Grieco, "Anarchy and the Limits of Co-operation: A Realist Critique of the Newest Liberal Institutionalism", (1988) 42 *International Organization* 485 at 485.
[10] K.N. Waltz, *Theory of International Politics* (Reading Mass.: Addison-Wesley, 1979) 118.

to the contention that principles, norms, rules, and decision making procedures have a significant impact on outcomes and behaviour."[11]

The weakness with this conception of the UN is that it ignores the sheer number of entities operating under the umbrella. States would not create so many 'costly' bodies simply out of self-interest, unless an extreme view is taken that such bodies do help cement the *status quo* in international relations, perpetuating dominance by nation states. Nevertheless, the inherent hierarchy and inequity recognised in this conception of the world does not really explain why disadvantaged states meet powerful states – the sole beneficiaries of such a conception – in these fora. To contend that international organizations perpetuate, indeed legitimate, Eurocentric dominance[12] is to deny smaller, developing or indeed enlightened states any free will, any ability to change the world. International bodies are potentially concrete mechanisms for checking the ambitions of powerful states. The plethora of bodies acting under the UN umbrella, some but not all of which are dominated by powerful states, cannot simply be explained as maintaining the *status quo*. This still leaves the possibility that the UN 'umbrella' conception still holds but that the unco-ordinated entities acting under it do affect state behaviour – each is "an intervening variable" which "stands between basic causal factors on the one hand and outcomes and behaviour on the other".[13] However, this ignores the fact that there does appear to be some co-ordination, indeed hierarchy, under the umbrella, which would suggest that there is not simply a jumble of bodies in which states meet and possibly regulate state behaviour, but that there are at least systems or networks, no matter how weak, within that mass of bodies. Simply put, the umbrella conception of the UN is unrealistic, despite its Realist underpinnings.

UN Systems

If the UN cannot be explained as a collection of entities acting in unco-ordinated ways, then there must be UN systems although not necessarily a UN system. One way of explaining the systems that operate under the rubric of the UN is simply to ask whether there are "persistent sets of rules that constrain activity, shape expectations, and prescribe roles"

---

[11] S. Krasner, "Structural Causes and Regime Consequences: Regimes as Intervening Variables", (1982) 36 *International Organization* 184 at 190.
[12] M. Koskenniemi (ed.), *International Law* (Dartmouth, Aldershot, 1992) xi.
[13] Krasner, *loc.cit.*, 189.

operating across UN bodies.[14] As has been seen above this analysis could be applied to each individual entity acting under a UN umbrella, but a more complete approach is to look for a "set of implicit or explicit principles, norms, rules and decision-making procedures around which actors' expectations converge *in a given area of international relations*".[15] Thus there could be systems which cut across bodies and institutions covering such areas as human rights, collective security, environmental matters, and labour conditions. Some of these may be dealt with *primarily* within one of the entities in the system such as the ILO as regards labour conditions, but others are more likely to be dealt with across those bodies – for instance human rights are dealt with by organs within the UN, many of the specialized agencies, many of the subsidiary organs, and by bodies created under UN sponsored treaties. Even a narrower function such as the improvement of labour conditions will involve not only the primary agency, the ILO, but others as well, such as the WHO, for instance, where oppressive labour conditions affect health. If there is some co-ordination of these institutions then it can be said that there are at least weak systems within the UN. The question then arises as to whether these are systems *per se* or are they simply subsystems within an overall UN system?

UN System

Whereas the depiction of the UN as a mere umbrella for groupings of states reflects a state dominated international system, viewing the UN as having systems within it is indicative of levels of co-operation and co-ordination which cannot purely be explained in terms of the self-interest of states. The "creation of rules that very deeply affect the domestic structures and organization of states, that invest individuals and groups within states with rights and duties, and seek to embody some notion of the common good (human rights, democratization, the environment, the construction of more elaborate and intrusive inter-state security orders)", raises issues of "society and community".[16]

Applying such a vision to the UN, it is possible to see it developing, evolving towards an integrated whole, not simply a series of meeting

---

[14] R.O Keohane, "International Institutions: Two Approaches", (1988) 32 *International Studies Quarterly* 379 at 384.
[15] Krasner, *loc.cit.*, 186. Emphasis added.
[16] A. Hurrell, "International Society and the Study of Regimes: A Reflective Approach", in V. Rittberger (ed.), *Regime Theory and International Relations* (Oxford: OUP, 1993) 49 at 63.

places, or indeed networks of such fora. Although the institutional framework of the UN is still grounded on the 1945 model, the powers of those institutions have developed just as the goals and values of the UN have changed over the years – there is organic and systemic development to the extent that there is a UN system, though not necessarily a strong one. There are mechanisms for co-ordination of the diverse activities of the system,[17] though their weaknesses are well known. One criticism goes as far as saying that these mechanisms do not provide for any co-ordination, serving "principally as occasions for long and generally inconclusive arguments over territory – unless common interests are perceived to be threatened". The end result, according to this view, is that there is no UN system as such, instead each agency "is primarily concerned to assert" its "unique competence", leading "to the sort of territorial and bureaucratic infighting that impels fifteen different UN organizations to involve themselves in ocean management" for instance.[18]

Nevertheless, mechanisms for co-ordination and direction are present. In other words at least there are the elements of a system present. Unless these elements fail to function at all, a possibility which must be recognised, it is valid to state that there is a weak system, no matter that it is fragmented and chaotic. The assertion that there is a UN system is not to be confused with an idealistic view "of the organic unity of space ship earth", not allowing "any intermediate level of competence" which would be "seen as permitting an unacceptable compromise with the integrity of the essential whole".[19] The contention is not one of world government, which clearly has not been achieved by the UN, but that the UN is a system, or has evolved into one, which has elements of global governance[20] in it and which may evolve further. In some ways this approach is similar to the middle way Grotius depicted between a Hobbesian vision of nation states unrestrained in a state of nature and the rationalist conception of a "central authority".

---

[17] For example the Administrative Committee on Co-Ordination (ACC), D.W. Bowett, *The Law of International Institutions* (London: Stevens, 4th ed., 1982) 68. Also the Joint Inspection Unit (JIU), W. Münch, "The Joint Inspection Unit of the United Nations and the Specialized Agencies: The Role and Working Methods of a Comprehensive Oversight Institution in the United Nations System", (1998)2 *Max Planck Yearbook of United Nations Law* 287.

[18] Righter, *op.cit.*, 47, 53.

[19] Taylor, *op.cit.*, 7.

[20] F.K. Lister, *The European Union, the United Nations, and the Revival of Confederal Governance* (Westport, Conn., Greenwood Press, 1996) 162-3.

Although Grotius' "international society" of the early seventeenth century did not include within it international organizations, it did recognise that states "are bound by rules and form a society and community with one another".[21]

One contradiction in the UN system is that it is a curious combination of centralization (for instance, at least on paper, in the area of collective security), and decentralization in most economic and social matters through the establishment of functional specialized agencies. Although these agencies have links with the UN centre, namely ECOSOC, they have a great deal of autonomy. To have created in 1945 "one central organization embracing all activities"[22] would have been too radical, so under the influence of functionalism,[23] the UN was arranged upon the basis of the decentralization of many of its functions. Indeed, the prematurity of centralization is shown by the fact that in the area of collective security which, according to the UN Charter should be centralized under the control of the UN Security Council, the practice has been one of decentralization.[24] A decentralized system may have weaknesses, particularly in overlap and co-ordination of the activities of the agencies and their relations to the main organs and their subsidiary bodies, but it is a system nonetheless, the aim of which is to fulfil the goals and values of the UN as formulated in the main by the centre. However, if that decentralized system collapses into "polycentrism" with no real co-ordination or central management, then, but only then, is it possible to state that the UN system is a "myth".[25]

A political system has been defined as existing "wherever and whenever a group of actors are caught up in a nexus of relationships, both conflictual and co-operative, generated by common problems and the need to deal with them".[26] The UN system is a product of the desire of the international community to deal with common problems, rang-

---

[21] H. Bull, "The Importance of Grotius in the Study of International Relations", in H. Bull, B. Kingsbury and A. Roberts (eds.), *Hugo Grotius and International Relations* (Oxford: Clarendon Press, 1992) 71-2.

[22] Schermers and Blokker, *op.cit.*, 1056.

[23] D. Mitrany, *A Working Peace System: An Argument for the Functional Development of International Organization* (London: Royal Institute for International Affairs, 1943).

[24] N.D. White and Ö. Ülgen, "The Security Council and the Decentralised Military Option: Constitutionality and Function", (1997) XLIV *Netherlands International Law Review* 378.

[25] Righter, *op.cit.*, 43-6.

[26] R.W. Gregg and M. Barkun (eds.), *The United Nations System and its Functions* (Princeton: Van Nostrand Co., 1968) 4.

ing from the prevention of war to the need to co-ordinate the use of radio frequencies. Furthermore, despite manifest deficiencies in the co-ordination of these disparate aims, the purpose of the system is to deal with these problems in a co-ordinated way so that there should be no contradiction between the UN's actions as regards the prevention of war and its directions of the use of radio frequencies, or the peaceful development of civil aviation, or the protection of the environment. Clearly the diverse goals of the UN make it an unwieldy system and there is a manifest difficulty in the co-ordination of all these activities in a consistent way, as well as there being a significant gap between the goals of the organization and its achievements.

Setting aside the first ('umbrella') conception which does not posit any system, neither the second ('systems') or third ('system') accords with the Court's view. The two views are both functionally driven in that institutions cluster round specific functions but there is much greater flexibility than accorded by the Court which equates each specialized agency with a particular function. A flexible approach accords more with the dictates of functionalism which argued against drawing rigid formal legal boundaries around organizations and institutions as this may prevent natural co-operation in order to meet common problems.[27] However, the proliferation of bodies dealing with the same problem could be said to be unnecessary, and thus the Court could be seen as trying to remedy this confusion by defining the competence of each organization operating within the system in a narrow way. This seems to ignore the reality of a multi-layered, and yes confused and often unco-ordinated, UN system.

The UN has evolved beyond the point of the UN organization dealing with general and security matters and the Agencies dealing with other functionally defined areas such as health, labour, education and agriculture. The issues define the system rather than the entities that make it up. Thus the UN's concern is with, *inter alia*, health and how it can be improved rather than with the precise mandate of the WHO. However, health is a potentially self-contained area, along with others such as telecommunications. In these areas the hard shell of the relevant organization could be seen as still intact, unaffected by the proliferation of bodies in other parts of the system. The question of whether this justifies a stricter interpretation of the competences of certain institutions than others will be returned to later in this paper. Certainly the issue of nuclear weapons concerns different parts of the UN system, the

---

[27] Mitrany, *op.cit.*, 43-4.

question is in what ways are they to be concerned. The use of nuclear weapons and their consequent impact on health is of course a direct concern to the WHO, but the question asked of the Court was not simply that of use but of the legality of use.[28] The Court, in disallowing the WHO's question stated that "whether nuclear weapons are used legally or illegally their effects on health would be the same".[29] The Court went on to state that the WHO's responsibilities "are necessarily restricted to public 'health' and cannot encroach on the responsibilities of other parts of the UN system". To allow the WHO to concern itself with the legality of nuclear weapons would be "to render meaningless the notion of a specialized agency".[30] The Court's vision of functionally limited agencies with consequently narrowly defined powers is perhaps more convincing in the case of the WHO than it is in other instances. The UN system may have evolved with cross-cutting concerns breaking down the original boundaries between many of the entities, but this does not mean that all entities have been so affected.

However, the major cross-cutting concern within the UN, and the issue which has broken down strict divisions between entities within the family, is the issue of human rights. The activities of all the elements in the UN system impact upon, concern, or indeed define or refine human rights. The practice of the UN has led to a re-statement of the purposes of the UN Charter and those of the various constituent documents of the agencies as human rights. Their degree of entrenchment as positive human rights varies – the right to peace is perhaps much less developed than the right to adequate working conditions.[31] In the case of the WHO the Preamble of the Constitution clearly states that "the enjoyment of the highest attainable standard of health is one of the fundamental rights of every human being". The WHO's central focus on protecting, improving, and preventing violations of this right, entitles it, indeed obliges it, to concern itself with legal as well as purely health matters. The use of nuclear weapons clearly concerns the WHO in terms of dealing with the effects of their use, but the protection of the

---

[28] On the question of whether the Court misinterpreted the WHO's question see V. Leary, "The WHO Case: Implications for Specialized Agencies", in De Chazournes and Sands (eds.), *op. cit.*, 112 at 114-17.

[29] *WHO Opinion*, 77.

[30] *Ibid.*, 80.

[31] But see S.S. Kim, "Global Rights and World Order" in R. Falk, S.S. Kim and S.H. Mendlovitz (eds.), *The United Nations and a Just World Order* (Boulder: Westview, 1991) 364-5.

human right to health concerns the WHO in terms of the legality of the use of such weapons.[32]

Furthermore, that the competence of the WHO in protecting this right can clearly overlap with the competence of another element in the system, whose primary concern is with security matters, is recognised in the Preamble of the WHO's Constitution when it states that "the health of all peoples is fundamental to the attainment of peace and security". The linkage of health and security signifies that although the regulation of armaments and the use of force is a central concern to the UN, they do not "lie outside" the competence of the WHO as stated by the Court.[33] Indeed, the more accurate view of the UN is to be found in the dissenting opinion of Judge Weeramantry, when he stated:

> The United Nations family of organizations today is widely expanded, closely knit, and works together, in developing areas of international activity, within the framework of the international rule of law. While each of these organizations has its specific functions, they all interlock in the common service of the ideals of the United Nations and they all operate under the common aegis of international law. Though each of them is given a particular sphere of activity, they do not necessarily function in closed compartments, for the complex nature of United Nations activities may often result in overlapping areas of interest. The work of one organization may interweave with that of other organizations, and hence would have repercussions on the work of other members of the United Nations family.[34]

---

[32] On the issue of whether the WHO's preventive function gives rise to concern with legality see D. Akande, "The Competence of International Organizations and the Advisory Jurisdiction of the International Court of Justice", (1998) 9 *European Journal of International Law* 437 at 446.

[33] *WHO Opinion*, 80.

[34] *Ibid.*, 107. See also his statement on the overlap between security and health at 133. See also his other examples of overlap in the UN system at 150-1 where he concludes by saying that "[c]omplex problems have ramifications in many specialized directions to which the specialists alone are most competent to draw attention. Such a view contributes to the richness of the United Nations system. To expect otherwise would be contrary to the essence and rationale of a complex organization which straddles all facets of human activity". See further the dissenting opinion of Judge Koromo at 195.

THE LEGAL BASIS OF THE UN SYSTEM

The Court's analysis of the UN system is arguably deficient. Furthermore, its analysis of the constituent treaties of organizations within the system seems also to be based on outdated presuppositions. Although the Court, in delineating the competence of an IGO started with its "constitution",[35] it did not treat the constituent document of the WHO as a constitution in the "stronger sense", only in the "weak sense" of a constitution which just constitutes an organization not a society.[36] This is reflected by the Court's statement that the constituent documents of organizations are "conventional and at the same time institutional".[37] Starting from a "formal standpoint", the Court treated constituent instruments as "multilateral treaties".[38] Such an approach will always tend to favour the state members, particularly the original members, in issues of whether the organization has the competence to take a particular course of action. Although the Court did recognise that the subsequent practice of an organization, along with its purposes and its effectiveness in carrying out its functions, were major factors to be taken into account when interpreting the treaty, the overriding importance of the states' intention when setting up the organization prevails.

The Court emphasised the fact that the parties had entrusted the organization with "the task of realising common goals".[39] That *original* intent is not embodied in the *travaux préparatoires*, which after all, under Article 32 of the Vienna Convention on the Law of Treaties, are simply supplementary means of interpretation, but in the text of the treaty which is interpreted in a formal way to preserve that intent. The International Law Commission stated in 1966 that "the text must be presumed to be the authentic expression of the intention of the parties; the starting point of interpretation is the elucidation of the meaning of the text, not an investigation *ab initio* into the intentions of the parties".[40] The Court, though it does have regard to the *current* intent of the members by examining and considering subsequent practice, places

---

[35] *WHO Opinion*, 74.
[36] J. Crawford, "The Charter of the United Nations as a Constitution", in H. Fox (ed.), *The Changing Constitution of the United Nations* (London: British Institute of International and Comparative Law, 1997) 3 at 8.
[37] *WHO Opinion*, 75.
[38] *Ibid.*, 74.
[39] *Ibid.*, 75.
[40] *Yearbook of the International Law Commission* 1966, vol.II, 220.

it below the original intent of the parties as contained in the text.[41] The textual analysis of the Court is illustrated when it examines the wording of Article 2 of the WHO's constitution, which lists the functions of the organization, to conclude that "none of these subparagraphs expressly refers to the legality of any activity hazardous to health; and none of the functions of the WHO is dependent on the legality of the situations upon which it must act".[42]

Though there are debates as to whether the UN Charter is a multilateral treaty or a constitution (in a more profound sense),[43] these do not appear to have filtered down, nor are they perhaps applicable, to the constituent documents of the specialized agencies. On this basis it is possible to argue that the Court could justifiably apply different, more formalistic, rules of interpretation to the WHO Constitution than it has appeared to do in the past as regards the UN Charter. However, the Court made no such distinction, applying the same principles of interpretation to all international organizations, citing a favourable passage in the *Expenses Case*.[44] The issue of the compatibility of the *WHO Opinion* with the Court's previous jurisprudence will be returned to when looking at the issue of powers.

The debate as to the Charter's legal status does affect the constituent treaties of the agencies. Even if the Charter was not intended in 1945 to be the constitution of the UN system then it has become so,[45] in a stronger sense than simply a document that constitutes an organization. Its principles have been recognised by its members as fundamental and its purposes as defining the political will of the UN community, as well as providing the legal framework within which the UN must operate. Under the general framework of the Charter a UN

---

[41] Compare the Court's treatment of the WHO's practice, *WHO Opinion*, 81-3, with Judges Weeramantry, 152-3; and Koroma, 198-9, 204-7 (both dissenting).

[42] *Ibid.*, 75-6. But see M.S. McDougal, H. D. Lasswell, and J.C. Miller, *The Interpretation of International Agreements and World Public Order* (New Haven: New Haven Press, 1994) 135.

[43] See for example G. Arangio-Ruiz, "The 'Federal' Analogy and UN Charter Interpretation: A Crucial Issue", (1997) 8 *European Journal of International Law* 1 at 9 where he refers to the Charter as a "mere inter-state compact". But see B. Fassbender, "The United Nations Charter as a Constitution of the International Community", (1998) 36 *Columbia Journal of Transnational Law* 375.

[44] *WHO Opinion*, 74-5, citing *Certain Expenses of the United Nations*, I.C.J. Reports 1962, 151 at 157 (hereinafter *Expenses Case*).

[45] R. Bernhardt, "On Article 103", in B. Simma (ed.), *The Charter of the United Nations: A Commentary* (Oxford: OUP, 1994) 1117. See also C. Tomuschat (ed.), *The United Nations at Age Fifty: A Legal Perspective* (The Hague: Kluwer, 1995) ix.

legal order has developed,[46] whereby more detailed rules are produced not only by the UN but also by its agencies. Indeed, in terms of law making and law compliance the specialized agencies are much more productive and effective than the UN itself – with the ITU, UPU, ICAO etc. regularly producing forms of legislation which states accept as regulatory.[47] In producing these rules and regulations, the agencies are fulfilling some of the purposes of the UN. Thus they are also operating within the framework of the UN Charter as well as their own constituent documents. These documents establish formal legal links with the Charter and its organs. Thus there appears to be a constitutional hierarchy within the UN system with the UN Charter at its apex.

The constitutional argument is strengthened further when looking at the purposes of the UN as defined in the Preamble and Article 1 of the UN Charter – peace and security, human rights, justice, and economic and social progress. The Charter is a "legal framework determining certain common values",[48] but these constitutional values are not to be achieved by the UN alone with its central concern with security matters. Although the General Assembly and ECOSOC have economic and social competence, the bulk of the work is carried out by the specialized agencies. Judge Koromo, in his dissent, seemed to make this point when he stated that it should be recalled that "the WHO is also part of the United Nations system, and that one of the main objectives of the Charter of the United Nations is not only to maintain international peace and security but to 'promote solutions to international, social, *health*, and related problems'".[49] Viewing the Charter and the constituent documents of the agencies together as forming a constitutional framework may be disputed, and it certainly does not seem to have been the view of the Court. However, "constitutions almost always present a complex of fundamental norms governing the organization and performance of government functions", and governing the relationship between the authoritative bodies and the members of the society, as well as containing "statements of policy goals (regarding for example, economic development, culture, international peace, and

---

[46] O. Schachter, "The UN Legal Order: An Overview" in O. Schachter and C.C. Joyner (eds.), *United Nations Legal Order: Volume 1* (Cambridge: Cambridge UP, 1996)1-23.
[47] H.G. Schermers, "We The Peoples of the United Nations" (1997) 1 *Max Planck Yearbook of UN Law* 117.
[48] C. Tomuschat, "Obligations Arising for States Without or Against their Will", (1993) 119 *Hague Recueil* 195 at 236.
[49] *WHO Opinion*, 194.

conservation)".[50] The UN Charter and the constituent documents of the agencies seem to fit this description of a constitution, particularly when account is taken of the Universal Declaration on Human Rights, and the International Covenants, which together provide the missing Bill of Rights element.

Constitutional deficiencies abound throughout the UN system, in particular, the lack of separation of powers, the democratic deficit (apart perhaps from the ILO), and deficits in legitimacy more so within particular organs in the system, and the lack of legal rather than political review. However, there any many indications that the UN system is governed by a rather elaborate constitution in the stronger sense of the term. The consequences of this are manifold. First of all, in terms of interpretation the emphasis turns to how the organs of the organization themselves have interpreted their competence, the overriding limitation then becomes not one of express grant but one of express denial – is there anything in the treaty which prohibits the action in question? The guiding lights become not what the body of the treaty expressly (or by necessary implication) permits, but instead focus on the object and purposes of the treaty.[51] Secondly, within the system there arise constitutional checks and balances between the different component parts. Some are recognised formally, as with ECOSOC's responsibilities as regards the agencies. Some emerge in practice, such as the General Assembly's role as the conscience of the Security Council during the Cold War.[52] In the case under discussion an example of review in practice can be seen in the General Assembly's endorsement of the WHO's request for an advisory opinion.[53] The Court considered that such "political support" could not confer on the WHO the competence to ask a question which was within the competence of the General Assembly.[54] However, as Judge Koromo stated, the issue was not simply one of politics but of law, and if the General Assembly had viewed the WHO's request as outside its competence it could have brought this "to the attention of the agency", or have exercised "its discretionary powers" and brought "the irregularity to an end".[55] Indeed, the Assembly's

---

[50] Fassbender, *loc.cit.*, 536.
[51] See dissenting opinion of Judge Weeramantry, *WHO Opinion*, 147-9.
[52] N.D. White, *Keeping the Peace: The United Nations and the Maintenance of International Peace and Security* (Manchester: Manchester University Press, 1997) 164-9.
[53] GA Res. 49/75K, 15 Dec.1994.
[54] *WHO Opinion*, 83-4.
[55] *Ibid.*, 220.

endorsement of the WHO's request, alongside the practice of the World Health Assembly itself, suggest subsequent practice in support of an interpretation of the WHO Constitution which permits the WHO to ask such a question.[56]

Mechanisms of accountability are present in the system, although there is the issue of lack of judicial review. While the *Lockerbie* cases themselves might not yet provide an answer as regards the Court's contentious jurisdiction,[57] certainly the Court in the advisory opinion itself was exercising powers of review in declaring the WHO incompetent to ask a question of the Court. The Court found that "the mere fact that a majority of States, in voting on a resolution, have complied with all the relevant rules of form cannot in itself suffice to remedy any fundamental defects, such as acting *ultra vires*, with which the resolution might be afflicted".[58] The Court in reaching the conclusion that the WHO had acted beyond its competence in requesting an opinion seems to pay undue attention to the express words of the treaty, and insufficient to the purposes of the treaty and to the practice of the organization. It is only after looking at all three together that the question of *vires* should have been answered. The text does not expressly grant the WHO the power, but neither does it expressly deny it. The purposes and the practice tend to support the fact that the WHO does have the competence. Interpretation in this constitutional sense produces a different conclusion than that reached by the Court.[59]

THE ISSUE OF POWERS

In the *WHO Opinion*, the Court reinforced its formal interpretation of the WHO Constitution with a correspondingly narrow view of powers. In so doing the Court apparently deployed a new concept in the law of

---

[56] See further E. Lauterpacht, "Judicial Review of the Acts of International Organizations", in De Chazournes and Sands (eds.), *op. cit.*, 92 at 101-2. On whether there was sufficient subsequent practice see generally C.F. Amerasinghe, *Principles of the Institutional Law of International Organizations* (Cambridge: Cambridge University Press, 1996) 48-55.

[57] *Cases Concerning Questions of Interpretation and Application of the Montreal Convention Arising From the Aerial Incident at Lockerbie (Libya v UK), (Libya v US)* I.C.J. Reports 1992, 3 and 114 (Provisional Measures Judgments); (1998) 37 *International Legal Materials* 587 (Preliminary Objections Judgments).

[58] *WHO Opinion*, 82.

[59] Leary, *loc.cit.*, 117-19.

international organizations, namely the "principle of speciality",[60] although this appears to simply be a new label used "to express a basic and uncontroversial rule of the law of international organizations, namely the principle of enumerated powers or attributed competences".[61] According to the Court, organizations do not have the general competence possessed by states, instead they are "invested by the States which create them with powers, the limits of which are a function of the common interests whose promotion the States entrust to them". Again, as with the issue of interpretation, the emphasis is upon the intention of the states that created the organization. This approach very tightly confines the powers of the organization to those expressly provided by constituent document, or exceptionally, given "the necessities of international life", to "subsidiary" or "implied" powers,[62] namely those that "are conferred upon it by necessary implication as being essential to the performance of its duties".[63] The emphasis is upon the state parties' intention, either express or implied.

The Court relied on the *Reparation Case* for its narrow view of implied powers. However, the World Court in that case was not averse, in 1949, to recognising a right which cannot be readily implied from any of the express provisions in the Charter, and in so doing recognised that the UN had rights of protection over individuals overlapping or in "competition" with those customarily belonging to states.[64] The Court deemed that it was necessary for the UN to be able to bring a claim on behalf of its employees, though it did not state from which express provision that implied power was derived. It appeared to be derived more from the general nature and purposes of the UN as an organization aiming at securing peace and security, an aim requiring the extensive use of personnel in dangerous situations. Judge Hackworth, in his dissenting opinion, could not see how such a power could be implied from those powers expressly delegated by member states. "Implied

---

[60] On the source of this concept see Lauterpacht, *loc.cit.*, 98-9.
[61] Bothe, *loc.cit.*, 106.
[62] *WHO Opinion*, 78-9.
[63] *Ibid.*, citing *Reparation for Injuries Suffered in the Service of the United Nations*, I.C.J. Reports 1949, 174 at 182-3 (hereinafter *Reparation Case*).
[64] The Court did attempt to distinguish "functional" protection offered by organizations from "diplomatic" protection offered by states – *Reparation Case*, 182-6. Furthermore, capacity to bring a claim may be viewed as a power "inherent" in legal personality rather than an implied power – see M. Rama-Montaldo, "International Legal Personality and Implied Powers of International Organizations", (1970) 44 *British Yearbook of International Law* 111 at 155.

powers flow from a grant of expressed powers, and are limited to those that are 'necessary' to the exercise of powers expressly granted. No necessity for the exercise of power here in question has been shown to exist".[65] While the Court in the *WHO Opinion* did not wholly adopt Judge Hackworth's approach, it did not seem to follow the majority opinion in the *Reparation Case* either despite citing it favourably. In the *Reparation Case*, the Court paid lip service to the doctrine of implied powers, but in reality applied it very liberally. In the *WHO Opinion* the Court repeated its 1949 formulation of the implied powers doctrine, and then proceeded to apply it in a narrow manner. It stated that "to ascribe to the WHO the competence to address the legality of the use of nuclear weapons ... would be tantamount to disregarding the principle of speciality; for such competence could not be deemed a necessary implication of the Constitution of the Organization in the light of the purposes assigned to it by its member States".[66]

The Court *seems* to be acting in accordance with its 1949 opinion by making reference to the purposes of the organization rather than to the express powers as Judge Hackworth did, but then it reads the term "necessary" in line with Judge Hackworth rather than the main opinion. The result seems not only out of line with the *Reparation Case* but also with the later jurisprudence of the Court. For instance, in 1971 the International Court found that the termination of South Africa's mandate over Namibia was within the competence of the General Assembly. There was no attempt to specify precisely the source of the power nor any real attempt to amplify the necessity criterion.[67] In the earlier *Expenses Case* the Court stated that the overall test of competence was by reference to the purposes of the UN, though it laid no emphasis on there being any proof of necessity.[68] Furthermore, the Court was prepared to assume that the creation of a peacekeeping force by the General Assembly was *intra vires*. The Court was of the opinion that the provisions of the Charter which distribute functions and powers to the Security Council and to the General Assembly did not support the view that such distribution excluded from the General Assembly the power to adopt measures designed to maintain peace and security. Although

---

[65] *Reparation Case*, 198.
[66] *WHO Opinion*, 79.
[67] *Legal Consequences for States of the Continued Presence of South Africa in Namibia (South West Africa) Notwithstanding Security Council Resolution 276 (1970)*, I.C.J. Reports 1971, 16.
[68] I.C.J. Reports 1962, 167-8.

the Court mentioned the possibility of implying the power to create a peacekeeping force from either Article 11(2), or more specifically from the word "measures" in Article 14 of the Charter, the overall emphasis was not on the implication of powers necessary to make an express provision effective, but on the absence of any provision in the Charter prohibiting the exercise of a power which fulfils the purposes of the UN. The only limitation on the powers of the General Assembly in the field of peace and security is that in the Court's words only the Security Council can "order coercive action".[69] In effect, the General Assembly's exercise of power is limited only by the necessity to show that it fulfilled the purposes of the United Nations and was not clearly prohibited by express provisions in the Charter.

It seems from these opinions of the Court that "powers relating to the purposes and functions specified in the constitution can be implied" rather than the formalistic proposition that "one can only imply such powers as arise by necessary intendment from the constitutional provisions".[70] The weaker the tie in reality between implied powers and express powers, the weaker seems to be the justification based on intent. Although the implication of powers from the purposes of the organization may have the appearance of being based on intent, since the founding states had expressly formulated those purposes, it is in fact a legal fiction since the founding members intended the organization to fulfil those purposes only by the powers expressly granted or those which have to be implied to fulfil those express powers. There was no real intention to create an organization which had general powers to fulfil the purposes whether by reason of necessity or not. It seems that the test for the existence of powers, like the test for the existence of legal personality,[71] is now an objective one; it does not depend upon stretching the notion of intent beyond breaking point. The tests to be passed are whether the action in question is taken in fulfilment of the purposes of the organization and whether there are any express limitations in the treaty which prohibit the action in question.[72] The founding states can thus restrict the powers of the organization by providing express limitations, but beyond that they cannot restrict its develop-

---

[69] *Ibid.*, 163-4. See Article 11(2) of the UN Charter.
[70] Bowett, *op.cit.*, 337-8.
[71] R. Higgins, *Problems and Process: International Law and How We Use it* (Oxford: Clarendon Press, 1994) 46-7. But see Schermers and Blokker, *op.cit.*, 979.
[72] F. Seyersted, *United Nations Forces* (Leyden: Sijthoff, 1966) 155.

ment by the practice of the organs within the framework of the constitution as established by the purposes.[73]

In the *WHO Opinion* the Court seemed to be redressing the trend of its previous jurisprudence towards liberal implied, arguably inherent, powers. The opinion certainly seems inconsistent with its jurisprudence where it was content if "the power claimed relate[d] to and [was] directed at achieving the purposes and functions given to the Organization by its constituent instrument".[74] In the case of the WHO's request, while it may not be strictly necessary for the WHO to know about the legal position relating to the use of nuclear weapons, it is certainly useful for the WHO's assessment of the likelihood of use of such weapons, which would in turn affect the agency's preparations. This of course rightly assumes that the use of such weapons is a great deal less likely if such use is illegal.[75] Secondly, a knowledge of the legal position is very useful, if not essential, if the WHO wishes to take steps to change the law. If the use of nuclear weapons is deemed lawful by the Court then the WHO may wish to prepare a treaty in accordance with Article 2(k) of its Constitution, to outlaw such use.[76]

The WHO's request was thus taken in pursuance of its purposes and was not prohibited by any express provision. It appears to be *intra vires*. Its dismissal by the Court appears unconvincing.[77] The conflation of the speciality principle with the idea of sectorality may suggest that the specialized agencies should be subject to a stricter regime than the UN itself. However, this does not convince, not only because the Court stated that the WHO's request violated the principle of speciality itself which was said to be applicable to the UN as well as its agencies, but also because, as has been seen, the view of the UN system taken by the Court was in itself inadequate. Why then did the Court take this apparently retrograde step?

---

[73] Pollux, "The Interpretation of the Charter", (1946) *British Yearbook of International Law* 54.
[74] Akande, *loc.cit.*, 445. See also Judge Koromo (dissenting), *WHO Opinion*, 198.
[75] Judge Weeramantry (dissenting), *WHO Opinion*, 128, 131, 134.
[76] Akande, *loc.cit.*, 447.
[77] See Judge Koromo (dissenting), *WHO Opinion*, 190-1 where he describes the Court's reasoning as "unduly formalistic and narrow".

THE PROBLEM OF POLITICIZATION

One possible answer is that the "Court seems to have been enticed by the argument that the WHO, in considering the issue of the legality of the use of nuclear weapons, was engaging in 'political' matters lying within the remit of the UN and therefore outside the competence of a specialized agency".[78] The Court found that the request constituted a "legal question" irrespective of the "political nature of the motives which may be said to have inspired the request".[79] However, when it came on to address the issue of whether the request was within the scope of the activities of the WHO, its notion of a specialized agency did seem to be premised on the technical/political dichotomy, with the UN having general political competence, and the specialized agencies having narrow technical competence – to confuse the two would be to "render virtually meaningless the notion of a specialized agency".[80] "[T]he Court seemed to be saying that specialized agencies should confine their attention to technical and functional matters ... this is a departure from previous cases where the notion of giving full effect to objects and purposes of the organization was paramount".[81] Although the desire to restrict the politicization of the agencies did not surface in the Court's reasoning, it is reflected in the Declaration of Judge Ferrari Bravo who stated that the Court should try "to prevent those political functions that the logic of the system has entrusted *only* to the United Nations from being usurped by other organizations which, to say the least, have neither the competence nor the structure to assume them".[82]

Matheson is certainly of the opinion that:

> The Court's decision should have a useful effect in restraining attempts to use the specialized agencies and other technical organs as launching pads for putting issues of general policy or a political character before the Court. The performance of the important technical functions of these bodies would be compromised by the persistent introduction of extraneous political issues, and the successful use of the WHO to introduce such an issue into the Court in this case could

---

[78] Akande, *loc.cit.*, 451.
[79] *WHO Opinion*, 73-4.
[80] *Ibid.*, 80.
[81] Akande, *loc.cit.*, 451.
[82] *WHO Opinion*, 87.

easily have led to an avalanche of similar efforts in organizations that are not well equipped to resist or deal with them.[83]

Furthermore, as well as deterring a proliferation of political requests to the Court, the opinion can also, according to Matheson, be cited more generally to oppose the "confusion and competition" which would arise among UN bodies "if those with peripheral expertise and responsibility could preempt those with predominant expertise and responsibility".[84]

Western states' concern with the politicization of the Agencies surfaced in the 1970s and 1980s with the US withdrawal from the ILO and the US and UK withdrawals from UNESCO.[85] In giving notice of its intent to withdraw from the ILO in 1975, the US stated that the "ILO has become increasingly and excessively involved in political issues which are quite beyond the competence and mandate of the organization".[86] The attempts by the ILO and UNESCO to condemn Israeli practices which violated labour rights or were deemed to damage cultural sites were clearly part of a desire by the majority of the United Nations, acting within the assemblies of the specialized agencies, to isolate Israel.[87] These condemnatory resolutions were clearly politically motivated but it is rather difficult to see how this made them *ultra vires*, given the wide nature of the purposes of both organizations, in particular the fact that the Preambles of both Constitutions made an express link between labour conditions (in the case of the ILO), and the "minds of men" (in the case of UNESCO), and the maintenance of international peace and security. A teleological interpretation of these constitutions would suggest that they are not confined by technical or narrowly functional considerations. The distinction between technical and political matters is collapsed even further when considering that many, if not all, technical issues, are actually very politicised. They are less publicised and perhaps more solvable but nonetheless they involve highly political issues concerning, *inter alia*, the distribution and allocation of finite resources. Curiously the Western approach and perhaps

---

[83] M.J. Matheson, "The Opinions of the International Court of Justice on the Threat of Use of Nuclear Weapons" (1997) 91 *American Journal of International Law* 417 at 420.

[84] *Ibid.* See also P.H.F. Bekker, "Legality of the Use by a State of Nuclear Weapons in Armed Conflict", (1997) 91 *American Journal of International Law* 134 at 137-8.

[85] F.L. Kirgis, *International Organizations in Their Legal Setting* (St. Paul Minn: West Publishing, 2nd ed., 1993) 260-70.

[86] UN Doc. A/C.5/1704 (1975).

[87] N.D. White, *The Law of Internationl Organisations* (Manchester: Manchester University Press, 1996) 149.

the underlying rationale behind the Court's reasoning in the *WHO Opinion* seems to reflect the Soviet Marxist division of matters into "class" matters upon which vacuous compromises may be reached, and "technical" matters upon which progress can be made even between states with opposing ideologies.[88] However, to state that the specialized agencies central concern is with technical matters does not mean that it does not have competence in "class" or "political" matters.

Furthermore, whether intended or not, the Court's attempted restriction of the activities of the agencies if accepted by the agencies, which admittedly is unlikely,[89] will perhaps make the UN system more attractive to functional or technical organizations operating outside it, who may fear political control or more generally the politicization which is perceived to be inherent within the system. While, for instance, the WTO may have developed some links with the UN system, particularly the Bretton Woods organizations since its inception in 1995,[90] it is not formally a part of the UN system. Whether this presents problems, for example in consistency between the WTO's dispute settlement jurisprudence and UN law, is beyond the remit of this paper. It may be argued that the WTO has respect for UN law anyway so there is no need for it to be brought within the system.[91] Further, the presence of the WTO within the UN family would not, by itself, ensure consistency within different branches of UN law. Nevertheless, the obvious way to create the framework to ensure consistency is to bring all universal functional agencies within the UN system. There is no doubt then that the true measure of an organization's activities is not simply its own constitution, but the constitution of the UN, with the Charter at its apex. It is only in this situation that a full evaluation of the

---

[88] V. Kartashkin, "The Marxist-Leninist Approach: The Theory of Class Struggle and Contemporary International Law", in R.J. MacDonald and D.M. Johnston (eds.), *Structure and Processes of International Law* (Dordrecht: Nijhoff, 1983) 84.

[89] Leary, *loc.cit.*, 126-7.

[90] D. Vines "The WTO in Relation to the Fund and the Bank: Competencies, Agendas and Linkages", in A.O. Krueger (ed.), *The WTO as an International Organization* (Chicago: University of Chicago Press, 1998) 59. See also the International Trade Centre – part of the UN system which, since 1968, has acted as a focal point between GATT/WTO and UNCTAD. It is a joint subsidiary organ of the WTO and UN – see http://www.intracen.org/.

[91] E-U. Petersmann, "How to Promote the International Rule of Law? Contributions by the WTO Appellate Review System" in J. Cameron and K. Campbell (eds.), *Dispute Resolution in the World Trade Organization* (London: Cameron May, 1998) 75 at 96-7. But see A. Enders, "The Role of the WTO in Minimum Standards", in P. Van Dijck and G. Faber, *Challenges to the New World Trade Organization* (Hague, Kluwer, 1998) 61 at 65-6.

entity's compliance and furtherance of the UN's fundamental values, in particular human rights, can be undertaken. Although an organization outside the system may strive to bring its actions into line with UN law, that would appear to be a voluntary,[92] and non reviewable decision on the part of the organization.

THE WHO OPINION: POSITIVE OR NEGATIVE?

On balance, the Court's opinion appears to do more harm than good. Any positive effects arising from the opinion seem remote. The restrictions suggested by the Court on the competence of the WHO fly in the face of that organization's practice. They also defy the reality of the UN system and the legal parameters within which it operates. The depoliticization of the UN system may make it more attractive to current or future organizations operating outside it. If brought within the system, the WTO for example, would then have to ensure that its dispute settlement jurisprudence was in complete conformity with the overriding constitutional principles governing the UN system, including human rights norms. It is desirable that the UN family be extended to cover such organizations, not for the sake of neatness or completeness, but for the sake of consistency. However, while this is a valid objective, the Court's approach is unlikely to achieve it as it is not reflective of the actual UN system as it exists today. It is more a nostalgic attempt to return to the blueprint of the immediate post-war era. The fact that the original system was so rapidly outdated shows that it was actually flawed in its inception so that the Court's opinion cannot be defended as an attempt to return to some sort of ideal. Unfortunately though, in attempting to turn the clock back to the original UN system, the Court also turned the clock back in terms of interpretation, where it adopted a narrow textual approach to a constituent treaty, and in terms of powers, where it regressed to a tightly subjective approach. While the Court's opinion on the UN system, treaty interpretation, and powers may be internally consistent, it is externally inconsistent with its own jurisprudence and with the nature of the UN system.

The Court's opinion though, does provoke a re-examination of the UN system. There is no doubt that there is tremendous room for

---

[92] Although states that are members of the UN and the functional organization are obliged to give precedence to the UN Charter in the event of incompatibility. See Article 103 of the UN Charter.

improvement, in particular in co-ordination and consistency. It is only by making improvements that the organization will become attractive to new recruits. Improvement in co-ordination and consistency between the various elements of the UN can better be achieved by recognising that there is a flexible system, where the issues define the structure rather than *vice versa*, and where above all the system is governed by a complex organic constitution, which has at its core the protection of human rights. To put it another way: "[t]he family of United Nations agencies, in working harmoniously for the common welfare of the global community, will need to work as a team, each helping the other with the special expertise that lies within its province", rather than confining "their vision within compartmentalized categories of exclusive activity".[93]

---

[93] Judge Weeramantry (dissenting), *WHO Opinion*, 170.

TECHNIQUES TO AVOID PROLIFERATION OF INTERNATIONAL ORGANIZATIONS – THE EXPERIENCE OF THE WORLD BANK

*Ibrahim F.I. Shihata**

INTRODUCTION

We live in a world seen by many to be saturated with international organizations, both universal and regional, yet lacking in several respects world regulatory and adjudicative agencies with compulsory jurisdiction and direct enforcement powers.

Some organizations, in spite of the great need for their activities, are under- resourced; they receive little or no support from the most affluent and influential countries.(e.g.,UNESCO). Other organizations, mainly the two Bretton Woods institutions, keep expanding and are requested by their members, especially the more affluent and influential ones, to continually take on new functions, including functions that may fall within the domain of the former organizations.

There are at least two related reasons for this phenomenon. The two organizations created at Bretton Woods in the mid-1940s are controlled by the richer and more developed countries, through their weighted voting system and the selection of their top management. They are also perceived to be more efficient. Part of this perception is due to the greater control by developed countries, and part to the nature of their work which is often easier to measure. They are action-oriented organizations dealing mostly with tangible issues and problems. They are not merely or mainly debating societies.

Questions were raised from the beginning regarding the reasons for creating two organizations at Bretton Woods, the International Monetary Fund (IMF) and the International Bank for Reconstruction and Development (IBRD). The answer given at the time was basically simple. The Fund would promote international monetary cooperation and exchange rate stability, assist in the establishment of a multilateral

---

* Former Vice President and General Counsel, World Bank.

system of payments for current transactions between members and in the elimination of foreign exchange restrictions which hamper the growth of world trade and provide temporary, i.e. short term assistance to correct balance of payments imbalances. The Bank, on the other hand, would focus on longer term concerns of reconstruction, development and stabilization.[1] The eloquent distinction has to a great extent proved to be academic, however. There is overlapping between the functions of the two organizations. More interestingly, each organization seems to have developed a propensity to deal increasingly with issues the other was particularly created to address. They have discovered, each on its own, that short and longer term issues always need to be balanced. Problems raised by these issues often require simultaneous actions. The rationale for this growing institutional duplication will, however, sooner or later raise serious questions.

---

[1] The distinction is based on the texts of Article 1 in the respective Articles of Agreement of the Fund and the Bank, complemented by a formal interpretation by the Bank's Board of Executive Directors adopted on September 20, 1946 to explicitly allow the Bank to make long term stabilization loans and an interpretation made by the Fund's Executive Board on September 26, 1946 restricting the use of Fund resources "to give temporary assistance in financing balance of payments deficits on current account for monetary stabilization operations." The first April 1942 US Treasury draft plan for what became the Fund and the Bank Articles of Agreement pointed to the possibility of a single institution to serve all these purposes but concluded that "the two tasks should be kept distinct" adding that "doubtless one agency with the combined functions of both could be set up, but it could operate only with a loss of effectiveness, risk of overcentralization of power, and danger of making costly errors of judgment." See "Proposal for United Nations Stabilization Fund and a Bank for Reconstruction and Development of the United and Associated Nations." Preliminary Draft (April 1942) at p. 5. At Bretton Woods, India made a proposal to add "development" to the Fund's purposes and Brazil suggested to add assistance in "the fuller utilization of the resources of economically underdeveloped countries and to contribute thereby to the maintenance in the world as a whole of a high level of employment and real income." In the final text "development" was mentioned in Article 1 (ii) of the Fund's Articles not as a purpose in itself but as a consequence of the Fund's facilitation of the growth of international trade. After the Bretton Woods Conference, the US banking community expressed fear to the US Congress about permitting the Fund to use its resources for long term stabilization loans. See House Hearings on HR 2211 at 734-35. Questions were raised again in the US Senate which ended with a request in the US Bretton Woods Act for a formal interpretation of the Articles of the two institutions as mentioned above. See Senate Hearings on H.R. 3314 at 224-25. Interestingly, 55 years later, the US Secretary of the Treasury in a speech in London on December 14, 1999, called for some reduction in the IMF's role as a steady provider of medium or long term finance. See Financial Times, 14 December 1999 at p. 1.

This chapter will try to describe first how the IBRD has repeatedly managed to persuade its members to form a network of legally separate institutions which together with the IBRD now form the "World Bank Group." It will then explain how the IBRD has expanded its own activities far beyond original expectations but within its basically unchanged legal framework. The latter great expansion has been and continues to be carried out without the creation of new international organizations with separate legal personalities. It has rather relied on the employment of two techniques, one of which is the product of the other. Each technique has its inherent limitations, however.

THE TRADITIONAL APPROACH – NEW ORGANIZATIONS FOR NEW FUNCTIONS

Over the years, the IBRD has sponsored the creation of new affiliated institutions. They are neither owned nor controlled by the IBRD which is not a member of any of them. Although not tied to the IBRD in a subsidiary-to-parent relationship, these institutions were brought to existence through pioneering efforts by the IBRD. They work with it to serve a common objective, the transfer of resources and the promotion of international investment for development purposes. In current language, this objective is articulated as "poverty reduction".

CREATION OF THE IFC

In its own charter (Articles of Agreement), the IBRD had a list of purposes to achieve, mainly to help the transition from a war to a peacetime economy and to facilitate and promote investment, foreign private investment in particular, for productive purposes, especially in its less developed members. The means envisaged in the charter to achieve such purposes include guarantees of foreign private loans, participation in such loans and, when borrowers are otherwise unable to receive financing on reasonable terms through private channels, the provision of direct loans by the Bank.[2] Any loan (or guarantee of a loan) provided by the Bank to an entity other than a member country has, however, to be backed by a guarantee (or a counter-guarantee) from that member

---

[2] See, IBRD Articles of Agreement, Article 1, published in SHIHATA, THE WORLD BANK IN A CHANGING WORLD, Vol. I, Appendix I at p. 345 (Martinus Nihoff, 1991).

(or its central bank or equivalent agency).[3] The IBRD is made to rely on the faith and credit of its members. Sovereign involvement was seen as an ultimate guarantee against default and an important assurance to the IBRD's own creditors. The latter requirement made it difficult for IBRD to finance private enterprises through direct loans or guarantees. Governments were more interested in borrowing directly from the Bank than in guaranteeing Bank loans to private enterprises in their territories. Reconstruction of their public services and building infrastructural projects typically implemented by their public sector enterprises were their priority. The Bank, whose primary function was meant to consist of guaranteeing private investment loans in fact provided its first guarantee in May 1984, forty years after its inception at Bretton Woods. With the mandatory requirement of the sovereign guarantee of all IBRD loans, other ways had to be found to provide funding and guarantees to private enterprises. All major Bank shareholders believed in private sector development as the major engine for growth.

Deliberations on the matter culminated in the establishment of the International Finance Corporation in 1956 as a legally separate organization whose Board of Directors and Board of Governors consist, however, of the same individuals serving as members of the IBRD respective Boards.[4] Although IFC could have a separate President (and had one at the beginning), the IBRD President has since been elected President of IFC. Unlike the IBRD, IFC is authorized, indeed required, to provide finance to private enterprises without any government guarantee. Its financing is not limited to loans and guarantees; it can take any appropriate form, including equity participation.[5]

The Articles of Agreement of the IFC were prepared in draft by IBRD staff, discussed and finalized by the IBRD Board of Executive Directors, then opened for signature by the IBRD Board of Governors. All members of the IBRD became eligible for IFC membership. The same pattern was followed in the creation of subsequent affiliates, without the typical time-consuming negotiation processes of multilateral conventions.

---

[3] *Id*, Article III, Section 4 (i).In practice, the Bank has always required this guarantee to be made by the member country involved.

[4] See IFC Articles of Agreement, Article IV, Section 2 (b) and Section 4 (b), published in Shihata, note 2 *supra*, Appendix II, at 373, 376.

[5] *Id*., Article III, Section 2.

A proposal by the IBRD/IFC President in the early 1960s to amend the IBRD charter so as to allow it to lend to private entities without government guarantee had not received support (mainly out of concern for the IBRD's standing in the market and for possible negative impact on IFC).[6] Instead, the IBRD Articles of Agreement were amended in 1965 to allow it to lend to the IFC – and the IFC Articles were also changed to limit its borrowing to four times its subscribed capital and surplus.[7] A Task Force of World Bank Group staff was also asked in the early 1990s to study the possibility of amending the IBRD Articles to allow lending to the private sector without government guarantee. The study assessed the policy, operational, financial and legal risks involved in such a change.[8] Although it did not rule out completely that possibility, its findings persuaded management not to pursue the matter further.

CREATION OF IDA

With the decolonization movement that started in the late 1950s, a large number of new countries became members, or candidates for membership, of the IBRD. Yet, one of the conditions of IBRD lending is that the Bank must pay due regard to the ability of the borrower, or its guarantor, to meet its obligations under the loan.[9] In practice, this meant that IBRD borrowers have to be "creditworthy," a description that would not readily apply to most, or any, of those new members. By subscribing to IBRD capital without being able to borrow from it, the poorest countries would in fact be in the unacceptable position of subsidizing the more creditworthy ones. However, the IBRD, which relies heavily in its operations on borrowing from the market, could not afford to do away with the creditworthiness requirement of its borrowers. Consideration of the creation of a new agency, not dependent on borrowing and in a position to provide concessional financing, had therefore to take place. The case was so compelling; in 1961 the International Development Association (IDA) was created for the purpose. Its initial capital resources consisted of subscriptions and contributions

---

[6] For a description of this episode, see DEVISH KAPUR, JOHN LEWIS AND RICHARD WEBB, THE WORLD BANK – ITS FIRST HALF CENTURY, Vol. I at 824-28, 1997.
[7] See IBRD Articles of Agreement, Article IV, section 6 and IFC Articles of Agreement, Article III, Section 6 (i) as amended.
[8] The Task Force had wide representation from different parts of the Bank and IFC. It was chaired by this writer.
[9] IBRD Articles of Agreement, Article III, section 4 (v).

paid mainly by the richer members and were envisaged to be periodically complemented by supplementary subscriptions and other contributions.[10] (Twelve such replenishments have taken place so far.) The IBRD has also contributed to IDA resources since 1964 through grants made out of its net income. IDA credits are interest free and repaid over a very long period (35 to 40 years), including a long grace period (10 years). Since the 11th replenishment, IDA is also authorized to use replenishment funds to make grants to its heavily indebted eligible recipients. Although some original IDA-eligible countries have since "graduated" and some of them have even become participants in the more recent IDA replenishments, changes in Eastern Europe and Central Asia in the early nineties and the subsequent impoverishment of a few "graduated" countries have brought forward a host of new IDA-eligible countries, thus increasing in fact the overall number of IDA recipients.

CREATION OF ICSID

The IBRD, or its President, became involved as a mediator in, or the appointing authority of arbitrators for, the resolution of some international investment disputes, most notably the dispute between Egypt and the shareholders of the Suez Canal Company after its nationalization in 1956. Demands for this kind of intervention at a time of rising nationalizations of foreign assets in many developing countries prompted the Bank to consider the establishment of a more elaborate facility for conciliation and arbitration to be readily available to resolve disputes between foreign investors and their host governments when both parties agreed to submit to it legal disputes resulting from such investments. Some IBRD members argued at the time that this matter should best be left to the parties to disputes, fearing that any Bank involvement was likely to strengthen the position of foreign investors against their host governments. The Bank, however, considered the creation of such a mechanism an important way to encourage the flow of foreign investment to countries that need them most. The Convention establishing the International Centre for Settlement of Investment Disputes (the ICSID Convention of 1965) was opened for signature after its finalization in the Bank's Board of Executive Directors. To

---

[10] See Articles II, Section (2) and III, Sections (1 and 2) of the IDA Articles of Agreement and Schedule A of these Articles listing "Initial Subscriptions." Published in Shihata, note 2 *supra*, Appendix II at 391, 392-95.

date, 132 Bank members are members of ICSID, including many countries that were initially opposed to the initiative. The Bank did not just help to bring this legally separate organization to existence; the latter's Administrative Council consists mainly of the same individuals serving as Bank Governors, as the latter serve *ex officio* as members of ICSID's Council in the absence of a contrary designation.[11] The President of the Bank is the Chairman of that Council,[12] and the Bank's General Counsel has traditionally been elected ICSID's Secretary-General. ICSID's Secretariat does not itself resolve the disputes submitted to it; it screens the requests to ensure they are not manifestly outside the jurisdiction of ICSID and it provides institutional support to ensure the efficient operation of ICSID's conciliation commissions and arbitral tribunals, constituted on the occasion of each case. Such support includes the appointment (by the ICSID Chairman) of arbitrators not otherwise appointed by the parties within predetermined time limits. By force of the ICSID Convention, arbitration awards of ICSID tribunals are not subject to judicial review by national courts (they could be subject to an internal annulment procedure through an *ad hoc* ICSID Committee).[13] They have the same finality accorded to final judgments of national courts in member countries -- a feature exclusive to ICSID arbitration.

ICSID's jurisdiction, like all conciliation and arbitration proceedings, is based on the mutual consent of the parties to a dispute. Almost sixteen hundred bilateral and multilateral investment and trade agreements have been concluded in recent years, of which some nine hundred provide for the *a priori* acceptance of the contracting parties of resort to ICSID arbitration as the sole or an alternative dispute settlement mechanism with nationals of the other parties. This has given ICSID what amounts to a compulsory jurisdiction once invoked by an eligible investor with respect to a legal dispute arising out of an investment in a country which is a party to such treaties.[14]

---

[11] See ICSID Convention, Article 4 (2). Published in Shihata, *id.* Note 2 *supra*, Appendix V at p. 446, 447.
[12] *Id.*, Article 5.
[13] *Id.*, Article 52 and 53.
[14] For a recent account of the ICSID experience in general, see Ibrahim F.I. Shihata, *The World Bank In A Changing World*, Vol. III, Chapters 20 and 21 (Kluwer International, 2000).

CREATION OF MIGA

The last separate organization created under the IBRD's auspices is the Multilateral Investment Guarantee Agency (MIGA). The idea of having a separate international organization to provide guarantees to foreign (mainly equity) investors against non-commercial risks preceded Bank deliberations on the establishment of IFC and IDA. Although the function could theoretically have been taken over by IFC (the Bank itself can provide guarantees only for loans and with a government counter-guarantee), lack of interest from IFC and the insistence of borrowing countries that any such organization should be separate from the Bank and IFC, led, after a long hesitation, to the establishment of MIGA, the Convention of which was opened for signature by the Bank's Board of Governors in 1985.[15]

Contrary to initial speculations, demand for MIGA's services has proved to be high and continued to rise with the unprecedented growth of foreign direct investment flows to developing and transition countries in the last decade. Ten years after the start of its operations, MIGA received its first capital increase, after having received grant support from IBRD (through the latter's net income). By its Convention, MIGA can have a President of its own and its Board of Directors need not consist of the members of the Bank's Board. The only required linkage is that the Bank President serves *ex officio* as the Chairman of MIGA's Board of Directors and nominates to that Board the President of MIGA.[16] In practice, however, Bank Executive Directors have been elected by their countries to serve as MIGA's Board (with two exceptions at present) and the Bank President has always been elected President of MIGA by the latter's Board.

A BANK'S BANK?

In addition to the four international organizations the IBRD helped establish, it considered in the mid-1980s the idea of establishing a bank to carry out some of its activities without the constraints provided for in the IBRD Articles of Agreement, e.g. the statutory "lending limit," that requires that the IBRD's outstanding loans and guarantees not exceed

---

[15] For details, see Shihata, *MIGA and Foreign Investment* (Martinus Nihoff, 1985).

[16] See the MIGA Convention, Article 32 (b) and 33 (b). Published in Shihata, note 2, *supra*, Annex IV, p. 413, 425-26.

at any time its capital, reserves and surplus.[17] Two novel ideas were considered. One was to establish a new international bank, through an agreement with another international financial institution, e.g., a joint venture with the Inter-American Development Bank. The other was to establish a wholly-owned national bank as a subsidiary of IBRD under the laws of a member country or in Switzerland (not then a member). Neither idea was acted upon, however. But the concept of an international organization establishing a private company to carry out part of the activities originally assigned to it was followed for a while by the International Telecommunications Satellite Organization (INTELSAT). The latter organization initially moved towards establishing a private company under Dutch law, in the capital of which it would have held ten per cent. The company was established in 1998 as NEWskies satellites N.V. with its shares held however by the signatories of the INTELSAT Agreement in the same proportion as their holdings in INTELSAT. Meanwhile, INTELSAT's Assembly has recently decided in favor of privatizing INTELSAT altogether while maintaining a supervisory inter-governmental agency "to protect lifeline connectivities and users.[18] Some see in this process a beginning of a possible privatization of operational activities of international organizations that compete with the private sector (as distinct from their regulatory, policy or other public purpose functions). A decision to privatize the European EUSAT has subsequently been made.

A Retrospective Outlook

Although the proliferation of World Bank Group institutions seemed perfectly justified at the time of the creation of each of them, with hindsight, other, perhaps more rational, approaches could have also been considered. It may still be possible, at least theoretically, to consider a merger of the IBRD, IFC and MIGA, while restructuring IDA as an international trust fund administered by the resulting mega institution.[19] The purpose would not only be cost reduction but also ensuring greater effectiveness, especially in dealing with the private sector. This could also limit the conditions that usually accompany the replen-

---

[17] See IBRD Articles of Agreement, Article III, Section 3.
[18] INTELSAT Assembly of Parties, Record of Decisions of the Twenty-fourth meeting, Penang, Malaysia, 28 October,1999
[19] The author first floated this question in his book *The World Bank in a Changing World*, Vol. II, p. 26 (Martinus Nihoff, 1995).

ishment of IDA resources to the activities of that institution, leaving the Bank policy to be determined, as it should be, by its Board of Executive Directors (not by the major donors to IDA, acting in informal fora outside the Bank).[20]

ADDITIONS THROUGH CREATIVE INTERPRETATION OF THE CONSTITUENT INSTRUMENT

Like other international organizations, the World Bank does not exist in a vacuum. It deals with a world that undergoes constant changes at an increasing pace. Changes occur not only in the conditions and relationships the Bank is meant to address with their complex political, economic, environmental and social underpinnings, but also in the expectations of its members, the ideological orientation of its work and evolving development economic theories pertaining to it. The Bank's ability to adapt to these changes and to remain relevant to the needs of its members calls for a functional, teleological approach in interpreting its charter, without necessarily being limited by the originally intended meaning of its words. This author, as the Bank's General Counsel for over fifteen years, has advocated this broader approach and applied it in his numerous legal opinions. The idea, of course, is not to use interpretation as a guise for amendment in violation of the basic text and its purposes. On the contrary. A teleological approach is perfectly in harmony with the basic text. Article 1 of the Bank's charter requires it to be guided in all its decisions by the purposes stated in that article. Decisions on interpretation are included in this directive. The charter also vests the power of interpreting its provisions in the Bank's Board of Executive Directors, not in a court of law. Interpretation under these circumstances can acquire a great measure of flexibility. Although it cannot substitute for amendment, it can be helpful in many other respects. It can complement the text to further enable the institution to achieve its ultimate objectives by addressing matters not explicitly mentioned but deemed relevant to serving the stated purposes. It can thus add new functions of the institution, even though they are not specifically stated in the Articles of Agreement. The limits to interpretation under this approach seem to be twofold: not to deviate from the

---

[20] For the role of the IDA Deputies, see Shihata, note 14, *supra* at pp 129-35.

Bank's purposes stated in its Articles of Agreement and not to violate explicit prohibitions of these Articles.[21]

Examples of expansion of Bank functions through a broad, purposive interpretation of the Articles of Agreement (rather than the creation of further affiliated organizations) are common in the practice of the Bank. Four examples may clearly illustrate this practice:[22]

Financing social and institutional development, including certain governance reforms and acting as a knowledge and advisory agency

A literal reading of the IBRD's purposes may restrict its role to financing or facilitating "investment for productive purposes" in a narrow sense. Article III, section 4 (vii) of the IBRD charter also provides that its loans and guarantees will be made for specific projects "except in special circumstances." In its initial years, the IBRD financed construction programs in Europe and economic development projects (mainly infrastructure and agricultural projects in developing countries). It slowly started to move, however, to financing social projects, following the example of IDA which began the trend since the early 1960s under the broader wording of its Articles of Agreement.

Under the "special circumstances exception" allowing loans for other than specific projects, the Bank started in 1980 to provide "structural adjustment loans" followed, as of 1984, by "sectoral adjustment loans." These loans basically provide cash to the borrowing country to support structural (policy and institutional) reforms in the economy as a whole or in a specific sector. Although the emphasis was placed at the beginning on macro- and micro-economic reforms, it was soon extended to certain issues of governance, considered in a legal opinion by the General Counsel to be closely related to, if not inherent in, the Bank's objective of facilitating investment for productive purposes. These included in particular legal, regulatory, judicial and civil service reforms that provide the institutional framework needed for private sector development.[23] For the same reason, the Bank (and IDA) provided loans to facilitate privatization of public enterprises.

---

[21] For details of this thesis, see Chapter One (Interpretation and Amendment of the IBRD Articles of Agreement) in Shihata, note 14, *supra*.

[22] For a more comprehensive description of the major changes in Bank activities, see, *id*, Chapter Three, (*Major Changes in the Bank's Activities*).

[23] See Chapter Two (The World Bank and Governance Issues in Borrowing Countries) in SHIHATA, *The World Bank in a Changing World*, Vol. I, pp 53-96 (1995). In the exceptional FY 98 and 99, following the Asian crisis, non-project lending constituted 47 percent and 63 percent, respectively, of Bank loans.

With its accumulated knowledge of development issues and its increased involvement in policy dialogues with borrowing countries, the Bank expanded also its non-financial products, mainly providing advisory services on appropriate policies and the design of development programs and projects. The latter expansion has been such that some Bank staff and others now emphasize its "knowledge" function as potentially becoming its more important activity.[24]

Lending and standard-setting for the environment

Although environment protection and conservation, like social and institutional development, are not mentioned in the Bank's or IDA's Articles of Agreement as a specific purpose to be served by the institutions, they have become a major concern in their work, both in terms of extending the scope of their lending and devising policies to conserve the environment and minimize pollution resulting from projects financed by them. In fact, the Bank stands today as the largest source of external finance for environmental purposes, including a large number of projects primarily or exclusively dealing with environmental concerns. These concerns have been "mainstreamed" in Bank operations as an integral part of the "sustainable development" concept. It was natural, therefore, as will be shown, for the Bank to become the financial mechanism under new multilateral environmental conventions, the accepted trustee of the Global Environment Facility Fund and the main implementing agency of this large facility.[25]

Financing debt and debt service reduction

With the eruption of the international debt crisis in the eighties, proposals were made for the creation of a separate international arrangement or organization that would have a decision-making power to restructure private sovereign debt within an overall plan to be devised and monitored for each country by such arrangement or organization. Instead, the Bank's charter, which certainly does not envisage for it a role in the refinancing of commercial debt, let alone debt that cannot otherwise be repaid, were interpreted to practically allow such course of action if it would result in a material positive impact on the debt burden

---

[24] See, generally, World Development Report 1998/99, (Knowledge for Development).

[25] See Chapter 15 (The Contribution of the Bank to the Progressive Development of International Environmental Law in SHIHATA, note 14, *supra*).

of a borrowing member country so as to allow it to regain creditworthiness and resume growth through new investment. Under "materiality criteria" adopted pursuant to this interpretation, Bank loans were thus made to allow borrowing countries to restructure their debt by drastically reducing its principal amount or the interest thereon or extending its payment period or by replacing existing debt by a smaller debt that could be serviced more readily, secured by a collateral financed by the Bank. IDA's recent replenishments also authorized for the first time IDA grants and not just highly concessional loans to heavily indebted poor countries. More recently, the Bank, in collaboration with the IMF and a host of other sources, established the Heavily Indebted Poor Countries (HIPC) trust fund to help ease the indebtedness of these countries in the context of an overall attempt to reduce their debt service burden to a sustainable level.[26] Practical solutions were thus found to the debt crisis without the creation of new institutions, although the crisis facing certain countries, e.g., Russia; F.R. Yugoslavia, etc., may require further innovative thinking in future.

Moving from a project-by-project approach in favor of a "comprehensive development framework"

The Bank's charter mandates, as mentioned, that except in special circumstances the Bank shall finance specific projects. This does not mean, however, that projects should be funded without consideration of the overall needs and priorities of the country and without knowledge of other possible or potential sources of financing projects, or other development objectives in the same country. On the contrary, the Bank's "consideration of the total external position of the prospective borrowing country, taking into account all the relevant economic factors" was mentioned in the early US Treasury documents on the establishment of the Bank.[27] The need for "country discussions" was also repeatedly raised throughout the Bank's history. And a practice of establishing a country assistance strategy (CAS) for each borrowing country was instituted in 1992. It was only in 1998, however, that the Bank President called for a new "Comprehensive Development Framework" where "the fate of the poor would no longer take a back seat to market stability" and where "the financial, the institutional and

---

[26] See Shihata, note 14, *supra* at 105-88 and summary of the *World Development Report 1999/2000* (Entering the 21st Century) at 3-4.

[27] See Questions and Answers on the Bank for Reconstruction and Development at 43 (US Treasury, June, 1944).

the social [would be taken] together."[28] The idea here is to agree with each country on an overall framework to be reviewed annually to allow it to develop in an integrated fashion. Within this strategic framework all the elements of development would be linked. The country and its external sources of assistance would move beyond typical indicators of economic performance to address "the fundamental long term issues of the structure, scope and substance of social development." This movement to a more holistic approach would not do away with the financing of specific projects. It would, on the contrary, further facilitate the cofinancing of such projects with other donors. More importantly, it would place project financing in the context of the overall needs of the country, including in particular the need for structural and social reforms. This approach is now operational on a pilot basis in twelve countries (and the West Bank and Gaza). It is adopted by the same institution, the Articles of Agreement of which simply envisaged its main function as the financing of specific projects that could not otherwise be financed on reasonable terms through normal channels.

EXPANSION OF BANK ACTIVITIES THROUGH THE MEDIUM OF INTERNATIONAL TRUST FUNDS

The creation of separate funds to finance specific activities that serve the Bank's purposes or closely related purposes started early on in the Bank's practice with the establishment of funds financed by other donors which the Bank accepted to administer. An early important example was the Indus Basin Development Fund established in 1960 by agreement between the Bank and a number of donor countries to finance projects agreed upon as part of the overall agreement between India and Pakistan on the use of the Indus Basin, mediated earlier by the Bank. An increasing number of separate funds, facilities and accounts administered by IBRD or IDA have mushroomed in practice. They included at the end of calendar 1998 over five thousand funds from which billions of dollars have been committed and disbursed over the years. The power to establish international trust funds was seen in some early doctrinal writings as "inherent" in international organizations to the extent needed to promote their purposes.[29] The Bank

---

[28] Speech by James D. Wolfensohn before the joint Annual Meetings of the Board of Governors of the Bank and the Fund, October 6, 1998.

[29] See C. Henry G. Schermers, *International Institutional Law*, Vol. II, 419-20 (1972); see *also*, C. Wilfred Jenks, *The Proper Law of International Organizations* 187 (1962).

started to use the Common Law term "trust fund" after the IMF established the International Monetary Trust Fund in 1976 for the use of the proceeds of certain gold sales. In all these trust funds, the Bank acts as the trustee (legal owner and administrator) of the funds it manages for the benefit of designated beneficiaries and purposes (trust beneficiaries) according to the terms of a resolution by its Board of Executive Directors or an agreement with donors.

Some of the trust funds administered by the Bank have their own administrative structures that resemble in many ways those of separate international organizations. This is particularly the case of the Global Environmentally Facility Trust Fund, the more recent Prototype Carbon Fund, and to a lesser extent, the HIPC Trust Fund. It is likely to be also the case of the projected trust fund for primary commodity price insurance, which is under consideration at present.

GLOBAL ENVIRONMENT FACILITY (GEF) TRUST FUND

The creation of the GEF Trust Fund in 1991 by decision of the Bank's Board proved that wide-scale and long-lasting international action could be undertaken multilaterally without the need to conclude a new treaty on such action or to establish a new international organization for that purpose. A total of 113 projects addressing biodiversity, global warming and ozone layer issues constituted the GEF pilot phase program which was implemented by the World Bank, UNDP and UNEP without any prior treaty or formal agreement among the contributing States on the establishment of that program. The formal agreement among the three agencies was concluded after the Facility became operational.[30] When the Facility was later reconstituted after lengthy negotiations involving 73 states, agreement was reached on a text, which was neither signed nor ratified as a treaty. The "Instrument" which resulted from these negotiations, as it is formally called,[31] was later incorporated in separate resolutions adopted by the Bank's Board and the governing councils of UNDP and UNEP (and endorsed by the

---

[30] The "tripartite procedural arrangements" agreed upon on October 28, 1991, took the form of an annex to the Resolution establishing the GEF on March 14, 1991, and replaced earlier arrangements included in a joint statement by the heads of agencies in September 1990.

[31] See Instrument for the Establishment of the Restructured Global Environment Facility, Report of the GEF Participants Meeting in Geneva, Switzerland, on 14-16 March, 1994, *printed in* 33 I.L.M. 1273 (1994).

UN General Assembly), without a formal agreement between the Bank and the UN on the establishment or legal status of the GEF.[32]

The GEF, as reconstituted, is an entity which has many of the attributes of an international organization, including a clear international mandate and well structured organs: (i) an Assembly of all participant states that reviews the general policy, evaluates the operations of the Facility and its membership and approves by consensus amendments to the "Instrument"; (ii) a Council of 32 members that approves the work program and the budget, appoints the Chief Executive Officer and keeps the Facility's operations under review (Council members may also comment on projects before they are sent to the implementing agency for approval); and (iii) a Secretariat headed by the Chief Executive Officer. GEF projects are approved by the implementing agencies according to their own procedures. In the case of the Bank, the main such agency, they require approval by the Executive Directors. Yet the GEF does not have a juridical personality and is not based on a binding convention in a legal sense. The GEF trust fund was re-established as such, pursuant to the Instrument, by a decision of the World Bank's Board of Executive Directors that accepted the roles assigned to the Bank in the Instrument.

Innovation in this approach extended to the decision-making process within the Facility. Rejecting both approaches of the UN Charter (one member, one vote) and the World Bank's Articles of Agreement (one share, one vote, in addition to a small equal number of votes for each member), the Instrument requires that decisions of the 32-member GEF Council be taken in the absence of consensus by a double majority consisting of two thirds of the votes of the participants in the GEF provided they represent two thirds of the financial contributions.[33] Eligibility for grants from the GEF trust fund is open to countries eligible to borrow from the World Bank (IBRD and/or IDA) and those eligible to receive UNDP technical assistance even if they are not Bank members (such as Cuba). New and additional concessional fund-

---

[32] Some UN documents referred to the GEF as a "joint subsidiary body" of the UN and the World Bank, a description which the Bank's Legal Department has formally disputed, as the Bank does not consider the GEF a subsidiary organ of the Bank or the UN and limits the responsibility for its activities for the GEF to its distinct roles as trustee and implementing agency.

[33] The formula was proposed by this author during the restructuring of the GEF, and was adopted earlier also at his suggestion in the agreement establishing the OPEC Fund. See Ibrahim Shihata et al., *The OPEC Fund for International Development – The Formative Years* 31, 36 (1983).

ing is provided by the GEF to meet agreed incremental costs of projects and programs aiming to achieve global environmental benefits in the four focal areas: climate change, biological diversity, international waters, and ozone layer depletion. However, GEF grants extended within the frameworks of the Climate Change Convention or the Biodiversity Convention are to be made only in conformity with the eligibility criteria decided by the Conference of the Parties of each convention. Also eligible for funding are the agreed incremental costs of activities concerning land degradation (primarily desertification and deforestation) as they relate to the above four areas, as well as such costs of other relevant activities under Agenda 21 of the UN Conference on Environment and Development that may be agreed by the GEF Council "insofar as they achieve global environmental benefits by protecting the global environment in the four focal areas."[34]

THE HIPC TRUST FUND

When calls were made on the Bank in the mid-nineties to help resolve the heavy indebtedness of the poorest countries to multilateral institutions (notably IDA and the IMF), the Bank, as already mentioned, in collaboration with the IMF, devised a comprehensive scheme that addresses the totality of the debt burden of these countries in an attempt to bring it back to a serviceable level in the context of reform programs certified by the Bank and the IMF.[35] It also established the HIPC Trust Fund, (by a joint resolution of the Executive Directors of the Bank and IDA) and designated IDA as the trustee. The purpose of the trust fund is to repay the debt which an eligible creditor has agreed to include under the HIPC initiative, to pay debt service as it falls due, to purchase at net present value (NPV) existing debt from an eligible creditor, then cancel that debt, or to make other financial commitments as IDA (as administrator and trustee) will reach with an eligible creditor which has the effect of reducing the present value of the debt service owed to such creditor

The trust fund accepts contributions from the IBRD and other donors (the Bank initially pledged $ 2 billion (in NPV terms) from its net

---

[34] Instrument, *supra* note 31, at para. 3. For details see L. Boisson de Chazournes, Le Fonds pour l'Environnement Mondial: Recherche et Conquête de son Identité, *XLI Annuaire Français de Droit International* 612-32 (1995).

[35] See a detailed description of the HIPC initiative in Shihata, note 14, *supra*, Chapter Eleven (The World Bank and the Debt Crises).

income and has recently raised this amount by $150 million). Amounts received are to be used for the purpose of providing to "eligible creditors," which include IBRD, IDA and any other multilateral creditor that is "either a donor to the trust fund or in respect of which another donor or donors have made contributions to the fund totaling at least one million US dollars." Eligible HIPC beneficiaries are countries determined by IDA's Executive Directors to qualify for benefits from the fund. Contributions by donors, other than the IBRD, are to be made through an agreement between IDA (as fund administrator) and each donor. At the election of the donor, contributions may be made either as (i) unrestricted (core) contributions; (ii) restricted contributions to be used to make payments to a specifically identified eligible creditor; or (iii) restricted contributions to be used to make payments with respect to debts owed by a specifically identified eligible HIPC beneficiary country either for payment of debt to one or more specific creditor or to all the country's creditors. A donor may also elect to make all its contributions as core contributions, one or more creditor-specific contribution or one or more country-specific contribution (in the absence of an election, the contribution is deemed to be a core contribution). All the income from the investment of trust fund money is credited to the fund's various components on a pro-rata basis and used for the purposes of the fund, except when a donor requires that income from its contribution should be paid to it.

Although IDA is the sole administrator of the trust fund, its actions are qualified in many ways by the actions of other parties. The debt sustainability analysis it prepares for the determination of a country's eligibility to benefit from the initiative must be made in consultation with the IMF and the debtor country concerned. It must then consult with the IMF, the debtor country and its creditors to ascertain the amount of debt relief projected to be needed from eligible creditors. Donors have great latitude concerning the use of their individual contributions and any subsequent increase to it. Following these consultations, IDA, as administrator, makes a preliminary determination of the maximum amount of resources that could be made available for the trust fund to assist eligible creditors to provide debt relief. In doing so, the administrator must consult with donors and potential donors to the fund, to the extent appropriate, to determine whether they are prepared to make additional contributions regarding debt owed by the HIPC country concerned to eligible creditors and must inform the IMF of the maximum amount involved. The amount of the relief made from core contributions to an eligible creditor must be approved by donors whose core contributions represent at least a majority of all core contributions. And the financing to be provided to an eligible creditor must be evidenced by an agreement with that creditor on its terms and conditions. IDA, as administrator of the trust fund, is obligated under such agreements to make the payment provided for in them subject to (i) the availability of funds in the trust fund and (ii) the fulfillment of the initially agreed upon conditions precedent for the provision of debt relief by the eligible creditor. The administrator may also enter into parallel arrangements with member countries or other entities prepared to make grants available directly to the eligible creditor or an eligible beneficiary country to cofinance debt relief in parallel with the financing provided by the trust fund. Interestingly, amendment of the resolution establishing the trust fund by the Executive Directors of the Bank and IDA is subject to agreement of donors whose contributions represent at least a majority of all contributions to the trust fund. Furthermore, IDA may be renewed as administrator upon a decision to this effect by the same majority of donors, in which case the successor administrator must be approved by donors having the same majority. The Executive Directors of the Bank and IDA can still terminate the function of IDA as administrator upon their finding that the trust fund has fulfilled its purpose or can no longer do so. Termination will be followed by a distribution of the assets of the trust fund to the donors on a pro-rata basis, except for the IBRD contribution whose share will go to IDA as part of its general resources.[36]

THE PROTOTYPE CARBON FUND

In July 1999, the Bank's Board of Executive Directors decided to establish a Prototype Carbon Fund (Carbon Fund) as a trust fund administered by the IBRD.[37] The idea of establishing a Carbon Fund derived from the 1992 UN Framework Convention on Climate Change

---

[36] The details mentioned above appear, among others, in the resolution establishing the HIPC debt initiative Trust Fund. For the text of this resolution, with an introduction by this author, see 36 ILM 990 (1997).

[37] See the Proposal to Establish a Prototype Carbon Fund (R99-130, dated July 1, 1999). The IBRD, in its capacity as trustee of the Carbon Fund, and thus as legal owner, holds in trust the Fund Property only for the purposes of, and in accordance with the provisions of the Instrument establishing the Carbon Fund. The Fund Property is kept separate and apart from all other accounts and assets of the IBRD. See IBRD Resolution No. 99-1 (Instrument Establishing the Prototype Carbon Fund), (M99-45 IDA / M99-44, IFC / M99-24, Annex I).

(UNFCCC) and its 1997 Kyoto Protocol.[38] The Convention and its Protocol were designed to stabilize Greenhouse Gas (GHG) concentrations "at the level that would prevent dangerous anthropogenic interference with the climate system."[39] The creation of the Prototype Carbon Fund reflects the World Bank's conviction that the impact of global climate change is an important factor in the economic development of the Bank's borrowing countries, as such change has a detrimental impact on their agricultural and health sectors and may even lead to natural disasters in these countries.

In order to reduce adverse effects of climate change and promote sustainable development in the Bank's borrowing countries, the Carbon Fund was set up to pursue three primary strategic objectives: (i) to promote a "High Quality"[40] reduction of "Greenhouse Gas"[41] emis-

---

[38] The Kyoto Protocol has not yet entered into force, but in the meantime the Parties to the United Nations Framework Convention on Climate Change (UNFCCC) have been negotiating the ways in which its mechanisms would operate if and when it does enter into force. The three major mechanisms the Parties to the UNFCCC agreed upon in the Kyoto Protocol for specific Quantified Emission Limitation and Reduction Commitments (QELROs) to be met by the countries listed in UNFCCC Annex I (OECD member countries and transition countries) were the Joint Implementation (Article 6 of the Kyoto Protocol), the Clean Development Mechanism (Article 12 of the Kyoto Protocol), and the Emission Trading Mechanism (Article 17 of the Kyoto Protocol). The Joint Implementation mechanism consists of the transfer of "Emission Reduction Units" among Annex I countries (defined developed and transition countries), on a project by project basis. The Clean Development Mechanism allows the transfer of "Certified Emission Reductions" to Annex I countries from non-Annex I countries. Emission Trading is a mechanism that allows the trading of parts of Assigned Amounts among Annex I countries (defined developed and transition countries). Assigned Amounts refers to the quantity of Greenhouse Gases (GHG) a party to the Kyoto Protocol is allowed to release in the global atmosphere as calculated on a yearly basis in Annex B of the Protocol. The Carbon Fund will be involved in activities related to the first two mechanisms.

[39] See Article 2 of the UNFCCC.

[40] The term "High Quality" reduction of Greenhouse Gases is used to express GHG reductions of a sufficient quality so that, in the opinion of the Trustee, at the time a Project is selected and designed, there will be a strong likelihood, to the extent it can be assessed, that Participants may be able to apply their share of emission reductions for the purpose of satisfying the requirements of the United Nations Framework Convention on Climate Change, relevant international agreement, or applicable national legislation.

[41] The term Greenhouse Gas(es)or GHG covers the six gases listed in Annex A of the Kyoto Protocol (the Protocol to the UNFCCC adopted at the Third Conference of the Parties to the UNFCCC in Kyoto, Japan on December 11, 1997); GHG are carbon dioxide, methane, nitrous oxide, hydrofluorecarbons, perfluorocarbons, and sulphur hexaflouride.

sions, (ii) to provide the Parties to the UNFCCC with an opportunity to "learn by doing" as they deliberate on the rules, regulations and procedures which will govern project-based emission reduction transactions under the framework of the UNFCCC/Kyoto Protocol,[42] and (iii) to illustrate how the Bank is capable of working in collaboration with both the public and private sectors to mobilize new resources for its borrowing member countries while addressing global environmental problems.[43] This form of collaboration may, in addition, become a contribution to the further development of a more comprehensive regulatory framework for the UNFCCC and/or the Kyoto Protocol to reduce global GHG concentrations.

The Carbon Fund consists of five main organs: a Fund Management Committee, a Fund Manager, a Meeting of the Participants, a Participants Committee, and a Host Country Committee. The Fund Management Committee is composed of four senior Bank staff, and the Fund Manager. It will be set up within the Bank and will be responsible for project approval and for overseeing the Fund Management Unit, which in turn is responsible for the overall administration and operation of the Carbon Fund. The meeting of the Participants, to be held at least once every year, is a forum where the annual budget of the Carbon Fund will be approved and the general policy and strategic guidance provided. The role of the Participants Committee (consisting initially of seven, to be reduced to five representatives of participating donors) is to advise on issues regarding the operation of the Carbon Fund, and to approve the budgetary overruns in excess of 10 percent. Furthermore, the Participants Committee has the authority to reject a project proposal. Finally, a Host Country Committee (consisting of each host country or potential host country which has signed a letter of endorsement or a memorandum of understanding with the Bank regarding the trust fund) will meet at least annually and advise on the appropriate development and implementation of the Carbon Fund,

---

[42] See the Proposal to Establish a Prototype Carbon Fund, *supra* note 37. Concerning the relation between the Carbon Fund and the Kyoto Protocol, the Fund is intended to provide the Parties to the UNFCCC with practical demonstrations of ways in which Projects designed to reduce and sequester GHG can be implemented and financed, as the Parties deliberate on the development of detailed modalities necessary for the efficient conduct of project-based Emission Reduction transactions under the framework of the mechanisms provided for in Article 6 and Article 12 of the Kyoto Protocol.

[43] See the Proposal to Establish a Prototype Carbon Fund, note 37, *supra*.

including proposed amendments to the criteria for project selection and project portfolio profile.[44]

As trustee of the Carbon Fund, the IBRD will place major emphasis on the development of projects in the area of renewable energy technology. All projects of the Carbon Fund are to be selected in accordance with the IBRD's Operational Policies and Procedures and the Carbon Fund's specific project selection and portfolio criteria. They require the Host Country's approval, and should contribute to sustainable development and comply with the guidelines, modalities and procedures provided by the emerging regulatory framework of the UNFCCC/ Kyoto Protocol.

The projects financed by the Fund will generate "Emission Reductions," to be certified by a third party. These reductions would be distributed to individual Participants in the Fund in accordance with their *pro rata* interest in it. In other words, each participating entity would receive a *pro rata* share of the "Emission Reductions" achieved through Fund activities to be used in meeting its respective country emission reduction commitments under the Kyoto Protocol.[45]

The Prototype Carbon Fund will terminate at the end of the year 2012 unless the Participants by unanimous vote decide to continue it "on such terms as they may determine" provided the Bank's Executive Directors have expressly agreed to the extension and its terms. The fund may also be terminated on an earlier date if this is decided by (i) the Participants in their meeting, by not less than a two-third majority of the votes cast or (ii) a unanimous consent in writing signed by all Participants. In deference to the fact that the Instrument Establishing the Prototype Carbon Fund is a negotiated instrument with potential Participants, it may only be amended by the Bank's Executive Directors "with the prior unanimous consent of Participants" except that the Bank may amend it without prior notice to supply any omission and cure, correct or supplement incorrect or obscure provisions. The trustee may also introduce amendments "for any other purpose which does not adversely affect the rights of any Participant, provided that all Participants are notified of any such amendment within 15 days after the effective date of such amendment." For the first time in a Board resolution establishing a trust fund, there is an arbitration clause for the

---

[44] For further details contact the website <http://www.esd.worldbank.org/html/esd/env/org/envgc/cc/>

[45] See reference to the Quantified Emission Reduction Limitations and Reduction Commitments (QELROs) in note 38, *supra*.

settlement of disputes between the trustee and a Participant arising out of or relating to the Instrument. This is also the first time interpretation of a resolution of the Board will be given by a third party. Strangely, the Instrument, which is formally a decision of the IBRD Executive Directors, places its provisions above those of the IBRD Articles of Agreement by stating that "[n]either the Trustee nor any Participant shall be entitled in any proceeding to assert any claim that any provision of this Instrument [and any agreement between the trustee and a Participant] is invalid or unenforceable because of any provision of the charter or consecutive documents of the Participant or the Articles of Agreement of the IBRD."[46] While a formal agreement between the Bank and a third party acting in good faith may prevail over the Bank's charter,[47] the same does not apply to a decision of the Bank's own Board of Executive Directors. The text seems to have paid greater attention to the fact that the Instrument was a negotiated document than to the more important fact that no organ of the Bank has the power to take decisions that prevail over its Articles of Agreement.

CONCLUSIONS – LIMITS ON INNOVATIVE TECHNIQUES

The above analysis shows how the World Bank has responded to the needs of the world it serves through diverse means that included both proliferation and containment of new organizations. By applying a purposive, teleological approach to the interpretation of its charter and resorting to the establishment of international trust funds controlled by their own constituent instruments where the Bank acts in a fiduciary capacity as trustee and in an agency capacity as implementing agency, the Bank has had a marked success in expanding the scope of its activities without either amending its Articles of Agreement or sponsoring the creation of new international organizations.

These useful techniques have their limitations, however. Interpretation cannot go so far as to deviate from the Bank's purposes stated in its charter or to contradict any of the charter's explicit provisions (such

---

[46] Section 18.1 of the Instrument.
[47] This is an extension of the principle now codified in Article 27 (2) of the 1986 Vienna Convention on the Law of Treaties between States and International Organizations or between International Organizations. UN Doc. A/CONF 129/15.

as those prohibiting interference in political affairs). If it does, it would amount to amending the charter through a process and a majority vote other than those specified in it. This would not only run counter to the Bank's own legal and good governance requirements, but would also undermine the rights of members secured by the very high majority required for charter amendments.

The proliferation of trust funds administered by the Bank, though useful in many ways, also has its risks. It taxes the Bank's managerial capacity and requires continuous staff expansion. More importantly, it introduces in the Bank's decision-making process the influence of individual donors in respect of specific funds thus possibly undermining the multilateral character of the Bank and the role of its Board, especially in the cases of funds financed mainly by one or a few countries. There is also increasing concern on the part of many developing countries that issues of great concern to their future should not always be left to institutions controlled by a weighted voting system tied to financial contributions.

There is a need therefore for some balance. Efforts to avoid proliferation should continue. It should be recognized, however, that there will be cases where an optimal solution would be the creation of a new agency, not the over-burdening of existing ones by tasks which may not be consistent with their mandate or a reasonable expansion of their capacity.

THE PROLIFERATION OF ARMS CONTROL ORGANIZATIONS

Paul C. Szasz[*]

INTRODUCTION

When considering the proliferation of international organizations in general or in a given field, the first question is: what exactly does the term "proliferation" mean? It evidently implies some growth in numbers; does it necessarily mean fast growth or excessive growth or even dangerous growth? The term appears to have entered the international vocabulary through the Non-Proliferation Treaty (NPT), which of course referred to the proliferation of nuclear weapons. As these weapons represent the ultimate in danger, their proliferation was understood to be bad, even potentially disastrous. But what if the term proliferation had first been attached to medical relief programmes – would it have acquired such a negative connotation? So, we must ask ourselves: is the proliferation of international organizations inherently bad, or does it not imply the positive factor that international problems are being increasingly tackled in a cooperative manner?

In any event, a careful examination of the annexed chart of "Multilateral Arms Control Regimes and Related Control Arrangements", suggests that there may be a clutter of Arms Control Organizations (ACOs) but hardly a real proliferation.

At present there exists only one major full-time ACO: The Organization for the Prohibition of Chemical Weapons (OPCW). Another is perhaps coming into being: the Comprehensive Test-Ban Treaty Organization (CTBTO) which, in view of the recent vote in the US Senate, will probably for a long time be represented only by its Preparatory Commission. A third one is at best in utero: the proposed Organization for the Prohibition of Bacteriological (Biological) and

---

[*] Adjunct Professor, New York University School of Law. Formerly Legal and Safeguards Officer, International Atomic Energy Agency; Legal Officer, World Bank; Deputy to the Legal Counsel, United Nations.

Toxin Weapons (OPBTW)[1] – whose birth, at best uncertain, is also likely to be set back by the disaster that has befallen the CTBTO. There are also a few very minor ACOs: The Organization for the Prohibition of Nuclear Weapons in Latin America (OPANAL – from the Spanish title), the Consultative Committee established by the Inter-American Convention for Illicit Trafficking in Firearms[2], and the Wassenaar Secretariat.[3]

There are a few other Inter-Governmental Organizations (IGOs) with major arms control activities: the International Atomic Energy Agency (IAEA), the European Atomic Energy Community (Euratom – a component of the European Communities), and the Organisation for Security and Cooperation in Europe (OSCE - technically a "non-organization").[4]

Finally, there are some political organizations, primarily the United Nations, that have a few peripheral arms control functions. For example, the UN Secretary-General has certain responsibilities for monitoring compliance with the 1925 Geneva Protocol,[5] for maintaining the General-Assembly mandated Registers of Military Expenditures[6] and of Conventional Arms Transfers[7] and in connection with the Oslo/Ottawa Landmines Convention;[8] considerably more ambitious functions are foreseen in the Secretary-General's 1990 "Study of the Role of the United Nations in the Field of Verification".[9] The UN Security Council has been assigned a task in connection with the entirely *ad hoc* monitoring of the Biological Weapons Convention,[10] and of course provides the fall-back in the event of violations of the IAEA's safeguards systems, including that for monitoring the NPT.[11] The General Secretariat of the Organization of American States (OAS)

---

[1] See endnote s to the Annex.
[2] See endnote kk to the Annex.
[3] Established by the agreement cited in endnote gg to the Annex.
[4] In changing the name of the Conference for Security and Cooperation in Europe (CSCE – originally established to implement the 1975 Helsinki Accords) to Organisation for Security and Cooperation in Europe (OSCE), it was explicitly decided that the change in name did not mean that OSCE would constitute an IGO.
[5] See endnote q to the Annex.
[6] See endnote ii to the Annex.
[7] See endnote q to the Annex.
[8] See endnote y to the Annex.
[9] UN doc. A/45/372 & /Corr.1.
[10] See endnote r to the Annex.
[11] See endnote c to the Annex.

collects information under the Inter-American Convention on Transparency in Conventional Weapons Acquisitions.[12]

Finally, there are also a number of multilateral arms control arrangements with no control regimes, such as the Partial Test Ban Treaty (PTBT),[13] the Environmental Modification Convention (ENMOD)[14] and the Seabed Placement Treaty.[15]

From all this it may be concluded that there is less proliferation of ACOs than meets the eye.

Incidentally, I am speaking here only of arms monitoring organizations – not those that perform merely legislative or quasi-legislative functions in connection with arms control. On the universal level, this of course is mainly the UN General Assembly, acting primarily through its First (Disarmament) Committee, but also through the Disarmament Commission (DC), the Conference on Disarmament (CD – technically not a UN organ), and the Ad Hoc Committee on the Indian Ocean; that machinery also includes the periodic (usually quinquennial or ad hoc) Review Conferences provided for by most major arms control agreements, as well as the episodic Special GA Sessions on Disarmament (SSODs); all these can receive technical support from the UN Institute for Disarmament Research (UNIDIR). On a regional level, there is the OSCE in Europe, and the General Assembly of the Organization of American States (OAS) in the Americas. Except for a brief mention in connection with a possible World Arms Control Agency (WACA – see below), these functions are not the subject of the present analysis.

POSSIBLE COMBINATION OF EXISTING ARMS CONTROL REGIMES OF DIFFERENT GEOGRAPHIC SCOPES

There is only one field in which there exist both worldwide and regional ACOs: that of nuclear non-proliferation, where the world-wide NPT is accompanied by some four regional ones: Tlatelolco (which actually preceded NPT),[16] Rarotonga,[17] Bangkok[18] and Pelindaba[19] –

---

[12] See endnote ll to the Annex.
[13] See endnote l to the Annex.
[14] See endnote z to the Annex.
[15] See endnote o to the Annex.
[16] See endnote g to the Annex.

and more are currently being negotiated. And there is also Euratom, which functions as a sub-regional non-proliferation regime, as well as in a sense the worldwide IAEA, which has some inherent though limited non-proliferation functions of its own (the prevention of proliferation through Agency-assisted projects)[20] even aside from having become the implementer of NPT.

In principle, there should be no difficulty in merging most of the regional non-proliferation organs into the IAEA. Most of these regional structures (except for Euratom) lead at most a shadow existence, as in practical terms all safeguards functions to implement them are carried out by the Agency. Indeed, the Tlatelolco Treaty was recently amended to deprive OPANAL of even the vestigial inspection functions with which it was originally endowed. By the same token, however, nothing much would be accomplished by such mergers, for the existing regional organs in practical terms consume no resources, nor do they distract from the central rôle of the IAEA. On the other hand, there may be some political advantage in maintaining nominal regional non-proliferation apparati, if for no other purpose than to serve as standbys should anything befall the worldwide regime.

The only difficulty – indeed at present a political impossibility – would be to merge the safeguards functions of Euratom into those of the IAEA. Until NPT, these two regimes operated side by side without significant interactions.[21] However, once NPT had been agreed to, the existence of Euratom safeguards did constitute a significant political obstacle to the establishment of a universal IAEA regime for implementing its control functions under the Treaty – but these matters were resolved through extensive negotiations and, after a somewhat uneasy start, the two systems now collaborate smoothly within the geographic scope of the European Union.[22] For the nonce, any disturbance of the current harmonious relationship in this respect seems undesirable – though if the IAEA were to take over all of Euratom's safeguards functions this might allay possible lingering concerns in

---

[17] See endnote i to the Annex.
[18] See endnote j to the Annex.
[19] See endnote k to the Annex.
[20] See IAEA Statute Arts. II, III.A.5 and XI.F.4.
[21] See Paul C. Szasz, *The Law and Practices of the International Atomic Energy Agency* (IAEA Legal Series No. 7, 1970), Section 21.11.
[22] See Reinhard H. Rainer & Paul C. Szasz, *The Law and Practices of the International Atomic Energy Agency 1970-1980* (IAEA Legal Series No. 7-S1, 1993), Section 21.11.3.

other parts of the world as to self-inspection by the Europeans and thus deprive some countries (i.e. Japan) of an excuse for insisting on corresponding treatment.[23]

POSSIBLE COMBINATION OF EXISTING ARMS CONTROL REGIMES RELATING TO DIFFERENT SUBJECTS

It is tempting to think that some savings or other practical advantages could be achieved by combining certain ACOs, as well as the arms control functions of some other IGOs. What comes to mind in particular are the safeguards functions of the IAEA and the control functions of the nascent CTBTO (as both deal with different aspects of nuclear proliferation), as well as the controls of OPCW and those of the proposed OPBTW (because of assumed similarities in the problems of controlling chemical and biological weapons). Indeed, why not combine all four organizations, or at least the three newer ones with the safeguards organs of the IAEA?

However, on closer examination it will be seen that there really are few similarities and overlaps in the operations of these four control regimes. There is of course the infrastructure of every IGO, in particular the secretariats, and perhaps some economies could be achieved by combining their administrative (e.g., financial, personnel, meeting servicing) organs. There is the intake for national reports, which all regimes require – though for some these are mostly routine to be submitted on agreed schedules, while for others they are principally or perhaps entirely *ad hoc*, triggered by the occurrence of specified events. And finally there are the formal arrangements concerning the inspectors: their appointment, their acceptance by states parties, their dispatch on routine and special inspections, and their control and protection – all of which are likely to have a number of similarities regardless of the particular control regime.

On the other hand, the substantive functions required by the various regimes are quite different. For example, even though both the IAEA and CTBTO deal with "nuclear" matters, the similarities stop with that word. The IAEA is ultimately concerned that certain critical "special fissionable materials" that constitute the "explosives" in any fission or fusion bomb, be closely monitored and in particular that

---

[23] *Ibid.*, Section 21.11.3.3.9.

those that are dedicated to peaceful uses do not enter military channels; its inspectors therefore visit places where nuclear materials are used or stored to conduct inventories and to gage production rates. The CTBTO, on the other hand, routinely monitors, or causes to be monitored, the earth as a whole by non-intrusive devices, such as seismic or hydrophonic monitors, to determine whether there are any disturbances that might signal hidden nuclear explosions; once a suspicious event is detected, inspectors may be despatched to the indicated area to see on the ground or by probing beneath it, whether indeed there was such an explosion. It will be seen that the training, skills and experience required in respect of these two regimes are completely different, so that the same persons could hardly serve as inspectors for both. Although the control of chemical and biological weapons are not as radically different, the actual requirements for chemists and biologists who would examine the reports received and perform inspections are again sufficiently different that no substantial personnel exchanges can be contemplated.

Finally, there is the question of the political control organ(s). As long as these several regimes have different participants, it is likely that these will insist that each of the regimes be governed by the parties thereto. This would, of course, not exclude a WIPO-like[24] structure whereby each regime is governed by its parties while the organization as a whole is governed by an organ in which all the states that participate in any of the regimes are represented. But it should be recognized that the types of decisions required in respect of each control regime are different. For some, inspectors are normally dispatched routinely by the Executive Head, without reference to any political organ except if extraordinary circumstances (usually opposition from the target state) should arise; in others, each or certain dispatches of inspectors require a political decision, whether positive or negative. Each regime requires a political decision to determine that there has been non-compliance, though in spite of differences as to the type of substantive violations to be prevented or detected, in practice it is most unlikely that a "smoking gun" will ever be found by any of the control regimes; rather at some point, when such a gun seems just beyond the next door, the target state will, without a sufficiently plausible excuse, prohibit further probing, and the international political organ will then have to determine whether under the circumstances this technical violation is meant to hide a substantive one. Once a determination of non-compliance has

---

[24] The World Intellectual Property Organization.

been made there arises the question of sanctions, for which each regime has its own provisions – though, ultimately, any serious substantive violation (whether actually found or merely presumed) will probably have to be referred to and dealt with by the UN Security Council. Altogether, it seems that while it may be difficult to ensure the proper political governance of each control system, their combination is not impossible.

To sum up: at this stage and in the foreseeable future, while it may be possible technically to combine one or all of the major control regimes over nuclear, chemical and biological weapons, there would on the one hand be political difficulties, while on the other no particular economies or other management advantages can be foreseen.

A WORLD ARMS CONTROL AGENCY

The idea of establishing a World Arms Control Agency (WACA) or a Universal Verification Organization[25] has been considered from time to time in academic circles, but apparently only once within an international diplomatic context.[26] However, the General Assembly did consider, and requested a comprehensive study on the establishment of an International Satellite Monitoring Agency (ISMA),[27] which came to a generally negative conclusion on various grounds, including the immense cost, the limited type of information to be gathered and, principally, because of the clear lack of enthusiasm of those states then monopolizing the launching and operation of satellites.

Should it be decided – in spite of the considerations advanced in the previous section – to establish a WACA, the first question would be: in what legal form should that be done?

The easiest course would be to establish it as a quasi-autonomous body within the UN itself, such as the High Commissioner for Refugees (UNHCR), the UN Development Programme (UNDP) or the UN Environment Programme (UNEP), with an executive head nominally appointed by the UN Secretary-General with the approval of the

---

[25] As referred to by Jozef Goldblat in *Arms Control: A Guide to Negotiations and Agreements* (PRIO, 1994) [hereinafter "Goldblat"], pp. 230-32, in which the author expresses a similar skeptical view as follows from the analysis in the present text.

[26] In the 1961 McCoy-Zorin Statement – see *ibid*, p. 230.

[27] UN doc. A/AC.206/14, later published as *Implications of Establishing an International Satellite Monitoring Agency* (UN Publications Sales No. E.83.IX.3).

General Assembly, a suitable political governing body, and a secretariat largely controlled by the executive head; all this would require is a resolution of the UN General Assembly. A more conventional route would be the creation of an IGO by a multilateral treaty, which could either just establish the organization and leave its tasks to be defined by separate treaties concerning different arms control regimes, or have such tasks included in the principal treaty itself or in protocols thereto. Finally, considering the absolutely crucial importance of these tasks, one could contemplate establishing a WACA as a new principal organ of the United Nations by suitably amending the UN Charter and thereby giving that organ the maximum international political clout available.

Such a WACA would presumably in the first instance absorb the existing world-wide arms control regimes: the IAEA's in connection with NPT, as well as OPCW, CTBT, the Landmines Convention, the UN Registers of Military Budgets and of Conventional Arms Transfers, and the UN Secretary-General's functions in monitoring compliance with the 1925 Geneva Protocol. Possibly, some of the few regional regimes, in particular those that parallel NPT, might also be absorbed. Moreover, WACA could also establish controls over some of the regimes that currently have none or only very primitive ones, such as the Biological Weapons Convention, ENMOD, Seabed Placement and possibly the Inhumane Weapons Convention[28] (though that falls more in the field of humanitarian than of arms control activities), and also carry out the functions tentatively foreseen in the above-mentioned 1990 study of the UN's rôle in verification.

A crucial question would be whether such an organization or organ should take over some or all of the arms control legislative functions at present carried out by the UN General Assembly or under its control. In part the answer to that would depend on the form of the proposed WACA: as a quasi-autonomous but still subsidiary organ of the General Assembly, as an independent IGO, or as a new principal UN organ. In a sense there may be an advantage in having a full-time consideration of these normative issues rather than the necessarily periodic ones that the General Assembly can give them -- which currently leads to a great deal of effort being put into the annual crafting of repetitive resolutions that admittedly normally accomplish very little. On the other hand, the General Assembly is becoming more and more the recognized central forum for all important international political

---

[28] See the Convention referred to in endnote x to the Annex.

questions, and consequently its rôle in respect of arms control should not be completely excluded, though it might be shared with a suitable WACA.

The principal advantage of a comprehensive WACA would be that it is likely to have more clout and gravitas than the existing separate regimes – but for serious enforcement in case of non-compliance it would still have to rely on the UN Security Council, which will necessarily retain the monopoly over the institutionalized use of force by the international community.

There may also be some economies of scale and the reduction in the task of coordinating different regimes (taking into account that not much coordination would appear necessary), though experience shows that larger organizations (whether private, governmental or international) tend to develop their own inefficiencies, in part because of the need to ensure internal coordination and in part because of the inevitable rigidities of larger structures.

Certainly the principal problems in establishing a WACA are political, and these have in part been discussed in the previous section dealing with the possible combination of some of the existing regimes. Though not insurmountable, there would have to be some very potent reason to move the world community in this direction.

CONCLUSION

The current system of multiple arms control regimes and control organs does not cause any real problems and combining them would probably be difficult and achieve no significant economies or increase in force or reliability. Nevertheless, ultimately a World Arms Control Agency might be contemplated, especially if the number of monitored arms control regimes should increase significantly.

ANNEX

MULTILATERAL ARMS CONTROL REGIMES AND RELATED CONTROL ARRANGEMENTS[a]

OBJECT	TREATY	CONTROL ARRANGEMENT[b]		OTHER
		INTER-GOVERNMENTAL ORGANIZATION		
		WORLD-WIDE	REGIONAL	
Mass Destruction				
Weapons				
Nuclear				
Proliferation				
	NPT[c]	IAEA[d]	Euratom	London Club[e]
				Zangger Com.[f]
	Tlatelolco[g]	IAEA	OPANAL[h]	
	Rarotonga[i]	IAEA	Consultative Com.	
			S. Pac. Bur. for	
			Economic Coop.	
	Bangkok[j]	IAEA	Commiss. for SE Asia	
			Nucl. Weap-Free Z.	
	Pelindaba[k]	IAEA	Afri. Commiss.	
			on Nucl. Energy	
Testing				
	PTBT[l]	---		
	CTBT[m]	CTBTO[n]		
		& PrepCom		
Seabed Placement				
	SBT[o]	---		
Biological				
Warfare				
	Geneva Prot.[p]	UN S-G[q]		

OBJECT	TREATY	CONTROL ARRANGEMENT[b]		
		INTER-GOVERNMENTAL ORGANIZATION		OTHER
		WORLD-WIDE	REGIONAL	

Biological
  Arms
    BWC[r]   UN Sec.Coun.
                 [OPBTW][s]

Chemical
  Warfare
    Geneva Prot.[p]   UN S-G[q]

  Arms
    CWC[t]   OPCW[u]

Ad hoc Controls
  Iraq
    [S/RES/687   UN Spec. Com.[v]
    (1990)   IAEA]
    S/RES/1784   UNMOVIC[w]
    (1999)   IAEA

Conventional
Weapons
  Landmines
    Mines Prot.[x]   ---

    Lndmi. Conv.[y]   UN-SG

  Environ. Mod.
    ENMOD[z]   Ad hoc Consult.
                      Comm. of Experts

  Armed Forces
    Europe
      CFE[aa]   Joint Consultative
                                      Group/OSCE[bb]

      CSBMs[cc]   OSCE

OBJECT	TREATY	CONTROL ARRANGEMENT[b]		
		INTER-GOVERNMENTAL ORGANIZATION		OTHER
		WORLD-WIDE	REGIONAL	
Central Asia				
	CBM[dd]	---		
	RAF[ee]	---		
Missile Technology				
	MTCR[ff]	---		
Arms Export & Trade				
World-Wide				
	Wassenaar[gg]	Wassenaar Secretariat		
	Milit.Expend.	UN S-G[hh]		
	Conv. Arms. Transf.Regis.	UN S-G[ii]		
Europe				
	EU CoC on Arms Exports[jj]		EC Commission	
Latin America				
	I-A Conv.Illicit Manuf.&Traffic.[kk] Firearms, etc.		Consult. Comm.	
	I-A Conv.Transpar. in Conv.Weap. Acquisition[ll]		OAS General Secret.	

---

a. Aside from omitting bilateral and very restricted multilateral arms control and disarmament treaties, this list also does not include some multilateral treaties that have arms control implications but that provide for no types of controls whatsoever (e.g, the Outer Space Treaty).

b. Only those that involve some type of international mechanism. Where there is no entry, any controls would be direct state-to-state ones, as provided for in the respective treaty.
c. Non-Proliferation Treaty = 1968 Treaty on the Non-Proliferation of Nuclear Weapons, UNTS vol. 729, p. 161; ILM vol. 7, p. 809; Goldblat (*supra* note 25) p. 343.
d. International Atomic Energy Agency.
e. London Nuclear Suppliers Group (NSG), see Goldblat pp. 86-88.
f. Zangger Committee = NPT Exporters Committee, see Goldblat p. 88.
g. 1967 Treaty for the Prohibition of Nuclear Weapons in Latin America [and the Caribbean], as amended in 1990, 1991 and 1992, original text in UNTS vol. 634, p. 281; ILM vol. 6, p. 521; Goldblat p. 326.
h. Organization for the Prohibition of Nuclear Weapons in Latin America (acronym from the Spanish).
i. 1985 South Pacific Nuclear Free Zone Treaty, ILM vol. 24, p. 1440; Goldblat p. 502.
j. 1995 Southeast Asia Nuclear Free Zone Treaty, ILM vol. 35, p. 641.
k. 1996 African Nuclear Weapons Free Zone Treaty, ILM vol. 35, p. 709.
l. Partial Test Ban Treaty = 1963 Treaty Banning Nuclear Weapons Tests in the Atmosphere, in Outer Space and Under Water, UNTS vol. 480, p. 43; ILM vol. 2, p. 883; Goldblat p. 318.
m. Comprehensive Test Ban Treaty = 1996 Comprehensive Nuclear Test-Ban Treaty, ILM vol. 35, p. 1443.
n. Comprehensive Test Ban Treaty Organization.
o. Seabed Treaty = 1971 Treaty on the Prohibition of the Emplacement of Nuclear Weapons and Other Weapons of Mass Destruction on the Seabed and the Ocean Floor and in the Subsoil Thereof, UNTS vol. 955, p. 115; ILM vol. 10, p. 145; Goldblat p. 349.
p. 1925 Geneva Protocol for the Prohibition of the Use in War of Asphyxiating, Poisonous or Other Gases, and of Bacteriological Methods of Warfare, LNTS vol. 94, p. 65; Goldblat 277.
q. UN Secretary-General, pursuant to UNGA resolution 44/115 B of 15 December 1989.
b. Only those that involve some type of international mechanism. Where there is no entry, any controls would be direct state-to-state ones, as provided for in the respective treaty.
r. Biological Weapons Convention = 1972 Convention on the Prohibition of the Development, Production and Stockpiling of Bacteriological (Biological) and Toxin Weapons and on Their Destruction, UNTS vol. 1015, p. 163; ILM vol. 11, p. 309; Goldblat p. 370.
s. "Organization for the Prohibition of Bacteriological (Biological) and Toxin Weapons", proposed name of the IGO that would be established by Art. IX of the Rolling Text of a Protocol to the BWC (BWC/AD HOC GROUP/45 (Part I), 14 April 1999).
t. Chemical Weapons Convention = 1993 Convention on the Prohibition of the Development, Production, Stockpiling and Use of Chemical Weapons and on Their Destruction, UNTS Reg. No. 33757; ILM vol. 32, p. 804; Goldblat p. 711.
u. Organization for the Prohibition of Chemical Weapons.

v. UN Special Commission, established by Security Council resolution 687 (1990), to be superseded by UNMOVIC.
w. UN Monitoring, Verification and Inspection Commission, established by Security Council resolution 1784 (1999) -- not yet operative as of July 2000.
x. 1981 Protocol II On Prohibitions or Restrictions on the Use of Mines, Booby-Traps and Other Devices (as amended in 1996) to the 1981 Convention on the Prohibition or Restrictions on the Use of Certain Conventional Weapons Which May be Deemed Excessively Injurious or to Have Indiscriminate Effects (Inhumane Weapons Convention), original text: UNTS vol. 1342, p. 137; ILM vol. 19, p. 1529; Goldblat p. 486; amended text, ILM, vol. 35, p. 1206.
y. 1997 Convention on the Prohibition of the Use, Stockpiling, Production and Transfer of Anti-Personnel Mines and on Their Destruction (Oslo/Ottawa Convention), ILM vol. 36, p. 1509.
z. Environmental Modification Convention = 1977 Convention on the Prohibition of Military or any Other Hostile Use of Environment Modification Techniques, UNTS vol. 1108, p. 151; ILM vol. 16, p. 88; Goldblat p. 419.
aa. Conventional Forces in Europe = 1990 Treaty on Conventional Armed Forces in Europe, and subsequent amendments and related agreements, Goldblat pp. 550, 668, 675, 693.
bb. Organization for Security and Co-operation in Europe.
cc. Confidence and Security Building Measures = Document on Confidence-Building Measures and Certain Aspects of Security and Disarmament, included in the 1975 Helsinki Act (Final Act of the Conference on Security and Cooperation in Europe), and subsequent related instruments, Goldblat pp. 405, 644.
b. Only those that involve some type of international mechanism. Where there is no entry, any controls would be direct state-to-state ones, as provided for in the respective treaty.
dd. 1996 Agreement Between Kazakhstan, Kyrgystan, Russia, Tajikistan and China on Confidence Building Measures in the Military Field in the Border Area, to be set out in Goldblat revised edition (2000).
ee. 1997 Agreement Between Kazakhstan, Kyrgystan, Russia, Tajikistan and China on the Mutual Reduction of Armed Forces in the Border Area, to be set out in Goldblat revised edition (2000).
ff. Missile Technology Control Regime = 1987/1992 Guidelines for Sensitive Missile-Related Transfers, Goldblat p. 683.
gg. 1996 Wassenaar Arrangement on Export Controls for Conventional Arms and Dual-Use Goods and Technologies, to be set out in Goldblat revised edition (2000).
hh. Pursuant to UNGA resolution 53/72 of 4 December 1998, incorporating resolution 35/142 B of 12 December 1980.
ii. UN Register of Conventional Arms, established pursuant to UNGA resolutions 46/36L ("Transparency in Armaments") of 9 December 1991.
jj. 1998 EU Code of Conduct on Arms Exports, to be set out in Goldblat revised edition (2000).
kk. 1997 Inter-American Convention Against Illicit Manufacturing of and Trafficking in Firearms, Ammunition, Explosives and Other Related Materials, http://www.oas.org/EN/PROG/JURIDICO/english/treaties/a-63/html, to be set out in Goldblat, revised edition (2000).

11. 1999 Inter-American Convention on Transparency in Conventional Weapons Acquisitions, http://www.oas.org/EN/PROG/JURIDICO /english/treaties/a-64/html, to be set out in Goldblat, revised edition (2000).

THE PROLIFERATION OF INTERNATIONAL INSTITUTIONS DEALING WITH INTERNATIONAL ENVIRONMENTAL MATTERS

Gerhard Loibl[*]

INTRODUCTION

When looking for international institutions dealing with environmental issues today it becomes obvious very quickly that nearly all international organizations within the United Nations system and numerous other international organizations have taken up the challenge of environmental protection and sustainable development. Moreover, most regional organizations are involved in environmental matters, as well as a large number of institutions, which have been set up on the bilateral or sub-regional level, such as river commissions.

Before analyzing why this situation has came about over the last decades the evolution of international environmental law should be recalled in order to provide a better understanding for the current institutional structure concerning environmental issues on the international level. Compared with other areas of public international law international environmental law is a relatively new area of international relations. Although a few international treaties, which deal with matters concerning the environment, have been concluded after the end of the Second World War, the broad public only paid close attention to environmental issues during the last third of the 20th century. The United Nations Conference on a Human Environment[1], which was held in Stockholm in 1972, has to be seen as the catalyst for the speedy evolution of environmental regulations, both on the national and international level. The United Nations Conference on Environment and Development, held in Rio de Janeiro in 1992, made it evident that a

---
[*] Professor, Institute of International Public Law and International Relations, University of Vienna; former director for international affairs, Federal ministry for the Environment.
[1] Cf. Declaration of the United Nations Conference on the Human Environment 1972 (ILM 11 (1972), 1416 ff.)

compromise was necessary between environmental protection and economic development. This was not only underlined in the Rio Declaration on Environment and Development[2] setting the aim of sustainable development, but is also clearly reflected in the large number of international regulations which have been adopted in the last decade.

International regulations dealing with issues of environmental protection and sustainable development have – like on the national level – been centred on a sectoral approach, i.e. regulations have been created when an environmental problem became evident and the international community felt that an international or regional treaty was necessary.[3] Moreover, when looking at the question of "proliferation of international institutions dealing with environmental matters" another factor has to be taken into account: international law making in the environmental area follows very often a framework approach, i.e. first basic principles and an institutional setting for the further elaboration of those basic principles are set up in an international agreement. Within this agreed framework more detailed provisions are to be elaborated. Examples for this approach are the ECE Convention on Long-range Transboundary Air Pollution 1979 and its Protocols or the United Nations Framework Convention on Climate Change 1992 (UNFCCC) and the Kyoto Protocol 1997.[4] Whereas the UNFCCC contains basic principles and institutional arrangements, more detailed rules to deal with climate change are set out in the Kyoto Protocol.[5] In other areas of international environmental law treaties containing general provisions have been supplemented by protocols dealing with specific questions. This approach has been followed e.g. in the fields of biodiversity or the transboundary movement of hazardous wastes.[6]

---

[2] ILM 31 (1992), 874 ff.

[3] Gehring, International Environmental Regimes: Dynamic Sectoral Legal Systems, YbIEL 1 (1990), 35 ff.

[4] The first time a framework convention approach was used in the context of the Barcelona Convention for the Protection of the Mediterranean Sea Against Pollution 1976.

[5] The central obligation contained in the Kyoto Protocol is Article 3 para. 1 which states that industrialised countries ("Parties included in Annex I") "shall, individually or jointly, ensure that their aggregate anthropogenic carbon dioxide equivalent emissions of the greenhouse gases listed in Annex A do not exceed their assigned amounts, calculated pursuant to their quantified emission limitation and reduction commitments inscribed in Annex B and in accordance with the provisions of this Article, with a view to reducing their overall emissions of such gases by at least 5 per cent below 1990 levels in the commitment period 2008 to 2012".

[6] Cf. also the Convention on Biological Diversity and the Cartagena Protocol on Biosafety to the Convention on Biological Diversity.

The proliferation of international institutions in the environmental field – in particular since 1992 – has also been pointed out in the report of the Secretary-General of the United Nations "Renewing the United Nations: A Programme for Reform"[7]:

> "In the United Nations, the Commission on Sustainable Development has become an important policy forum; environmental capacities within major United Nations bodies and specialized agencies have been developed; and the number of international environmental conventions with autonomous governing bodies and secretariats has been growing".[8]

In the area of international environmental regulations various questions are raised in regard to the institutional arrangements. Among the issues which have come to the attention of the public and which need to be addressed are the following:

- the relationship between the various institutions (in particular UNEP and CSD) which have been created within the United Nations system;
- the relationship to other international organizations which deal with international environmental matters; and
- the role and status of the institutions which have been established by multilateral environmental treaties.

In discussing institutional arrangements concerning international environmental issues it has to be borne in mind that the evolution of international environmental law – as has been shown above – has already established a pattern which has some impact on the institutional arrangements concerning environmental matters on the international level.

---

[7] A/51/950 dated 14 July 1997.
[8] A/51/950, para. 173.

INTERNATIONAL INSTITUTIONS WHICH HAVE BEEN ESTABLISHED WITHIN THE UNITED NATIONS ORGANIZATION TO DEAL WITH GLOBAL ENVIRONMENTAL AND SUSTAINABLE DEVELOPMENT ISSUES

Both at the Stockholm Conference 1972 and the Rio Conference 1992 institutional arrangements to deal with the further implementation of the programmes adopted by those Conferences were discussed. In the aftermath of the two UN-Conferences new institutions were set up: in 1972 UNEP was established by the General Assembly and in 1992 the Commission of Sustainable Development was created by the General Assembly.

UNEP (UNITED NATIONS ENVIRONMENT PROGRAMME)

The United Nations Environment Programme was established by the United Nations General Assembly in 1972 upon the recommendation of the Stockholm Conference.[9] UNEP reports through the ECOSOC to the GA. The functions of UNEP include promoting international co-operation in the field of the environment and providing general policy guidelines for the formulation and co-ordination of the UN's environmental programmes.[10] UNEP has in the past been the main UN body to deal with environmental issues. It has played a decisive role in elaborating new international regulations to deal with upcoming environmental challenges and has – by its Montevideo Programme 1982 as well as the Revised Montevideo Programme 1993 – set the stage for the development of international law on environmental issues.[11] These programmes were the basis for the successful negotiation of a number of multilateral environmental agreements such as the Basel Convention on the Control of Transboundary Movements of Hazardous Wastes and Their Disposal 1989 and the Vienna Convention for the Protection

---

[9] GA-Res. 2997 (XXVII) dated 15 December 1972; ILM 13 (1974) 234; see Kiss/Shelton, International Environmental Law (1991), 59 ff.

[10] Cf. Simma (ed.), The Charta of the United Nations – A Commentary (1995), Art. 55 (a) and (b), 759 ff., at 775.

[11] On the Montevideo Programmes see UNEP, Development and Periodic Review of Environmental Law at the United Nations Environment Programme: Programmes, Implementation and Reviews – Compilation of Documents (1997). Currently the Montevideo III Programme is under consideration. It is planned to be adopted at the next session of the Governing Council in 2001.

of the Ozone Layer 1985. The success of these activities under the auspices of UNEP have been one of the causes for the proliferation of international institutions, as each of these conventions set up their own separate institutional arrangements.[12]

CSD (COMMISSION ON SUSTAINABLE DEVELOPMENT)

The CSD was created as a suborgan of ECOSOC upon request of the General Assembly in accordance with the recommendations of the Rio Conference.[13] As was stated in Chapter 38 of Agenda 21 a "high-level Commission on Sustainable Development should be established in accordance with Article 68 of the Charter of the United Nations".[14] Furthermore, Agenda 21 stated that the Commission was created

> "in order to ensure the effective follow-up of the Conference, as well as to enhance international co-operation and rationalise the intergovernmental decision-making capacity for the integration of environment and development issues and to examine the progress in the implementation of Agenda 21 at the national, regional and international levels"[15].

General Assembly Resolution 47/191 reaffirmed the functions as have been set out in Agenda 21 Chapter 38[16] but recommended furthermore that the Commission should also promote the incorporation of the principles of the Rio Declaration in the implementation of Agenda 21, the incorporation of the

> "Non-legally Binding Authoritative Statement of Principles for a Global Consensus on the Management, Conservation and Sustainable Development of All Types of Forests"

and keep under review the implementation of Agenda 21.[17] Moreover, the General Assembly also decided that the Commission should

---

[12] See below Part 4.
[13] GA-Res. 47/191 dated 22 December 1992.
[14] Para. 38.11 of Agenda 21. Art. 68 of the UN-Charta authorises ECOSOC to "set up commissions in economic and social fields for the promotion of human rights, and such other commissions as may be required for the performance of its functions". Cf. Simma (ed.), The Charta of the United Nations – A Commentary (1995), Art. 68, 875 ff.
[15] Para. 38. 11 of Agenda 21.
[16] Cf. GA-Res. 47/191 op. para. 3.
[17] See GA-Res. 47/191 op. para. 4.

"monitor progress in promoting, facilitating and financing, as appropriate, the access to and the transfer of environmentally sound technologies and corresponding know-how, in particular to developing countries, on favourable terms, including on concessional and preferential terms, as mutually agreed, taking into account the need to protect intellectual property rights as well as the special needs of developing countries for the implementation of Agenda 21" and

"should consider issues related to the provision of financial resources from all available funding sources and mechanisms".[18]

It has to be noted that the Commission of Sustainable Development itself is not a forum for the negotiation of multilateral environmental agreements.

Relationship between UNEP and CSD – Institutional Framework

The relationship between UNEP and CSD raised a number of questions as early as the preparatory process of the Rio Conference. Agenda 21 states in its Chapter 38 that the institutional arrangement of the United Nations has to be adjusted in order to ensure the implementation of Agenda 21. It states that the objectives of the institutional arrangements dealing with environment and development issues should be

"to enhance the role and the functioning of the United Nations system [...]. All relevant agencies, organizations and programmes of the United Nations system should adopt concrete programmes for the implementation of Agenda 21 and also provide policy guidance for the United Nations activities or advice to Governments, upon request, within their areas of competence."

Furthermore, the co-operation and co-ordination on environment and development in the United Nations system should be strengthened. Agenda 21 lists the following bodies within the United Nations system as having a function in its implementation: the General Assembly, the Economic and Social Council, the Commission on Sustainable Development and the Secretary-General. Furthermore, the United Nations Environment Programme, the United Nations Development Programme, the United Nations Conference on Trade and Development

---

[18] GA-Res. 47/191 op. para.5.

and the United Nations Sudano-Sahelian Office are named as having an important role in the implementation of Agenda 21. Whereas, the General Assembly[19] and ECOSOC have mainly a review role in the environmental field, the respective roles of CSD and UNEP, as well as their relationship in the implementation of Agenda 21, need to be further scrutinized. As was set out in Chapter 38 of Agenda 21 the CSD should mainly consider and review information provided by governments and make recommendations to ECOSOC and the General Assembly, whilst UNEP should concentrate on a number of priority areas such as

> "strengthening its catalytic role in stimulating and promoting environmental activities and considerations throughout the United Nations system; promoting international co-operation in the field of environment and recommending, as appropriate, policies to this end" and "co-ordination and promotion of relevant scientific research with a view to providing a consolidated basis for decision making."[20]

The relationship between UNEP and CSD was also discussed at the Earth Summit +5 in 1997 which adopted a "Programme for the Further Implementation of Agenda 21".[21] In regard to UNEP's further goal the Programme states:

> "The role of UNEP, as the principal United Nations body in the field of the environment, should be further enhanced. Taking into account its catalytic role, and in conformity with Agenda 21 and the Nairobi Declaration on the Role and Mandate of the United Nations Environment Programme, adopted on 7 February 1997, UNEP is the leading global environmental authority that sets the global environmental dimension of sustainable development within the United Nations system, and serves as an authoritative advocate for the global environment."[22]

---

[19] Para. 38. 9 states that the General Assembly, "as the highest intergovernmental mechanism, is the principal policy-making and appraisal organ on matters relating to the follow-up of the Conference" and it should consider "holding a special session not later than 1997 for the overall review and appraisal of Agenda 21". This special session was held in 1997 and is known as the Rio+5 Summit.

[20] Cf. Para. 38.22 of Agenda 21.

[21] For an analysis of the Rio+5 Summit see Freudenschuss-Reichl, The 19th Special Session of the United Nations General Assembly "Rio+5", Austrian Review of International and European Law 2 (1997), 425 ff.

[22] Para. 123.

With regard to the CSD the Programme deals both with the future role and programme of work of the CSD[23] as well as the methods of work of the CSD.[24]

---

[23] Paras. 130 – 132.
These paragraphs read in their relevant parts as follows:
"130. The Commission on Sustainable Development, within its mandate as specified in General Assembly resolution 47/191, will continue to provide a central forum for reviewing progress and for urging further implementation of Agenda 21 and other commitments made at the United Nations Conference on Environment and Development or as a result of it; for conducting a high-level policy debate aimed at consensus-building on sustainable development; and for catalysing action and long-term commitment to sustainable development at all levels. It should continue to undertake these tasks in complementing and providing interlinkages to the work of other United Nations organs, organisations and bodies acting in the field of sustainable development. The Commission has a role to play in assessing the challenges of globalisation as they relate to sustainable development. The Commission should perform its functions in co-ordination with other subsidiary bodies of the Economic and Social Council with related organisations and institutions, including making recommendations, within its mandate, to the Economic and Social Council, bearing in mind the interrelated outcomes of recent United Nations conferences.
131. The Commission should focus on issues that are crucial to achieving the goals of sustainable development. It should promote policies that integrate economic, social and environmental dimensions of sustainability and should provide for integrated consideration of linkages, both among sectors and between sectoral and cross-sectoral aspects of Agenda 21. In this connection, the Commission should carry out its work in such a manner as to avoid unnecessary duplication and repetition of work undertaken by other relevant forums."

[24] Paras. 133 – 137. The relevant parts of the programme reads:
"133. Based on the experience gained during the period 1993-1997, the Commission, under the guidance of the Economic and Social Council, should:
Make concerted efforts to attract the greater involvement in its work of ministers and high-level national policy makers responsible for specific economic and social sectors, who, in particular, are encouraged to participate in the annual high-level segment of the Commission, together with the ministers and policy makers responsible for environment and development. The high-level segments of the Commission should become more interactive, and should focus on the priority issues being considered at a particular session. The Bureau of the Commission should conduct timely and open-ended consultations with a view to improving the organisation of the work of the high-level segment;
Continue to provide a forum for the exchange of national experience and best practices in the area of sustainable development, including through voluntary national communications or reports. Consideration should be given to the results of ongoing work aimed at streamlining requests for national information and reporting and to the results of the "pilot phase" relating to indicators of sustainable development. In this context, the Commission should consider more effective modalities for the further implementation of the commitments made in Agenda 21, with the appropriate emphasis on the means of implementation. Countries may wish to submit to the Commission, on a voluntary basis, information regarding

Thus, the Earth Summit + 5 underlined the distribution of work between the two organs which have been set up following the two UN-Conferences dealing with environmental matters: UNEP is to concentrate on its catalytic role, whereas CSD should give policy guidance for the implementation of Agenda 21. This statement on the relationship between UNEP and CSD may be seen as clarifying *in abstracto* the different roles of these institutions, but whether it will lead to the avoidance of duplications and a coherent approach to environmental issues in their practical work remains to be seen. A number of issues still need to be tackled, such as the input to be made by UNEP to the annual sessions of CSD or the follow-up to the documentation prepared for CSD by the UN-Secretariat on the annual topics in the work of UNEP.

In general, it has to be noted that neither the UNEP-Governing Council nor the CSD have the competence to adopt legally binding decisions. Decisions or resolutions adopted by them are indicators of the will of the member States on how to tackle environmental issues in the future. They determine the direction these international bodies should take in their future activities.

INTERNATIONAL ORGANIZATIONS DEALING WITH ENVIRONMENTAL MATTERS

The increasing awareness of environmental issues, which became manifest in the Rio Declaration 1992, is also reflected in the work programmes of other international organizations. Agenda 21 has set such a wide field for activities that in principle all international organizations have included issues on environment and sustainable development in their respective work programmes. E.g. the World Meteorological Organization (WMO), the World Health Organization, the International Maritime Organization (IMO), the Food and Agri-

---

their efforts to incorporate the relevant recommendations of other United Nations conferences in national sustainable development strategies;
[...]
(d) Establish closer interaction with international financial, development and trade institutions, as well as with the relevant bodies within and outside the United Nations system, including the World Bank, GEF, UNDP, the World Trade Organisation, UNCTAD and UNEP, which, in turn, are invited to take full account of the results of the policy deliberations in the Commission and to integrate them in their own work programmes and activities; [....].

culture Organization (FAO)[25] and the World Bank Group[26] have taken up the challenge of sustainable development in their activities.[27] Moreover, at the regional level a large number of organizations deal with environmental matters. In Europe, environmental issues are discussed e.g. within the UNECE, the Council of Europe, OSCE and NATO.[28] Moreover, OECD plays a leading role in developing policies concerning environmental issues.[29]

This large number of international organizations dealing with environmental matters run the risk of duplication of work and the creation of numerous regulations which even might be contradictory. Thus, co-ordination between the various international organizations is essential. Within the United Nations system the co-ordination between the UN and its specialized agencies and other intergovernmental bodies – although the General Assembly and ECOSOC are primarily responsible for performing these tasks – takes place within the Administrative Committee on Co-ordination (ACC) which is chaired by the Secretary-General.[30]

---

[25] Birnie/Boyle, International Law and the Environment (1992), 53 ff.

[26] For a detailed description of the activities of the World Bank Group see Shihata, The World Bank's Contribution to the Development of International Environmental Law, in: Hafner/Loibl/Rest/Sucharipa-Behrmann/Zemanek (eds.), Liber Amicorum Seidl-Hohenveldern (1998), 631 ff.; Loibl, The World Bank Group and Sustainable Development, in: Weiss/Denters/de Waart (eds.), International Economic Law with a Human Face (1998), 513 ff.

[27] Cf. the annual reports in the Yearbook of International Environmental Law (since 1990) which give an overview of the activities of the various international organisations and bodies in the environmental field.

[28] Cf. Kiss/Shelton, International Environmental Law (1991), 59 ff.

[29] See Birnie/Boyle, International Law and the Environment (1992), 71 ff.; for the ongoing activities of OECD in the environmental area cf. the annual reports in YbIEL.

[30] Simma (ed.), The Charta of the United Nations – A Commentary (1995), Art. 99, 1033 ff, at 1041.

INTERNATIONAL INSTITUTIONS ESTABLISHED WITHIN THE FRAMEWORK OF MULTILATERAL ENVIRONMENTAL TREATIES – COMMON FEATURES

The Institutional Arrangements of Multilateral Environmental Treaties

As has been shown above – a number of international institutions (both organs within the UNO and specialized agencies) deal with environmental matters and questions of sustainable development, the question of the proliferation of international institutions has been made evident by the increase of separate institutional arrangements within multilateral environmental conventions.

International environmental agreements, which have been adopted in the last decades, have followed a certain pattern with regard to their institutional arrangements: most of these treaties have established at least two institutions:

- a Conference of the Parties (so-called COP), and
- a Secretariat.

Furthermore, a number of them have in addition established subsidiary bodies to deal with such issues as scientific and technological advice or implementation (e.g. the United Nations Framework Convention on Climate Change established SBI and SBSTA).

Each of these institutions have been entrusted with different tasks under the respective international treaties dealing with environmental issues.

Under the UNFCCC the Conference of the Parties is entrusted in accordance with Article 7

> "as the supreme body of this Convention" to keep "under regular review the implementation and any related legal instruments that the Conference of the Parties may adopt, and shall make, within its mandate, the decisions necessary to promote the effective implementation of the Convention".[31]

To this end, it shall, among other matters, "periodically examine the obligations of the Parties and the institutional arrangements under the Convention", "consider and adopt regular reports on the implementation of the Convention", "make recommendations on any matters

---

[31] Art. 7 para. 2.

necessary for the implementation of the Convention" and "seek and utilise, where appropriate, the services and co-operation of, and information provided by, competent international organizations and intergovernmental and non-governmental bodies".

According to Article 8 paragraph 2, the functions of the Climate Change Secretariat shall be

> "to make arrangements for sessions of the Conference of the Parties and its subsidiary bodies established under the Convention and to provide them with services as required; to compile and transmit reports transmitted to it; to facilitate assistance to the Parties, particularly developing country Parties, on request, in the compilation and communication of information required in accordance with the provisions of the Convention; to prepare reports on its activities and present them to the Conference of the Parties; to ensure the necessary co-ordination with the secretariats of other relevant international bodies;" and

> "to enter, under the overall guidance of the Conference of the Parties, into administrative and contractual arrangements as may be required for the effective discharge of its functions."

Similar provisions concerning the functions of the Conference of the Parties, as well as of the secretariat are to be found in other multilateral environmental agreements, e.g. the Basel Convention on the Control of Transboundary Movements of Hazardous Wastes and their Disposal 1989[32], the Vienna Convention for the Protection of the Ozone Layer 1985[33] and the Montreal Protocol on Substances that Deplete the Ozone Layer 1987[34], the Convention on Biological Diversity 1992[35] and the Cartagena Protocol on Biological Safety 2000[36], the United Nations Convention to Combat Desertification in Countries Experiencing Serious Drought and/or Desertification, Particularly in Africa 1994 or the Rotterdam Convention on the Prior Informed Consent Procedure for Certain Hazardous Chemicals and Pesticides in International Trade 1988[37]. Such arrangements are also found in the

---

[32] Article 15 (Conference of the Parties) and Article 16 (Secretariat).
[33] Article 6 (Conference of the Parties) and Article 7 (Secretariat).
[34] Article 11 (Meeting of the Parties) and Article 12 (Secretariat).
[35] Article 23 (Conference of the Parties) and Article 24 (Secretariat).
[36] Article 29 (Conference of the Parties serving as the meeting of the Parities to the Protocol) and Article 31 (Secretariat).
[37] Article 18 (Conference of the Parties) and Article 19 (Secretariat).

multilateral environmental agreements which have been elaborated within the framework of the United Nations Economic Commission for Europe, such as the Espoo Convention on Environmental Impact Assessment in a Transboundary Context 1991[38] or the Helsinki Convention on the Protection and Use of Transboundary Watercourses and International Lakes 1992[39].

Regarding the establishment of secretariats two approaches may be distinguished: a number of multilateral environmental agreements provide that "the Conference of the Parties, at its first session, shall designate a permanent secretariat and make arrangements for its functioning." This approach has been followed in the UNFCCC[40] and the United Nations Convention to Combat Desertification[41].

Other multilateral environmental agreements determine that "the secretariat functions [...] shall be performed by an existing organization" or an organ. This approach has been followed in two ways in multilateral environmental agreements. Whereas the Convention on Biological Diversity[42] stated that the first Conference of the Parties will at its first ordinary meeting designate the secretariat amongst existing competent international organizations, the Rotterdam Convention 1998[43] and the draft Convention on Persistent Organic Pollutants, which is currently being negotiated, already determine in the Convention itself the international organization which is to be the secretariat.[44] The latter method

---

[38] Article 11 (Meeting of the Parties) and Article 13 (Secretariat).
[39] Article 17 (Meeting of the Parties) and Article 19 (Secretariat).
[40] Article 8 para. 3.
[41] Article 23 para. 3.
[42] Article 24 para. 2 reads:
"At its first ordinary meeting, the Conference of the Parties shall designate the secretariat from amongst those existing competent international organisations which have signified their willingness to carry out the secretariat functions under the Convention."
[43] Art. 19 pares 3 and 4 read as follows:
"3. The secretariat functions for this Convention shall be performed jointly by the Executive Director of UNEP and the Director-General of FAO, subject to such arrangements as shall be agreed between them and approved by the Conference of the Parties.
4. The Conference of the Parties may decide, by a three-fourths majority of the Parties present and voting, to entrust the secretariat functions to one or more other competent international organisations, should it find that the Secretariat is not functioning as intended."
[44] See Draft Article P para. 3 which reads:
"The secretariat functions for this Convention shall be performed by the Executive Director of the United Nations Environment Programme, unless the Conference

is also used by Conventions, which have been elaborated under the auspices of the United Nations Economic Commission for Europe.[45]

Following the first approach the United Nations Framework Convention on Climate Change states in its Article 8 that the Conference of the Parties, at its first session, shall designate a permanent secretariat and make arrangements for its functioning. Consequently the COP dealt with the status of the Secretariat at its first session in 1995. In its Decision 14/CP.1 op. para. 2, adopted at the first session of the Conference of the Parties, it was stated:

> "Decides that the Convention secretariat shall be institutionally linked to the United Nations, while not being fully integrated in the work programme and management structure of any particular department or programme".[46]

It was further agreed that the functioning of the institutional linkage set up was to be reviewed no later than 31 December 1999. [47] Although the question of the legal status was raised and debated at some length at COP2, a decision on the legal status of the Secretariat was deferred to be discussed at a later date, but not later than 31 December 1999.[48]

At its fifth session the Conference of the Parties[49] in 1999 decided that consideration of the juridical personality of the Convention secretariat on the international plane should be deferred and taken up in 2001 in conjunction with the review of the overall linkage of the Con-

---

of the Parties decides, by a three-fourths majority of the Parties present and voting, to entrust the secretariat functions to one or more other international organizations". (UNEP/POPS/INC.3/4).

[45] These conventions provide that the "Executive Secretary of the Economic Commission for Europe shall carry out" the secretariat functions.

[46] Cf. FCCC/CP/1995/7/Add.1, p. 42

[47] Cf. Decision 14/CP.1 op.para. 4 (FCCC/CP/1995/7/Add.1). The relevant paragraphs of this decision read as follows:

"4. Decides further, to review the functioning of the institutional linkage referred to in paragraph 2 above, not later than 31 December 1999, in consultation with the Secretariat-General, with a view to making such modifications as may be considered desirable by both parties".

[48] Cf. Decision 15/CP2 op. para. 2 (FCCC/CP/1996/15/Add.1) which reads:

"Concludes that the Conference of the Parties should consider, in the context of the review of the functioning of the institutional linkage of the Convention secretariat to the United Nations, whether the functions that have to be carried out by the secretariat necessitate that it be given juridical personality on the international plane."

[49] The fifth session of the Conference of Parties took place in November 1999 in Bonn, Germany.

vention secretariat to the United Nations, which is to be completed by 31 December of that year.[50] By adopting this decision the Conference of the Parties underlined that the existing institutional arrangement, which avoids addressing the question of the legal status of the Secretariat, has not given rise to problems in practice and has worked satisfactorily for the Parties and the Secretariat alike. Furthermore, it should be noted that by establishing the above described institutional arrangements, the creation of a new international organization could be avoided. Thus, the Secretary-General of the United Nations and the Executive Director of the Climate Change Secretariat signed the headquarters agreement for the Climate Change Secretariat with the Federal Republic of Germany.[51]

A different approach has been taken under the Convention on Biological Diversity. Following Article 24 para. 2 the COP decided at its first session to designate UNEP as the secretariat of the Convention[52] and it decided to locate the secretariat in Montreal, Canada at its second session[53]. The COP took its decision based on a "note" prepared by the interim secretariat which contained the recommendations made by the Intergovernmental Committee concerning the secretariat[54] and the proposals which had been received by UNEP, the World Conservation Union (IUCN), UNDP, the Intergovernmental Oceanographic

---

[50] Cf. FCCC/SBI/1999/L.11, p. 16.

[51] Cf. FCCC/CP/1996/MISC.1. A similar pattern has been followed within United Nations Convention to Combat Desertification. Article 23 para. 3 states that "the Conference of the Parties, at its first session, shall designate a Permanent Secretariat and make arrangements for its functioning".

[52] Cf. Decision I/4 entitled "Selection of a competent international organisation to carry out the functions of the Secretariat of the Convention" (UNEP/CBD/COP/1/17).

[53] See Decision II/19 op.para.2

[54] The Intergovernmental Committee recommended a lost of attributes an other considerations which might be used to indicate a range of suitable organisations to be considered by the Conference of the Parties when determining the international organisation to perform the secretariat function under the Convention. Among them the Committee listed the following: relevance of the mandate, general objectives and substantive activities of the organisation to the purpose and objectives of the Convention; extent to which the organisation could provide technical support to the substantive work to be undertaken under the Convention and co-ordinated by the Secretariat; demonstrated effectiveness of the organisation in its own sphere of activities; and experience in providing secretariat functions to an intergovernmental process ((UNEP/CBD/COP/1/9, para.6).

Commission (IOC) and FAO.[55] The "headquarters agreement" concerning the Biodiversity Secretariat was negotiated and signed by the Executive Director of UNEP. Thus, the secretariat of the Convention on Biological Diversity, which has been established in accordance with Article 40, is part of UNEP and has no juridical personality of its own.

Furthermore, the memoranda of understanding between the Conference of the Parties and the Council of the Global Environmental Facility (GEF) underline that the member States will not give a legal status to institutions created by the multilateral environmental agreements. These memoranda have been adopted by decisions of the COP and the language used in them indicates that they are not legally binding instruments, but non-legal instruments on co-operation between these institutions.[56] This is also demonstrated by the Memorandum of understanding between the Conference of the Parties to the United Nations Convention to Combat Desertification and the International Fund for Agricultural Development regarding the modalities and administrative operations of the Global mechanisms which was adopted by Decision 10/COP.3 on 26 November 1999. The terminology used – e.g. it "enters into operation" – is an indication of the Parties' will that the memorandum shall not constitute a treaty under international law.[57]

A Legal Appraisal of the Institutional Arrangements Set up under International Environmental Agreements

Generally an "international organization" is understood to be a form of co-operation founded on an international agreement creating at least one organ with a will of its own, established under international law, i.e. that the organ has the competence to express its will vis-à-vis the member States.[58] Moreover, such an international organization set up would

---

[55] UNEP/CBD/COP/1/9. Cf. Report of the First Meeting of the Conference of the Parties to the Convention on Biological Diversity (UNEP/CBD/COP/1/17, paras. 63 – 69).

[56] Cf. e.g. the Memorandum of Understanding between the Conference of the Parties to the Convention on Biological Diversity and the Council of the Global Environmental Facility (Decision III/8) and the Memorandum of Understanding between the Conference of the Parties to the United Nations Framework Convention on Climate Change and the Council of the Global Environmental Facility (Decision 12/CP.2).

[57] See ICCD/COP (3)/20/Add.1, 37 ff.

[58] Cf. Blokker/Schermers, International Institutional Law, 3 ed. (1995), § 33; Seidl-Hohenveldern/Loibl, Das Recht der Internationalen Organisationen

have legal personality under international law, in particular, in relationship to its member States within its area of competence. It would, e.g. be entitled to enter into international agreements governed by international law with other subjects of international law.[59]

Taking into account the above given definition of an international organization an analysis demonstrates that the Conference of the Parties – under each of the international environmental agreements – has a will independent from its member States. Although so far, no agreement has been reached under most multilateral environmental agreements on the question of the voting rules applicable to adoption of COP decisions, it has to be borne in mind that all draft rules of procedure provide for majority decisions on those matters which fall within the competence of the respective Conference of the Parties.[60] Thus, Parties have accepted that the Conference of the Parties has a will independent of that of its members. Furthermore, the structure of the secretariat follows along the lines known within international organizations such as the United Nations Organization. Although, in principle the elements for an international organization would be fulfilled, Parties determined during the negotiations not to grant international legal personality to the "organization" or secretariat in the Convention itself. Moreover, Parties have withheld such personality from the "organization" itself or the Secretariat by not adopted relevant COP decisions. Therefore, it would not reflect political or legal reality if the conclusion were to be drawn by an academic analysis that an international organization, i.e. a subject of international law, was created in any of these international environmental agreements. As the example of the headquarters agreements shows the Parties to the multilateral environmental

---

einschließlich der Supranationalen Gemeinschaften, 6. Auflage (1996), Rz 111; see also Abi-Saab (ed.), The concept of international organization (1981), 11 f.

[59] Cf. Reparations for Injuries suffered in the Service of the United Nations, Advisory Opinion ICJ Reports (1949), 174 ff. See also Brownlie, Principles of Public International Law, 5th ed. (1998) who states that "the criteria of legal personality may be summarised as follows:

"a permanent association of states, with lawful objects, equipped with organs;

a distinction, in terms of legal powers and purposes, between the organisation and its member states;

the existence of legal powers exercisable on the international plane and not solely within the national systems of one or more states." (679 f.).

[60] Cf. e.g. the rules of procedure "applied" under the UNFCCC. So far no agreement could be reached concerning majority decisions under the Convention (see Report of the President of the Conference of the Parties at its second session, on his informal consultations on the draft rules of procedure (FCCC/CP/1997/5)).

agreements have found ways to avoid the expression that subjects of international law exist or have been established.

A tendency emerges which can be found also in other areas of international law and international relations: States are reluctant to create new international organizations for a number of reasons.[61] They might – although States are rather cautious about expressing their concerns – include the following: the creation of new international organizations would add new international administrations to the already existing ones; duplication of work should be avoided and the already undertaken efforts in existing international organizations should be used in the most efficient manner for the implementation of new international agreements; implications for already existing international organizations and institutions and their work programmes would need to be taken into account. It seems that the international community has taken a rather cautious and practical approach to new international institutional arrangements. Taking these developments into account it may be concluded that States would like to see whether there is a need for further international organizations or whether a rather limited approach proves to be sufficient to deal with the challenges for the international community raised by environmental issues.

As has been described above, if such an institution created by an international environmental agreement would be given legal personality under international law it would be such a subject and able to enter into a host country agreement in its own name. In each case the Secretariat has been able to derive its international juridical personality, through its parent body – the UNO – and enter into the host country agreement for and on behalf of the UNO. But as practice shows, member States of international environmental agreements have refrained from taking such a step and have rather found other constructions to "side-step" the question of whether a new subject of international law has been created or needs to be created. So far, this has not lead to problems in practice or in law, it could be an incentive to academic analysis of this state practice, which does not follow the classical theories of international law on organizations.

Academic writings have not taken much notice of the trend of institutional arrangements within the framework of international envi-

---

[61] Cf. e.g. the history of the Organisation of Security and Cooperation in Europe (OSCE). So far – although it is called an organisation and various organs have been established (see e.g. the Paris Charta for a New Europe 1990) – no international agreements could be reached to establish an international organisation in accordance with international law.

ronmental agreements; nor have they developed a theoretical approach to deal with this new phenomenon. Although in other areas of international law a reluctance to create new international organizations has also been witnessed[62], no other area of international law has seen such a similar general trend as in the area of multilateral environmental agreements. International institutions, but no new subjects of international law have been established, have been created to operate in the environmental field.

ISSUES RAISED BY THE PROLIFERATION OF INTERNATIONAL INSTITUTIONS IN THE ENVIRONMENTAL FIELD

The large number of international organizations dealing with environmental issues and the institutional arrangements set up by multilateral environmental agreements raise a number of issues. Although no subjects of international law have been set up by the multilateral environmental agreements the number of such treaties has grown enormously in the last years. This development raises a number of issues:
- not only has the number of international institutions and thus the number of international meetings grown in the last years, but also the amount of documents and information provided to States have increased enormously;
- governments, thus, face the challenge of having to attend an ever larger number of international meetings, which also requires preparation and co-ordination on the national level; this may not only be difficult for smaller countries and developing countries, but has become a challenging task for all countries; and
- the growing number of agreements also leads to increased reporting requirements, which might be difficult to fulfil for smaller, and developing countries.

Thus, the currently applied methods of law making in the environmental area as well as the consequential institutional arrangements have to be questioned. The sectoral approach that has been followed and has been successful in so far as the international community was able to address emerging environmental problems quickly might have

---

[62] Cf. the development of the CSCE and the creation of the OSCE, which also falls short of an international organisation in the classical sense.

to be changed in the future. The decentralized law-making process of international environmental law should be adapted in order to avoid the above raised matters. It seems unlikely that the pattern of environmental law making on a sectoral basis will be changed in the near future, but a more coherent and co-ordinated approach seems to be necessary and has been used already in recent years. Certain questions, such as information sharing and clearing-house mechanisms, dispute settlement procedures, compliance procedures or financial resources, technology transfer and capacity buildings, have arisen under most multilateral environmental agreements. Although, it has proven that – due to the different structure of the various instruments – it is not possible to elaborate a "model provision" which could be incorporated into future multilateral environmental agreements, some common features may be elaborated and synergies may be used. As the example of dispute settlement mechanisms and compliance procedures demonstrate they have to be adapted to the specific circumstances under each multilateral environmental agreement.[63] Issues such as financial resources have shown that a common and coherent approach could be beneficial. The use of the Global Environmental Facility (GEF) as the main financial instrument for most multilateral environmental agreements negotiated in the last years has proven to be a helpful means to provide financial means for the implementation of the international environmental agreements[64], although it has to be borne in mind that criticism has been raised by developing countries sometimes on the role of GEF.[65] Thus, a multiplication of administrative structures in the

---

[63] Cf. e.g. the compliance provisions elaborated under UNFCCC and the Kyoto Protocol (see Loibl, Compliance with International Environmental Law – The Emerging Regime under the Kyoto Protocol, in: Benedek/Isak/Kicker (ed.), Development and Developing International and European Law – Essays in Honour of Konrad Ginther on the Occasion of his 65th Birthday (1999), 263 ff.; Werksman, Compliance and the Kyoto Protocol: Building a Backbone into a "Flexible" Regime, YbIEL 9 (1999), 48 ff.

[64] In the last years GEF was not included as the financial instrument under the international agreements dealing with the protection of the ozone layer and desertification. Article 10 of the amended Montreal Protocol sets up a Multilateral Fund, whereas the Global Mechanism set up by Article 21 para. 4 of the Desertification Convention is hosted by the International Fund for Agricultural Development.

[65] Developing countries have critizied that GEF only meets costs for the protection of the global environment and not for the sometimes pressing needs for local environmental protection. Moreover, it has been stated that the restriction to the four main areas of activities excludes new emerging environmental issues from the scope of GEF. In the context of the negotiations for an Internationally Binding Instrument for Implementing International Action on Certain Persistent Organic

financial field – as would have been the result if the example of the Montreal Protocol's Multilateral Fund[66] had been taken up – was avoided. The close co-operation between GEF[67] and the institutions established by the various multilateral environmental agreements – set out in the memoranda of understanding – ensures that the tasks set by the various international environmental agreements are fulfilled.[68]

The question of a better co-ordination between the various activities concerning environmental issues and sustainable development has also been addressed in the Task Force on Environment and Human Settlements set up by the Secretary-General and chaired by the Executive Director of UNEP. The General Assembly took note of its report in Res. 53/242 dated 10 August 1999 and established a framework for the further activities in the area of the environment. It set up an "Environmental Management Group for the purpose of enhancing inter-agency co-ordination in the field of the environment and human settlements, and request[ed] the Secretary-General to develop, in consultation with the Member States and the members of the Administrative Committee on Co-ordination, the mandate, terms of reference, appropriate criteria for membership and flexible, cost-effective working methods of the proposed environment management group and to

---

Pollutants the question whether GEF could be designated as the financial mechanism under the new instrument was raised. Representatives of GEF declared the readiness of GEF to act as the financial mechanism, but it should be borne in mind that such a decision would request increased financial resources for GEF.

The scepticism of developing countries towards GEF is also reflected in the decision of the Conference of the Parties under UNFCCC that GEF "shall be the entity entrusted with the operation of the financial mechanism referred to in Article 11" of UNFCCC, but agreeing that this arrangement is to be reviewed in four years time (Decision 3/CP.4). Thus, GEF was not given a "permanent" status under UNFCCC as the donor countries were seeking (YbIEL 9 (1998), 554).

[66] A Multilateral Fund to meet the incremental costs of developing countries and countries with economies in transition in order to enable them to fulfil their commitments under the Montreal Protocol was set up by the 1990 Amendment the Montreal Protocol. For a detailed description and analysis of the development of the international regime dealing with ozone depletion cf. Benedick, Ozone Diplomacy: New Directions in Safeguarding the Planet (1991). See also Franck, Fairness in International Law and Institutions (1995), 385 f. On the operation of the Multilateral Fund see annual reports in YbIEL.

[67] The funding provided by GEF primarily falls within our "focal areas" – climate change, biological diversity, international waters, and ozone layer depletion. On the structure and activities of GEF after the second replenishment of the GEF Trust Fund in 1998 see report in YbIEL 9 (1998), 550 ff.

[68] Cf. Report on GEF activities in 1998 (YbIEL 9 (1998), 550 ff.).

submit them to the General Assembly for consideration at its fifty-fourth session."[69]

CREATION OF A WORLD ENVIRONMENTAL ORGANIZATION AS A WAY TO DEAL WITH THE INSTITUTIONAL QUESTIONS IN THE ENVIRONMENTAL AREA?

In recent years proposals have been made to create a World Environment Organization encompassing the existing international institutions dealing with environmental issues. In particular, the growing number of international environmental agreements and the setting up of new international institutions have raised concerns on the fragmentation of international law dealing with environmental issues and on the consistency of international environmental regulations. Moreover, the aim of "sustainable development" set by the United Nations Conference on Environment and Development 1992 has underlined the close relationship between environment and economic issues.[70] Furthermore, the use of trade-related instruments in international environmental agreements as a means to achieve environmental goals has given rise to an on-going debate on the relationship between environment and trade rules in a large number of international fora.[71] In particular, the question of the relationship between the rules of GATT/WTO and international environmental regulations has been debated both in academic writings and practice.[72] It was felt that one of the shortcomings of the environmental field was that no overall institutional body existed which would ensure that a comprehensive system of international environmental law was developed as was secured by GATT/WTO. Among the arguments which have been put forward in favour for an attempt of "GATTing the

---

[69] A/RES/53/242, para. 5. Cf. GA Res. 54/217 dated 3 February 2000 which requests the Secretary-General to report on this matter to the 55th session.

[70] See in particular Principle 12 of the Rio Declaration on Environment and Development 1992.

[71] Cf. the discussions in the Committee on Trade and Environment of GATT/WTO, UNEP Governing Council and the work undertaken within UNCTAD and OECD (see annual reports in YbIEL).

[72] Cf. YbIEL 9 (1999). This volume centres on the question of the relationship between trade and environment taking the dispute concerning the United States Import Prohibition of Certain Shrimp and Shrimp Products as the starting point of the discussion.

Greens"[73] into one singular international organization are the following:
- a universal approach to environmental matters would be ensured which might result in dealing with environmental challenges in a more holistic manner;
- "common elements" concerning environmental issues could be elaborated in a structured way, such as provisions on dispute settlement or compliance;
- a balance in the relation with universal economic organizations, such as GATT/WTO could be achieved; and
- common services could be provided to the numerous multilateral environmental agreements, thus saving administrative costs in the nearby future.

Although these arguments for the creation of a World Environment Organization carry some weight they have to be discussed in more detail. A first scrutiny – no detailed proposal has been put forward so far – indicates that a closer analysis is needed. E.g. in the area of dispute settlement and compliance experience demonstrates that "common elements" are found in all international environmental treaties, nevertheless the procedures and mechanisms for each individual agreement has to be tailor-made depending on the stringency of the normative obligations and their structure.[74] Thus, the positive effects of a newly created World Environment Organization might be more limited than envisaged.

In case such a new global international organization is to be established, a number of issues have to be addressed in order to make it a success:
- the diversity of environmental problems has proven the need for specified approaches on the various environmental issues. Therefore, the solutions taken within international environmental instruments differ to a certain extent as the example of the "prior informed consent under the Basel Convention 1989, the Rotterdam Convention 1998 and the Cartagena Protocol 2000 show. A more universal approach in law making would be needed;

---

[73] Cf. Esty, GATTing the Greens, Foreign Affairs 72 (1993), 32 ff.
[74] Cf. Loibl, Compliance with International Environmental Law – The Emerging Regime under the Kyoto Protocol, in: Benedek/Isak/Kicker (eds.), Development and Developing International and European Law – Essays in Honour of Konrad Ginther on the Occasion of his 65th Birthday (1999), 263 ff., 282 f.

- States so far have followed a sectoral approach in the environmental field. Creating a new universal organization to deal with environmental matters would raise a number of legal and institutional questions: in particular, it has to be borne in mind that membership of international environmental agreements varies – not all States have become parties to all international agreements. Thus, a solution would have to be found how to deal with this different number of members to international agreements. It would need a detailed scrutiny whether the approach taken within GATT/WTO to ensure uniform membership to all agreements of the GATT/WTO system[75] is a possible solution for the environmental field;
- Existing international institutional structures would have to be altered quite radically as not only those institutions which have been created within the framework of international environmental agreements would be affected, but also international organizations within the United Nations system would need to be adapted. A World Environment Organization would have to have influence on the work of other international organizations in order to ensure that duplications of activities are avoided.

Taking into account these issues it is not likely that a World Environment Organization will be able to address all the questions in the environmental field. It could – in the unlikeness of its establishment – be a first step in the evolution of a comprehensive and coherent international framework to deal with environmental matters and issues of sustainable development.

CONCLUDING REMARKS

The evolution of international environmental law has been based on a sectoral approach. This approach has not only influenced the creation of substantive regulations dealing with environmental matters, but has also shaped the institutional arrangements. Furthermore, the framework approach taken in international-law-making has increased the number of international institutions both on the regional and international level.

---

[75] Cf. Article II of the Marrakech Agreement on the Establishment of the World Trade Organisation 1994.

As has been shown above it is unlikely that the features of the elaboration of international environmental law will change dramatically in the near future. The growth of these institutions will, almost certainly, maintain the same pattern – each treaty establishes its own Conference of Parties as well as creates its own Secretariat. The proposal to create a "World Environment Organization" is unlikely to be implemented as it would require a total change of the structure of today's approach to international environmental law: The sectoral approach would have to be replaced by a more holistic approach both for substantive provisions and institutional arrangements. Such a radical change seems very unlikely, as the difficulties, which would have to be overcome, are numerous. Established structures would have to be abolished not only within the institutional framework of international environmental agreements but would also affect the United Nations system as a whole. Taking into account the difficulties encountered in the discussions on the reform of the United Nations system it seems unlikely that such a change can be accomplished in the environmental field in the near future.

Thus, the current situation is likely to remain and will provide a challenge for the international community. As has been demonstrated the international community has been creative to tackle a number of problems concerning the proliferation of international institutions in the environmental field by following a cautious and practical approach. Although the number of Conferences of the Parties and secretariats under international environmental agreements has increased in the last decade the international community has found ways and means to tackle problems in a pragmatic and solution-oriented manner. The increased co-operation between the various institutions might prove to be a successful tool. This might help to demonstrate that an "acquis of international environmental law" has been elaborated in the last decades and avoid duplications of efforts under the various international environmental instruments. As the field of international financial instruments has demonstrated that the use of existing institutions as well as making use of synergies could be a useful means to add to the goal of achieving environmental protection. But it has to be borne in mind that the various challenges in the environmental field require different solutions and therefore limits exist for such an approach.

UNEP and CSD – as the main UN institutions to deal with environmental issues and sustainable development – could help to ensure the necessary coherence in the environmental field.

ORGANIZATIONAL PROLIFERATION AND CENTRALIZATION UNDER THE TREATY ON EUROPEAN UNION

Armin von Bogdandy[*]

A PARADOXICAL DEVELOPMENT?

States have recognized that there are many public tasks which they cannot fulfil alone. The proliferation of common transnational organizations as an institutional response to this need is the subject of this book.[1] In this contribution, organizational proliferation under the Treaty on the European Union shall be addressed. The apparently paradoxical simultaneous development of organizational proliferation *and* unity-building, of fragmentation *and* centralization within the European Union shall be examined.

This paradoxical development has been conspicuous for the last ten years. On the one hand, the creation of unity has been a strong undercurrent of the Union's recent development. The Union, as guarantor of the European collective order, bundles together almost all integration enterprises in Europe and *fuses the Communites into one organization*. The Union sees itself as a unitary *polity*. Consequently, it makes claims on its *citizens* and on territory. Thus, European integration does not – as the functionalist or a postmodernist approach suggest – lead towards the political rule of different and primarily functionally oriented, partially overlapping organizations, for which territory and citizenship are negligible elements. On the other hand, elements of proliferation and fragmentation abound: they can be found in the internal, i.e. organizational, framework of the central institutions, the increasing number of independent or semi-independent agencies

---

[*] Professor for European Law and International Economic Law, Frankfurt am Main; Judge at the European Atomic Energy Tribunal, Paris.
[1] The term "proliferation" is used loosely in this text. It covers any development which entails the creation of new transnational public bodies. Since organizational proliferation and fragmentation are often linked – the fragmentation of an organization often leads to the development of a separate organizational unit – processes of fragmentation are also addressed.

and the "underworld" of committees. Moreover, an ever increasing number of substantial law applies only to parts of the Union, and flexibility has become a buzzword of the constitutional discourse.

This contribution will outline these apparently contradictory developments and will demonstrate that they can be construed as rational responses to the challenges of European integration. An overarching legal approach is proposed which may help to meet the requirements of efficient and constitutional government within the Union.

UNITY-BUILDING BY FUSION OF THE COMMUNITIES INTO THE UNION

The thesis of unity building presented here must begin by addressing a fundamental question: Does the core of the European Union consist of one, three or four organizations? If the organizational set-up of the Union consisted of four different organizations, the constitutional development within the Union would evidence a significant amount of organizational proliferation at a fundamental level. As will be demonstrated, the Union is, however, a single organization which encompasses the Communities and does not evidence this type of proliferation.

THE THESIS AND ITS IMPLICATIONS

The origins of the theory of unity can be traced to the Treaty of Maastricht.[2] The Treaty of Amsterdam adds further evidence and allows the substantiation and development of the thesis.[3] These two treaties permit the four European institutions[4] be understood as parts of

---

[2] In detail v. Bogdandy/Nettesheim, *Ex Pluribus Unum – Fusion of the European Communities into the European Union*, 2 ELJ (1996), 267 et. Seq.

[3] Therefore, the Treaty is more important than is generally assumed. For the majority opinion see Europäische Kommission, *Der Vertrag von Amsterdam: Ergebnisse, Erläuterungen, Vertragsentwurf*, EU-Nachrichten 3/1997, VI; Langrish, *The Treaty of Amsterdam: Selected Highlights*, 23 ELR (1998), 3 at 18 et seq.; Louis, *Le traité d'Amsterdam: une occasion perdue?*, (1997) Revue du Marché unique européen, 5; Manin, *The Treaty of Amsterdam*, 4 CJEL (1998), 1; Morata, *La Unión Europea. Procesos, actores y politicas* (1998), 80 et seq.; Streinz, *Der Vertrag von Amsterdam*, (1998) EuZW, 137 at 147; Weiler, *Bread and Circus: The State of the European Union*, 4 CJEL (1998), 223 et seq.; and *Amsterdam, Amsterdam*, 3 ELJ (1997), 309 et seq.; Delors, in: International Herald Tribune 23 June 1997, 2.

[4] Those based on the Treaty on European Union (TEU), the Treaty establishing the European Community (TEC), the Treaty establishing the European Atomic Energy Community (TEAC) and the Treaty establishing the European Coal and Steel Community (TECSC), respectively.

one single organization called the "European Union".[5] The European Community, Euratom and the ECSC as independent organizations were, on this reading, absorbed by the new organization, i.e., the Union. The terms "Communities" and "pillars of the European Union" do not demarcate different organizations but only describe different capacities and partially specific legal instruments and procedures of a single organization, namely, the Union.[6] All the Treaties and the secondary law form a single legal order.

This thesis has several consequences. It clarifies political accountability and legal responsibility. It allows all rules enacted by the institutions to be considered as part of a single legal order. Therefore it is perhaps the only legal construction that can explain the ECJ's recent landmark decision, *C-170/96 Commission v. Council*, where the Court held itself competent under the procedure of Art. 230 (ex 173) TEC[7] to declare an act pursuant to Art. K.2 lit. b TEU (Maastricht version) void.[8] The thesis can be employed in the practical simplification and consolidation of the law concerning the European institutions *de constitutione lata* in several ways. Unity can be expressed by the institutions describing themselves as institutions of the European Union.[9] It can also be expressed in legislation and in inter-institutional

---

[5] This name is laid down in the Treaty (Art. 1 (ex A) TEU) and is commonly used. For an early usage of this, see The Economist, *EU fugaces labuntur communitates*, 20 Nov. 1993, 28.

[6] For a similar view cf. Pernice, in: Dreier (Ed.), *Grundgesetz Kommentar* (1998), Vol. 2, Art. 23, note 42; de Witte, *The Pillar Structure and the Nature of the European Union: Greek Temple or French Gothic Cathedral?*, in: Heukels/Blokker/Brus (Eds.), *The European Union after Amsterdam* (1998), 51 at 55 et seq.; Zuleeg, *Die Organizationsstruktur der Europäischen Union*, EuR Beiheft 2/1998, 151 at 152 et seq.; and most recently Curtin/Dekker, *The EU as a "Layered" International Organization: Institutional Unity in Disguise*, in: Craig/de Búrca (Eds.), *The Evolution of EU Law* (1999), 55 et seq. Curtin/Dekker and de Witte distinguish themselves from my approach as they argue in favour of a "layered organization". In my understanding, they do not give, however, any reason that leads to an organizational distinction between the Union and the Community, given the identity of their institutions, in detail see below, II 4 c.

[7] All Treaty references apply the numbering of the new consolidated version of the Treaties unless otherwise stated. The old numbering is added in parenthesis where it is thought to be helpful.

[8] Case C-170/96, *Commission v. Council*, ECR [1998] I-2763. (All page references relate to the German version of the ECR); similarly the thrust of the argument in EFI, judgment of 19 July 1999, case T-14/98, *Hautala/Council*, the CFI applies a right to information established under the TEC to a policy under title V TEU.

[9] See, for example, the Council renaming itself as the Council of the European Union, Decision of 11 Aug. 1993, O.J. 1993, L 281/18; O.J. 1993, L 285/41, Art. 13 Council's Rules of Procedure (6 Dec. 1993), O.J. 1993, L 304/1. (All page references relate to the German version of the Official Journal.) Under different

agreements.[10] These possible courses of action complement the formal treaty revision procedure provided for in Art. 48 TEU.[11] Consolidating measures may hereby become part of the *acquis* prior to formal treaty revision. This might decrease the political controversy involved in consolidation on a treaty law level and should simplify the taking of such initiatives. Another consequence is that the thesis makes it possible *cum grano salis* to apply the legal principles developed on the basis of the EC Treaty with regards to the Treaty on European Union and secondary law adopted under it.[12] Finally the Short Basic Treaty aspired to by the European Parliament[13] can be marked out *de constitutione lata* in Arts. 1-7, 43-49 and 51-53 TEU on the basis of the thesis.

THE "LEGALITY" OF THE PROPOSED INTERPRETATION

Limits of interpretative construction

This article submits that the Treaty on European Union merges the Union and the Communities. This interpretation is neither self-evident from the treaty text, nor does it correspond with the widespread legal understanding of the European organizational structure. Therefore it has to be asked whether such a construction of the Treaties (especially of Arts. 3-5 TEU) is admissible at all.

The proposed construction would be inadmissible if it were to contravene the intention of the norm-enacting *pouvoir*, i.e. the totality of the Member States or, to be more precise, the majority of the Union's citizens organized through the Member States' constitutional

---

constructions of the relationship between the Union and the Community one is tempted to consider that the Council is acting under a wrong and perhaps illegal designation when enacting legislation under the EC Treaty. By now, all institutions represent themselves on most occasions as institutions of the Union as can be seen e.g. from their website (http://europa.eu.int/).

[10] Cf. European Parliament, *Rapport sur les améliorations pouvant être apportées au fonctionnement des institutions sans modifier le traité*, rapporteur: Fernand Herman, 23 March 1998, PE 225.909/déf.; for the last inter-institutional agreement on the financing of the CFSP, see O.J. 1997, C 286/80.

[11] The fusion of the provisions in Art. 237 TEEC, Art. 205 TEAC and Art. 98 TECSC into Art. O TEU (Maastricht version) was of little political significance because of the fact that prospective new Member States could only join all three Treaties together that were, at that time, part of the *acquis communautaire*. Equally Art. F (2) of the Treaty of Maastricht merely extended the ECJ's decisions on fundamental rights and the Council Decision of 5 March 1977.

[12] However, care has to be taken to respect the differences in competence, procedure and forms of legislation and the institutions' autonomy.

[13] Tsatsos, *Die Europäische Unionsgrundordnung*, (1995) EuGRZ, 287.

systems.[14] Therefore the norm-enacting *pouvoir*'s reluctance to fully harmonize procedures and legal instruments under the different Treaties, to formulate a specific and unified international legal personality and to enact a single constitutional document consolidating all treaty law has to be considered.[15] It shows that the norm-enacting *pouvoir* does not want identical organizational and legal dynamics in all the areas of the Union's competence. However, this reluctance does not impede interpreting the Treaty on European Union as giving rise to the unity of the organization and its single legal system. On the contrary, this article will make it clear that the various innovations and alterations of the Amsterdam Treaty signify the norm-enacting *pouvoir*'s intention to organize more effectively and to develop further what had already with the Maastricht Treaty become a single organization.[16] Merely the explicit statement of this intention within the Amsterdam Treaty was omitted. The strategy of allowing room for dynamic development and of waiting for the stabilization of the interactions between the constituent parts of the Union may have played a part in this omission. Moreover, the diffuse provisions in the EU Treaty are due to the lack of an explicit decision as regards the organizational shape of the Union which is the result of the need to accommodate different views on where European integration should lead. Given this situation there is scope to clarify the present organizational structure.

The vexed question of legal personality

Most legal scholars regard the proposed thesis as being refuted by the continuing existence of Art. 281 TEC, Art. 184 TEAC and Art. 6 TECSC. These articles grant legal personality to the EC, EAC and ECSC, respectively. Regardless of the question whether the TEU bestows a legal personality on the Union, it is the conventionally held

---

[14] For an analysis of the relevant competences see European Parliament, *de Vigo-* and *Tsatsos-Report* on the Treaty of Amsterdam; 5 Nov. 1997, (1998) EuGRZ, 72, note 1.

[15] For the different positions and the debate during the Intergovernmental Conference see Droutsas/Griller et.al., *Regierungskonferenz 1996: Ausgangspositionen*, IEF Working Paper No. 20 (Diskussionspapier des Forschungsinstituts für Europafragen an der Wirtschaftsuniversität Wien), July 1996; ibid : *Regierungskonferenz 1996, Der Vertragsentwurf der irischen Präsidentschaft*, IEF Working Paper No. 25, Febrary 1997; ibid: *Regierungskonferenz 1996: Der Vertrag von Amsterdam im der Fassung des Gipfels vom Juni 1997*, IEF Working Paper No. 27, July 1997.

[16] This concern had been dominant in the political preparations of the 1996 IGC, see in particular Secretary General of the Council of the European Union, *Intergovernmental Conference 1996*, Report of the Reflection Group (Westendorp Group) (1996), 19 et seq., at 25 et seq., at 38 and at 60.

view that those provisions lead to the conclusion of separate organizations.[17] The following analysis shows that such a conclusion is not as obvious as it appears.

The mentioned treaty provisions only conflict with the thesis if legal personality is the crucial aspect in determining the legal structure of an organization.[18] This view was extremely important in continental European public law as legal personality was held to be the decisive element in the public law understanding of the state.[19] Public law as an autonomous science found its origin in this concept which was at the same time the juridical cornerstone of the bureaucratic state. The importance of this formula was the result of the historical conflict between the monarchical and the democratic principles. This central conflict was "overcome" – at least in terms of jurisprudence – by viewing sovereignty as originating from the legal entity called "the state" and not from the monarch or the people. Since this conflict has been completely resolved through the democratization process, the concept of legal personality has lost much of its practical importance in national law.[20] In the light of this development it is not convincing to discuss the whole question of the organizational constitution primarily as a question of legal personality.

The "legal personality" approach also contains certain epistemological problems. The term "legal personality" is epistemologically a theoretical notion.[21] Thus, it is epistemologically problematic as it entails the danger of reification. To avoid such a danger, epistemologists generally suggest reducing theoretical notions to empirical ones. This course, however, cannot be pursued in the legal field due to the normative function of legal notions. Nonetheless a functional interpretation is possible whereby a legal notion is used as the nodal point where the requirement of applicability and legal consequences intersect. Employing legal notions in this way enables the

---

[17] Explicit Oppermann, *Europarecht* (2. ed. 1999), 75, note 154.

[18] This is a frequently held view, Benedek, *Die Rechtsordnung des GATT aus völkerrechtlicher Sicht* (1990), 255; Brownlie, *Principles of Public International Law*, (4. ed. 1990), 681 et seq.

[19] Stolleis, *Geschichte des öffentlichen Rechts in Deutschland* (1992), Vol. 2, 108, who also explains the background.

[20] Similarly, legal personality in international law is no longer an issue frequently discussed, Schermers/Blokker, *International Institutional Law* (3.ed. 1995), § 1567.

[21] Neumann, *Wissenschaftstheorie und Rechtswissenschaft*, in: Kaufmann/Hassemer (Eds.), *Einführung in die Rechtsphilosophie und Rechtstheorie der Gegenwart* (6. ed. 1994), 422 at 430 et seq.

elimination of theoretical terms to a large extent or at least allows controlling their use in legal arguments.[22]

In public international law the majority of scholars consider an organization's status as a subject of international law to be vital because it normally constitutes the *conditio sine qua non* of its capacity to act. This capacity to act is, however, in most cases limited to the international plane. It enables the organization's organs to interact with other subjects of international law, allows for international law actions against the organization and determines the organization's consequential liability.[23] It is not appropriate to deduce the European Union's legal organizational structure from its international law status, because the EU's capacity to interact with other subjects of international law is only *one* aspect amongst its competences. An internal competence of the Union can be found, for example, in Art. 7 TEU or Art. 34 TEU read in conjunction with Art. 32 TEU. In addition, as will be shown below, the legal personality of the organization, irrespective of whether one considers the EU or the EC, has little bearing on the internal relations of the organization with the Union's citizens and the Member States. For all practical purposes the European institutions fulfil the function of the holder of authority and bearer of duties. Thus, it can be concluded that, although the analysis of the organization's legal personality is of relevance, it should not be the crucial element in the legal understanding of the organizational make-up of the Union.

On a more general level it has to be stressed that conclusions reached solely on the basis of legal personality are not suitable for determining the legal nature of an association and its organizational structure because they do not extend beyond a formalistic legal understanding. Such an understanding, limiting itself to the fiction of the subject's legal personality, neglects the necessity of understanding the association within the context of the concrete world; in other words, the formalistic understanding does not meet the need of integrating reality. In an area as vague as the constitutional structure of the Union, traditional jurisprudence has to be integrated with insights from sociological jurisprudence and other sciences such as political science.[24]

---

[22] Neumann, ibid.

[23] Moreover, even under international law the legal status as an organization and the international law status can be separated, see the ICJ's Bernadotte decision of 11 April 1949. The ICJ uses the concept of an organization independently from the concept of legal personality in international law, ICJ Rep. 1949, 174 at 178.

[24] Koch/Rüßmann, *Juristische Begründungslehre* (1981), 227 et seq., 373 et seq.

The process of legal construction requires the consideration of established constitutional practices, as well as empirical structures and possible empirical consequences of a proposed legal understanding. In conclusion, the provisions on legal personality do not settle the question of the legal organizational structure.

3. Applying Traditional Interpretative Instruments

Through the looking-glass of international institutional law

The thesis that the formerly independent European organizations have been fused into a single organization must be analyzed in light of the above conclusions. After the Maastricht Treaty, there was uncertainty as to the legal nature of the EU as founded by Art. A(1) TEU. The German *Bundesverfassungsgericht* ruled that the Union lacked the character of an organization.[25] However, an open-minded reading of Arts. A - F, N and O of the Maastricht Treaty indicates the inadequacy of this understanding.[26] Later developments in the Union's constitutional practice further support the thesis of the Union being one over-arching organization. For example, the Council, the institution bound closest to the interests of the Member States, has given itself the name "Council of the European Union" and acts under this title in all its areas of competence. Although the Union is thought to be a mere international conference of Member States, according to the prevailing opinion in legal literature,[27] the Council assumed as early as 1994 that the Union (sic!) can be bound by international norms,[28] and even that it can take over the administration of a city.[29] What was formerly the Budget of the European Communities had already become the all embracing Budget of the European Union under the Maastricht

---

[25] BVerfGE 89, 155 at 195. This opinion is shared by many scholars, cf. Pliakos, *La nature juridique de l'Union européenne*, 22 RTDE (1993), 187 at 213.

[26] For a more detailed analysis see v. Bogdandy/Nettesheim, *supra* note 2, 5 et seq., 13 et seq.; Dörr, *Zur Rechtsnatur der Europäischen Union*, (1995) EuR, 334 et seq.; Ress, *Ist die Europäische Union eine juristische Person?*, EuR-Beiheft 2/1995, 27 et seq.; Seidl-Hohenveldern/Loibl, *Das Recht der Internationalen Organizationen einschließlich der Supranationalen Gemeinschaften* (6. ed. 1996), note 0119e, 1505, 2213i.

[27] In detail Pechstein/Koenig, *Die Europäische Union* (2. ed. 1998), para. 81.

[28] 3. Consideration of the Regulation (EU) 3381/94, O.J. 1994, L 367/1 (dual use goods). For an extensive survey see Curtin/Dekker, *supra* note 6, at 104 et seq.

[29] Decision of the Council 94/308/CFSP of 16 May 1994; O.J. 1994, L 134/1, Art. 1: 'The Administration of the Town Mostar by the European Union': see also Decision of the Council 94/790/CFSP of 12 Dec. 1994, O.J. 1994, L 326/2.

Treaty,[30] although according to conventional understanding the Union cannot establish any legal acts relating to the budget.

Post-Amsterdam it is even more evident that the Union with its single institutional framework constitutes an international organization; it suffices to apply the conventional legal criteria for such organizations.[31] The criterion of the organization's competences, fulfilment of which was debated with respect to the Maastricht Treaty, has now evidently been settled by a number of provisions such as Arts. 7 and 34 TEU, which constitute the EU as a legal entity in relation to the Member States and the citizens. Art. 24 TEU also provides a strong basis for the view that the EU has international law status.[32] Declaration 4 to the Treaty of Amsterdam only states that this specific external competence is shared with Member States and not exclusive to the Union. It does not put into question the Union's external competence as such.

Important developments can also be seen in the area of the CFSP in which the Union on its own, i.e. no longer in concert with the Member States, is authorized to formulate and enforce policies (contrast Art. 11(1) TEU with J.1(1) TEU).[33] The function of the notion of an international organization should be recalled: it is employed to demarcate forms of close inter-state co-operation from forms of looser co-operation. Those forms of co-operation which constitute an international organization are regarded separately because they are particularly problematic with respect to the principles of democracy and the rule of law, given the possibility of autonomous developments on the international level. The powers of the EU stated in the TEU extend far beyond what is normally considered the standard for an international organization. Arts. 23(2) and 35(1) TEU, for example, show that the EU post-Amsterdam even includes supranational elements.

---

[30] O.J. 1998, L 44/1.

[31] Schermers/Blokker, *supra* note 20, § 33, in more detail: Trüe, *Verleihung von Rechtspersönlichkeit an die Europäische Union und Verschmelzung zu einer einzigen Organization* (1997), 11 et seq.

[32] In detail Blokker/Heukels, *The European Union: Historical Origins and Institutional Challenges*, in: Heukels/Blokker/Brus (Eds.), *supra* note 6, 9 at 31et seq.; Langrish, *supra* note 3, at 14; Thun-Hohenstein, *Der Vertrag von Amsterdam* (1997), 75 et seq.; R. Wessel, *The European Union's Foreign and Security Policy*, 1999, at 242 et seq.; Zuleeg, *supra* note 6, 151 at 153; for the opposite view Manin, *supra* note 3, at 16.

[33] In detail De Zwaan, *Community Dimensions of the Second Pillar*, in: Heukels/Blokker/Brus (Eds.), *supra* note 6, at 179 et seq.; Wessel, *supra* note 32, at 71 et seq.

A systematic interpretation of the Treaties

So far our analysis has not specified the relationship between the Union and the Communities. The strong interconnection of the founding Treaties through the Treaty of Amsterdam provides further indications for the supposition that the EU is a single organization with a single legal system. Indicative of this development are hereby the treatment of fundamental rights which now find explicit application to all acts of the institutions including those taken under the EC treaties (Arts. 6(2), 46(d) TEU), the single framework for closer co-operation (Art. 43 et al. TEU)[34] as well as the single budget (Arts. 28, 41 TEU). Moreover, the thesis is also supported by the partial consolidation of the various legal instruments in Art. 34 TEU and the extension of the competences of important supranational institutions, namely the increase in competence of the European Parliament, of the European Court of Justice (Art. 46 TEU) and of the Ombudsman.[35] Some areas, e.g. foreign and trade policies, can only be regulated efficiently by using competences from the EC Treaty and the EU Treaty in unison.

The imagery of the three- or even five-pillared temple cannot reflect this situation accurately because the metaphor implies a strict separation.[36] The reality is a continuum with interpenetration of procedures and legal instruments.[37] This continuum begins with the "supranational standard procedure" of formulating policy and passing legislation interlacing "exit" and "voice"[38] of the Member States (e.g. Art. 95 (ex 100a) TEC). Further along in this continuum are the traditionally "sensitive" competences (Art. 93 (ex 99) TEC) where the "voice" of the Member States is enshrined with the unanimity

---

[34] As Ehlermann points out, the new provisions on flexibility ensure that the danger of fragmentation inherent in many projects is avoided, Ehlermann, *Engere Zusammenarbeit nach dem Amsterdamer Vertrag: Ein neues Verfassungsprinzip?*, (1997) EuR, 362 at 394 et seq.; see also Kortenberg, *Closer cooperation in the Treaty of Amsterdam*, 35 CML Rev. (1998), 833 at 854; for the earlier discussion see Ehlermann, *Increased differentiation or stronger uniformity*, in: Winter/Curtin/Kellermann/de Witte (Eds.), *Reforming the Treaty on European Union* (1996), 27 et seq.

[35] For more detail see Harings, *Die Zusammenarbeit in den Bereichen Justiz und Inneres*, EuR Beiheft 2/1998, 81 et seq.; Kugelmann, *Die Gemeinsame Außen- und Sicherheitspolitik*, EuR Beiheft 2/1998, 99 et seq.; Zuleeg, *supra* note 6, at 151 et seq.

[36] de Witte, *supra* note 6, at 66.

[37] Cf. Weiler, *The Trinity Structure of the Treaty on the European Union*, in Monar/Ungerer/Wessels (Eds.), *The Maastricht Treaty on European Union* (1993), 49 at 60 seq.

[38] In detail Weiler, *The Transformation of Europe*, 100 YLJ (1991), 2403 at 2412 et seq.

requirement in the Council. It continues with other EC Treaty provisions where Member States are left with the right to initiate legislation (Art. 67 TEC). The next shade in the continuum would be the co-operation in the fields of justice and home affairs, which now includes the ECJ as adjudicator (Art. 35(6) and (7) as well as optionally Art. 35(2) TEU) and which conforms with the forms of legislation under the EC Treaty but which lacks direct applicability, thus enabling "exit". Finally, the spectrum ends with the CFSP, where both "exit" and "voice" are easier. The main emphasis and centre of gravitation is the "supranational standard procedure". This shows that the norm-enacting *pouvoir* has brought about a situation that is far removed from the rhetoric of the inter-governmental conference which depicted the three-pillar model as sacrosanct.[39]

RE-CONSTRUCTING THE UNION IN THE TRADITION OF THE THEORY OF STATE

The above findings on the Treaty of Amsterdam show closer links between the Treaties and lead to a revaluation of the Union. They cannot, however, provide a final determination of the organization's shape and form. To interpret the relevant treaty provisions recourse has to be taken to further premises. The following analysis is based on the development of these premises from the discussions relating to the unity of the state, in general, and the unity of administration, in particular.

Borrowing from this complex body of knowledge requires some introductory explanations. First of all, this article does not suggest that the creation of a unity in the sense of state- or nation-building is taking place. Moreover, the focus of any research into the unity of the state and the unity of administration differs from the focus required to determine the European Union's shape and form. The former usually asks whether it is still appropriate to employ the traditional understanding of such unity, considering the plurality of administrative bodies and of legal entities exercising sovereign rights in the contemporary state.[40] In this context, the fact that the various bodies act under one single legal personality is one of the crucial unifying elements. The situation in the European organization stands in stark contrast to this. Here, the constellation is as follows: the acting

---

[39] Cf. Bardenhewer, *Die Einheitlichkeit der Organizationsstruktur der Europäischen Union*, EuR Beiheft 2/1998, 125 et seq.
[40] Bryde, *Die Einheit der Verwaltung als Rechtsbegriff*, 46 VVDStRL (1988), 181 et seq.

institutions of the organization are always the same, i.e. the EP, the Council of Ministers, the Commission and the ECJ, irrespective of the pillar under which they are acting. Only the legal personality varies according to the legal area in which the particular institution exercises its functions.

When discussing unity, one has to inquire into the reasons for the differentiation which makes unity questionable. Here, another important difference between the unity of the state and the European situation comes to the fore. Within the state context, the differentiation of the state into a variety of different bodies, which are sometimes even endowed with their own legal personality, is commonly acknowledged to be indispensable for a political and administrative system in order to allow it to efficiently manage the demands of a highly complex environment.[41] The same explanation cannot be employed within the context of the European organization as regards the differentiation of legal personalities. Since the Merger Treaty of 1965 at the latest, the legal personalities cannot be explained as based on the specific needs required for the accomplishment of tasks since the same institutions act under all the competences. Instead, the retention of the different legal personalities and the diffuse architecture of the Union is entirely due to political differences regarding integration.[42] This background is relevant when considering the consequences of the thesis, for the unity thesis does not lead to a loss in functional efficiency.

The following considerations build upon the established knowledge acquired in the discussion on the unity of the state and the unity of administration. One might challenge this analogy by pointing out that the European Union is neither a state nor solely an administrative body. The Union is not just an administration because it does not only command administrative organs, but also, even primarily, has at its disposal parliamentary, governmental and judicial organs. Furthermore, a national administration presupposes the presence of a state, of which it is part and parcel.[43] Although the European Union is fundamentally dependent on the political, administrative and legal systems of the Member States, it is nonetheless far more independently developed than a national administration. Similarly, the discussion on unity of the state can only partially be applied to the European organization, since it

---

[41] ibid., at 182 et seq.
[42] This discussion does not deal with the question of the EU outsourcing parts of its area of competence to legally independent bodies such as the European Patent Office.
[43] Becker, *Öffentliche Verwaltung* (1989), 110.

can not be conceived of as a state. Again, it has to be emphasized that the unity thesis does not presuppose or entail the creation of a political and social system as integrated as a state-system is assumed to be. The European Union is the remarkable attempt to provide for political order under the principles of pluralism and despite the dearth of substantial homogeneity. Nevertheless, the analogy is permissible since the Union, the state and the national administration all have the authority to issue *unilaterally binding decisions*. With respect to international organizations which do not have this competence, the point of comparison might be their duty to further public tasks.

Unitary legitimation

Wherein lies the ultimate reason for the quest for unity? Unity of the state and unity of administration are both based on the unity of the democratic origin of all sovereign power.[44] All public authority originates with the people. With the constitution's enactment, continuation and development, this authority is passed on to the various organs within the constitutional framework. All bodies exercising sovereign power continue to be dependant on the unifying origin of that power.[45]

Whether the founding Treaties of the Union make up a constitution may be debatable[46] but it is difficult to contest that they pass on to the institutions original authority and not derivative national powers.[47] This original authority is based on a collective act of the citizens (now of the Union) in which they constituted this authority through the relevant procedures set out in their national constitutions.[48] Initially, there were different authorities founded separately by the procedures required in Art. 247 TEEC, Art. 224 TEAC and Art. 99 TECSC although political links were already present at the inception of the Communities and their integration soon became part of the *acquis communitaire*. The Maastricht Treaty incorporated this *acquis*: Art. N

---

[44] Schuppert, *Die Einheit der Verwaltung als Rechtsproblem*, (1987) DöV, 757 at 760.
[45] Hesse, *Grundzüge des Verfassungsrechts der Bundesrepublik Deutschland* (19. ed. 1993), note 27.
[46] See, for example, Läufer, *Zur zukünftigen Verfassung der Europäischen Union*, (1994) integration, 204 et seq.; Weiler, *The Constitution of Europe* (1998).
[47] Ipsen, *Europäisches Gemeinschaftsrecht* (1972), 62 et seq.; for a contrary view see Schilling, *The autonomy of the Community Legal Order*, 37 Harv. Int. LJ (1996), 389 et seq.; see also the convincing reply of Weiler/Haltern, *Response: The autonomy of the Community Legal Order*, Harv. Int. 37 LJ (1996), 411 et seq.
[48] On the collective act see *Ipsen, supra* note 47, at 58 et seq.; Rodriguez Iglesias, *Gedanken zum Entstehen einer Europäischen Rechtsordnung*, (1999) NJW, 1 at 3.

TEU lays out the *only* procedure that can now be used for the confirmation and development of the supranational authority whatever its Treaty base. The second usage of the collective act procedure has just occurred, and a substantial extension of authority (e.g. Art. 7 TEU, EMU, CFSP, PJCC) and procedures (e.g., EP's co-decision) took place in both the Maastricht Treaty and the Treaty of Amsterdam. The Maastricht Treaty is especially important in this context because it provoked the first important public discussion of integration, which lead to three referenda and to changes in several of the Member States' constitutions. Therefore, the legitimizing force of the collective act which always changed all the Treaties (see Arts. G, H and I Maastricht Treaty and Arts. 1, 2, 3 and 4 Treaty of Amsterdam), feeds the Union *as a whole*. Art. 52 TEU, read in conjunction with Arts. 6(1) and 7(1) TEU,[49] accounts for the democratic origin of the sovereign power founded in the Treaties. Today, there is *only one source of constitutional legitimacy* in the European Union. The unity of the organization on this fundamental level thus results from the fact that its legitimization flows from the citizens of the Union to the organization as a whole. Its component parts, i. e. the EU, the EC, Euratom and the ECSC, obtain their legitimation only through it. All the Treaties are now legitimized through a single constitutional "legitimation-chain".[50]

Furthermore, not only does the legitimacy of the primary treaty provisions flow from a unitary source of legitimacy; the legitimacy of all legislation emanating from the European institutions is identical insofar as such legislation is enacted through the same organs.[51]

A lesson from the theory of organizations

So far, the unity of the organization has been demonstrated from a first and fundamental perspective, but that is not in itself sufficient proof. The aspect of unity shown in the unitary origin of democratic legitimation is only of limited practical relevance, as it leaves a number of possible ways to legally organize the Union. However, the Treaty on European Union does not integrate the Treaties merely on this level. Instead, the integration of the component parts of the organization, as

---

[49] The respective national ratification procedures all have to embody the democratic principle. The Union could not accept a state as a Member which did not fulfil this requirement.

[50] For this concept, central to German public law, cf. Böckenförde, *Demokratie als Verfassungsprinzip*, in: Isensee/Kirchhof (Eds.), *Handbuch des Staatsrechts* (1987), Vol. I, 953.

[51] This will be further illustrated below in the context of political accountability and legal responsibility.

begun in the Maastricht Treaty and furthered in the Treaty of Amsterdam, takes place in a multiplicity of ways.

In order to evaluate the changes, it is helpful to examine whether the Union and the Communities can be seen as a single organization from a sociological perspective.[52] Of course there is no single sociological concept of "organization"[53] and different dimensions of the term have to be considered. In particular three aspects have to be differentiated: firstly, the organizational macro-system; secondly, the organizational units which are in themselves (part-)organizations; and, thirdly, the internal organization of such organizational units.[54] Following *Renate Mayntz*, the first dimension – the organizational macro-system – is present where the social construct (a) demarcates itself from its social environs through an ascertainable group of members, (b) possesses a differentiated internal structure and (c) pursues specific aims.[55] The main function of an organization consists of a purposive and permanent regulation of its agents in their performance of its tasks and their fulfilment of its aims.[56]

Employing this usage of the term "organization", it becomes clear that the construct called European Union, which encompasses all the Treaties, is an organization in the sociological sense. There is an ascertainable, and of necessity in all the Treaties identical, group of Members, namely the Member States and the citizens of the Union. The differentiated internal structure exists between the institutions of the EU, which are identical in all areas of the organization's activity. These institutions constitute the framework for their agents' acts and

---

[52] This analysis by no means aims to use empirical data to arrive at normative conclusions. Instead, it is important to regard empirical aspects in order to avoid the risk inherent in a purely legal analysis which may arrive at abstruse results. For the necessity of extending legal analysis to these sociological aspects see Böckenförde, *Organ, Organization, Juristische Person*, in: *Festschrift Wolff* (1973), 269 at 294.

[53] Hoffmann, *Stichwort: Organization, Begriff der*, in: Grochla (Ed.), *Handbuch der Organization* (2. ed.1980), column 1424; in detail Groß, *Grundzüge der organizationswissenschaftlichen Diskussion*, in: Schmidt-Aßmann/Hoffmann-Riem (Eds.), *Verwaltungsorganizationsrecht als Steuerungsressource* (1997), 139 et seq.; Walter-Busch, *Organizationstheorien von Weber bis Weick* (1996), 93 et seq., 208 et seq.

[54] Becker, *supra* note 43, at 190 et seq.

[55] Mayntz, *Soziologie der öffentlichen Verwaltung* (1997), 82; similarly Schmidt-Aßmann, in: Schmidt-Aßmann/Hoffmann-Riem, *supra* note 53, at 34.

[56] Hoffmann, *supra* note 53; for our purposes it is irrelevant whether the organization is the *system itself* (Mayntz) or its *structure* (Luhmann).

the agents are selected according to the rules of the organization.[57] The internal structure manifests itself through the effective co-ordination of the institutions in all their areas of authority (cf. Art. 3 et al., Art. 46 et al. TEU as well as the inter-institutional agreements). Finally, the social system of the Union is purposive, as can be seen from the over-arching aims in Art. 2 TEU, which show the Union as a historically unprecedented peace-ensuring and wealth-creating polity.[58]

This empirical notion of organization meets the legal understanding employed to determine the legal unity of a public authority. In the continental tradition of legal thought the state is conceived as an organized decision and action "unit".[59] More precisely, and in the context of administration, unity results from the legal requirement of a coherent programme of public action and its establishment.[60] It is in particular this requisite that has been decisively developed since the Merger Treaty of 1965.[61] Even though the ECJ had already begun in the 1960s to connect the Communities and their institutions to a functional unit,[62] it was only the Maastricht Treaty that placed all activity founded in the treaties within a single substantive framework: Art. B of the Maastricht Treaty (Art. 2 TEU) formulated over-arching aims which encompassed the entire aims pursued within the three Community Treaties (Arts. 1(3) and 2 (1st hyphen) TEU, Art. 2 TEC). Moreover, Art. 6(2) TEU now clearly formulates an over-

---

[57] Schwarz, *Aufgabenträger*, in: Grochla, *supra* note 53, column 217 et seq.; Schnapp, *Grundbegriffe des öffentlichen Organizationsrechtes*, (1980) Jura, 68 at 70: An important element of the law of organizations is regulating when the acts of natural persons working for public authorities can be attributed to the organization.

[58] Müller-Graff, *Einheit und Kohärenz der Vertragsziele von EG und EU*, EuR Beiheft 2/1998, 67 et seq. This explains why political science had no difficulty in exchanging the Union for the European Communities as the object of their analysis: see Wallace, *Dynamik des EU-Institutionsgefüges*, in: Jachtenfuchs/Kohler-Koch (Eds.), *Europäische Integration* (1996), 141.

[59] Heller, *Allgemeine Staatslehre* (1983), 228; Böckenförde, *supra* note 52, at 298; in more detail v. Bogdandy/Nettesheim, *supra* note 2, at 16 et seq.

[60] Bryde, *supra* note 40, at 190.

[61] The development of this substantive framework is what differentiates the present situation from the merger of the institutions in the Merger Treaties in the 1960s. According to C. D. Ehlermann, the Commission had already then considered the thesis formulated in this article, but these thoughts were not pursued for political reasons.

[62] Joined Cases C-27/59 and C-39/59, *Campolongo*, [1960] ECR 819 at 849; Case C-221/88, *Busseni*, [1990] ECR I – 495, paras. 13, 16.

arching framework for the application of fundamental rights in all areas of activity.[63]

Another central element in the assessment of unity is centralized law-making.[64] This leads to the most important argument in favour of the unity thesis: the central institutions of the Communities and the Union are identical.

Fusion due to the lack of organizational autonomy

So far, it has been shown that, both from an empirical and from a legal perspective, it would be appropriate to treat the Union and the Communities as a single organization. Therefore, the essence of the pillar structure is nothing but a variation in the allocation of powers amongst the institutions.[65] However, the degree of unity remains to be determined. One might argue that the Communities form partly or completely independent organizations within the over-arching association of the Union. If this were the case a semi-autonomous or gradational arrangement would be the suitable conception of the Union.[66] Such an internal differentiation is theoretically easy to conceive on the basis of the distinction between the macro-structure of the organization, its organizational units and their internal organization.[67]

The discussion of this aspect has to bring out the most forceful argument in favour of the proposition that the EU is a single organization: the (unitary) identity of its central institutions (Parliament, Council, Commission, ECJ and Court of Auditors, Art. 5 TEU) in all areas of activity of the Union. In empirical terms their identity is the result of the fact that they perceive themselves and are perceived by others as being the same irrespective of the area of

---

[63] It was possible to infer this already from Art. F para. 2 TEU (Maastricht version). The provision in Art. 6 para. 2 TEU, read in conjunction with Art. 46 (d) TEU, leaves no room for doubt, whereas the Maastricht Treaty provision lacked such explicitness.

[64] Bryde, *supra* note 40, at 190.

[65] de Witte, *supra* note 6, at 66.

[66] On this type of organization see further Wolff, *Verwaltungsrecht II* (2. ed. 1967), § 71; v. Bogdandy/Nettesheim, *supra* note 2, 274; the concept is mainly developed by Curtin/Dekker, *supra* note 6; Dörr, *supra* note 26, 344 et seq.; Schroeder, *Die Rechtsnatur der Europäischen Union und verwandte Probleme*, in: Hummer/Schweitzer (Eds.), *Österreich und das Recht der Europäischen Union* (1996), 3, at 6 et seq.; C. Wichard, *Wer ist Herr im europäischen Haus?*, (1999) EuR, 170; de Witte, *supra* note 6.

[67] See above the text accompanying footnotes 61 to 66.

competence and treaty base under which they are acting.[68] In legal terms, their identity results from Art. 9 Amsterdam Treaty (and prior to the Amsterdam Treaty from the two Merger Treaties).

A closer analysis can again start with an empirical sociological approach: here the degree of unity of an organization is determined by its degree of centralization and decentralization. A decentralized organization is present when the decision-making authority is organizationally independent, i.e. competences and thereby decision-making is delegated to *parts* of the organizational system.[69] Thus, an institutionally decentralized organization requires decision-making power to be allocated to separate institutions[70] with a certain degree of independence.[71]

At this point the incoherence of the prevailing view of the organizational set-up of the European Union becomes apparent. A differentiation of competences can certainly be found amongst the EU's institutions (Parliament, Council, Commission, ECJ and Court of Auditors)[72] but this differentiation does not correspond to the various Treaties and areas of competence: EU, EC, Euratom and ECSC[73]. None of the institutions has exclusive authority regarding a particular area. On the contrary, the same institutions exercise the decision-making authority under all the Treaties, i. e., in all areas of competence. Therefore, the very opposite of decentralization is present. The only mechanism of independence is the various areas' separate legal personalities. But this in itself cannot lead to decentralization, as independence can only exist where there is some real separation. Separation is not primarily attained through legal personality but instead through organizational autonomy and through independence in their personnel.

---

[68] The most problematic institution in this context is the Council, given its changing composition of national ministers according to the area of competence. Nevertheless it is considered as one single institution in all areas, see Dashwood, *The Council of the European Union in the Era of the Amsterdam Treaty*, in: Heukels/Blokker/Brus (Eds.), *supra* note 6, 117 at 126.

[69] Mayntz, *supra* note 55, at 26.

[70] Becker, *supra* note 43, at 195 et seq.

[71] Mayntz, *supra* note 55, at 83.

[72] In the Union there is, of course, an autonomy of organizational units, i.e., the various institutions are independent of each other.

[73] It would be different if the Council were only to be responsible for the EU, the Commission in charge of the ECSC, and the Parliament were only to deal with the EC. However, since none of the institutions has an exclusive competence as regards to any one of these areas, the independence of the institutions does not lead to an autonomous organizational status of the areas (EU or EC etc.).

This can be further illustrated by a comparison of the Council, Commission, Court of Justice and Parliament, on the one hand, with the partial autonomy of the ECB and the separate organizations within the World Bank Group on the other hand. The ECB in fact constitutes an independent sub-organization of the Union because it is independent with regard to its personnel, its finances and its legal personality (Arts. 107, 108 TEC, Arts. 26 et al. ESCB Statute). Similarly, the World Bank Group's organizations do not merely possess separate legal personalities but also, at least to a certain extent, separate personnel and a strict separation of capital (see Art. IV part 5, 6 and 7 IFC Agreement).

The sociological analysis and the legal analysis again lead to similar results. The branch of jurisprudence concerned with international organizations considers the ability to independently formulate a decision to be a constitutive prerequisite for the existence of an international organization. This prerequisite requires at least a certain degree of autonomy.[74] This criterion demarcates international organizations from other forms of international co-operation, where the execution of tasks is assigned to a governmental body of one of the parties to the agreement.[75] If this criterion is used to clarify the internal relations of the different areas of activity of the Union, it supplies strong evidence for the unity thesis. Not only is there no independence within the Union regarding the building and formulation of a political will between the different areas of activity under the various Treaties, but such independence would also be contrary to the Treaty on European Union in the light of Arts. 3 and 5 TEU.

Another public law aspect is also of relevance in this context, namely that the division of a sovereign organization into part-organizations and sub-organizations normally serves useful purposes under the doctrine of separation of powers.[76] From a constitutional point of view, the division aims to prevent the abuse of power and thereby to protect the individual. Its democratic purpose is to facilitate participation in political processes and, from a functional perspective, division attempts to ensure and increase efficiency by creating bodies focussed on their specific tasks.[77] None of these three purposes can be

---

[74] Schermers/Blokker, *supra* note 20, § 33.
[75] Schermers/Blokker, *supra* note 20, § 30, § 34.
[76] *Locus classicus* Locke, *Two Treatises of Government* (1690), Ch. XII and Ch. XIII; Lenaerts, *Some Reflections on Separation of Powers in the European Community*, 28 CML Rev. (1991), 11 et seq.
[77] Hesse, *supra* note 45, note 233 et seq.

promoted by clinging on to the formal separation of EU, EC, Euratom and ECSC, because their respective institutions and their personnel are identical.

In conclusion, it is not convincing – neither from an empirical nor from a legal perspective – to interpret the activities of the European institutions (Council, Parliament, Commission, ECJ and Court of Auditors) as the acts of separate organizations, according to the Treaty on which the activity in question is founded. Due to the lack of organizational independence of the different areas EU, EC, Euratom and ECSC, a fusion of the organizations has taken place. What remains are different capacities with partially specific legal instruments and procedures.

5. Meeting Possible Objections

Unity of the association and legal personality

A unique situation in the European Union results from the fact that identical institutions with identical finality, and within an identical fundamental rights framework, use competences from the diverse Treaties and thereby also the different legal personalities. The ensuing question is how to interpret those provisions which, according to the conventionally held view, establish independent organizations (Art. 281 TEC, Art. 184 TEAC and Art. 6 TECSC).

There are several ways to respond to this question. First, however, it should be recalled that, irrespective of the preferred approach the problem of legal personality, the answer is not decisive for the question of unity within the organization. Unity of an organization does not depend on the association as a whole having the status of a legal subject, as the public law of the United Kingdom demonstrates.[78] One approach would be to read the provisions in question within the context of the (over-arching) Union and to conclude that the diverse provisions regarding legal personality are the expression of *one* over-arching and unitary legal personality.[79] A more pragmatic and consensus seeking construction leads one to consider the practical implications of the division of the Communities and Union and their respective legal personalities. The significance of the retention of formal separation

---

[78] The British system shows that the state vis-à-vis its citizens does not need to have an over-arching legal personality, see Turpin, *British Government* (2. ed. 1990), 139.

[79] v. Bogdandy/Nettesheim, *supra* note 2, at 23.

within the Treaties depends on the legal significance attributed to the legal personality within the context of the law of the Union.

At this point the structures of political accountability and legal responsibility have to be investigated. In the European arena such accountability and responsibility do not correspond with the divisions between the EU, the EC, Euratom and the ECSC. Instead, political accountability, which is institutionalized in elections, is specific to the different institutions. Elections to the European Parliament ensure its accountability and also vicariously at least in part the accountability of the Commission (Art. 201, 214 TEC). Political accountability of the other institutions is ensured via national parliamentary elections.[80] The formal separation of EU, EC, Euratom and ECSC tends to obscure political accountability of the institutions which are involved in all the areas. The political structures of accountability are specific to the institutions, not the areas of competence (EU, EC, EAC and ECSC).

From the perspective of legal responsibility, the significance of the differentiation between institution (organ) and a legal person lies in the following aspect: that the legal responsibility for an institution's acts belongs to the legal person represented by the institution. Therefore, the legal person will bear the responsibility vis-à-vis the citizens, e.g., in a court room situation.[81] Thus, in practice, the legal function of the concept of legal personality lies in most legal systems in its determination of who bears legal responsibility.[82]

The situation within the Union is different. In its internal context, the institutions of the Union are the relevant subjects and directly accountable in law for their acts. Once again, the legal personality of the association is irrelevant. Its institutions can sue and be sued; they may benefit from material entitlements, as well as incur liabilities.[83] Although the ECJ in its judgements generally refers to the "institutions

---

[80] The political accountability of the Council of Ministers, the European Council, the unanimously appointed ECJ judges, the Commissioners and ECB Directors is ensured via the national governments' accountability to the Member States' Parliaments. In the case of national semi-presidential systems, such as France, presidential elections also contribute to the institutions' political accountability.

[81] Schnapp, *Zu Dogmatik und Funktion des staatlichen Organsisationsrechts*, (1978) Rechtstheorie, 275 at 282.

[82] Koenig, *Die Europäische Union als bloßer materiellrechtlicher Verbundrahmen*, EuR Beiheft 2/1998, 139 et seq.

[83] It is beyond the scope of this article to analyze in how far – in the light of the outlined developments – the EU institutions can still be thought of as "organs" in the traditional legal sense. All in all, one might discern a movement towards a structure similar to the one present in the United Kingdom where only the acting institution and not the state features in the internal legal relations.

of the Community", where legal personality is of relevance, only the individual institution and not the association (EC or EU) is held responsible. In internal European legal actions (i.e., involving a Member State or private party), the relevant party is thus the institution involved and only that institution is the addressee of the court's decision.[84] For some of the procedures this is expressly provided for by the EC Treaty (e.g. Art. 230 (ex 173) TEC). But also in other cases, such as that of an action for damages (Arts. 235, 288 (2), (ex 178, 215 (2)) TEC), the party is the individual institution and not the Community (or Union) according to the more recent case law of the Court.[85] Where a claim is granted, the ECJ holds the responsible institution liable and not the Community (or Union) as a whole.[86] This is a pragmatic solution, given the single budget and in the light of the disputed organizational structure.[87]

Legal personality is to a very large extent irrelevant for the political accountability and legal responsibility in the internal European context. As astonishing as this may seem to lawyers brought up in the continental tradition, this only refers back to the long advocated opinion that legal systems are free in their classification of relationships and systems of responsibility.[88]

With regard to public international law, the situation is different because, in the international context, the institutions act as representatives of the European Community, insofar as their competence results out of the EC Treaty.[89] However, the significance

---

[84] Case C-285/94, *Italy/Commission*, [1997] ECR I – 3519; Joined Cases T-70/92 and T-71/92, *Florimex and VGB/ Commission*, [1997] ECR II-693.

[85] Joined Cases C-104/89 and C-37/90, *Mulder*, [1992] ECR I - 3061; it is impossible to take legal action for damages against the Community as such, Case T-572/93, *Odigitria*, [1995] ECR II - 2025, para 22; in detail v. Bogdandy in: Grabitz/Hilf (Eds.), *Kommentar zur Europäischen Union* (1997), Art 215 TEC, note 39 et seq.

[86] Joined Cases C-104/89 and C-37/90, *Mulder*, [1992] ECR I – 3061, 3138. The same is true for contractual claims: Case C-42/94, *Heidemij Advies*, [1995] ECR I - 1417.

[87] This approach is also revealing from another point of view: the significance of an organization's legal personality is related to its individual assets available to satisfy any financial liability. Such individual assets do not exist since the Union has a single budget (Arts. 28 II - IV, 41 II – IV TEU, Art. 9 VI Amsterdam Treaty). In this respect, the company law discussion is enlightening, cf. Mülbert, *Aktiengesellschaft, Unternehmensgruppe und Kapitalmarkt* (1995), 20 et seq., see also AG *Darmon*, final submissions in case C-241/87, *Watson*, [1990] ECR I - 1797, 1821;

[88] Schnapp, *supra* note 81, 238 et seq.

[89] See, for example, O.J. 1998, L 118/3; inconsistency between internal and external legal relations does not cause legal problems, see Schnapp, *supra* note 81, 284.

of this is diminished by the fact that the international legal personality is not the cornerstone of the Union's ability to act. Instead, it can be seen as only one of its many competences. In addition, the actual practice suggests that the appropriate institution avails itself of the EC's legal personality, just as it exercises other internal EC competences. On this level, there is – as pointed out by the ICJ – no difference between a competence and legal personality.[90] The Union thus acts through the legal personality of the EC in international contexts.[91] According to this understanding, the European Union is responsible for all public international law obligations resulting from the institutions' usage of the international legal personality of one of the Communities. Encroachment on the rights of other legal subjects can therefore be excluded.

It can be concluded that the proposed construction does not give rise to any modification as regards the many aspect of legal responsibility, that it clarifies the situation for third states and that it increases transparency in the field of political accountability.

Unity of the association and substantive unity

The analysis so far has shown how the whole of the Union and the Communities can be seen *de lege lata* as a single organization and therefore – in a more doctrinal view – a single association. However, this does not imply a unitary organizational structure in the sense of there being only one form of interaction between the different institutions in all areas and under all competences. Even in consolidated constitutional states that is not the case.[92] The unity thesis is also not contradicted by the differences between the law founded in the Treaties of the Communities and the law of the EU Treaty outside the Communities' sphere. The unity of the organization does not require or imply unity of procedural law, law-making or legal instruments in all areas of competence. Organizational unity is a prerequisite for substantial homogeneity a the constitution, but such constitutional homogeneity is not a requirement for organizational unity as outlined in this article.

One might consider one of the differences between the law under the Community Treaties and under Titles V and VI TEU to be so

---

[90] See ICJ Rep. 1949, 174 at 178.
[91] v. Bogdandy/Nettesheim, *supra* note 2, at 23 et seq.; similarly Schermers/Blokker, *supra* note 20, § 1562.
[92] As the government's preponderance in external attests.

important as to become a criterion for organizational separation.[93] This would be convincing if a difference were to be so grave that it hits the vital nerve of integration. The problem lies, though, in deciding what makes up this vital nerve and how to formulate the *Leitidee*[94] on which it is based. One possibility would place the emphasis on the concentration of political and administrative entwinement, embodied by the intensity of interaction in the Union.[95] The operative idea, the *Leitbild*, would be an organization which meets the need and desire for co-operation of the societies joined in the organization by way of producing unilaterally binding decisions within a over-arching framework through functionally differentiated institutions. When using this *Leitbild*, demarcation between the Union and the Communities is no longer possible. Procedural forms as well as forms of law-making and legal instruments can also no longer be strictly separated. It is certainly true that supranational features vary within the Union and that the direct applicability of law is excluded in Art. 34 TEU. Nonetheless, in the light of the continuum[96] explored earlier on, after Amsterdam it has become virtually impossible to define useful criteria for a demarcation.

Summing up, the Treaty on European Union, particularly after the Treaty of Amsterdam, and the constitutional practice of the Union's institutions provide strong reasons for considering the Union as a single organization fusing the different Communities within this single entity. On this basis, coherence and transparency of the organizational set-up of the Union can *de constitutione lata* be further pursued. All Treaties and all rules created by the institutions under their competences form a single legal order. This results in important consequences for the legal practitioner. Most significantly the Court hereby has at its disposal a mechanism for the furtherance of legal coherence. For example, conflicts between different rules of a legal system normally lead to the nullity of one of the rules. Therefore the ECJ is right – on the basis of the unity thesis – in its assumption that it can declare a legal act void which had been taken under Art. K.3 II lit. b) TEU.[97] Moreover, as a

---

[93] On this see Kadelbach, *Einheit der Rechtsordnung als Verfassungsprinzip der Europäischen Union*, EuR Beiheft 2/1998, 51 et seq.

[94] Cf. Caporaso, *The European Union and Forms of State*, 34 JCMSt (1996), 29 et seq.; Schneider, *Leitbilder der Europapolitik* (1977); Zuleeg, *Wandlungen des Begriffs der Supranationalität*, (1988) integration, 103 et seq.

[95] Schreckenberger, *Von den Schengener Abkommen zu einer gemeinsamen Innen- und Justizpolitik*, 88 VerwArch (1997), 389 at 394.

[96] Cf. above II.4.

[97] For the opposite view see Pechstein, *Die Justiziabilität des Unionsrechts*, (1999) EuR, 1 at 3.

presumption, the legal principles developed in the context of the EC-Treaty can be extended to the EU-Treaty as long as they are not expressly excluded.[98] The principle of direct effect, for example, is excluded, but the principle of European Law's supremacy is not. The case-law on supremacy also covers provisions that are not directly applicable.[99] The critical case might be where a legal act under Title VI TEU which requires the adoption of a national law is in conflict with a Member State's constitution. Here, the national law can be adopted if the European act is considered supreme. A careful extension of the ECJ's case law might bridge many *lacunae* in the EU Treaty.

FURTHER ELEMENTS OF UNITY-BUILDING

THE UNION AS GUARANTOR OF A COLLECTIVE ORDER

Unity-building is not limited to the fusion of the Communities into the Union. Of numerous further developments which aim into the same direction, the most notable will now be discussed. A remarkable innovation of the Treaty of Amsterdam consists in the introduction of requirements for structural compatibility. Art. 6 sec. 1 TEU, read together with Art. 7 sec. 1 TEU, enshrines unitary standards of democracy and the rule of law for all public authority in the multilevel constitutional system, i.e., also for the Member States. But not only that: Art. 7 TEU gives the Union sanctions against a Member State that seriously and persistently violates the principles of Art. 6 sec. 1 TEU. The Treaty thus entrusts the Union with the protection of the liberal-democratic constitutions. The Union, as the last instance, is supposed to guarantee the essentials of the constitutional network and thereby also of the national legal orders, if all national safeguards fail.

Thus it becomes an organization of collective order which stabilizes the constitution of its Member States. This innovation is a change in quality as the previous situation was characterized by fragmentation:[100] provisions overarching the entire multilevel system

---

[98] In detail Everling, *Folgerungen*, EuR-Beiheft 2/1998, 185, at 192 and 194.
[99] It is established case law that European norms can be of relevance in national law even though they are not directly applicable and do not provide for subjective rights; see case C-431/92, *Commission/Germany (Wärmekraftwerk Großkotzenburg)*, [1995] ECR I – 2189.
[100] For the centralizing effects of the human rights decisions of the US Supreme Court see Jacobs/Karst, *The "Federal" Legal Order: The U.S.A. and Europe Compared – A Juridical Perspective*, in: Cappelletti/Seccombe/Weiler (Eds.),

were missing. Now the Union has been given the power for developing a human rights policy in relation to the Member States. In this development, one can see an even wider process of unity-building, namely, the creation of a unity which encompasses the Union and the Member State. Certainly, grasping this overall European system remains a challenging task. This is particularly evident when one considers the as yet unchristened Union-Member States complex. The Union does not represent the Member States and the Union in their entirety, as a nation-state represents itself and its constituent elements, for example, the German federation (*Bund*) with respect to the *Länder*. Such a high degree of federal unity has not been reached and its realization seems improbable in light of the principal structures. Further research will be needed to develop an adequate conceptual construction for this form of unity.

CONCENTRATING INTEGRATION ON THE UNION

European integration is a societal evolution that reaches beyond the political and legal processes of the European Union. However, not all the legal and the political processes have been monopolized by the Union; one has but to recall the prominent role of the European Court of Human Rights (ECHR). Even in the more narrow context of EU-Member States, co-ordination has not been achieved solely through the European Community's and later the Union's institutions. The relevant category of the so-called complementary (international) law, as well as a number of other co-ordinating organs, institutions and legal instruments, have also played key roles in efforts towards co-ordination. Prominent examples include the *Schengen-acquis*[101] as well as the Convention on jurisdiction and the enforcement of judgements in civil and commercial matters.[102]

These additional organizations and legal instruments established a solid basis for the understanding that the Communities (and later the Union) would deal only with some – albeit important – aspects of

---

Integration Through Law (Vol 1, 1986) 169, at 205 et seq.; Kutscher, *Thesen zu den Methoden der Auslegung des Gemeinschaftsrechts aus der Sicht eines Richters*, in: EuGH, *Begegnung von Justiz und Hochschule am 27. und 28. Sept.1976* (Luxemburg 1976) I-8; for the earlier discussion of how to respond if a Member State were to become a dictatorship, see Hilf, in: von der Groeben/Thiesing/Ehlermann, *Kommentar zum EU-/EG-Vertrag* (5 ed. 1997) Vol. 5, Art. 240 TEC para. 13.

[101] See Art. 2 of Protocol (No 2) integrating the Schengen acquis into the framework of the European Union.

[102] O.J. 1972 L 299/32.

European co-ordination. Therefore, the Union is perceived as a functionally-oriented form of political and legal organization rather than as a territorially-oriented one. With this in mind, the implications of the following provisions of the Amsterdam Treaty become more evident. These provisions transfer various political and legal processes of Europeanisation, which were hitherto independent of the European Union, to the Union's institutional framework.[103]

Thus, European integration is now to a large extent concentrated on the Union – a direction that had been established by the Maastricht Treaty and has been carried forth by the Treaty of Amsterdam. Important European legal bodies that had previously not found themselves within the Union's legal framework have been integrated. Of these, the most impressive is the transfer of the *Schengen-acquis*.[104] Similarly, Art. 31 lit a. TEU enhances the Union competences to include the Convention on Jurisdiction and the Enforcement of Judgements in Civil and Commercial Matters. Also of high relevance are the above-mentioned competences that allow the Union to regulate horizontal networking. As a result, the Union has become the central organization for legal and political Europeanisation. In other words, we are witnessing a further form of unity-building and centralization.

Territory and Citizenship

The influential definition of the state by Georg Jellinek provides a further tool for examining the building of unity within the Union. According to Jellinek's primarily static definition, the essential criteria for a state are a defined territory, a permanent population and an effective government.[105] These "three elements" are useful as rough indicators when analyzing the development of a unified polity. Viewed comprehensively, a unifying orientation becomes evident.

The most impressive development is the evolution of the Union's territorial nexus and thus the territorial dimension of integration. The weight of this evolution can be appraised retrospectively. The Common

---

[103] And thereby at least partially realizing a project which the Member States have worked at for a considerable time, see Piris, *After Maastricht, are the Community Institutions More Efficacious, More Democratic and More Transparent?*, 19 ELR (1994), 449 et seq.

[104] For a thorough review Wagner, *The Integration of Schengen into the Framework of the European Union*, LIEI 25 (1999), 1.

[105] Jellinek, *Allgemeine Staatslehre* (reprint of the 3. ed. 1976), 179 et seq.; on its influence see Brownlie, *Principles of Public International Law* (5. ed. 1998), at 70 et seq.

Market (which was the central term used to describe integration until 1993) rests on a concept of integration that emphasizes the functional over the territorial component. According to this approach to integration, the organization administering the Common Market can be understood as an example for the "de-bordering of the nation-state."[106] Further, the new transnational organization would allegedly not become an authority characterized by a unitary structure and the principal territorially founded identity of rulers and subjects, but would instead result in co-operative problem-solving within a variety of global spheres of functional Cupertino.[107] Transnational authority is seen in this light at best as a plurality of overlapping institutions, memberships and interests.[108] In the legal debate these questions have often been implicitly discussed in the context of rendering the Union more flexible, through, for example, "variable geometry", "concentric circles" or a "multi-speed Europe".[109]

The developments under the Maastricht and now the Amsterdam Treaty point, at least in some respects, in the opposite direction and suggest unity-building. The Treaty on European Union promulgates objectives and competences for the creation and preservation of a unitary territory. Until the Treaty of Amsterdam, the creation of a unitary area, at which Art. 8a of the Treaty of the European Economic Community (EEC) had aimed since the Single European Act (now Art. 18 TEC), had been outside the competences of the Community.[110] Now, through the integration of the *Schengen-acquis*, it has become a central part of the Union's activities. This territorial orientation is already evident in the actual choice of words; for example Art. 11 TEU refers to safeguarding the Union's integrity and preserving its *external borders*.

---

[106] Mitrany, *The prospect of integration: federal or functional?*, 4 JCMSt (1965) 119; Albert/Brock, *Debordering the world of states*, 35 New Political Science (1996), 69 et seq; Schmitter, *Representation and the Future Euro-Polity*, (1992) Staatswissenschaft & Staatspraxis, 379, at 385; Ladeur, *Towards a Legal Theory of Supranationality – The Viability of the Network Concept*, 3 ELJ (1997) 33, at 51; Zürn, *Jenseits der Staatlichkeit. Über die Folgen der ungleichzeitigen Denationalisierung*, 4 Leviathan (1992), 490 et seq.

[107] Elkins, *Beyond Sovereignty: Territory and Political Economy in the Twenty-First Century* (1995), especially at 45 et seq.; Zellentin, *Der Funktionalismus – eine Strategie gesamteuropäischer Integration?*, 23 PVS special issue (1992) 62, at 71.

[108] Ladeur, *supra* note 106, at 51: "Overlapping Transnational Networks of Law-making".

[109] Illuminating Stubb, *A Categorization of Differentiated Integration*, 34 JCMSt (1996), 283 et seq.

[110] Trumpf, *Vom Binnenmarkt zur politischen Union*, Schriftenreihe des Zentrums für Europäisches Wirtschaftsrecht, Heft 21 (1992), at 14.

Alongside the territorial element in Jellinek's classic concept is the personnel component: the people, which in a democratic reading refers to the entirety of citizens that constitute the polity. The initial treaties did not provide for a European citizenship. Even national citizenship is not central to the Common Market. Two of the freedoms of the TEC (free movement of goods and of capital) are applicable regardless of the nationality of the person claiming these rights. Thus the idea of the "market citizen",[111] the central concept of the early era, was and still is partially independent from citizenship. In addition, those freedoms that are linked to citizenship – the freedoms of providing services, of establishment and of free movement of workers – are extended to non-EU nationals through a series of treaties with third countries. A clear delineation between citizens and non-citizens is not known to the logic of the Common Market: it protects whomever advances the association's function to generate wealth.

In the further development of the EU, this personnel aspect continues to gain importance. The personal aspect initially gained visibility via the Act that provided for direct elections to the European Parliament[112] and is significantly enhanced by the introduction of Union citizenship. Even though the material content of this citizenship may be weak,[113] the concept as such is important to the classification of the Union's structure as a supranational federation, as it shows that the Union is framed as a political community having a direct nexus with its citizens.

The Amsterdam Treaty establishes competences for a massive strengthening of Union citizenship, albeit in a surprising area. It does not strengthen civil or political rights but rather creates unitary mechanisms for exclusion. Articles 62 and 63 TEC provide for – and even require (Art. 61 lit. a. TEC) – a policy which allows the Union in many respects to distinguish between Union citizens and non-EU nationals inside the Union. The implications of these extended powers manifest themselves when one examines the foundations of real citizenship. This "real citizenship" is not so much a formal legal concept. At its centre lies the social identity of the individual.[114] As

---

[111] The concept was invented by Ipsen, *supra* note 47, 42/1 et seq.; for the current debate see Shaw, *The Interpretation of European Union Citizenship*, 61 Modern Law Review (1998), 293, at 300.

[112] O.J. 1976, L 278/1

[113] See Weiler, *European Citizenship and Human Rights*, in Winter at al., *supra* note 34, 57, at 65: „little more than a cynical exercise of public relations".

[114] Wiener, *"European" Citizenship Practice. Building Institutions of a Non-State* (1998), at 228 et seq., 286 et seq.

formation of social identity results in exclusion,[115] the Union's competence for exclusion along its outer borders includes a possible strengthening of its own citizenship. Exclusion may have other, stronger effects (whether or not they are positive, shall not be discussed) than the difficult and disputed extension of political participation. The amendment of Art. 17 sec. 1 TEC reflects the fact that that Union citizenship merely complements national citizenship and as such does not replace it, as citizenship in the European Union can only be conceptualized by means of multiple identities and memberships. When analyzing the Union's competences with respect to territory and citizenship, one finds clear federal dynamics in the sense that a government for a defined territory and that a defined citizenship exists and the sovereign authority defines itself in these terms.

PROLIFERATION, FRAGMENTATION, AND FLEXIBILITY

The previous section provides evidence of unity-building within the Union as opposed to organizational proliferation and fragmentation. Given the above analysis, one could even be tempted to assume that the Union is becoming a state. After all, the emergence of a state to a large extent consists in the building of unity: it is the unification of previously dispersed authority under a central political-administrative system, the framing of a unitary legal order[116] and a process aspiring to subordinate all other societal systems to under the territorial logic of the nation-state.[117] However, other elements in the legal set up of the Union strongly counteract such a conclusion. In the context of this study, only those will be mentioned which are due to organizational proliferation and fragmentation. Another important point regards flexibility. However, since this book contains a paper whose idea I largely share,[118] I will address flexibility only in my concluding remarks.

---

[115] Habermas, *Die postnationale Konstellation* (1998), at 122 et seq., 161.
[116] Compare Baldus, *Die Einheit der Rechtsordnung* (1995), esp. at 121 et seq.
[117] See the classical formulation by Hegel, *Rechtsphilosophie* (1820, reprinted 1971), § 257 et seq.
[118] Dekker/Wessel, *Proliferation of Legal Systems within International Organizations: The European Union and the Concept of Flexibility.*

The Proliferation of Council-formations as Polycentric and Fragmented Negotiating Systems

A closer look at the Union's institutions reveal important signs of internal fragmentation into sub-units which can be read in the light of organizational proliferation. According to *Carol Harlow*, even the Commission can be seen „as a bundle of regulatory agencies represented by the Directorates General."[119]. It is beyond doubt that the Commission is characterized by a strong sectoral bias.[120] However, institutional fragmentation and polycentricity at the level of the Union's general institutions is most evident in the internal structure of its most powerful organ, the Council. It deliberates in over twenty constellations and does not possess the primary unifying mechanism of institutions, a hierarchy. In many respects the Council appears rather more like a multi-faceted and fragmented processes of consensus-building between 16 different political-administrative systems (15 states and the Commission) than a solid, independent institution.[121] Moreover, depending on the participation in the policy area, not all Member States are represented in the respective Council.[122] The resulting problems for the coherence of European Union law, required by Art. 3 TEU, are well known. The innovations of Art. 207 sec. 2 TEC and the strengthening of the administrative competence of the General Secretariat of the Council change nothing in this respect.[123] The implication of this fragmentation for the nature of the Union becomes evident if one compares the Council with those national organs which have similar power. In this context, only the executive (cabinet) and parliament are relevant. The executive and parliament,

---

[119] Harlow, *European Administrative Law and the Global Challange*, in: Craig/de Burca, *supra* note 6, 261, 273.

[120] Mazey/Richardson, *EU policy-making. A garbage can or an anticipatory and consensus style policy?*, in: Mény/Muller/Quermonne (Eds.), *Adjusting to Europe. The impact of the European Union on national institutions and policies* (1996), 53.

[121] Wuermeling, *Streicht die Räte, rettet den Rat! Überlegungen zur Reform des EU-Ministerrats*, (1996) EuR, 167, at 168 et seq. Even the unifying roll of the so-called General Council, which is composed of the Member States' foreign ministers, is endangered, cf., Secretary General of the Council of the European Union, *Intergouvernemental Conference 1996*, Report of the Reflection Group (Westendorp Group) (1996), Para.106.

[122] On the ECOFIN-Council The Economist, *Coreper, Europe's managing board*, 8 August 1998, 27.

[123] For the relevant debate see Dashwood, *Effectiveness and Simplification of Decision-Making by the Council*, in: Winter et al., *supra* note 34, 147, at 156 et seq., referring especially to a proposal for a "presidency of the Council" at 158.

the latter due to its partisan structure, are much more solid and hierarchical institutions. Of particular significance is the governing majority, which – like the opposition – has a more or less evident hierarchy of individuals. A structure along party lines as well as a personification hardly exist on the European level.[124] One might argue that even in the national systems a strict hierarchy no longer exists. Still, there remains a qualitative difference, as the national legal orders generally have a tendency to concentrate political power in the cabinet. In fact, the participation of states in the fragmented and polycentric system of the Union promotes the centralization of authority at the top of the executive.[125]

PROLIFERATION OF PROCEDURES

Fragmentation and polycentricity are magnified by the Union's decision-making processes. Practically all important decisions are made on a basis of participation by various organs, and co-operation among these organs is not centrally led: even the European Council lacks the legal instruments as well as the real powers for orchestrating the co-operation of the different organs.[126] In addition, the decision-making procedures have different structures. There are procedures of a "constitutional" nature which include not only the Union institutions but national organs as well (Art. 17 sec. 1, Art. 48 TEU, Art. 190 sec. 4 TEC). However, even the procedures in which only Union institutions participate are generally opaque, multifaceted, and confusing.[127] Moreover, the applicable form of co-operation of the various organs often does not follow from a clear correlation between the procedure and the field of activity.[128] Depending on the procedure, the structures of political accountability and legal responsibility change considerably.

---

[124] To change this is important to many reform projects, compare Commissariat Général du Plan, *L'Union européenne en quete d'institutions légitimes et efficaces, Rapport du groupe présidé par Jean-Louis Quermonne* (1999), at 41, 55, 61 et seq.; Grevisse, *A propos de quelques institutions*, Revue du Marché commun et de l'Union européenne (1998), 569, 572 et seq.

[125] Moravcsik, *Warum die Europäische Union die Exekutive stärkt*, in: Wolf (Ed.), *Projekt Europa im Übergang?* (1997), 211 et seq.

[126] Wallace, *supra* note 58, at 159.

[127] Piris, *supra* note 103, at 469 et seq.

[128] Timmermans, *The Effectiveness and simplification of decision-making*, in: Winter et al., *supra* note 34, 133, at 145.

In this respect, even though the Treaty of Amsterdam has led to several improvements,[129] fragmentation, opacity and polycentricity remain.

If one compares these results with the situation in the Member States, one will certainly find different law-making procedures as well. However, at the Member State level fragmentation is avoided, since generally all law-making procedures are built around the legislative process which lies at the centre of the Member States' law-making-procedures.[130] At the European level, in contrast, the co-decision procedure does not play such a centralizing role, despite its expansion through the Treaty of Amsterdam.

Organizational Proliferation: ECB, CoR, Committees and Agencies

Even though the organizational set up has been remarkably stable when looking at the main institutions as named in Art. 7 TEC (only the Court of Auditors has been added), a closer look reveals an astonishing organizational development. Three levels can be distinguished: the constitutional level, the substructure of the Commission and the Council, and the creation of new bodies.

At the constitutional level, two developments are to be mentioned: the creation of the Committee of the Regions, and, even more important, the creation of the European Central Bank. Whereas the Committee of the Regions[131] has not gained the importance the German Länder in particular wished,[132] the creation of the European Central Bank can be seen as the most important single step since the inception of the Communities.

The autonomy of the ECB is enshrined in Art. 108 (ex 107) TEC. However, neither this nor any other provision define clearly the legal position of the Bank in the overall framework of the Treaties. The attempts of determination have given rise to a vivid and controversial

---

[129] E.g. the co-decision procedure of Art. 251 TEC has been streamlined; for the problems of the previous procedure see European Parliament, Resolution on the functioning of the EU-Treaty (A.4-0102/95), para. 30; Lipsius, *The 1996 Intergovernmental Conference*, 20 ELR (1995) 235, at 264.

[130] This is true also for France, in contrast to the text of Art. 34 CF, *cf.* Boulouis, *L'influence des articles 34 et 37 sur l'équilibre politique entre les pouvoir*, in: Favoreu (Ed.), *Le domaine de la loi et du règlement* (2 ed. 1982), at 195.

[131] For considering it an organization see above section II + b.

[132] On this Blanke, in: Grabitz/Hilf, *supra* note 85, vor Art. 198a-c EGV, note 8 et seq.

debate.[133] In my understanding, any theory will get into serious difficulties if it tries to determine the constitutional position of the ECB in respect to the three organizations EC, EAC and ECSC, simply because these organizations have ceased to exist. EC, EAC and ECSC are only areas of activity and competences of the Union's institutions. The constitutional position of the ECB has to be determined not with respect to the Communities, but within the organizational framework of the European Union which has fused the Communities as independent organizations.

On the basis of the assumption of this paper, the ECB can only be considered as the central bank of the European Union. It is set up through the Union's primary law, is subject to the ECJ's control and can only be changed through the procedure of Art. 48 (ex Art. N) TEU. Consequently it is subject to all primary law (e. g. Art. 6 (ex Art. F) TEU) which is not specific to a particular body or institution. Hereby the ECB is solidly bound into the Union's constitutional framework which distinguished it radically from the Worldbank with its loose relationship to the United Nations. This solid constitutional basis provided by the unity thesis allows for far reaching organizational and operational autonomy, such as the ECB's international legal personality, its non-contractual liability and its partial independence from secondary legislation by other institutions.[134]

Organizational growth is even more important below the constitutional level. One aspect which has recently drawn much attention has been the so called *comitology*.[135] Around the Commission, a great number of committees has been established. They consist of national officials and experts, who are appointed according to provisions by the Council to oversee the Commission's implementing legislation. According to research for the year 1990, there were more than 600 groups comprising annually over 17,000 national officials and over 10,000 other experts.[136] A similar structure, with sometimes

---

[133] See Zilioli/Selmeyr, *The external relations of the Euro area: legal aspects*, CMLRev. 36 (1999), 273; Torrent, *Whom is the European Central Bank the central bank of?: Reaction to Zilioli and Selmayr*, CMLRev. 36 (1999), 1229, with further references.

[134] In detail Zilioli and Selmayr, *supra* note 133.

[135] On this in detail Vos/Joerges (Eds.), *EU Committees: Social Regulation, Law and Politics* (1999).

[136] Wessels, *Comitology: fusion in action: Politico-administrative trends in the EU system*, Journal of European Public Policy 5 (1998), 171et seq.; Falke/Winter, *Management and regulatory committees in executive rule-making*, in: Winter (Ed.), *Sources and Categories of European Union Law* (1996); Glatthaar, *Einflußnahme auf Entscheidungen der EG durch die Ausschüsse der EG-Kommission*, (1992) RIW, 179 et seq.

identical participants, can be found below the Council. The decision-making process is heavily influenced by the meetings of the Permanent Representative's *advisory board* and the Council's working groups which precedes it.[137] As early as 1990 the frequency of ca. 40 meetings per week had been reached. This helps to clarify the singular volume of transnational administrative communication achieved by the Union. It is estimated that in 1990 ca. 25% of all Bonn ministerial officials of high rank participated directly and personally in the EU administration, and 40% of them had EU issues as an integral part of their responsibilities.[138] In view of the enormous expansion of tasks created by the Maastricht and Amsterdam Treaties, as well as the post cold war aspects of relations with the EU's eastern neighbours, one can expect that this number has substantially increased. The proliferation of committees within the organizational sub-structure of the Commission and the Council is a central element of the European Union's politico-administrative system. These committees have a direct impact on the legislative outcome, which receives very little control once unanimity has been achieved among the members.

This development may endanger the principle of democracy. The informational exchanges and communications within these committees are not neutral social operations. Decision-making processes are significantly influenced by the nature of the information, its construction and its presentation.[139] The administrative information and communications network is thus largely independent. Through its control of the information the political bodies receive, it pre-programmes their debates. Although the professional ethics of most of the officials involved should be above attempting to institute an authoritarian bureaucracy, there is a justified concern that a one-sided view of reality may result.[140]

Another important development which can come under the heading "proliferation" consists in the creation of agencies. Until today, agencies have only limited competences. That does not mean that they are negligible. Of particular interest are those agencies which aim at a

---

[137] This phase has heretofore been studied primarily from a political science perspective, cf. Ayes-Renshaw/Wallace, *The Council of Ministers* (1997); Pedler/Schäfer (Eds.), *Shaping European Law and Policy* (1996).
[138] Wessels, *supra* note 134, 178 et seq.
[139] Berger/Luckmann, *Die gesellschaftliche Konstruktion der Wirklichkeit* (5. ed. 1977), 49 et seq.
[140] Joerges/Neyer, *Transforming Strategic Interaction into Deliberative Problem-Solving*, Journal of European Public Policy 4 (1997), 609 et seq.; Scharpf, *Regieren in Europa. Effektiv und demokratisch?* (1999), 143.

new form of supranational guidance: guidance by the provision of information. They serve a steering function by binding the Member State's governmental administrative bodies and their officials to a European database and communications network and to European programmes and projects. Of the 14 agencies so far created, five can be considered as specific information agencies.[141]

The agencies are usually created as independent legal entities for the fulfilment of specific tasks.[142] The organizational structure usually consists of three organs: the administrative council, director and the complementary board. The leading organ of the three is the administrative council, which is responsible for naming the director. The director implements the directives of the Council, organizes the on going administration and makes the personnel decisions.[143] He or she is responsible to the administrative council and must report to them on a regular basis.[144] Thus the administrative council controls the person who runs the day-to-day business of the agency. Furthermore, the council is obliged to make those decisions which are of critical importance to the agency's mission. These decisions are set out in various programme resolutions, first as a draft resolution for the next several years[145] and then concretized in annual work programmes.[146] There is a corresponding requirement that the summaries of the progress reports on the implementation of the programmes be made to the council and, furthermore, be made available to the public.[147] Finally, the administrative council participates in the planning and approval of

---

[141] European Environment Agency (established by Regulation 1210/90 of 7 May 1990, O.J. 1990, L 120/1, following EEA), European Monitoring Centre for Drugs and Drug Addition (established by Regulation 302/93 of 8 Feb. 1993, O.J. 1993, L 036/1, following EMCDDA), European Foundation for the Improvement of Living and Working Conditions (established by Regulation 1365/75 of 26 May 1975, O.J. 1975, L 139/1, following EFILWC), European Agency for Safety and Health at Work (established by Regulation 2062/94 of 18 July 1994, O.J. 1994, L 216/1, following EASHW), European Monitoring Centre on Racism and Xenophobia (established by Regulation 1035/97 of 2 June 1997, O.J. 1997, L 151/1, following EMCRX).

[142] Most important is the discussion whether the administration of European competition law should be devolved to a semi-independent agency along the lines of the German Bundeskartellamt, on this Ehlermann, *Reflections on a European Cartel Office*, CML Rev. 32 (1995), 471.

[143] Art. 9 EEA, Art. 9 EFILWC.

[144] Art. 9 I EMCDDA; Art. 9 I, II EEA; Art. 8 III c, 10 EMCRX; 11 EASHW; Art. 9 EFILWC.

[145] Art. 8 III EMCDDA, Art. 12 EFILWC, Art. 8 IV EEA.

[146] Art. 8 III a EMCRX; Art. 10 I EASHW.

[147] Art. 8 III b EMCRX, Art. 13 EFILWC.

the agency's budget.[148] This body, which is responsible for the critical decisions concerning the agency, is mainly composed of representatives of the Member States,[149] each of whom generally sends one or two representatives as opposed to the one or two usually sent by the Commission. Thus, in practice, the Member States dominate the administrative councils[150] and are directly involved in the formation of the agencies' programmes and in controlling the agencies. Consequently, the agencies do not act as remote agents with respect to the Member States because they and their specialized ministries are deeply integrated into their operations. Furthermore, the agencies necessarily maintain close ties to the relevant national interest groups and science, and some even integrate representatives from affected interest groups into their administrative council.[151] The agencies are, moreover, obliged to co-ordinate their programmes and policies with those of the Member States.[152] The Commission, by contrast, while integrated into the structure, is not usually a primary actor.[153] The Commission has a limited right to make recommendations for nominations[154] and to dispatch its own members. While it remains largely an observer, it can, under certain circumstances, take part in the agency's supervision.[155] Organizing the agencies' general framework remains, of course, the responsibility of the Union. The agencies are thus subject to financial control by the Union, may avail themselves of the Union's law concerning employment and civil servants and utilize the Union's translation services.[156] The agencies generally fall within the jurisdiction of the European Court.[157]

The reaction in legal scholarship to this development has been mixed. Some argue that organizational proliferation in the sense of

[148] Art. 8 III d EMCRX; Art. 13 EASHW, Art. 12, 13 EEA.
[149] Art. 8 EASHW; Art. 8 EMCRX; Art. 8 EEA.
[150] Kreher, *Agencies in the European Community: A Step towards Administrative Integration in Europe*, JEPP 4 (1997), 238 et seq.
[151] Art. 8 I EASHW, 6 EFILWC. The information agencies, or, more precisely, their administrative councils, are, on the whole, astonishingly open to other members. Thus, third States or other organizations (e.g., the Council of Europe) are admitted. (Art. 19 EEA, Art. 9 EASHW, Art. 8 EMCRX).
[152] For example, Art. 7 EMCRX.
[153] On the Commission's role in general see Wallace, *The Institutions of the EU: Experience and Experiments*, in: Wallace/Wallace, *Policy-Making in the European Union* (1996), at 57 et seq.
[154] Art. 10 EMCRX; 11 I EEA; 9 EMCDDA; Art. 10 EFILWC.
[155] Art. 22 EASHW.
[156] Art. 13 EMCRX; Art. 11 EMCRX; 20 EASHW; Art. 12 IX EMCRX.
[157] Art. 15 EMSRX, Art. 18 EEA.

functional differentiation is inherent: a complex world needs a complex, i.e., differentiated institutional response.[158] Moreover, the creation of specific agencies with specific regulatory powers which involve interested parties along the lines of the American regulatory agencies has been seen by some as a way to cope with the problem of democratic participation within the Union.[159] Organizational proliferation would therefore resolve some of the Union's most urgent problems. Other, however, fear for the constitutional integrity of the Union.[160] To me, doubts remain as to what extent the Union should emulate American regulatory agencies, given their many problems.[161] On the other hand, the constitutional concerns appear exaggerated: the agencies in themselves doe not pose a constitutional problem, but rather a question of administrative law. From this perspective, increasing the Union's coherence through the mechanism of the administrative legal regime appears desirable.

CONCLUSIONS

This paper has focused on the astonishing phenomena of the simultaneous development of organizational proliferation and fragmentation on the one side, unity-building and centralization on the other side. It remains to be clarified how the apparently contradictory developments fit together.

With respect to the proliferation of more or less autonomous bodies such as the ECB and some agencies it can be argued that they are mainly a by-product of the deepening integration process. If the Union has become – through diverse developments of unity building and centralization – the main organization of transnational co-operation in Europe and even some kind of a new polity, it has also had to adapt organizationally. The Union required new, differentiated

---

[158] Majone, *Regulating Europe* (1996), 15 et seq.; Kreher, *supra* note 148, 225; in general see Bryde, *supra* note 40; Fischer-Appelt, *Agenturen der Europäischen Gemeinschaft (1999)*.

[159] On this Dehousse, *Regulating by Networks in the European Community: The Role of Agencies*, JEPP 4 (1997), 246.

[160] See the not very convincing critique of de Burca, *Institutional Development of the EU: A constitutional Analysis*, in: Craig/de Burca, *supra* note 6, 75 et seq.; Shapiro, *The Problems of Independent Agencies in the United States and the European Union*, JEPP 4 (1997), 276.

[161] On this Shapiro, *APA:Past, Present and Future*, Virginia Law Rev. 72 (1986), 447; Pierce Jr., *Rulemaking and the Administrative Procedure Act*, Tulsa Law Journal 32 (1996), 185.

organizational responses to meet the challenges posed by increasingly complex tasks. This type of organizational proliferation presents therefore basically a process by which the polity adapts to new tasks and more complex environments. It is, to a large extent, parallel to intra-state developments. On all levels of government there is a general trend of public tasks being fulfilled by non-centralized, more or less autonomous sub-bodies. Studies which have examined this intra-state development may provide insights that can be used on the transnational level to shape these sub-bodies according to basic constitutional principles.[162]

Similar conclusions may be reached with respect to the committees. Their proliferation is a central feature of the Union's development since they provide the institutional framework for close collaboration between all interested actors. Nevertheless, their procedures are cause for concern; much has to be done to better realize the principle of democratic accountability in their proceedings.

If the above mentioned forms of organizational proliferation are necessary in order to cope with complex environments under the premise of supranational or co-operative federalism in a polycentric constitutional framework, the drive toward basic unity becomes a fundamental constitutional urgency. A complex public organization which is divided into numerous sub-parts and bodies needs a strong encompassing constitutional system which provides for democratic legitimacy by guiding and controlling the diverse parts.[163] That institutional core within the Union is provided for by the central institutions of Art. 4 TEU and Art. 5 TEU if one follows the unity thesis presented here. On all of the other interpretations of the relationship between the EU and the Communities, transparency, coherence and most forms of political and legal responsibility would be endangered. It would be detrimental to the Union, and probably unconstitutional on both the national and the Union level, if its development did not concentrate its mission(s) and competences in a single organization. The unhappy development of the United Nations "family" may serve as proof of this thesis. The UN "family" presents the case of an organizational set-up in which the competences are dispersed between several agencies and entities, rather than being

---

[162] Dreier, *Hierarchische Verwaltung im demokratischen Staat* (1991), 19 et seq., 211 et seq.; Schlink, *Die Amtshilfe* (1982), 62 et seq.

[163] The charter of the ECB represents a particular type of economic thinking. As written into the EC Treaty it is, from a constitutional perspective, highly questionable, because an ammendment affecting this aspect of the ECB has been rendered all but impossible, even if a majority of the Union's citizens desire it.

concentrated in one. The core mission remains the maintenance of peace (Art. 1 UN Charter)[164] and is mostly handled by the Security Council. Further public missions are scattered among a large number of loosely co-operating and badly co-ordinated organizations.[165] The regrettable results of this arrangement are all too obvious.

We must now turn to the question of procedural proliferation. Given the basic structure of the Union as a polycentric political and institutionally fragmented entity, the institutions must draw up decisions via complicated procedures and an even more complicated political processes. Actors with different backgrounds and with quite different interests participate in these procedures. There appears little remedy to this situation. The traditional mechanism for managing complexity – hierarchy – is generally not available due to the polycentric structure of the Union. It would be unthinkable for a single Member State to exercise a leading (hegemonic) function in the Union and it does not appear likely that a hierarchy rooted in solid transnational party-politics will develop. The reform proposals aiming[166] in this direction will be neither effective nor desirable if they are meant to change this structure fundamentally. The mechanisms for dealing with Member State differences and complexities arising out of their national systems are best handled by contractual and co-operative relations in the sense of co-operation between different political-administrative systems.[167] Since no strong hierarchy will develop within the European political system, fragmentation will remain a durable feature which should not be viewed as *a priori* detrimental. Rather, those aspects of fragmentation which are due to the polycentric and non-hierarchical nature of the Union should be formulated in a constitutional principle through which the unique features of the Union's constitution with respect to Member States' constitutions gain legal substance.

Flexibility and centralization form another dialectic pair. First, flexibility – meaning that not all Member States participate in all policies at a given moment, or, to put it differently, that the Union's

---

[164] Insofar as it has assumed further responsibilities, in particular economic ones, the reform movements have been pressing for a massive reduction, The Economist, *Reforming the United Nations*, 8. August 1998, 17, 18.

[165] Overview in Hüfner, *UN-System*, in: *Handbuch Vereinte Nationen*, 1991, § 133; Schermers/Blokker, *supra* note 20, 1194 et seq.

[166] On the proposals on future institutional changes cf. Blokker/Heukels, *supra* note 32, 38 et seq.

[167] Scharpf, *Introduction. The Problem Solving Capacity of Multi-Level Governance*, 4 Journal of European Public Policy (1997), 520 et seq.

law is not the same everywhere in the Union – needs a strong institutional base if it is not to imperil basic constitutional values.[168] The solution in the Amsterdam Treaty in this respect is convincing: closer co-operation is only permissible while preserving institutional unity.[169] At the same time, the development of the Union into an overarching European federation requires mechanisms of flexibility if it is to remain the dominant organization through which the participating societies co-ordinate themselves.[170] This is particularly evident in light of the prospect of 20 or even 25 members. The solution in Art. 11 TEU is probably too strict, given the veto-power in para. 2. Therefore the danger remains that ad hoc, problematic, partial "solutions" such as the Maastricht Social protocol or the Schengen Agreement – will be taken in the future. Constitutional politics here approaches flexibility on an ad hoc basis, which can lead to solutions that bring with them all the dangers of unprincipled *proliferation*, resulting in legal regimes which are uncoordinated, in-coherent and divisive. The legal community is called on to identify acceptable, sound solutions to the challenges facing the European Union and to participate in the construction of convincing forms of flexibility which will contribute to define the singular constitution of the European Union.[171]

---

[168] Commissariat du Plan, *supra* note 124, at 78.

[169] Ehlermann, *Increased Differentiation or Stronger Uniformity*, in: Winter et al., see *supra* note 34, 27 at 43; Kortenberg, *Closer Cooperation in the Treaty of Amsterdam*, 35 CML Rev. (1998), 833, at 854.

[170] Early on Grabitz (Ed.), *Abgestufte Integration. Eine Alternative zum herkömmlichen Integrationskonzept?* (1984).

[171] For examples cf. Tuytschaever, *Differentiation in European Union Law* (1999); Shaw and Wiener, *The Paradox of the "European Polity"*, in: Green Cowles/Smith (Eds.), *State of the European Union 5: Risks, Resistance, and Revival* (2000).

THE PROLIFERATION OF LAW-MAKING ORGANS: A NEW ROLE FOR THE INTERNATIONAL LAW COMMISSION?

*Rosanne van Alebeek**
(in co-operation with John Dugard) [1]

INTRODUCTION

In 1928 Brierly wrote that "an international legislature, in the sense of a body having the power to enact new international law binding on the States of the world or on their peoples, does not exist".[2] This observation still holds true today. After the Second World War it was commonly felt that the international peace and security would benefit from extensive and effective co-operation between states on issues of international law. Proposals for a legislative role for the General Assembly (GA) of the United Nations (UN) to enact or revise binding rules of international law were nevertheless rejected at the San Francisco Conference.[3] Instead, article 13(1)(a) of the UN Charter was adopted. It imposes the obligation on the Assembly to "initiate studies and make recommendations for the purpose of promoting international co-operation in the political field and encouraging the progressive development of international law and its codification". The GA established a Committee for the Progressive Development of International Law and its Codification to study the methods by which article 13(1)(a) could be implemented. That Committee recommended the establishment of the International Law Commission (ILC).[4] The GA adopted the Statute of the

---

[*] Law Degree Leiden University, M.Jur. (Oxon), M.St. in Legal Research (Oxon), Doctoral Research Fellow at the Meijers Institute for Legal Research, Leiden University.
[1] Professor Dugard delivered a paper at the conference which reflected many of the views in this article.
[2] J.L. Brierly, *The Law of Nations, An Introduction to the International Law of Peace* (1st edn. 1928) p. 96.
[3] M.R. Anderson et al. (eds), *The International Law Commission and the Future of International Law* (1998) p. xiv.
[4] Report of the Committee, Doc. A/331, GA Official Records, Second Session (1947), Sixth Committee, p. 173-182.

International Law Commission by Resolution 174 (II) on 21 November 1947. Article 1(1) of the Statute provides that "The International Law Commission shall have for its object the promotion of the progressive development of international law and its codification."

At its inception, the Commission was seen as "the principal instrument for the codification of international law" and it was optimistically held that "[t]here is ... no reason why in two decades or so ... the results of the work of the International Law Commission should not cover practically the entire field of international law."[5] Since then the ILC has undeniably made a substantial contribution to the codification of international law by drafting some of the most important conventions in modern international law. The Vienna Conventions on Diplomatic Relations (1961) and Consular Relations (1963), the Vienna Convention on the Law of Treaties (1969) and the Geneva Conventions on the Law of the Sea (1958) were all based on drafts prepared by the ILC. However, it has also been remarked that the ILC "has been excluded from preparation of some of the most important law-making conventions of our time".[6] Conventions in the field of human rights law, economic or environmental law for example, are usually concluded without any involvement of the ILC.

This paper examines the role of the United Nations International Law Commission in the international law-making process in light of the proliferation of other law-making bodies. Particular attention will be given to the question whether the proliferation of law-making bodies and the consequent bypassing of the ILC in the preparation of certain conventions is a negative development that should be countered or an inevitable process which forces the ILC to reconsider its position. For a clear understanding of the position of the Commission within the international legal order an introduction to its composition and working methods is required. It is emphasized that this paper does not aspire to give a comprehensive overview of ILC practice but will only highlight those features relevant for the question under consideration.[7]

---

[5] Sir Hersch Lauterpacht in the Survey of International Law in Relation to the Work of Codification of the International Law Commission, UN Doc. A/CN.4/1/Rev.1 of 10 February 1949 reproduced as Appendix 2 in M.R. Anderson et al. (eds) *The International Law Commission and the Future of International Law* (hereinafter "The Survey"), para. 22.

[6] H. Owada, in *Making Better International Law: The International Law Commission at 50* (1998) p. 70, p. 71.

[7] See for general literature on the ILC e.g. H.W. Briggs, *The International Law Commission* (1965); B.G. Ramcharan, *The International Law Commission, Its Approach to the Codification and Progressive Development of International Law* (1977); I. Sinclair, *The International Law Commission* (1987). See *Analytical Guide to the Work*

COMPOSITION AND WORKING METHODS ILC

Although the Committee for Progressive Development had suggested that a full-time body might be desirable, the Sixth-Committee decided that ILC members be appointed on a part-time basis. Originally, the Commission was composed of fifteen members. The number has been increased on several occasions and since 1981 the Commission consists of 34 members.[8] The Commission's members are elected on basis of their "recognized competence in international law" (article 2(1) Statute). Moreover, article 8 of the Statute emphasizes that in the Commission as a whole "representation of the main forms of civilization and of the principal legal systems of the world should be assured". ILC members are not state representatives but sit in an individual capacity.[9] However, the seats are distributed on the basis of strict geographical guidelines. General Assembly Resolution 36/39 paragraph 3 prescribes that there will be:

> Eight nationals from African States;
> Seven nationals from Asian States;
> Three nationals from Eastern European States;
> Six nationals from Latin American States;
> Eight nationals from Western European or other States;
> One national from African States or Eastern European States in rotation, with the seat being allocated to a national of an African State in the first election held after the adoption of the present resolution;
> One national from Asian States or Latin American States in rotation, with the seat being allocated to a national of an Asian State in the first election held after the adoption of the present resolution.

It has been suggested that "the basic requirement that the members of the Commission 'shall be persons of recognized competence in international law' has, on occasion, been minimized in the preoccupation with

---

of the International Law Commission 1949-1997 (1998) for information on all the documents discussed and prepared by the ILC.

[8] GA Res. 1103 (XI) of 18 December 1956; GA Res. 1647 (XVI) of 6 November 1961; GA Res. 36/39 of 18 November 1981.

[9] This is generally accepted although the ILC Statute itself is silent on the subject: for a recent confirmation of this principle see the Report of the International Law Commission on the Work of its Forty-Eighth Session (1996), reproduced as Appendix 5 in M.R. Anderson et al. (eds) *The International Law Commission and the Future of International Law* (1998) (hereinafter the 1996 Report), para. 175.

political and geographical factors."[10] However, it is also argued that the advantages of the politicization of elections outweigh the disadvantages. It has been held that "by bringing the political element into the Commission, the chances of successful completion in an accepted international instrument are considerably enhanced."[11] Moreover, it has to be realized that although ILC members are independent from the state of their nationality, the ILC as a whole is not entirely independent from the General Assembly in which all UN member states are represented; it is a subsidiary organ.

This is manifested in the procedures applicable to the selection of topics and in the Commission's working methods. The distinction between codification and progressive development was endorsed in the Statute of the ILC. The Statute provides that progressive development, or "the preparation of draft conventions on subjects which have not yet been regulated by international law or in regard to which the law has not yet been sufficiently developed in the practice of States", relies on proposals to that effect from the General Assembly, members of the United Nations or any principal organ of the United Nations, specialized agencies, or official intergovernmental bodies established to encourage the progressive development of international law (articles 15 and 17 Statute). The Commission itself can take the initiative for codification, or "the more precise formulation and systematization of rules of international law where there has already been extensive State practice, precedent and doctrine", but its agenda for codification will be determined in consultation with the General Assembly (articles 15 and 18 Statute). Hence, the Commission's agenda is significantly influenced by decisions made within the intergovernmental structure of the General Assembly. Moreover, individual governments are regularly asked to provide the Commission with information during the drafting process. When the Commission as a whole has approved a first draft on first reading, usually prepared by a Special Rapporteur appointed for this specific topic, governments can study the draft and prepare their comments. The Special Rapporteur takes these comments together with the comments made in the debates in the Sixth Committee into account when he prepares a further draft. The Commission then adopts a final

---

[10] H.W. Briggs, *The International Law Commission* (1965) 42. See also S. Rosenne, "The International Law Commission, 1949-59", (1960) 36 *BYIL* p. 104, p. 125-130.

[11] B.G. Ramcharan, *The International Law Commission, Its Approach to the Codification and Progressive Development of International Law* (1977) 34.

draft, which it submits to the General Assembly with a recommendation for further action. Finally, the General Assembly is to decide on the course of action to be taken with regard to the reports submitted to it by the Commission.[12]

Article 18(1) of the Statute provides that "[t]he Commission shall survey the whole field of international law with a view to selecting topics for codification." A "Survey of International Law in relation to the work of the Codification of the International Law Commission" (the Survey) was prepared by Sir Hersch Lauterpacht before the first session of the ILC in 1949.[13] Twenty-two topics were suggested for codification. The Survey was premised on the ambitious idea that the ILC would eventually codify "the entire field of international law".[14] On the basis of the Survey the Commission selected a provisional list of 14 topics for codification.[15] The Survey emphasized that the topics selected should not be regarded as exhaustive.[16] They were held not to be more suitable for codification than other topics.[17] Moreover, although Lauterpacht did emphasize that codification necessarily entails development in case of gaps and did discuss the Commission's task in the development of rules *de lege ferenda*[18], a possible independent role for progressive development was disregarded in the list of topics; the Survey focused exclusively on the formulation of a list of topics for codification.

Nevertheless, this document "has defined much of the Commission's agenda until now".[19] Topics like the law of sea, the law of nationality, the law of diplomatic and consular intercourse and immunities, the law of treaties, succession of states and governments and the law of state responsibility were already identified in the Survey. In 1971 the majority of ILC members maintained "that the Commission's essential function [is] to codify and illuminate the major aspect of traditional international law."[20] This focus on the initial, non-exhaustive list of

---

[12] See I. Sinclair, *The International Law Commission* (1987) p. 32-44 for more specific information on the Commission's working methods.
[13] See n. 5 above.
[14] The Survey, para. 22.
[15] *ILC Yearbook* 1949, p. 281.
[16] The Survey, para. 25.
[17] The Survey, para. 103.
[18] The Survey, para. 109-112.
[19] M.R. Anderson et al. (eds), *The International Law Commission and the Future of International Law* (1998) p. 3.
[20] *ILC Yearbook* 1971 vol. I, p. 376, para-. 51.

topics suitable for codification as produced by Lauterpacht and the omission to consider taking up work on topics suitable for progressive development has been fiercely criticized from an early date onwards. As early as 1960, Rosenne questioned whether "the provisional list is not too conservative".[21]

Article 1 of the Statute reflects the distinction made in article 13(1)(a) of the UN Charter between codification and progressive development. The Commission itself at a very early stage rejected a clear distinction between codification and progressive development.[22] The Committee on the Progressive Development of International Law had already recognized in its final report that "the terms employed are not mutually exclusive, as, for example, in cases where the formulation and systematization of the existing law may lead to the conclusion that some new rule should be suggested for adoption by States."[23] Article 13(1)(a) UN Charter was at its inception thought to strike "a nice balance between stability and change".[24] However, in practice no balance has been achieved. It is clear that codification rather than progressive development has dominated the Commission's agenda in the past half-century. Progressive development has in effect been limited to what the Committee had merely indicated was the grey area between codification and progressive development: the progressive development of details of a traditional topic in general ripe for codification (e.g. the *jus cogens* provision in the Vienna Convention on the Law of Treaties and the provisions on the continental shelf in the Geneva Conventions on the Law of the Sea). The Formulation of the Principles recognized in the Charter of the Nürnberg Tribunal and it the Judgment of the Tribunal in 1950, the Draft Statute for an International Criminal Court and the Draft Code of Offences against the Peace and Security of Mankind as revised in 1996 are exceptions to this rule. The Commission's work on the law of the Non-Navigational Uses of International Watercourses resulting in a Convention in 1997, may also not be called a traditional codification topic.

---

[21] S. Rosenne, "The International Law Commission, 1949-59", (1960) 36 *BYIL* p. 104, p. 160.

[22] Compare *ILC Yearbook* 1956 vol. II, p. 256, para. 26. In the 1996 Report the ILC recommended the elimination of the distinction, para. 148 & 243.

[23] Report of the Committee, Doc. A/331, GA Official Records, Second Session (1947), Sixth Committee, p. 173, p. 175, para. 7.

[24] UNCIO IX, 177-178, Doc. 848 II/2/46, 7 June 1945, Summary Report of Twenty-first Meeting of Committee II/2.

Progressive development projects are in principle dependent on initiatives from outside the ILC. However, the close working relationship the Commission has with the General Assembly gives it the opportunity to suggest suitable projects for the progressive development of international law. There is ample evidence in practice that the Commission itself is reluctant to engage in less traditional and politically sensitive areas of law. It is for example instructive to see that the Commission has not taken up some of the more political topics of the fourteen topics it had selected for codification at its first session in 1949. It is suggested that it is no coincidence that the three topics the Commission has avoided - Recognition of States, Jurisdiction with regard to Crimes Committed Outside National Territory and the Right to Asylum - all relate to fundamental sovereign powers of states. The work on the topic of State Responsibility is another example. The first Special Rapporteur on the topic, Garcia-Amador, started his work in 1956. He received fierce criticism for his focus on the treatment of aliens as part of state responsibility.[25] In 1970, the then Special Rapporteur on State Responsibility, Ago, introduced the distinction between primary rules of state responsibility "defining the rules of international law which ... impose particular obligations on states" and secondary rules "concerned with determining the consequences of failure to fulfil the obligations established by the primary rules".[26] Since then the ILC has moved away from the drafting of substantive rules laying down the obligations of states but has focused exclusively on the so-called secondary rules. The denounced suggestions of Garcia-Amador have, however, been taken up outside the ILC. In 1985 the General Assembly adopted the Declaration on the Human Rights of Individuals who are not Nationals of the Country in which They Live.[27] Although the Declaration is a non-binding document, it was a valuable step on the way to an effective protection of individuals abroad. In 1990 the International Convention on the Protection of the Rights of All Migrant Workers and Members of Their Families (ICMW) was adopted by the General Assembly.[28] Although the Convention does not provide rights to all aliens and has only secured 9 ratifications until now, it is potentially an important tool for the future protection of the substantial group of aliens that work in a state of which they are not a

---

[25] I. Sinclair, *The International Law Commission* (1987) p. 61-62.
[26] *ILC Yearbook* 1970, vol. II, p. 179, para. 11.
[27] GA Res. 40/144 of 13 December 1985.
[28] GA Res. 45/158 of 18 December 1990. See (1991) 30 ILM 1517.

national. The topic that was too hot to handle for codification by the ILC proved to be suitable for a convention after several non-binding documents had paved the way. Recently, the Draft Statute for an International Criminal Court evinced once again the Commission's conservative approach. The ILC draft formed the blueprint for the negotiations on the 1998 Rome Statute on an International Criminal Court but the final provisions of the Rome Statute went much further than the Commission's draft proposal. It can be asserted that the ILC seriously miscalculated the mood of the international community on this issue. Another opinion would be that the ILC was very realistic on the will of states to bind themselves to a truly progressive document. After all, the Rome Statute has secured only 13 ratifications until now. Irrespective of the question which approach is more effective in the long run; fact is that the ILC did not dare to engage in progressive development but rather drafted a statute in accordance with perceived political reality. The lack of balance between codification and progressive development projects is therefore something for which both the General Assembly and the Commission can be held responsible. A UNITAR Study commented in this respect that "[t]he Commission has eschewed, for the most part, areas of international law which for one reason or another would have required primarily progressive development as that term is used in the Statute."[29]

In 1982 the comment was made that the Commission's agenda had "become a veritable *What's What* of drafting trivia, a parody of the world's urgent agenda".[30] The current agenda still displays a preference for more traditional topics of international law, unconnected to major political controversies or technical specialist knowledge and not subject to the dilemma of cultural relativism. Topics under consideration include for example State Responsibility, Diplomatic Protection and Reservations to Treaties. At its 1998 session, the ILC did agree that "it should not restrict itself to traditional topics, but could also consider those that reflect new developments in international law and pressing concerns of the international community as a whole".[31] Concrete pro-

---

[29] M. ElBaradei, T.M. Franck & R. Trachtenberg, "The International Law Commission: The Need for a New Direction", (UNITAR 1981) (hereinafter cited as UNITAR Study) p. 4.

[30] T.M. Franck & M. ElBaradei, "The Codification and Progressive Development of International Law: A UNITAR Study of the Role and Use of the International law Commission", (1982) 76 *American Journal of International Law* p. 630, p. 634.

[31] Report of the International Law Commission on the Work of its Fiftieth Session (1998), para. 553.

posals to give effect to this intention were however lacking and have also not been made at the 1999 session.

A final observation on the practice of the Commission's working methods concerns the end product. In 1987 Sinclair pointed out that "[t]he practice of the Commission, at least in recent years, has been invariably to recommend, in accordance with Article 23(1)(d), that a conference be convoked to conclude a convention." [32] The Commission does indeed usually aspire to prepare draft articles that can serve as the basis of a multilateral convention. Already in 1977 this practice was held to be "unduly rigid" and to deprive "the Commission of avenues for influencing the development of the law in subjects which have not yet reached the stage for the conclusion of a convention."[33] The ancient chicken and egg riddle manifests itself in the necessary link between the focus on the eventual conclusion of a convention and the failure to include topics for progressive development. Which of the two phenomena is cause and which is effect is not that interesting; crucial is that a vicious circle is the result.

SOME OBSERVATIONS ON INTERNATIONAL LAW-MAKING

As stated above, the ILC has made a substantial contribution to the codification of international law by drafting some of the most important conventions in modern international law.[34] It is important to realise though that the Commission's influence on the international legal order is not limited to those drafts that eventually result in a multilateral convention. In this respect some elementary observations regarding international law-making are warranted. Treaties are, formally speaking, sources of obligation rather than sources of law.[35] When a treaty only

---

[32] I. Sinclair, *The International Law Commission* (1987) p. 36.

[33] B.G. Ramcharan, *The International Law Commission, Its Approach to the Codification and Progressive Development of International Law* (1977) p. 76.

[34] See *Analytical Guide to the Work of the International Law Commission 1949-1997* (1998) for a comprehensive overview of the work of the ILC. Also M.R. Anderson et al. (eds), *The International Law Commission and the Future of International Law* (1998) 157-169.

[35] G.G. Fitzmaurice, "Some Problems Regarding the Formal Sources of International Law", in *Symbolae Verzijl* (1958) p. 153, p. 157; G.G. Fitzmaurice; "The General Principles of International Law Considered from the Standpoint of the Rule of Law", 92 *Recueil des Cours* 1957-II p. 1, p. 98; R.Y. Jennings, "Recent Developments in the International Law Commission: its Relation to the Sources of

codifies existing law, it is obvious that the treaty itself is merely a reflection of the original source. When a treaty, however, creates new obligations for the parties to it, it is not a source of general international law but a source of obligation. Of course, these obligations can obtain the status of customary international law when they gain general acceptance. However, the source of law is then the relevant state practice and the *opinio juris* rather than the initial treaty.[36]

Most scholars agree that the reports of the Commission and of its Special Rapporteurs constitute a source of international law at least equivalent to the most highly qualified publicists.[37] However, the influence of the ILC's work on the source "customary international law" is more important. The observation that it is not decisive for the influence on the international law-making process whether or not the ILC's work actually results in the adoption of a multilateral treaty is true for both mechanisms of "law-making". The work of the ILC can of course not itself amount to state practice since its members sit in an individual capacity. However, its work often influences the legal opinion of states, courts and scholars long before states have ratified the resulting conventions and even when no convention has been concluded (yet).[38] The Commission's Draft Articles on State Responsibility, for example, were invoked as evidence of customary international law even before their first reading was completed.[39] The International Court of Justice also regularly relies on the Commission's work even when no convention has as yet been concluded, as was recently exemplified in the *Gabcíkovo-Nagymaros* case.[40]

---

the Sources of International Law", (1964) 13 *International and Comparative Law Quarterly* p. 385, p. 390; I. Sinclair, *The International Law Commission* (1987) p. 123.

[36] Compare e.g. *North Sea Continental Shelf* cases, ICJ Reports 1969, para. 71-75.

[37] I. Sinclair, *The International Law Commission* p. 121-122. Compare C. Parry, *The Sources and Evidences of International Law* (1965) p. 23-24 & p. 114; I. Brownlie, *Principles of Public International Law* (5th edn.) 1998) p. 25.

[38] It should also be noted that the ILC's work retains independent value also after a convention has been concluded. See *Making Better International Law: The ILC at 50* (1998) p. 10-11 and the examples mentioned there. Compare the *North Sea Continental Shelf* cases, ICJ Reports 1969, para. 48-50: the ICJ attached decisive weight to the debates in the ILC on the equidistance rule when it concluded that the rule had no customary status prior to the 1958 Geneva Convention.

[39] *Making Better International Law: The ILC at 50* (1998) p. 11, footnote 80-81.

[40] 25 September 1997. See on this S.M. Schwebel, "The Influence of the International Court of Justice on the Work of the International Law Commission and the Influence of the Commission on the Work of the Court", in *Making Better International Law: The International Law Commission at 50* (1998) p. 161-164.

OTHER LAW-MAKING BODIES

As stated in the introduction, the ILC is not the only body concerned with the codification and development of international law. The proliferation of ad hoc and specialist bodies with a law-making mandate, within the UN system and outside, has resulted in many international conventions concluded without the involvement of the ILC.[41] They are prepared, discussed and concluded within specialist intergovernmental bodies. The 1947 idea that the ILC be the principal international institution responsible for the codification of international law seems therefore no longer tenable.

Human rights treaties, for example, are usually concluded within the framework of the Third Committee (e.g. The Convention on the Prevention and Punishment of the Crime of Genocide; International Covenant on Economic, Social and Cultural Rights (1966) International Covenant on Civil and Political Rights (1966) or the Commission on Human Rights (e.g. the Convention on the Rights of the Child (1989). The International Labour Organization (ILO) has adopted numerous conventions relating to labour issues, like health and safety in the work place, equal opportunity and freedom of association. Rules and procedures in the field international trade law are discussed, prepared and adopted by the United Nations Commission on International Trade Law (UNCITRAL) while treaties on environmental law are usually prepared within the framework of the United Nations Environment Programme (UNEP). Conventions in the field of disarmament, e.g. the Treaty on the Non-Proliferation of Nuclear Weapons (1968), the Convention on the Prohibition of the Development, Production and Stockpiling of Bacteriological (Biological) and Toxin Weapons and on Their Destruction (1972) and the Convention on the Prohibition of the Development, Production, Stockpiling and Use of Chemical Weapons and Their Destruction (1992), are negotiated within the permanent multilateral disarmament negotiating forum of the United Nations: the Conference on Disarmament. Often ad hoc bodies are established especially for the preparation of the specific convention. For example, the International Convention Against the Taking of Hostages (1979) was prepared by the ad hoc Committee on

---

[41] See for a comprehensive overview of law-making processes in the UN system P.C. Szasz, "General Law-Making Processes" and F.L. Kirgis, "Specialized Law-Making Processes", in O. Schachter & C.C. Joyner (eds), United Nations Legal Order (1995) p. 35-108 & p. 109-168.

the Drafting of an International Convention against the Taking of Hostages and the Treaty on Principles Governing the Activities of States in the Exploration and Use of Outer Space, including the Moon and Other Celestial Bodies (1967) was prepared by the Committee on the Peaceful Uses of Outer Space. Sometimes an ad-hoc intergovernmental conference is organized in order to conclude a specific treaty. For example the United Nations Conference on the Law of the Sea (III) resulting in the United Nations Convention on the Law of the Sea (1982); the Uruguay Round of Multilateral Trade Negotiations resulting in the 1994 Marrakech Agreement and the UN Conference on the Environment and Development resulting in e.g. the United Nations Framework Convention on Climate Change (1992). Finally, it is interesting that the Sixth Committee itself has prepared the 1997 International Convention for the Suppression of Terrorist Bombing and the 1999 International Convention for the Suppression of the Financing of Terrorism, which have been adopted by the General Assembly.

Moreover, it has to be noted that many conventions are concluded on a regional level as well. Regional bodies as for example the Organization of Security and Co-operation in Europe, the Council of Europe, the European Union, the Commonwealth of Independent States, the Organization of American States and the Organization of African Unity all serve as negotiating forums that prepare influential regional treaties.

THE DEMANDS OF MODERN INTERNATIONAL LAW-MAKING: A NEW ROLE FOR THE ILC?

As a result of this proliferation of law-making bodies it has been argued that "the Commission is no longer playing the central role in the law-making process that it could and should play"[42], and proposals have been forwarded to restore the Commission's central role in international law-making. However, it is submitted in this paper that that line of reasoning disregards the essential, preliminary question. Not the preservation of the centrality of the position of the ILC, but rather the objective of an effective and thorough international law-making process should be the basis of any proposal. In this regard the demands of modern international law-making and both strengths and weaknesses of the Commission will be discussed in order to arrive at a conclusion that

---

[42] UNITAR Study, p. 2.

aspires to optimize the balance between the ILC and other law-making bodies.

It is important to realize that the international community in 1945 was a very different one from that today. In the first place, the perception and manifestation of that community differs significantly from the contemporary one. A disproportionate focus on the major western states and their ideas of what the international community should look like characterized the post-war era. As a result, a deceptive homogeneity dominated discussions on the codification and development of international law. It is now generally recognized that international law should serve the international community as a whole, including developing states and non-state actors like individuals as well. Consequently, new, or rather previously disregarded, interests and views, often conflicting with the traditional interests of states, have entered the arena of international law-making. Apart from this shift in perception, the international community has effectively undergone some considerable changes. The proliferation of (independent) states is one. Most importantly, the globalization and consequent increasing interdependence of states has initiated co-operation between states on an unanticipated diversity of subjects and causes problems not foreseen in 1945. Moreover, the advances in technology and science have introduced issues that require consideration and regulation on the international level.

This paper proceeds from the proposition that the challenge facing bodies engaged in the preparation of multilateral conventions in contemporary international law practice is essentially twofold. In the first place, treaty-drafting is nowadays not predominantly the codification of already existing customary international law as was the case with the law of treaties and the law of diplomatic relations. Often, the law under consideration is evolving. No consensus exists as yet and drafting consists for a substantial part of progressive development of the law. Additionally, it is more difficult to reach consensus in the contemporary pluralistic negotiating environment. Because of this heterogeneity in legal opinions and the consequent unpredictability of the result of any drafting process, states are increasingly reluctant to leave that process to an essentially independent body. This is especially true when politically sensitive issues are under consideration. States may want to be directly involved in and exercise political control over the elaboration of conventions especially when vital interests are at stake or when politically sensitive topics are at issue and the state of the law is uncertain. Although the ILC does have some political authority behind it, states cannot directly influence the Commission's work. States may therefore prefer intergovernmental bodies, whether ad hoc or permanent, to engage in the negotiation and preparation of legal texts on certain issues. The advantage of a more overtly political law-making process is however not limited to greater control of the states involved. Effective tools like political horse-trading and "package deal" diplomacy can also only be employed in a political negotiating environment.

Another consequence of the lack of widespread consensus is the resort of states to regional solutions for international problems. The ILC is primarily a universal body. It is therefore inevitable that certain controversial topics are better suited to be treated on a regional level by a body with a regional mandate. However, the ILC might be said to take its universal mandate too far. It has been said to follow a "tone of resolute universalism".[43] The Commission rarely recognises special subcategories of states in its drafts. It has avoided partial and particularistic categories.[44] The Draft Articles on the Most-Favoured Nation Clauses (1978) and the work on State Succession (in which special provision is made for "newly-independent" states) are exceptions to this rule. It has to be noted however, that no convention on these two topics has entered into force yet. The ILC has never included special provisions for developing countries in its work, while for example the 1982 Law of the Sea Convention, prepared by the Third United Nations Conference on the Law of the Sea, does.[45] Of course, this is to some extent the inevitable consequence of the lack of political bargaining and the absence of lobbying and pressure-diplomacy by blocks of like-minded states. However, it is carefully suggested that, additionally, the ILC may itself be too focused on the type of standards that has brought it glory and esteem some decades ago: the completely general and reciprocal norms of the law of treaties and diplomatic and consular relations.

The second main challenge facing bodies engaged in the drafting of treaties today is the increase in specialist and technical issues that require regulation on an international level. International trade, the protection of the environment and the regulation of arms are examples of interdisciplinary topics. These are essentially non-legal issues that require legal regulation. The ILC is pre-dominantly a body of general-

---

[43] J. Crawford, "Universalism and Regionalism from the Perspective of the Work of the International Law Commission", in *International Law on the Eve of the Twenty-first Century, Views from the International Law Commission* (1997) p. 99, p. 103.
[44] Ibid 108.
[45] Ibid 104.

ists. The Commission's members are elected on basis of their "recognized competence in international law". The force of the ILC lies exactly in this unrivalled and broad legal knowledge of its members, representing legal systems from over the world. Although article 16(e) of the Statute allows the ILC to consult scientific institutions and individual experts, these experts are not part of the actual negotiating and drafting process. Many bodies with a law-making mandate have been established over the years to deal with this need of specialist knowledge on confined areas of the law. These bodies consist of specialists; lawyers as well as others. Examples are the UN Commission for International Trade, the UN Environmental Programme, the International Labour Organization, the World Trade Organization and the International Atomic Energy Agency. An important feature of these bodies is that they are formally a diplomatic intergovernmental negotiation forum but that technical experts play a crucial role in the preparation of legal texts. Moreover, the participation of NGO's (representing e.g. industry or activists) is commonly accepted within many of these bodies while the ILC has always been immune from pressure exercised by NGO's. The importance of these non-governmental bodies in the contemporary treaty-drafting process should not be underestimated as was for example exemplified in the drafting process of the Ottawa Convention on Landmines and the Rome Statute on the International Criminal Court. It is submitted here that the ILC, notwithstanding their pre-eminency in legal issues, can usually not compete with these specialist bodies when it comes to the actual regulation of specialist and technical issues. This in light of the knowledge required to adequately deal with these issues as well as the time and funds available for study and exploration of the topic.

Many scholars have argued that the ILC should undergo significant changes in order to be able to draft treaties on political sensitive and technical issues as well. The 1981 UNITAR Study, for example, asserted that "the Commission is no longer playing the central role in the law-making process that it could and should play".[46] The focus of the UNITAR Study was therefore to restore the ILC's central position in the international law-making process. Several proposals were made to accomplish that. Among others it was suggested that the Commission should become a full-time body, or should at least appoint full-time Rapporteurs for certain topics.[47] Moreover, the use of Chambers was

---

[46] UNITAR Study p. 2.
[47] *Ibid* p. 13-15, p. 15-16.

recommended.[48] The establishment of an International Legal Research Centre for background research and technical support that could guard against overlap with other bodies and preserve the uniformity in legal terminology was suggested.[49] Finally, the Commission was urged to undertake more effective consultations with governments.[50] The Study concluded with the observation that the ILC should not avoid areas of economic and technological development, environmental protection, violence control and human rights. These topics were held to be "more important than the status of the diplomatic pouch".[51]

A similar line of reasoning can be found in Hafner's 1996 article on the future of the ILC.[52] With regard to the drafting of treaties on technical issues he asserted that "there is no reason why the ILC members should not become capable of acquiring such technical knowledge either directly or by the use of resource persons. There is only the need to establish appropriate communication with the experts in the relevant fields so that instruments also of technical nature could emerge from this body."[53] With regard to the progressive development of politically sensitive issues he maintains that this requires "a changed communication between the States and the ILC. The communication channels between them must be improved so that the ILC can take the different positions of the States abroad and serve as a honest broker of these positions."[54]

This paper proposes a different approach. Rather than trying to counter the proliferation of specialist intergovernmental bodies in order to preserve the central position of the ILC, it is suggested that in light of the changed demands of international law-making the Commission's strengths should be exploited to the fullest while its comparative weaknesses should be acknowledged at the same time. It is moreover suggested that the proposals for change, as described above, might harm the Commission's position rather than further it. The ILC has many assets that have proven to be invaluable for the law-making process.

---

[48] Ibid p. 21-22.
[49] Ibid p. 23-24.
[50] Ibid p. 24-25.
[51] Ibid p. 26.
[52] G. Hafner, "The International Law Commission and the Future Codification of International Law", (1996) 2 *ILSA Journal of International and Comparative Law* p. 671-677.
[53] Ibid p. 672.
[54] Ibid p. 675.

This paper will divide its proposal for a possible "new role" for the ILC in separate, though related conclusions, each based on the optimisation of these assets.

In the first place it is asserted that the ILC should remain the principal legal body responsible for the codification of traditional international law. Even international law norms that are undisputed at a given time and that are sometimes already codified, evolve. Take for example the rule of state immunity. Until 50 years ago most states considered state immunity to be absolute, no exceptions to the rule were recognized. Today, it is generally accepted that states are not protected by immunity when they act in their "private capacity". The rapidly increasing trading activities of states made that "economic reality" left "no alternative" but to adopt the restrictive theory of immunity.[55] The reality of the international community is always developing. When new, widely accepted norms of international law emerge in the field of general international law, the ILC should be the body to codify these principles. In this respect, it can be questioned why the ILC was not involved in the preparation of the 1979 International Convention against the Taking of Hostages. A very similar convention – the 1973 Convention on the Prevention and Punishment of Crimes against Internationally Protected Persons, Including Diplomatic Agents – had after all been drafted by the Commission at the request of the General Assembly. There does not seem to be an obvious reason why the ILC was excluded from the preparation of the Hostages Convention. This example has been said "to indicate the need for greater attention to be paid to coordination between the General Assembly and the International Law Commission".[56] The ILC might have to take a somewhat less absolute universalistic approach in its codification projects since, as Crawford recently noted, "the scope for new international standards of a general and reciprocal character ... is limited."[57]

It is submitted further though that the ILC should not engage in the preparation of treaties that are either too specialist or too politically sensitive. Specialist and intergovernmental bodies are much better

---

[55] M.B. Feldman, "The United States Foreign Sovereign Immunities Act of 1976 in Perspective: A Founders View", (1986) 35 *International and Comparative Law Quarterly* p. 302, p. 302.

[56] H. Owada, "The International Law Commission and the Process of Law-Formation", in *Making Better International Law: The International Law Commission at 50* (1998) p. 167, p. 175.

[57] J. Crawford, "Universalism and Regionalism from the Perspective of the Work of the International Law Commission", in *International Law on the Eve of the Twenty-first Century, Views from the International Law Commission* (1997) p. 99, 120.

equipped to deal with the regulation of those issues and have proven to be often less conservative than the ILC in the regulation of politically sensitive topics. I wholeheartedly agree with Crawford when he commented: "Certainly, the Commission will never be the principal mechanism for legislative preparation within the United Nations system. It is absurd to think otherwise."[58] Moreover, where technical issues are admittedly better regulated on a universal level, the regulation of politically sensitive issues like human rights protection should not be limited in that way. The ILC, or any other universal body, can only offer a lowest common denominator approach in the preparation of human rights treaties where regionally higher standards may be adopted.

It is time to link this conclusion to a truth introduced earlier in this paper. The fact that the Commission is not involved in the preparation of conventions in the field of for example human rights law does not mean that it cannot influence the development of international human rights norms. The task of progressive development of international law has never been taken seriously by the Commission. It has even recently proposed to abolish the distinction between codification and progressive development.[59] It is obvious that this lack of "progressive development" projects is necessarily linked to the Commission's preference to work on draft articles that will result in a widely accepted multilateral convention. Many scholars have urged the ILC to "move away from its implicit focus on producing draft conventions in favour of more flexible instruments".[60] International law-making is not confined to treaty-drafting. The Commission's potential to influence the process of custom-formation with regard to less traditional international norms should not be underestimated. The Model Rules on Arbitral Procedures, the 1996 Draft Code of Crimes against the Peace and Security of Mankind of 1996, the Guidelines on Reservations to Treaties that are currently under consideration and the discussion on whether the work on State Responsibility will eventually result in a multilateral convention or a Restatement of the Law indicate the variety of possible different instruments. The ILC is however still too focused on influencing international law through conven-

---

[58] J. Crawford, in *Making Better International Law: The International Law Commission at 50* (1998) p. 130.

[59] The 1996 Report, para. 148 & 243.

[60] M.R. Anderson et al. (eds), *The International Law Commission and the Future of International Law* (1998) p. 23. See also The UNITAR Study, p. 20-21 and G. Hafner, "The International Law Commission and the Future Codification of International Law", (1996) 2 *ILSA Journal of International and Comparative Law* p. 671, p. 676.

tions rather than through other, more flexible means. Only recently a Commission member commented that: "[u]ltimately, the ILC's efforts are wasted if, after some five or ten years of work, a broad majority of states in the General Assembly cannot be persuaded to support the draft or to convene an international diplomatic conference to conclude a convention on the subject."[61] The focus on treaty-drafting is evident and the statement indicates the fundamental change of attitude that is needed within the Commission.

The second conclusion of this paper is therefore that the Commission should draft reports on pressing, developing issues of international law. The example of the General Assembly's work on the rights of migrant workers epitomizes that non-binding documents like resolutions and declaration of principles may significantly benefit the eventual treaty-drafting process. The Commission's undisputed status as a body consisting of the most learned international lawyers has always influenced legal opinion and therewith state practice. Although the ILC should not engage in the codification of politically sensitive issues, there is no reason why it should stay clear from the discussions on more political international law issues. On the contrary, that would be an unacceptable waste of legal expertise. Reports of the Commission in the field of "progressive development" of international law do not always have to offer definite answers to the questions it addresses; the manifestation of contrasting legal opinions can also be influential. The influence of the Commission in this field is not only possible but it is also indispensable. The independence of the ILC members makes it less suitable to political negotiating. It was therefore concluded that treaty-drafting in certain areas of law is sometimes better left to more political bodies. However, the undisputed independence of the Commission's members does guarantee the development of coherent, well-reasoned legal principles. Political pressure often results in inconsistencies in the legal texts produced. The ILC's opinions are not obscured by political representation and can be said to have therefore more legal authority than the opinions of government representatives. At the Commission's twenty-fifth anniversary Waldock observed "If ... the Commission's work [has] come to have its own measure of authority in its own right, it [is] because of the sheer quality of that work".[62] Any proposal involving the politicization of the

---

[61] B. Graefrath, "The International Law Commission Tomorrow: Improving its Organization and Methods of Work", (1991) 85 *American Journal of International Law* p. 595, p. 600.

[62] *Yearbook ILC* 1974, vol. I, p. 70, para. 27.

Commission so that it can serve as a "broker" of states' views necessarily compromises this quality and is therefore vigorously rejected here. The ILC's high-quality work should be used to guide the political negotiating process instead of vice versa.

This conclusion needs to be qualified. The ILC itself has displayed an apparent reluctance to engage in politically sensitive questions. The issue of non-discrimination, for example, was recently rejected as a possible new agenda item. ILC members themselves argued that a lack of both expertise and commitment makes the ILC unsuitable for discussing the topic. Another incident confirms the trend. When the Sixth Committee asked the ILC to inform it on recent developments in the area of jurisdictional immunities, the ILC preferred not to consider important developments in the field of human rights and confined its report to the immunity of states for commercial acts.[63] This merits the conclusion that, apart from a change in attitude towards the end product, the ILC needs a fundamental change in perception of its own role within the international legal order before it can successfully embark on the task envisaged for it in this paper.

Finally, it has been proposed that the ILC should co-operate more closely with other law-making bodies.[64] It is suggested that the ILC's comparative strengths should be employed to assist other law-making bodies and maybe even co-ordinate and supervise the international law-making process. The conclusion that the bypassing of the ILC is an inevitable consequence of the changed demands of international law-making does not mean that proliferation of law-making bodies does not have any detrimental consequences. In the first place, bodies codifying technical and politically sensitive issues do encounter questions of general international law. It has been suggested that the ILC could function as an advisory body on general international law, assisting other bodies in their codification efforts when requested to do so. One step further would be to grant the ILC a supervisory role in the international law-

---

[63] State immunity for violation of core human rights norms has been the subject of academic and political discussion for more than a decade. Cases like *Siderman de Blake v. Republic of Argentina*, 965 F.2d 699 (9th Cir. 1992); *Princz v. Federal Republic of Germany*, 26 F.3d 1166 (D.C. Cir. 1994) indicate that, under international law, states may not enjoy immunity when *jus cogens* norms have been violated. In the recent *Pinochet* decision of the UK House of Lords, [1999] 2 All ER 97, [1999] 2 WLR 827 HL, (ex-head of state) immunity was denied for the allegations of torture.

[64] e.g. M.R. Anderson et al. (eds), *The International Law Commission and the Future of International Law* (1998) p. 47-48. See also the 1996 Report, para. 241.

making process. Proliferation of law-making bodies leads inevitably to the fragmentation of the law-making process. Fragmentation endangers the uniformity of the corpus of international law. The ILC has been held to be "the only body capable of consolidating and developing a coherent corpus of general international law on a systematic basis."[65] It could be envisaged that the Commission has a task in co-ordinating these widely diverging and in essence often unrelated law-making processes. A central body that keeps track of relevant activity in all international bodies with a law-making mandate would counter, at least partially, the drawbacks inherent in the fragmentation of law-making procedures. It could guard the uniformity of legal terminology, prevent overlap (and the inherent waste of time and resources) and locate gaps.[66]

However, this paper is reluctant to propose that the ILC could find a new role as an advisory or supervisory body. Apart from the practical problems, the ILC being a part-time body with limited research facilities, the suggestion is troubled by an ideological problem. It is doubtful whether other law-making bodies will accept the ILC as the formal authority on the more general international law aspects of their work, as was epitomized by the commotion caused by General Comment 24 of the UN Human Rights Committee.[67] This Comment effectively proposes that the regime with regard to reservations to human rights treaties is different than the general regime codified in the Vienna Convention on the Law of Treaties. It is stressed that "[i]t necessarily falls to the Committee to determine whether a specific reservation is compatible with the object and purpose of the Covenant." The ILC responded to this Comment by asking the HRC to seriously reconsider its views in light of the general applicability of the regime as codified by the Vienna Convention. The reaction of the Committee representing the human rights treaty bodies showed that it was not particularly concerned with the views of the

---

[65] M.R. Anderson et al. (eds) *The International Law Commission and the Future of International Law* (1998) p. 4.

[66] See P. Tomka, "Major Complexities Encountered in Contemporary International Law-Making", in *Making Better International Law: The International Law Commission at 50* p. 209, p. 212-213 for criticism on this proposal. He also argues that in light of the principles of interpretation as *lex specialis derogat legi generali* and *lex posterior derogat legi priori* fragmentation of the law-making process is not really a problem even when contradiction occurs.

[67] General Comment No. 24 (52) of 2 November 1994 on issues relating to reservations made upon ratification or accession to the Covenant or the Optional Protocols thereto, or in relation to declarations under article 41 of the Covenant. See on this problem in general and for a reproduction of the Comment: C. Chinkin et al., *Human Rights as General Norms and a State's Right to Opt Out* (1997)

ILC. In view of the reputation of the ILC as a rather conservative body, unsympathetic to human rights law, this cannot be said to come as a surprise. When Blokker introduced the topic of the Conference he argued in favour of the "inter-organization principle of good neighbourliness".[68] In a reaction to this, Alston claimed that, although the idea is appealing in theory, it is more likely that the Darwinian principle reigns in practice. I agree, and it is therefore asserted that law-making bodies will most probably strive to enlarge their mandate rather than effectively transfer part of their mandate to the Commission.

CONCLUSION

One scholar once suggested that the ILC might assume "the role of an International Law Research Center".[69] When change is proposed one should however always be careful not to throw the proverbial baby out with the bath water. The ILC's unique position and great scholarship could still have significant value for the codification and progressive development of international law. In its 1996 report the ILC explicitly recognized that Lauterpacht's ambition to codify the whole of international law is no longer considered feasible.[70] This paper does not really propose a new role for the ILC but essentially proposes a reconsideration of the Commission's working methods and a shift in focus within the existing mandate: the promotion of the progressive development of international law and its codification. The comparative strengths of specialist, intergovernmental bodies with regard to drafting technical and politically sensitive conventions should be accepted. A shift in focus from codification in conventions to progressive development through other means would ensure that the Commission retains its influence on the law-making process. Its vast and unrivalled legal expertise should guide the political negotiating process and may benefit the coherent and well-reasoned development of both politically sensitive and technical issues. Although the idea of the ILC as an advisory or supervisory body is appealing in theory, it is doubtful whether it would function in practice.

---

[68] See the contribution by Blokker to this book, p. 29-33.
[69] J. Stone, "On the Vocation of the International Law Commission", (1957) 57 *Colombia Law Review* p. 16, p. 49-50.
[70] 1996 Report, para. 168-170.

THE PROLIFERATION OF ADMINISTRATIVE TRIBUNALS

Paul C. Szasz [*]

Any apparent proliferation of international administrative tribunals (ATs)[1] is a direct consequence of the so-called proliferation of international inter-governmental organizations (IGOs). In principle, each IGO should make available a judicial organ to which its staff members can appeal adverse administrative decisions. This obligation was recognized by the International Court of Justice in its *Effect of Awards* Advisory Opinion to the UN General Assembly[2], and can be derived from the general obligation of organizations that enjoy immunity from national judicial processes to provide some means of settling disputes to those who have claims against them[3].

To the extent that the number of ATs is less than that of IGOs, this is due to two factors, one positive and one negative. The latter is that some IGOs, generally smaller ones but regrettably also including some recently established larger ones (such as OSCE), have not provided such a facility to their staffs. The positive phenomenon is that a

---

[*] Adjunct Professor, New York University School of Law. Formerly Legal Officer, International Atomic Energy Agency and World Bank; Deputy to the Legal Counsel, United Nations. Acting Executive Secretary, United Nations Administrative Tribunal; Legal Advisor, IAEA and UNIDO Staff Councils, and of the International Civil Service Commission.

[1] There are about thirty such bodies, though some (particularly those of the European coordinated organizations) are called Appeals Boards; in the European Communities it is the Court of Justice that fulfills, *inter alia*, this function. See J. Moussé, *Le contentieux des organisations internationales et de l'Union européenne* (1997), p. 129, note 43 and Annex. The governing instruments of 16 of these (including the defunct LNAT) are set out by C.F. Amerasinghe in *Statutes and Rules of Procedure of International Administrative Tribunals* (Revised ed., vols. I and II, World Bank, 1983), and the judgments of 13 of them are analyzed by the Office of the Executive Secretary of The World Bank Administrative Tribunal in *Index of Decisions of International Administrative Tribunals* (3rd ed., 1991).

[2] *Effect of Awards of Compensation Made by the United Nations Administrative Tribunal, Advisory Opinion*, I.C.J. Reports 1954, p. 47, at 57.

[3] See, e.g., Article 29(a) of the Convention on the Privileges and Immunities of the United Nations, UNTS vol. 1, p. 15.

number of IGOs have arranged to use ATs established by another organization, thus somewhat reducing the clutter of largely inactive tribunals while at the same time strengthening the one to which they adhere. Aside from situations such as that of the World Bank, whose Tribunal (WBAT) has jurisdiction over the staffs of all its related organizations (IFC, IDA, ICSID, MIGA) because these cannot readily be distinguished from the staff of the Bank itself, the principal collective tribunal is that of the International Labour Organization (ILOAT), which was originally established as the successor to the first such court, that of the League of Nations (LNAT) to continue its services to the ILO staff, and whose jurisdiction was then extended to most of the other UN specialized agencies (e.g., WHO, UNESCO) and later to many other IGOs, mostly in Europe.[4]

GENERAL CONSIDERATIONS REGARDING THE PROLIFERATION OF ATs

In principle, there appears to be no fundamental objection to having the number of ATs generally match the number of IGOs, or rather of IGO secretariats. After all, ATs are IGO organs, and once one has reconciled oneself to the number of IGOs one cannot specifically object that there are therefore a similar number of plenary political organs, or credentials committees, etc.

One objection that might be raised is that if every small IGO has its own AT, the latter are likely to be mostly inactive. Evidently this represents some waste of infrastructure – though not much, for normally an inactive tribunal simply does not meet. However, there is another drawback: on the few occasions when such a tribunal must be convened to hear one or more cases, the judges are likely to be quite inexperienced in dealing with international staff disputes and with the general growing administrative jurisprudence, so that their judgments are more likely to be arbitrary than those of more experienced adjudicators. As pointed out below, such tribunals may also be or at least appear to be less independent than more active and prominent bodies.

The normal excuse for maintaining separate tribunals for separate IGOs is that each organizations has its own relevant constitutional provisions, its own staff regulations and rules and other administrative issuances, and in deciding disputes between the organization and its

---

[4] The jurisdiction of ILOAT currently extends to 37 IGOs (including ILO itself).

staff only these instruments should be relied on.[5] However, certain domestic courts, for example federal appeals courts in the USA, are used to deciding cases under several legal systems (federal plus that of each state under their jurisdiction, involving civil, criminal and all types of administrative law). Also ILOAT has long demonstrated that it can adjudicate disputes under the separate rules applicable to the almost two score organizations under its jurisdiction, some of which (e.g., the UN common system organizations) have rather similar though not identical legal regimes, while others are in many ways quite different.

Even if the functioning of many small, separate tribunals weakens these only marginally, it can be argued that consolidating them into one or more "super tribunals" would notably strengthen these – as already illustrated by the example of ILOAT. Such strengthening would have several aspects. In the first place, the judges of such a tribunal would acquire a great deal of experience, which should improve their decisions. Secondly, to the extent certain matters cannot be decided just based on the wording of the relevant instruments of the IGO whose staff have brought a claim, reference to general principles of law and particularly of international civil service law may become necessary or at least useful[6] – and this can more easily and fruitfully be done by a tribunal having multiple jurisdictions. Finally, there is always the danger that a lesser tribunal, serving only a single organization, may in spite of its nominally autonomous status, fall too much under the sway of the executive head (who may have a role in nominating the judges) or of the political organs, so that true independence is impaired[7]; such danger can largely be eliminated by having an AT that is in fact entirely independent of all organs of most of the IGOs it serves, because it is established and maintained solely by the competent organs of its own parent IGO.

It should, incidentally, be noted that if this logic is pursued to its extreme, i.e., if all or most of the ATs of the ever more numerous and generally expanding IGOs were to be consolidated, one would be faced

---

[5] See Jonathan L. Charney, *Is International Law Threatened by Multiple International Tribunals?*, *Recueil des cours*, vol. 271 (1998), p. 221, citing C.F. Amerasinghe, *The Law of the International Civil Service*, vol. I, p. 47 (2nd ed., 1994).

[6] See, Charney, *supra* note 5, pp. 227-28 and 232-33.

[7] This is particularly likely to be the case if the staff challenge is not against a true administrative decision but rather against the administration's implementation of a legislative decision that might violate staff rights; see Paul C. Szasz, "Adjudicating Staff Challenges to Legislative Decisions of International Organizations", Ch. 36 in *Liber Amicorum Professor Seidl-Hohenveldern* 699-720 (1998).

with a potentially quite different court. Instead of being a part-time institution (as even ILOAT is)[8] with judges who are substantially unremunerated, one would have tribunal that could probably function full-time with full-time and fully remunerated judges – though that would not necessarily be so, for one could simply expand the number of part-time ones. Arguably such a full-time tribunal would be a better one than the current arrangements, if for no other reason than that cases could then be heard as soon as the written pleadings are concluded, rather than having to wait many months until the next tribunal session. Quite possibly, however, such a super tribunal would be viewed as too powerful and independent by the political organs of at least some of the IGOs potentially under its jurisdiction.

PARTICULAR CONSIDERATIONS REGARDING CERTAIN ATs

It would thus appear that in general there are few significant drawbacks from a proliferation of ATs, though there may be some distinct advantages in their consolidation. However, there are situations in which the arguments against particularism and for merger become more persuasive. These are the ones in which IGOs maintain separate ATs even though their staff regimes are closely related. The principal examples are: the two tribunals of the UN common system of staff administration (ILOAT and UNAT); the two tribunals of the Bretton Woods institutions (WBAT and IMFAT); and the several adjudicative bodies of the European coordinated system of organizations (Appeals Boards of the Council of Europe, ESA, NATO, OECD, WEU). Of these only the former will be discussed in some detail.

The United Nations common system of staff administration is based on provisions included in most of the relationship agreements concluded between the UN and its specialized agencies (except the Bretton Woods IFIs) pursuant to Article 63 of the UN Charter.[9] It is currently exemplified principally through participation in the International Civil Service Commission (ICSC), the United Nations Joint Staff

---

[8] This, of course, is not true of the First Instance of the European Court of Justice which decides most staff appeals against all organs of the European Community, whose judges are full-time and fully remunerated.

[9] The International Atomic Energy Agency (IAEA), though technically not a specialized agency, has concluded a similar Relationship Agreement and participates fully in the common system.

Pension Fund (UNJSPF), the Consultative Committee on Administrative Questions (Personnel) (CCAQ(PER)) of the Administrative Committee on Co-ordination (ACC), and substantial adherence to General Assembly resolutions relating to the common system. Though the Staff Regulations and Rules of the several common system organizations are not identical, they are substantially similar and in many instances their wording is the same. Furthermore, the remuneration levels of both their Professional and their other staffs (in particular the General Service) is established on the basis of determinations and recommendations by the ICSC, which in turn bases these on an elaborate set of rules, in part specifically approved by the UN General Assembly.

The common system organizations are, largely for historical reasons, served by two ATs: ILOAT and UNAT. The latter has jurisdiction over the UN, ICAO and IMO, and over all appeals against UNJSPF from any of the common system organizations. ILOAT has jurisdiction, except in respect of Pension Fund disputes, over all the other common system organizations (as well as in respect of a number of other, non-common system IGOs). It is easy to see that this arrangement can easily lead to two sorts of difficulties:

(a) Different interpretation of identically or similarly formulated staff regulations and rules, one subject to ILOAT and the other to UNAT. (In principle this could of course also occur within a single tribunal, as neither applies the principle of *stare decisis*; nevertheless, except in the rarest instances, neither tribunal consciously disregards its prior decisions, though infrequently they may deliberately overrule one.)[10]

(b) Different decisions as to the legality of a challenged determination of the ICSC setting salary levels at a particular duty station, which could result in different IGOs in that location paying staff members at the same occupational level differently – precisely the outcome that the common system is designed to prevent.[11]

Although these situations have so far generally been avoided, this sometimes required one of the IGOs to refrain from defending a case in

---

[10] See Charney, *supra* note 5, Ch. III.G.2, "Citation of administrative tribunals' case law as authority for their decisions".

[11] See the study cited in note 7 *supra*.

one of the tribunals, to prevent the possibility of an explicit divergence.[12]

Staff members and associations are, of course, under no such institutional constraints. Although an individual staff member cannot "forum shop" as there is always only a single judicial forum available for a given appeal, staff associations that wish to sponsor a challenge to a particular system- or duty-station-wide measure can sometimes choose the tribunal to which the issue will first be submitted, in the hope that if there is a favourable judgment that will also be accepted either by the other tribunal or by the organizations subject to it. Though such a selection is likely to be largely speculative as there are few detectable differences in the approach of the two tribunals, it could make sense if there may be an issue of "acquired rights".[13]

---

[12] For example, when ILOAT in its Judgments Nos. 1000 (concerning IAEA) and 1001 (concerning UNIDO) invalidated a particular determination of ICSC to include certain Commissary benefits in its calculation of General Service salaries in Vienna, the UN, against which a similar case was pending in UNAT in respect of its Vienna Office (UNOV), decided to concede the issue, even though oral argument in UNAT had been completed, and thus prevented a possible UNAT determination in its favour, which would have resulted in two GS salary scales in Vienna.

[13] It appears that a true divergence of jurisprudence has developed between the two Tribunals in respect of the meaning of the term "acquired rights": UNAT considers this term to refer, in addition to the protection of so-called "contractual rights", merely to rights flowing from past service, so as to prohibit any retroactive changes to the detriment of the staff but allowing almost any type of prospective change (e.g, UNAT Judgements Nos. 82 (*Puvrez v. SG/ICAO*), No. 202 (*Quéguiner v. SG/UN*), 273 (*Mortished v. SG/UN*), 395 (*Oummih, Gordon, Gruber v. SG/UN*), 478 (*Sundaram v. SG/ICAO*)); in the view of ILOAT such a right must relate to a significant term of service (and in practice it has set a high threshold) that may have motivated a person to become or to remain a staff member, and of which he therefore cannot be deprived through subsequent changes in the terms of service (e.g., ILOAT Judgments Nos. 61 (*Lindsey v. ITU*), 357 (*Asp v. ILO*), 666 (*Chomentowsky v. EPO*), 751 (*Alders-Meewis v. EPO*)). The contrast between these two approaches can best be observed when the two Tribunals were faced with an identical issue: can an organization that has reimbursed national income taxes imposed on certain payments from UNJSPF change that policy with effect on staff members who have already retired and applied for that reimbursement; UNAT answered that this would violate their acquired rights (Judgement No. 237, *Powell v. UN/SG*, para. XVI), while ILOAT, though aware of the *Powell* decision, specifically stated there was no acquired right but held for complainants on another ground (Judgment No. 1053, *Beetle et al v. IAEA*, para. 5). Although Jean-Didier Sicault argues in "L'evolution recente de la jurisprudence des tribunaux administratifs des Nations Unies et de l'OIT en matière de droits acquis", *Revue générale de droit international public*, 1990:I, p. 7, that there are indications of a rapprochement between the jurisprudence of the two tribunals on this point, his UNAT examples relate principally to cases involving pension rights, in which even

Evidently, this is not a satisfactory situation, and in 1978 the UN General Assembly (under the erroneous impression that a split had developed between ILOAT and UNAT concerning the possibility of reversing an agreement as to GS salary levels in Geneva that had been reached in order to settle a strike) requested the Secretary-General to explore the possibility of merging the two common system tribunals.[14] The latter reported the next year that this was not feasible, largely because of the opposition of ILO and of most of the IGOs over which ILOAT had jurisdiction and the need to achieve agreement with all of these through extensive negotiations,[15] and that in fact there was no significant discrepancy in their jurisprudence.[16] The Assembly therefore accepted the Secretary-General's suggestion that arrangements be made to pursue a progressive harmonization and further development of the statutes,[17] rules[18] and practices[19] of the two Tribunals with the

---

apparently purely prospective changes may effect pension payments based in part on past service.

[14] UN doc. A/RES/33/119 of 19 December 1978, para. I.2. The previous year the Federation of International Civil Servants' Associations (FICSA – at that time the union of all UN common system staff associations) had already suggested a study on the establishment of a single administrative tribunal for the UN system as a whole (FICSA, "Recourse procedures in the organizations of the United Nations system", Geneva, 1977).

[15] UN doc. A/C.5/34/31 (1979), paras. 10, 13. This opposition was, aside from the normal but unfortunate "territoriality" of many IGOs, apparently largely motivated by the fear that a combined tribunal would largely be based on the UNAT model, which for various reasons was considered inferior to the ILOAT one, and also because it was felt that a single tribunal might be less able to stand up to the General Assembly than under the then and still existing arrangement under which substantial jurisdiction rests in a forum over which the Assembly has at best indirect influence.

[16] UN doc. A/C.5/34/31 (1979), paras. 6, 11-12. Actually, even at that time and certainly since then the divergent approach as to acquired rights (note 13 *supra*) was becoming apparent.

[17] There are at least two important differences between the ILOAT and UNAT Statutes: (1) ILOAT is normally to require specific performance (ILOAT Statute Art. VIII), though it may award compensation (without any statutory limit) if in the Tribunal's view such performance is not possible or advisable; UNAT in effect must always give the executive head a choice between specific performance or the payment of an alternative compensation fixed by the Tribunal, and the amount of such compensation is subject to some statutory restraints (UNAT Statute Art. 9.1); this difference presumably flows from the more political nature of the UN, where the Secretary-General must have the right to fire a staff member unconditionally. (2) ILOAT judgments may be challenged in the International Court of Justice on the ground that the Tribunal exceeded its jurisdiction or that it committed a major procedural fault; from 1955 until 1995 UNAT judgments could also be referred to the ICJ on these and two other grounds (UNAT Statute Art. 11, as it appeared in UN doc. AT/11/Rev.4) but the UN General Assembly abol-

ultimate aim of establishing a single tribunal.[20] However, when the Secretary-General some years later reported that he had succeeded in negotiating a considerable degree of harmonization, and asked the Assembly to approve those changes relating to UNAT and to recommend corresponding changes to ILO in respect of ILOAT,[21] the Assembly had lost interest and after some years buried the proposals.[22]

During the past several years, the Legal Advisers of the common system organizations considered the possibility of establishing a special "advisory organ" to review and render opinions concerning proposed ICSC decisions under certain circumstances, which organ was to consist of one ILOAT judge and one UNAT judge, with a neutral chair. It was expected that this arrangement would, *inter alia*, serve to reduce the possibility of divergent judgments concerning ICSC determinations.[23] However, the ICSC opposed this arrangement,[24] and the General Assembly took no action on it.[25] Of course, such an advisory organ would have been only a partial safeguard against true divergences of jurisprudence, which could probably be best handled by a formal joint appeals body incorporated into the statutes of both Tribunals – a proposal that the Legal Advisers are currently considering.[26]

Turning now to the Bretton Woods institutions, when consideration was first given, in the late 1960s, to arrangements for World Bank staff to appeal administrative decisions, various alternatives were con-

---

ished this possibility by resolution 50/54 of 11 December 1995, thereby widening the gap between the two Statutes.

[18] For example, ILOAT normally allows four written pleadings, ending with a surrejoinder by the defendant organization (ILOAT Rules Arts. 6-9), while UNAT normally allows only three, ending with observations by the applicant on the defendant organization's reply (UNAT Rules Arts. 7-9).

[19] For example, ILOAT always meets in Geneva while UNAT alternates between New York and Geneva; although oral proceedings are rare in either Tribunal, they are somewhat more generously granted by UNAT.

[20] UNGA decision 34/438 of 17 December 1979.

[21] The original report was set out in UN docs.A/C.5/39/7 and /Corr.1 (1984). In subsequent years the Secretary-General submitted similar though slightly more developed reports: UN docs. A/40/471 (1985) and A/42/328 (1987).

[22] UNGA decision 44/413 of 22 November 1989.

[23] UN doc. A/C.5/54/24.

[24] UN doc. A/54/30 (GAOR 54th Session, Suppl. No. 30), paras. 206-15.

[25] UNGA resolution 54/238 of 20 December 1999, Part IV.

[26] Such a body was apparently first suggested by the representative of Canada in 1979 (UN doc. A/C.5/34/L.21, para. (a)). Proposals along that line were incorporated in the reports of the Secretary-General cited in note 21 *supra*, and were also made by the present author in the study cited *supra* note 7, p. 719.

sidered, including submission to UNAT or ILOAT. However, when the Bank finally concluded that it needed an appeals body, it decided to establish its own, that is WBAT, presumably because it felt that its staff regime was sufficiently and consciously different from that of most other IGOs that it required its own Tribunal, and wished to have one that meets in Washington (without, however, associating itself with the Tribunals of OAS and the I-ADB). Partly because of the continued growth of the Bank and the rather frequent drastic reorganizations of its staff, WBAT has become a relatively active body, with over 200 Decisions rendered between 1981 and 1998.

For a dozen years after WBAT was established in 1980, the International Monetary Fund still failed to provide any judicial appeals machinery to its staff. When it finally decided that it, too, needed one, it disregarded advice that it join up with WBAT (which could have been renamed the Bretton Woods AT) and established IMFAT. So far, that body has had only a trickle of cases that could easily have been accommodated by the already established institution. This move can really only be explained by pure territorialism and the habitual bad blood between the administrations of these closely related and located institutions, but should have been prevented by the respective Executive Directors of the two institutions, whose membership overlaps to a considerable extent. Because their staff regimes (including pension funds) are in many ways quite similar, there is a real danger that eventually divergences will arise between WBAT and IMFAT concerning corresponding provisions. This is clearly one example where proliferation of ATs should not have been allowed to occur.

CONCLUSION

Although any perceived proliferation of administrative tribunals does not constitute a serious problem, advantages could be derived from some further consolidation of these bodies in order to create a few stronger judicial institutions. In some cases, when related organizations have different appeals bodies, their joinder – or at least formal coordination through a common appeals body – would appear highly desirable.

THE PROLIFERATION OF INTERNATIONAL JUDICIAL ORGANS: INSTITUTIONAL AND SUBSTANTIVE QUESTIONS

THE INTERNATIONAL COURT OF JUSTICE AND OTHER INTERNATIONAL COURTS

Hugh Thirlway[*]

International law, because it lacks a centralized structure, does not provide for an integrated judicial system operating an orderly division of labour among a number of tribunals, where certain aspects of components of jurisdiction as a power could be centralized or vested in one of them but not the others. In international law, every tribunal is a self-contained system (unless otherwise provided).
International Tribunal for the Former Yugoslavia, Appeal Chamber, *Prosecutor* v. *Dusko Tadic*, Judgment of 2 October 1995.

INTRODUCTION

The Phenomenon

It has become trite to observe that there is a modern trend towards what is often called the proliferation of international tribunals[1], the creation of international judicial bodies with general or specialized competence, applying international law[2]. What do we mean by "international tribunals"? For the purposes of this discussion, the following definition may be given: a judicial or arbitral body, either standing or capable of being constituted according to pre-existing and

---

[*] Professor of International Law, Graduate Institute of International Studies, Geneva: former Principal Legal Secretary, International Court of Justice.
[1] Whether the appropriate term is "proliferation", whose root meaning is "the production of offspring", and hence "the budding off of cells", may perhaps be doubted, since new tribunals do not grow in a family or in a derivative way out of existing tribunals, even if their constitutive statutes may often present common features.
[2] For a useful list of tribunals created over the last 50 years, see Guillaume, "The Future of International Judicial Institutions", 44 *I.C.L.Q.* (1995), pp. 848-9.

compulsory mechanisms, empowered and required to give binding decisions on the basis of international law, between parties one or more of whom are States.

This definition requires a few glosses. Standing tribunals obviously include (*inter alia*) the International Court of Justice, the International Tribunal for the Law of the Sea, and the two International Criminal Tribunals for the Former Yugoslavia and for Ruanda; this part of the definition will also cover the International Criminal Court provided for in the Rome Statute once it becomes established. The United States/Iran Claims Tribunal is also included, since it is a standing body though not a permanent one; a more doubtful candidate is the United Nations Claims Commission[3]. Also included are the panels and the appeals body provided for in the Disputes Settlement Understanding of the World Trade Organization[4], which are established for each dispute individually, but from an existing body of arbitrators and according to a procedure which, once invoked by one party to a dispute, has to be followed. The Permanent Court of Arbitration does not however fall within the definition, since although a Secretariat and an extensive list of possible arbitrators are available, there is no mechanism entailed in the PCA as such to enable one party to a dispute to require the establishment of an arbitral tribunal. The reference to decisions on the basis of international law refers primarily to general international law, but the fact that, for example, the Yugoslav and Ruanda Tribunals are dealing with international crimes, and the Hamburg Tribunal with the law of the sea, does not prevent those bodies from having to examine and rule on questions of general international law in the course of giving their decisions: as witness the examination of the powers of the Security Council by the ICTFY in the *Tadic* case, and the examination of the law relating to the use of force by ITLOS in the case of the *M/V Saiga (No. 2)*.

Arbitral tribunals pure and simple, established by agreement between the parties to deal with one or more specific disputes, do not seem to attract the suspicion attaching to new standing tribunals: they have always (or at least for some 150 years or more) been with us, and they do not seem to be seen as any threat to the unity of international

---

[3] See Wuehler, "*The United Nations Claims Commission: a new contribution to the process of international claims resolution*", 2 Journal of International Economic Law (1999), p. 249.

[4] Whether the decision of the Disputes Settlement body is a "binding decision" in the same sense as, for example, a judgment of the ICJ, is unsettled: such decisions have been referred to as "almost binding"(see note 22 below).

law. They will therefore not be placed in the "proliferating" category[5], even though their existence is of some significance for our study.

RELATIONSHIP BETWEEN ORGANIZATIONS AND TRIBUNALS

The present conference has as its main subject the proliferation of international organizations, international tribunals being seen as merely one aspect of this phenomenon. There have however been less new tribunals than organizations: a new organization does not necessarily entail the immediate creation of a new disputes settlement mechanism[6]. It may be correct that *ibi societas, ubi jus*, and that *ibi jus, ubi judex*, but an international organization is not *per se* a society in need of a judiciary. The initial stages of the drafting of the Covenant of the League of Nations did not contemplate a permanent international tribunal; it was only the final text of the Covenant which provided that the Council of the League should formulate plans for a Permanent Court of International Justice.

In some cases, however, the creation of the organization has been seen as automatically involving the creation of a tribunal: for example the European Communities, springing from the original Coal and Steel Community, which had from the outset its own Court[7]; and the WTO may also be mentioned, since one of the advances intended to be secured over the old GATT system was the inclusion of a more effective means of dispute settlement[8]. The International Court itself could hardly have been omitted from the post-war United Nations

---

[5] Though, as Judge Guillaume has observed, "in recent years, arbitration in public international law has been expanding as [the]courts have been created": "The Future of International Judicial Institutions", 44 *I.C.L.Q.* (1995), P. 859.

[6] The World Intellectual Property Organization can, it is said, trace its existence back to the 1883 Paris Convention for the Protection of Industrial Property; yet it st up its own disputes resolution service only in 1994: see Gurry, "The Disputes Resolution Services of the World Intellectual Property Organization", 2 *Journal of International Economic Law* (1999), p. 385.

[7] Established by Articles 31-45 of the Paris Treaty of 18 April 1951 creating the ECSC.

[8] The original GATT, in contrast to the Havana Charter, contained no provision for dispute settlement as such, but a system for such settlement grew out of the provision in Articles XXII and XXIII for bilateral and multilateral "consultations". Successive subsequent texts refined and elaborated this system, but it remained based essentially on consensus. See Petersmann, *The GATT/WTO Dispute Settlement System*, Kluwer 1996, pp. 70-71, and "The Transformation of the World Trading System through the 1994 Agreement Establishing the World Trade Organization", 6 *European Journal of International Law*, pp. 207-210.

system, if only because of the precedent of the Permanent Court of International Justice, and the influential 1944 Report of the Informal Inter-Allied Committee on the future of the Permanent Court[9]. The General Assembly found it necessary as early as 1949 to create a tribunal to determine disputes between its own staff and the administration, in this following the example of the ILO; and other bodies have done the same, except where they have found it a more satisfactory solution to make use of the United Nations or the ILO Administrative Tribunals[10]. In the case of the OSCE, the original Helsinki Act (1975) provided in Principle V for peaceful settlement of disputes, but the creation of a disputes settlement mechanism had to await the Stockholm Conference of 1992[11]

The relationship of the European Court of Human Rights to the Council of Europe is less direct: the Court is often considered an organ of the Council of Europe, but is not a statutory organ, having been created by a treaty, the European Convention on Human Rights, some 18 months after the establishment of the Council; however, the Congress of Europe held in May 1948 had called for a United Europe including, *inter alia*, a charter of human rights and a court of justice.

The International Tribunal for the Law of the Sea came into existence along with the International Seabed Authority, but its creation was less attributable to the needs of the Authority than to the desire to create a new specialized tribunal for inter-State disputes in the field of the law of the sea, the International Court of Justice being then temporarily in the doldrums and out of favour[12]. It was the substantive requirements of the Law of the Sea Convention (which of course

---

[9] British Parliamentary Paper, Cmd. 6531; 39 *AJIL* (1945).

[10] There has in fact been a very marked proliferation of administrative tribunals, which, with the exception of the UN and ILO Tribunals have not contributed to a unified jurisprudence: see the criticisms of Thierry at the 1993 Forum of the American Society of International Law and the Graduate Institute of International Studies, quoted in Jennings, "The Role of the International Court of Justice", 68 *BYBIL* (1998), p. 60.

[11] See Laurence Cuny, *L'OSCE et le règlement pacifique des différends: La Cour de conciliation et d'arbitrage*, IUHEI Geneve, 1997.

[12] The offence has been attributed to the decisions in the *South West Africa* and *Northern Cameroons* cases (Guillaume in 44 *I.C.L.Q.* (1995), p. 854, and Oda, ibid., p. 865); however, the 1974 decisions of the Court in the two *Fisheries Jurisdiction* cases have also been mentioned as having had considerable influence on a number of delegations to UNCLOS which regarded the decisions as lagging behind the development of the law of the sea: see Ranjeva, "Quelques observations sur l'intérêt à avoir une juridiction internationale unique", *International Law Forum, Journal of the International Law Association*, "Zero Issue", July 1998, p. 11.

included an appreciable element of innovation, likely to require judicial clarification) which rendered a tribunal necessary, rather than the simultaneous creation of an organization[13].

If new tribunals have been associated with new organizations, the reason is often an economic one: a tribunal has to be paid for, and as was discovered with the League of Nations and the Permanent Court of International Justice, the most practical method of financing a tribunal is through the budget of an international organization, thus tapping the purses of member States who may not be interested in contributing to an international judiciary as such.

THE BENEFITS AND THE DISADVANTAGES

BENEFITS

An international judicial or arbitral body has in itself some claim to be regarded as a good thing: opposition to the establishment of such a body has more to be based on questioning whether it is actually needed rather than on any denial of its virtues. The creation of new tribunals may indeed be regarded as an encouraging sign, as amounting to the "expression d'adhésion plus grande des acteurs de la vie internationale à la doctrine de la primauté de la règle de droit dans les rapports internationaux; juridicisation croissante du règlement des différends"[14]. It is to be supposed that more tribunals will lead to more justice; that a multiplication of peaceful means of settling international disputes will result in a higher proportion of such disputes actually being settled peacefully[15]. To prove that this is so might however be difficult. At one time, one could point to the gross under-use of the International Court

---

[13] It is however true that the creation of the Seabed Disputes Chamber with its specialised jurisdiction was clearly bound up with the establishment of the Seabed Authority: see Boyle, "Dispute Settlement and the Law of the Sea Convention: Problems of Fragmentation and Jurisdiction", 46 I.C.L.Q., p. 39.

[14] Raymond Ranjeva, "Quelques observations sur l'intérêt à avoir une juridiction internationale unique", *International Law Forum, Journal of the International Law Association*, "Zero Issue", July 1998, p. 10.

[15] Thus President Schwebel of the ICJ, addressing the General Assembly on 26 October 1999, expressed the view that "A greater range of international legal fora is likely to mean that more disputes are submitted to international judicial settlement. The more international adjudication there is, the more there is likely to be; the 'judicial habit' may stimulate healthy imitation."

of Justice to argue that States were disinclined to submit their disputes to judicial settlement, and thus that the creation of other tribunals would serve no useful end, but the situation had at that time been distorted by the violent negative reaction to the 1966 Judgment of the Court in the *South West Africa* case. As a result of this, there was then some force in the argument that alternative methods of judicial or arbitral settlement should be provided, in order that the unpopularity of the specific Court should not impede the progress made toward acceptance of judicial settlement of disputes as a normal feature of international relations.

At the present time, the unprecedentedly heavy workload of the International Court suggests that that particular battle has been won, that there is now a real demand for the services of international judges; and that since the 15 judges of The Hague are now so overburdened that they cannot keep up with their workload, some other tribunal is desirable if only as a relief solution. Clearly however to set up a sort of deutero-ICJ would be impracticable: it would have to be a United Nations organ like the existing Court, and an amendment of the Charter on these lines would both present insoluble problems of constitutional structure, and require the opening of the Pandora's box of Charter amendment – an operation whose results are too unforeseeable to be contemplated, and which is therefore generally considered to be impracticable[16].

If more tribunals are desirable simply to meet a demand for more judicial disputes-settlement, the creation of the International Tribunal for the Law of the Sea may prove to be a benefit for reasons other than those which inspired its inclusion in the Montego Bay Convention. It is not that the Hague court is still regarded as politically unsatisfactory, or as unable to handle law of the sea problems competently[17], but simply that that Court has too much to do. At the same time, it is noticeable that no maritime delimitation case has yet been submitted to ITLOS, while several have in recent years been presented to the ICJ[18]. This may

---

[16] But see the interesting suggestion of Petersmann that, instead of trying to achieve the consensus necessary to amend the Charter, "following the example of the replacement of the 'GATT 1947' by the 1994 WTO Agreement, the 1945 UN Charter should be replaced by a new Charter": "How to Reform the UN System? Constitutionalism, International Law, and International Organizations", 10 *Leiden Journal of International Law* (1997), p. 424.

[17] See above, note 11.

[18] The Tribunal came into existence with the coming into force of the Montego Bay Convention on 16 November 1984; but the first election of judges did not take place until 1 August 1996. Since the coming into force of the Convention, the

represent no more than a preference for the known to the unknown, but it is perhaps not a favourable augury for the creation of specialized tribunals in parallel to the universal jurisdiction of the ICJ.

Among the possible advantages which States may see in the creation of new tribunals, there is first of all the obvious one of specialisation. This is one justification for the International Tribunal on the Law of the Sea[19]; the fact that its Statute provides that the judges are to be expert in the law of the sea has been seen by some as a negative characteristic, but in the thinking of the authors of the text it was clearly an advantage. Secondly, there is the simple point to which Sir Robert Jennings has drawn attention. – an important limitation on the otherwise universal international jurisdiction of the International Court of Justice: the fact that "Only States may be parties in cases before the Court"; thus, for example, disputes between States and international organizations do not fall within the competence of the Court[20]. The International Tribunal for the Law of the Sea, for example, is not subject to this limitation[21], but in general it does not appear that provision for litigation by or against international organizations has been a significant motive in the creation of new judicial bodies.

The assumption that more tribunals means more peaceful settlement also presupposes that the submission of a dispute to a tribunal will necessarily result, first in a binding decision, and subsequently in the peaceful settlement of the dispute, normally in accordance with that decision. If there is a present willingness on both sides to see the dispute settled on a basis of law, no problem arises; but

---

following cases affecting maritime delimitation have been submitted to the ICJ: *Kasikili/Sedudu Island (Botswana/Namibia)*, 29 May 1996; *Land and Maritime Boundary between Cameroon and Nigeria*, 29 May 1994; *Sovereignty over Pulau Ligitan and Pulau Spadan (Indonesia/Malaya)*, 2 November 1998. The case concerning *Maritime Delimitation and Territorial Questions between Qatar and Bahrain* is also pending, having been submitted on 8 July 1991.

[19] Cf Fleischhauer, "The Relationship between the International Court of Justice and the Newly Created International Tribunal for the Law of the Sea in Hamburg", 1 *Max Planck Yearbook of United Nations Law*, (1997), p. 327.

[20] Jennings, "The Role of the International Court of Justice", 68 *BYBIL* (1998), p. 58. See also Charney, "Third Party Dispute Settlement and International Law", 36 *Columbia Journal of International Law*, 1997, p. 74.

[21] The Tribunal is open, under Article 20 of its Statute, to "entities other than States Parties in any case expressly provided for in Part XI" of the Convention (e.g. to the Council of the Seabed Authority under Article 162 (1) (*u*)), "or in any case submitted pursuant to any other agreement conferring jurisdiction on the Tribunal which is accepted by all the parties to that case".

by the same token, no new tribunal is needed, as the same end can be achieved without standing mechanisms, through the submission of the dispute to an *ad hoc* arbitral tribunal. To obtain full benefit from new tribunals, they should be standing tribunals with a provision for advance acceptance, like the optional clause of Article 36, paragraph 2, of the ICJ Statute, or Article 287 of the Convention on the Law of the Sea. The object of such provisions is to make possible judicial settlement, the delivery of a binding decision[22] when one party is less than enthusiastic – possibly because of doubts in the strength of its case – and would therefore be reluctant to conclude a *compromis* for arbitral settlement[23]. If however one party is reluctant to have the dispute judicially heard and determined, it will similarly be reluctant to put the decision into execution, assuming that that decision is not in its own favour; thus some mechanism of execution, even if as ineffective and symbolic as Article 92 of the Charter, is needed[24].

It should not be overlooked that the creation of more tribunals, if it is to have an effective positive impact on State practice in the field of peaceful dispute-settlement, must be accompanied by adequate publicity and even education. Philippe Sands, Co-Director of the Project on International Courts and Tribunals, has given expression, in the light of personal experience, to "growing concern about the implications of the trend toward international adjudication", with the question: "are governments and other international actors (particularly those from the developing world and from economies in transition) adequately informed about and able to participate effectively in

---

[22] One possible weakness of the WTO Disputes Settlement Understanding is that there is doubt how far the ultimate decision can be said to be binding: for Judge Guillaume, it is "*almost* a binding decision" : "The Future of International Judicial Institutions", *44 I.C.L.Q.*, (1995), p. 860 (emphasis added).

[23] In the case of the ITLOS, it has been pointed out by Judge Oda that the extent to which the disputes-settlement provisions of UNCLOS commit States parties to acceptance of compulsory jurisdiction is in fact less that an initial reading of the text might suggest: see Oda, "Disputes Settlement Prospects in the Law of the Sea", *44 I.C.L.Q.*, (1995), p. 863.

[24] This is, or may become, a problem with the WTO disputes settlement system: under the Disputes Settlement Understanding, "compensation is voluntary" (Art. 22), and both compensation and suspension of concessions or other obligations are regarded only as "temporary measures" pending compliance with rulings of the Disputes Settlement Body. In the event of persistent non-compliance, it is unclear whether or not general international law as to State responsibility and the lawfulness of counter-measures may be appealed to.

proceedings of international litigation?"[25]. States in the categories referred to may also have problems financing international litigation, though the Secretary-General's fund may go some way to assist, at least as regards ICJ proceedings[26].

DISADVANTAGES

The mere creation of a new tribunal is harmless enough, though it may involve financial commitments for the States that establish it[27]: it is when it starts to operate that problems may arise!

Essentially two problems have been identified as related to the establishment of a number of international tribunals operating in parallel. The first, of lesser gravity, is that of conflict of jurisdictions: that for a given dispute, the constitutional system of more than one tribunal may, in conjunction with the pre-established consent of the parties to the dispute, by whatever means given, entitle both tribunals to assert jurisdiction if invited to do so by one party. The conditions of operation, or the means of enforcement, may however differ from the one tribunal to the other, thus offering one or other party to a dispute an inducement to indulge in a sort of international "forum-shopping" in order to seise the instance the more favourable to its case or its interests. Furthermore, it would be possible for one party to seise one of the possible fora, and the other party the other, or one of the others. For each tribunal, once informed of the situation, a problem of positive conflict of jurisdictions would arise; and in the absence of some power to resolve the conflict, the consequence could be two rival decisions on the same dispute, possibly - probably - not identical, or even mutually contradictory.

The other problem is that of inconsistency of decision on questions of law. This could, as just noted, occur as a result of a simultaneous

---

[25] Philippe Sands, "Work in Progress: Project on International Courts and Tribunals", *International Law Forum (Journal of the International Law Association)*, "Zero Issue", July 1998, p.21. For information on the project, Dr. Sands can be contacted at <ps12@soas.ac.uk>.

[26] The Secretary-General's Trust Fund to Assist States in the Settlement of Disputes through the International Court of Justice is designed, as its name implies, to encourage States to settle their disputes peacably by submitting them to the Court by Special Agreement, and offers financial assistance to this end to States that need it. See UN doc. A/44/PV.43 (1989).

[27] The delay in electing the first judges to establish the ITLOS has been attributed to financial considerations being allowed to over-ride the terms of the Convention.

conflict of jurisdictions: but it could also occur without any such conflict arising. All that is needed for a conflict to arise is that there be more than one tribunal empowered to give a decision in the same field or fields of international law; and the more tribunals there are that can decide matters of general international law, the greater the risk of such conflict. This is one reason why the principal source of concern observed by commentators is the jurisdiction of the ITLOS; not only may it be called upon to decide matters of general international law in the course of deciding a law-of-the-sea dispute, as indicated by the *M/V Saiga (No. 2)* case, but it has been suggested that it may also decide general international law disputes[28]. We may in fact distinguish three categories of conflict-of-judicial-decision problems.

There is first the situation in which an international tribunal called upon to determine, for the purposes of the case before it, a particular controverted point of international law, finds that that point has already arisen in a different case before another international tribunal, and has been determined in a sense which the second tribunal regards as erroneous[29]. If the International Court of Justice in one case decides that international law on a specific point is thus and thus; and at the same time, or at a later date, another tribunal (say, the Law of the Sea Tribunal) decides in a different case that international law on that specific point is not what the ICJ has stated it to be, the result is, at the least, doubt on what international law *does* provide on that point, and at worst a step towards a fragmentation of international law. Such inconsistency of decision could indeed produce a self-maintaining trend. Let it be supposed that on an issue affecting the respective rights of coastal States and long-distance fishing States the Law of the Sea Tribunal gave a decision giving more satisfaction to the coastal States; and that the International Court of Justice, in a case involving the same elements, decided differently, and in a way more pleasing to the fishing

---

[28] See Alan Boyle, "Dispute Settlement and the Law of the Sea Convention: Problems of Fragmentation and Jurisdiction", 46 *I.C.L.Q.*, (1997), p. 49; contrasting Article 288 of the Convention with Article 21 of the Tribunal's Statute, he considers that "Although it might be argued that it was never intended for the Tribunal to be a court of general jurisdiction, the Convention provides little warrant for confining the Tribunal's consensual jurisdiction to law of the sea cases"

[29] For completeness, the case should also be recalled in which a tribunal is asked to say that an earlier decision *of its own* either was wrongly decided, or is obsolete and should not be followed, as occurred in the *Cameroon* v.*Nigeria* case *I.C.J. Reports 1998*, pp. 290 ff., paras. 21-35. This however is not a consequence of multiplication of tribunals.

States. Whenever a similar question underlay a dispute between two States, the coastal State would be inclined to bring the matter to Hamburg, and the fishing State to The Hague, so that a conflict of law would result in a conflict of jurisdictions.

Secondly, the same situation may present itself, but with the additional embarrassment that the previous tribunal, while seised of a different case, was dealing with the same factual background as the second tribunal, so that a different decision on the law would have a greater degree of inconsistency with the earlier decision: this is the problem presented by the question of the international or other character of the conflict in the former Yugoslavia, mentioned below. Thirdly, the second tribunal may find that an element of the case before it is a decision of some other tribunal on one of the legal questions arising in that very case: this was the situation that faced the ICJ Chamber in the *Land, Island and Maritime Frontier Dispute* between El Salvador and Honduras, inasmuch as the status of the waters of the Gulf of Fonseca had been the subject of a decision in 1917 of the Central American Court of Justice; fortunately, as there was not the identity of parties required for strict application of *res judicata*, the Court, while reaching essentially the same conclusion as the Central American Court, was able to avoid having to decide the exact impact of the earlier decision on the legal position[30].

Another possible effect of the multiplication of alternative tribunals that has been mentioned with disapproval is its impact on the position and status of the International Court of Justice. This is one of the objections of Judge Oda to the establishment of the Law of the Sea Tribunal[31]; but even Professor Charney, when refuting Judge Oda's criticisms, declared that he believed "that it is valuable to maintain the predominance of the ICJ in public international law", and that competition form other tribunals might "diminish the importance of the Court" as well as encouraging uneven development in the jurisprudence[32]. Expressed in more practical terms is the concern of Judge Schwebel, President of the Court, that proliferation of international tribunals might lead to "evisceration of the docket of the

---

[30] See *I.C.J. Reports 1992*, pp. 600-601, paras. 402-3.
[31] See in particular Oda, "The International Court of Justice from the Bench", 244 *Recueil des Cours*, 1993-VII, pp. 144 ff.
[32] Charney, "The Implications of Expanding International Dispute Settlement Systems: the 1982 Convention on the Law of the Sea", 90 *AJIL* (1996), pp. 70, 71.

International Court of Justice"[33]. The present writer believes that in this respect, quality will tell; that so long as the decisions of the International Court remain worthy of its status, States will continue to refer matters to it, whatever specialized alternatives may be available. At all events, if this is a naïve and over-simplified view, it is not evident what means could be adopted to keep the ICJ docket filled, nor can that objective constitute a worthy end in itself.

How great is the danger that the theoretical problems, of conflict of jurisdictions and fragmentation of international law, will arise in practice – or have they arisen already? And how are these disadvantages to be avoided, or if unavoidable, palliated? For the problem of divergent case-law and possible fragmentation of international law, apart from the radical solution of refraining from creating rival tribunals in parallel to the ICJ – for which it is obviously too late –, the only suggestion that has been made has been to provide for an international judicial structure, a hierarchy of courts, with possibilities of appeal. In the municipal sphere, it is one of the functions of courts of appeal or of cassation to iron out differences of approach or of interpretation of the law by lower courts. The creation of such a structure would also afford the opportunity to foresee and exclude possible conflicts of jurisdiction.

We shall thus examine successively the dangers of fragmentation of substantive law which, it has been suggested, flow from the proliferation of tribunals; the problems of conflicts of jurisdiction; and the remedies which have been adumbrated.

TOWARD FRAGMENTATION OF INTERNATIONAL LAW?

Two principles may be noted at the outset as defining the scope of the problem. First, that of the unity of international law: while there may be specialized areas of international law, and even "self-contained regimes", whatever that expression may mean[34], general international

---

[33] Address to the United Nations General Assembly, 26 October 1999.
[34] The origin of the concept, which has been asserted in connection with WTO law, seems to be the decision of the ICJ in the case of *United States Diplomatic and Consular Staff in Tehran*, which considered the rules of diplomatic law as such a regime, with the consequence that Iran's only remedy for alleged abuses of diplomatic privilege by US diplomats was to declare them *personae non gratae*. Simma has defined the category of such regimes as "a certain category of subsystems [of law], namely those embracing, in principle, a full (exhaustive and

law must be the same for all States at any given moment[35]. Secondly, the principle well stated by Sir Robert Jennings "that the *primary* task of a court of justice is not to "develop" the law, but to dispose, in accordance with the law, of that particular dispute between the particular parties before it"[36]. Sir Robert continues: "This is not to say that development is not frequently a secondary part of the judge's task", provided it is "integral and incidental to the disposal according to law of the actual issues before the court"[37]. Thus conflict, if it is to arise, should in principle only result from two disputes, brought before different tribunals, raising, *for the purpose of settlement*, identical legal problems. Inconsistency of *obiter dicta* as between two tribunals is or should be immaterial[38]; but at the same time, the more tribunals there are, the more judges should exercise self-restraint, and not touch unnecessarily in their decisions on matters which may arise directly for determination before another judicial body.

In the light of these principles, how great is the danger of fragmentation? The views of commentators differ considerably. Thus Judge Guillaume, writing in 1995, emphasized what he saw as the under-rated danger "of divergences resulting from the proliferation of tribunals courts and quasi-judicial bodies", and insisted that while international law must "take into account the problems arising in specific regions or in specific fields", it "must not be broken up in such a way as to jeopardize its unity"[39]. Professor Charney, in 1997, referred to the possibility that "Decisions reaching different conclusions on the same international law subject by a variety of tribunals may undermine the appearance, if not the fact, of a unitary system of international law", so much so as to "damage the coherence of the international legal

---

definite) set of secondary rules": "Self-contained Regimes", *Netherlands Yearbook of International Law*, 1985, p. 117.

[35] For a powerful defence of this view, see Charney, "Universal International Law", 87 *AJIL* (1993), p. 522.

[36] "The Role of the International Court of Justice", 68 *BYBIL* (1998), p. 41 (emphasis original).

[37] *Ibid.*

[38] In view of the absence of any system of binding precedent in international tribunals, the distinction between *ratio decidendi* and *obiter dicta* is not generally regarded as relevant on the international level; but note the reference, in the decision of the ICJ Chamber in the *Land, Island and Maritime Frontier* case, to the *ratio decidendi* of the 1917 decision of the Central American Court of Justice (*I.C.J. Reports, 1992*, p. 599, para. 401).

[39] "The Future of International Judicial Institutions", *44 I.C.L.Q.*, (1995), p. 862.

system itself". Yet, in his view, "based on the available information, a serious problem does not appear likely"[40].

The existence of the theoretical risk cannot of course be denied; has the threat already been fulfilled? Attention has already been drawn in legal literature, for example, to two areas in which there is either an actual or a potential conflict between decisions of the International Court of Justice and those of Chambers of the International Criminal Tribunal for the former Yugoslavia. In the first place, the International Court, concerned with the conflict in the former Yugoslavia by virtue of the proceedings instituted by Bosnia-Herzegovina against Yugoslavia, has so far been able to refrain from ruling on the question whether that conflict is or is not of an international character; it has indicated that the Genocide Convention applies whether or not the conflict is international[41]; whereas Chamber II of the ICTFY, in its decision of 13 September 1996 in the *Rajic* case[42], following in this Chamber I in its decision of 11 July 1996 in the *Karadzic-Mladic* case[43], has decided that, for the purposes of the jurisdiction of the Tribunal under Articles 2, 3 and 5 of its Statute, the conflict is international because of the involvement of more than one State[44]. Here is a conflict perhaps narrowly avoided; and yet it would not have been a head-on collision, since the two tribunals would have been examining whether, *for the purposes of a particular treaty*, and not the same treaty, the conflict should be regarded as international. Can international law not permit that a conflict may be international for some purposes, but not for others?

The decision in the *Rajic* case however goes further, and bases the conclusion that the conflict is an international one also on the finding that the Bosnian Croats were acting, in the relevant activities, as agents of Croatia. This conclusion, it has been suggested, is difficult to reconcile with the finding of the International Court in the case

---

[40] "Third Party Dispute Settlement and International Law", *36 Columbia Journal of Transnational Law*, (1997), p. 77. In the same sense: Boisson de Chazournes, "Multiplication des instances de règlement des différends: vers la promotion de la règle de droit", *International Law Forum, Journal of the International Law Association*, "Zero Issue", July 1998, p. 14.

[41] *I.C.J. Reports 1996*, pp. 615, 621, paras. 31, 43.

[42] Case no. IT-95-12-R61.

[43] Cases nos. IT-95-5-R61 and IT-95-18-R61.

[44] See the very interesting discussion of what is seen as a very real potentiality for conflict in Christakis, "Les relations entre la CIJ et le Tribunal pénal: les premières fissures à l'unité du droit?", *L'Observateur des Nations Unies*, No. 1 (1996), pp. 53-58.

concerning the *Military and Paramilitary Activities in and against Nicaragua* that, notwithstanding the activities of the United States in arming, financing and supplying the *contra* forces, they were not acting on behalf of the United States so as to render that State responsible for their activities[45]. Again: provide the same principles are recognized as governing, an apparent inconsistency in their application to two different sets of circumstances is not so grave a matter.

An earlier decision which, it has been suggested, involved a divergence from the established case-law of the International Court was that of the European Court of Human Rights in the case of *Loizidou* v. *Turkey*[46]. The European Court there interpreted its own Statute, which, so far as relevant, is in terms identical to those of the ICJ Statute, as not permitting a reservation by Turkey limiting application of the European Convention to metropolitan Turkey (i.e., excluding the "Turkish Republic of Cyprus"); this in stark contrast to the liberal attitude of the Permanent Court and the postwar Hague Court to the making of reservations to optional-clause acceptances of jurisdiction[47].

It must be conceded that whether these specific cases are true examples of conflict is not here to the purpose[48]: they do serve to make clear that the possibility of conflicting decisions by two or more international tribunals on the same point of international law is more than a *hypothèse d'école*. In view of the recognition, by Article 38, paragraph 1 (*d*), of the ICJ Statute, that "judicial decisions" constitute a subsidiary source, or more precisely a "subsidiary means for the

---

[45] *I.C.J. Reports 1986*, pp. 64-5, para. 115.

[46] 23 March 1995, Judgement No. 40/1993/435/514. For the view that this decision conflicts directly with ICJ case-law, see Jennings, "The Proliferation of Adjudicatory Bodies: Dangers and Possible Answers", *ASIL Bulletin No. 9* (1995), pp. 5-6.

[47] The present writer has examined the *Loizidou* case and concluded that there is no real conflict: see Thirlway, "The Proliferation of International Judicial Organs and the Formation of International Law" in *International Law and The Hague's 750th Anniversary*, T.M.C. Asser Institute, 1999.

[48] As the *Loizidou* case shows, a conflict may only apparent (see previous note). Another example is the finding of the WTO panel in the *Grey Portland Cement* case that, in the WTO context that the absence of reference in the texts to the rule of the exhaustion of local remedies signified that the rule was not to apply (GATT doc. ADP/82, para. 5.9), in contrast to the finding of the ICJ in the *Elettronica Sicula* case that it was "unable to accept that an important principle of customary international law [i.e. the local remedies rule] should be held to have been tacitly dispensed with, in the absence of any words making clear an intention to do so": *I.C.J. Reports 1989*, p. 42, para. 50.

determination of rules of law", this is perhaps a prospect not to be viewed with equanimity.

At the same time, the matter should be kept in proportion. The "judicial decisions" referred to in Article 38 are not limited to those of major standing international tribunals: they include arbitral decisions[49], and even the decisions of municipal courts. Such decisions might well not coincide with the view of international law stated subsequently by the International Court; and an arbitral tribunal or municipal court might even choose to differ *ex post facto* from that august body[50]. The modern development is therefore one merely of degree: a conflict between decisions of the ICJ and the ICTFY, or the ITLOS, is both more conspicuous and more disturbing than the differences which might previously have been encountered. Furthermore, judicial decisions, even those of the ICJ itself, are not more than "subsidiary means for the determination of rules of law"; inconsistent decisions do not *make* incoherent law, but show that it is not easy correctly and coherently to declare the law.

Nor should our attachment to the ideal of the unity of international law blind us to the fact that that unity is to some extent a fiction – a valuable fiction, and one to be cherished, but a fiction. Article 59 of the Statute of the International Court implicitly recognizes the possibility of divergences between successive decisions of the Court itself, even though the Court in practice clearly endeavours to avoid, or if not, to mask, such inconsistencies. What is more, the provision in the ICJ Statute for its Members to attach separate or dissenting opinions to its decisions is a recognition that there may not be unanimity among the most authoritative exponents of international law as to what that law is in specific cases. While it is only the judgment of the Court that attracts the force of *res judicata*, and binds the parties to the case, the view of the law expounded in a separate or dissenting opinion may be highly influential for its subsequent development, or even become recognized

---

[49] In the specific field of the law of the sea, where both the ICJ and arbitral tribunals have been active, there has, in the view of Prof. Alan Boyle, been "no overt conflict" between their decisions: "Dispute settlement and the Law of the Sea Convention: Problems of fragmentataion and Jurisdiction". *46 I.C.L.Q.*, (1997), p. 41.

[50] The jurisprudence of the US/Iran Claims Tribunal adopts a more flexible approach to the nationality of claims rule than would be recognized by writers following strictly the established arbitral case-law; the United Nations Compensation Commission has abandoned the rule on humanitarian grounds. The International Court has however not yet had occasion to take a position in the matter.

subsequently as a more accurate analysis of it than that given in the decision itself – or so the authors of such opinions hope.... Nor have judges been reluctant to take advantage of the opportunity to indicate in what way the majority of the Court has mis-stated international law[51].

The question is thus not: can we live with a fragmented international law? but is the proliferation of tribunals such as to lead to a greater or more marked fragmentation than that which has always existed?

D. THE PROBLEM OF CONFLICTS OF JURISDICTIONS

Private international lawyers have always had to face the problems of two, or even more, courts being seised of the same dispute, and the various national systems of conflict of laws have worked out certain rules and principles to govern the matter, such as those of litispendence, *forum non conveniens*, etc. At the level of public international law and inter-State disputes, this is a field of study which has up to now not required great attention[52], and there is a consequent dearth of clear rules on the subject.

The Permanent Court had occasion to consider the matter briefly on two occasions only. In the *Chorzów Factory* case, there were proceedings, parallel to those brought before the Court, pending before a Germano-Polish Mixed Arbitral Tribunal. The Court observed that "when it has to define its jurisdiction in relation to that of another tribunal", it could not "allow its own competence to give way unless confronted with a clause which it considers sufficiently clear to prevent the possibility of a negative conflict of jurisdiction involving the danger of a denial of justice"[53]. In the case of the *Minority Schools in Upper Silesia*, the question was the relevance of the jurisdiction of the League of Nations Council to receive petitions; the Court referred to the definition of its jurisdiction in Article 36 of the Statute, and continued:

---

[51] For an extreme example, see the advisory opinion on the *Legality of the Threat or Use of Nuclear Weapons* (1996), to which were attached declarations or opinions by every single Member of the Court.

[52] With the notable exception of the specialised problem of the relationship between the International Court of Justice and the United Nations Security Council, when the same matter has been brought before both: see the cases of *United States Diplomatic and Consular Staff in Tehran, Aegean Sea Continental Shelf*, and the current *Lockerbie* cases.

[53] *Chorzów Factory (Jurisdiction) P.C.I.J. Series A, No. 9*, p. 30.

"This principle only becomes inoperative in those exceptional cases in which the dispute which States might desire to refer to the Court falls within the exclusive jurisdiction reserved to some other authority"[54]

Thus if this jurisprudence is to be followed (as it should be, in the name of the unity of international law!), the International Court will not insist on its pre-eminence to other tribunals so far as to decline to yield to their competence, but will require to be satisfied that it was the intention of the parties to the dispute that the other tribunal was to have *exclusive* competence, and that that tribunal will be available to deal with the dispute, so that there will be no negative conflict of jurisdictions. A negative conflict is perhaps *a priori* unlikely; in the *Electricity Company* case the Permanent Court (followed in *Border and Transborder Armed Actions* by the post-war Court) emphasized that where parallel titles of jurisdiction existed, the intention was presumed to be to open up fresh avenues, rather than closing existing ones[55]; and although these dicta relate to alternative avenues leading to the competence of the International Court (or Permanent Court) itself, the same reasoning would surely apply where there were alternative tribunals.

The effect of the application of this principle will be to avoid the risk of competing (and possibly inconsistent) decisions by the ICJ and another tribunal; but at the same time to increase the likelihood that it will be the specialized tribunal, rather than the ICJ, which will deal with the case. Unless one has a firm and unbending faith in the superiority of legal reasoning of the IC J in all matters, this seems a desirable result – that specialized cases should be decided by specialized tribunals.

The extent to which other tribunals do in fact have exclusive jurisdiction under their constituent instruments is a matter requiring further study. The provisions of Article 287 of UNCLOS are designed to ensure a single identifiable tribunal for any given dispute, through a system of interlocking declarations referring either to the ITLOS, the ICJ, an arbitral tribunal or a "special arbitral tribunal"[56]; and paragraph 4 of the Article provides that "If the parties to a dispute have accepted

---

[54] *P.C.I.J. Series A, No. 15*, p. 23.
[55] *P.C.I.J. Series A/B, No. 77*, p. 76
[56] The so-called "smorgasbord" or "cafeteria" system: see Charney, "The Implications of Expanding International Dispute Settlement Systems: The 1982 Convention on the Law of the Sea", *90 AJIL* (1996), p.71; and Boyle, "Dispute Settlement and the Law of the Sea Convention: Problems of Fragmentation and Jurisdiction, *46 I.C.L.Q.*, (1997), P. 40.

the same procedure for the settlement of the dispute, it may be submitted *only* to that procedure, unless the parties otherwise agree" (emphasis added). Similarly if the parties have made different choices, the dispute may be submitted "only to arbitration". It is however arguable that this only commits the parties within the context of UNCLOS, and that if there is in existence (for example) an unconditional acceptance of ICJ optional-clause jurisdiction by both parties, this may be relied on to seise the ICJ even if the parties have, under Article 287, made a different choice or choices. Article 299 (2) provides that "Nothing in this section impairs the right of the parties to the dispute to agree to some other procedure for the settlement of such dispute or to reach an amicable settlement"; can such agreement be general, and made in advance of any dispute arising?

The WTO Disputes Settlement Understanding does not provide in so many words that the system established by it excludes other means of settlement; but Article 23 of the DSU does provide that "When Members seek redress of a violation of obligations ... under the covered agreements..., they *shall* have recourse to, and abide by, the rules and procedures of this Understanding""(emphasis added). The question may shortly acquire some actuality in the context of disputes relating to Bilateral Investment Treaties, since a number of such treaties contain compromissory clauses conferring jurisdiction on the ICJ.

While only the International Criminal Tribunals for the Former Yugoslavia and Ruanda can try individuals for crimes committed in those regions, there seems no reason why the ICJ could not rule on whether or not such crimes had or had not been committed if the point arose in the course of determination of an inter-State dispute, as in fact it has done in the case concerning *Application of the Genocide Convention.* The Court did not see any need to question its own jurisdiction on the basis of any exclusivity of jurisdiction of the ICTFY, or some rule of *forum non conveniens.*

In the field of declarations under the ICJ optional clause, it is common for a reservation to be made excluding disputes for which the parties "have agreed or shall agree another means of pacific settlement"[57]; thus where such a reservation exists, the jurisdiction conferred on whatever other means of settlement has been agreed on

---

[57] Of the 59 declarations reproduced in *ICJ Yearbook 1995-1996*, 32 contain a proviso on these lines.

becomes exclusive, at least in relation to the optional-clause jurisdiction of the ICJ[58].

With regard to the possibility of "forum-shopping", this cannot yet be regarded as a serious danger, in view of the presently restricted range of jurisdictions available[59], nor is it necessarily to be regarded as a bad thing. What has brought the concept into disrepute at the private law level has been the quest by plaintiffs for the court awarding the highest scale of damages, not a likely consideration at the international level. Insofar as there may be a choice, the determining factor may however be the *type* of remedies available, a consideration likely to favour use of the ICJ, with the possibility, limited as it is, of recourse to the Security Council under article 94 of the Charter. The ITLOS already enjoys a privileged position in this respect, in view of the possibility afforded by Article 292 of UNCLOS (and taken advantage of in the recent case of the *M/V Saiga (No. 1)*) of securing the prompt release of vessels and crews.

Possibly a more sophisticated system of rules of conflict of jurisdictions needs to be developed; but in the last resort, it should not be overlooked that it will be the individual tribunals which would have to apply them, and there can be no greater guarantee of consistency in this field of law than in any other.

STRUCTURE OF TRIBUNALS: SUPERVISION BY THE INTERNATIONAL COURT?

Within a given municipal system, it is possible to regulate the relationships between various courts and tribunals, and between the courts established by the State, on the one hand, and *ad hoc* arbitrations on the other, by legislative means, according to a planned pattern. It may therefore appear desirable to achieve the same result on the international plane, both to regulate conflicts of jurisdiction and to resolve contradictory decisions by referral of the case, or the

---

[58] If the Court could be seised under some other title of jurisdiction, it does not appear that the restriction in the optional-clause declaration could be "read into" that other title, as representing the basic limitation imposed by that party on the Court's jurisdiction: see the attempt of Honduras to present an argument of this kind in *Border and Transborder Armed Actions, I.C.J. Reports 1988*, p. 83, paras. 30-31; and the similar argument of France (not examined by the Court) in the *Nuclear Tests* cases: *Pleadings, Vol. II*, pp. 356-7.

[59] But see the suggestion above, as to the effect of divergent policies in law of the sea matters of the ICJ and the ITLOS.

controversy, to a superior court[60]. It is however clearly too late to restructure the international straggle of different tribunals, and to incorporate them into some pre-established plan[61]; but may there be possible methods of defining, if only in a piecemeal manner, their relations with each other, or of establishing a court enjoying a supervisory function over them?

For the avoidance of conflicts of jurisdiction, it is necessary to decide on a policy: are specialist tribunals to be given priority over general ones, including the ICJ? Or is the ICJ at least to preserve its universal jurisdiction, coupled with a discretion to disseise itself in the event that proceedings before a specialist tribunals are to be preferred? The latter course would involve the development of a principle of *forum non conveniens*.

For the avoidance, or at least the remedying, of conflicts of decisions, there seems no substitute for a system of appeal, review, or cassation; and the obvious body to exercise such powers is the International Court of Justice[62]. In many areas of law the Court has already contributed through its decisions to the establishment of what are now recognized rules and principles; and, as Judge Ranjeva has put it, "La conservation de ce legs amène une juridiction qui a une longue expérience judiciaire, à veiller aux développements qui pourraient être

---

[60] As was recalled by Prof. Georges Abi-Saab in 1993, the "Draft Model Rules on Arbitral Procedure" introduced by Prof. Georges Scelle in the ILC would have resolved problems of this kind by an automatic reference to the ICJ: see *ASIL Bulletin No. 9* (November 1995); and for the Scelle draft, *Yearbook of the ILC, 1952-II*, pp. 60-67.

[61] Apart from any other problem, the existing members of the various bodies might well have strong feelings as to their relative importance and ranking in the international order: cf. the "bataille de préeminence" between the ICTFY and the ICJ (the term is that of Christakis, "Les relations entre la CIJ et le Tribunal pénal: les premières fissures à l'unité du droit", *L'Observateur des Nations Unies*, No. 1, 1996, p. 51).

[62] Judge Guillaume argues that "Courts and tribunals must... be very cautious in developing their case-law, which must remain consonant with the jurisprudence of the International Court, which, after all, is the 'principal judicial organ of the United Nations', and to which 'legal disputes should as a general rule be referred', under Article 36, paragraph 2, of the Charter" ("The Future of International Judicial Institutions", *44 I.C.L.Q.* (1995), p. 862). It may however be questioned whether these texts confer on the ICJ any inherent superiority of wisdom, let alone any aura of infallibility. As Charney has pointed out, at the San Francisco Conference the participants deliberately chose not to give the ICJ ultimate authority to interpret the Charter ("Third Party Dispute Settlement and International Law ", *36 Columbia Journal of Transnational Law*, p. 71, footnote 26).

déduits de ses propres propositions"[63]. A practical problem, to which there is no obvious solution, is however the already overburdened docket of the Court, and its increasing difficulty, with its present means and methods of work[64], in deciding cases as fast as new ones are submitted to it. Assuming however that the ICJ can take on a supervisory role, the next question is whether that role should or could be exercised by advisory opinion or through the exercise of its contentious jurisdiction.

Supervision through the Contentious Procedure of the ICJ

That the Court can, in the framework of a contentious case, exercise a purely appellate jurisdiction is clear from the example of the *Appeal Relating to the Jurisdiction of the ICAO Council* [65] in 1972; shortly afterwards the Court deleted from its 1946 Rules the Article (Article 67) dealing with appeals, replacing it with an article (Article 87 of the 1978 Rules) under the section heading "Special Reference to the Court", but it does not appear that the intention was to abolish the appellate jurisdiction, - which, indeed, is conferred on the Court by other instruments[66], and therefore beyond the reach of amendments of the ICJ Rules.

It should however perhaps be emphasized that any appellate jurisdiction has to be agreed to specifically by the parties, through acceptance of a convention enshrining it or otherwise. No appeal lies to the Court against the decision of some other judicial or arbitral body simply by way of a complaint that that body made a wrong decision. The matter is not a jurisdictional one: even if the parties concerned are linked by a general jurisdictional title (e.g. two optional-clause

---

[63] "Quelques observations sur l'intérêt à avoir une juridiction internationale unique", *International Law Forum, Journal of the International Law Association*, "Zero Issue", July 1998, p. 13. The idea of long experience has to be treated with caution, since the composition of the Court changes over time (as was only too evident in 1966 in the *South West Africa* case!), but there is a certain coherent and continuing spirit discernible in the Court's jurisprudence.

[64] For a thorough study of the Court's current working methods, and of the possibilities (which proved to be very limited) of enabling it to get through more cases, see the publication of the British Society of International and Comparative law, *The International Court of Justice: Process, Practice amd Procedure*, BIICL 1997.

[65] I.C.J. Reports 1972, p. 46.

[66] E.g., the 1947 Chicago Convention on Civil Aviation, under which the *ICAO Appeal* was brought: or Articles 29 (2) and 32 of the ILO Constitution, providing for appeals to the Court against the decision of a Commission of Enquiry concerning an alleged failure to comply with the Convention.

declarations without reservations), the Court cannot be asked to declare, in the application of international law, that the previous decision was wrong. In the case concerning the *Arbitral Award of 31 July 1989*, the Court was careful to emphasize that it was not acting as a court of appeal, but hearing an application alleging that the decision of the arbitral tribunal was a nullity, i.e. not that the tribunal had decided wrongly on the merits, but that it had committed an error in the assessment of its own jurisdiction[67]. The reason, it is submitted, why the Court cannot in such circumstances simply re-open the decision, and substitute its own view (even where the error of law on the merits may be regarded as flagrant), derives from the principle of *res judicata*. The parties having agreed that the first tribunal shall decide with binding force what their legal relationship is as regards the matter in dispute, that decision represents the law between them: thus, it might be more accurate to say, not that the Court cannot be asked to give its own view of the legal position, but that if so asked, its reply would have to be that the legal position is as the first tribunal found it to be – that is the *lex inter partes* [68]. This is not to say, of course, that the parties cannot *by agreement* bring an appeal to the International Court, and ask it to re-judge the matter *de novo*; but any unilateral attempt to impeach the original decision before the ICJ must be limited, as in the case of the *Arbitral Award of 31 July 1989*, to a request for a declaration of the nullity of the decision. Such a request cannot validly be based on a mere allegation that the original arbitrator made an error, of law or of fact, on the merits of the dispute, since even if this were correct, the decision would be a regular and proper one. It is only if the arbitrator exceeded his jurisdiction (which he may do, paradoxically enough, by failing to exercise it properly or fully) that it can be claimed that there is no valid decision. The consequence may be a fresh decision *by the arbitrator*: all the ICJ can do is declare the nullity of the original decision. Thus this possibility does not serve to remedy any possible conflict of decisions on matters of merits.

The agreement of the parties that appeal shall lie against an initial decision may be *ex post facto*, in relation to a particular decision; but it is more appropriate that it be provided for in general and in advance. This was of course the situation in the *Appeal Relating to the Jurisdiction of the*

---

[67] *I.C.J. Reports 1991*, p. 62, para. 25.

[68] For a fuller discussion of this problem, see the present writer's article on "The Law and Procedure of the International Court of Justice: Part Nine", in 69 *BYBIL* (1998), at pp. 66-7.

ICAO Council, where the provision for appeals to the Court from decisions of the Council was made in the 1947 Chicago Convention on Civil Aviation and in the related Transit Agreement. A similar provision is to be found in, for example, Articles 29 (2) and 32 of the ILO Constitution.

It follows that the creation of appellate jurisdiction has to be "bottom-up" rather than "top-down": for the ICJ to declare in its Rules a power of entertaining appeals from any tribunal whatsoever would be ineffective; an amendment of the Statute could have the desired effect, but only through the consent of States to an appeal system, given by accession to the revised Statute. It would however be perfectly possible, as a legal matter, to amend individually the various constituent instruments, such as the Statute of the International Tribunal for the Law of the Sea, the Statutes of the two International Criminal Tribunals, or the WTO Disputes Settlement Understanding, to add an appeal provision. As already observed, even in the absence of such provisions, the parties to a given dispute could agree to have the first decision re-examined by the ICJ by way of a contentious procedure; but by definition the successful party at the first stage would be likely to be reluctant to agree. Only in a case where the first decision was satisfactory to neither party would this course have a chance of being followed.

Supervision through the ICJ Advisory Procedure

An alternative method whereby the International Court of Justice could play a role in securing consistency of international law as expressed in judicial and arbitral decisions would be by a request made to it, by an organ possessing the necessary competence, for an advisory opinion. Such a request could be made either *ante factum* or *ex post facto*: i.e., the ICJ could be asked by the tribunal itself to rule on a doubtful point before the tribunal delivered its own judgment; or an appropriate organ could ask for an advisory opinion on the correctness of a decision of another tribunal as to which doubts had been raised. In the first case, the tribunal would put a case for opinion; in the second, the question submitted for opinion would presumably be on the lines of "Is the decision of the [specified tribunal] of [date] in the case concerning [etc.] in accordance with international law?"; or it might be limited to asking whether a particular finding in the challenged decision was in accordance with law[69].

The idea of making use of the Court's advisory function *ante factum* enjoys the support of Judge Schwebel, currently President of the ICJ; in his address of 26 October 1999 to the General Assembly, he suggested that

"in order to minimize such possibility as may occur of significant conflicting interpretations of international law, there might be virtue in enabling other international tribunals to request advisory opinions of the International Court of Justice on issues of international law that arise in cases before those tribunals that are of importance to the unity of international law."

President Schwebel goes on to discuss the constitutional possibilities for requests for advisory opinion, taking into account Article 96 of the Charter; but if the proposal is that such a procedure is authorized under international law as it now stands, it is suggested that there is a more fundamental difficulty.

The jurisdiction of international tribunals depends on the consent of States, and its scope and extent is determined by that consent. If States entrust the decision of a particular question to a given tribunal, it is the decision of that tribunal that they have consented to accept. (On the practical level, the States parties may not be best pleased to see the tribunal which they have chosen – possibly in order to obtain a speedy decision – suspend the proceedings pending a reference to the overburdened Court at The Hague.) But as a matter of legal principle, can the tribunal, to which they have delegated the power to determine their mutual rights and obligations, delegate[70] in its turn some part of that decision-making power to some other body, however competent? It may be argued that an advisory opinion is of its nature non-binding, and therefore the tribunal retains the power of decision which the parties have entrusted to it; but the whole purpose of the procedure is to obtain an authoritative ruling from the principal judicial organ of the United Nations, and if, not merely in theory but as a practical matter, the tribunal is free to depart from that ruling, there seems little point in asking for it. If therefore the advisory opinion is to be made binding by

---

[69] The first technique is of course already recognized in the context of the European Union, where a national court may, and in some cases must, refer a point of Community Law to the European Court of Justice for a ruling under Article 177 of the Treaty of Rome.

[70] The principle *delegatus non potest delegare* is recognized in some systems of administrative law.

some form of international agreement, it must apparently be an agreement of the parties, or a general instrument by which both they and the tribunal itself are bound, e.g. a revision of the statute of the tribunal in question.

Furthermore, a request for advisory opinion is only likely to be made where the point of law is doubtful, admitting of more than one view, and not (for example) where there is a already a clear decision of the ICJ. Thus by definition, whichever way the tribunal decides, the problem will not be one of conflict of decisions or fragmentation of law: at most, one side in a controversy will have received some judicial support. Can it be assumed, even by those who take the opposite view, that the ICJ would have decided the other way had it been asked to do so?

Turning to the constitutional question of the mechanism of requests for opinion, President Schwebel observes that the Yugoslavia and Ruanda tribunals are organs of the United Nations, and could request the Security Council to request opinions on their behalf; to this may be added the apparent possibility of their being authorized, under Article 96, paragraph 2, of the Charter to request such opinions themselves. The President continues:

> "There is room for the argument that even international tribunals that are not United Nations organs, such as the International Tribunal for the Law of the Sea, or the International Criminal Court when established[71], might, if they so decide, request the General Assembly – perhaps through the medium of a special committee established for the purpose – to request advisory opinions of the Court."

Apart from being cumbersome, this procedure reinforces the difficulty as to the impact of the opinion on the tribunal concerned; is it to be regarded as bound by an opinion not even given directly to the tribunal, but to an intermediary organ? One may recall the anomalies and difficulties attaching to the procedure (now abolished) of requests for advisory opinion under Article 11 of the Statute of the United Nations Administrative Tribunals. Once again, it would seem essential at least that there exist a text, binding on the tribunal and on the parties

---

[71] It would seem that the International Criminal Court is not, and cannot be, a subsidiary organ of the United Nations, but could become a "treaty organ": see Sarooshi, "The Statute of the International Criminal Court", 48 *ICLQ* (1999), p. 394.

before it, requiring the tribunal to respect the opinion and give judgment in accordance with it.

The other possible use – *ex post facto* – of the advisory competence of the International Court is today a possibility if the opinion is requested by the Security Council or the General Assembly, since they are empowered to ask for opinion on "any legal question". Such a procedure is at first sight attractive as a means of resolving a conflict of decisions between two courts other than the ICJ, or of correcting what has been widely regarded as an erroneous decision. Nothing however can be done if the Court advises that a given decision of another tribunal is unsound, as being not in accordance with international law; not merely will the decision impeached still stand as *res judicata* between the parties, but in fact a conflict of interpretation of international law will have been created. Again, the original decision is most unlikely to have been flagrantly in contradiction with a rule of law clearly established, by judicial decision or otherwise; it is more likely to have chosen one side – arguably the wrong side – in an existing controversy. Thus while publicists may criticise the decision severely, no judicial conflict will, as things now stand, come into existence until the same point arises in a case before another tribunal. It is also not unknown for a judicial decision regarded, on its delivery, as out of step with existing accepted law, to prove influential as a pioneering operation[72].

There is also, once again, the problem of consent as basis of jurisdiction. It is established in the case-law of the ICJ that the consent of States concerned in the matter is not a condition for the exercise of the advisory jurisdiction; but that it is a relevant consideration as regards the propriety of giving effect to the request, and in particular, it is relevant to enquire whether the advisory procedure is being used to get round the consent principle[73]. What weight is to be given to the consent, or lack of it, on the part of the parties to the original case, when determining whether it is proper to give an advisory opinion assessing the validity of the judgment given? Assuming that one party is a clear winner and the other a clear loser, the former is unlikely to favour a possible condemnation of the decision, even if its force as *res judicata* is unaffected.

---

[72] One may think of the ICJ decision on the effect of reservations in the case of *Reservations to the Genocide Convention*.

[73] See *Western Sahara*, I.C.J. Reports 1975, pp. 24-25, paras. 32-33; the "Mazilu" case. *Applicability of Article VI, Section 22, of the Convention on Privileges and Immunities*, I.C.J. Reports 1989, pp. 190-192, paras. 37-39.

CONCLUSION

In brief, the suggestion of this paper is that the dangers of fragmentation of international law and of conflict of decisions have not been under-estimated but, if anything, exaggerated: such dangers certainly exist in theory, but there is little trace at present of their becoming realized. The fact that two tribunals apply the same principles and rules to situations which bear an apparent close resemblance, and yet come up with different answers, is a tribute to the flexibility of those principles and rules rather than a sign of fragmentation. Conflicts of jurisdiction are not excluded by the texts currently in force governing the various international tribunals, but it is doubtful whether they could be, without a restructuring of international judicial organs which is in practice not feasible. The solution of supervision by the International Court of Justice, of such theoretical attractiveness, presents more complications, practical and legal, than might at first be apparent.

THE PROLIFERATION OF INTERNATIONAL JUDICIAL ORGANS: THE ROLE OF THE INTERNATIONAL COURT OF JUSTICE

Dietmar W. Prager *

THE BENEFITS OF PROLIFERATION

The creation of new international tribunals is a positive development which reflects the vitality and maturity of today's international life. As President Schwebel has pointed out, it "evidences the understanding that the effectiveness of international law can be increased by equipping legal obligations with means of their determination and enforcement"[1].

It is one of the merits of proliferation that it has broadened the access of actors to the international judicial system. International litigation is no longer a matter over which States have a monopoly, as more international tribunals grant standing to individuals, corporations, NGOs and international organizations. Proliferation also contributes to the process of making international law more objective, by reducing the power of sovereign States to appreciate themselves the legality of their acts.

An increase in international litigation is likely to promote the evolution of public international law. The growing number of judicial decisions will enrich the body of jurisprudence which interprets and develops the international legal system. This has become evident above all in the field of human rights, where major legal developments are the result of the jurisprudence of human rights tribunals. Similar

---

* At the time of writing, Legal Officer at the Registry of the International Court of Justice. The views expressed are solely those of the author and do not engage the responsibility of the International Court of Justice

[1] Schwebel, S., Address by the President of the International Court of Justice to the General Assembly of the United Nations, 27 October 1998, www.icj-cij.org

developments are presently unfolding in other specialized areas, such as international criminal law or international economic law.

As a positive side effect, proliferation is likely to further the acceptance by the public of international law as a true system of law. Today, international litigation is found in headline news. The rapidly growing number of applications filed at the human rights tribunals are another sign of an increased public awareness.

The International Court of Justice does not appear so far to have been negatively affected by the existence of other adjudicatory bodies. This is in particular true with regard to those international judicial bodies with a distinct jurisdiction *ratione personae* or *ratione materiae*. While standing before the Court is limited under Article 34, paragraph 1, of its Statute, to States, several judicial bodies grant access to other actors in the international field. The most notable examples are the regional human rights courts, but there are also claims and compensation bodies, the ICSID, the World Bank Inspection Panel, the family of international administrative tribunals and the group of quasi-judicial human rights bodies. International criminal tribunals, such as the International Criminal Tribunal for the Former Yugoslavia (ICTY) and for Rwanda (ICTR) and the future International Criminal Court (ICC), determine the responsibility of individuals under international law. Tribunals of more advanced regional economic integration agreements, while usually allowing access both to State and non-State actors, chiefly apply the legal norms of their integration scheme, which are generally recognized to have a *sui generis* character[2].

But even with regard to those international judicial bodies which do settle inter-State disputes on questions of international law, it appears that the International Court of Justice has so far not been negatively affected. The option to refer a dispute to an arbitral tribunal rather than to the World Court has existed ever since its creation. It may well be that a number of cases, which could have been brought to the Court since 1922, were submitted to arbitration instead. This has, for example, been suggested particularly with regard to the *Beagle Channel* case[3] and most recently, the *Eritrea/Yemen* case[4]. In both cases,

---

[2] Ipsen, H.P.: Europäisches Gemeinschaftsrecht (1972) at 62 *et seq.*; ECJ, Rs 11/70 Internationale Handelsgesellschaft/Einfuhr – und Vorratsstelle für Getreide und Futtermittel, Slg 1970, 1125; With regard to the Mercosur, see for example, Viterbori, J.C.: Solución de controversias en el Mercosur, 59 La Ley (1995), No.20, 1.

[3] Case concerning a dispute between Argentina and Chile concerning the Beagle Channel, R.I.A.A. Vol.XXI, 55.

the arbitral panels were entirely or almost entirely constituted by current or former members of the International Court of Justice. On the other hand, it may equally be suggested that some of the cases which were submitted to an *ad hoc* Chamber of the Court, might have gone to arbitration instead if the revision of the Rules of Court in 1972 or 1978 had not granted the parties more influence with regard to the composition of the *ad hoc* Chamber[5]. In the large, international arbitration and international adjudication have co-existed peacefully and there is little indication that the one has negatively affected the other. On the contrary, the case-law of the Court has been supportive of the processes of international arbitration.

The fact that regional human rights courts may also settle inter-State disputes has likewise not decreased recourse to the International Court of Justice. So far, only two inter-State cases have been submitted to the European Court of Human Rights and none to the Inter-American Court of Human Rights. At the same time, quite a number of cases before the World Court have dealt with human rights issues and the Court has made important contributions to the development of human rights law[6].

It is too early to speculate whether the recent creation of regional judicial bodies with wide subject matter jurisdiction on questions of international law would affect the International Court of Justice. The Central American Court of Justice, *inter alia*, has general jurisdiction *ratione materiae* in international legal disputes, including any frontier or maritime disputes arising between its Member States[7]. Prior to the creation of the Central American Court, boundary disputes between

---

[4] Eritrea/Yemen case, for the text of the two awards, see www.pca-cpa.org

[5] Valencia-Ospina, E.: The use of Chambers of the International Court of Justice, in: Lowe, V. and Fitzmaurice, M.: Fifty years of the International Court of Justice: essays in honour of Sir Robert Jennings (1996), 503; Schwebel, S.M.: Chambers of the ICJ formed for particular cases, in: Justice in international law (1994), 93; Mosler, H.: The ad hoc Chambers of the International Court of Justice: evaluation after five years of experience, in: Dinstein, Y.: International law at a time of perplexity: essays in honour of S. Rosenne (1989), 449.

[6] Schwebel, S.: Human Rights in the World Court, in: Pathak, R.S. and Dhokalia, D.P. (eds.): International Law in Transition, Essays in Memory of Judge Nagendra Singh, New Dehli, 1992; and idem: The contribution of the International Court of Justice to the development of human rights; address on the occasion of the opening ceremony of the fifth session of the International Bioethics Committee of UNESCO, Nordwijk, 2 December 1998, www.icj-cij.org

[7] See Article 12, paragraph a), of the Statute of the Central American Court of Justice. Unlike other disputes, frontier, territorial or maritime disputes may only be brought before the Central American Court of Justice by special agreement.

States of the region had been submitted to the International Court of Justice and successfully resolved. Although the Central American Court has otherwise had an active start, no disputes of this kind have as yet been submitted to it. The OSCE Court of Conciliation and Arbitration likewise enjoys wide subject matter jurisdiction over questions of general international law[8]. To date, no cases have been brought before it.

The International Tribunal for the Law of the Sea has just started its judicial activity, so that here too, any effects on the International Court of Justice are conjectural. Cases involving questions of maritime delimitation nevertheless continue to be brought before the International Court of Justice. There are currently four such cases on the Court's docket[9].

In view of these developments, President Schwebel was right in pointing out that concerns that the proliferation of international tribunals might produce "evisceration of the docket of the International Court of Justice have not materialized". Indeed, there are more cases pending before the Court than ever before in the Court's history. In 1998, four disputes were submitted to the Court and in 1999, seventeen new cases were filed before the Court. By the end of 1999, the Court's general list includes twenty-four cases. There is reason to surmise that the Court will continue to remain busy.

It thus appears that the increasing choice between different judicial bodies does not necessarily lead to a diversion of cases from one court to another. Instead, these developments – as preliminary as they are – appear to confirm that the increase in the number of international judicial bodies has also led to an increase in the overall number of cases submitted to international adjudication. The greater the number of disputes submitted to adjudication, the more States will become

---

[8] See Articles 18 and 26, paragraph 2, of the Convention on Conciliation and Arbitration within the OSCE; printed in 32 I.L.M. (1993), 557. The OSCE Court is not a standing judicial body. States may, however, accept its jurisdiction as compulsory (see Article 26, paragraph 2, of the Convention). The Convention provides for a mechanism which enables a party to a dispute to require, under certain circumstances, the establishment of an arbitral tribunal. The OSCE Court is therefore covered by Professor Thirlway's definition of an "international tribunal".

[9] Maritime Delimitation and Territorial Questions between Qatar and Bahrain; Land and Maritime Boundary between Cameroon and Nigeria (*Cameroon v. Nigeria*); Sovereignty over Pulau Ligitan and Pulau Sigatan (*Indonesia/Malaysia*). On 8 December 1999, Nicaragua filed an application instituting proceedings against Honduras concerning "legal issues subsisting between the Republic of Nicaragua and the Republic of Honduras concerning maritime delimitation".

inclined to follow that example. While twenty years ago, recourse to adjudication was considered as a "last resort" if all other means of dispute settlement had failed, it has now become more of a routine matter in international relations and is often used complementarily to other methods of dispute settlement.

THE NEED FOR INTERNATIONAL JUDICIAL BODIES TO GIVE DUE WEIGHT TO EACH OTHER'S DECISIONS

A major concern has been that the multiplication of international judicial bodies might lead to a fragmentation of international law. While it would be desirable that general international law was the same for all States at any given moment[10], complete unity has never existed in international law[11]. Processes of the development of customary international law are neither uniform nor unified. Many customary norms have developed on a regional or a sub-regional, rather than a universal level. States may also unilaterally exclude themselves from the application of new customary international law. Treaty-making is bilateral as well as multilateral, and many multilateral treaties fail to attract universal adherence. There is also some diversity among different regional traditions in international law, among competing ideologies, and between the approaches of developed and less developed States of the international community. Diverging views not only exist among States, but one observes occasionally considerable gaps between State practice. Divergent views of international lawyers on questions of international law are obvious. This does not exclude the judges sitting on the Bench of the International Court of Justice. Most decisions are not taken unanimously and judges are free to state their views in separate and dissenting opinions, a right of which they make ready use.

It is reasonable to suggest that these diverse elements may have contributed to the development of international law rather than

---

[10] Charney, J.I.: Universal International Law, 87 *AJIL* (1993), 522
[11] On the problem of the fragmentation of international law and its effects on the coherence of the international legal system, see: Valticos, N.: Pluralité des ordres juridiques internationaux et unité du droit international, in: Makarczyk, J. (ed.): Theory of international law at the threshold of the 21st century (1996), 301; Barnhoorn, L.A. and Wellens, K.C.: Diversity in secondary rules and the unity of international law (1995); Jessup, P.C.: Diversity and Uniformity in the Law of Nations, 58 *AJIL* (1964), 341.

impeded it. Proliferation of tribunals adds an additional element to this already existing diversity. There is some possibility that different tribunals might reach different conclusions on the same international legal questions. Is this additional element likely to upset the balance by increasing diversity to such a degree as to jeopardize the coherence of international law?

The possibility of conflicting decisions between different judicial bodies cannot be excluded, but it should not be assumed or magnified. It is important that international judicial bodies do not seek to establish their identity by deliberately developing distinctive viewpoints. Rather they share not only the common purpose of judicially settling disputes, but also that of developing international law. They can best do so if they give due weight to the decisions of other international courts and tribunals.

Several examples of such mutual respect may already be found in the jurisprudence of most international judicial bodies. International arbitral tribunals, for instance, have amply relied on the jurisprudence of the Permanent Court of International Justice and the ICJ. The fast growing jurisprudence of the ICTY also reveals a notable reliance on the case-law of other international judicial bodies, such as the ICJ, the European Court for Human Rights and the Inter-American Court for Human Rights[12]. The WTO dispute settlement panels and its Appellate Body have occasionally referred to the jurisprudence of the ICJ when clarifying provisions of WTO agreements in accordance with customary rules of interpretation of public international law in accordance with Article 3, paragraph 2, of the WTO Dispute Settlement Understanding[13].

---

[12] See, for example, *The Prosecutor v. Dusko Tadic*, Judgment of 2 October 1995, reprinted in 35 I.L.M. 32 (1996), with reference to Effect of Awards of Compensation Made by the United Nations Administrative Tribunal, Advisory Opinion, I.C.J. Reports 1954, and Nottebohm, Preliminary Objection, Judgment, I.C.J. Reports 1953; see also *The Prosecutor v. Anto Furundzija*, Judgment of 10 December 1998, reprinted in 38 *I.L.M.* 317 (1999), paras.144,160 and 163.

[13] United States – Import Prohibitions of Certain Shrimp and Shrimp Products, WT/DS58/R, reprinted in 37 *I.L.M.* (1998), 834; at para. 7.41 and United States – Import Prohibitions of Certain Shrimp and Shrimp Products, WT/DS58/AB/R, 12 October 1998, reprinted in 38 *I.L.M.* (1999), 121, para. 130, with reference to Legal Consequences for States of the Continued Presence of South Africa in Namibia (South West Africa) notwithstanding Security Council Resolution 276 (1970), Advisory Opinion, I.C.J. Reports 1971; and at para. 158 with reference to: Border and Transborder Armed Actions (*Nicaragua v. Honduras*), Jurisdiction and Admissibility, Judgment, I.C.J. Reports 1988; Rights of Nationals of the United

The International Tribunal for the Law of the Sea, in its Judgment of 1 July 1999 in the *M/V "Saiga" (No.2)* case, referred to the ICJ's recent case concerning the *Gabcíkovo-Nagymaros Project (Hungary/Slovakia)*[14], when establishing the conditions for the defense based on state of necessity to justify an otherwise international wrongful act[15], and to the PCIJ's well-known holding in the *Factory at Chorzów* case[16], when defining the nature of reparation[17]. The arbitral award in the *SS. "I'm Alone"* case[18] served as precedent for the finding that, in case of use of force in enforcement operations at sea, appropriate warning had to be issued to the ship and all efforts should be made to ensure that life is not endangered[19]. In its recent Order indicating provisional measures in the *Southern Bluefin Tuna* case, the Tribunal relied on the World Court's jurisprudence regarding the definition of a dispute[20].

The ICJ has referred in some of its recent cases to several arbitral awards. In the case concerning the *Gabcíkovo-Nagymaros Project (Hungary/Slovakia)*, for example, the Court relied *inter alia* on a decision of the arbitral tribunal in the *Air Service Agreement* case[21] when establishing the conditions a counter-measure must meet[22].

These examples mark a positive trend which future decisions would do well to develop. Such mutual reliance on each other's decisions might be further increased by affording members of the diverse courts and tribunals better access to the case-law of the international judiciary.

States of America in Morocco *(France v. United States of America)*, Judgment, I.C.J. Reports 1952; Fisheries, Judgment, I.C.J. Reports 1951.

[14] Gabcíkovo-Nagymaros Project *(Hungary/Slovakia)*, Judgment, I.C.J. Reports 1997, 7.

[15] M/V "Saiga"(No.2) *(Saint Vincent and the Grenadines v. Guinea)*, Judgment, para. 133.

[16] Factory at Chorzów, Merits, Judgment No.13, 1928, P.C.I.J. Series A, No.17.

[17] M/V "Saiga"(No.2) *(Saint Vincent and the Grenadines v. Guinea)*, Judgment, para. 170.

[18] SS "I'm Alone", R.I.A.A., Vol. III, 1609.

[19] M/V "Saiga"(No.2) *(Saint Vincent and the Grenadines v. Guinea)*, Judgment, para. 156.

[20] Southern Bluefin Tuna *(New Zealand v. Japan; Australia v. Japan)*, Provisional Measures, Order of 27 August 1999, para.44, citing: Mavrommatis Palestine Concessions, Judgment No.2, 1924, P.C.I.J. Series A, No.2, 11; South West Africa, Preliminary Objections, Judgment, I.C.J. Reports 1962, 328.

[21] Air Service Agreement of 27 March 1946 between the United States of America and France, R.I.A.A., Vol. XVIII, 443 *et seq*.

[22] Gabcíkovo-Nagymaros Project *(Hungary/Slovakia)*, Judgment, I.C.J. Reports 1997, 7, at 55, para 83.

In this connection, it would be helpful to create a data-base containing the jurisprudence of all international judicial bodies.

Nonetheless, there have also been several examples where different judicial bodies have reached diverging conclusions. I agree with Professor Thirlway that the example most often cited in this connection, namely the *Loizidou v. Turkey* case[23] of the European Court of Human Rights, does not fall into this category. A human rights court should be free to apply a different standard of interpretation of its optional clause system than a court of general international law, in particular as regards the validity of reservations. In general, questions of jurisdiction are proper to each court and are not of such a character as to pose a threat to the unity of substantive international law.

Professor Thirlway mentions several examples of apparent inconsistencies between the jurisprudence of the ICTY and the ICJ[24]. In the recent judgment of the ICTY in the *Tadic* case[25], these apparent inconsistencies crystallized into a real conflict of jurisprudence. The Appeals Chamber of the Tribunal, in determining whether the armed conflict had an international character, had to establish under what legal conditions armed forces might be regarded as acting on behalf of a foreign power. It decided to examine this matter by applying the rules of state responsibility establishing the conditions under which an individual might be held to act as a *de facto* organ of a State. It questioned a finding of the ICJ in the case concerning *Military and Paramilitary Activities in and against Nicaragua (Nicaragua v. United States of America)*, in which the Court required that, in order for a State to be held responsible for violations of international humanitarian law committed by individuals, the State not only had to be in effective control of a military or paramilitary group but that the control be exercised with respect to the specific operation in the course of which the breaches may have been committed. The ICTY Appeals Chamber found that the ICJ's finding did "not seem to be consonant with the logic of the law of State responsibility"[26] and was "at variance with judicial and State practice"[27]. It then established some less stringent conditions, requiring an "overall control" by the State of the actions of

---

[23] Judgment of 23 March 1995, No.40/1993/435/514.
[24] Prosecutor v. Karadzic – Mladic, IT-95-5-R61 and IT-95-18-R61, decision of 11 July 1996; and *Prosecutor v. Rajic*, IT-95-12-R61, decision of 13 September 1996.
[25] *Prosecutor v. Dusko Tadic*, IT-94-1-A, Judgment of 15 July 1999
[26] *Ibid.*, para. 116 *et seq.*
[27] *Ibid.*, para. 124 *et seq.*

the military or paramilitary group which did not need to extend to the issuance of specific orders or instructions relating to single military actions[28]. The Appeals Chamber came to its decision after closely examining State practice and various decisions of municipal courts.

The principle that international judicial organs should mutually respect each other's decisions does not prevent a judicial organ from exceptionally coming to a different conclusion than another organ, if it is convinced that the previous ruling was erroneous or that, due to subsequent developments in international law, the previous decision no longer reflects the current law. It is desirable that such findings contain sufficient reasoning specifying the grounds on which a diverging conclusion has been reached.

THE SUPERVISORY FUNCTION OF THE INTERNATIONAL COURT OF JUSTICE

The current international legal order has not devised any hierarchical order among international judicial bodies and thus no system of appeal or of cassation. It has nonetheless been observed that there exists a need to define some sort of legal relationship between the different courts and tribunals, which could strengthen the coherence of international law and avoid the danger of developing autonomous sub-systems[29]. Any solution which could be achieved only through an amendment of the UN Charter appears, however, to be unlikely in view of the present political circumstances. It will therefore probably be necessary for the participants in the international process to design such a system within the existing constitutional framework.

In this connection, Professor Thirlway discusses a supervisory role of the International Court of Justice, which he recognizes to be the "obvious body to exercise such powers". While the UN Charter designates the ICJ as the "principal judicial organ of the United Nations", it has not endowed the Court with the status of a supreme

---

[28] *Ibid.*, para. 145.

[29] Abi-Saab, G.: Fragmentation or Unification: Some Concluding Remarks, 31 NYU *JILP* (1999), 919; Orrego Vicuña, F. and Pinto, C.: The Peaceful Settlement of Disputes: Prospects for the Twenty-First Century, Preliminary Report for the 1999 Centennial of the First International Peace Conference, paras. 103 *et seq.*; Petersmann, E.-U.: Constitutionalism and International Adjudication: How to Constitutionalize the U.N. Dispute Settlement System, 31 NYU *JILP* (1999), 753; Jennings, R.: The Role of the International Court of Justice, 68 *BYIL* (1997), 62.

court of international law with review authority. However, the meaning of the phrase "principal judicial organ of the United Nations" has acquired practical importance in the context of the proliferation of international judicial bodies.

The ICJ enjoys general jurisdiction over all questions of international law and all member States of the United Nations are *ipso facto* parties to its Statute. Its Bench represents, in accordance with Article 9 of the Court's Statute, "the main forms of civilization" and "the principal legal systems of the world", which enables the Court to develop principles of international law from a universalist perspective, taking account of the various legal traditions. The international community has taken the Court's findings on general international law seriously. The Court's decisions continue to be the most frequently analyzed by legal scholars and the most frequently relied upon by other international judicial bodies. As Professor Charney put it: "The ICJ's decisions reflect a perspective of a Court unsullied by narrow limitations that a special regime may impose on a forum. Thus, its pronouncements on general international law necessarily are more persuasive than similar pronouncements given by tribunals with specialized jurisdiction and narrow perspectives"[30].

SUPERVISION THROUGH THE ICJ ADVISORY PROCEDURE

Professor Thirlway examines the question of whether a possible supervisory role by the ICJ could best be exercised through its advisory or its contentious jurisdiction. I shall first comment on the idea of making use of the Court's advisory function in order to secure consistency in international law. It has been suggested by various authors[31] that a tribunal might request an advisory opinion from the ICJ on certain points of general international law arising in a dispute before it that are of importance to the unity of international law. This suggestion is inspired by Article 234 (former Article 177) of the Treaty of Rome, which allows national courts to refer certain questions of EC

---

[30] Charney, J.I.: The Impact on the International Legal System of the Growth of International Courts and Tribunals, 31 NYU *JILP* (1999), 697, at 706.

[31] Orrego Vicuña, F. and Pinto, C., *op.cit.*, paras. 138 *et seq.*; Sohn, L.B.: Important Improvements in the Functioning of the Principal Organs of the United Nations that can be made without Charter Revision, 91 *AJIL* (1997), 652; Guillaume, G.: The future of international judicial institutions, 44 *ICLQ* (1995), 848; Szasz, P.C.: Enhancing the Advisory Competence of the World Court, in: Gross, L.: The Future of the International Court of Justice, Vol.II, 1976, 499.

law to the European Communities Court of Justice, a mechanism which is recognized to have significantly contributed to the uniform interpretation of European Community law[32]. The idea was recently taken up by President Schwebel in his address of 26 October 1999 to the General Assembly[33].

If the international judicial organ is an organ of the United Nations (e.g. ICTY, ICTR, UN Administrative Tribunals), the General Assembly could authorize it under Article 96, paragraph 2, of the UN Charter to request advisory opinions of the ICJ. The tribunals could then, if they wish, refer certain questions of general international law directly to the ICJ. However, none of the United Nations judicial organs has so far been authorized by the General Assembly to request advisory opinions.

A second possibility is that international judicial organs transmit their request to the ICJ via an organ duly authorized under Article 96 of the UN Charter to request advisory opinions from the Court. For example, the ICTY and the ICTR might request the Security Council to request an advisory opinion on their behalf. The United Nations Administrative Tribunals might request the General Assembly or comparable organs of specialized agencies to request advisory opinions on their behalf. In the view of President Schwebel:

> "there is room for the argument that even international tribunals that are not UN organs, such as the International Tribunal for the Law of the Sea or the International Criminal Court when established, might, if they so decide, request the General Assembly - perhaps through the medium of a special committee established for that purpose – to request advisory opinions of the Court"[34].

The General Assembly has competence to request advisory opinions on behalf of international judicial bodies that are not UN organs, since it is empowered to request advice "on any legal question" and has also the broad mandate, under Article 13, paragraph 1 (a) of the

---

[32] See, for example, Dauses, M.: Das Vorabentscheidungsverfahren nach Artikel 177 EG-Vertrag, 2nd ed. (1995), at 43 *et seq.*; Andenas, M.: Article 177 References to the European Court – Policy and Practice (1994); Bebr, G.: Examen en validité au titre de l'article 177 du traité CEE et cohésion juridique de la communauté, 11 *Cahiers de droit européen* (1975), 379.

[33] Schwebel, S.M.: Address by the President of the International Court of Justice to the General Assembly of the United Nations, 26 October 1999, www.icj-cij.org

[34] *Ibid.*

UN Charter, to "encourage the progressive development of international law".

Professor Thirlway suggests that the procedure of reference raises a number of difficulties. He first voices doubt as to whether the consent of the parties to submit a dispute to one particular tribunal would also cover the reference by that tribunal of certain questions arising out of that dispute to the International Court of Justice. This problem does not arise with regard to the international criminal tribunals, such as the ICTY, the ICTR and the future ICC. With regard to other international judicial bodies, the consent of parties is certainly an important matter. In the first instance, it should be for the judicial body to which the parties have submitted the dispute to ensure the parties' consent for the reference of certain points of law to the Court. Here, one should not assume that parties would always be opposed to the procedure of reference, in particular, since the tribunal of their choice retains the power of decision which the parties have entrusted to it. Moreover, "consent" does not necessarily mean the current agreement of all parties that a particular question be referred to the ICJ. For example, a provision might be included in a Statute to allow for reference of certain questions of general international law to the ICJ. In ratifying or acceding to that Statute, a State *ipso facto* would consent to the procedure of reference. Consent of States may also be implied if the international judicial body was authorized by the UN General Assembly in accordance with Article 96, paragraph 2, of the UN Charter, to request advisory opinions from the Court.

As regards the International Court of Justice, it is not certain whether it would insist on the consent of the parties. Its jurisprudence suggests that it would not. In its Opinion on the *Interpretation of Peace Treaties*, the Court held that:

> "the consent of States, parties to a dispute, is the basis of the Court's jurisdiction in contentious cases. The situation is different in regard to advisory proceedings even where the Request for an Opinion relates to a legal question actually pending between States [...] The Court's Opinion is given not to the States, but to the organ which is entitled to request it"[35]

---

[35] Interpretation of Peace Treaties with Bulgaria, Hungary and Romania, First Phase, Advisory Opinion, I.C.J. Reports 1950, at 71. The Court further held that: "[t]he existence, in the background, of a dispute the parties to which may be affected as a consequence of the Court's opinion, does not change the advisory nature of the Court's task, which is to answer the questions put to it", Application

In the *Western Sahara* Opinion, the Court further found that a State which

> "is a Member of the United Nations and has accepted the provisions of the Charter and Statute [...] has thereby in general given its consent to the exercise of the Court of its advisory jurisdiction"[36].

In this connection, it should be noted that the parties to the dispute would be allowed to participate in the ICJ's advisory procedure and would thus have the opportunity to fully defend their views. Under Article 66, paragraph 2, of the Statute, any State entitled to appear before the Court may file written statements and possibly present oral arguments.

Professor Thirlway also addresses the question of the non-binding nature of advisory opinions. While advisory opinions are indeed non-binding, they are nonetheless considered to be highly authoritative statements of general international law. If an international judicial body decides to refer certain points of international law to the ICJ, it has to be supposed that it intends to follow the ruling of the Court, otherwise the request would make little sense. The same holds true if the opinion is not formally requested by the judicial body itself, but on its behalf by a "transmitting organ", such as the General Assembly or the Security Council.

There is therefore little point in making the Court's opinions binding by means of an international agreement. To do so would nevertheless be possible, for example by agreement of the parties or by a general instrument by which both the parties and the international judicial body itself are bound, such as an amendment to the Statute of the international judicial body in question. In the view of the ICJ, it is irrelevant to the Court's own functions what the parties do or agreed to do with an advisory opinion[37].

A third problem raised by Professor Thirlway is that reference to the "overburdened Court in The Hague" might result in an unduly prolonged suspension of the proceedings before the tribunal chosen by the parties "possibly in order to obtain a speedy decision". This concern

---

for Review of Judgment No. 158 of the United Nations Administrative Tribunal, Advisory Opinion, I.C.J. Reports 1973, at 173.

[36] Western Sahara, Advisory Opinion, I.C.J. Reports 1975, at 30.

[37] Difference relating to Immunity from Legal Process of a Special Rapporteur of the Commission on Human Rights, Advisory Opinion, I.C.J. Reports 1999, para. 25; Judgments of the Administrative Tribunal of the ILO upon complaints made against UNESCO, Advisory Opinion, I.C.J. Reports 1956, 77, at 84.

appears, however, not to be justified. Pursuant to Article 103 of the Rules of Court, the body requesting an advisory opinion may inform the Court that "its request necessitates an urgent answer". The Court shall then "take all necessary steps to accelerate the procedure, and it shall convene as early as possible for the purpose of proceeding to a hearing and deliberation on the request". The Court has shown on various occasions that, despite its heavy workload, it can act fast if the circumstances so require. In the *LaGrand* case[38], for example, the Court agreed unanimously on an indication of provisional measures within less than twenty-four hours of receipt of the Application. It should also be taken into account that the Court's advice would be requested only on one or a few particular points of general international law. The Court would thus not have to tackle a whole range of complex factual and legal issues and its opinion could therefore be relatively brief.

While the procedure of reference represents a new and yet untested use of the Court's advisory function, there have already been several examples of what Professor Thirlway calls an *ex post facto* use of the Court's advisory function, i.e. the request for an advisory opinion on the correctness of a decision of another international judicial body. Until recently, the Statute of the UN Administrative Tribunal (UNAT) provided for a system of recourse through the Court's advisory jurisdiction if a judgment of the Tribunal was challenged on the ground that the Tribunal had exceeded its jurisdiction, or that it had failed to exercise jurisdiction vested in it, had erred on a question of law relating to provisions of the Charter, or had committed a fundamental error in procedure which occasioned a failure of justice[39]. The challenge could be made by a member State, the Secretary-General or the staff member concerned. A special Committee for Review of Administrative Tribunal Judgements was established to filter applications for review and was authorized by the General Assembly to request advisory opinions from the Court. The Committee has on three occasions requested advisory opinions for the review of UNAT Judgements No.158[40], No.273[41] and

---

[38] LaGrand (*Germany v. United States of America*), Order indicating provisional measures, I.C.J. Reports 1999.

[39] See former Article 11 of the Statute of the UN Administrative Tribunal. The system of recourse through the advisory function of the International Court of Justice was established by General Assembly resolution 957 (X) of 8 November 1955 and abolished by General Assembly resolution 50/54 of 11 December 1995.

[40] Application for Review of Judgement No.158 of the United Nations Administrative Tribunal, Advisory Opinion, I.C.J. Reports 1973, 166.

No.333[42]. The UNAT Statute determined that the Court's advisory opinion would be considered as binding.

The Statute of the Administrative Tribunal of the International Labour Organization (ILOAT) also establishes a mechanism under which the ILO Governing Body or the Executive Board of an international organization, having recognized the Tribunal's jurisdiction, might submit the question of the validity of an ILOAT decision for an advisory opinion to the ICJ[43], if that decision had been challenged on certain grounds. One such opinion was requested by the Executive Board of UNESCO[44]. The ILOAT Statute also provides that the opinion given by the Court should be binding. If an advisory opinion is requested, the Tribunal's decision does not become *res judicata* between the parties until the Court has rendered its opinion concerning the validity of that decision.

SUPERVISION THROUGH THE CONTENTIOUS PROCEDURE OF THE ICJ

The supervisory function of the International Court of Justice, in the framework of its contentious procedure, has been developed with respect to international arbitration. At the core of these developments was the question whether a State might challenge the validity of a final and binding arbitral award by means of an unilateral application under the optional clause system of the Court's Statute. In the case concerning the *Société Commerciale de Belgique*[45], the Permanent Court of International Justice, viewing itself as *pars inter parem* with arbitral tribunals, refused to accept a general jurisdictional clause as a sufficient conferral of jurisdiction to do anything with respect to an international arbitral award, not even to confirm it, let alone to examine its validity. Instead, it required a clear manifestation of the parties' agreement to have the award examined by the Court.

The International Court of Justice has, however, assumed a different relationship towards international arbitral tribunals. In the

---

[41] Application for Review of Judgement No.273 of the United Nations Administrative Tribunal, Advisory Opinion, I.C.J. Reports 1982, 325.
[42] Application for Review of Judgement No.333 of the United Nations Administrative Tribunal, Advisory Opinion, I.C.J. Reports 1987, 18.
[43] See Article XII of the ILOAT Statute and the Annex to the ILOAT Statute.
[44] Judgments of the Administrative Tribunal of the ILO upon Complaints Made against UNESCO, Advisory Opinion, I.C.J. Reports 1956, at 77.
[45] Société Commerciale de Belgique, Judgment, 1939, P.C.I.J., Series A/B, No.78, 160.

case concerning the *Arbitral Award Made by the King of Spain on 23 December 1906*, it took a less stringent approach than the Permanent Court[46]; and in the case concerning the *Arbitral Award of 31 July 1989*[47], the Court took another decisive step by examining for the first time the validity of an arbitral award on the basis of an unilateral application filed under the optional clause system.

In this key decision, the Court appears to draw a distinction between a request to declare the nullity of an award (*recours en nullité*), under which the Court would examine, in interpreting the arbitral agreement, whether the arbitral tribunal correctly exercised its competence, and an appeal properly speaking, under which the Court would examine whether the arbitral award was right on the merits[48]. While the Court's jurisdiction for the former might be based on an unilateral application under the optional clause system, the latter requires a manifest agreement of the parties.

This is in line with Article 87, paragraph 1, of the Rules of Court, which requires "a treaty or convention in force" in order to have the Court decide on "a matter which has been the subject of proceedings before some other international body". The right to appeal against a previous decision on the merits might accordingly be agreed on by the parties in the post-adjudication phase[49]. It may also be included in an arbitral agreement or in a jurisdictional clause of an international convention providing for recourse to arbitration. Moreover, an appeal

---

[46] Arbitral Award Made by the King of Spain on 23 December 1906, Judgment, I.C.J. Reports 1960, 192. In that case, the parties had submitted the dispute on the validity of an arbitral award rendered by the King of Spain in 1906 to the ICJ on the basis of a common agreement through the instrument of the Washington Agreement. The legal significance of that agreement was far from clear and the Court did not explicitly confirm it as an adequate basis for its exercise of supervisory jurisdiction. The Court nonetheless proceeded to the merits of the dispute before it and confirmed the award. See Reisman, W.M.: The Supervisory Jurisdiction of the International Court of Justice: International Arbitration and International Adjudication, 258 RdC (1996), at 253 *et seq*.

[47] Arbitral Award of 31 July 1989, Judgment, I.C.J. Reports 1991, 53. The Court did so on the basis of a unilateral application, adding that the respondent had not disputed "that the Court had jurisdiction to entertain the application under Article 36, paragraph 2, of the Statute" (at 62, para.24). The judgment, however, left open whether this was a constituent fact for the jurisdiction over that matter, in the form of forum prorogatum. A number of individual opinions suggest that it was not.

[48] *Ibid.*, at 62, para. 24; and at 69, para. 47.

[49] See Guyomar, G.: Commentaire du Règlement de la Cour internationale de Justice (1983), at 560.

to the ICJ may be provided for in model laws for arbitration[50], or eventually, in the Statute of an international judicial body.

It follows that the development of a supervisory role of the International Court of Justice in the framework of its contentious procedure has to be a combined process in which both the International Court of Justice and States partake. The Court may define its relationship with other international judicial bodies through its jurisprudence. As shown above, the Court has so far moved steadily towards a vision of a broader political role which, according to Professor Reisman, is "likely to change the nature of its supervisory relationship to international arbitration"[51]. It remains, however, unclear whether this jurisprudence, which has been developed with respect to arbitral awards, would also apply to decisions of other international judicial bodies. Moreover, the Court's future role in this process is dependent on the kind of cases which will be submitted to it. States, on the other hand, may contribute to this process of further developing the supervisory function of the Court by providing, on a consensual basis, for a system of appeal to the International Court of Justice.

CONCLUSIONS

In sum, proliferation of international judicial bodies has so far yielded more benefits than disadvantages. The dangers of a further fragmentation of international law and of conflict of decisions could be mitigated if (a) international judicial bodies give due weight to the decisions of other international courts and tribunals and (b) if the supervisory function of the International Court of Justice, the "principal judicial organ of the United Nations" is further gradually developed. The development of the Court's supervisory function, in the framework of both its advisory function and its contentious procedure, may be achieved without an amendment of the international constitutional framework, but requires a combined effort of both the Court and the international community.

---

[50] The Model Rules on Arbitral Procedure, adopted by the ILC at its tenth session in 1958, provide for recourse to the ICJ if the validity of an award is challenged on certain grounds and, if it is not possible to submit the application to the tribunal which rendered the award, in cases of interpretation or revision. However, the Model Rules met with much criticism in the General Assembly.

[51] Reisman, W.M., op.cit., at 378.

THE DISPUTE SETTLEMENT SYSTEM OF THE WORLD TRADE ORGANIZATION: INSTITUTIONS, PROCESS AND PRACTICE

Florentino P. Feliciano and Peter L.H. Van den Bossche [1]

INTRODUCTION

Since its establishment on 1 January 1995, the World Trade Organization (the "WTO"), now 136 Members strong, has been the focal point of action and reaction by governments and civil society concerning international trade and economic globalization. Perhaps more than any other international organization in recent years, the WTO has engaged popular and scholarly attention. Much of that attention has been and is focused upon the WTO's unique dispute settlement system. The issues involved in some of the disputes brought to the WTO for resolution have deeply engaged public opinion in the countries concerned and have precipitated political debate. This has been the case, for example, with regard to the dispute on the European Union's preferential import

---

[1] Hon. Florentino P. Feliciano is Chairman of the Appellate Body of the World Trade Organization. He was Senior Associate Justice of the Supreme Court of the Philippines. Dr. Peter L.H. Van den Bossche is Counsellor at the Appellate Body Secretariat and Professor of International Trade Law at the University of Maastricht, the Netherlands. The views expressed in this article are the views of the authors and do not represent the views of the Appellate Body or the World Trade Organization. The authors thank Debra Steger for her invaluable insights and advice. They also thank Peter Morrison, Petina Gappah and Mariano Garcia Rubio for their comments on a draft of this article.

The scholarly literature on the WTO dispute settlement system has reached very impressive proportions. The limited objectives of the authors' presentation and practical constraints prevent, however, any systematic reference to this important literature. Accordingly, the authors have opted to focus instead on the growing WTO jurisprudence and to refer the interested reader to the selected bibliography appended to this article. This article covers developments until January 2000 although occasionally reference is made to later developments.

regime for bananas[2], the dispute on the European Union's import ban on meat from cattle treated with growth hormones[3], the dispute on the United States' import ban on shrimp harvested with nets not equipped with turtle excluder devices (TEDs)[4], the dispute on the United States' special tax treatment of export-related earnings of foreign sales corporations (FSCs)[5], the dispute on India's import restrictions for balance-of-payments purposes on 2700 different products[6], the disputes on Canada's and Brazil's subsidies for the export of aircraft[7] and the disputes on Japan's, Korea's and Chile's domestic taxes on alcoholic beverages.[8]

During the first five years of its operation, the WTO dispute settlement system has in many respects been a remarkable success and has become the "centrepiece" of the WTO. As of 1 January 2000, WTO Members had made 185 requests for consultations, the first and indispensable step in the WTO dispute settlement process[9] and the Dispute Settlement Body of the WTO had adopted the recommendations and rulings set out in Appellate Body and/or panel reports in 27 distinct

---

[2] *European Communities - Regime for the Importation, Sale and Distribution of Bananas* ("*European Communities - Bananas*"), complaints by Ecuador, Guatemala, Honduras, Mexico and the United States (WT/DS27).

[3] *EC Measures concerning Meat and Meat Products (Hormones)* ("*European Communities - Hormones*"), complaints by the United States (WT/DS26) and Canada (WT/DS48).

[4] *United States - Import Prohibition of Certain Shrimp and Shrimp Products* ("*United States - Shrimp*"), complaint by India, Malaysia, Pakistan and Thailand (WT/DS58).

[5] *United States - Tax Treatment for "Foreign Sales Corporations"* ("*United States - FSC*"), complaint by the European Communities (WT/DS108).

[6] *India - Quantitative Restrictions on Imports of Agricultural, Textile and Industrial Products* ("*India - Quantitative Restrictions*"), complaint by the United States (WT/DS90).

[7] *Brazil - Export Financing Programme for Aircraft* ("*Brazil - Aircraft*"), complaint by Canada (WT/DS46) and *Canada - Measures Affecting the Export of Civilian Aircraft* ("*Canada - Aircraft*"), complaint by Brazil (WT/DS70).

[8] *Japan - Taxes on Alcoholic Beverages* ("*Japan - Alcoholic Beverages*"), complaints by the European Communities (WT/DS8), Canada (WT/DS10) and the United States (WT/DS11); *Korea - Taxes on Alcoholic Beverages* ("*Korea - Alcoholic Beverages*"), complaints by the European Communities (WT/DS75) and the United States (WT/DS84); and *Chile - Taxes on Alcoholic Beverages* ("*Chile - Alcoholic Beverages*"), complaint by the European Communities (WT/DS110).

[9] The number of requests for consultations increased from 25 in 1995 to 39 in 1996 and 50 in 1997 and then fell in 1998 to 41and in 1999 to 30.

disputes.[10] During the same five-year period, a total of 24 international disputes were brought to the International Court of Justice and the Court delivered 6 judgments and 1 advisory opinion.[11] The International Tribunal for the Law of the Sea delivered one judgment.[12] Of all international dispute settlement systems, the WTO system appears at present to be the most frequently used system.

The WTO dispute settlement system has been used intensively by the major trading powers, and, in particular, the United States and the European Communities.[13] Of the 185 requests for consultations made over the past five years, 30 percent were made by the United States and 24 percent by the European Communities. Developing country Members have, however, also had recourse to the WTO dispute settlement system, both to challenge trade measures of major trading powers[14] and

---

[10] The Dispute Settlement Body adopted the recommendations and rulings set out in Appellate Body and/or panel reports in 2 disputes in 1996, 5 disputes in 1997, 11 disputes in 1998 and 10 disputes in 1999.

[11] See: http://www.icj_cij.org.

[12] "Saiga" case between Saint Vincent and Grenadines v. Guinea, Judgment on the merits rendered on 1 July 1999. During the same period the ITLOS rendered two Provisional Measures Orders: a) M/V "Saiga" (No. 2) Provisional Measures Order of March 11, 1998 (37 I.L.M. 1202 [1998]); and b) Southern Bluefin Tuna Cases No. 3 (New Zealand v. Japan) and No. 4 (Australia v. Japan) Provisional Measures Order of August 27, 1999 (38 I.L.M. 1624 [1999]).

[13] Pursuant to Article XI of the *Marrakesh Agreement Establishing the World Trade Organization* (the "*WTO Agreement*"), the European Communities is a Member of the WTO. We will, therefore, refer to the European Communities, rather than the European Union, as an actor within the WTO dispute settlement process. The 15 Member States of the European Union are also Members of the WTO. None of the EU Member States has ever brought a complaint to the WTO for resolution. A number of complaints, however, have been brought against individual EU Member States. See for example, *United Kingdom – Customs Classification of Certain Computer Equipment*, complaint by the United States (WT/DS62); and *Ireland – Customs Classification of Certain Computer Equipment*, complaint by the United States (WT/DS67).

[14] See for example: *United States – Standards of Reformulated and Conventional Gasoline* ("*United States – Gasoline*"), complaints by Venezuela (WT/DS2) and Brazil (WT/DS4), *United States – Restrictions on Imports of Cotton and Man-Made Fibre Underwear* ("*United States – Underwear*"), complaint by Costa Rica (WT/DS24), *United States – Measure Affecting Imports of Woven Wool Shirts and Blouses from India* ("*United States – Shirts and Blouses*"), complaint by India (WT/DS33), *European Communities – Bananas*, complaints by Ecuador, Guatemala, Honduras, Mexico and the United States (WT/DS27) and *United States – Shrimp*, complaints by India, Malaysia, Pakistan and Thailand (WT/DS58). In all these disputes the complainants successfully challenged the trade measure of a major trading power.

to settle trade disputes with other developing countries.[15] Of the 185 requests for consultations, 45 were requests from developing countries.[16] The most active users of the dispute settlement system among developing country Members are India, Brazil and Mexico. Thus far, no least developed country has brought a complaint to the WTO. During the period from 1 January 1995 to 31 December 1999, a total of 33 WTO Members brought at least one complaint to the WTO by making a request for consultations.[17] The relatively frequent recourse to the WTO dispute settlement system during the first five years of its operation is commonly taken as a reflection of the confidence of WTO Members in this system and as one measure of its utility for such Members.

Another, and perhaps more important, aspect of the WTO dispute settlement system has been its ability to bring disputes to a resolution. While in a fair number of the 185 disputes brought to the WTO over the past five years, consultations are still being held or adjudication proceedings still pending, on 31 December 1999, 77 disputes (41.7 percent) have been resolved. Of these 77 disputes, 41 disputes (22.2 percent) were resolved without actual recourse to adjudication, usually through a mutually agreed solution reached between the parties[18], and 36 disputes (19.5 percent) resulted in the adoption by the Dispute Settlement Body of legally binding recommendations and rulings set out in Appellate Body and/or panel reports. In a few highly visible disputes, such as the disputes on the European Union's preferential

---

[15] See, for example, *Brazil – Measures Affecting Desiccated Coconut* ("*Brazil – Coconut*"), complaint by the Philippines (WT/DS22) and *Guatemala Anti-Dumping Investigation Regarding Portland Cement from Mexico* ("*Guatemala – Cement*"), complaint by Mexico (WT/DS60).

[16] The number of requests for consultations by developing country Members has remained more or less stable over the past five years: 1995, 11 requests, 1996, 9 requests, 1997, 10 requests, 1998, 8 requests and 1999, 7 requests. The number of requests of developed country Members, on the contrary, has had a less tranquil evolution: 1995, 13 requests, 1996, 27 requests, 1997, 40 requests, 1998, 33 requests and 1999, 22 requests.

[17] The most frequent respondents are the United States and the European Communities. 19 percent of all complaints concern trade measures of the United States and 16 percent concern trade measures of the European Communities or of the Member States of the European Union. Of all complaints brought to the WTO, 38 percent concerned trade measures of developing country Members. India, Korea, Argentina and Brazil have been the most frequent respondents among the developing country Members.

[18] Mutually agreed solutions were reached in 30 disputes. In other disputes, the contested measure or the request for the establishment of a panel was withdrawn.

import regime for bananas and its import ban on meat from cattle treated with growth hormones, the implementation of the recommendations and rulings of the DSB has been problematic. For these situations, the WTO dispute settlement system provides a special mechanism to encourage a reluctant Member to implement the recommendations and rulings of the DSB.[19] However, in most disputes in which the time for implementation of the recommendations and rulings has expired, compliance with the DSB's recommendations and rulings has been timely and to the satisfaction of the complaining party.

The WTO dispute settlement system, set out in 1994 *Understanding on Rules and Procedures Governing the Settlement of Disputes* (the "DSU") is one of the most important results of the GATT Uruguay Round of negotiations on the liberalization of international trade (1986-1994).[20] The WTO dispute settlement system is, however, not a totally novel system for the resolution of trade disputes. It is built on the dispute settlement system of the GATT, which over a period of almost 50 years evolved in a most pragmatic manner on the basis of Articles XXII and XXIII of the GATT 1947 from diplomatic, power-based dispute settlement towards a more judicial, rules-based dispute resolution system.[21] The WTO system has taken on board the invaluable experience of the GATT with trade dispute settlement.[22] In Article

---

[19] See *infra*. p. 337.

[20] The *Understanding on Rules and Procedures Governing the Settlement of Disputes*, commonly referred to as the *Dispute Settlement Understanding* or DSU, is attached as Annex 2 to the *Marrakesh Agreement Establishing the World Trade Organization* (the "*WTO Agreement*"), done 15 April 1994, published in *The Legal Texts: The Results of the Uruguay Round of Multilateral Trade Negotiations* (Cambridge University Press, 1999), 354-379. The rules and procedures of the WTO dispute settlement system are further set out in the *Rules of Conduct for the Understanding on Rules and Procedures Governing the Settlement of Disputes*, WT/DSB/RC/1, 11 December 1996, and the *Working Procedures for Appellate Review*, WT/AB/WP/3, 28 February 1997.

[21] On the GATT 1947 dispute settlement system and its development, see Hudec, R., *Enforcing International Trade Law: The Evolution of the Modern GATT Legal System* (Butterworth, 1993), 630 p.; and Petersmann, E-U., "International Trade Law and the GATT/WTO Dispute Settlement System 1948-1996: An Introduction", in Petersmann, E-U. (ed.), *International Trade Law and the GATT/WTO Dispute Settlement System* (Kluwer Law International, 1997), 3-122.

[22] We note that in the period from 1948 to 1994, there was significant recourse to this system: a total of 250 complaints were brought under the GATT 1947 and the 1979 Tokyo Round Codes and 115 panel reports were rendered. Of these 115 panel reports, 91 reports were rendered under Article XXIII of the GATT 1947, and 24 reports were rendered under the equivalent provision of a Tokyo Round Code.

3.1 of the DSU, WTO Members explicitly "affirm their adherence to the principles for the management of disputes ... applied under Articles XXII and XXIII of GATT 1947". The adoption of the DSU and the introduction of the WTO dispute settlement system constituted, however, a dramatic development in the process of judicialisation of the settlement of international trade disputes. The WTO system continues to move towards a more judicial type of process. The rulings of the Appellate Body on a large number of procedural and systemic issues constitute an increasing body of judicial practice and procedure tending to fortify the rules-based character of the WTO system.[23]

In this article we propose to examine the basic and distinctive characteristics of the WTO dispute settlement system. We will discuss *seriatim* the compulsory jurisdiction of the system, its object and purpose, its political and judicial-type institutions, access to the system, the mandate of panels and the scope of appellate review, panel and Appellate Body proceedings and the implementation and enforcement of recommendations and rulings of the Dispute Settlement Body. Some of the characteristics of the WTO system clearly distinguish it from other forms of international dispute settlement and may have contributed to its apparent success thus far. Other characteristics underscore the need for further development.

THE COMPULSORY JURISDICTION OF THE WTO DISPUTE SETTLEMENT SYSTEM

The WTO dispute settlement system has compulsory jurisdiction over any dispute between WTO Members arising under what is called the covered agreements. The covered agreements are the WTO agreements listed in Appendix 1 of the DSU, including the *WTO Agreement*, the *General Agreement on Tariffs and Trade 1994* (the "GATT 1994") and all other Multilateral Agreements on Trade in Goods, the *General Agreement on Trade in Services*, the *Agreement on Trade-related Aspects of*

---

[23] Steger, D. and Hainsworth, S., "World Trade Organization Dispute Settlement: The First Three Years", *Journal of International Economic Law*, 1998, 199-226; Steger, D. and Van den Bossche, P., "WTO Dispute Settlement: Emerging Practice and Procedure", *Proceedings of the 92⁷ Annual Meeting ASIL (1998)*, 79-86, and Steger, D., and Lester, S., "WTO Dispute Settlement: Emerging Practice and Procedure in Decisions of the Appellate Body", in Schütte, M. and Reisenfeld, K. (eds.), *The WTO Dispute Settlement System* (Oxford University Press), forthcoming.

Intellectual Property Rights and the DSU.[24] A complaining Member is obliged to bring a dispute arising under any of the covered agreements to the WTO dispute settlement system and a responding Member has, as a matter of law, no choice but to accept the jurisdiction of the WTO dispute settlement system.

Pursuant to Article 23 of the DSU, when a WTO Member seeks redress of a violation of obligations or other nullification or impairment of benefits under the covered agreements or an impediment to the attainment of any objective of the covered agreements, it must have recourse to, and must abide by, the rules and procedures of the DSU.[25] Members have to have recourse to the DSU dispute settlement system to the exclusion, in particular, of any mode of unilateral enforcement of WTO rights and obligations. Members are prohibited from making a determination to the effect that a violation has occurred, that benefits have been nullified or impaired, or that the attainment of any objective of the covered agreements has been impeded, *except* through recourse to dispute settlement in accordance with the rules and procedures of the DSU.[26]

Article 1.1 of the DSU establishes "an integrated dispute settlement system" which applies to all of the covered agreements.[27] The DSU provides for a single, coherent system of rules and procedures for dispute settlement applicable to disputes arising under any of the covered agreements. However, some of the covered agreements provide for a few special and additional rules and procedures "designed to deal with the particularities of dispute settlement relating to obligations

---

[24] Plurilateral Trade Agreements are covered agreements subject to the adoption of a decision by the parties to these agreements setting out the terms for the application of the DSU (Appendix 1 of the DSU).

[25] Article 23.1 of the DSU. The only exception to this provision are the special or additional rules and procedures contained in other covered agreements and identified in Appendix 2 of the DSU (see *infra*). On the interpretation and application of Article 23 of the DSU, see Panel Report, *United States – Sections 301-304 of the Trade Act of 1974* ("*United States – Section 301*"), WT/DS152/R, adopted 27 January 2000.

[26] Article 23.2 (a) of the DSU. Article 23.2 also stipulates that to determine the reasonable period of time for implementation (see *infra*) or to determine the level of suspension of concession or other obligations and to obtain DSB authorization for such suspension (see *infra*), Members must also follow the rules and procedures set out in the DSU.

[27] Appellate Body Report, *Guatemala – Anti-Dumping Investigation Regarding Portland Cement from* Mexico ("*Guatemala – Cement*"), WT/DS60/AB/R, adopted 25 November 1998, para. 64.

arising under a specific covered agreement".[28] Pursuant to Article 1.2 of the DSU, these special or additional rules and procedures, which are listed in Appendix 2 of the DSU, prevail over the DSU rules and procedures to the extent there is a difference between the DSU rules and procedures and the special and additional rules and procedures. As the Appellate Body ruled in *Guatemala - Cement*, "it is only where the provisions of the DSU and the special or additional rules and procedures of a covered agreement *cannot* be read as *complementing* each other that the special additional provisions are to *prevail*."[29] A special or additional provision should only be found to prevail over a provision of the DSU "in the case of a *conflict* between them".[30] The special and additional rules and procedures of a particular covered agreement combine with the generally applicable rules and procedures of the DSU "to form a comprehensive, integrated dispute settlement system for the *WTO Agreement*."[31]

Just as the complaining Member must bring a dispute arising under any of the covered agreements to the WTO dispute settlement system, so also must the responding Member accept the jurisdiction of the WTO dispute settlement system. The responding Member cannot prevent the establishment of a panel to adjudicate the dispute. As discussed below, the Dispute Settlement Body will establish a panel if requested to do so by the complaining party unless there is a consensus among WTO Members against establishment. Unlike in other international dispute settlement systems, there is no need for the parties to a dispute arising under the covered agreements specially to recognize the jurisdiction of the WTO dispute settlement system to adjudicate that dispute. Accession to membership in the WTO constitutes consent to and acceptance of the compulsory jurisdiction of the WTO dispute settlement system.

It should be noted that the DSU provides in fact for a multitude of dispute settlement procedures. Apart from the procedure which is set out in considerable detail in Articles 4 to 20 of the DSU and which is the procedure primarily discussed below, Article 5 of the DSU provides the possibility for the parties to a dispute -- if they all agree to do so --

---

[28] *Ibid.*, para. 66.
[29] *Ibid.*, para. 65.
[30] *Ibid.*, para. 65 and Appellate Body Report, *Brazil – Export Financing Programme for Aircraft* ("*Brazil – Aircraft*"), WT/DS46/AB/R, adopted 20 August 1999, para. 192.
[31] Appellate Body Report, *Guatemala – Cement*, para. 66.

to enter into good offices, conciliation and mediation to settle a dispute.[32] Thus far, there has been no formal recourse to any of these procedures. Furthermore, the DSU, and, in particular, Article 25 thereof, provides for expeditious arbitration within the WTO as an alternative means of dispute settlement.[33] Subject to mutual agreement, parties to a dispute arising under a covered agreement may decide to resort to arbitration, rather than follow the procedure set out in Articles 4 to 20 of the DSU. In that case, the parties must clearly define the issues referred to arbitration and agree on the particular procedure to be followed.[34] The parties must also agree to abide by the arbitration award.[35] By resorting to such arbitration, parties do not, however, put themselves outside the WTO dispute settlement system. The DSU itself explicitly provides for the possibility of resort to arbitration. Furthermore, the arbitration award must be notified to the DSB and the relevant Council or Committee, where the award may be subjected to scrutiny by any WTO Member.[36] The arbitration award must be consistent with the covered agreements.[37] The provisions of Article 21 of the DSU concerning the surveillance of implementation and Article 22 of the DSU concerning compensation and the suspension of concessions, apply *mutatis mutandis* to arbitration awards under Article 25.[38] During the first five years of operation of the WTO dispute settlement system, no use has been made of Article 25.

THE OBJECT AND PURPOSE OF THE WTO DISPUTE SETTLEMENT SYSTEM

WTO Members consider the dispute settlement system "central" to the overall task of "providing security and predictability to the multilateral trading system."[39] The prompt settlement of disputes arising under the covered agreements "is essential to the effective functioning of the WTO and the maintenance of a proper balance between the rights and

---

[32] Pursuant to Article 5.6 of the DSU, the Director-General of the WTO may, acting in an *ex officio* capacity, offer good offices, conciliation or mediation.
[33] Article 25.1 of the DSU.
[34] *Ibid.* and Article 25.2 of the DSU.
[35] Article 25.3 of the DSU.
[36] *Ibid.*.
[37] Article 3.5 of the DSU.
[38] Article 25.5 of the DSU.
[39] Article 3.2 of the DSU.

obligations of Members."[40] The dispute settlement system is designed "to preserve the rights and obligations of Members under the covered agreements, and to clarify the existing provisions of those agreements in accordance with customary rules of interpretation of public international law."[41] The goal of the dispute settlement system is "to secure a positive solution to a dispute."[42] The DSU thoughtfully provides that the use of the dispute settlement procedures "should not be intended or considered as contentious acts" and that all Members must "engage in these procedures in good faith in an effort to resolve the dispute."[43]

The DSU expresses a clear preference for solutions mutually acceptable to the parties to the dispute, rather than solutions resulting from adjudication.[44] Accordingly, each dispute settlement proceeding must start with consultations by one with the other party with a view to reaching a mutually agreed solution.[45] As noted above, in a number of disputes, it has indeed been possible to reach a solution acceptable to both parties to a dispute.[46] In other disputes recourse to adjudication, however, was necessary in order to secure actual resolution of the dispute. Adjudication will result in recommendations and rulings by a panel, and possibly the Appellate Body. These recommendations and rulings, the DSU states, cannot add to or diminish the rights and obligations provided in the covered agreements. This warning appears in two different provisions of the DSU.[47]

The declared object and purpose of the WTO system is to achieve a satisfactory settlement of the dispute *in accordance with* the rights and obligations established by the covered agreements.[48] All resolutions of

---

[40] Article 3.3 of the DSU.
[41] Article 3.2 of the DSU. In *United States – Shirts and Blouses*, the Appellate Body found that, given the explicit aim of dispute settlement that permeates the DSU, it did not consider that Article 3.2 of the DSU is meant to encourage either panels or the Appellate Body to "make law" by clarifying existing provisions of the covered agreements outside the context of resolving a particular dispute (Appellate Body Report, *United States – Measures Affecting Imports of Woven Wool Shirts and Blouses* ("*United States – Shirts and Blouses*"), WT/DS33/AB/R, adopted 23 May 1997, p. 20).
[42] Article 3.7 of the DSU.
[43] Article 3.10 of the DSU. On the role of good faith in such effort, see Appellate Body Report, *United States – Tax Treatment for "Foreign Sales Corporations"* ("*United States – FSC*"), WT/DS108/AB/R, adopted 20 March 2000, para. 166.
[44] Article 3.7 of the DSU.
[45] Article 4.3 of the DSU.
[46] See *supra*, p. 300.
[47] Articles 3.2 and 19.2 of the DSU.
[48] Article 3.4 of the DSU.

matters formally raised under the consultation and dispute settlement process, including arbitration awards, must be consistent with those agreements and must not nullify or impair benefits accruing to any Member under those agreements, nor impede the attainment of any objective of those agreements.[49]

ACCESS TO THE WTO DISPUTE SETTLEMENT SYSTEM

Normally a State has recourse to an international dispute settlement system only when it considers that another State has violated its international obligations. A WTO Member may have recourse to the WTO dispute settlement system, however, when it considers that a benefit accruing to it directly or indirectly under a covered agreement is being nullified or impaired or the attainment of any objective of a covered agreement is being impeded. The nullification or impairment of a benefit or the impeding of realization of an objective may, and most often will, be the result of a violation of an obligation prescribed by a covered agreement.[50] In fact, when the complaining Member can demonstrate that the responding Member has violated an obligation under a covered agreement, a *prima facie* presumption arises that this violation constitutes nullification or impairment of a benefit under that agreement.[51] Such nullification or impairment or the impeded attainment of objectives may, however, also be the result of "the application by another [Member] of any measure, whether or not it conflicts with the provisions" of a covered agreement[52] or of "the existence of any other situation".[53] Unlike other international dispute settlement systems, the WTO system, therefore, provides for three types of complaints: "violation" complaints, "non-violation" complaints and "situation" complaints.[54] Violation complaints are by far the most common type of

---

[49] Article 3.5 of the DSU.
[50] Article XXIII:1 (a) of the GATT 1994 and Article 3.8 of the DSU.
[51] Article 3.8 of the DSU. It is then on the responding Member to rebut this presumption.
[52] Article XXIII:1 (b) of the GATT 1994 and Article 26.1 of the DSU
[53] Article XXIII:1 (c) of the GATT 1994 and Article 26.2 of the DSU.
[54] Pursuant to Article XXIII.3 of the GATS, situation complaints are not possible in disputes arising under the GATS. Pursuant to Article 64.2 of the *TRIPS Agreement* non-violation complaints and situation complaints were not possible in disputes arising under the *TRIPS Agreement* during a period of five years from the date of entry into force of the *WTO Agreement*. Article 64.3 provides that the Ministerial

complaints. During the first five years of the operation of the WTO system, there have, in fact, been few non-violation complaints and no situation complaints.[55] The difference between the WTO system and other international dispute settlement systems on this point may, therefore, be of little practical significance.

There is no explicit provision in the DSU requiring a Member to have a "legal interest" in order to have recourse to the WTO dispute settlement system. It has been held that such a requirement is not implied either in the DSU or any other provision of the *WTO Agreement*.[56] Article XXIII:1 of the GATT 1994 and Article 3.7 of the DSU clearly indicate that a Member has broad discretion in deciding whether to bring a case against another Member under the DSU, and that a Member is expected to be largely self-regulating in determining whether any such action would be "fruitful".[57]

Access to the dispute settlement system of the WTO is limited to Members of the WTO.[58] This access is not available, under the *WTO Agreement* and the other covered agreements as they are currently written, to individuals or international organizations, whether governmental or non-governmental. It is clear from Articles 4, 6, 9 and 10 of the DSU that only Members may become parties to a dispute and only Members "having a substantial interest in a matter before a panel" may become third parties in the proceedings before that panel. As the Appellate Body ruled in *United States – Shrimp*, under Articles 10 and 12 and Appendix 3 of the DSU, only Members who are parties to a dispute, or who have notified their interest in becoming third parties in such a dispute to the DSB, have a legal right to make submissions to, and have a legal right to have those submission considered by, a panel.[59] Individuals, companies or organizations are not accorded such legal

---

Conference can only extend this period by consensus. No such decision has been taken and, therefore, both types of complaint are now possible.

[55] See, for example, *Japan – Measures Affecting Consumer Photographic Film and Paper*, complaint by the United States (WT/DS44) and *Korea – Measures Afffecting Government Procurement*, complaint by the United States (WT/DS163).

[56] Appellate Body Report, *European Communities – Regime for the Importation, Sale and Distribution of Bananas* ("*European Communities – Bananas*"), WT/DS27/AB/R, adopted 25 September 1997, paras. 132 and 133.

[57] Appellate Body Report, *European Communities – Bananas*, para. 135.

[58] Appellate Body Report, *United States – Import Prohibition of Certain Shrimp and Shrimp Products* ("*United States – Shrimp*"), WT/DS58/AB/R, adopted 6 November 1998, para. 101.

[59] *Ibid.* A panel is obliged in law to accept and give due consideration only to submissions by parties and third parties to the dispute.

rights. They do not, as such, have direct access to the WTO dispute settlement system.[60]

THE POLITICAL AND JUDICIAL-TYPE INSTITUTIONS OF THE WTO DISPUTE SETTLEMENT SYSTEM

While the WTO has entrusted the adjudication of disputes to independent judicial-type institutions, the *ad hoc* panels at the first instance level and the standing Appellate Body at the appellate level, the political institutions of the WTO and, in particular, the Dispute Settlement Body, continue to play a vital role in the WTO dispute resolution process. We will briefly discuss the main features of the Dispute Settlement Body, the first instance panels and the Appellate Body.

THE DISPUTE SETTLEMENT BODY OF THE WTO

The Dispute Settlement Body of the WTO (the "DSB") is composed of representatives of all the WTO Members and administers the WTO dispute settlement rules and procedures set out in the DSU.[61] The main responsibilities of the DSB are the establishment of the *ad hoc* panels, the adoption of the reports of the panels and the Appellate Body, the surveillance of implementation of the adopted reports and the authorization of the suspension of concessions or other obligations in case of non-implementation. The DSB meets as often as necessary to carry out its functions within the time-frames provided in the DSU.[62] The decisions on the establishment of panels, on the adoption of panel and Appellate Body reports and on the authorization of the suspension of concessions or other obligations in case of non-implementation are adopted by *reverse consensus*, i.e., these decisions are adopted by the DSB

---

[60] On the authority of panels and the Appellate Body to consider *amicus curiae* briefs, see *infra*, p. 328.

[61] Article 2.1 of the DSU. Pursuant to Article III:3 of the *WTO Agreement*, the General Council of the WTO shall convene as appropriate to discharge the responsibilities of the DSB. The DSB, however, has its own chairman and may establish such rules of procedure as it deems necessary for the fulfillment of its responsibilities.

[62] Article 2.3 of the DSU. The DSB has a regular meeting each month; special meetings may be convened pursuant to footnote 5 to Article 6.1, footnote 7 to Article 16.4 and footnote 11 to Article 21.3 of the DSU.

unless the DSB decides by consensus *not* to adopted them.[63] Since there will usually be at least one Member with a strong interest in the adoption of these decisions, it is highly unlikely that there will ever be a consensus not to adopt these decisions.[64] As a result, decision-making by the DSB on these matters is, for all practical purposes, automatic and a matter of course. A party to the dispute is disabled from blocking the establishment of a panel, the adoption of a panel or Appellate Body report or the suspension of concessions or other obligations in case of non-implementation of DSB recommendations and rulings.

WTO Dispute Settlement Panels

At the first instance level, the actual adjudication of disputes brought to the WTO is done by panels. If consultations between the parties to a dispute fail to settle the dispute within 60 days of the receipt of the request for consultations, the complaining party may request the DSB to establish a panel to adjudicate the dispute.[65] The request for establishment of a panel must be made in writing and must indicate whether consultations were held, identify the specific measures at issue and provide a brief summary of the legal basis of the complaint sufficient to present the problem clearly.[66] If the complaining party so requests, a panel is established, by reverse consensus, at the latest at the DSB meeting following the meeting at which the request for the establishment first appears as an item on the agenda.[67]

---

[63] See Articles 6.1, 16.4, 17.14 and 22.6 of the DSU. Other decisions of the DSB, such as the appointment of the Members of the Appellate Body, are taken by normal consensus. See Article 2.4 of the DSU. Note that the DSB shall be deemed to have decided by consensus on a matter submitted for its consideration, if no Member, present at the meeting of the DSB when the decision is taken, formally objects to the proposed decision. See Footnote 1 to Article 2.4 of the DSU.

[64] Note, however, that if all parties to a disputes are very dissatisfied with a report, it is possible that the report is not put on the agenda of the DSB for adoption and thus remains unadopted.

[65] Article 4.7 of the DSU. Under certain circumstances set out in Articles 4.3, 4.7 and 4.8 of the DSU, the complaining party may request the establishment of a panel earlier.

[66] Article 6.2 of the DSU.

[67] Article 6.1 of the DSU. A panel can be established at the DSB meeting at which the request for the establishment first appeared on the agenda if the responding party does not object to the establishment. This has occurred on a few cases to date.

Once a panel is established by the DSB, the parties to the dispute try to reach agreement on the composition of the panel. In that context, the Secretariat proposes nominations for the panel to the parties.[68] In principle, the parties should not oppose these nominations except for compelling reasons.[69] In practice, the composition of the panel is often a difficult and contentious process. If, however, the parties are unable to agree on the composition of the panel within 20 days of its establishment by the DSB, either party may request the Director-General to determine the composition of the panel.[70] Within ten days of such a request, the Director-General shall – after consulting the parties to the dispute and the Chairmen of the DSB and of the relevant Council or Committee – appoint the panelists whom he considers most appropriate.[71] During the first five years of WTO dispute settlement, the Director-General decided on the composition of a fair number of panels.[72] To assist in the selection of panelists, the Secretariat maintains an indicative list of government and non-government individuals from which panelists may be drawn as appropriate.[73] Parties or the Director-General are free, however, to select panelists whose names do not appear on the Indicative List.

Panels are normally composed of three persons.[74] With regard to the qualifications of panelists, the DSU requires that panels be composed of well-qualified governmental and/or non-governmental individuals, including persons who have served on a panel, presented a case to a panel, served as a representative of a Member to the WTO, served in the Secretariat, taught or published on international trade law, or served as a senior trade policy official of a Member.[75] Members have

---

[68] Article 8.6 of the DSU.
[69] Ibid.
[70] Article 8.7 of the DSU.
[71] Ibid.
[72] Between January 1995 and April 1999, the Director-General decided on the composition of 16 panels.
[73] Article 8.4 of the DSU. Members periodically suggest names of individuals for inclusion on this list, providing relevant information on their knowledge of international trade and the *WTO Agreement*. These names shall be added to the list upon approval by the DSB.
[74] Article 8.5 of the DSU. The parties to the dispute can agree, within 10 days from the establishment of the panel, to a panel composed of five panelists. Since 1995, however, parties have not agreed to do so.
[75] Article 8.1 of the DSU. When a dispute is between a developing country Member and a developed country Member the panel shall, if the developing country Mem-

agreed that, as a general rule, they will permit their officials to serve as panelists.[76] During the period 1995-1999, most panelists were government trade officials with legal training, many among them Geneva-based trade diplomats. Increasingly, however, law professors and practitioners familiar with international trade law have been appointed to panels. Panelists are to be selected with a view to ensuring their independence, a sufficiently diverse background and a wide spectrum of experience.[77] It should be stressed that nationals of Members who are parties to the dispute or third parties may *not* serve on a panel seized with that dispute, unless the parties agree otherwise.[78] As a result, nationals of a number of smaller Members, such as Switzerland, New Zealand, Norway, the Czech Republic and Hong Kong, China, have frequently been chosen as panelists. Panelists serve in their individual capacities and not as government representatives, nor as representatives of any organization.[79] Members may not give panelists instructions nor seek to influence them as individuals with regard to matters before a panel.[80] Panelists are subject to the *Rules of Conduct for the Understanding on Rules and Procedures Governing the Settlement of Disputes* (the "*Rules of Conduct*").[81] These *Rules of Conduct* address the need to preserve the integrity and impartiality of panelists and the confidentiality of panel proceedings.[82] Panelists' expenses, including travel and subsistence

---

ber so requests, include at least one panelist from a developing country Member. See Article 8.10 of the DSU.

[76] Article 8.8 of the DSU.
[77] Article 8.2 of the DSU.
[78] Article 8.3 of the DSU. Thus far, the parties to the dispute have never agreed to allow nationals of parties to the dispute to serve on a panel.
[79] Article 8.9 of the DSU.
[80] Article 8.9 of the DSU.
[81] WT/DSB/RC/1, 11 December 1996.
[82] The *Rules of Conduct* also apply to other persons involved in the panel proceedings, such as the staff of the WTO Secretariat and experts consulted by the panel. Under the *Rules of Conduct*, prospective panelists must disclose the existence or development of any interest, relationship or matter that is likely to affect, or give rise to justifiable doubts as to his or her independence or impartiality. If a party to the dispute possesses information indicating a breach of the obligations of independence, impartiality or confidentiality on the part of a panelist, or has knowledge of direct or indirect conflicts of interest, it must submit this information promptly to the Chairman of the DSB. If the panelist does not withdraw, the Chairman of the DSB may, after consultations, revoke the appointment of the panelist.

allowances, are met from the WTO budget.[83] The Secretariat assists panels and provides them with secretarial and technical support.[84]

THE APPELLATE BODY

Appeals from the reports of dispute settlement panels are heard by the Appellate Body. Unlike panels, the Appellate Body is a permanent, standing international tribunal.[85] It is composed of seven Members who are appointed by the DSB.[86] The Appellate Body composition is broadly representative of the Membership of the WTO.[87] Each year the Appellate Body Members elect a Chairman from among themselves.[88]

The Members of the Appellate Body serve a term of four years, which can be renewed once.[89] As to the qualifications of Appellate Body

---

[83] Article 8.11 of the DSU.

[84] Article 27.1 of the DSU. Article 27.2 recognizes that there may be a need to provide additional legal advice and assistance in respect of dispute settlement to developing country Members. To this end, the Secretariat makes available legal experts to any developing country which so requests. However, the availability of these experts is currently limited to one day a week each and they have to assist the developing country Member in a manner ensuring the continued impartiality of the Secretariat.

[85] Article 17.1 of the DSU.

[86] Article 17.2 of the DSU. Pursuant to Article 2.4 of the DSU, the DSB takes the decision on the appointment of the Appellate Body by consensus.

[87] Article 17.3 of the DSU. During its first four years (December 1995-December 1999), the composition of the Appellate Body was as follows: James Bacchus (United States), Christopher Beeby (New Zealand), Claus-Dieter Ehlermann (Germany), Said El Naggar (Egypt), Florentino Feliciano (the Philippines), Julio Lacarte-Muró (Uruguay), and Mitsuo Matsushita (Japan).

[88] Rule 5(1) of the *Working Procedures*. The Chairman is responsible for the overall direction of the activities of the Appellate Body. His responsibilities comprise, in particular, the supervision of the internal functioning of the Appellate Body, and such other duties as the Members of the Appellate Body may agree to entrust to him or her.

[89] Article 17.2 of the DSU. In order to stagger the terms of office of the Members of the Appellate Body, three of the original seven Members (Mr. Ehlermann, Mr. Feliciano and Mr. Lacarte) served an initial term of two years. In 1997 these three Members were appointed for a second term, which will expire in December 2001. The first four-year term of the other four original Members expired in December 1999. On 3 November 1999, Mr. Bacchus and Mr. Beeby were re-appointed for a second term. Mr. El-Naggar and Mr. Matsushita did not seek a second term but they agreed to an extension of their first term to 31 March 2000 in order to allow the DSB time to reach a decision on the appointment of two new Members. On 7 April 2000, the DSB appointed Mr. Georges Abi-Saab (Egypt) and Mr. Arumugamangalam Ganesan (India) to serve on the Appellate Body. On 19 March 2000, Mr. Beeby passed away. On 25 May 2000, the DSB appointed Mr. Yasuhei Taniguchi (Japan) to serve for the remainder of the term of Mr. Beeby.

Members, the DSU provides that the Appellate Body shall comprise persons of recognized authority, with demonstrated expertise in law, international trade and the subject matter of the covered agreements generally.[90] Appellate Body Members must be unaffiliated with any government and must exercise their office without accepting or seeking instructions from any international governmental or non-governmental organization or any private source.[91] During their term of office, Members shall not accept any employment nor pursue any professional activity that is inconsistent with their duties and responsibilities.[92] Like panelists, the Members of the Appellate Body are subject to the *Rules of Conduct* and are required "to disclose the existence or development of any interest, relationship or matter" that "is likely to affect, or give rise to justifiable doubts" as to, his or her "independence or impartiality".[93] They may not participate in the consideration of any appeal that would create a direct or indirect conflict of interest.[94] Appellate Body Members are not required to reside permanently or continuously in Geneva. They are required, however, to be available at all times and on short notice to hear and decide appeals.[95] The Appellate Body Members convene on a regular basis to discuss matters of policy, practice and procedure.[96] The Appellate Body has its own Secretariat, which provides it with legal and administrative support.[97]

The Appellate Body hears and decides appeals in Divisions of three Members.[98] The Members constituting the Division hearing and deciding a particular appeal are selected on the basis of rotation, while

---

[90] Article 17.3 of the DSU.
[91] Article 17.3 of the DSU and Rule 2(3) of the *Working Procedures*.
[92] Rule 2(2) of the *Working Procedures*.
[93] Article III.1 of the *Rules of Conduct*. Annex 2 of the *Rules of Conduct* contains an illustrative list of information to be disclosed.
[94] A request from a party to the dispute for the disqualification of an Appellate Body Member should be presented to the Appellate Body itself, which decides whether to accept or reject the request (Rule VIII(14)-(17) of the *Rules of Conduct* and Rule 10(5) of the *Working Procedures*).
[95] Article 17.3 of the DSU. To this end, Members keep the Appellate Body Secretariat informed of their whereabouts at all times (Rule 2(4) of the *Working Procedures*).
[96] Rule 4 of the *Working Procedures*.
[97] Article 17.7 of the DSU. The Appellate Body Secretariat, directed by Ms. Debra Steger, consists of two counsellors, four legal advisors and four secretaries. The *Rules of Conduct* and the requirements of independence, impartiality and confidentiality also apply to the staff of the Appellate Body Secretariat.
[98] Article 17.1 of the DSU and Rule 6(1) of the *Working Procedures*.

taking into account the principles of random selection and unpredictability and opportunity for all Members to serve regardless their nationality.[99] The Members of a Division select their Presiding Member.[100] Decisions relating to an appeal are taken by the Division assigned to that appeal. However, to ensure consistency and coherence in decision-making, and to draw on the individual and collective expertise of all seven Members, the Division responsible for deciding an appeal exchanges views with the other Members on the issues raised by the appeal.[101] A Division shall make every effort to take its decision on the appeal by consensus. However, if a decision cannot be reached by consensus, the *Working Procedures* provide that the matter at issue shall be decided by a majority vote.[102] To date, all decisions of the Appellate Body have been taken by consensus.[103]

THE MANDATE OF PANELS AND THE SCOPE OF APPELLATE REVIEW

Before discussing the mandate of panels and the scope of appellate review, it should be noted that two important prescriptions are addressed to both panels and the Appellate Body. First, pursuant to the last sentence of Article 3.2 and Article 19.2 of the DSU, a panel or the Appellate Body, in their findings and recommendations, cannot add to or diminish the rights and obligations provided in the covered agreements. Second, pursuant to the second sentence of Article 3.2 of the DSU, panels and the Appellate Body are bound to interpret the provi-

---

[99] Article 17.1 of the DSU and Rule 6(2) of the *Working Procedures*. Unlike panelists, Appellate Body Members who are citizens of the parties to the dispute are not excluded from serving on the Division hearing and deciding the appeal. A member selected in the manner set out in Article 17.1 of the DSU and rule 6(2) of the *Working Procedures* shall serve on that Division unless he is excused pursuant to the *Rules of Conduct*, is prevented from serving because of illness or other serious reasons (Rule 6(3) of the *Working Procedures* referring to Rules 9, 10, 12 and 14 thereof). Where a Member is unable to serve on the Division for one of these reasons, he will be replaced by another Member, selected in the same manner (Rule 13 of the *Working Procedures*).
[100] Rule 7 of the *Working Procedures*.
[101] Rule 4(3) of the *Working Procedures*. Each Member shall receive all documents filed in an appeal. A Member who has a conflict of interest, shall not take part in the exchange of views.
[102] Rule 3(2) of the *Working Procedures*.
[103] The DSU provides that opinions expressed in an Appellate Body report by individual Members shall be anonymous (Article 17.11 of the DSU).

sions of the covered agreements in accordance with customary rules of interpretation of public international law.[104] As the Appellate Body found in *United States – Gasoline* and *Japan – Alcoholic Beverages*, the rules embodied in Articles 31 and 32 of *the Vienna Convention on the Law of Treaties* (the *"Vienna Convention"*) form part of the customary rules of interpretation of public international law.[105] Consequently, panels and the Appellate Body commonly interpret provisions of the covered agreements in accordance with the ordinary meaning of the words of the provision taken in their context and in the light of the object and purpose of the agreement involved. Interpretation must start with and be based on the text of the agreement.[106] Pursuant to Article 31 of the *Vienna Convention*, the duty of a treaty interpreter is to examine the words of the treaty to determine the common intentions of the parties.[107] One of the corollaries of the general rule of interpretation in the *Vienna Convention* is that interpretation must give meaning and effect to all terms of the treaty. An interpreter is not free to adopt a reading that would result in reducing whole clauses or paragraphs of a treaty to redundancy or inutility.[108] On the other hand, the general rule of treaty interpretation neither requires nor condones "the imputation into a treaty of words that are not there or the importation into a treaty of concepts that were not intended."[109]

---

[104] Article 3.2 of the DSU.

[105] Appellate Body Reports: *United States – Standards for Reformulated and Conventional Gasoline* ("*United States – Gasoline*"), WT/DS2/AB/R, adopted 20 May 1996, p. 17; and *Japan – Taxes on Alcoholic Beverages* ("*Japan – Alcoholic Beverages*"), WT/DS8/AB/R, WT/DS10/AB/R, WT/DS11/AB/R, adopted 1 November 1996, p. 10.

[106] See, for example, Appellate Body Reports: *Japan – Alcoholic Beverages*, p. 11; and *United States – Shrimp*, para. 114.

[107] See, for example, Appellate Body Reports: *India – Patent Protection for Pharmaceutical and Agricultural Chemical Products* ("*India – Patents*"), WT/DS50/AB/R, adopted 16 January 1998, para. 45; and *European Communities Customs Classification of Certain Computer Equipment* ("*European Communities – Computer Equipment*"), WT/DS62/AB/R, WT/DS67/AB/R, WT/DS68£/AB/R, adopted 22 June 1998, para. 84.

[108] Appellate Body Report, *United States – Gasoline*, p. 23. See also, for example, Appellate Body Reports: *Japan – Alcoholic Beverages*, p. 12; and *Korea – Definitive Safeguard Measure on Imports of Certain Dairy Products* ("*Korea – Dairy Safeguards*"), WT/DS98/AB/R, adopted 12 January 2000, para. 81.

[109] Appellate Body Report, *India – Patents*, para. 45. See also Appellate Body Report, *EC Measures Concerning Meat and Meat Products* ("*European Communities – Hormones*"), WT/DS26/AB/R, WT/DS48/AB/R, adopted 13 February 1998, para. 181.

The Mandate of Panels

The jurisdiction of a panel is established by that panel's terms of reference, which are governed by Article 7 of the DSU.[110] As the Appellate Body stated in *Brazil – Dessicated Coconut*, the terms of reference of the panel are important for two reasons.[111] First, terms of reference fulfil an important due process objective – they must give parties and third parties sufficient information concerning the claims at stake in the dispute in order to allow them an opportunity to respond to the complainant's case. Second, they establish the jurisdiction of the panel by defining the precise claims at issue in the dispute, i.e., the matter before it. A panel may consider only those claims that it has authority to consider under its terms of reference.[112] A panel is bound by its terms of reference.[113] Unless the parties agree otherwise within 20 days from the establishment of the panel, a panel is given the following standard terms of reference:

> To examine in the light of the relevant provisions in (name of the covered agreement(s) cited by the parties to the dispute), the matter referred to the DSB by (name of party) in document ... and make such findings as will assist the DSB in making the recommendations or in giving the rulings provided for in that/those agreement.[114]

The document referred to in these standard terms of reference is usually the request for the establishment of a panel.[115] Hence, a claim falls within the panel's terms of reference only if that claim is identified in the request for the establishment of a panel.[116] It is, therefore, important that a request for the establishment of a panel be sufficiently

---

[110] Appellate Body Report, *India – Patents*, para. 92.
[111] Appellate Body Report, *Brazil – Measures Affecting Desiccated Coconut* ("*Brazil – Dessicated Coconut*"), WT/DS22/AB/R, adopted 20 March 1997, p. 22.
[112] Appellate Body Report, *India – Patents*, para. 92. A panel cannot assume jurisdiction that it does not have (*Ibid.*).
[113] Appellate Body Report, *India – Patents*, para. 93.
[114] Article 7.1 of the DSU. In case the complaining party requests the establishment of a panel with other than standard terms of reference, the request of the establishment of the panel shall include the proposed text of the special terms of reference. See Article 6.2 of the DSU. In establishing a panel, the DSB may authorize its Chairman to draw up the terms of reference of the panel in consultation with the parties to the dispute. See Article 7.3 of the DSU.
[115] Note that the request for consultations may also be referred to.
[116] If the panel has special terms of reference, a claim will not fall within the terms of reference of the panel unless that claim is contained in these special terms of reference or identified in the documents referred to in these special terms of reference.

precise.[117] Pursuant to Article 6.2 of the DSU, a panel request must "identify the specific measures at issue" and "provide a brief summary of the legal basis of the complaint sufficient to present the problem clearly".[118] As the Appellate Body ruled in *European Communities – Bananas*, Article 6.2 requires that "the *claims*, but not the *arguments*, must all be specified sufficiently in the request for the establishment of a panel".[119] With regard to the requirement that the request must "identify the specific measures at issue", the Appellate Body ruled in *European Communities – Computer Equipment*, that "measures" within the meaning of Article 6.2 are not only normative rules or measures of general application, but also can be, for example, the application of tariffs by customs authorities.[120] In the same case, the Appellate Body found that although Article 6.2 does not require that the products to which the "specific measures at issue" apply be identified, with respect to certain WTO obligations, in order adequately to identify "the specific measures at issue" it may also be necessary to identify the products subject to the measures in dispute.[121] Whether the "specific measures at issue" are sufficiently identified as required by Article 6.2 relates to the ability of the responding party to defend itself given the actual reference to the measure complained about.[122] With regard to the requirement that the request for a panel must "provide a brief summary of the legal basis of the complaint sufficient to present the problem clearly", we note that Article 6.2 demands only a *brief* summary of the legal basis of the complaint which summary must, however, be one "sufficient to present the problem clearly".[123] In *European Communities – Bananas*, the

---

[117] Appellate Body Report, *European Communities – Bananas*, para. 142. The request for the establishment of a panel must also be sufficiently precise because it informs the defending party and the third parties of the legal basis of the complaint (*Ibid.*).

[118] In *India – Patents*, the Appellate Body ruled that the convenient phrase, "including but not necessarily limited to", is simply not adequate to "identify the specific measures at issue" and to "provide a brief summary of the legal basis of the complaint sufficient to present the problem clearly" (Appellate Body Report, *India – Patents*, para. 90).

[119] Appellate Body Report, *European Communities – Bananas*, para. 143. If a *claim* is not specified in the request for the establishment of a panel, then a faulty request cannot be subsequently "cured" by a complaining party's argumentation in its first written submission to the panel or in any other submission or statement made later in the panel proceedings.

[120] Appellate Body Report, *European Communities – Computer Equipment*, para. 65.

[121] *Ibid.* para. 67.

[122] *Ibid.* para. 70.

[123] Appellate Body Report, *Korea – Dairy Safeguards*, para. 120.

Appellate Body found that in view of the particular circumstances of that case, the listing of the articles of the agreements alleged to have been breached satisfied the *minimum* requirements of Article 6.2 of the DSU.[124] Whether the mere listing of the articles claimed to have been violated actually meets the standard of Article 6.2 must, however, be examined on a case-by-case basis. In *Korea – Dairy Safeguards*, the Appellate Body stated that in resolving that question, one must take into account "whether the ability of the respondent to defend itself was prejudiced, given the actual course of the panel proceedings, by the fact that the panel request simply listed the provisions claimed to have been violated."[125]

In the language of Article 11 of the DSU, the function of panels is to make an objective assessment of the matter before it, including an objective assessment of the facts of the case and the applicability of and conformity with the relevant covered agreements, and make such other findings as will assist the DSB in making the recommendations or in giving the rulings provided for in the covered agreements. In *European Communities – Hormones*, the Appellate Body noted that Article 11 of the DSU "articulates with great succinctness but with sufficient clarity the appropriate standard of review for panels in respect of both the ascertainment of facts and the legal characterization of such facts under the relevant agreements."[126] So far as fact-finding is concerned, the appropriate standard is neither a *de novo* review of the facts nor "total deference" to the factual findings of national authorities. Pursuant to Article 11 of the DSU, panels have rather "to make an *objective assessment* of the facts". With regard to legal questions, i.e., the consistency or inconsistency of a Member's measure with the specified provisions of the relevant agreement, Article 11 imposes the same standard on panels, i.e., "to make an *objective assessment* of ... the applicability of and conformity with the relevant covered agreement".

In *European Communities – Hormones*, the Appellate Body addressed for the first time the question when a panel may be regarded as having failed to discharge its duty under Article 11 of the DSU to make an objective assessment of the facts before it. According to the Appellate

---

[124] Appellate Body Report, *European Communities – Bananas*, para. 141.
[125] Appellate Body Report, *Korea – Dairy Safeguards*, para. 127.
[126] Appellate Body Report, *European Communities – Hormones*, para. 116. We observe, however, that there is one covered agreement, the *Anti-dumping Agreement*, which sets out in Article 17.6 thereof, a special standard of review for disputes arising under that agreement.

Body, "not every error in the appreciation of the evidence ... may be characterized as a failure to make an objective assessment of the facts."[127] The Appellate Body stated:

> The duty to make an objective assessment of the facts is, among other things, an obligation to consider the evidence presented to a panel and to make factual findings on the basis of that evidence. The deliberate disregard of, or refusal to consider, the evidence submitted to a panel is incompatible with a panel's duty to make an objective assessment of the facts. The willful distortion or misrepresentation of the evidence put before a panel is similarly inconsistent with an objective assessment of the facts. "Disregard" and "distortion" and "misrepresentation" of the evidence, in their ordinary signification in judicial and quasi-judicial processes, imply not simply an error of judgment in the appreciation of evidence but rather an egregious error that calls into question the good faith of a panel.[128]

An allegation that a panel has failed to conduct the objective assessment of the matter before it as required by Article 11 of the DSU is a very serious allegation. Such an allegation goes to "the very core of the integrity of the WTO dispute settlement process itself."[129] So far, no claim that a panel violated its obligation under Article 11 of the DSU has been successful.

If a panel concludes that a Member's measure is inconsistent with a covered agreement, it shall recommend that the Member concerned bring that measure into conformity with that agreement.[130] In addition to making recommendations, the panel may suggest ways in which the Member concerned could implement those recommendations.[131] These suggestions are not legally binding on the Member concerned but because the panel making the suggestions might later be called upon to assess sufficiency of the implementation of the recommendations, such suggestions are likely to have a certain impact.[132] Thus far, a few panels

---

[127] Appellate Body Report, *European Communities – Hormones*, para. 133.

[128] *Ibid.* The Appellate Body considered that "a claim that a panel disregarded or distorted the evidence submitted to it is, in effect, a claim that the panel, to a greater or lesser degree, denied the party submitting the evidence fundamental fairness, or what in many jurisdictions is known as due process of law or natural justice." *Ibid.*

[129] Appellate Body Report, *European Communities – Measures Affecting the Importation of Certain Poultry Products ("European Communities – Poultry")*, WT/DS69/AB/R, adopted 23 July 1998, para. 133.

[130] Article 19.1 of the DSU.

[131] *Ibid.*

[132] See *infra*, p. 339.

have made use of this authority to make suggestions regarding implementation of their recommendations.[133]

Panels are not required to examine each and every one of the legal claims that a complaining party might be minded to make. Since the aim of dispute settlement is to secure a positive solution to a dispute, panels "need only address those claims which must be addressed in order to resolve the matter in issue in the dispute."[134] A panel has discretion to determine the claims it must address in order actually and effectively to resolve the dispute between the parties.[135] Panels are, however, cautioned to be careful when applying the principle of judicial economy. To provide only a partial resolution of the matter at issue may be false judicial economy since the unanswered issues may well give rise to a new dispute. A panel has to address "those claims on which a finding is necessary in order to enable the DSB to make sufficiently precise recommendations and rulings so as to allow for prompt compliance by a Member with those recommendations and rulings 'in order to ensure effective resolution of disputes to the benefit of all Members '."[136]

SCOPE OF APPELLATE REVIEW

Only parties to the dispute may appeal a panel report.[137] Third parties or other WTO Members cannot appeal a panel report. However, WTO Members which have notified their interest to the DSB under Article 10.2 of the DSU, can participate in the appellate review proceedings as third participants, and make written submissions to the Appellate Body and appear at the oral hearing.[138]

An appeal is limited to issues of law covered in the panel report and legal interpretations developed by the panel.[139] Factual findings and

---

[133] See, for example: Panel Report, *United States - Underwear*, Panel Report, *Guatemala - Cement*, Panel Report, *India - Quantitative Restrictions*, and Panel Report, *United States – Imposition of Countervailing Duties on Certain Hot-Rolled Lead and Bismuth Carbon Steel Products Originating in the United Kingdom* ("*United States – Leaded Bars*"), WT/DS138/R.

[134] Appellate Body Report, *United States – Shirts and Blouses*, p. 19.

[135] Appellate Body Report, *India - Patents*, para. 87.

[136] Appellate Body Report, *Australia – Measures Affecting Importation of Salmon* ("*Australia – Salmon*"), WT/DS18/AB/R, adopted 6 November 1998, para. 223. See also Appellate Body Report, *Japan – Measures Affecting Agricultural Products* ("*Japan – Agricultural Products*"), WT/DS76/AB/R, adopted 19 March 1999, para. 111.

[137] Article 17.4 of the DSU.

[138] Article 17.4 of the DSU and Rules 24 and 27(3) of the *Working Procedures*.

[139] Article 17.6 of the DSU.

conclusions of the panel are, in principle, non-appealable. In order to determine the scope of its mandate, it is therefore necessary for the Appellate Body to distinguish between questions of law and questions of fact. In practice, the distinction is not always readily discernible. This problem is, of course, not uncommon and many national appellate courts with jurisdiction limited to questions of law have confronted it. In *European Communities – Hormones*, the Appellate Body found:

> The determination of whether or not a certain event did occur in time and space is typically a question of fact; for example, the question of whether or not the Codex [Alimentarius] has adopted an international standard, guideline or recommendation on MGA is a factual question. Determination of the credibility and weight properly to be ascribed to (that is, the appreciation of) a given piece of evidence is part and parcel of the fact finding process and is, in principle, left to the discretion of a panel as the trier of facts. The consistency or inconsistency of a given fact or set of facts with the requirements of a given treaty provision is, however, a legal characterization issue. It is a legal question.[140]

Although the panel's examination and weighing of the evidence submitted are, in principle, within the scope of the panel's discretion as the trier of facts and, accordingly, outside the scope of appellate review, the panel's discretion as trier of facts is not unlimited. The panel's discretion "is always subject to, and is circumscribed by, among other things, the panel's duty to render an objective assessment of the matter before it."[141] Whether the Panel has made such an objective assessment is itself a legal question.[142]

The legal findings and conclusions of the panel subject to appeal may be upheld, modified or reversed by the Appellate Body.[143] The Appellate Body cannot, however, remand a dispute to the panel for further or additional fact-finding or for the examination of legal issues not addressed by the panel. This lack of remand power is considered by some to be a major shortcoming of the current dispute settlement system. It should be noted, however, that in a number of cases the Appellate Body has examined legal issues which the panel had not

---

[140] Appellate Body Report, *European Communities – Hormones*, para.132.
[141] Appellate Body Report, *Korea – Taxes on Alcoholic Beverages* ("*Korea – Alcoholic Beverages*"), WT/DS75/AB/R, WT/DS84/AB/R, adopted 17 February 1999, para.162.
[142] Appellate Body Report, *European Communities – Hormones*, para. 132.
[143] Article 17.13 of the DSU.

addressed. The Appellate Body considered it to be within its competence to examine and decide these issues in order to complete the legal analysis and thus effectively resolve the dispute between the parties.[144] The Appellate Body has stressed, however, that it is possible to complete the legal analysis only where there are sufficient factual findings by the panel or undisputed facts in the panel record.[145]

PANEL AND APPELLATE BODY PROCEEDINGS

One of the most striking features of the WTO dispute settlement system is the short time-frames within which the proceedings of both panels and the Appellate Body must be completed. The period in which a panel shall conduct its examination, from the date that the composition and terms of reference of the panel have been agreed upon until the date the final report is issued to the parties to the dispute, shall, as a general rule, not exceed six months.[146] When a panel considers that it cannot issue its report within six months, it shall inform the DSB in writing of the reasons for the delay together with an estimate of the period within with it shall issue its report. In no case *should* the period from the establishment of the panel to the circulation of the report to the Members exceed nine months.[147] With regard to the Appellate Body proceedings, the DSU provides that, as a general rule, the proceedings shall not exceed 60 days from the date a party to the dispute formally notifies its decision to appeal to the date the Appellate Body circulates its report.[148] When the Appellate Body believes that it cannot render its report within 60 days, it shall inform the DSB in writing of the reasons for the delay together with an estimate of the period within

---

[144] Appellate Body Report, *Australia – Salmon*, para. 117. The Appellate Body completed the legal analysis in, for example: *United States – Gasoline*; *Canada – Certain Measures Concerning Periodicals* ("*Canada – Periodicals*"), WT/DS31/AB/R, adopted 30 July 1997; *European Communities – Poultry*; *United States – Shrimp*; and *Australia – Salmon*.

[145] Appellate Body Report, *Australia – Salmon*, paras. 241, 242 and 255.

[146] Article 12.8 of the DSU. In cases of urgency, including those relating to perishable goods, the panel shall aim to issue its report to the parties to the dispute within three months and shall make every effort to accelerate the proceedings to the greatest extent possible (Articles 12.9 and 4.9 of the DSU).

[147] Article 12.9 of the DSU.

[148] Article 17.5 of the DSU. In cases of urgency, including those which concern perishable foods, the Appellate Body shall make every effort to accelerate the proceedings to the greatest extent possible (Articles 17.5 and 4.9 of the DSU).

which it will submit its report. In no case *shall* the proceedings exceed 90 days. No other international court or tribunal operates under such severe time limits. These time limits, and in particular the time limits for the Appellate Body, have been criticized as excessively short and demanding for both the parties to the dispute and the Appellate Body. As a result of these time limits, however, there is no backlog of cases either at the panel or appellate level. While panels frequently go beyond the time limits imposed on them by the DSU, the Appellate Body has thus far been able to complete all but two appeals within the maximum period of 90 days.[149]

PANEL PROCEEDINGS

The basic rules governing panel proceedings are set out in Article 12 of the DSU. Article 12.1 of the DSU directs a panel to follow the Working Procedures contained in Appendix 3 of the DSU, but at the same time authorizes a panel to do otherwise after consulting the parties to the dispute. Since the Working Procedures contained in Appendix 3 are quite rudimentary, many panels have been obliged to adopt *ad hoc* procedures, which often differ from case to case and, therefore may leave an impression with the parties of procedural uncertainty. Panel procedures should provide sufficient flexibility so as to ensure high-quality panel reports, while not unduly delaying the panel process.[150] The Appellate Body has repeatedly observed, however, that detailed, standard working procedures for panels, including rules on preliminary rulings, fact-finding and the submission of evidence, would help to ensure due process and fairness in panel proceedings.[151]

After consulting the parties to the dispute at what is called the organizational meeting, the panel, as soon as practicable, fixes the timetable for the panel process, indicating *inter alia* precise deadlines for written submissions, and adopts, where necessary, *ad hoc* working pro-

---

[149] For panel reports circulated to WTO Members in the period from 1 January 1995 to 31 August 1998, the median time-period from the establishment of the panel to the circulation of the panel report was 10 months. The time-period ranged from 7 months to 17 months. In *European Communities – Hormones* and *United States – Leaded Bars*, the Appellate Body went beyond the 90-day time-limit due to extraordinary circumstances.

[150] Article 12.2 of the DSU.

[151] Appellate Body Reports: *European Communities – Bananas*, para 144; *India – Patents*, para. 95; and *Argentina – Measures Affecting Imports of Footwear, Textiles, Apparel and Other Items* ("*Argentina – Textiles and Apparel*"), WT/DS56/AB/R, adopted 22 April 1998, para. 79 and footnote 68.

cedures.[152] The complaining party makes its first submission in advance of the responding party's first submission unless the panel decides, after consultation with the parties, that the parties should submit their first submissions simultaneously. In their first written submissions, the parties present the facts of the case and their arguments. The rebuttal submissions, in which each party replies to the arguments and evidence submitted by the other parties, are submitted simultaneously.[153] Written submissions to the panel are treated as confidential and are not made available to the public.[154] Recognizing that parties have a legitimate interest in protecting sensitive business confidential information submitted to a panel, the Panels in *Canada - Aircraft* and *Brazil - Aircraft* adopted special procedures governing business confidential information.[155]

The panel meets in closed session.[156] After the filing of the first written submissions of the parties, the panel holds its first substantive meeting with the parties.[157] At this meeting, the panel asks the complaining party to present its case. At the same meeting, the respondent party is asked to present its own point of view.[158] Any Member having a substantial interest in a matter before a panel and having notified its interest to the DSB at the time of the establishment of the panel, is given an opportunity to be heard by the panel and to make written

---

[152] Articles 12.3 and 12.5 of the DSU. Paragraph 12 of Appendix 3 to the DSU contains a proposed timetable for panel work. In determining the timetable for the panel process, the panel must provide sufficient time for the parties to the dispute to prepare their submissions (Article 12.4 of the DSU).

[153] Article 12.6 of the DSU. Each party to the dispute shall deposit its written submissions with the WTO Secretariat for immediate transmission to the panel and to the other party or parties to the dispute.

[154] Article 18.2 of the DSU. However, nothing in the DSU precludes a party to a dispute from disclosing statements of its own positions to the public. A party to a dispute shall also, upon request of a Member, provide a non-confidential summary of the information contained in its written submissions that could be disclosed to the public (Article 18.2 of the DSU and paragraph 3 of Appendix 3 of the DSU). See also paragraph 10 of Appendix 3 of the DSU.

[155] Panel Reports: *Canada - Measures Affecting the Export of Civilian Aircraft* ("*Canada - Aircraft*"), WT/DS70/R, adopted 20 August 1999, Annex 1; and *Brazil - Export Financing Programme for Aircraft* ("*Brazil - Aircraft*"), WT/DS46/R, adopted 20 August 1999, Annex 1. These procedures concerned, *inter alia*, the storage of and access to business confidential information as well as the return and destruction of such information.

[156] Paragraph 2 of Appendix 3 of the DSU.

[157] Paragraph 4 of Appendix 3 of the DSU.

[158] Paragraph 5 of Appendix 3 of the DSU.

submissions to the panel.[159] Third parties are invited to present their views during a session of the first substantive meeting of the panel set aside for that purpose.[160] After the filing of the rebuttal submissions, the panel holds a second substantive meeting with the parties. At this meeting the respondent party is given the right to take the floor first, to be followed by the complaining party.[161] The panel may at any time put questions to the parties and ask them for explanations either in the course of a meeting or in writing.[162] No *ex parte* communications with the panel are allowed concerning matters under consideration by it.[163] The meetings of the panel with the parties are open only to WTO Members which are a party to the dispute. Panel meetings are not open to the general public.

The DSU does not explicitly address the issue of representation of the parties before panels. In *European Communities – Bananas*, the issue arose whether private counsel, not employed by government, may represent a party before the Panel and the Appellate Body. In a brief and matter of fact ruling, the Appellate Body noted that nothing in the *WTO Agreement* or the DSU, nor in customary international law or the prevailing practice of international tribunals, prevents a WTO Member from determining for itself the composition of its delegation in Appellate Body hearings. A party can, therefore, decide that private counsel forms part of its delegation and will represent it before the Appellate Body. In practice, private counsel now routinely appear in panel proceedings as well as in Appellate Body hearings.

In recognition of the fact that disputes brought to panels for adjudication often involve factual, technical and scientific issues, Article 13.1 of the DSU gives panels "the right to seek information and technical advice from any individual or body which it deems appropriate".[164]

---

[159] Article 10 of the DSU. Third parties shall receive the submissions of the parties to the dispute to the first meeting with the panel.

[160] Paragraph 6 of Appendix 3 of the DSU. In a few cases, panels have given third parties more extended rights of participation in the panel proceedings. In *European Communities – Bananas*, the Panel granted the third parties the right to attend both the first and second substantive meeting of the panel with the parties.

[161] Paragraph 7 of Appendix 3 of the DSU. Additional meetings with the parties may be scheduled if required (Paragraph 12 of Appendix 3 of the DSU). In practice, however, very few panels have had additional meetings with the parties.

[162] Paragraph 8 of Appendix 3 of the DSU. During panel proceedings parties may also question each other.

[163] Article 18.1 of the DSU.

[164] Pursuant to Article 13.1 of the DSU, "before a panel seeks such information or advice from any individual or body within the jurisdiction of a Member it shall

Panels may "consult experts to obtain their opinion on certain aspects of the matter" under consideration.[165] As the Appellate Body ruled in *Argentina - Textiles and Apparel*, "this is a grant of discretionary authority: a panel is not duty-bound to seek information in each and every case or to consult particular experts under this provision."[166] The panel's authority to seek information and technical advice is "comprehensive" and "embraces more than merely the choice and evaluation of the *source* of the information or advice which it may seek."[167] It includes the "authority to decide *not to seek* such information or advice at all."[168] In *United States - Shrimp*, the Appellate Body further stated:

> ... a panel also has the authority to *accept or reject* any information or advice which it may have sought and received, or to *make some other appropriate disposition* thereof. It is particularly within the province and the authority of a panel to determine *the need for information and advice* in a specific case, to ascertain the *acceptability* and *relevancy* of information or advice received, and to decide *what weight to ascribe to that information or advice* or to conclude that no weight at all should be given to what has been received.[169]

Panels thus have significant authority to ascertain facts relating to the dispute. A panel is entitled to seek information and advice from experts and from any other relevant source it chooses to help the panel to understand and evaluate the evidence submitted and the arguments made by the parties, but not, however, to make the case for one or the other party.[170] During the period 1995-1999, panels have consulted

---

inform the authorities of that Member. A Member should respond promptly and fully to any request by a panel for such information as the panel considers necessary and appropriate." Article 11.2 of the *SPS Agreement* also provides for the right of a panel to seek the advice of experts.

[165] Article 13.2 of the DSU. With respect to a factual issue concerning a scientific or other technical matter raised by a party to the dispute, a panel may request an advisory report in writing from an expert review group. Rules for the establishment of such a group and its procedures are set forth in Appendix 4 of the DSU. Thus far, panels have not made use of the possibility to request an advisory report from an expert review group. Panels have preferred to consult experts on an individual basis. The DSU leaves to the sound discretion of a panel the determination of whether the establishment of an expert review group is necessary or appropriate (Appellate Body Report, *European Communities – Hormones*, para. 147).

[166] Appellate Body Report, *Argentina - Textiles and Apparel*, para. 84.

[167] Appellate Body Report, *United States - Shrimp*, para. 104.

[168] *Ibid.*

[169] *Ibid.*

[170] Appellate Body Report, *Japan – Measures Affecting Agricultural Products* ("*Japan – Agricultural Products*"), WT/DS76/AB/R, adopted 19 March 1999, para. 129

experts in, for example, *European Communities – Hormones*, *Australia – Salmon* and *Japan – Agricultural Products*, all disputes involving sanitary or phytosanitary measures which required an understanding of complex scientific issues.

With regard to the issue whether panels may consider unsolicited *amicus curiae* briefs, the Appellate Body noted in *United States – Shrimp* the comprehensive nature of the authority of a panel under Article 13 of the DSU as well as the authority under Article 12.1 of the DSU to depart from, or to add to, the Working Procedures set forth in Appendix 3 of the DSU.[171] According to the Appellate Body,

> "the thrust of Articles 12 and 13, taken together, is that the DSU accords to a panel established by the DSB, and engaged in a dispute settlement proceeding, ample and extensive authority to undertake and to control the process by which it informs itself both of the relevant facts of the dispute and of the legal norms and principles applicable to such facts."[172]

That authority, and the scope thereof, is

> "indispensably necessary to enable a panel to discharge its duty imposed by Article 11 of the DSU to 'make an objective assessment of the matter before it, including an objective assessment of the facts of the case and the applicability of and conformity with the relevant covered agreements ...'."[173]

The Appellate Body came to the conclusion that panels have "the discretionary authority either to accept and consider or to reject information and advice submitted to it, *whether requested by a panel or not.*"[174]

The DSU does not establish precise deadlines for the presentation of evidence by a party to the dispute. The DSU contemplates two distinguishable stages in a panel proceeding: a first stage during which the complaining party should set out its case in chief, including a full presentation of the facts on the basis of submission of supporting evi-

---

[171] Appellate Body Report, *United States – Shrimp*, para. 105.
[172] *Ibid.*, para. 106.
[173] *Ibid.* The Appellate Body reversed the Panel's reasoning that the authority to *seek* information under Article 13 of the DSU implied a *prohibition* on accepting information which has been submitted without having been requested by a panel (Appellate Body Report, *United States – Shrimp*, para. 108).
[174] Appellate Body Report, *United States – Shrimp*, para. 108. The amplitude of the authority vested in panels to shape the process of fact-finding and legal interpretation makes clear that a panel will not be "deluged" with non-requested materials, unless that panel allows itself to be so "deluged" (*Ibid.*).

dence; and a second stage which is generally designed to permit "rebuttals" by each party of the arguments and evidence submitted by the other party.[175] However, in the absence of hard and fast DSU rules on deadlines for submitting evidence and in the absence of specific deadlines in *ad hoc* working procedures, a panel has discretion to admit or refuse evidence submitted late in the panel proceeding. The panel must of course be careful constantly to observe due process, which, *inter alia*, entails providing the parties adequate opportunity to respond to the evidence submitted.[176]

The DSU does not contain any specific rules concerning the burden of proof in panel proceedings. However, in *United States – Shirts and Blouses*, the Appellate Body noted:

> In addressing this issue, we find it difficult, indeed, to see how any system of judicial settlement could work if it incorporated the proposition that the mere assertion of a claim might amount to proof. It is, thus, hardly surprising that various international tribunals, including the International Court of Justice, have generally and consistently accepted and applied the rule that the party who asserts a fact, whether the claimant or the respondent, is responsible for providing proof thereof. Also, it is a generally-accepted canon of evidence in civil law, common law and, in fact, most jurisdictions, that the burden of proof rests upon the party, whether complaining or defending, who asserts the affirmative of a particular claim or defence. If that party adduces evidence sufficient to raise a presumption that what is claimed is true, the burden then shifts to the other party, who will fail unless it adduces sufficient evidence to rebut the presumption.[177]

These rules on the burden of proof also apply in panel proceedings. The Appellate Body further added that "precisely how much and precisely what kind of evidence will be required to establish a presumption that what is claimed is true, will necessarily vary from measure to measure, provision to provision, and case to case."[178]

As with a court or tribunal, the panel deliberations are confidential.[179] The reports of panels are drafted without the presence of the parties to the dispute in the light of the information provided and the

---

[175] Appellate Body Report, *Argentina – Textiles and Apparel*, para. 79.
[176] Appellate Body Reports: *Argentina – Textiles and Apparel*, paras. 80-81; and *Australia – Salmon*, para. 272.
[177] Appellate Body Report, *United States – Shirts and Blouses*, p. 14.
[178] *Ibid.*
[179] Article 14.1 of the DSU.

statements made.[180] Opinions expressed in the panel report by individual panelists must be anonymous.[181] Thus far, there has been only one panel report setting out an anonymous "dissenting opinion".[182]

Having completed a draft of the descriptive (i.e., facts and argument) sections of its report, the panel issues this draft to the parties for their comments.[183] Following the expiration of the time period for comments, the panel subsequently issues an interim report to the parties, including both the descriptive sections and the panel's findings and conclusions.[184] A party may submit a written request to the panel to review particular aspects of the interim report. At the request of a party, the panel may hold a further meeting with the parties on the issues identified in the written comments.[185] The findings of the final panel report commonly include a discussion of the arguments made at the interim review stage.[186] The need for and utility of this interim review procedure has been the subject of debate. The final panel report is first issued to the parties to the dispute and some time later, once the report is available in the three working languages of the WTO, circulated to the general WTO Membership.[187] Once circulated to WTO Members, the panel report is an unrestricted document available to the public. Within 60 days after the date of circulation of the panel report to the Members, the report is adopted at a DSB meeting unless a party to the dispute formally notifies the DSB of its decision to appeal, or the DSB decides by consensus not to adopt the report.[188]

---

[180] Article 14.2 of the DSU.
[181] Article 14.3 of the DSU.
[182] Panel Report, *European Communities – Poultry*.
[183] Article 15.1 of the DSU. We note that recently some panels have attached the submissions, the written versions of oral statements and answers to questions to their report, rather than summarizing these documents in the descriptive sections of the report. See, for example, Panel Report, *United States – Leaded Bars*.
[184] Article 15.2 of the DSU.
[185] *Ibid*.
[186] Article 15.3 of the DSU. If no comments are received from any party within the comment period , the interim report shall be considered the final panel report (Article 15.3 of the DSU).
[187] The working languages of the WTO are English, French and Spanish. The parties may use any of the three languages in the proceedings. During the period 1995-2000, however, English was the language commonly used by the panel, the parties and third parties in panel proceedings.
[188] Article 16.4 of the DSU. In order to provide sufficient time for the Members to consider panel reports, the reports shall not be considered for adoption by the DSB until 20 days after they have been circulated (Article 16.1 of the DSU). The parties to a dispute have the right to participate fully in the consideration of panel

It should be noted that, at the request of the complaining party, the panel may at any time during the panel proceedings suspend its work for a maximum period of 12 months.[189] If the work of the panel has been suspended for more than 12 months, the authority of the panel lapses.[190]

APPELLATE BODY PROCEEDINGS

The Appellate Body has detailed standard working procedures set out in the *Working Procedures for Appellate Review* (the *"Working Procedures"*).[191] Pursuant to Article 17.9 of the DSU, these *Working Procedures* were drawn up by the Appellate Body in consultation with the Chairman of the DSB and the Director-General. In addition, where a procedural question arises that is not covered by the *Working Procedures*, the Division hearing the appeal may, in the interest of fairness and orderly procedure in the conduct of the appeal, adopt an appropriate procedure for the purpose of that appeal.[192]

Pursuant to Rule 20(1) of the *Working Procedures*, an appellate review process commences with a party's notification in writing to the DSB of its decision to appeal and the simultaneous filing of a notice of appeal with the Appellate Body. The notice of appeal must adequately identify the findings or legal interpretations of the panel which are being appealed as erroneous.[193] A party can appeal a panel report as

---

reports by the DSB, and their views shall be fully recorded (Article 16.3 of the DSU).

[189] Article 12.12 of the DSU. See, for example, *United States – The Cuban Liberty and Democratic Solidarity Act* (*"United States – Helms-Burton Act"*) complaint by the European Communities, WT/DS38, and *European Communities – Measures Affecting Butter Products*, complaint by New Zealand, WT/DS72.

[190] See, for example, *United States – Helms-Burton Act*.

[191] *Working Procedures for Appellate Review*, WT/AB/WP/3, dated 28 February 1997. This is a consolidated, revised version of the *Working Procedures for Appellate Review*, WT/AB/WP/1, dated 15 February 1996.

[192] Rule 16(1) of the *Working Procedures*. Such procedure must, however, be consistent with the DSU, the other covered agreements and the *Working Procedures*.

[193] Pursuant to Rule 20(2)(d) of the *Working Procedures*, the notice of appeal must include "a brief statement of the nature of the appeal, including the allegations of errors in the issues of law covered in the panel report and legal interpretations developed by the panel." The notice of appeal is not expected to contain the reasons why the appellant regards those findings or interpretations as erroneous. The notice of appeal is not designed to be a summary or outline of the arguments to be made by the appellant. The legal arguments in support of the allegations of error are, of course, to be set out and developed in the appellant's submission. See Ap-

soon as the report is circulated to WTO Members and it can do so as long as the report has not yet been adopted by the DSB. In actual practice, parties usually appeal shortly before the meeting of the DSB that is to consider the adoption of the report.

Upon the commencement of an appeal, the Appellate Body Division responsible for deciding the appeal draws up an appropriate working schedule in accordance with the time periods stipulated in the *Working Procedures*.[194] In exceptional circumstances, where strict adherence to such a time-period would result in manifest unfairness, a party or third party to the dispute may request modification of such time period.[195] Within 10 days after filing of the notice of appeal, the appellant must file a written submission.[196] The written submission sets out a precise statement of the grounds of appeal, including the specific allegations of legal errors in the panel report, and the legal arguments in support of these allegations.[197] Within 15 days after the filing of the notice of appeal, other parties to the dispute may, by filing an appellant's submission, join in the original appeal or appeal on the basis of other alleged legal errors in the panel report.[198] Within 25 days after

---

pellate Body Reports: *United States – Shrimp*, paras. 92-97; and *European Communities – Bananas*, paras. 148-152.

[194] Rule 26(1) of the *Working Procedures*. The Appellate Body Secretariat shall serve forthwith a copy of the working schedule on the appellant, the parties to the dispute and any third parties (Rule 26(4) of the *Working Procedures*). The working schedule sets forth precise dates for the filing of documents and includes a timetable of the Division's work (Rule 26(2) of the *Working Procedures*). In appeals of urgency, including those which concern perishable goods, the Appellate Body shall make every effort to accelerate the appellate proceedings to the greatest extent possible (Rule 26(3) of the *Working Procedures*). Where possible, the working schedule will include the date for the oral hearing. Where a participant fails to file a submission within the required time periods, the Division shall, after hearing the views of the participants, issue such order, including dismissal of the appeal, as deems appropriate (Rule 29 of the *Working Procedures*).

[195] Rule 16(2) of the *Working Procedures*.

[196] Rule 21(1) of the *Working Procedures*. Pursuant to Rule 31 and the Timetable for Prohibited Subsidies Appeals set out in Annex I of the *Working Procedures*, the appellant's submission in proceedings involving prohibited subsidies shall be filed within 5 days after the date of the filing of the notice of appeal.

[197] Rule 21(2) of the *Working Procedures*. The submission also includes a precise statement of the provisions of the covered agreements and other legal sources relied on, as well as the nature of the decision or ruling sought.

[198] Rule 23(1) of the *Working Procedures*. Any written submission by such other appellants is subject to the same format requirements as the submission of the original appellant (Rule 23(2) of the *Working Procedures*). Pursuant to Rule 23(4) of the *Working Procedures*, parties may also, however, exercise their own right of appeal pursuant to Article 16.4 of the DSU. In such case a single Division shall ex-

the filing of the notice of appeal, any party that wishes to respond to allegations of legal errors, whether raised in the submission of the original appellant or in the submission(s) of other appellants, may file an appellee's submission.[199] The appellee's submission shall set out a precise statement of the grounds for opposing the specific allegations of legal errors raised in the appellant's submission, and include legal arguments in support thereof. Within 25 days after the date of the filing of the notice of appeal, any third party may file a written submission stating its intention to participate as a third participant in the appeal and presenting legal arguments in support of its position.[200]

The Division responsible for deciding the appeal holds an oral hearing. As a general rule, the oral hearing is held 30 days after the filing of the notice of appeal.[201] However, for practical and organizational reasons, the hearing is often held at a somewhat later date. The purpose of the oral hearing is to provide participants with an opportunity to present and argue their case before the Division, in order to clarify and distil the legal issues in the appeal. At the hearing, the appellant(s) and appellee(s) first make brief oral arguments focusing upon

---

amine the appeals (Rule 23(5) of the *Working Procedures*). In all appellate review proceedings to date, other parties have preferred to submit another appellant's submission within 15 days after the notice of appeal of the original appellant rather than exercising their own right of appeal. Pursuant to Rule 31 and the Timetable for Prohibited Subsidies Appeals set out in Annex I of the *Working Procedures*, the other appellant(s) submission(s) in proceedings involving prohibited subsidies shall be filed within 7 days after the date of the filing of the notice of appeal.

[199] Rule 22(1) and Rule 23(3) of the *Working Procedures*. Pursuant to Rule 31 and the Timetable for Prohibited Subsidies Appeals set out in Annex I of the *Working Procedures*, the appellee(s) submission(s) in proceedings involving prohibited subsidies shall be filed within 12 days after the date of the filing of the notice of appeal.

[200] Rule 24 of the *Working Procedures*. Pursuant to Rule 31 and the Timetable for Prohibited Subsidies Appeals set out in Annex I of the *Working Procedures*, the third participant(s) submission(s) in proceedings involving prohibited subsidies shall be filed within 12 days after the date of the filing of the notice of appeal.

[201] Rule 27(1) of the *Working Procedures*. Where possible in the working schedule or at the earliest possible date, the Appellate Body Secretariat shall notify all parties to the dispute, participants, third parties and third participants of the date for the oral hearing (Rule 27(2)). In exceptional circumstances, where strict adherence to a time period set out in the *Working Procedures* would result in manifest unfairness, a party to the dispute, participant, a third party or a third participant may request that a Division modify the date set out in the working schedule for the oral hearing (Rule 16(2)). Pursuant to Rule 31 and the Timetable for Prohibited Subsidies Appeals set out in Annex I of the *Working Procedures*, the oral hearing in proceedings involving prohibited subsidies shall be held an approximate 15 days after the date of the filing of the notice of appeal.

the core legal issues raised in the appeal. Any third participant may also make oral arguments.[202] The Presiding Member may, as necessary, set time limits for oral arguments.[203] As a rule, the appellant and appellee are given 30 minutes and the third participants 15 minutes each for their oral arguments. After the oral presentations, the participants (and the third participants) answer detailed questions posed by the Division regarding the issues raised in the appeal. At the end of the oral hearing, the participants and the third participants are given the opportunity to make a brief concluding statement. In oral hearings, participants and third participants are entitled to be represented by counsel of their own choice; they may, therefore, be represented by private lawyers rather than, or in addition to, government officials if they so wish.[204] The oral hearing is usually completed in one day. In complex cases, however, the oral hearing may take longer. In *European Communities – Bananas* and *European Communities – Hormones*, for example, the oral hearing took two and a half days and two days, respectively.

At any time during the appellate proceedings, the Division may address questions to, or request additional memoranda from, any participant or third participant, and specify the time periods by which written responses or memoranda shall be received.[205] Any such questions, responses or memoranda are simultaneously made available to the other participants and third participants in the appeal, who are given an opportunity to respond.[206] Throughout the proceedings, the participants and third participants are precluded from having *ex parte* communications with the Appellate Body in respect of matters concerning the appeal. Neither a Division nor any of its Members may meet with, or contact, one participant or third participant in the absence of the other participants and third participants.[207]

As noted above, the Division responsible for deciding an appeal will exchange views on issues raised by the appeal with the other Members

---

[202] Rule 27(3) of the *Working Procedures*.
[203] Rule 27(4) of the *Working Procedures*.
[204] Appellate Body Report, *European Communities – Bananas*, paras. 10-12.
[205] Rule 28(1) of the *Working Procedures*.
[206] Rule 28(2) of the *Working Procedures*.
[207] Rule 19(1) of the *Working Procedures*. No Member of the Division may discuss any aspect of the subject matter of an appeal with any participant or third participant in the absence of the other Members of the Division (Rule 19(2)). A Member of the Appellate Body who is not assigned to the Division hearing the appeal shall not discuss any aspect of the subject matter of the appeal with any participant or third participant (Rule 19(3)).

of the Appellate Body before finalizing its report. When finalized, the report is signed by the three Members of the Division. The report is then translated so that it is available in all three languages of the WTO.[208] After translation, the report is circulated to the WTO Members and is an unrestricted document, available to the public, as from that moment. Appellate Body reports shall, in no case, be circulated later than 90 days after the filing of the notice of appeal.[209] It is noteworthy that this 90-day period includes the time devoted to translation of the original version into the two other official languages of the WTO. Effectively, the 90-day period is, therefore, reduced to an 80-day period maximum by the requirement of translation.

The proceedings of the Appellate Body are confidential.[210] Therefore any written submission, legal memoranda, written responses to questions, and oral statements by the participants and the third participants; the conduct of the oral hearing before the Appellate Body, including any transcripts or tapes of that hearing; and the deliberations, the exchange of views and internal workings of the Appellate Body are confidential.[211] Furthermore, Members of the Appellate Body and its staff are covered by Article VII:1 of the *Rules of Conduct*, which provide that they shall at all times maintain the confidentiality of dispute settlement deliberations and proceedings together with any information identified by a party as confidential.[212]

---

[208] During the period 1995-1999, in all appellate review proceedings English has been the working language of the Appellate Body and the Appellate Body reports were all drafted in English and then translated into French and Spanish. In a few appellate review proceedings, participants or third participants filed submissions or made oral statements in French and Spanish. When requested, interpretation is provided at the oral hearing.

[209] Article 17.5 of the DSU. At any time during the appeal, the appellant may withdraw its appeal by notifying the Appellate Body, which shall forthwith notify the DSB (Rule 30(1) of the *Working Procedures*). Where the parties to a dispute reach a mutually agreed solution during the appellate review process, which is the subject of an appeal that has been notified to the DSB pursuant to Article 3.6 of the DSU, it too shall be notified to the Appellate Body (Rule 30(2)).

[210] Article 17.10 of the DSU. See also Article 18.2 of the DSU concerning the confidentiality of written submissions and information submitted to the Appellate Body.

[211] Appellate Body Reports in *Canada – Aircraft*, para. 143 and *Brazil – Aircraft*, para. 121.

[212] *Ibid.* We note that for these reasons, the Appellate Body did not consider it necessary in *Canada – Aircraft* and *Brazil Aircraft*, under all the circumstances of these cases, to adopt *additional* procedures for the protection of business confidential information in the appellate proceedings, and declined the request of Canada

Within 30 days following circulation, the Appellate Body report and the panel report as upheld, modified or reversed by the Appellate Body, are adopted by the DSB, unless the DSB decides by consensus not to adopt the reports.[213] The adopted Appellate Body report is accepted unconditionally by the parties to the dispute. The adoption procedure is, however, without prejudice to the right of Members to express their views on an Appellate Body report and parties to the dispute commonly avail themselves of this right.[214]

WTO Members have made extensive use of the possibility to appeal panel reports. Of the 33 panel reports circulated to WTO Members during the period 1995 – 1999, 27 were appealed.[215] During this period, the caseload of the Appellate Body has also steadily increased. In 1996, four appeals were filed, in 1997, five, in 1998, eight and in 1999, nine.

IMPLEMENTATION AND ENFORCEMENT OF RECOMMENDATIONS AND RULINGS

Where a panel or the Appellate Body rules that a measure is inconsistent with a covered agreement, it recommends that the Member concerned bring the measure into conformity with that agreement.[216] In

---

and Brazil for such additional procedures. See the Appellate Body Reports in *Canada – Aircraft*, paras. 141-147 and *Brazil – Aircraft*, paras. 119-125.

[213] Article 17.14 of the DSU. In accordance with Article 4.9 of the *SCM Agreement*, Appellate Body reports concerning prohibited subsidies shall be adopted by the DSB unless the DSB decides by consensus not to adopt the report within 20 days following its issuance to the Members.

[214] Article 17.14 of the DSU.

[215] The following panel reports were not appealed: *Japan – Measures Affecting Consumer Photographic Film and Paper* ("*Japan – Film*"), WT/DS44/R, adopted 22 April 1998; *India – Patent Protection for Pharmaceutical and Agricultural Chemical Products* ("*India – Patents (EC)*), complaint by the European Communities, WT/DS79/R, adopted 22 September 1998; *Indonesia – Certain Measures Affecting the Automotive Industry* ("*Indonesia – Automobile Industry*"), WT/DS54/15, WT/DS59/13, WTDS64/12, adopted 7 December 1998; *United States – Anti-Dumping Duty on Dynamic Random Access Memory Semiconductors /DRAMS) of One Megabit or Above from Korea* ("*United States – DRAMS*"), WT/DS99/R, adopted 19 March 1999; *Australia – Subsidies Provided to Producers and Exporters of Automotive Leather* ("*Australia – Automotive Leather*"), WT/DS126/R, adopted 16 June 1999; and *United States – Section 301*, WT/DS152/R adopted 27 January 2000.

[216] Article 19.1 of the DSU. However, if, in cases involving a "non-violation" complaint, a measure is found to nullify or impair benefits under, or impede the attainment of objectives of, a covered agreement without violation thereof, there is no obligation to withdraw the measure. In such cases, the panel or the Appellate

addition to its recommendations, the panel or Appellate Body may suggest ways in which the Member concerned could implement the recommendations.[217] The panel and Appellate Body reports, and the rulings and recommendations contained therein, become binding on the parties to the dispute after they have been adopted by the DSB, but not on Members that are not a party to the dispute. There is no *stare decisis* or binding precedent rule in the WTO dispute settlement system. However, in *Japan – Alcoholic Beverages*, the Appellate Body found with regard to adopted GATT 1947 panel reports that these reports "are an important part of the GATT *acquis*" and that "they are often considered by subsequent panels".[218] According to the Appellate Body, adopted GATT 1947 panel reports "create legitimate expectations among WTO Members, and therefore, should be taken into account where they are relevant to any dispute."[219] Similarly, adopted WTO panel reports and Appellate Body reports are taken into account where they are relevant to subsequent disputes.

Prompt compliance with recommendations or rulings adopted by the DSB is essential in order to ensure effective resolution of disputes to the benefit of all Members.[220] At a DSB meeting held within 30 days after the date of adoption of the panel or Appellate Body report, the Member concerned must inform the DSB of its intentions in respect of implementation of those recommendations and rulings.[221] If it is impracticable to comply immediately with the recommendations and rulings, and this may often be the case, the Member concerned has a reasonable period of time in which to do so. The reasonable period of time is defined as the period of time proposed by the Member concerned and approved by the DSB, or in the absence of such approval, the period of time mutually agreed by the parties to the dispute within

---

Body shall recommend that the Member concerned make a mutually satisfactory adjustment. See Article 26.1 of the DSU. With regard to cases involving a "situation" complaint, see Article 26.2 of the DSU.

[217] Article 19.1 of the DSU. See, for example, Panel Report, *United States – Leaded Bars*, para. 8.2.

[218] Appellate Body Report, *Japan – Alcoholic Beverages*, p. 14.

[219] *Ibid.* Unadopted reports, on the contrary, "'have no legal status in the GATT or WTO system since they have not been endorsed through decisions by the CONTRACTING PARTIES to the GATT or WTO Members'." (*Ibid.*) Nevertheless, a panel could find "useful guidance in the reasoning of an unadopted panel report that it considers to be relevant."(*Ibid.*, p 15).

[220] Article 21.1 of the DSU.

[221] Article 21.3 of the DSU.

45 days after the adoption of the recommendations and rulings.[222] If the parties are unable to agree on a reasonable period of time for implementation, the applicable period of time may be, at the request of either party, determined through binding arbitration within 90 days after adoption of the recommendations and rulings.[223] If the parties do not agree on an arbitrator within 10 days after referring the matter to arbitration, the arbitrator is appointed by the Director-General within 10 days, after consulting the parties.[224] During the period 1995-1999, the reasonable period of time was fixed by an arbitrator in 6 cases.[225] In all these cases, the arbitrator, chosen by mutual agreement of the parties or appointed by the Director-General, was a Member of the Appellate Body.[226] In deciding on the reasonable period of time for implementation, a principal guideline has been that such period "should not exceed 15 months from the date of adoption of a panel or Appellate Body report"; however, that period "may be shorter or longer, depending upon the particular circumstances." [227] In *European Communities – Hormones*, the arbitrator found that the reasonable period of time, as determined under Article 21.3 (c), should be the shortest period possible within the legal system of the Member to implement the recommendations and rulings of the DSB.[228] In the same case, the arbitrator noted that when implementation does not require changes in legislation but can be effected by administrative means, the reasonable period of time "should be considerably less than 15 months".[229] In past arbitration awards, the reasonable period of time for implementation has

---

[222] Article 21.3 (a) and (b) of the DSU. Parties to the dispute have mutually agreed on the reasonable period of time for implementation in, for example, *Canada –Periodicals* (15 months), *India – Patents* (15 months), *United States – Shrimp* (13 months), *Japan – Agricultural Products* (9 months and 12 days) and *United States – DRAMS* (8 months).

[223] Article 21.3 (c) of the DSU.

[224] Footnote 12 of the DSU.

[225] *Japan – Alcoholic Beverages*, *European Communities – Bananas*, *European Communities – Hormones*, *Indonesia – Automobile Industry*, *Australia – Salmon* and *Korea – Alcoholic Beverages*. During the first half of 2000, a seventh arbitration took place in *Chile – Alcoholic Beverages*.

[226] This has been so even in a case where no appeal from the panel report was taken. See: *Indonesia – Automobile Industry*.

[227] Article 21.3 (c) of the DSU.

[228] Arbitration Award under Article 21.3 (c) of the DSU, *European Communities – Hormones*, para. 26.

[229] *Ibid.*, para. 25. See also Arbitration Award under Article 21.3 (c) of the DSU, *Australia – Salmon*, para. 38.

ranged from 8 months in *Australia - Salmon* to 15 months and one week in *European Communities - Bananas*.

The DSB keeps under surveillance the implementation of adopted recommendations and rulings.[230] At any time following adoption of the recommendations or rulings, any WTO Member may raise the issue of implementation at the DSB. Starting six months after establishment of the reasonable period of time, the issue of implementation of the recommendations or rulings is placed on the agenda of each DSB meeting and remains on the DSB's agenda until the issue is resolved. At each DSB meeting, the Member concerned provides a status report on of its progress in implementing the DSB recommendations or rulings.[231]

Where there is disagreement as to whether the Member concerned has indeed taken measures to comply with the recommendations and rulings, or whether these measures are consistent with a covered agreement, Article 21.5 of the DSU provides that such disagreement shall be resolved through recourse to the DSU dispute settlement procedures. If possible, the original panel adjudicates this subsequent dispute. The panel must circulate its report within 90 days after referral of the matter to it.[232] During the period 1995-1999, 6 such implementation disputes under Article 21.5 of the DSU were referred to the original panel.[233]

In the event that the Member concerned fails to bring the WTO-inconsistent measure into conformity with, or otherwise fails to comply with the DSB recommendations and rulings within the reasonable period of time, such Member must, if so requested, and no later than the expiry of the reasonable period of time, enter into negotiations with the complaining party with a view to developing mutually acceptable compensation.[234] Compensation is voluntary and , if granted, must be consistent with the covered agreements.[235] If no satisfactory compensa-

---

[230] Article 21.6 of the DSU.
[231] Article 21.6 of the DSU.
[232] Article 21.5 of the DSU. When the panel considers that it cannot provide its report within this time frame, it shall inform the DSB in writing of the reasons for the delay together with an estimate of the period within which it will submit its report.
[233] *European Communities – Bananas* (recourse by Ecuador), *European Communities – Bananas* (recourse by the European Communities), *Australia – Salmon* (recourse by Canada), *Australia – Leather* (recourse by the United States), *Brazil – Aircraft* (recourse by Canada) and *Canada – Aircraft* (recourse by Brazil).
[234] Article 22.2 of the DSU.
[235] Article 22.1 of the DSU

tion has been agreed on within 20 days after expiry of the reasonable period of time, the complaining party, upon its request, may be granted authorization by the DSB to suspend the application to the Member concerned of concessions or other obligations under the covered agreements.[236] The request for authorization to suspend is granted within 30 days of the expiry of the reasonable period of time unless the DSB decides by consensus to reject the request.[237]

However, if the non-complying Member objects to the level of suspension proposed or claims that the principles and procedures for suspension have not been followed, the matter may be referred to arbitration before the DSB takes a decision.[238] The level of the suspension of concessions and other obligations to be authorized by the DSB must correspond to the level of the nullification or impairment.[239] The general principle is that the complaining party should first seek to suspend concessions or other obligations with respect to the same sector(s) as that in which the panel or Appellate Body found a violation or other nullification or impairment. However, if the complaining party considers that it is not practicable or effective to suspend concessions with respect to the same sector(s), it may seek to suspend concessions or other obligations in other sectors under the same agreement, or if that too is not practicable or effective and the circumstances are serious enough, concessions or other obligations under another covered agreement.[240] The arbitration on the level of the suspension or on the compliance with the suspension principles and procedures is carried out

---

[236] Article 22.2 of the DSU.
[237] Article 22.6 of the DSU.
[238] Article 22.6 of the DSU. Concessions or other obligations shall not be suspended during the course of the arbitration.
[239] Article 22.4 of the DSU. The arbitrator shall not examine the nature of the concessions or other obligations to be suspended but shall determine whether the level of such suspension is equivalent to the level of nullification of impairment (Article 22.7 of the DSU). The arbitrator may also determine if the proposed suspension of concessions or other obligations is allowed under the covered agreement (Article 22.7 of the DSU).
[240] Article 22.3 (a) to (c) of the DSU. For further principles and procedures, see Article 22.3 (d) and (e). See also: Decision by the Arbitrators, *European Communities – Bananas*, recourse to arbitration by the European Communities under Article 22.6 of the DSU, WT/DS27/ARB/ECU, 24 March 2000. With respect to goods, "sector" means all goods. With respect to services, "sector" means one of the 11 principal sectors identified in the current "Services Sectoral Classification List" (MTN.GNS/W/120). With respect to TRIPS, "sector" means each of the categories of intellectual property rights covered in Part II or the obligations under Part III or Part IV of the *Agreement on TRIPS* (Article 22.3 (f) of the DSU).

by the original panel, if the members thereof are available, or by an arbitrator appointed by the Director-General.[241] The arbitration must be completed within 60 days after expiry of the reasonable period of time[242] and no second arbitration is possible.[243] The DSB is informed promptly of the decision of the arbitrator and grants, by reverse consensus, the requested authorization to suspend concessions or other obligations, where the request is consistent with the decision of the arbitrator.[244] During the period 1995-1999, the DSB has granted authorization to suspend concessions and other obligations in two disputes. In *European Communities – Bananas*, the DSB authorized the United States to suspend concessions to the European Communities in an annual amount of US$ 191.4 million.[245] In *European Communities – Hormones*, the DSB authorized Canada and the United States to suspend concessions to the European Communities in an amount of CAN$ 11.3 million and US$116.8 million per year, respectively.[246] In both disputes, propriety of the proposed level of suspension was referred to the original panel for arbitration under Article 22.6 of the DSU.[247]

---

[241] Article 22.6 of the DSU.
[242] Article 22.6 of the DSU.
[243] Article 22.7 of the DSU.
[244] Article 22.7 of the DSU.
[245] Decision by the Arbitrators, *European Communities – Bananas*, recourse to arbitration by the European Communities under Article 22.6 of the DSU, WT/DS27/ARB, 9 April 1999. Note that on 8 November 1999, Ecuador requested authorization from the DSB to suspend the application to the EC of concessions or other obligations in an amount of US$ 450 million. The European Communities requested arbitration on the level of suspension requested by Ecuador. See: Decision by the Arbitrators, *European Communities – Bananas*, recourse to arbitration by the European Communities under Article 22.6 of the DSU, WT/DS27/ARB/ECU, 24 March 2000.
[246] Decision by the Arbitrators, *European Communities – Hormones* (original complaint by the United States), recourse to arbitration by the European Communities under Article 22.6 of the DSU, WT/DS26/ARB, 12 July 1999 and Decision by the Arbitrators, *European Communities – Hormones* (original complaint by Canada), recourse to arbitration by the European Communities under Article 22.6 of the DSU, WT/DS48/ARB, 12 July 1999.
[247] In both cases, the level of nullification suffered by the party requesting the suspension was found to be significantly lower than the proposed level of suspension In *European Communities – Bananas*, for example, the United States had proposed a level of suspension equal to US$ 520 million. The arbitrators determined that the level of nullification suffered by the United States to be equal to US$ 191.4 million.

It is arguable that neither compensation nor the suspension of concessions or other obligations is properly regarded as an alternative to compliance. WTO Members have an international law obligation to comply with the recommendations and rulings adopted by the DSB. Compensation and the suspension of concessions or other obligations are *temporary* measures available as a last resort in the event that the recommendations and rulings are not implemented by the defaulting Member within the reasonable period of time.[248] The suspension of concessions and other obligations are authorized only as long as justified by the failure of implementation.[249] The DSB continues to keep the matter under surveillance.[250]

The relationship between an Article 21.5 procedure regarding the implementation and an Article 22 request for authorization to suspend concessions or other obligations has been the source of considerable controversy. In *European Communities – Bananas*, the question arose whether, in a case where the parties disagree as to the consistency with the covered agreements of the measures taken to comply with the DSB recommendations and rulings, a party can request, and be granted, authorization to suspend concessions or other obligations before a panel under Article 21.5 has ruled on the WTO-consistency of the implementation measures.[251] Many Members have taken the position

---

[248] Articles 22.1 and 22.8 of the DSU. Article 3.7 of the DSU states with regard to compensation that the provision of compensation should be resorted to only if the immediate withdrawal of the measure is impracticable and as a temporary measure pending the withdrawal of the measure which is inconsistent with a covered agreement.

[249] Article 22.8 of the DSU.

[250] Article 22.8 of the DSU.

[251] In *European Communities – Bananas*, the DSB agreed on 12 January 1999, at the request of Ecuador, to reconvene the original panel to examine whether the measures taken by the European Communities to implement the DSB recommendations were WTO consistent. On 14 January 1999, the United States requested, pursuant to Article 22.2 authorization from the DSB to suspend concessions to the European Communities in an amount of US$ 520 million. On 26 January, the European Communities requested, pursuant to Article 22.6, arbitration on the level of suspension of concessions requested by the United States. The arbitrators under Article 22.6, who were the original panelists, determined the level of nullification suffered by the United States to be equal to US$ 191.4 million. The Article 21.5 panel requested by Ecuador found that measures taken by the European Communities to implement the DSB recommendations were not fully compatible with the WTO. The arbitrators' report and the report of the 21.5 panel were issued to the parties on 6 April 1999, and circulated to Members on 9 and 12 April 1999, respectively. On 9 April 1999, the United States requested the DSB to authorize suspension of concessions to the European Communities in an amount

that pursuant to Article 23 of the DSU, a Member cannot be granted authorization to suspend concessions or other obligations until after the WTO-inconsistency of the measures taken to comply with the DSB recommendations and ruling has been established through recourse to Article 21.5 of the DSU. However, it is possible to argue from the text of Article 22.6 of the DSU that the time-frame within which to obtain authorization to suspend concessions or other obligations, does not allow for recourse to Article 21.5 of the DSU after the expiry of the reasonable period of time for implementation. It is clear that the relationship between recourse to Article 21.5 and recourse to Article 22 of the DSU will need to be clarified.

CONCLUDING REMARKS

At the time of adoption of the *WTO Agreement*, it was agreed that the WTO Ministerial Conference would complete a full review of the DSU within four years after the entry into force of the *WTO Agreement*, and subsequently take a decision on whether to continue, modify or terminate the DSU.[252] In the context of this review of the DSU which took place in 1998 and 1999, Members made a large number of proposals and suggestions for further improvement of the dispute settlement system. In the run-up to and during the Seattle Ministerial Conference in December 1999, Members made a considerable but unsuccessful effort to reach agreement on modifications to be made to the DSU. While during the first five years of its operation the dispute settlement system has functioned reasonably well and has shown itself capable of handling complex and sensitive disputes, it is clear that some elements and characteristics of the current dispute settlement system underscore the need for further development. We are confident, however, that in view of the need for an effective dispute settlement system to provide predictability and stability to the multilateral trading system, the system will continue to develop on the basis of the experience that is gradually being acquired.

---

of US$ 191.4 million. On 19 April 1999, the DSB authorized the United States to suspend concessions to the European Communities in that amount.

[252] *Decision on the Application and Review of the Understanding on Rules and Procedures Governing the Settlement of Disputes*, published in *The Legal Texts: The Results of the Uruguay Round of Multilateral Trade Negotiations* (Cambridge University Press, 1999), 465.

ANNEX: SELECTED BIBLIOGRAPY

Bello, J., "The WTO Dispute Settlement Understanding: Less is More", *American Journal of International Law*, 1996, 416.

Bourgeois, J., "GATT/WTO Dispute Settlement Practice in the Field of Anti-dumping Law", in Petersmann E-U. (ed.), *International Trade Law and the GATT/WTO Dispute Settlement System* (Kluwer Law International, 1997), 283.

Brewer, T. and Young, S., "WTO Disputes and Developing Countries", *Journal of World Trade*, 1999, No. 5, 169.

Bronckers, M. and Jackson, J., "Outside Counsel in WTO Dispute Processes", *Journal of International Economic Law*, 1999, 155.

Bronkers, M. and McNelis, N.; "Fact and Law in Pleadings before the WTO Appellate Body", *International Trade Law and Regulation*, 1999, 118.

Cameron, J. and Campbell, K. (ed.), *Dispute Resolution in the World Trade Organisation* (Cameron May, 1998), 421 p.

Canal-Forgues, E., "La Procédure d'examen d'appel de l'Organe de règlement des différends de l'Organisation mondiale du commerce", *Annuaire français de droit international*, 1996, 845.

Cavalier, G., "A Call for Interim Relief at the WTO Level-Dispute Settlement and International Trade Diplomacy", *World Competition*, September 1999, 103.

Cho, S., "GATT Non-Violations Issues in the WTO Framework: Are They the Achilles' Heel of the Dispute Settlement Process?", *Harvard International Law Journal*, 1998, 311.

Chua, A., "The Precedential Effect of WTO panel and Appellate Body Reports", *Leiden Journal of International Law*, 1998, 45.

Chua, A., "Precedent and Principles of WTO Panel Jurisprudence", *Berkeley Journal of International Law*, 1998, 171.

Collier, J., *The Settlement of Disputes in International Law: Institutions and Procedures* (Oxford University Press, 1999), 395 p.

Cone, S., "The Appellate Body, the Protection of Sea Turtles and the Technique of 'Completing the Analysis'", *Journal of World Trade*, 1999, No. 2, 51.

Cottier T. and Schefer K., "Non-Violation Complaints in WTO/GATT Dispute Settlement: Past, Present and Future", in Petersmann E-U. (ed.), *International Trade Law and the GATT/WTO Dispute Settlement System* (Kluwer Law International, 1997), 143.

Cottier, T., "Dispute Settlement in the World Trade Organization: Characteristics and Structural Implications for the European Union", *Common Market Law Review*, 1998, 325.

Cottier, T., "The WTO Dispute Settlement System: New Horizons", *Proceedings of the 92ˢᵗ Annual Meeting ASIL (1998)*, 86.

Covelli, N., "Public International Law and Third Participation in WTO Panel Proceedings", *Journal of International Economic Law*, 1999, 125.

Croley, S., and Jackson, J., "WTO Dispute Panel Deference to National Government Decisions: The Misplaced Analogy to the U.S. Chevron Standard-of-Review Doctrine", in Petersmann E-U. (ed.), *International Trade Law and the GATT/WTO Dispute Settlement System* (Kluwer Law International, 1997), 185.

Davey, W., "The WTO Dispute Settlement System", *Journal of International Economic Law*, 2000, 15.

Davey, W., "Issues of WTO Dispute Settlement", *Proceedings of the 91ˢᵗ Annual Meeting ASIL (1997)*, 279.

Desmedt, A., "Hormones, 'Objective Assessment' and (or as) Standard of Review", *Journal of International Economic Law*, 1998, 695.

Ehrenhaft, P., "'Right to Counsel' in WTO Dispute Settlement Proceedings: a 1998 Resolution of the American Bar Association", *Journal of International Economic Law*, 1999, 159.

Feliciano, F., "Dispute Settlement under the Aegis of the World Trade Organization", in *Odyssey and Legacy: Chief Justice Andreas R. Narvasa Centennial Lecture Series* (Supreme Court Printing Services, 1999), 179.

Footer, M., "Some Aspects of Third Party Intervention in GATT/WTO Dispute Settlement Proceedings", in Petersmann E-U. (ed.), *International Trade Law and the GATT/WTO Dispute Settlement System* (Kluwer Law International, 1997), 211.

Hudec, R., "The New WTO Dispute Settlement Procedure: An Overview of the First Three Years", *Minn. J. Global Trade*, 1999, 1.

Jackson, J., "The WTO Dispute Settlement Understanding – Misunderstanding of the Nature of Legal Obligation", *American Journal of International Law*, 1997, 60.

Jackson, J., "Process, Compliance and Implementation Issues in WTO Dispute Settlement" *Proceedings of the 91" Annual Meeting ASIL (1997)*, 277.

Jackson, J., "Dispute Settlement and the WTO: Emerging Problems", *Journal of International Economic Law*, 1998, 329.

Joergens, K., "True Appellate Procedure or Only a Two-Stage Process?: a Comparative View of the Appellate Body under the WTO Dispute Settlement Understanding", *Law and Policy In International Business*, 1999, 193.

Kim, H., "The WTO Dispute Settlement Process: A Premier", *Journal of International Economic Law*, 1999, 477.

Komuro, N., "The WTO Dispute Settlement Mechanism : Coverage and Procedures of the WTO Understanding", *Journal of World Trade*, 1995, No.4, 5.

Kufuor, K., "From the GATT to the WTO: the Developing Countries and the Reform of the Procedures for the Settlement of International Trade Disputes", *Journal of World Trade*, 1997, No. 5, 117.

Kupfer Schneider, A., "Getting Along: The Evolution of Dispute Resolution Regimes in International Trade Organizations", *Michigan Journal of International Law*, 1999, 697.

Kuruvila, P., "Developing Countries and the GATT/WTO Dispute Settlement Mechanism", *Journal of World Trade*, 1997, No. 6, 171.

Lichtenbaum, P., "Reactions to Seattle: Dispute Settlement and Institutional Issues", *Journal of International Economic Law*, 2000, 173.

Ligustro, A., "La soluzzione delle controversie nel sistema dell' Organizzazione Mondiale del Commercio: problemi interpretativi e prassi applicativa.", *Rivista di diritto internazionale*, 1997, 1053.

Lugard, M., "Scope of Appellate Review: Objective Assessment of the Facts and Issues of Law", *Journal of International Economic Law*, 1998, 323.

Marceau, G, "NAFTA and WTO Dispute Settlement Rules – A Thematic Comparison", *Journal of World Trade*, 1997, No. 2, 25.

Marceau, G., "Rules on Ethics for the New World Trade Organization Dispute Settlement Mechanism – The Rules of Conduct for the DSU", *Journal of World Trade*, 1998, No.3, 57.

Marceau, G., "A Call for Coherence in International Law: Praises for the Prohibition Against "Clinical Isolation" in WTO Dispute Settlement", *Journal of World Trade*, 1999, No. 5, 87.

Martha, R., "Representation of Parties in World Trade Disputes", *Journal of World Trade*, 1997, No. 2, 83.

Morrison, P., "WTO Dispute Settlement in Services: Procedural and Substantive Aspects ", in Petersmann E-U. (ed.), *International Trade Law and the GATT/WTO Dispute Settlement System* (Kluwer Law International, 1997), 375.

Ni Chathin, C., "The European Community and the Member States in the Dispute Settlement Understanding of the WTO: United or Divided?", *European Law Journal*, 1999, 461.

Palmeter, D., "The WTO Appellate Body Needs Remand Authority", *Journal of World Trade* 1998, No. 1, 41.

Palmeter, D. and Mavroidis, P.; "The WTO Legal system: Sources of Law", *American Journal of International Law*, 1998, 398.

Pauwelyn, J., "Evidence, Proof and Persuasion in WTO Dispute Settlement: Who Bears the Burden?", *Journal of International Economic Law*, 1998, 227.

Petersmann, E-U., *The GATT/WTO Dispute Settlement System: International Law, International Organizations and Dispute Settlement* (Kluwer Law International, 1996), 344 p.

Petersmann, E-U. (ed.), *International Trade Law and the GATT/WTO Dispute Settlement System* (Kluwer Law International, 1997), 704 p.

Petersmann, E-U., "International Trade Law and the GATT/WTO Dispute Settlement System 1948-1996: An Introduction", in Petersmann, E-U. (ed.), *International Trade Law and the GATT/WTO Dispute Settlement System* (Kluwer Law International, 1997), 3.

Petersmann, E-U., "How to Promote the International Rule of Law ? Contributions by the World Trade Organization Appellate Review System", *Journal of International Economic Law*, 1998, 25.

Petersmann, E-U.; "From the Hobbesian Law of Coexistence to Modern Integration Law: the WTO Dispute Settlement System", *Journal of International Economic Law*, 1998, 175.

Petersmann, E-U., "Dispute Settlement in International Economic Law – Lessons for Strengthening International Dispute Settlement in Non-Economic Areas", *Journal of International Economic Law*, 1999, 189.

Porges, A., "The New Dispute Settlement: From the GATT to the WTO", *Leiden Journal of International Law*, 1995, 115.

Roessler, F., "The Concept of Nullification and Impairment in the Legal System of the World Trade Organization", in Petersmann, E-U. (ed.), *International Trade Law and the GATT/WTO Dispute Settlement System* (Kluwer Law International, 1997), 123.

Ruiz-Fabri, H., "Le règlement des différends dans le cadre de l'Organisation mondiale du commerce", *Journal du Droit International*, 1997, 709.

Ruiz-Fabri, H., "L'appel dans le règlement des différends de l'O.M.C.: trois ans après, quinze rapports plus tard", *Revue Générale de Droit International Public*, 1999, 47.

Sacerdoti, G., "Appeal and Judicial Review in International Arbitration and Adjudication: The Case of the WTO Appellate Review", in Petersmann E-U. (ed.), *International Trade Law and the GATT/WTO Dispute Settlement System* (Kluwer Law International, 1997), 245.

Salas, M. and Jackson, J.H., "Procedural Overview of the WTO EC-Banana Dispute", *Journal of International Economic Law*, 2000, 145.

Schede, C., "The Strengthening of the Multilateral System. Article 23 of the WTO Dispute Settlement Understanding: Dismantling Unilateral Retaliation under Section 301 of the 1974 Trade Act?", *World Competition*, 1996/7, 109.

Schleyer, G., "Power to the People: Allowing Private Parties to Raise Claims Before the WTO Dispute Resolution System", *Fordham Law Review*, 1997, 2275.

Schoenbaum, Th., "WTO Dispute Settlement: Praise and Suggestions for Reform", *ICLQ*, 1998, 647.

Schloemann, H. and Ohloff, S, "Constitutionalization and Dispute Settlement in the WTO: National Security as an Issue of Competence", *American Journal of International Law*, 1999, 424.

Shoyer, A., "The First Three Years of the WTO Dispute Settlement: Observations and Suggestions", *Journal of International Economic Law*, 1998, 277.

Shoyer, A., "The Future of WTO Dispute Settlement", *Proceedings of the 92st Annual Meeting ASIL (1998)*, 75.

Steger, D., "WTO Dispute Settlement: Revitalization of Multilateralism after the Uruguay Round", *Leiden Journal of International Law*, 1996, 319.

Steger, D. and Hainsworth, S., "World Trade Organization Dispute Settlement: The First Three Years", *Journal of International Economic Law*, 1998, 199.

Steger, D. and Van den Bossche, P., "WTO Dispute Settlement: Emerging Practice and Procedure", *Proceedings of the 92ⁿᵈ Annual Meeting ASIL (1998)*, 79.

Steger, D., "WTO Dispute Settlement", in Ruttley, Ph., Macvay, I., and George C. (eds.), *The WTO and International Trade Regulation* (Cameron May, 1998), 53.

Steger, D., and Lester, S., "WTO Dispute Settlement: Emerging Practice and Procedure in Decisions of the Appellate Body", in Schütte, M. and Reisenfeld, K. (eds.), *The WTO Dispute Settlement System* (Oxford University Press), forthcoming.

Stewart, T., and Burr, M.; "The WTO's First Two and a Half Years of Dispute Resolution", *North Carolina Journal of International Economic Law*, 1998, 161.

Symposium on the First Three Years of the WTO Dispute Settlement System, *The International Lawyer*, 1998, 609.

Thomas, C., "Litigation Process Under the GATT Dispute Settlement System: Lessons For the World Trade Organization?", *Journal of World Trade*, 1996, No. 2, 53.

Thomas, C., "The Need for Due Process in WTO Proceedings", *Journal of World Trade*, 1997, No. 1, 45.

Trachtman, J., "The Domain of WTO Dispute Resolution", *Harvard International Law Journal*, 1999, 333.

Van den Bossche, P. and Marceau, G., "Le système de règlement des différends de l'Organisation mondial du commerce: Analyse d'un système particulier et distinctif", *Revue du Marché Unique Européen*, 1998, 29.

Van den Bossche, P., "Appellate Review in WTO Dispute Settlement", in Weiss, F. (ed.), *Improving WTO Dispute Settlement Procedures: Issues and Lessons from the Practice of Other International Courts and Tribunals*, forthcoming.

Van der Borght, K., "The Advisory Center on WTO Law: Advancing Fairness and Equality", *Journal of International Economic Law*, 1999, 723.

Vermulst, E., Mavroidis, P. and Waer, P., "The Functioning of the Appellate Body After Four Years – Towards Rule Integrity", *Journal of World Trade*, 1999, No 2, 1.

Wiers, J., "The WTO's Rules of Conduct for Dispute Settlement", *Leiden Journal of International Law*, 1998, 265.

Zdouc, W., "WTO Dispute Settlement Practice Relating to the GATS", *Journal of International Economic Law*, 1999, 295.

Zonnekeyn, G., "The Banana Dispute in the WTO: the DSU Conundrum", *International Trade Law & Regulation*, 1999, 83.

Zonnekeyn, G., "Strechting the Limits of the WTO Dispute Settlement Mechanism", *International Trade Law & Regulation*, 1999, 31.

COMMENTS

Thomas A. Mensah *

I wish to associate myself with the expressions of thanks and congratulations to the organizers of the conference, first for the invitation to me to participate in this very interesting seminar and, secondly, for the efficient organization of the event. I have read with great interest the paper of Professor Thirlway, and I have listened with equal interest to his exposition this afternoon which clarified some important points in the paper and amplified some others. I am pleased to say that I agree in general with his arguments and conclusions. I would like to make a few comments on the contents of the paper and on the basic approach of the theme of the conference. Without too much elaboration I wish to emphasize the point made by Professor Szasz yesterday and repeated this morning by Mr. Alston concerning the pejorative implication of the term "proliferation". With them I think that the use of the term appears to suggest that we have already come to the conclusion that the increase in the number of international judicial bodies is undesirable. I believe that the point has been sufficiently clarified , so we may proceed on the understanding that no such conclusion has been reached. As I understand it, the basic concern behind the theme of the conference is that there has been an increase in the number of international judicial bodies, that this increase may have been far more than necessary and that it may have undesirable consequences, especially in the development of a uniform system of international law.

When we speak of an increase in the number of international judicial bodies what bodies do we have in mind? First there is the International Court of Justice. Then there is the International Tribunal for the Law of the Sea of which I have the great honour to be a member. There are also the arbitral tribunals and special arbitral tribunals to be composed under Annexes 7 and 8 to the Law of the Sea Convention. Although these tribunals are not standing judicial institutions I believe they can rightly be considered as international judicial bodies for the

---

* Judge, International Tribunal for the Law of the Sea, Hamburg.

purpose of the present discussion. Finally we have to consider the new criminal law tribunals, namely, the Yugoslav and the Rwanda Criminal Tribunals and, of course, the newly created International Criminal Court. We may also include in the list the World Trade Organization (WTO) dispute settlement mechanism. While there are special features of this mechanism which may distinguish it from the ICJ and the Law of the Sea Tribunal, it is also undeniable that the bodies within that mechanism perform judicial functions in the sense that they decide disputes by reference to legal rules and principles. The same may also be said about the World Bank Center for Settlement of Disputes. It is possible that the concern reflected in the theme of this conference extends to the establishment and activities of all these various institutions, since their existence results in the number of venues and procedures for settling disputes under international law between different subjects of international law.

As I see it, the question that we must first ask is: Are these different judicial bodies and mechanisms necessary or are they undertaking functions that can appropriately and conveniently be performed by already existing bodies? Because, if the new institutions are not really required, then the concern about "proliferation" may well be justified. In answering this question I think we must bear in mind that one of fundamental principles of the international judicial process is that states have the right to determine the mechanisms for settling disputes between them. To put it another way, a State cannot be forced to accept the jurisdiction of any court in a dispute between it and another state or other subject of international law. As we know, one of the major objectives of the recent increase in the number of available international judicial bodies has been to ensure that, as far as possible, international disputes are settled peacefully and, where necessary, by recourse to a judicial body acceptable to the parties in the dispute. I am pleased to note that this point has been so clearly made by President Schwebel, not only in the intervention that has just been made on his behalf, but also in other previous statements. This objective, which I personally consider to be laudable and legitimate, motivated the drafters of the Law of the Sea Convention when they decided to make provision for a number of alternative procedures for the settlement of disputes concerning the interpretation or application of the provisions of the new Convention. In this connection I think it is important to note that, although the International Court of Justice is described and designated in the Charter of the United Nations as the "principal judicial organ of the UN", the Court does not have automatic jurisdiction over disputes between Member States of the United Nations, except to the extent that those states have accepted the jurisdiction in the manner provided for in the Statute of the Court. And it is also a fact that not all Member States have accepted the jurisdiction of the Court. Indeed a number of States have made it a point to stress that they are unwilling to accept the Courts's jurisdiction in any circumstances. We are not concerned here with whether or not these states are justified in refusing to accept the jurisdiction of the principal judicial body of the United Nations. The point is that, because of this attitude of some States to the Court, it is not realistic to insist that the ICJ should be prescribed as the only judicial body for the settlement of disputes between states. Where a dispute involves a State that has not accepted the jurisdiction of the Court or is unwilling to accept the jurisdiction for the particular dispute, the dispute cannot be dealt with by the ICJ. That being the case we cannot prudently leave the ICJ as the sole mechanism for the world community if we also want as many international disputes as possible settled by judicial means.

Another fact worth noting is that that, pursuant to its Statute, the International Court of Justice is not able to deal with disputes in which one or more of the parties are not states. It is now generally accepted that the international community has developed to a point where it is necessary that suitable arrangements should be made available not only for non-state actors to have access to the international judicial process, but also for them to be made subject to that process. This objective cannot be attained if the International Court of Justice is the only international body.

Hence we must ask ourselves whether the International Court of Justice would have been in a position to deal with the cases and disputes that are the subjects of the new judicial institutions whose creation has raised the issue of "proliferation"?. We have heard from Judge Feliciano about the WTO Dispute Settlement process. We have also been informed by Mr. Shihata about the World Bank Dispute Settlement mechanism. I believe we should ask ourselves whether the ICJ would have received the consent of the parties that would have given the Court competence to deal with all these cases. And, even if all the state involved in the disputes had accepted the Court's jurisdiction, would the Court have been able to dispose of the cases in the time required, having regard to its preset workload and the resources available to it. Finally, do we seriously believe that the Court, with its special and rules and procedures, would be an appropriate and effective mechanism for dealing with all the various disputes that come before these specialized judicial bodies?

As far as the International Tribunal for the Law of the Sea is concerned, I think it is useful to recall that it was not established as a "competitor" to the International Court of Justice. Rather it is intended to be an alternative to the Court in one respect, and a "supplement" to it in another. It is an alternative because it offers a forum for judicial settlement for those States which, for whatever reasons, are not willing to accept the jurisdiction of the ICJ. An it is a supplement because it provides a judicial avenue for the settlement of certain types of disputes that the International Court of Justice would not have been able to deal with because of the constraints imposed on it by its Statute. An example of this is the "compulsory" jurisdiction that is granted to the International Tribunal for the Law of the Sea under article 292 of the Convention in respect of the "prompt release" of arrested ships or crews. In theory, it is possible for a flag State to apply to the ICJ for the prompt release of its ship if both the flag State and the arresting State have accepted either the jurisdiction of the ICJ under article 287 of the Convention or the compulsory jurisdiction of the Court under article 36 of the Statute of the Court. However, a flag State cannot apply to the ICJ for the prompt release of a ship by a port State if that State does not recognize the competence of the Court. In such a situation, unless the two states involved agree to a mutually acceptable court or tribunal, the application can only be dealt with by the International Tribunal for the Law of the Sea. In effect, the International Tribunal becomes endowed with compulsory jurisdiction if and when the parties do not agree on another court or tribunal to deal with the dispute. This arrangement was instituted because the international community has concluded that it is not permissible for the arresting state to keep the ship and its crew in detention for long periods without the possibility of review at the international level. This function of the Tribunal could not have been performed by the International Court of Justice precisely because it is based on compulsory jurisdiction that does not depend on the consent of the state that arrested the ship.

The same applies to the jurisdiction of the Tribunal for the prescription of provisional measures under article 290(5) of the Convention. Here too, the competence of the Tribunal does not derogate from the right of states in a dispute to apply to the International Court of Justice for provisional measures. However, where the states involved in the case have not accepted the jurisdiction of the International Court of Justice, it may not be possible for the matter to be brought before the Court. In such a situation, the Convention makes it possible for the Tribunal to step in. For example, where a dispute is being submitted to an arbitral tribunal under Annex VII to the Convention and the tribunal has not yet been constituted, the Convention provides that a request for provisional measures may be made to the International Tribunal for the Law of the Sea. This is to enable urgent issues of provisional measures to be dealt with pending the constitution of the arbitral tribunal which may take some time. Thus the parties are able to ensure the preservation of rights that might have been irreparably damaged if they had been obliged to wait until a decision of the arbitral tribunal. This jurisdiction is given to the Tribunal to deal with situations where speed and urgency are of the essence, without being subjected to the restriction which is inherent in the International Court of Justice regime – the requirement that the consent of both parties must be available before the Court can deal even with a request for provisional measures.

The role of the International Tribunal for the Law of the Sea as an alternative dispute settlement procedure becomes even more important when one considers the function and competence of the Seabed Disputes Chamber. This Chamber, which operates within the Tribunal, is intended to settle disputes arising under Part XI of the Convention, where a large number of the operators are likely to non-state entities. Here too, there is no way that the particular jurisdiction could have been exercised by the International Court of Justice since the Court is precluded by its Statute from dealing with disputes involving non-state entities.

So, if we consider just these two features of the Tribunal (and there are others), we may come to the conclusion that the establishment of the new Tribunal was by no means an exercise in the "proliferation" of international judicial bodies, but rather the creation of new mechanisms to ensure that, where disputes arise, there will be effective avenues which the states involved will find appropriate and acceptable to them for the judicial and binding settlement of those disputes.

Looked at in that way, the Tribunal, as well as the other courts and tribunals that have been established in recent years, are not unnecessary or superfluous just because the ICJ exists. This is because, for the most part, they are dealing with situations for which the International Court of Justice might have been considered to be either inappropriate because of the nature of the issues to be resolved or not competent because one or more of the parties to the dispute was unwilling to submit to its jurisdiction. This is also true of the international criminal courts whose fields of competence would appear to be largely outside the purview of the ICJ.

So I think the question we should ask ourselves is: if these judicial bodies are dealing with matters that could not have been dealt with by the International Court of Justice, why is there so much concern that their creation somehow has resulted in a "proliferation" of courts?

There surely is some merit in the view that new mechanisms must be devised to deal with new situations if existing procedures are not adequate or appropriate. Given the role assigned to the ICJ in its Statute and the basis on which the Court exercises jurisdiction, it is not easy to see how the international community could have dealt with the new requirements for dispute settlement without the establishment of new procedures to deal with cases that could not be handled by the Court. Every international lawyer knows that the function of the Court is important and indispensable. Like other international lawyers I recognize that the International Court of Justice is the senior international judicial body in the international community. About that I am in no doubt at all. But this does not mean that it must also be the ONLY judicial body of the international community. Nor does it mean that other international judicial bodies, assigned important functions in specific situations, must necessarily be subordinate to the International Court of Justice. I think this point needs to be borne firmly in mind when we consider the recent suggestions that some supervisory role over other international courts and tribunals might be given to the ICJ.

I will not dwell very long on the question of fragmentation of jurisprudence or conflict of jurisdiction because I believe Professor Thirlway has dealt with it very well and comprehensively. I just want to touch briefly on the issue of "supervision". It has been suggested, and it has been mentioned again by the representative of the President of the ICJ, that consideration be given to an arrangement under which some of the existing international judicial bodies, such as the International Tribunal for the Law of the Sea or the international criminal tribunals, might ask the International Court of Justice for advisory opinions on legal questions arising in the course of their work. A number of mechanisms for doing this have been suggested, and Professor Thirlway has commented on some of them in his paper.

There are two ways of looking at these suggestions: the theoretical and the practical. Theoretically, one must accept that in international law and politics nothing is impossible or inconceivable. If all states, or a large majority of them, really desire a particular outcome, they will always find a way to achieve it, regardless of what the current legal provisions may be. It is therefore entirely possible for the international community to organize matters in such a way that existing and future international courts are made subject to some form of supervision by the ICJ. But, theory aside, I believe there are serious legal and practical obstacles in the way of any such arrangement. Professor Thirlway has pointed out some of the difficulties that may need to be overcome before the International Court of Justice can effectively exercise a supervisory role over other judicial bodies, either by way of appeals to the court through a contentious procedure or through advisory opinions from the Court to the respective tribunals. With regard to a possible appeals procedure, there is nothing in principle to prevent parties to a case from agreeing to refer a judgment rendered by a court or tribunal to the ICJ for review or other action. It is a cardinal principle of international law that states have the sovereign right to choose their own procedures for the settlement of disputes between them. By virtue of this principle, nothing can prevent two states which have had a case decided in one court to decide, by agreement between them, to refer the decision to another court - national or international. There is, however, the important question whether it is realistic to expect that a party that has "won" a case before one court will be agreeable to referring the matter once again to another court? I personally have my doubts. In any case, if that were to happen, it is possible that such recourse will not be restricted to the ICJ. Some states may prefer to go elsewhere.

With respect to the use of the advisory opinion route it must be admitted, as has been pointed out by President Schwebel, that the possibilities exist in theory. The question is whether any of the other courts and tribunals will feel disposed to go to the ICJ for advisory opinions. And if a tribunal were to decide to request an advisory opinion from the Court, there would be the question of what the legal effect of such advisory opinion would be. Thus, let us assume that the International Tribunal for the Law of the Sea has agreed to seek the opinion of the ICJ on a legal issue that has arisen in the course of its consideration of a dispute between two states submitted to it. Under its current Statute, there would appear to be no bar to the Tribunal availing itself of an opinion of the Court. On the other hand there is no mechanism by which the Tribunal may make a direct request to the Court. It has been suggested that the Tribunal might request the General Assembly for permission to bring such requests to the Court or, alternatively, it might ask the General Assembly to make the request to the Court on its behalf. I can foresee numerous obstacles in the way of either of these procedures but I am willing, for the sake of argument, to assume that a request has been submitted to the ICJ and the Court has seen fit to respond to it. The question I ask is: what would be the attitude of the states which have deliberately chosen to bring a dispute to the Tribunal instead of the ICJ to a situation in which the Tribunal decides to remit a part of the decision process to the ICJ? The next question is: what will be the effect of the Court's advisory opinion on the Tribunal as a whole and on the individual Judges? In more specific terms, will the advisory opinion be binding on the Tribunal collectively or the Judges individually? What would happen if the majority of the Judges of the Tribunal were to come to the view that they are unable to accept the opinion of the Court? If, as I suspect, the conclusion is that an advisory opinion of the Court in such a situation is not binding on the Tribunal or its individual Judges (and presumably also not binding on the states parties to the dispute before the Tribunal), we would be faced with an advisory opinion whose effect is not easy to predict and whose value to the Tribunal and the international community may not be so certain. When I consider all the legal and practical hurdles that would need to be overcome to obtain such an advisory opinion and the difficulties that would have to be faced in determining the effect of an opinion, I come to the conclusion that, interesting as the idea may be, it does not appear to be feasible and, in any case, it is very unlikely that it will solve the problem with which it is intended to deal.

On the issue of the possible fragmentation or conflict of jurisdiction I share Professor Thirlway's conclusion that the fears are, perhaps, a trifle exaggerated. I do not believe that a really serious case has been made for the possibility that international jurisprudence will be fragmented because of the existence of more than one court of competent jurisdiction. Indeed the evidence available appears to prove the contrary. In the intervention on his behalf, President Schwebel has pointed to the many instances in which the International Tribunal for the Law of the Sea has, in the two judgments and two orders that it has issued so far, made references to and followed the dicta and reasoning of the ICJ, the Permanent Court and even of arbitral tribunals. This is likely to continue. I do not think that the integrity of international jurisprudence is likely to be seriously or even significantly undermined by the existence of the International Tribunal for the Law of the Sea or other courts and tribunal operating independently of the ICJ. There is, of course, no denying the fact that, in deciding law of the sea cases, the International Tribunal may on occasions have to deal with issues of general international law. I am quite sure that the Tribunal and other tribunals will exercise restraint when they deal with points of law that have already been dealt with by the International Court of Justice or by the Permanent Court. There may be situations, as has been suggested in the *Tadic case* in the Yugoslav Tribunal, where the Tribunal might come to the conclusion that on a particular point it is not able to agree with the International Court of Justice. But, as Professor Thirlway has quite pertinently pointed out, Judges of the International Court of Justice often announce, in dissenting or separate opinions, that they do not agree with decisions of the Court. So there is nothing really new in having a disagreement between two tribunals or courts or, indeed, between two members of the same court.

That having been said, I do not wish to discount altogether the possibility of conflicts arising on important points of international law as a result of the increase in the fora in which disputes involving such points may be judicially considered . For that reason, I believe it would be useful to consider some ways by which the possibility of such conflicts might be reduced, if not eliminated completely.

Reference has been made in the discussion to the ACC, the Administrative Committee on Coordination. This is the body in which the heads of the organizations, agencies and other bodies of the United Nations system meet, under the chairmanship of the Secretary General of the United Nations, to consider issues of coordination of the various complementary programmes of the organizations of the United Nations system. The ACC does not issue edicts that are binding on the organizations and agencies nor are its decisions legally binding on the participating Executive Heads. But it is generally agreed that the ACC provides a very useful forum for discussions of common problems. By the same token, a useful and non-controversial way of dealing with the potential problem of conflict of jurisdiction or fragmentation of jurisprudence in international law may be to organize an informal arrangement which brings together the heads (presidents or chairpersons) of the various international judicial bodies. Such meetings could be under the chairmanship of the President of the International Court of Justice, as the head of the most senior judicial body. At such meetings participants could examine the areas in which conflicts in jurisdiction and jurisprudence might arise, the nature and extent of such conflicts and possible ways of eliminating or at least minimizing them.

I believe that such an arrangement could provide a useful means by which the members of the various courts and tribunals would be encouraged to exercise appropriate restraint in the discharge of the respective judicial mandates. In my view this restraint is all that can be asked of them since, technically, they are independent of each other by virtue of their respective constitutional and legal mandates. But the exercise of restraint is essential because, in another sense the Judges of the different international courts are not really "independent". As judges they have a common obligation to the same body of international law, and their professional destinies are, therefore, intertwined. They share one fundamental objective – to decide disputes by elucidation of the law applicable to them; but in the process also to provide guidance to those who may face similar situations in the future. For it is important to remember at all times that the function of international judicial bodies is not merely to decide cases, but also to provide guidance to those who want to avoid litigation and conflict. Hence the courts and tribunals do not exist merely to resolve conflicts but they are also intended to be part of the conflict avoidance regime of the international community. For that reason all engaged in the settlement of disputes have the same obligation to the international community: the obligation to elucidate the law and to make it more possible for those concerned to determine the nature and extent of their legal rights and obligations.

COMMENTS

Christos Rozakis [*]

Thank you very much Mr. Chairman. Allow me to thank Professor Thirlway for his excellent presentation and his stimulating ideas which have given me the opportunity to enter directly into the particular theme of my intervention without making long introductory remarks. I shall still underline from the outset that some of his remarks do not necessarily apply to the European Court of Human Rights – which is the theme of my intervention – because of the specific nature of this institution. Indeed the European Court of Strasbourg is not an international court mainly settling disputes between States, and it does not work at the universal level as a mechanism partaking in the promotion of international peace and security. Although it may, very indirectly, serve such a function, its nature is that of a supranational organ, working within a relatively coherent and homogeneous regional system, and having as its main function the respect of human rights in Europe as part and parcel of the latter's process of integration. In other words, the European Court of Human Rights has been conceived as one of the tools of European integration within the wider context of other organizations and organs serving the same ultimate goal, and with a division of labour which for a number of years had been unexceptionably respected.

Indeed there had been a period in the operation of the European organizations where each one of them was fulfilling a particular role in the European construction and served the role of the integration of the, then, Western European States into a socially, culturally and politically homogeneous entity. One can easily discern the distinct competence of the main three traditional European organizations, looking at both their constitutional texts and their early operation in the European affairs: the Council of Europe was the mechanism to assist the social,

---

[*] Vice-President of the European Court of Human Rights, Professor of International Law, University of Athens.

political and cultural rappochement of these States, the European Communities were the mechanism of economic integration, while NATO – a not altogether European mechanism – provided the defense limb of the "union". Later on in the history of European organizations, the picture was completed by the entry of the Conference (and later organization) for Security and Cooperation in Europe, a forum of European States together with their transatlantic counterparts (USA and Canada) which aimed to facilitate the peaceful coexistence of the East and West on the continent.

This division of labour is no longer rigorously respected by the European mechanisms. There are now serious overlappings in their operation; and there are, at least, two factors which have contributed to this new situation: the first is the gradual expansion of the European communities (today European Union), related to both membership and competence. The second is the dramatic political change which has occurred in Central and Eastern Europe since the late 1980's. The result of these two developments is that the overlapping of certain activities of the European organizations has reached a level sometimes undermining the coherence and effectiveness of their endeavour ; equally the interference of one organization with the traditional affairs of another has created, in certain cases, a degree of antagonism between them which seems to impede the possibility of sound cooperation and the search for practical solutions to deal with the problems.

One of the fields which has not remained immune against the transformation of the respective spheres of competence is the interstate protection of human rights. In the traditional division of labour the monitoring of the respect of human rights by States – basically civil and political and, to a smaller extent, social rights – had been fulfilled by the Council of Europe, having been the sole designated mechanism designed to promote the coordination of democracy, the respect of the rule of law and the harmonization of the application of human rights in the then Western European States belonging to the same geopolitical system and being members of the organization.

That pattern is, as I have already said, in the process of changing. The protection of human rights at the European level is no longer the exclusive responsibility of the Council of Europe and of the organs which were instituted to deal specifically with a rigid legal control of the States' compliance, namely the European Commission and Court of Human Rights (today these organs are replaced by a single Court). Both the European Union and the Organization for Security and

Cooperation in Europe are increasingly interfering with questions of human rights protection on the continent.

There seems to be a contradiction in this course of action which is leading to a reappraisal of the traditional division of labour enshrined, explicitly or implicitly, in the constitutional texts of the basic European organizations: there is no question that the pivotal role of these organizations remains the gradual integration of, now, all the European States into a system with commonly shared values which, although allowing the retention of local differences to its participants, would cover instrumental aspects of life and human activities. There is no question, also, that the entry of new States into the European system of integration requires a coordination of efforts of all the European mechanisms to assist the transition of these States from the old regime to a stage of respect of the values of democracy, the rule of law, and human rights; and that this coordination could have been better achieved with the traditional division of labour of the European organizations. What the new States really want is effective and efficient assistance from various sources, which each one of them has a clear mandate and clearly determined field of competence.

These primary goals ought therefore to determine the piecemeal moves of the European organizations. Instead, and here lies the contradiction, the entire situation has recently developed towards a centrifugal, uncoordinated (or coordinated in an elementary manner) activity of the mechanisms, only abiding by some fundamental features of the system, rather than by a well-orchestrated and disciplined action in pursuance of the same goal. In these circumstances the conclusion is that there is a visible danger of a diffusion of goals at this particular crucial period of European integration and the creation of undue delays in the achievement of the main original aims.

What may be proposed, specifically in the field of protection and promotion of human rights, is the taking of initiatives on the part of the European organizations for a reappraisal of their work and the search for ways of cooperation and coordination both in the political and the legal field. The Council of Europe, the European Union, the Organization of Security and Cooperation in Europe – one may add NATO because of some of its activities which are relevant to the matter – should sit together and establish the necessary infrastructure. They may even start with the reallocation of their jurisdictional limits – in accordance with the original division of labour or on the basis of the present effectiveness of each of them to deal successfully with the matter –, and it might be necessary to create organs that will coordinate these measures. Such a move seems to me to be indispensable in order to put back in track the institutional protection of human rights in Europe, and to prevent damages to its effective application mainly in the States which have recently joined the system.

FLEXIBILITY AND THE INTERNATIONAL LABOUR ORGANIZATION

Dominick Devlin[*]

In the programme for today's session of the Conference on the Proliferation of International Organizations: Legal Issues, relating to the *ILO and flexibility*, the following questions appear:

> "Proliferation of standards? More members of international organizations: lower but uniform standards, or different standards?"

They suggest as a possibility that in the International Labour Organization there could have been a proliferation of standards, due to the advent of new members and a consequent need for flexibility, leading to a lowering of standards or different concepts. There is indeed a proliferation of standards in the ILO, giving rise to certain problems which the Organization has been addressing over the past decades and which it should resolve if it is to have a coherent body of standards as we cross into the next millennium. As will be seen from the second section of this paper, these problems are to some extent attributable to some inflexibility in the standard-setting mechanism. Flexibility - the subject of the first section – has always been part of the standard-setting philosophy of the ILO and cannot therefore be said to have resulted from the various increases in membership over the years.

---

[*] The author is the Legal Adviser of the International Labour Office (ILO). This article reflects his own views which are not necessarily those of the ILO. It has also benefited from the ideas of his predecessor, Francis Maupain, contained in a course entitled "L'OIT, la justice sociale et la mondialisation" to be published in the *Collected Courses, Hague Academy of International Law*, 1999, as well as from the assistance of Juan Llobera in the ILO Office of the Legal Adviser. The classic work on international labour standards is *International Labour Law*, by Nicolas Valticos and G. Von Potobsky, 2nd Ed. - Deventer : Kluwer Law and Taxation Publishers, 1995.

FLEXIBILITY

The ILO has a tradition of providing for flexibility in the Conventions that it adopts with the aim of making them not only ratifiable by all its Members, at their very different stages of economic and social development, but also adaptable to those different conditions. This tradition has been with it since its creation, is firmly rooted in its Constitution and is evidenced from the very first international labour Conventions. The Organization was founded in 1919, as part of the League of Nations[1], on the premise that universal and lasting peace can be established only if it is based upon social justice[2]. At that time, the main arm for implementing its objectives was the establishment of international labour standards in the form of Conventions and Recommendations. These are adopted by the ILO's supreme organ, the International Labour Conference, consisting of all the Member States with their tripartite representation: made up of four delegates, two for the government, one for the employers and one for the workers of the country concerned. Each delegate has one vote. As will be seen below, tripartism – the great particularity of the International Labour Organization – is a significant element of flexibility in the standard-setting process.

After adoption by the International Labour Conference, the Conventions and Recommendations are submitted to the Members of the Organization under constitutional provisions which require Governments to bring them to the attention of their legislative or other competent authorities and to inform the Director-General of the measures taken in this respect[3]. If as a result the country ratifies an international labour Convention, it will be bound by its provisions as soon as it enters into force in accordance with those provisions as well as by the obligation under the Constitution[4] to submit regular reports on implementation. Reports may also be required "at appropriate intervals" by the executive organ of the ILO, the Governing Body, with respect to the effect given by Members to Conventions that they have not ratified[5] and to International labour Recommendations.[6]

---

[1] Under Part XIII (Labour), Treaty of Peace signed at Versailles on 28 June 1919.
[2] See the Preamble to Part XIII of the Treaty of Versailles.
[3] Article 19, paragraph 5 (b) and (c), Constitution of the ILO.
[4] Article 22, Constitution of the ILO.
[5] Article 19, paragraph 5 (e).
[6] Article 19, paragraph 6 (d).

The Constitution thus provides flexibility through the non-binding Recommendations for which it makes provision and above all in the principle that each Member is bound only by those Conventions which it has decided to ratify. Indeed, were it not for the principle of good faith and for two very important qualifications – one procedural and the other substantive – to be explained later, one might be tempted to equate flexibility in the ILO with laxity.

With respect to the flexibility or rigidity in the content of international labour Conventions, there is a Constitutional dialectic: on the one hand, the principles laid down in the Constitution, and in the Declaration of Philadelphia annexed to it in 1946, "are fully applicable to all peoples everywhere"[7] and, as a matter of longstanding practice, ratifying Members are not permitted to make reservations. On the other hand, "the manner of their application must be determined with due regard to the stage of social and economic development reached by each people"[8]. In this connection, paragraph 3 of Article 19 of the Constitution (almost identical to Article 405 of the Treaty of Versailles) provides: "In framing any Convention or Recommendation of general application the Conference shall have due regard to those countries in which climatic conditions, the imperfect development of industrial organisation or other special circumstances make the industrial conditions substantially different and shall suggest the modifications, if any, which it considers may be required to meet the case of such countries."

This last instruction was immediately applied: the original Members of the new Organization comprised countries at very different stages of development and even a country under colonization, India (now covering Bangladesh, Myanmar, India and Pakistan); many of them were the subject of tailor-made provisions in the Conventions adopted at the time. Convention No. 1 is a good example, the Hours of Work (Industry) Convention, 1919: various countries were excluded from the general standard of an eight-hour a day or a 48-hour week (Siam, China, Persia)[9] and different standards were set for other countries: Greece, Japan, "British India".[10] Similar provisions are to be found in the Night Work (Women) Convention, 1919 (No. 4) and the

---

[7] Part V, Declaration concerning the aims and purposes of the International Labour Organisation, adopted at Philadelphia on 10 May 1944.
[8] *Ibid.*
[9] See Convention No. 1, article 11.
[10] *Ibid*, article 10 for British India, article 12 for Greece and article 9 for Japan.

Night Work of Young Persons Convention, 1919 (No. 6)[11]. In 1946, a provision was added to the Constitution (as Article 35) with respect to non-metropolitan territories; it allows the metropolitan powers to decide whether and to what extent a Convention that they had ratified would also apply to a territory specified by them in a declaration addressed to the Director-General of the International Labour Office.

At the same time, it should be noted that the flexibility provided for in the Constitution operates within a firm legal framework. As indicated above, there is no binding requirement on Members to ratify any international labour Conventions, but Members are required to take the necessary action for their consideration with a view to ratification and, if they do ratify, to regularly report on the implementation of the Conventions concerned in law and practice. They are also, if requested, bound to submit reports on Conventions that they have not ratified. Examination of the reports on ratified Conventions was initially carried out by the Governing Body, but the growing number of reports and the expertise required to examine them led to the creation in 1926 of a Committee of Experts on the Application of Conventions and Recommendations, now consisting of 20 legal experts acting in an individual capacity. The Committee's report to the Governing Body on the implementation of specific Conventions by ratifying Members is transmitted to the International Labour Conference, where it is discussed by a tripartite committee on the application of international labour standards. This practice in monitoring has been developed to a point which may well justify a claim by the International Labour Organization to have the most effective supervisory machinery at the universal level[12].

The ILO's survival of the Second World War was the occasion for a renewed standard-setting activity. In fact, during the thirteen years following the end of it, all but three of what are known as the "fundamental Conventions"[13] were adopted. These Conventions cover the

---

[11] An even more specific exception is to be found in the Minimum Age (Trimmers and Stokers) Convention, 1921 (No. 115), relating to "trimmers or stokers on vessels exclusively engaged in the coastal trade of India and of Japan".

[12] For information on this machinery, reference could be made to N. Valticos, "Un système de contrôle international: la mise en oeuvre des conventions internationales du travail", *Recueil des Cours de l'Académie de droit international*, 1968; N. Valticos, "Once More about the ILO System of Supervision: In what respect is it Still a Model?", *Towards a More Effective Supervision by International Organizations, Essays in Honour of H. Schermers*, Nijhoff, (1994).

[13] See paragraphs 1(b) and 2 of the ILO Declaration on Fundamental Principles and Rights, referred to below.

fundamental principles and rights within the ILO's sphere of action in the following four areas:

Convention	No.	Date
Freedom of Association and the Right to Collective Bargaining	No. 87 No. 98	1948 1949
Elimination of Forced or Compulsory Labour	No. 29 No. 105	1930 1957
Abolition of Child Labour	No. 138 No. 182	1973 1999
Elimination of Discrimination in Respect of Employment and Occupation	No. 100 No. 111	1951 1958

From the mid-1950s, the ILO had the same influx of new Members from the developing world as other organizations in the United Nations system and wide use was made of the Organization's flexibility techniques realized through particular phrases designed to enable the standard to fit in with national conditions (in the more recent Conventions, for example, certain entitlements of workers are to be determined "in accordance with national law and practice"[14]) and especially through provisions giving options concerning the manner in which or the extent to which the standard is to be implemented. But the main consequence of the advent of these new Members was rather a revision of basic priorities under which technical cooperation activities came to have the

---

[14] See for instance Article 12, Occupational Safety and Health Convention, 1981 (No. 155); Article 12.1, Termination of Employment Convention, 1982 (No. 158); Article 11, Private Employment Agencies Convention, 1997 (No. 181).

same importance as the traditional activity of the setting of standards and the supervision of their application.

These provisions, in many if not most cases, do not result in any lowering of standards, but could be considered as ledges on which countries unable to reach the full level may rest on the way forward. A good example is the Minimum Age Convention, 1973 (No. 138, one of the "fundamental Conventions" referred to above), which requires countries, at the time of ratification, to specify the minimum age for admission to employment, which must not be lower than the country's minimum school-leaving age and in no case less that 15, except that Members may initially set an age of 14, which is to be raised when conditions permit[15]. Progress in this respect will be monitored in the reporting system already referred to. Provisions of this kind are most frequent in Conventions relating to social security. Under Convention No. 130 (medical care and sickness benefit), for example, there is a general obligation for a certain percentage of the population to be covered by medical care (75% of the active population), but countries whose economy and medical facilites are not sufficiently developed may initially limit the acceptance of obligations to a lower percentage (25%).[16] Some Conventions provide flexibility enabling the ratifying Member to set higher standards. Thus another of the fundamental Conventions, the Discrimination (Employment and Occupation) Convention, 1958 (No. 111), gives a basic list of the forms of discrimination to be eliminated (in particular, race, sex, colour, religion and national extraction), leaving other forms to be determined by the Member, "after consultation with the representative employers' and workers' organizations".[17]

Convention No. 111 also provides a general obligation on ratifying Members to promote equality of treatment in employment and occupation.[18] It thus exemplifies another flexibility technique, found in many standards, under which the main requirement is for Members to pursue a policy aimed at promoting the principles and rights embodied in the Convention. The example frequently cited of what might be termed a "procedural" Convention of this kind is the Employment Policy Convention, 1964 (No. 122), under which "each Member shall

---

[15] Convention No. 138, article 2, paragraphs 4 and 5.
[16] Convention No. 130, article 2.
[17] Convention No. 111, article 1.1(b).
[18] Convention No. 111, article 2.

declare and pursue, as a major goal, an active policy designed to promote full, productive and freely chosen employment".[19]

It is also common for Conventions to be composed of various parts not all of which need be accepted. The social security Conventions Nos 102, 118 and 128[20] allow a choice of various parts on, for instance, old-age benefit, unemployment benefit, medical care benefit and invalidity benefit. Sometimes, the ultimate objective is not affected as the different parts are simply different means of attaining the same end. Thus under the Workers' Claims (Employer's Insolvency) Convention, 1992 (No. 173) a ratifying State may choose between the acceptance of Part II of the Convention (protection of workers' claims by means of a privilege) or Part III (protection by means of a guarantee institution), or have both. Nevertheless, it is clear that this technique often leads to different levels of standards as between ratifying States.

This is clearly also the case with some of the Conventions (and there are many examples) that allow ratifying Members to exclude specific branches of the economy or sectors of activity or categories of workers from the application of the Convention concerned, even on a more permanent basis. This has however always been the case and one could cite two fundamental Conventions adopted prior to 1950, Nos 87 and 98 (on freedom of association and collective bargaining), under which it is left to each ratifying State to decide upon the extent to which they will be applied to the armed forces and the police.[21] Under other Conventions exclusions are permitted but only on a transitional basis. Thus, under the Minimum Age Convention (No. 138), a ratifying State whose economy and administrative facilities are insufficiently developed may initially limit the application of the Convention to certain sectors of the economy, some of which however must necessarily be covered. In addition, limited categories of work in which special or substantive problems of application arise may be excluded from the scope of the Convention.

There is however another procedural qualification (in addition to the obligation to refer to such exclusions in the reports submitted to the ILO) in that, before excluding or not including various provisions of a Convention, the Member will be required – sometimes by the

---

[19] Convention No. 122, article 1, paragraph 1.
[20] Social Security (Minimum Standards) Convention, 1952 (No. 102); Equality of Treatment (Social Security) Convention, 1962 (No.118) and Invalidity, Old-Age and Survivors' Benefits Convention, 1967 (No. 128).
[21] Convention No. 87, article 9, and Convention No. 98, article 5.

terms of the Convention itself or by the provisions of the Tripartite Consultation (International Labour Standards) Convention, 1976 (No. 144)[22] if the Member has ratified it or by the general philosophy of the ILO – to hold prior consultations with the most representative organization of employers and workers in their country. A large number of Conventions rely on tripartism in this way, not simply as a check on the flexibility for limiting the scope of application of standards, but also for providing flexibility in cases where the precise terms of a Convention are difficult to define, especially on a universal basis. Thus, the Minimum Age Convention and the very recent Abolition of the Worst Forms of Child Labour Convention, 1999 (No. 182), require ratifying States to prohibit persons under 18 from engaging in hazardous work. They are required to draw up a list of what constitutes "hazardous work" after consulting the organizations of employers and workers concerned. Indeed, it has been pointed out that the principle of freedom of association and the right to bargain collectively are at the heart of all the obligations accepted by Members of the ILO.[23]

PROLIFERATION OF STANDARDS

To come back now to the main theme of the Conference held in Leiden, one can indeed speak of a proliferation of international labour standards – not however due to their flexibility, but rather to the passage of time and the indestructibility of the legal instruments created over the years. 182 Conventions have been generated since 1919. The present rate is at least one per year. A number of the older ones (and even not so old) have become obsolescent, either because times and conditions have changed or thinking has changed. This is a problem with other organizations too, especially the older ones: after a decade or two, revisions are necessary, a revision conference has to be called, the modifications negotiated, the amended act needs then to be submitted for ratification, and will in most cases only bind the Members that have ratified it. Thus different Members will be bound by different versions of the same instrument.

---

[22] See article 2, Convention No. 144.
[23] Wilfred Jenks, "The International Protection of Freedom of Association for Trade Union Purposes", *Collected Courses, Hague Academy of International Law*, (1955), pp. 7-115.

The ILO is in the same position as the others as far as the substantive situation is concerned, and probably in a worse one from a formal point of view. It has made no provision for the amendment of its standards as in other fora. The normal way of revising its Conventions is by way of adoption of a new Convention (or occasionally) a protocol, with the old Convention not only remaining in existence, but also still open to ratification. This latter aspect was cured (in the 1930s) by final clauses, so that ratification of a revising Convention will constitute denunciation of the revised Convention (if post 1929) and entry into force of the revision will close such Convention to further ratification. Other measures have been taken at the practical level to ensure, in particular, that Members are not requested to provide reports on obsolete Conventions[24] and finally, in 1997, after decades of discussions, the Constitution was amended to allow any Convention, whatever its final clauses, to be abrogated by the International Labour Conference if it has become obsolete. But several years will be needed before the amendment receives the number of ratifications required for it to enter into force.[25] In the meantime, provision has been made for the withdrawal of obsolete Conventions that have not entered into force and of recommendations.

At present therefore, the ILO has a disparate body of standards; in spite of a trend towards codification and a preference for standards of general application over ones of a sectoral nature, the same basic standard may be formulated in different ways, or overlap with or even contradict other standards, sometimes providing different solutions in regard to each other or in regard to a later Convention of general scope, with outdated standards (sometimes no longer even consistent with the values of today) coexisting with more modern ones. Thus, for example, 20 Members are required to take measures (subject to certain safeguards) for the progressive integration of indigenous and tribal

---

[24] Requests for reports under article 22 of the ILO Constitution have been discontinued for 27 Conventions. These are known as "shelved Conventions". For more details, see ILO document GB.276/LILS/WP/PRS/1.

[25] Under Article 36 of the Constitution of the ILO : *"Amendments to this Constitution which are adopted by the Conference by a majority of two-thirds of the votes cast by the delegates present shall take effect when ratified or accepted by two-thirds of the Members of the Organization including five of the ten Members which are represented on the Governing Body as Members of chief industrial importance in accordance with the provisions of paragraph 3 of article 7 of this Constitution."*

populations into the life of their countries,[26] whereas 13 others are to guarantee respect for the integrity of such peoples.[27]

In addition to the efforts that are needed to bring consistency as between the standards adopted in the past, a host of questions are pushing their way to the fore with respect to the future: is it useful – in this era of deregulation and reliance on market forces – to continue the adoption of instruments in the traditional form? Should the ILO not rather be concentrating on the revision of the old Conventions and on limiting the new instruments adopted to broad principles? Should more use be made of other legal or legally relevant media? These are only a few of the questions that may be discussed in the context of a general review by the Organization on its standard-setting policy. But questions like this have been the subject of study over the decades and will be touched upon in the following section of this paper in so far as they appear relevant to the subject of flexibility in the ILO.

FLEXIBILITY IN THE INSTRUMENTS USED

The non-binding international labour Recommendations, giving guidance on what "should" be done rather than "shall", have of course an inbuilt flexibility. In recent decades, efforts have been made to convince the Members of the value of setting certain standards in autonomous Recommendations, rather than – as is normally the case – using the Recommendation as ancillary to an international labour Convention adopted at the same time. The question arises as to how far the standards need to be set out in binding instruments, particularly since binding provisions exist with respect to the reporting requirements that are parallel to those applicable in the case of Conventions. Under paragraphs 6 and 7 of article 19 of the ILO Constitution, as amended in 1946, Members must submit the Recommendations to their competent legislative or other authority, normally within one year (or at most 18 months) from their adoption, and inform the ILO of the action taken by those authorities. When requested to do so by the ILO Governing Body, they must report on the position of their country's law and practice in relation to the subject matter, showing the extent to which effect is being given to them or is proposed to be given. However, the latter possibility has not yet been resorted to.

---

[26] See the Indigenous and Tribal Populations Convention, 1957 (No. 107).
[27] See the Indigenous and Tribal Peoples Convention, 1989 (No, 169).

On the other hand, deviations from a Recommendation cannot be considered *per se* as violations of international law. Nor can they be the subject of the two adversarial procedures provided for by the ILO Constitution in the case of ratified Conventions: these take the form of "representations" by employers' or workers' organizations (Article 24) or "complaints" initiated by other Members that have also ratified the Convention concerned or by the ILO Governing Body on the motion of a delegate to the International Labour Conference or on its own motion (Article 26). Although in principle, the possible sanctions under Article 26 (see Article 33 of the Constitution[28]) can be more severe and embody a higher degree of solemnity, in practice the sanction under those procedures is of the same kind as that which may result from the Organization's supervisory procedures, namely adverse publicity, which Governments will normally go out of their way to avoid. Moreover in practice, the parties normally bringing the adversarial proceedings (representatives of employers and workers) are also enabled to initiate requests for reports from a Member on a Convention that it has ratified.

In cases in which Members consider that precise standards should apply, the "shall" of Conventions[29] is obviously preferable to the "should" of Recommendations. But where it is considered difficult or inappropriate to draft precise norms that are universally applicable, the Recommendation provides a medium which, if it were brought within the normal supervisory procedures, could be used as a means to assess the progress of each Member towards the fulfilment of the Organization's objectives, having regard to that Member's particular circumstances and capabilities.

Now at the end of 1999, the ILO has a mass of Conventions some of them regulating details and some providing for fundamental principles of human rights. As indicated at the beginning of this paper, each Member decides whether or not it is in a position to ratify a particular Convention. Thus, flexibility in the ILO appears so extensive as to impeach the very credibility of the Organization: what is the use of

---

[28] Article 33 provides: *"In the event of any Member failing to carry out within the time specified the recommendations, if any, contained in the report of the Commission of Inquiry, or in the decision of the International Court of Justice, as the case may be, the Governing Body may recommend to the Conference such action as it may deem wise and expedient to secure compliance therewith."*

[29] An unratified Convention however is considered to have the same legal force as a Recommendation.

having a sophisticated supervisory system in which the progress towards social justice comes under scrutiny, to the last detail, for some Members, when other Members can tranquilly violate the most fundamental rights, without any scrutiny, as they have not ratified the Conventions concerned? As stated earlier part of the answer to this apparent incongruity is the principle of good faith as well as the procedural possibility of requesting reports on the effect given even to Conventions that have not been ratified.

A first answer from the viewpoint of substantive law was given in the 1950s, with the establishment of institutions, which developed into a "Committee on Freedom of Association", a subsidiary organ of the Governing Body hearing complaints of violations of that freedom[30]. Unlike the representation and complaints procedures provided for under the Constitution, complaints may be made to the Committee by relevant national or international organizations even where the country concerned has not ratified the Conventions based on the right to freedom of association. The justification is that an obligation to respect this fundamental right is inherent in membership of the Organization, upon acceptance of the ILO Constitution.

Another answer has taken the form of a campaign to achieve universal ratification of the (then seven) Conventions setting out fundamental human rights principles, which has been quite successful. Of these, the Convention that is perhaps the most difficult to implement in countries whose economic and social systems are less developed, is the Minimum Age Convention, 1973 (No. 138). The subsequent eighth fundamental Convention – the Worst Forms of Child Labour Convention, 1999 (No. 182) – takes account of this situation, by focusing on action that is attainable and essential whatever the stage of development, namely the immediate elimination of the forms of child labour that are recognized as intolerable. From this point of view and having regard to the other developments referred to below that are designed to ensure a continual progress, the new Convention exemplifies a form of flexibility (restriction of scope to essentials) that has been used to promote the universal application of a fundamental right.

The previous year 1998 had seen what may well be the best answer to the apparent uneven playing field: the adoption by the International Labour Conference of the "ILO Declaration on Fundamental Princi-

---

[30] See W. Jenks, *op. cit.*; Nicolas Valticos "Les méthodes de la protection internationale de la liberté syndicale", Collected Courses, Hague Academy of International Law, (1975-I), pp. 77-138.

ples and Rights at Work and its Follow-Up".[31] This solemn Declaration took part of the philosophy of the Freedom of Association procedure, but then continued in a different direction: in addition to freedom of association, the Conference identified other fundamental principles and rights specified in the ILO Constitution (including the 1944 Declaration of Philadelphia) and declared that all Members, even if they have not ratified the Conventions based on those principles,"have an obligation arising from the very fact of membership in the Organization" to respect, to promote and to realize those principles, in good faith and in accordance with the Constitution: the principles identified were those in the four categories listed above: freedom of association and to bargain collectively, elimination of forced labour, abolition of child labour and elimination of discrimination in employment and occupation.

The essential departure from the earlier philosophy is that the Declaration is promotional rather than supervisory or adversarial in nature. There is no complaints procedure, but a follow-up under which Members which have not ratified the fundamental Conventions concerned will be asked (in accordance with Article 19.5(e) of the Constitution) to annually report on progress in giving effect – not to the Conventions themselves – but to the fundamental principles and rights on which they are based. Information gathered from those reports will be discussed in the Governing Body and, together with information taken from the reports from countries that have ratified the Conventions, will form the subject of a periodic Global Report on the situation of each of the four categories of fundamental rights, which will be discussed in the International Labour Conference itself.

The Declaration does not recognize simply the obligations of Members flowing from their acceptance of the Constitution of the ILO, but also the obligation on the Organization itself "to assist its Members, in response to their established and expressed needs," to attain the Constitutional "objectives". Consequently, while still remaining "obligations" inherent in membership, their full implementation is recognized as an "objective" on which some countries may need assistance. The ILO has thus stepped beyond the traditional supervisory system – beyond the verification of compliance with treaty obligations. It is a step beyond, not a turning away from the supervisory system, which will remain in place for ratifying countries. Indeed, one of the consequences of the Follow-up should be to help Members to be

---

[31] See Record of Proceedings, International Labour Conference, 86th session, 1998.

in a position to ratify the fundamental Conventions, although the main purpose is to review the general situation and to identify specific needs. It will be interesting to see how far the forthcoming discussions on the future of standards, referred to above (top of p. 374), will be permeated by the philosophy of the Declaration.

CONCLUSION

A comparison of the trend of flexibility in the ILO's standard-setting activity with the situation in European institutions, which were the subject of very interesting lectures at the session on flexibility of the Conference on the Proliferation of International Organizations, indicates that the whole question is necessarily linked to the objectives of the organization concerned, and not only the standard-setting objectives[32]. The objective in the ILO is not unity among its Members, nor uniformity, nor fairness in trade[33], nor even the harmonization of laws. Members "have undertaken to work towards attaining the overall objectives of the Organization to the best of their resources and fully in line with their specific circumstances".[34] They are not asked to accept standards that are beyond their means but efforts are made to design standards that fit their economic and social situation as closely as possible, in that they make frequent reference to the law and practice of the country concerned and allow governments considerable latitude provided that this is exercised in consultation with the representatives of employers and workers. The great flexibility that exists as far as substantive obligations are concerned, operating within a firm procedural structure, provides a legal framework that is consistent with the philosophy of the International Labour Organization: a dynamic framework providing a flow towards the social objectives, in which all Members are legally caught up in a system of international cooperation

---

[32] The four strategic objectives defined in the Director-General's report (Decent Work) to the 87th Session of the International Labour Conference (1999) are the following: the promotion of fundamental principles and rights at work; the creation of greater employment and income opportunities for women and men; the strengthening of social protection and the strengthening of social dialogue and tripartism.

[33] An aspect of fair trade has however been an important consideration. The third paragraph of the Preamble to the ILO Constitution reads: *"Whereas also the failure of any nation to adopt humane conditions of labour is an obstacle in the way of other nations which desire to improve the conditions in their own countries"*.

[34] 1998 Declaration referred to above, para. 1(a).

and monitoring. Each Member chooses (preferably on a tripartite basis) the extent to which it will move with the flow or beyond it, but the rest of the international community, including the social forces, are on the bank, looking on and, ideally, encouraging and assisting the Member's progress.

THE EUROPEAN UNION AND THE CONCEPT OF FLEXIBILITY: PROLIFERATION OF LEGAL SYSTEMS WITHIN INTERNATIONAL ORGANIZATIONS

Ige F. Dekker and Ramses A. Wessel[1]

INTRODUCTION

European Community law traditionally builds on the principle of uniformity. This principle implies that all member states reach a certain objective at the same time and that measures discriminating between member states are not adopted. Community law is the same for all member states under all circumstances.[2] However, from the outset exceptions to this rule were accepted, and related to either 1) the participating states, 2) the moment of entry into force of a measure, and/or 3) the attainment of the objective of a measure. Thus, the original EEC Treaty acknowledged closer co-operation between the Benelux countries; transition arrangements were accepted for new member states and certain member states were allowed to refrain from participation in the European Monetary System or other areas of co-operation.[3] Secondary legislation as well revealed temporary differences between member states as it sometimes allowed for alternative, optional or minimum national measures.[4] In addition Article 220 (now 293) of

---

[1] Mr. I.F. Dekker and Dr. R.A. Wessel are both researcher and lecturer at the Department of the Law of International Organizations of Utrecht University, the Netherlands. The authors wish to thank Maaike de Langen and Marieke van Lenten for research assistance and Niels Blokker, Ton Heukels, Eric Myjer, Ronald van Ooik, Helen Stapels and Wouter Werner for their helpful comments on an earlier version.

[2] *Cf.* European Court of Justice, Case 166/73, *Rheinmühlen*, [1974] ECR, p. 19. The principle of uniformity runs through the entire case law of the Court. See Barents (1999), at 85.

[3] Examples of the latter include the Protocols to the original EEC Treaty on Luxembourg Agriculture of German Internal Trade.

[4] See for instance the Groundwater Directive 80/68 (OJ 1980, L 20/43) and the Capital Movements Directive 88/361 (OJ 1988, L 178/5).

the Treaty establishing the European Community (TEC) allowed for separate treaties to be concluded between member states on subjects connected with the development of the Community.

The past decade presents further examples of an erosion of the principle of uniformity. In 1985 a Community-related matter – the dissolution of border controls – became subject of an extra-Community arrangement between a restricted number of member states: the Schengen agreement. In 1986 the Single European Act extended and strengthened the harmonization competences of the EEC, while at the same time allowing member states to continue to apply national measures on certain grounds and under specified procedures.[5] The 1992 Treaty on European Union (TEU) allows for different speeds to reach the objectives of a Economic and Monetary Union (EMU) as well as for member states not to participate at all in the EMU. Comparable exceptions were for instance allowed in the fields of social policy (United Kingdom) and the development of a defence policy (Denmark).

The idea of a possible fragmented Union played an important role during the negotiations on the Amsterdam Treaty in 1996/97. The different variations of flexibility were frequently presented as harmful to the Union's unity. Thus concepts like *variable geometry*, *concentric circles*, a *multiple-speed Europe*, or a *Europe à la carte* all seemed to prelude the end of the Union. While as such these concepts did not make it to the final draft of the Treaty, the development towards a more flexible approach of the co-operation within the European Union is reflected in the modifications to the TEU introduced by the 1997 Amsterdam Treaty. The concept of flexibility is rightly considered to be the *Leitmotiv* of the Amsterdam Treaty.[6]

The 1997 Treaty on European Union as well as the modified EC Treaty provide for a number of general and specific arrangements allowing for forms of flexible co-operation between a limited number of member states. For the first time in the Unions' legal history, the Treaties contain general clauses on the possibility for further integration between some but not all member states, under the new heading of "closer co-operation". In addition, the Amsterdam Treaty introduced new specific examples of flexibility, in particular with regard to the new Title IV inserted into the EC Treaty on the free movement of persons, asylum and immigration and the Protocol incorporating the

---

[5] See the old Art. 100A(4) TEC. The Treaty of Amsterdam extended and to some extent clarified its elements. See the new Art. 95 TEC.

[6] See Editorial (1997), at 768.

Schengen *acquis* into the Unions' legal system. In some cases these forms of flexible co-operation allow for even further closer co-operation between some members of the already restricted group of member states.[7] Many view this development as an undesired, but nevertheless unavoidable, solution to problems related to the social-economic and political differences between the EU member states. It is generally expected that this problem will only become more apparent once the Union has completed its proclaimed extension to Central- and Eastern European states.

The aim of the present contribution is not to analyze the various forms of flexibility as such. This has been done quite extensively already by others.[8] Rather we have taken up the task of studying the legal institutional implications of the various forms of flexible co-operation for the unity of the European Unions' legal system. By making use of insights offered by legal theorists – in particular those who are active in the field of institutional legal theory – we will make an attempt to shed a light on the legal possibilities and impossibilities of the emergence of limited (in the sense that not all member states participate) legal systems within the framework of the European Union. This proliferation of legal systems within the framework of a more comprehensive legal system is, of course, not a new phenomenon, an obvious example being formed by the United Nations family of organizations. A major difference, however, is that in the case of the European Union the principle of uniformity is traditionally presented as fundamental to the co-operation and that forms of flexible co-operation clearly change this fundamental starting point. Despite the division in different areas of co-operation, its constituent treaty presents the European Union as a legal unity in which the principle of consistency plays a major role.[9] It is believed that a proliferation of legal sub-systems may affect this unity and that the concept of legal unity, in turn, may set limits to the existence of legal sub-systems.

In this context, two questions in particular emerge: *1* to what extent does the legal unity of the European Union put limitations to the legal

---

[7] See Article 1 of the Schengen Protocol, authorising the signatories to the Schengen agreements to establish closer co-operation among themselves within the scope of the Schengen acquis. See also Wagner (1998), at 33.

[8] See for instance Barents (1999), Curtin (1995), Edwards & Philippart (1997), Ehlermann (1996 and 1998), Gaja (1998), Kortenberg (1998), Shaw (1998), Usher (1999), Wouters (1999), De Zwaan (1999).

[9] See on this topic some earlier publications of the authors: Dekker & Wessel (1997), Curtin & Dekker (1999), Wessel (1999), Chapter 7.

validity of forms of flexible co-operation? and 2 to what extent do forms of flexible co-operation potentially harm the unity of the Union? Keeping in mind the discussions during the Amsterdam Intergovernmental Conference on the link between flexibility and the unity of the union, we aim to investigate to what extent the current provisions on flexibility pose a threat to the Union's legal unity.

Section 2 will first of all try to make the concept of flexibility more concrete by pointing to a number of provisions in the Treaty on European Union allowing for co-operation between a limited number of member states. This section will also provide a survey of the Treaty requirements for the establishment of the most general form of flexibility, labelled "closer co-operation", as well as of the role of the Union's institutions in this form of co-operation. In section 3 the theoretical tools are developed for analyzing the unity as well as forms of flexibility within the legal system of the European Union. Section 4 will focus on the main research question of this paper by attempting to look at the legal implications of the emergence of legal sub-systems within the overall legal system of the European Union. Section 5, finally, will be used to draw the main conclusions.

FLEXIBILITY IN THE EUROPEAN UNION

The concept of "flexible co-operation" or "flexibility" in the context of the present paper concerns the situation in which the fifteen member states do not necessarily participate to the same extent in every policy or activity of the Union.[10] The Treaty on European Union nowhere explicitly refers to the notion of flexibility.[11] However, one can distinguish between at least two broad categories of flexibility within the Unions' legal system. The first category contains the general *enabling clauses* on the basis of which the Council has a competence – through the adoption of secondary legislation – to decide on the establishment of "closer co-operation". The second category harbors a variety of forms of flexible co-operation linked to specific fields of EU/EC competence, including the so-called *pre-determined* forms of

---

[10] *Cf.* Usher (1999), at 253. *Cf.* also De Zwaan (1999), at 13.
[11] See Edwards & Philippart (1997), at 12: "During the legal and linguistic revision of the text agreed in June (1997), the word 'flexibility' disappeared. The need for it was no longer important in the domestic politics of the UK." See also Shaw (1998), at 69.

flexibility, i.e. forms of differential treatment of certain member states as laid down in the treaties themselves or in protocols.

General Forms of Flexibility: Closer Co-operation

The first category of flexibility provisions is contained in the new Title VII TEU and introduces a general competence for member states to use the mechanism to establish "closer co-operation" in yet unidentified areas. Article 43 TEU states: "Member states which intend to establish closer co-operation between themselves may make use of the institutions, procedures and mechanisms laid down by this Treaty and the Treaty establishing the European Community [...]". Article 43 refers to Article 11 TEC and to Article 40 TEU (on police and judicial co-operation) for additional criteria, which forms the reason why it is generally held that the general provisions on closer co-operation may only be applied in the framework of the Community and under Title VI TEU (police and judicial co-operation), and not under the provisions on a common foreign and security policy (Title V TEU).[12]

The concept of "closer co-operation" is nowhere defined in the Treaties. However, it follows from the general provisions that the core of the concept concerns a competence of the Council to decide on measures for further integration between some but not all of the member states which, to that end, may make use of "the institutions, procedures and mechanisms" laid down in the Treaties. This competence is subject to a number of general and specific conditions – as listed in Article 43 TEU, Article 11 EC and Article 40 TEU – which to a large extent determine the feasibility of the mechanism of closer co-operation. On first sight these conditions may seem to be obvious, but in fact they raise a lot of still unsettled questions of interpretation.[13]

Article 43 TEU lists a number of conditions that must be fulfilled in order to render closer co-operation valid.[14]

• First of all the co-operation must be aimed at furthering the objectives of the Union and at protecting and serving its interests.

• Secondly, the co-operation must respect the principles of the Treaties and the single institutional framework of the Union. These

---

[12] Gaja (1998), at 856; Kortenberg (1998), at 844; Ehlermann (1998), at 264. However, the TEU does not exclude the possibility of flexibility within the second pillar (see *infra* at 391).

[13] See also, Shaw (1998), at 70-76; Ehlermann (1998), at 253-259; Usher (1999), at 263-264.

[14] See also Usher (1999), at 263-264.

principles thus seem to include, at least, the principles of consistency, transparency, subsidiarity and attribution of competences. But one could also mention the principles of democracy and respect for human rights and national identities.[15] Regarding the Community, one could argue that the principle of non-discrimination on grounds of nationality (or: the uniformity principle) also seems to be covered by this requirement,[16] although it seems that this principle can only have a function between the participating states in a closer co-operation régime, as the very notion of closer co-operation implies a discrimination between member states.[17]

- The third condition stipulates that closer co-operation is only to be used as a last resort, where the objectives of the Treaties could not be attained by applying the relevant procedures laid down therein. It thus seems that there should have been prior attempts to enact legislation on the basis of the regular provisions, before a fall back on Article 43 is allowed.

- The fourth condition requires that at least a majority of member states participates in the closer co-operation; so, closer co-operation should at least concern eight member states.[18] The obvious reason is to prevent the establishment of conflicting closer co-operation groups.

- The fifth condition purports to safeguard the *"acquis communautaire"* in that it stipulates that the *acquis* is not to be affected by forms of closer co-operation. This condition seems to aim at the prevention of a negative affection of the *acquis* only; it does not seem to prevent closer co-operation at all in areas which are thought to fall under the *acquis*, although it is still difficult to fix the *acquis* in general terms and thus to determine concrete areas for further co-operation. One could also ask the question of whether the safeguarding of the *Union acquis* is intended as well. The first condition mentioned above –

---

[15] Articles 3, 5 and 6 TEU.
[16] See for instance De Zwaan (1999), at 16.
[17] It seems that the requirement of non-discrimination – in line with the Court's case law (*cf.* Kapteyn & VerLoren van Themaat (1998), at 168) – should not be regarded as ruling out any form of differentiation, but rather concerns the prohibition of treating similar situations differently, and different situations in the same manner. It is in that sense conceivable that citizens in non-participating states are in an objectively different situation than citizens in participating states. *Cf.* Wouters (1999), at 36.
[18] It would thus not have been possible to adopt the original Schengen Agreement under the current provisions.

which explicitly refers to the Union – indeed seems to point in this direction. Furthermore, "measures adopted under the other provisions *of the said Treaties*" are explicitly referred to.

• According to the sixth condition, closer co-operation may not affect the competences, rights, obligations and interests of those member states which do not participate therein. One could say that this condition is balanced by the obligation of the non-participating states not to impede the implementation of closer co-operation by the participating member states (laid down in Article 43(2) TEU). Some authors hold that these requirements are nothing more than a specification and generalisation of the principle of good faith, contained in Article 10 TEC.[19] However, when taken strictly, this condition seems not only extremely difficult to meet, but it also seems to provide to unwilling member states a wide range of arguments to oppose a specific proposal for closer co-operation. In one way or another, each instance of closer co-operation is likely to affect, at least, the "interests" of the non-participating states.

• The seventh condition stipulates that closer co-operation be open to all member states and allows them to become parties to the co-operation at any time, provided that they comply with the basic decision and with the decisions taken within that framework. It has been argued that a consequence of this condition may be that member states wishing to set up closer co-operation abstain from doing so. After all, when three people who want to play tennis or bridge are joined by a fourth person who would spoil the game, the first three may prefer not to play at all.[20]

• The eighth and final condition in Article 43 in fact refers to specific additional criteria for the application of closer co-operation in the EC and PJCC legal systems, as formulated in Article 11 TEC and Article 40 TEU. The additional requirements in the EC Treaty are partly a reaffirmation of the conditions laid down in Article 43 TEU, "but in other ways add extra and more precise conditions which closer co-operation must satisfy before it can validly be authorized."[21] They concern the conditions that closer co-operation does not take place in areas which fall within the exclusive competence of the Community, that it does not affect Community policies, actions or programmes, and that it does not concern the citizenship of the Union or discriminate

---

[19] See Ehlermann (1998), at 254; Shaw (1998), at 71.
[20] Gaja (1998), at 860.
[21] Shaw (1998), at 72.

between nationals, or between member states when issues of trade or competition are at stake. Furthermore, it is made clear once more that closer co-operation can only take place when a Community legal basis exists ("remains within the powers conferred upon the Community").[22] Regarding PJCC, Article 40 TEU repeats that closer co-operation respects the powers of the Community and stipulates that it must have the aim of enabling the Union to develop more rapidly into an area of freedom, security and justice.

In making use of the institutions, the states participating in closer co-operation are furthermore bound by Article 44 TEU, which provides that the relevant institutional provisions apply. An exception is made with regard to the adoption of decisions by the Council. While all states may take part in the deliberations, only the states participating in closer co-operation take part in the adoption of decisions, which implies a *de facto* derogation from the unanimity rule on issues where it would normally be applied (since it is not required to have *fifteen* votes in favour, despite the fact that the legal basis remains the same). In case of qualified majority voting, the rules are adapted according to the number of participating member states. Except for the administrative costs of the institutions, expenditure is to be borne by the participating member states, unless the Council unanimously decides otherwise.

With regard to the *authorization* for the establishment of closer co-operation on a certain issue the procedures of the EC and the PJCC regulations differ in some respects. As far as closer co-operation within the Community is concerned, an authorization from the Council is needed, which acts by a qualified majority on a proposal from the Commission and after consulting the European Parliament. This means that initiatives for closer co-operation may be blocked by the Commission. But despite the reference to qualified majority voting, even member states may block further initiatives as they may have "important and stated reasons of national policy", in which case a vote shall not be taken and the Council may decide (by qualified majority) to (unanimously) decide on the matter in the composition of the Heads of State and Government. Under the PJCC provisions, the authorization is also granted by the Council (using the same procedures), but the Commission is merely invited to present its opinion and the EP only gets to see the request.

---

[22] According to Gaja (1998) this does not rule out the use of Article 308 (ex 235) TEC.

In case a non-participating member state wishes to accede to an ongoing form of closer co-operation within the EC, Article 11(3) TEC demands a prior notification of the Council and the Commission. Within three months of receipt of the notification, the Commission gives its opinion on the request, and within four months it has to decide on the application. Under the PJCC regulation laid down in Article 40(3) TEU, it is not the Commission but the Council which takes the decision on a request for accession.

SPECIFIC FORMS OF FLEXIBILITY

The second category of flexibility within the EU/EC legal systems first of all contains the aforementioned *pre-determined* forms of flexible co-operation. While one could say that these forms of flexibility are instances of the concept of closer co-operation,[23] it must be taken into account that these instances are not established through secondary law but find their basis in primary law, and that some of the specific rules governing these instances differ from the rules attached to the mechanism of closer co-operation.

Pre-determined flexibility may either take the form of a permission granted by all member states to a group of member states to act together through Union institutions and legislation (e.g. the Social Protocol under the Maastricht regime), or it is reflected in the permission given to member states *not* to participate in an activity in which they should in principle participate as a matter of Union or Community law (e.g. the 1991 Protocols on the basis of which Denmark and the United Kingdom are not obliged to take part in the third phase of the EMU; the 1991 Protocol concerning Denmark's non-participation in the elaboration or implementation of measures having defence implications).[24] This last sub-category has gained some popularity under the Treaty of Amsterdam, especially in the context of the new Title in the EC Treaty on the free movement of persons and the integration of the Schengen *acquis* into the legal framework of the Union. The following examples were introduced by the Amsterdam Treaty.[25]

---

[23] See, in this context Article 11(5) TEC.
[24] *Cf.* Usher (1999), at 254-256.
[25] *Cf.* Usher (1999), at 267-271. The position of Norway and Iceland with regard to their participation in the Schengen *acquis* is not mentioned here, because this concerns a form of flexible co-operation outside the Union's legal system. On 17 May 1999 the Council concluded international agreements with these two

1. The Protocol annexed to the TEU and to the EC Treaty which entitles the United Kingdom and Ireland, notwithstanding Article 14 TEC on "an area without internal frontiers", to maintain border controls and to continue to make arrangements on their own "Common Travel Area".

2. The Protocol on the basis of which the United Kingdom and Ireland do not take part in the adoption by the Council of proposed measures pursuant to Title IV of the EC Treaty on visas, asylum, immigration and other policies related to free movement of persons. Measured adopted under this Title do not form part of community law as it is applied in the UK and Ireland. An "opting-in" on a case-by-case basis is possible, but the procedure is more restrictive than it is with regard to the general clauses on closer co-operation, as the Council shall unanimously decide on such request.[26] On the basis of another Protocol Denmark is not bound by Title IV TEC and by the measures adopted pursuant to that Title, except for measures that were already adopted under the old Article 100C TEC. In addition, as Title IV TEC allows for a compulsory but specific system of preliminary rulings in this area (Article 68 TEC), this system not applicable to the United Kingdom, Ireland and Denmark.

3. The Protocol integrating the Schengen *acquis* (the Agreements and decisions on a gradual abolition of checks at common borders) into the framework of the European Union is binding on Denmark as far as the Schengen provisions have become part of Community law, but Denmark does not participate in the elaboration of new measures (except those concerning visas); it may nevertheless exercise its right to opt in within six month after the Council has adopted a measure which builds upon the Schengen *acquis*. In that case an obligation "under international law" is created between Denmark and the other Schengen states, as well as with the UK and Ireland when these states have opted in. As far as the parts of the Schengen *acquis* are concerned that have been placed under the header of Title VI of the TEU concerning police and judicial co-operation in criminal matters (PJCC), Denmark will fully participate – not only on the basis of international law, but on the basis of Union law. The Schengen *acquis* is not binding on the United

---

countries on their involvement in the Schengen *acquis*. See *OJ* L 176/35, 10.7.1999.

[26] See also Wagner (1998), at 39.

Kingdom and Ireland, but these states may request to take part in some or all of the provisions. [27]

Beside these pre-determined forms of flexibility, the Treaties harbour a variety of provisions which in one way or another result in a permeation of the principle of uniformity in a specific area the Unions' legal system. Without attempting to be complete, the following new examples may be discovered in the TEU.[28]

1. The possibility of "constructive abstention" on the basis of Article 23 TEU allows for coalitions of able and willing member states to emerge in the field of foreign and security policy. Member states may qualify their abstention in a formal declaration, in which case they shall not be obliged to apply the adopted decision.

2. On the basis of Article 24 (and Article 38) TEU, the Council may decide that international agreements with third states or international organizations may provisionally apply to certain member states.

3. On the basis of Article 34 TEU, PJCC agreements may enter into force when they are accepted by at least half of the member states.

4. Judicial flexibility is the result of variations on the system of preliminary rulings. Article 35 TEU provides that the Court has jurisdiction on PJCC matters to the extent that a member state declares that it has jurisdiction; each member state may determine whether the power to make a reference is to be made available to all courts or limited to courts of final appeal.

---

[27] The Schengen Agreement was originally concluded between Germany, France, and the Benelux countries and was later succeeded by Italy, Spain, Portugal, Greece, Austria, Denmark, Sweden and Finland. The UK and Ireland never participated. See on the integration of the Schengen *acquis* in the Union's legal system: Staples (1999), Toth (1999), Wagner (1998).

[28] Before 'Amsterdam', the EC Treaty already contained such forms of flexibility, for instance those included in Article 95 with regard to the harmonization of national legislation, and in Articles 168 and 169 concerning the area of research and technological development on the basis of which multi-annual framework programmes may be implemented through supplementary programmes involving the participation of certain member states only.

FORMS OF CO-OPERATION AS "LEGAL INSTITUTIONS"

THE EUROPEAN UNION AS A LEGAL UNITY

The media, public opinion, and third states relatively quickly regarded the European Union as a new entity on the international plane. As from the entry into force of the TEU at the end of 1993, the label "European Union" was accepted rather smoothly, regardless of the issue area at stake.[29] The European Union was seen as a "unity", replacing the old three European Communities, which were now part of the Union alongside the two other "pillars" on a Common Foreign and Security Policy (CFSP) and the Co-operation in the Fields of Justice and Home Affairs (JHA). What we see here, however, is a reference to "unity" in a political sense. In contrast, it took much more time for European *legal* circles to accept the legal unity of the Union. At first, the three-pillar structure of the Union proved to be an obstacle in viewing the legal system established by the TEU as a legal unity. As stated in a well-known and often cited critical article, the "constitutional structure of the Union" consisted of "bits and pieces" which would prevent the very Union from developing.[30] Of course, it cannot be denied that the Treaty on European Union indeed separates the three issue areas: the CFSP and the JHA — by the Treaty of Amsterdam renamed to PJCC — provisions can be found in separate titles (Titles V and VI respectively) of the Treaty which are meant to "supplement" the European Communities (Article 1 TEU). Despite some links with the legal orders by which they are surrounded, Titles V and VI of the TEU present the CFSP and the PJCC as more or less autonomous sets of rules, meant to lead to a policy which, *prima facie*, is not by definition connected to the policies of the Community, and which is clearly not to be equalled with the national policies of the member states.

However, this paper starts from the presumption that the Union can be qualified as a legal unity.[31] The foundation for this conclusion

---

[29] See for instance Koenig & Pechstein (1995), at 22: "Jedenfalls im nichtjuristischen Sprachgebrauch hat sich sehr rasch eine Redeweise verbreitet, die den Begriff der 'Europäischen Union' im Sinne einer eigenständigen Einheit verwendet, welche die bisherigen Gemeinschaften vollständig ersetzt hat".

[30] See Curtin (1993).

[31] See also Dekker & Wessel (1998). *Cf.* also Dörr (1995), at 336: "eine eigenrechtliche Einheit"; and De Witte (1999), at 59: "a unified international

can *inter alia* be found in the provisions in the Treaty on European Union that are common to all Union areas, and which for instance relate to common objectives (Articles 1 and 2), a single institutional framework together with a requirement for consistency (Articles 3 and 5), common values (Article 6) and common rules of change (Articles 48 and 49). Moreover, the establishment of the European Union through the Treaty on European Union points to the existence of a Union legal system, since it may be asserted that the conclusion of a treaty implies the creation of a legal system, in the sense of a system of valid legal norms derived from the competence of states to conclude international legal agreements. While this may very well be one single system, the possibility of sub-systems existing within the framework of the treaty is not excluded. It may be argued that the norms in the TEU are not merely to be seen as a loose "set", but indeed form a system with mutual dependencies. Hence, the entry into force of the Treaty on European Union marked the coming into being of a new legal system, comprising a number of sub-systems (the different "pillars" of the Union as well as the sub-legal systems developed within these areas).

The consequences of viewing the European Union as a legal unity are at least twofold. A first consequence is that the norms in the unitary legal system of the Union are inter-related. This in turn implies that the different parts of the Union cannot be viewed as isolated regimes, but that the interpretation of the norms should take into account their setting within the legal system of the Union, which reveals the necessity to establish a hierarchy of norms within the legal system of the European Union. The second consequence is related to the external relations of the European Union. When the Union is qualified as a legal unity that is capable of acting within the international legal system, this implies that its external policy be consistent in the sense that it does not "blow hot and cold at the same time". In other words: the internal unity should also "be worn inside out". In their legal relations with the Union third parties must be able to rely on the fact that they have one counterpart only.

A new stream of literature on the legal unity of the European Union seems to take account of the fact that both the internal and the external dimension of the unitary nature of the Union call for an interpretation of any EU, EC, CFSP and PJCC provision in the context of

---

organization". Some authors have even argued that the existence of a Union legal order implies a *fusion* of the three pillars. See in particular Von Bogdandy & Nettesheim (1996) and the contribution of Von Bogdandy in the present volume.

the overall legal system as presented in the TEU.[32] Admittedly, this system at certain points hints at a hierarchy between its norms in favour of the *acquis communautaire*, but examples can also be pointed out in which an unconditional preference for the Community rules would simply neglect key provisions in the other areas.[33] As Trüe has stated: "Die grundsätzliche Gleichrangigkeit folgt aus dem Kohärenzgebot: Das Kohärenzgebot verlangt [...] nicht eine Anpassung des Rechts der einen Säule an das Recht einer anderen, sondern eine gegenseitige Abstimmung der Säulen".[34] The practice of Union decision-making – with institutions being increasingly active in all Union areas – seems to have confirmed this constitutional element.[35]

INSTANCES OF FLEXIBLE CO-OPERATION AS LEGAL INSTITUTIONS

Our starting-point in analyzing the European Union as a legal unity in relation to the concept of flexibility is the so-called "institutional theory of law", as developed in the works of MacCormick & Weinberger, Ruiter, Wróblewski and others.[36] A key concept in the institutional theory of law is the "legal institution". Legal institutions in this discipline are not to be seen as a synonym to (international) organizations. The concept has a broader, but nevertheless well-defined, meaning. Legal institutions are viewed as the building blocks of legal systems, which at the same time harbour their own legal system. In that sense they can be roughly characterized as distinct legal systems governing specific forms of social conduct within the overall legal system.[37] Legal institutions are a specific type of normative institutions, namely normative institutions which derive their validity from a legal

---

[32] See, for instance, Dörr (1995), Devroe & Wouters (1996), Klabbers (1997), Trüe (1997), Wessel (1997), De Witte (1998), Curtin & Dekker (1999) and Wessel (1999). In contrast to their earlier focus on the 'intergovernmental' aspects of the non-Community areas of the Union (1995), Koenig and Pechstein now also seem to have accepted the existence of a Union legal order (*'Unionsrechtsordnung'*); see Koenig & Pechstein (1998).

[33] See Wessel (1999), Chapter 7.

[34] Trüe (1997), at 61.

[35] See, in particular, Curtin & Dekker (1999), at 104-131. On the hierarchy of norms in relation to constitutional questions also Gaudin (1999). Gaudin in particular pointed to the question as to what extent the Union constitution is bound to the 'supra-constitutional' principles referred to in Article 6 TEU.

[36] MacCormick & Weinberger (1986), Weinberger (1991), MacCormick (ed.) (1997), Ruiter (1993), Ruiter (1997), Ruiter (1998), and Wróblewski (1992).

[37] Ruiter (1997), at 358.

system. Ruiter defines a legal institution as "... a régime of legal norms purporting to effectuate a legal practice that can be interpreted as resulting from a common belief that the régime is an existent unity."[38] In other words, a legal institution does not refer to an existent entity, but to a presentation of a phenomenon that ought to be made true in the form of social practices. Thus, legal institutions have their counterparts in social reality, often referred to as "real" institutions.

Inherent in the concept of legal institutions is its *unitary* character, which has the purpose of indicating that the institution can be dealt with as a more or less autonomous phenomenon within the over-all legal system of which it forms part and that it can be distinguished from other legal institutions within that system. According to MacCormick's definition of legal institutions, their autonomous character is determined

"by sets of institutive, consequential, and terminative rules, with the effect that instances of them are properly said to exist over a period of time, from the occurrence of an institutive act or event until the occurrence of a terminative of a terminative act or event."[39]

The autonomous character of legal institutions implies a minimum of consistency and coherence within the legal régime of the institution. In relation to law, "coherence" not only means the absence of contradiction – often referred to as "consistency" – but also the presence of a positive connection between the different parts of a legal system.[40] Thus, unity tests of legal institutions also depend on the question whether and how the legal regime of a legal institution binds together its different parts by common legal norms, rules and competences. This aspect is relevant in particular when the legal institution itself is at the same time a legal system, i.e. the legal framework of other legal institutions, as is the case with the legal institution "European Union", harbouring other legal institutions.

Apart from making sense of the different issue areas foreseen in the Treaty on European Union, the concept of legal institutions also seems to be relevant in relation to forms of flexible co-operation within the Union. The legal institutional approach provides a number of theoretical tools to analyze at least two questions that emerge in this

---

[38] Ruiter (1997), at 358.
[39] MacCormick & Weinberger (1986), at 53.
[40] See, on the concept of coherence in law, e.g. Van der Velden (1992), at. 257; Tietje (1997), at. 211.

context: *1* what possible shapes may forms of flexible co-operation within the Union have? and *2* what is the legal régime of forms of flexible co-operation established under the umbrella of the Unions' legal system?

Regarding the first question, Ruiter distinguishes between seven categories of legal institutions.[41] Only two of these seem to be *prima facie* relevant to the concept of flexibility: personal legal connections and legal persons. The first category is defined as "a valid legal régime with the form of a connection between subjects". The bottom line is that a legal institution in this form reflects a legal relation between legal persons. Most types of flexibility mentioned above will have this shape, as they are or will be based on agreements between states or decisions of the Council. The second appropriate category is the legal person. A legal person is defined as "a valid legal régime with the form of an entity that can act". In this case it is not so much the relation between legal persons that counts, but rather the establishment of a new legal person, a new international legal entity. The most well-known example in this respect is the European Central Bank (ECB). One could even go as far as to argue that every form of closer co-operation decided on by the Council on the basis of the general clauses will result in at least one new legal person, namely a "Council" in the composition of the participating member states. After all, Article 44 TEU provides that only those members of the Council representing the participating states take part in the adoption of decisions. This in clear contrast to the general Community provisions on the Council stating that the Council shall consist of a representative of each member state and that all members take part in the decision-making (Articles 203 and 205 TEC). An interesting example in this respect is the so-called "Euro-11 Council", established on the basis of a resolution of the European Council as an "informal" body, but with some decision-making capacity.[42] A somewhat similar situation occurs whenever the "Councils" act on the basis of the aforementioned pre-determined forms of flexibility introduced by the Amsterdam protocols relating to Article 14 TEC, the

---

[41] *Legal persons* (representing a subject); *legal objects* (representing an object); *legal qualities* (representing a property of a subject); *legal status* (representing a property of an object); *personal legal connection* (representing connection between subjects); *legal configurations* (representing a connection between objects); *objective legal connections* (representing a connection between a subject and an object). Ruiter (1997), at 365-369.

[42] See Wouters (1998), at 39-40.

new Title IV TEC on visas, asylum and immigration, and the Schengen Protocol.[43]

With regard to the legal régime of legal institutions, MacCormick's definition of legal institutions reveals that they are determined by sets of institutive, consequential, and terminative rules. To this list Ruiter added constitutive, content and invalidating rules.[44] These rules determine the autonomous character of a legal institution within the surrounding legal system. In our attempt to present forms of flexible co-operation within the European Union as legal institutions a concretization of these rules as to the subject before us may therefore give an indication of the autonomous character of the legal institutions based on the concept of flexible co-operation. For reasons of simplicity, we will restrict ourselves to the rules related to the general form of flexibility: closer co-operation, and we will disregard the specific forms of flexible co-operation.

A *constitutive* rule presents the creation of a legal concept. The concept of "closer co-operation" in the Unions' legal system is constituted through Article 43 TEU, although the article gives no definition of the concept. Article 44 TEU in particular implies that closer co-operation is a form of decision-making between some but not all member states of the Union, based on existing legal competences provided for by the Treaties and resulting in secondary legislation. The way in which member states may establish instances of this general concept is laid down in *institutive* rules, regulating the valid creation of a new legal institution. We can find these rules in Article 11 TEC and Article 40 TEU authorizing the Council to establish, under certain procedural conditions, instances of closer co-operation.

Consequential rules "attach legal consequences to the validity of a legal institution of a certain category" and these legal consequences "do not enjoy validity as part of the legal institution itself but as part of the encompassing legal system."[45] They form no prerequisite for the validity of an institution and can be violated without affecting that validity. Two consequential rules explicitly relate to closer co-operation. The first one concerns the application of the principle of good faith in relation to the creation and implementation of instances of closer co-operation, as formulated in Article 43(1)f and Article 43(2) TEU. The second one concerns the rule that non-participating member

---

[43] See *supra* at 390.
[44] Ruiter (1998), at 218-221.
[45] Ruiter (1998), at 227.

states can, at any time, become parties to an established form of closer co-operation, "provided that they comply with the basic decision and with the decisions taken within that framework"(Article 43(10(g) TEU).

Content rules define the (valid) content of legal institutions, i.e. "what legal conditions must, may or cannot be part of legal institutions".[46] The most basic content rule is, of course, the application of the principle of the attribution of powers, as expressed in general terms in Article 43(1)(b) TEU and more specifically in Article 11(1)(d) TEC: the co-operation must remain "within the limits of the powers conferred upon the Community by this Treaty". In addition, most of the requirements mentioned in Article 43(1) TEU and the additional criteria mentioned in Article 11(1) TEC and Article 40(1) TEU are content rules, such as the conditions that forms of closer co-operation may not affect the *acquis communautaire*, may not concern the exclusive competence of the Community or may not exclude certain member states.

Finally, (norms making up) legal institutions may cease to exist because of invalidating and terminative rules. *Invalidating* rules establish the defectiveness of legal institutions. No explicit example of this rule can be found in the TEU, but it seems that an implied rule exist, reading something like: "If the Council decides to establish an instance of closer co-operation between member states which is not in accordance with the rules laid down in the Treaty on European Union or the Treaty establishing the European Community, this form of closer co-operation is invalid". This rule follows in particular from the competence of the Court of Justice with regard to closer co-operation as laid down in Article 46 TEU. It may form the basis for the Court to invalidate acts of the Council on closer co-operation. *Terminative* rules regulate the termination of a legal institution. It is unclear whether a terminative rule exists in relation to closer co-operation within the European Union. In contrast to the substantive number of institutive rules, the Treaties do not indicate the way in which member states are to make an end to their closer co-operation. In line with the spirit of the concept of closer co-operation one could only come up with one (implied) terminative rule: "a legal institution harbouring a legal régime of closer co-operation ceases to exist once all members of the European Union participate in it".

---

[46] Ruiter (1998), at 230.

FLEXIBLE CO-OPERATION AND THE UNIONS' LEGAL SYSTEM

The foregoing analysis leads to the conclusion that the general provisions concerning flexibility, as explicitly or implicitly expressed in the Treaties, provide a sufficient basis to view the concept of closer co-operation as an institutional legal concept in its own right. This implies that instances of closer co-operation can be dealt with as legal institutions, i.e. as independent legal entities within the encompassing legal system of the EU. Against this background we will try to go into the main research questions posed in the introduction to the present contribution.

INSTITUTIONAL LIMITATIONS OF FLEXIBLE CO-OPERATION

Regarding the first question – whether and to what extent the legal system of the European Union puts limitations to the legal validity of forms of flexible co-operation – the general answer is rather clear. One could say that the EU's legal system has given birth to this new institutional concept but at the same time entangled it in almost every possible way in order to ensure the Union's legal unity. The different kinds of rules determining the establishment, validity and operation of legal institutions based on the concept of flexible co-operation all point to an existing unity of the Union's legal system. After all, they only make sense when their relation to the unity of that encompassing legal system is taken into account. This not only holds true for the *constitutive* rule regarding the concept of flexible co-operation, but equally for most of the *institutive, consequential* and *content* rules.[47]

As pointed out earlier, valid legal institutions of flexible co-operation either exist on the basis of previously adopted provisions in the Treaties – the so-called pre-determined (or primary) forms of flexible co-operation – or they can be established through the mechanism of closer co-operation in secondary Union law. The introduction of the concept of closer co-operation in the TEU does not seem to exclude the capacity of the member states to create new *ad hoc* forms of flexible co-operation through new amendments of the Treaty, as was done in "Maastricht" as well as in "Amsterdam". The member

---

[47] The invalidating and terminative rules are dealt with in the next section.

states are still the "Herren der Verträge".[48] However, it is far more difficult to accept the idea that the provisions on closer co-operation do not exclude the possibility for two or more member states to establish other forms of flexible co-operation on issues within the competence of the Union while disregarding the new "rules of the game". One could of course argue, that Article 43 TEU only formulates the *right* of member states to use the institutions and procedures of the EU and EC whenever they intend to embark on closer co-operation between themselves, and that they are thus free to take another road. However, this interpretation not only misconceives the word "right" as a subjective right instead of a competence. Moreover, it does not seem to be in line with the unitary character of the legal system of the Union as defined by, in particular, the principles of a single institutional framework (Article 3 TEU) and the principles of consistency and loyalty (Articles 3 and 11 TEU, Article 10 TEC). In a legal sense, the main purpose of inserting a regulation on closer co-operation in the Treaties is to uphold the unity of the Union's legal system and at the same time to meet the future needs for further integration on a flexible basis. That means, at least, that member states intending to establish closer co-operation, have the *duty* first to try to apply the specific provisions on closer co-operation. If they do not succeed in their attempts – for instance, because only six member states are interested – they will seriously have to investigate the possibility to establish a primary form of flexible co-operation through an amendment of the Treaties. Only in a situation where both "internal" ways prove to be inadequate, one might accept the possibility of member states being free to apply the general rules of international law to achieve the goal that could not be attained on the basis of the special rules.[49]

Further limitations follow from the *institutive* rules on closer co-operation. The purpose of these rules seems to be to uphold the single institutional framework of the Union to the largest possible extent, in the sense that member states wishing to cooperate more closely have to use the existing institutions of the Union. In fact, the possibility of using these institutions forms the very essence of the mechanism of closer co-operation. The composition and the voting rules of the

---

[48] See, on the 'rules of change' of the Union's legal order, especially De Witte (1994).

[49] This interpretation applies also to those other elements of the Union's legal system, which define its highly self-sufficient character. See on the issue of the Union's legal system as a 'self-contained regime' in international law, Marschik (1997).

Commission and the Parliament remain the same, and even in the Council the non-participating states have a right to participate in the deliberations on the establishment and implementation of instances of closer co-operation. Through the application of the regular decision-making procedures, and the supervisory role of the European Court of Justice, the existing "institutional balance" – sometimes considered to be one of the fundamental constitutional principles of the Community[50] – is only marginally affected. Nevertheless, the position of the Commission with regard to closer co-operation within the Community seems to be strengthened, in that it not only has retained its exclusive right of initiative but also has the final say in the accession procedure. Regarding the decision to start closer co-operation on a specific issue, the position of the Parliament is rather weak since it has an advisory role only.

The unitary character of the EU's legal system is further safeguarded by the limitations following from the *consequential* rules, taking into account the fact that that seems to be the main purpose of these rules. As noted earlier, the general provisions on closer co-operation harbour explicit consequential rules which closely tie this new legal institution to the ground rules of institutional European law. Regarding a first consequential rule – the application of the principle of good faith[51] – there was a good reason to specify explicitly its significance for the new institutional concept of closer co-operation. This holds true in particular for the application of this principle to the position of the non-participating states.[52] According to Article 43(2) TEU, these states have a duty not to impede the implementation of closer co-operation by the participating states. At the same time, non-participating states always have the right to opt-in in established forms of closer co-operation (as well as in other forms of flexibility), although they will have to accept the *acquis* produced by the closer co-operation concerned.[53] In both ways – the openness of the co-operation and the closeness of the *acquis* – this rule purports to guarantee the effectiveness of uniformity principle to the largest extent possible.

---

[50] Cf. Jacqué's note under Case C-70/88, Parliament v. Council, [1990] ECR I-2041 (Chernobyl), 26 RTDE (1990), p. 620. See in general on the institutional balance: Prechal (1999), at 273-294.

[51] See Art. 43(1)f and 43(2) TEU.

[52] Cf. Ehlermann (1998), at 254.

[53] See Art. 43(1)(g) TEU, Art. 11(3), TEC Art. 40(3) TEU.

The *raison d'etre* of most of the limitations on the creation and realization of closer co-operation laid down in the *content* rules, also seems to be related to safeguarding the Union's legal unity. As already mentioned, one of the most fundamental conditions in this respect is that decisions taken in the framework of closer co-operation – or flexibility in general – must be based on one of the existing legal bases in the Union or Community Treaties.[54] This means that the competences of the Union and the Community cannot be extended through the application of the (general or specific) provisions on flexible co-operation. More or less the same holds true for the content rules referring to the "untouchability" of the principles laid down in the Treaties,[55] as well as of the *acquis communautaire*,[56] of the areas falling under the "exclusive competence" of the Community,[57] of the EU citizenship,[58] and of the "internal market".[59] In the same sense, the rule that no member state can be excluded from participation in a instance of closer co-operation, purports to prevent the establishment of "closed circles" within the Union. But regardless of the rather self-evident character of these conditions, most of them at the same time raise a series of questions of interpretation which cannot be answered easily. We already noted that the EU legal concept "principles" is far from clear and in that respect the reference in Article 43 TEU to "the principles of the said Treaties" is not very helpful either.[60] Does Article 43 merely refer to the principles mentioned in Article 6 TEU – the "principles of liberty, democracy, respect for human rights and fundamental freedoms, and the rule of law" – or are the principles concerning, for instance, proportionality, subsidiarity, and non-discrimination included as well? In the same sense, the notions of the "*acquis communautaire*", the "exclusive competence" and the "internal market" are rather imprecise, at least as far as their margins are concerned.[61] Moreover, these notions are not static but rather dynamic in character. For example, it is generally held that the *original* exclusive

---

[54] See Art. 11(1)(d) TEC, Art. 40(1)(a) TEU.
[55] See Art. 43(1)(b) TEU.
[56] See Art. 43(1)(e) TEU.
[57] See Art. 11(1)(a) TEC.
[58] See Art. 11(1)(c) TEC.
[59] See Art. 11(1)(c)&(e) TEC.
[60] Also because Article 43(1)(b) TEU refers to 'the principles of the said Treaties and the single institutional framework of the Union', implicating that the single institutional framework is not a principle of EU law.
[61] See Shaw, (1998), at 71-75; Wouters (1999), at 35-38.

competences of the Community are restricted to trade, fisheries and monetary matters.[62] But in other areas, such as agriculture and transport, the competences of the Community have, to a large extent, become exclusive because of their use by the EC institutions.

A "unity" perspective on closer co-operation would lead to a rather strict interpretation of the content rules, with the clear risk of making closer co-operation almost impossible in practice, at least within the Community's legal system. Particularly problematic in this respect are the conditions related to the safeguarding of the "internal market". These concern in particular the rules requiring that closer co-operation "does not discriminate between nationals of member states" and that it "does not constitute a discrimination or a restriction of trade between member states and does not distort the conditions of competition between the letter".[63] It seems that in the framework of a closer co-operation these principles of non-discrimination are applicable only between the participating states, as the very notion of closer co-operation implies a discrimination between member states. However, one can argue that these principles at least imply that in implementing instances of closer co-operation member states may not discriminate between nationals of participating states and nationals of non-participating states.

On the basis of the foregoing general analysis, it becomes clear that the "autonomy" of newly established legal institutions based on the concept of closer co-operation seems severely restricted by the encompassing legal system of the European Union. At the same time, and due to the rather general and sometimes vague notions used, it remains difficult to define the institutional as well as substantial limits posed by the EU legal system on closer co-operation in a more decisive manner. This leaves it to practice, if any, to come up with legal solutions. For, as Shaw rightly states, most of these notions "are certainly capable of application by a court even if the determination of their precise meaning would undoubtedly offer a considerable challenge to any judicial instance."[64]

---

[62] See Wouters (1999), at 35; Barents (1999), at 105-107.
[63] Article 11(1)(c)&(e) TEC.
[64] Shaw (1998), at 72.

The Operation of Flexible Co-operation

The second question posed above concerns the extent to which forms of flexible co-operation potentially harm the unity of the Union. On the basis of the conclusions drawn with regard to the sub-ordination of closer co-operation régimes to the overall legal system of the Union the answer to this second question is obvious at first sight. After all, how could closer co-operation ever affect the unity of the Union's legal system when the validity of this co-operation depends on norms defined by that system? However, the essence of a legal norm is that it *purports* to be made true. Institutional legal theorists have constantly emphasized the difference between "normative" and "real" institutions. The first are defined as systems of rules, whereas the latter are social practices corresponding with the former.[65] Legal institutions are a specific type of normative institutions, namely normative institutions which derive their validity from a legal system.[66] Legal norms present a situation which they want to become reality. Nevertheless, everyone is aware of the fact that legal norms do not always achieve this end. The classic discussion in legal theory concerns exactly this possible friction between the validity and the effectiveness of a norm. Keeping in mind this friction, could it be possible that a closer co-operation régime (in due time) develops rules that do not correspond with the rules set by the legal system of the European Union?

Theoretically, an affirmative answer to this question seems justified. When it is accepted that social practice does not always answer to the pressure put on it by legal norms, one can also imagine a limited number of member states taking decisions that conflict with the higher norms of the Union's legal system. The question, however, is whether the latter system contains invalidating rules to revoke a legal institution. It has already been asserted that no explicit invalidating rule can be found in the Union's legal system. However, an implied rule was already assumed to exist, reading something like: "If the Council decides to establish a form of closer co-operation between member states which is not in accordance with the rules laid down in the Treaty on European Union or the Treaty establishing the European Community, this form of closer co-operation is invalid". This rule may be applied by the European Court of Justice in case this institution enjoys jurisdiction. According to Article 46 TEU the Court's jurisdiction

---

[65] See for instance Ruiter (1997), at 72; Weinberger (1991), at 158.
[66] Ruiter (1997), at 360. See also Weinberger (1991), at 20.

extents to "provisions of Title VII, under the conditions provided for by Article 11 of the Treaty establishing the European Community and Article 40 of this Treaty". This means that the Court may rule on the validity of the establishment of closer co-operation under Article 43 TEU (including the requirements for the establishment and the operation of closer co-operation) and on the procedural requirements in Article 44 TEU. In addition, the Court has a competence to review closer co-operation established and implemented under the PJCC provisions (Article 40 TEU) and the Community provisions (Article 11 TEC).[67]

However, for our purpose these provisions are particularly helpful when they can be invoked by non-participating states, the Commission or the European Parliament. And, moreover, when they can be invoked, not only to question the validity of the establishment of closer co-operation, but also to question the validity of secondary legislation adopted within the framework of the new legal institution. It seems that with regard to the *establishment* of instances of closer co-operation (the *institutive* rules) no restrictions to the jurisdiction of the Court are envisaged.[68] This means that the Court can make full use of the regular direct legal remedies, including those based on Article 230 TEC.[69] Actions of non-participating states could for instance be based on the requirement that their competences, rights, and interests are not to be affected by the establishment of closer co-operation. While Article 230 thus seems to provide an opening for member states to question established forms of closer co-operation, it is highly inconceivable that decisions on this matter are of "direct and individual concern" to individuals, which limits the options of these actors.

Regarding the *implementation* of instances of closer co-operation it seems that the Council, the Commission and the European Parliament may bring a case before the Court on the basis of Article 230 TEC (under the conditions laid down therein). The Commission – as the

---

[67] See also Pechstein (1999), at 12.
[68] See also Tuytschaever (1999), at 275-276; Barents (1999), at 111.
[69] Examples could include an action by a member state against a Council decision based on Article 11, par. 2 TEC regarding a refusal to establish a form of closer co-operation, or an action directed towards a Commission decision based on Article 11, par. 3 TEC concerning the request of a member state to participate in an existing form of closer co-operation. But even an action against a failure to act on the basis of Article 232 TEC is conceivable, once the Commission ignores a request of a number of member states to forward an initiative to that end to the Council. See Wouters (1999), at 45.

traditional watchdog of the Community principles – in particular could be expected to make use of the infringement procedure of Article 226 TEC.[70] But taken into account the fact that in most cases the Commission is supposed to be involved in the decision-making within the régime of closer co-operation, it may also be useful to investigate whether non-participating states have a possibility to bring an action before the Court. After all, these states (or their nationals) will most probably suffer the risk of being negatively affected by forms of closer co-operation.

The Treaties do not explicitly clarify the position of non-participating states before the Court. Nevertheless, the Treaties do not exclude actions by these states concerning the implementation of closer co-operation in which they do not participate.[71] As far as Community law is concerned, it could be argued that closer co-operation cannot alter the territorial scope of Community law (Article 299 TEC). After all, Article 299 TEC cannot be modified through closer co-operation decisions. This would mean that the decision to establish closer co-operation as well as the implementation decisions based on it are to be regarded as Community law which enjoys validity in all member states. These decisions are, however, probably *not applicable* in non-participating states. This implies that non-participating states can bring actions before the Court based on the implementation of closer co-operation, by making use of Article 227 TEC, and that the Court's interpretations of Community law remain binding for all member states. On the other hand, regardless of the fact that preliminary rulings of judges in non-participating states would be admissible, provisions in the decision involved could probably not be invoked.[72]

While these conclusions may apply to closer co-operation established under the general provisions in the Treaties, exceptional situations can be found in the pre-determined forms of flexibility based on the Protocols. The Protocol on the Position of the United Kingdom and Ireland states that "none of the provisions of Title IV TEC [on visas, asylum and immigration], no measure adopted pursuant to that Title, no provision of any international agreement concluded by the

---

[70] *Cf.* Wouters (1999), at 44.
[71] It could, however, be argued that in that case non-participating states do no longer enjoy a privileged status under Article 230 EC and that actions therefore will have to be aimed at the protection of their 'prerogatives'. See also Usher (1999). *Contra* Wagner (1998) at 37: "Non-participating Member states may not challenge measures which are adopted under a legally established closer co-operation".
[72] Barents (1999), at 111.

Community pursuant to that Title, and no decision of the Court of Justice interpreting any such position or measure shall be binding upon or applicable in the United Kingdom or Ireland". In fact, the Protocol states that "these measures or decisions do not form part of Community law as they apply to the United Kingdom or Ireland". A similar provision can be found in the Protocol on the Position of Denmark. In addition, the latter Protocol provides that in the case of an opt-in by Denmark, "an obligation under international law" between Denmark and the other states will be created. These cases seem to hint in the direction of a fragmentation of Community law. After all, it seems that the uniformity principle (the same application of Community law in all member states at all times) is affected. One could, however, also argue that Community law is not fragmented at all, since it is simply *not applied* in the situations described above. Practical consequences may be that the non-participating states may not challenge the validity of measures adopted under Title IV TEC before the Court and that non-participating states remain free to conclude agreements with third states in this area even when this competence under Community law is reserved to the Community.[73]

Under the PJCC provisions the Treaty provides no reasons to approach the jurisdiction of the Court regarding the implementation of closer co-operation in any other way than what counts for regular co-operation in that area. This means that all actions of institutions and member states would be subject to the Court's scrutiny (Article 40 TEU refers to Article 35 on the Court's jurisdiction).[74] Under Title V TEU (CFSP) the general exclusion of the Court's jurisdiction obviously applies to any coalition of "able and willing" member states established under that Title.

The conclusion regarding the extent to which forms of flexible co-operation potentially harm the unity of the Union should therefore probably be that invalid developments within a closer co-operation régime are in general subject to a correction by the Court of Justice. This is not to say that differences between participating and non-participating member states do not exist. In particular some situations of pre-determined flexibility based on the Protocols reflect the novelty that Community law is not applicable in a member state of the European Union. Similar cases occur when judges in non-participating states cannot make full use of the system of preliminary rulings. The

---

[73] *Cf.* Gaja (1998), at 868-869.
[74] Barents (1999), at 113; Tuytschaever (1999), at 277.

question, however, is whether the unitary character of the Union's legal system is harmed by situations in which Union law is not at all applicable. These situations may certainly be harmful for the political unity of the Union, but it is more difficult to find arguments indicating that developments taking place outside the Union's legal system pose a threat to the unity of that system.[75]

CONCLUDING OBSERVATIONS

The purpose of the present paper was to shed light on the legal institutional implications of the various forms of flexible co-operation for the unity of the European Union's legal system. In answering the question of whether the initial fears that flexibility would mean the end of the Union's unity have become real, our method was to find an answer to two related questions: *1* to what extent does the legal unity of the European Union limit the legal validity of flexible forms of co-operation?; and *2* to what extent do flexible forms of co-operation potentially harm the unity of the Union?

Regarding the first question, our main conclusion is that – despite the fact that the concept of "unity" cannot explicitly be found in the Treaty on European Union – a *presumed* unity is obviously accepted. The basis for this conclusion is to be found in the fact that the strict requirements for establishing and implementing closer co-operation all point in the direction of an existing unity. In other words: the rules on flexibility *strengthen* the notion of the unity of the Union's legal system rather than that they weaken it. As far as closer co-operation within the Community is concerned, the uniformity of Community law does not seem to be affected, but here too the importance of the concept is strengthened through the requirements laid down in Article 11 TEC. These requirements are quite strict and it is not yet clear whether it is possible at all to establish instances of closer co-operation on the basis of Community competences.

Taking account of the requirements for closer co-operation – and in particular the institutive and content rules related to the validity of instances of closer co-operation – the concept of closer co-operation implies the existence of a hierarchy of norms within the European

---

[75] A comparable situation can be found in the position of Norway and Iceland which since 1996 participate in Schengen and the position with regard to the new régime is laid down in a separate international agreement.

Union. One could argue that the rather undefined principle of consistency is further filled-in through this hierarchy of norms. The "higher" Union norms on the validity of instances of closer co-operation serve to solve problems of consistency and coherence within the Union's legal system. The application of institutive as well as content rules by the Court – but also by the other institutions – may cause the invalidity of forms of closer co-operation. While the obvious reason may be the protection of consistency, it is also conceivable that the less strict concept of coherence is used, in which case the Court may seek a balance between the unity of the Union's legal system and the preference for closer co-operation.

This latter point brings us to the second question: to what extent do forms of co-operation potentially harm the unity of the Union? As far as closer co-operation based on Article 43 TEU is concerned, all arguments hint in the direction of a superior status of the Union's legal system and of the competence of the Court that is not restricted when compared to the regular system of legal protection. As far as the pre-determined forms of flexible co-operation are concerned one could argue that in general these are harmless to the extent that they form part of Community/Union law. This leads to the overall conclusion that, in contrast to what was expected by some member states during the IGCs of 1991 and 1996, the forms of flexible co-operation do not seem to pose a direct threat to the unity of the Union's legal system.

This is not to say that there are not at all negative effects of the current provisions on flexibility. An obvious example in that respect is the situation of Denmark once that state opts-in in the area of Title IV TEC. In that case "an obligation under international law" is created between one member state of the Union and the others. Its is highly questionable whether the Treaties allow for a possibility of Union member states to engage in separate legal relationships on areas covered by the Union and thus to act as regular states, instead of *member* states. A fact is that the Denmark Protocol reflects this situation, resulting in a legally unclear and thus unpreferred relationship.

Keeping in mind our assertion that the unity of a legal system has an external dimension as well, a second problem is posed by the external relations of the Union in areas where not all member states participate. Apart from the fact that it may not always be clear to outsiders that certain member states do not participate in all Union actions or positions, the legal difficulties in case of Community agreements with third states on issues subject to flexibility are obvious.

In most cases the Community and the participating member states will make use of a so-called mixed agreement, but taking into account the fact that agreements concluded by the Community form an integral part of Community law it is hard to imagine the different status of the non-participating member states. In the case of the Economic and Monetary Union, where some member states enjoy derogations and others do not participate at all, the external relations also lack clarity. The EMU agreements with third states (or organizations) will not apply to the non-participating member state or to those with a derogation, which means that these states will retain their freedom to conclude their own agreements. On the other hand, competences may become exclusive once they are used by the Community, which certainly changes the autonomous status of the non-participating states. In that respect Tuytschaever warned that this differentiated integration *in foro interno* may lead to an unprecedented Babylonic situation *in foro externo*.[76]

After a long academic and political discussion on the definition and varieties of flexibility in the context of the European Union, the Amsterdam Treaty in 1997 finally made an end to all confusion by allowing flexibility on a restricted number of issues laid down in Protocols annexed to the TEU and by introducing a new concept of "closer co-operation". These days a new Intergovernmental Conference is faced with the task of finding a solution to the problem of reconciling the proclaimed extension of the Union and the wish of some member states to deepen their co-operation. As shown in this contribution, the current Treaty is based on the idea of a single legal system, which sets the limits for closer co-operation within that system. A more loose approach to the requirements to establish closer co-operation, as proposed by some member states, does not seem to be in line with this idea. The conclusions drawn in this article thus depend on the extent to which member states are willing to uphold the choice made in Amsterdam. While history shows that outcomes of IGC's are almost never predictable, the past decade we can surely witness a trend towards a recognition – both by the EU's institutions and most member states – of the unity of the EU's legal system and of the implications of this unity for the ways in which member states are allowed to deviate in their bi- or multilateral relations from the fundamental principles set by the Union's legal system.

---

[76] Tuytschaever (1997), at 319.

BIBLIOGRAPHY

Barents, R. (1999), Het Verdrag van Amsterdam in werking, Europese Monografieen, nr. 62, Deventer, 1999

Curtin, D.M. (1993), "The Constitutional Structure of the Union: A Europe of Bits and Pieces", 30 CMLRev 1993, 17

Curtin, D.M. (1995), "The shaping of a European constitution and the 1996 IGC: 'Flexibility' as a key paradigm?" Aussenwirtschaft 1995, 238

Curtin, D.M. & Dekker, I.F. (1999), "The EU as a 'Layered' International Organization: Institutional Unity in Disguise", in: P. Craig & G. de Burca (eds.), The Evolution of EU Law, Oxford, 1999, 83-136

Devroe, W. & Wouters, J. (1996), De Europese Unie. Het Verdrag van Maastricht en zijn uitvoering: analyse en perspectieven, Peeters, 1996

De Witte, B. (1994), "Rules of Change in International Law: How Special is the European Community?" 25 NYIL 1994, 299-334

De Witte, B. (1999), "The Pillar Structure and the Nature of the European Union: Greek Temple or French Gothic Cathedral?", in: T. Heukels, N.M. Blokker, M.M.T.A. Brus (eds.), The European Union after Amsterdam, A Legal Analysis, Deventer 1999

Dekker, I.F. & Wessel, R.A. (1998), "The Union's Unity Unveiled, A Legal Institutional Approach", Unpublished paper, 1998

Dörr, O. (1995), "Zur Rechtsnatur der Europaischen Union", EuR 1995, 334-348

Editorial (1997), "The Treaty of Amsterdam: Neither a bang nor a whimper", 34 CMLRev 1997, 767

Edwards G. & Philippart, E. (1997), "Flexibility and the Treaty of Amsterdam: Europe's New Byzantium?", CELS Occasional Paper, no. 3, Cambridge 1997

Ehlermann, C.D. (1984), "How flexible is Community law? An unusual approach to the concept of 'two speeds'", Michigan Law Review 1984, 1275

Ehlermann, C.D. (1996), "Increased differentiation or stronger uniformity" in: J.A. Winter e.a. (eds.), Reforming the Treaty on European Union, 1996, Asser Instituut, Den Haag, 27

Ehlermann, C.D. (1998), "Differentiation, Flexibility, Closer Co-operation:The New Provisions of the Amsterdam Treaty", 4 European Law Journal 1998, 246-270

Feenstra J.J. & Mortelmans, K.J.M. (1985), Gedifferentieerde integratie en Gemeenschapsrecht. Institutioneel- en materieelrechtelijke aspecten, Den Haag, 1985

Gaja, G. (1998), "How Flexible is Flexibility under the Amsterdam Treaty?", 35 CMLRev 1998, 855-870

Gaudin, H. (1999), Amsterdam: L'échec de la hiérarchie des normes?, Rev. trim. de droit eur., No 1, 1-20

Grabitz, E. (Hrsg.) (1984), Abgestufte Integration. Eine Alternatieve zum herkömmlichen Integrationskonzept?, Engel Verlag, 1984

Kortenberg, H. (1998), "Closer Co-operation in the Treaty of Amsterdam", 35 CMLRev 1998, 833-854

Manin, Ph. & Louis, J.V. (1996), Vers une Europe différenciée? Possibilité et Limite, Paris 1996

MacCormick, N. (ed.) (1997), Constructing Legal Systems, "European Union" in Legal Theory, The Hague 1997

MacCormick, N. & Weinberger, O., An Institutional Theory of Law, Reidel, 1986

Marschik, A. (1997), Subsysteme im Volkerrecht, Ist die Europaische Union ein "self-contained regime"?, 1997

Pechstein, M. (1999), "Die Justitiabilität des Unionsrecht", 34 Europarecht 1, 1-26

Prechal, S. (1999), "Institutional balance: a fragile principle with uncertain contents", in: T. Heukels, N.M. Blokker, M.M.T.A. Brus (eds.), The European Union after Amsterdam, A Legal Analysis, Deventer 1999

Rapport Reflectiegroep, Intergovernementele Conferentie 1996, Brussel, 1996

Ruiter, D.W.P. (1993), Institutional Legal Facts, Legal Powers and their Effects, The Hague 1993

Ruiter, D.W.P. (1997), "A Basic Classification of Legal Institutions", 10 Ratio Juris 1997, 357-371

Ruiter D.W.P. (1998), "Structuring Legal Institutions" 17 Law and Philosophy 1998, 215-232

Shaw, J. (1998), "The Treaty of Amsterdam: Challenges of Flexibility and Legitimacy", ELJ 1998, 63

Staples, H. (1999), The Legal Status of Third Country Nationals Resident in the European Union, The Hague, 1999

Tietje, C. (1997), "The Concept of Coherence in the Treaty on European Union and the Common Foreign and Security Policy", European Foreign Affairs Review 1997, 211-233

Tindemans, L. (1976), "Rapport over de Europese Unie", Bull. EG 1/76 (Supplement), p. 22

Toth, A.G., "The legal effects of the Protocols relating to the United Kingdom, Ireland and Denmark", in: T. Heukels, N.M. Blokker, M.M.T.A. Brus (eds), The European Union after Amsterdam, A Legal Analysis, The Hague 1999, pp. 227-252

Tuytschaever, F. (1999), "Nauwere samenwerking volgens het Verdrag van Amsterdam", SEW 1999, 270

Tuytschaever, F. (1997), "Omtrent EMU, gedifferentieerde integratie en de externe betrekkingen van de EG", SEW 1997, 313

Usher, J.A. (1997), "Variable geometry or concentric circles: patterns for the European Union", ICLQ 1997, 243

Usher, J.A. (1999), "Flexibility: The Amsterdam Provisions", in: T. Heukels, N.M. Blokker, M.M.T.A. Brus (eds.), The European Union after Amsterdam, A Legal Analysis, The Hague 1999

Van der Velden, W. (1992), "Coherence in Law. A Deductive and a Semantic Explication of Coherence", in: P.W.Brouwer *et.al.* (eds.), Coherence and Conflict in Law, Kluwer, 1992, 279

Von Bogdandy, A. & Nettesheim, M. (1996), "Die Europaische Union: Ein einheitlicher Verband mit eigener Rechtsordnung", EuR 1996, 3-26

Wagner, E. (1998), The Integration of Schengen into the Framework of the European Union, LIEE, 1-60

Weinberger, O. (1991), Law, Institution and Legal Practice. Fundamental Problems of Legal Theory and Social Philosophy, The Hague 1991

Wessel, R.A. (1997), "The International Legal Status of the European Union", 2 EFAR 1997, 109-129

Wessel, R.A, (1999), The European Union's Foreign and Security Policy. A Legal Institutional Perspective, The Hague 1999

Wouters, J. (1999), Flexibiliteit in de Eerste Pijler, in: Flexibiliteit en het Verdrag van Amsterdam, Den Haag: TMC Asser Press, 1999, pp. 29-46

Wroblewski, J. (1992), The Judicial Application of Law, The Hague 1992

EXTENDING THE EUROPEAN FAMILY OF NATIONS: THE RESPONSE OF THE COUNCIL OF EUROPE TO GROWING MEMBERSHIP

Rick Lawson[*]

INTRODUCTION: ON FEATHERED FRIENDS AND UNIVERSAL VALUES

On 22 August 1992, a grouse shoot was held in Wheeldale Moor, Yorkshire. Together with some 60 others, Helen Steel took part in a protest action. She tried to obstruct and distract the hunters and jumped up and down in front of anyone lifting a shotgun.

The hunters were apparently unable to settle this situation, for instance by *using* their shotguns, and called for the police. Thus Ms Steel was arrested for breach of the peace (although she was not the one carrying weapons) and detained. Eventually she was convicted. A fine of 70 pounds sterling was imposed and she was ordered to be "bound over" for a period of twelve months. This meant that she had to promise not to engage in similar conduct for a year. As she refused to consent to this order, she was committed to prison for 28 days.

Ms Steel lodged a complaint with the European Commission of Human Rights, arguing *inter alia* that her conviction entailed a disproportionate interference with her freedom of expression, as guaranteed by Article 10 of the European Convention on Human Rights (ECHR). When her case finally came before the European Court of Human Rights, a majority found that no violation of Article 10 had occurred. But Judges Valticos and Makarczyk disagreed:

> to detain for forty-four hours and then sentence to 28 days' imprisonment a person who, albeit in a extreme manner, jumped up and down in front of a member of the shoot in order to prevent him from killing a feathered friend is so manifestly extreme, particularly in a

---

[*] Dr R.A. Lawson is senior lecturer in the Europa Instituut, University of Leiden, the Netherlands.

country known for its fondness for animals, that it amounted, in our view, to a violation of the Convention.[1]

It is, of course, the last part of the quote that intrigues us here: "particularly in a country known for its fondness for animals". Would the outcome be different in a country where our feathered friends are not so popular? In other words, is the European Court free to apply different standards according to the circumstances prevailing in the States parties to the Convention?

This question is not new. It reminds us of the debate on the universality of human rights, which has been going on for at least two decades. But in a way this debate never seemed to relate to Strasbourg: the Member States of the Council of Europe represented a fairly homogeneous group where cultural relativism was not so relevant. Yet, since 1989 the membership of the Council of Europe has doubled. Some 20 States from Central and Eastern Europe have joined the Council. And it cannot be denied that most of them brought poverty in their trail, economic and political instability, fragile democratic institutions and a poor judicial infrastructure, a legal tradition that had lost contact with the developments in the West. How does Strasbourg respond to this new situation?

In their introduction to the conference which laid the foundations for the present volume, the organizers assumed that "the more variety there is amongst the members of an organization, the more the question becomes relevant whether the organization should maintain lower but at least uniform standards, or whether it is preferable to have different standards". This seems to be a logical assumption – but in this contribution I will argue that in fact the growing membership of the Council of Europe has *not* led to a lowering or a fragmentation of its standards. On the contrary: as will be illustrated below, the Council has developed a detailed policy to deal with requests for membership and it has clearly and deliberately intensified its methods to supervise compliance with its standards. As to the European Court of Human Rights generally speaking its settled case-law has been applied to new Member States without any distinction. But some recent judgments do give rise to the impression that the Court is willing to make special exception for the new Member States. I will argue that it should be careful not to do so.

---

[1] European Court of Human Rights [hereinafter: ECtHR], 23 September 1998, *Steel a.o. v. the UK* (Reports of Judgments and Decisions [hereinafter: RJD] 1998, p. 2719), at p. 2751.

THE RESPONSE OF THE COUNCIL OF EUROPE TO GROWING MEMBERSHIP

FLEXIBILITY: THE NATURE OF THE COUNCIL OF EUROPE

Our starting point should be the loose nature of cooperation taking place within the Council of Europe. Unlike the European Union, there is no traditional drive for uniformity and harmonization of legal rules. According to Article 1 of its Statute, the aim of the Council of Europe is "to achieve a greater unity between its Members" – not uniformity. The European Convention on Human Rights does not seek to establish a single market for fundamental freedoms: it seeks to uphold international minimum norms. States are free to offer a higher level of protection.[2] This holds true for the European Social Charter as well.

Flexibility is thus allowed for. The very way in which the Council of Europe operates, underlines this. No regulations, directives and decisions are imposed from above. The Committee of Ministers, the main policy-making body, does not have supranational powers; it essentially organizes intergovernmental co-operation in the areas of interest to the Council. It may adopt agreements and conventions – such as the European Convention on Human Rights – that are binding on those States which are prepared to ratify them subsequently. Unlike the case of the ILO, there is no obligation for the Member States to submit these texts to their national parliaments with a view to possible ratification.

In addition, and again unlike the ILO, most conventions concluded within the framework of the Council of Europe allow for reservations to be made.[3] Along these lines, Article 57 ECHR enables States to make reservations when signing or ratifying the Convention. It may be true that this right is not unlimited[4], and it may be equally true that the

---

[2] Cf. Article 53 ECHR: "Nothing in this Convention shall be construed as limiting or derogating from any of the human rights and fundamental freedoms which may be ensured under the laws of any High Contracting Party or under any other agreement to which it is a Party".

[3] The European Convention for the Prevention of Torture and Inhuman or Degrading Treatment or Punishment (CPT, 1987) is an exception: see Article 21. See generally S.S. Akermark, "Reservation Clauses in Treaties Concluded within the Council of Europe", in *ICLQ* vol. 48 (1999), pp. 479-514, and, by the same author, "Reservations: breaking new grounds in the Council of Europe", in *ELR* vol. 24 (1999), pp. 499-515.

[4] Notably reservations of a general character are not permitted.

European Court of Human Rights has assumed the power to determine the validity of reservations.[5] But the point is that, from a legal perspective, Member States are free to accept legal obligations – and *if* they do, they are free, to some extent at least, to customize these obligations to their particular needs.

POLITICAL REALITY: A PRESSURE TO CONFORM

However, the Council of Europe Member States are not so free as might seem at first sight.

For one thing, Article 3 of the Council's Statute stipulates that every Member State must accept the principles of the Rule of Law and of the enjoyment by all persons within its jurisdiction of human rights and fundamental freedoms. Such a general, if somewhat imprecise, obligation is not often found in the constitutions of international organizations.[6] Article 8 adds that any Member which has "seriously violated" these principles may be suspended or even expelled from the organization. Admittedly, the Council of Europe will not easily evict one of its members, and the criterion of "serious violations" allows for great latitude. Nevertheless, Article 8 is not a dead letter: in response to Russia's conduct in the Chechen conflict the Parliamentary Assembly recommended in April 2000 that the Committee of Ministers initiate the procedure for the suspension of Russia from its rights of representation in the Council of Europe.[7]

But there is more. In the years following the fall of the Berlin Wall, when many States sought admission to the Council of Europe, the organization became increasingly demanding.[8] It required from each

---

[5] See esp. ECtHR, 29 April 1988, *Belilos v. Switzerland* (Series A, vol. 132), § 50, and ECtHR, 23 March 1995, *Loizidou v. Turkey (prel. obj.)* (Series A, vol. 310), § 65 *et seq.*

[6] Until recently, it was unique. Since 1 May 1999 (the date of entry into force of the Treaty of Amsterdam), Article 49 of the Treaty of European Union (ex Article O) provides that any European State may apply to become a member of the Union if it respects the principles mentioned in Article 6 (including democracy and human rights). Article 7 allows for suspension of certain rights of EU Members following serious and continuous violations of these principles.

[7] Recommendation 1456 (2000) of 6 April 2000. Greece withdrew from the organisation in 1969, when it was about to be expelled in response to widespread violations of human rights perpetrated by a military junta.

[8] See, e.g., J.F. Flauss, "Les conditions d'admission des pays d'Europe centrale et orientale au sein de Conseil de l'Europe", in *EJIL* vol. 5 (1994), pp. 401-422; H. Winkler, "Democracy and Human Rights in Europe – A Survey of the Admission Practice of the Council of Europe", in *Austrian Journal of Public and International*

applicant country that the principles of pluralist parliamentary democracy be implemented, that the legislative and judicial system be brought in line with the Rule of Law, and that the domestic legal order ensured respect for human rights and fundamental freedoms. In practice this led to extensive cooperation programmes and lengthy negotiations during which the domestic legal order of each candidate was carefully scrutinized. In addition new Members were required to sign the European Convention on Human Rights upon accession and to ratify it speedily. They also had to commit themselves to recognize, upon ratification, the right of individual application and to accept the compulsory jurisdiction of the European Court of Human Rights.[9] It could thus be said that the new Member States were required to accept the *"acquis conventionnel"*.[10]

Closely related to these developments is the introduction in the last few years of monitoring procedures of a new sort. A need was felt to ensure that the new Members would really keep the promises made at the moment of their accession. Indeed, doubts were expressed in some quarters about the ability and willingness of countries like Romania, the Russian Federation, Ukraine and Croatia to comply fully with their commitments.

A problem in this connection is that the commitments entered into – leaving obligations under specific legal texts, such as the European Convention on Human Rights, aside for a second – are to a large extent of a political nature. Whether the principles of pluralist parliamentary democracy have been implemented in a satisfactory fashion, is not a black-and-white question. Or to give another example: until 4 April 2000 Ukraine failed to ratify Protocol No. 6 to the European Convention – which abolishes the death penalty – although it committed itself in 1995 to do so within three years.[11] Obviously, it is not so easy to

---

Law vol. 47 (1995), pp. 147-172; E. García Jiménez, *El Convenio Europeo de Derechos Humanos en el umbral del siglo XXI* (València, 1998), pp. 53-88.

[9] A striking example is offered by the accession of Croatia. When the Committee of Ministers invited Croatia to become a member of the Council of Europe, it expressly indicated that it might *reconsider* this decision in the light of the manner in which Croatia had respected its obligations deriving from the Dayton Peace Agreement, had demonstrated its willingness to honour all its commitments, and was cooperating "with the Council of Europe *inter alia* in applying the Constitutional Law on Human Rights and Freedoms and the Rights of National and Ethnic Communities or Minorities" (Resolution (96)31 of 2 July 1996).

[10] See P. van Dijk, "Distinguished Lecture", to be published in the 1999 issue of the Collected Courses of the Academy of European Law.

[11] See Resolution (95) 22 of the Committee of Ministers (*Invitation to Ukraine to become a member of the Council of Europe*) of 19 October 1995, in conjunction with

enforce such a commitment in a legal way. In this respect the Council of Europe differs from the European Communities, where the question of compliance with the *acquis communautaire* is usually a legal one which may well be brought before the European Court of Justice (Article 226 EC, the former Article 169).

Be that as it may, in the mid-1990s the Committee of Ministers adopted a monitoring procedure, which applies by the way to *all* Member States.[12] Another monitoring procedure was established by the Parliamentary Assembly in 1993. In 1997 a special committee was set up for this purpose.[13] Again both old and new Member States are examined.

Conclusion

To conclude this brief overview of the Council of Europe's general policy in the face of growing membership: what we see here is not a lowering of standards. If there was disagreement surrounding the admission of specific States, this related to their ability or willingness to meet the standards; the standards themselves were not a subject of discussion. The following passage (taken from Recommendation 1456, in which the Parliamentary Assembly pressed for the suspension of Russia) illustrates the point:

> The Assembly recalls that Russia, upon its accession to the Council of Europe, committed itself in writing to observe the principles and standards of the Organization and to fulfil all obligations arising from the Statute of the Council of Europe and its most important conventions. In particular, Russia's accession, it was assured, would not result in the lowering of the high standards of the Organization. In keeping with these assurances the Assembly insists on the maintenance and respect of the standards of the Council of Europe [...].[14]

Individualized commitments have been introduced and special mechanisms have been devised to ensure compliance therewith. It is interesting to recall that the founding Members of the Council of

---

Opinion 190 (1995) of the Parliamentary Assembly *(on the application by Ukraine for membership of the Council of Europe)* of 26 September 1995, point 12 (ii).

[12] See the *Declaration on compliance with commitments accepted by the Member States of the Council of Europe*, adopted by the Committee of Ministers on 10 November 1994, as well as the *Procedure for Implementing the Declaration of 10 November 1994*, adopted 20 April 1995.

[13] See Resolution 1115 of 29 January 1997.

[14] See *supra* note 7, § 14.

Europe were allowed much more freedom. France, for instance, became a party to the Council's Statute in 1949, but it ratified the Convention only in 1974 and waited until 1981 before recognizing the right of individual petition! And when Liechtenstein ratified the Convention in 1982, it was allowed to make far-reaching reservations, aiming to neutralize the famous *Marckx* and *Dudgeon* judgments.[15] Clearly this would be inconceivable today.

THE EUROPEAN COURT OF HUMAN RIGHTS FACING DIVERSITY AMONGST THE MEMBER STATES

It may be interesting to focus in more detail on the European Court of Human Rights. How does the Court respond to the presence of new States parties to the Convention? I will not discuss the organizational measures which had to be taken in order to cope with the growing number of applications (or with the growing number of judges in the Court). The emphasis will be on the dilemma mentioned in the introduction: "the more variety there is amongst the members of an organization, the more the question becomes relevant whether the organization should maintain lower but at least uniform standards, or whether it is preferable to have different standards".

No Lowering of the Standards

At the outset it may be observed that the Court itself insists that it has *not* lowered its standards in any way. The Court's president, Mr Wildhaber, said at a press conference:

> The Court has had a difficult year, but we finished on an optimistic note. Firstly, the judgments delivered last year speak for themselves and indicate not only that there has been no lowering of standards, but indeed that the Court intends to apply the rights and freedoms

---

[15] According to the Liechtenstein reservation, "le droit au respect de la vie familiale, garanti dans l'article 8 de la Convention, s'exercera, en ce qui concerne l'enfant illégitime, en conformité avec les principes qui trouvent actuellement leur expression dans les dispositions du (...) Code civil lichtensteinois (...)". In addition "le droit au respect de la vie privée, garanti dans l'article 8 de la Convention, s'exercera, en ce qui concerne l'homosexualité, en conformité avec les principes qui trouvent actuellement leur expression dans les dispositions du (...) Code pénal lichtensteinois (...)". The reservation was withdrawn in 1991 (*Yearbook ECHR* vol. 34 (1991), p. 5).

guaranteed by the European Convention on Human Rights with greater firmness.[16]

There are various judgments which lend support to this contention. In July 1999 the Court found a systematic breach of Article 6 § 1 of the Convention in Italy – the first time in more than 20 years that a systematic violation was found.[17] On the very same day the Court took the view in the case of *Selmouni* that

> the increasingly high standard being required in the area of the protection of human rights and fundamental liberties correspondingly and inevitably requires greater firmness in assessing breaches of the fundamental values of democratic societies.[18]

There are no signs to date that the Court softened its interpretation and application of the Convention in a general way. The question remains whether the Court took the alternative road by applying different standards to different States.

The European Family of Nations

By their very nature, human rights have a universal aspiration. "*All human beings are born free and equal in dignity and rights*". "*No one shall be subjected to torture*". "The enjoyment of the rights and freedoms shall be secured *without discrimination on any ground*". Against this background it is hard to accept that different standards would apply to States Parties to the same Convention.

In the well-known case of *Tyrer* a boy had been subjected to judicial corporal punishment on the Isle of Man. The Court observed that:

> the Convention is a living instrument which must be interpreted in the light of present-day conditions. In the case now before it the Court cannot but be influenced by the developments and commonly accepted standards in the penal policy of the member States of the Council of Europe in this field. [...] in the great majority of the member States of the Council of Europe, judicial corporal punishment is

---

[16] Press release 50 ("Court making steady progress in the face of continuing rise in case-load") of 24 February 2000.
[17] ECtHR, 28 July 1999, *Ferrari v. Italy* (n.y.r.). The breach concerns the length of proceedings in civil cases.
[18] ECtHR, 28 July 1999, *Selmouni v. France* (n.y.r.), § 101.

not used and, indeed, in some of them, has never existed in modern times.[19]

When the Manx authorities relied on support for corporal punishment amongst the local population, and argued that local requirements demanded this deterrent, the Court responded:

> The Isle of Man not only enjoys long-established and highly-developed political, social and cultural traditions but is an up-to-date society. Historically, geographically and culturally, the Island has always been included in the European family of nations and must be regarded as sharing fully that "common heritage of political traditions, ideals, freedom and the rule of law" to which the Preamble to the Convention refers.[20]

This "European family of nations" may not be a strictly legal concept. But it is a nice expression of one the basic ideas underlying the Convention, which is also reflected in its Preamble:

> the governments of European countries which are like-minded and have a common heritage of political traditions, ideals, freedom and the rule of law, [are resolved] to take the first steps for the collective enforcement of certain of the rights stated in the Universal Declaration.

It is this common heritage of the "European family of nations" which enabled the Court in *Tyrer* to disregard local opinion and to follow a harmonizing, integration-oriented approach. A similar line of reasoning was followed on many occasions.[21] In 1998 the Court used comparable language when it referred to "the Convention community".[22]

On a somewhat different level the principle of equality may have harmonizing effects too. In its 1999 *Pellegrin* judgment the Court attempted to put an end to the uncertainty which surrounded the application of the guarantees of Article 6 § 1 to disputes between States and public servants. It considered

> that it is important, with a view to applying Article 6 § 1, to establish an autonomous interpretation of the term "civil service" which would make it possible to afford equal treatment to public servants per-

---

[19] ECtHR, 25 April 1978, *Tyrer v. the UK* (Series A, vol. 26), §§ 31, 38.
[20] *Ibidem*, § 38.
[21] See notably ECtHR, 13 June 1979, *Marckx v. Belgium* (Series A, vol. 31), § 41, and ECtHR, 22 October 1981, *Dudgeon v. the United Kingdom* (Series A, vol. 45), § 60.
[22] ECtHR, 28 July 1998, *Loizidou v. Turkey (Art. 50)* (RJD 1998, p. 1807), § 48.

forming equivalent or similar duties in the States party to the Convention, irrespective of the domestic system of employment and, in particular, whatever the nature of the legal relation between the official and the administrative authority.[23]

Referring to this passage Mr Martens, the former Dutch judge in the Court, has argued that the principle of equality among the Contracting Parties may well play a more prominent role in the future case-law of the Court.[24]

The Margin of Appreciation

But this is not to say that uniform application of the Convention is required under all circumstances. In particular, by allowing States a certain "margin of appreciation", the Court gave national authorities some space to manoeuvre. The margin was introduced in the famous *Handyside* case, in which the Court observed:

> it is not possible to find in the domestic law of the various Contracting States a uniform European conception of morals. The view taken by their respective laws of the requirements of morals varies from time to time and from place to place, especially in our era which is characterized by a rapid and far-reaching evolution of opinions on the subject. By reason of their direct and continuous contact with the vital forces of their countries, State authorities are in principle in a better position than the international judge to give an opinion on the exact content of these requirements as well as on the "necessity" of a "restriction" or "penalty" intended to meet them.[25]

Consequently, the Court found that, particularly in the case of protection of morals, a margin of appreciation is to be left to the Contracting States. This has been confirmed on several occasions.[26] The Court has likewise accepted that national authorities enjoy a wide margin of appreciation when implementing social and economic policies. In a recent Italian case on tenancy legislation, the Court went quite far (or rather: it did not go far at all) when it considered:

---

[23] ECtHR, 8 December 1999, *Pellegrin v. France* (n.y.r.), § 63.

[24] S.K. Martens, speech held in Leiden on 3 March 2000, published in *NJCM-Bulletin* vol. 25 (2000), no. 3. pp. 756-757.

[25] ECtHR, 12 December 1976, *Handyside v. the United Kingdom* (Series A, vol. 24), § 48.

[26] See, e.g., ECtHR, 24 May 1988, *Müller v. Switzerland* (Series A, vol. 133), § 35; ECtHR, 20 September 1994, *Otto Preminger v. Austria* (Series A, vol. 295-A), § 50.

In spheres such as housing, which plays a central role in the welfare and economic policies of modern societies, the Court will respect the legislature's judgment as to what is in the general interest unless that judgment is manifestly without reasonable foundation.[27]

Much more could be said about the margin of appreciation doctrine, the coherency of its application and the Court's review methods more in general. But for present purposes it may suffice to note (a) that there is a clear tendency towards uniform standards, but (b) that the European Court has never required full uniformity in all respects, and (c) that there has always been a certain balance between European standards and supervision on the one hand, and national particularities and a margin of appreciation on the other. The question is: was this balance affected following the accession of new Member States? Are they entitled to a wider margin, due to specific problems which they encounter?

THE COURT AND "OLD" NEW MEMBER STATES: PORTUGAL AND SPAIN

These questions arose already prior to the accession of States from Central and Eastern Europe. When Portugal and Spain joined the Council in the late 1970s, both countries were in a process of transition. The Court did not, however, display a specific degree of flexibility, as a brief review of case-law will illustrate.

In 1976 Mr Guincho was involved in a car accident in Portugal. He tried to obtain damages, but the proceedings took almost four years. When Mr Guincho brought a complaint in Strasbourg about the length of the proceedings, the Government stressed that at the relevant time the Portuguese legal system had to operate under exceptional circumstances: democracy had been restored recently; newly set up institutions had to be consolidated; almost a million people had repatriated from the former colonies. In addition, the domestic courts had to be reorganized in a period of serious economic recession. Several measures relating to the administration of justice were taken, but from 1974 to

---

[27] ECtHR, 28 July 1999, *Immobiliare Saffi v. Italy* (n.y.r.), § 49. The Court referred to two previous judgments (amongst which ECtHR, 19 December 1989, *Mellacher a.o. v. Austria* (Series A, vol. 169), § 48), but on these occasions the Court actually did not limit its review to manifest unreasonableness. On the scope of the margin of appreciation, see also the well-reasoned passage in ECtHR, 27 April 2000, *L. v. Finland* (n.y.r.). §118.

1979, the volume of litigation almost doubled. The Court recognized the value of this argument:

> The Court cannot overlook that the restoration of democracy as from April 1974 led Portugal to carry out an overhaul of its judicial system in troubled circumstances which are without equivalent in most of the other European countries and which were rendered more difficult by the process of decolonization as well as by the economic crisis. [...] Nonetheless, ... in ratifying the Convention, Portugal guaranteed to "secure to everyone within [its] jurisdiction the rights and freedom defined in Section I" (Article 1). In particular, Portugal undertook the obligation of organizing its legal system so as to ensure compliance with the requirements of Article 6 § 1, including that of trial within a reasonable time.

The Court accepted that a temporary backlog of court business does not engage the international responsibility of the State concerned under the Convention, provided that the State takes effective remedial action with the requisite promptness. However, the measures adopted to strengthen the administration of justice were, in the eyes of the Court "evidently insufficient and belated". The Court unanimously found a breach of Article 6 of the Convention.[28]

A similarly uncompromising line was followed in the case of *Castells*. Mr Castells, a Basque nationalist senator, wrote a newspaper article about a series of murders in the Basque country. He alleged that the perpetrators of these murders enjoyed total impunity as the authorities were unwilling to investigate the crimes; he even claimed that "behind these acts can only be the Government". Mr Castells was subsequently convicted for insulting the Government. He argued that this violated his freedom of expression.

When his case came before the European Commission of Human Rights, two of its members (Mr Frowein and Sir Basil Hall) emphasised that, in the late 1970s, Spain was in a process of transition from an authoritarian State into a democracy. Against this background, and taking into account the terrorist attacks prevailing in the Basque provinces, they felt that Mr Castells had failed to assume the responsibilities inherent in the exercise of the freedom of expression. They considered therefore that the conviction of Mr Castells was justified.[29] This line of reasoning was rejected, however, by a large majority of the Commission

---

[28] ECtHR, 10 July 1984, *Guincho v. Portugal* (Series A, vol. 81), § 41.

[29] ECtHR, 23 April 1992, *Castells v. Spain* (Series A, vol. 236), dissenting opinion annexed to the Report of the Commission, at p. 41.

and by a unanimous Court. Both found a violation of the Convention, without giving Spain any margin of appreciation at all.

The Court and new Member States: Central and Eastern Europe

Now let's turn to the members who were admitted most recently, the countries from Central and Eastern Europe. So far, there is not so much case-law available: the first judgment against one of these countries dates from March 1997. As it happened, it was quite a delicate case, relating to criminal proceedings brought against the former Prime Minister of Bulgaria, Mr Lukanov. The Government of Bulgaria, however, conceded that a violation of the Convention had taken place and the Court did not apply any 'special' standards.[30]

The same picture emerges from a series of cases against Poland concerning the right to a fair trial within a reasonable time. In one of these cases, *Podbielsky v. Poland*, the Court observed that

> the delay in the delivery of a final decision on the applicant's action has been caused to a large extent by the legislative changes resulting from the requirements of the transition from a state-controlled to a free-market system and by the complexity of the procedures which surrounded the litigation and which prevented an expeditious decision on the applicant's claim. The Court recalls in this respect that Article 6 § 1 imposes on Contracting States the duty to organize their judicial systems in such a way that their courts can meet each of its requirements, including the obligation to decide cases within a reasonable time [...]. Therefore the delay in the proceedings must be mainly attributed to the national authorities.[31]

The Court clearly followed the strict line of *Guincho v. Portugal*. In the other cases the Polish Government apparently did not seek to argue that it was entitled to more lenient standards because of transitional problems, and the Court applied its regular standards.[32]

In some other cases too, the Court entertained complaints under various provisions of the Convention without making any special allow-

---

[30] ECtHR, 20 March 1997, *Lukanov v. Bulgaria* (RJD 1997, p. 529).
[31] ECtHR, 30 October 1998, *Podbielsky v. Poland* (RJD 1998, p. 3387), § 38.
[32] See, e.g., ECtHR, 16 December 1997, *Proszak v. Poland* (RJD 1998, p. 2765), § 33; ECtHR, 30 October 1998, *Styranowski v. Poland* (RJD 1998, p. 3367), § 47; ECtHR, 15 October 1999, *Humen v. Poland* (n.y.r.), § 60; ECtHR, 4 April 2000, *Dewicka – Poland* (n.y.r.), § 44. See also, under Art. 5 § 4, ECtHR, 25 March 1999, *Musial v. Poland* (n.y.r.), § 43.

ance for possible transitional problems.³³ In the recent case of *Brumarescu* the Court even seemed to display extra sensitivity for the past: it strongly criticized the power of the Procurator-General of Romania to challenge final judgments before the Supreme Court of Justice.³⁴

SIGNS OF LENIENCY

There have, however, also been a few signs of leniency. A – German! – example is offered by the case of *Süßmann*. Mr Süßmann complained about the length of a procedure before the German Federal Constitutional Court *(Bundesverfassungsgericht)*. The European Commission of Human Rights unanimously agreed that Article 6 § 1 had been violated. The Court, however, found by 14 votes to 6 that there had been no violation. It took into account that Mr Süßmann had filed his appeal at the same time as a large number of former civil servants of the German Democratic Republic. They challenged a provision of the Treaty on German Unification, terminating the employment contracts of around 300,000 persons. In this connection the Court found that

> bearing in mind the unique political context of German reunification and the serious social implications of the disputes which concerned termination of employment contracts, the Federal Constitutional Court was entitled to decide that it should give priority to those cases.³⁵

Now what is a "unique political context"? States may be tempted to perceive their own situation as truly unique. Applicants too.

In 1994 the Hungarian Constitution was amended to the effect that members of the armed forces, the police and the security services were prohibited from joining any political party and from engaging in any political activity. Yet in the case of *Rekvényi* the Court, unlike the

---

³³ See for instance ECtHR, 22 May 1998, *Vasilescu v. Romania* (RJD 1998, p. 1064): unlawful seizure of gold coins by the *militia* in 1966 and lack of tribunal that could order their return; ECtHR, 28 October 1998, *Assenov a.o. v. Bulgaria* (RJD 1998, p. 3264): alleged ill-treatment by police and pre-trial detention; ECtHR, 25 March 1999, *Nikolova v. Bulgaria* (n.y.r.): lack of judicial review of detention on remand; ECtHR, 25 January 2000, *Ignaccolo-Zenide v. Romania* (n.y.r.): failure to end situation of child abduction; ECtHR, 18 May 2000, *Velikova v. Bulgaria* (n.y.r.): death of Romany in police custody; ECtHR, 27 June 2000, *Constantinescu v. Romania* (n.y.r.): conviction following trial *in absentia*.
³⁴ ECtHR, 28 October 1999, *Brumarescu v. Romania* (n.y.r.), § 62.
³⁵ ECtHR, 16 September 1996, *Süßmann v. Germany* (RJD 1996, p. 1158), § 60. Cf. also ECtHR, 25 February 2000, *Gast & Popp v. Germany* (n.y.r.), § 75 *et seq.*

Commission, accepted that no violation of the Convention had occurred:

> The Court observes that between 1949 and 1989 Hungary was ruled by one political party. Membership of that party was, in many social spheres, expected as a manifestation of the individual's commitment to the regime. This expectation was even more pronounced within the military and the police, where party membership on the part of the vast majority of serving staff guaranteed that the ruling party's political will was directly implemented. This is precisely the vice that rules on the political neutrality of the police are designed to prevent. It was not until 1989 that Hungarian society succeeded in building up the institutions of a pluralistic democracy, leading to the first multi-party parliamentary elections in more than forty years being held in 1990. [...]
>
> Regard being had to the margin of appreciation left to the national authorities in this area, the Court finds that, especially against this historical background, the relevant measures taken in Hungary in order to protect the police force from the direct influence of party politics can be seen as answering a "pressing social need" in a democratic society.[36]

This judgment is surprising for several reasons. It fits ill into the Court's existing case-law. The Court has held that freedom of political debate is at the very core of the concept of a democratic society.[37] The Convention applies equally to civil servants and members of the military,[38] and whereas it is open to the authorities to impose restrictions, for instance, to protect army discipline and operational effectiveness, they may not frustrate the exercise of their rights.[39] An absolute and general ban on "political activities" – a vague and sweeping notion – is not compatible therewith and disproportionate in a democratic society. Is it not one of the basic conditions of a modern pluralistic democracy that, regardless of profession or status, every citizen can freely express his political convictions, in particular through elections, but also by

---

[36] ECtHR, 20 May 1999, *Rekvényi v. Hungary* (n.y.r.), §§ 47-48.
[37] See, e.g., ECtHR, 8 July 1986, *Lingens v. Austria* (Series A, vol. 103), § 42; ECtHR, 27 April 1995, *Piermont v. France* (Series A, vol. 314), §§ 51-53; ECtHR, 26 September 1995, *Vogt v. Germany* (Series A, vol. 323), § 44.
[38] See e.g. ECtHR, 28 August 1986, *Glasenapp v. Germany* (Series A, vol. 104), § 49.
[39] See e.g. ECtHR, 25 November 1997, *Grigoriades v. Greece* (RJD 1997, p. 2589), § 45, and ECtHR, 27 September 1999, *Lustig-Prean & Beckett v. United Kingdom* (n.y.r.), §§ 82, 86.

adhering to political parties? Political parties are the major instrument for the citizen to participate in the political life of a nation.[40]

A judgment like this risks to serve as a standing invitation to Governments from Central and Eastern European Member States to invoke their recent past when defending themselves in Strasbourg.

Indeed, this is what seems to have happened in the recent cases of *Špacek v. the Czech Republic* and *Majaric v. Slovenia*. The *Špacek* case, decided on 9 November 1999, concerns a rather technical matter. Additional tax and a penalty were imposed upon the *Špacek* company, because it had not applied certain regulations concerning the determination of the income tax base. *Špacek* complained in Strasbourg these regulations had never been published or announced in the Official Gazette. It alleged a violation of its right to property as it was taxed and fined without proper legal basis. And what did the Czech Government submit?

> after a long period with a centrally planned economy, private business activity was a novelty which had required speedy adaptation to new accounting and tax rules.[41]

As it happened the Court did not find a violation. In reaching this conclusion it did not expressly deal with the 'transition' argument – so we have to guess whether it influenced the Court's position. In my opinion, if the Court considered it persuasive, it should have explained why it did so. And if it did not subscribe to it, it would have been better to say so expressly. The Court should take great care to avoid the impression that it applies double standards vis-à-vis two or three groups of States.

A similar a-mbiguity may be traced in the *Majaric* case. A complaint was brought against Slovenia about the length of criminal proceedings. The Government advanced several arguments why, in their view, no breach of Article 6 § 1 of the Convention had taken place. Interestingly, the Government maintained that

> any delays imputable to the domestic authorities were to be considered in the context of radical changes in the legal and economic system in Slovenia at the relevant period which brought about an increase of the courts' workload.[42]

---

[40] ECtHR, 30 January 1998, *TBKP v. Turkey* (RJD 1998, p. 1), § 42 *et seq.*
[41] ECtHR, 9 November 1999, *Špacek v. the Czech Republic* (n.y.r.), § 48.
[42] ECtHR, 8 February 2000, *Majaric v. Slovenia* (n.y.r.), § 30.

One might have expected the Court to reject that argument offhand, as it had done in *Podbielsky v. Poland*, quoted above. In fact, however, the Court did not dismiss this argument completely:

> The Court has before it no information which would indicate that the difficulties encountered in Slovenia during the relevant period were such as to deprive the applicant of his entitlement to a judicial determination within "a reasonable time".[43]

It is hard to shake off the impression that the Court was signalling its willingness to take into account transition difficulties, if sufficient information is provided by the respondent Government.

CONCLUSION

All in all, a mixed picture emerges. In the face of its growing membership, the Council of Europe has become more demanding of its Members; new monitoring mechanisms have been devised; the importance of uniform application of the law is emphasized increasingly.[44] The European Court of Human Rights applies its existing case-law without much ado, although in a few cases it seemed prepared to make special exception for the political situation in the new Member States.

How should this result be assessed? Organizations like the Council of Europe face a dilemma. On the one hand they will wish to expand, so as to include as many countries as possible. It can only be welcomed that the European Convention on Human Rights now applies to 700 million people; stability in Europe is furthered by the integration of Russia and other Central and East European States into European structures. On the other hand: as the European family of nations extends, there is a growing risk that unstable countries, some of which may be too big to be open to persuasion, are admitted. By continuing to apply high standards international organizations are seemingly bound for confrontations. Yet, to accommodate these standards may entail that they loose their authority and, in the end, their legitimacy.

To some extent, the European Court of Human Rights may solve this dilemma by allowing – by continuing to allow – a certain margin of

---

[43] *Ibidem*, § 39.
[44] Further evidence of this trend can be found in Recommendation 1458 (2000) of 6 April 2000. As there is "a need for uniform interpretation and application of the Council of Europe conventions in the different member states", the Parliamentary Assembly calls for the creation of a 'General Judicial Authority'.

appreciation to the national authorities. In principle there is nothing wrong with that. It seems (still) unavoidable that some margin is left to the Contracting States as a recognition of the diversity of political, economic and cultural situations. However, one should not ignore the fact that the Convention contains minimum standards which all Contracting Parties have accepted. The application of the margin of appreciation doctrine should not, in fact, lead to the application of double standards. There is no better way to express this than to quote one of the editors of this volume, professor Henry Schermers:

> indeed, every State, every nation, in Europe has its own standard of morality. In that sense, we do not have an integrated Europe, but we do have some common basis. There would be no Europe at all if there were not some common features, some basic standards, which are the same in all countries. [...] We do accept that there are differences in level, differences in feelings, but, for the Convention to function at all, we must accept some minimum which all countries have to stay above.[45]

---

[45] Speaking as delegate of the European Commission of Human Rights in the case of *Lingens v. Austria*; see ECtHR, Series B, vol. 86, p. 118.

THE PRIMARY MODEL RULES OF ACCOUNTABILITY OF INTERNATIONAL ORGANIZATIONS: THE PRINCIPLES AND RULES GOVERNING THEIR CONDUCT OR THE YARDSTICKS FOR THEIR ACCOUNTABILITY

*Karel Wellens**

INTRODUCTION

Although everything seems to have been said about them "an impression of dissatisfaction remains on the state of international law with respect to international organizations".[1] The fact that "despite the rapid proliferation of these organizations during the last (60) years, relatively little is known about (them) or how they operate"[2] could only partly explain this state of affairs. The exclusive objective of the ILA-Committee on Accountability of International Organizations is to consider what measures should be adopted to ensure their accountability. The Committee's activities are thus measure-oriented. The identification and formulation of a pragmatic and feasible set of such measures has to be the final outcome of the Committee's work.[3]
The set of model rules should be elaborated in such a way as to rightfully claim widespread and general applicability to their addressees:[4] in order to achieve this, the process of elaboration should not only be firmly based upon a careful analysis of existing practices and mecha-

---

* Professor of International Law, Nijmegen University, The Netherlands; Chairman of the Netherlands Advisory Committee on Issues of Public International Law; Co-rapporteur, Committee on Accountability of International Organizations of the International Law Association.
[1] Smouts used this assessment in 1993 but with regard to international relations theory: D. Dijkzeul, *The Management of Multilateral Organizations*, Kluwer Law International, The Hague, Boston, London, 1997, 241 pages, at p.14.
[2] Cooperrider and Pasmore writing in 1991 as cited by Dijkzeul, *op.cit.*, at p.20.
[3] ILA, Report of the Sixty-eighth Conference, Taipei, Taiwan, Republic of China, 1998, at p. 588.
[4] *Ibid.*

nisms, but it has also to be properly embedded in an encompassing doctrinal framework on the various complex aspects of accountability as such. The latter will function as signposts in the interpretation of a consistent pattern surfacing in the relevant practice of IO-s.

Mapping the territory of relations of accountability between the IO-s, Member States and third parties requires the drawing up of an inventory of existing practices but also further reflection on the principles and limitations constraining the exercise of the ever expanding institutional and operational authority and powers of IO-s i.e. the yardsticks for their accountability.[5]

Accountability of IO-s covers both secondary rules to render operational the accountability towards those entitled to raise it (its *mise-en-oeuvre*) and primary rules or yardsticks governing the conduct of IO-s. The Committee's mandate covers both set of rules.

The present study is aimed at contributing to further progress in two of the Committee's main areas of concern: looking more closely into and eventually suggesting the adjustment of the legal parameters governing activities of IO-s and making useful suggestions as to the adoption by IO-s of new operating procedures.

An attempt will be made to explore in more detail two of the yardsticks referred to by the Committee in its First Report .[6]

In Part One we will look at the principle of good governance which is of an evolving nature and comprises such elements as a transparent and democratic decision-making process, access to information, well-functioning of the international civil service, sound financial management and reporting and evaluation.

Part Two will be devoted to objectives and principles common to all IO-s (the principle of good faith in international law; the principle of constitutionality; the principle of institutional balance; the principle of subsidiarity; the principle of supervision and control; the principle of stating the reasons for decisions or a particular course of action; the principle of the protection of legitimate expectations; the principle of proportionality; the principle of procedural regularity; the principle of objectivity and impartiality; the principle of due diligence; the principle of promoting justice; the concept of functional necessity and propositions on financial accountability).

---

[5] *Ibid.* at p. 601.
[6] *Ibid.* at pp. 601-602.

The secondary rules or the *mise-en-oeuvre* of accountability of IO-s i.e. the mechanisms available to ensure accountability of IO-s will be dealt in a further publication.

When looking more closely into the different yardsticks which the Committee has tentatively identified in its First Report one should be constantly aware that the envisaged model rules will have to keep the balance between preserving the necessary autonomy in decision-making of IO-s and guaranteeing that they will not be able to avoid accountability.[7] This vital balancing act is bound to permeate any useful discussion on the headings listed by the Committee as yardsticks. The reading and use for instance of the principle of good governance or principles common to all IO-s should be carried out in such a way that the balance is maintained. Existing principles may have to be reformulated or re-orientated to avoid becoming counter-productive as a result of an unqualified transposition into the area of accountability.

One should also reckon with the more general problem that Member States are already perceived as dominating IO-s to such an extent that these are unable to exercise maximum control over their environment. The considerable influence exercised by Member States constrains autonomous behaviour by IO-s.[8]

The variety of legal layers providing flexibility for IO-s when conducting their multilevel operations[9] has to be matched by a comprehensive set of yardsticks leaving no loopholes at each individual legal level. Both parties involved – the IO-s concerned and the entities asserting control and supervision – although for different reasons, are looking for a certain degree of predictability and consistency in the way the multiple yardsticks are put into operation: any attempt to impose too rigid a system of accountability would not survive the complexities of international reality.[10]

---

[7] *Ibid.* at p.602.
[8] Haas as cited by Dijkzeul, *op.cit.*, at p. 33.
[9] ILA, Report of the Sixty-eighth Conference, *op. cit.*, at p. 591
[10] *Ibid.* at p.598.

PART ONE:
THE PRINCIPLE OF GOOD GOVERNANCE

The principle of good governance (or of good administration) as it is commonly understood includes the following: transparency in both the decision-making process and the implementation of the ensuing institutional and operational decisions, a large degree of democracy in the decision-making process, access to information open to all potentially concerned and/or affected by the decisions at stake, the well functioning of the international civil service, sound financial management, reporting and evaluation.

Although these elements will be reviewed separately below, it is clear that their close interconnection, also in practical terms, is vital to procure good governance by IO-s. In his report on the work of the Organization the UN Secretary-general, in contrast to the Committee's approach, appears to consider good governance as the overarching term when he wrote: "By good governance is meant creating well-functioning and accountable institutions – political, juridical and administrative – that citizens regard as legitimate, through which they participate in decisions that affect their lives, and by which they are empowered. Good governance also entails a respect for human rights and the rule of law generally."[11]

TRANSPARENCY IN BOTH THE DECISION-MAKING PROCESS AND THE IMPLEMENTATION OF INSTITUTIONAL AND OPERATIONAL DECISIONS.

As in any other kind of organization, working methods of an organ of an IO should be continuously reviewed in a way "that will further strengthen its capacity and effectiveness, enhance its representative character and improve its working efficiency and transparency".[12]

The basic standard undoubtedly has to be total transparency of the quasi-legislative procedure followed by decision-making organs of an

---

[11] A/53/1, Report of the Secretary-general on the Activities of the Organization, para. 114.

[12] Declaration on the Occasion of the Fiftieth Anniversary of the United Nations, A/Res 50/6 of 9 November 1995, para. 14.

IO whereas the adoption of all normative decisions in a public vote is a condition sine qua non of democracy and transparency.[13]

Even within an IO lacking a mechanism providing for judicial review, transparency of the decision-making process would be increased if its organs would refer to the applicable provisions of the constitution attributing their power to take the decision in question.[14] The choice of the legal basis may also be important because it could determine what procedure for decision-making applies.[15]

Timely notification to interested parties or in some circumstances to the public at large of projects envisaged by an IO could further contribute to genuine transparency and by the same token increase the chances of a more democratic decision-making process.

The following observation made by Bailey and Daws in connection with the UN Security Council[16] applies unreservedly to all IO-s: a special obligation to act as transparently as possible is incumbent upon non-plenary organs acting on behalf of the whole membership under the governing provisions of an Organization's constituent instrument. The more extensive powers are bestowed upon a non-plenary organ, the more compelling the imposition of such a special obligation from the perspective of effective accountability.

The self-interest for any such non-plenary organ operating in a *generally* (emphasis added) transparent and open manner has clearly to be found in the ensuing additional legitimization and support as it was rightly pointed out by Winkelman.[17]

Such a special obligation however should not be unlimited; indeed, as Bailey and Daws have observed, measures to maximize transparency should not interfere with such an organ's primary responsibility in a field of the Organization's main purposes.[18]

---

[13] Based upon the Resolution of the European Parliament on Democracy, transparency and subsidiarity and the Interinstitutional Agreement on procedures for implementing the principle of subsidiarity, adopted on 17 November 1973, OJEC, C 329/132, at p.132.

[14] See also Henry G. Schermers and Niels M. Blokker, *International Institutional Law. Unity within diversity*, Third revised Edition, Martinus Nijhoff Publishers, The Hague, London, Boston, 1995, 1305 pp., at para.16.

[15] *Ibid.* at para. 218.

[16] Sydney D. Bailey and Sam Daws, *The Procedure of the UN Security Council*, Third Edition, Clarendon Press Oxford, 1998, 689 pp., at 393.

[17] Ingo Winkelmann, Bringing the UN Security Council into a New Era, *Max Planck Yearbook of United Nations Law*, Volume I, 1997, Kluwer Law International, London, The Hague, Boston, pp.35-90, at 37.

[18] *Op. cit.*, at p. 393.

Winkelman[19] has drawn a very useful distinction as to the obligation of transparency imposing itself upon non-plenary organs.

General transparency is aimed at by improved information for all Member States about the work of non-plenary organs.

Individual transparency may be provided by an enhanced status of Member States who consider themselves to be particularly affected by decisions to be taken by a non-plenary organ.

Collective transparency will result from improved co-operation between the non-plenary organ and groups of interested Member States.

Along these lines the following observations may be made.

In general, transparency could only benefit form an increase in the number of public meetings – depending on the issue at hand – "coupled with genuine consultations with concerned non-members at early stages in the deliberations".[20]

Countries contributing to operational activities of a military, technical or humanitarian nature by providing personnel or otherwise, should be fully informed and genuinely consulted by an non-plenary organ having executive power before the actual decision to launch the operation is being taken, and thereafter at regular intervals, upon their own requests, or as a matter of standard practice. The genuine character of consultations may be tested by including issues such as policy and mandate and operational aspects.

Private (closed) meetings of non-plenary organs possessing extensive executive powers have been considered to be unconstitutional and contrary to the provisions of the Organization's constituent instrument, as all Members of an IO should have the right to be acquainted with the proceedings of such a non-plenary organ.[21] However, the practice of hearing comments by States and organizations concerned during closed meetings raises similar objections as with regard to broadening access to informal closed consultations.[22]

The draft-programme of work for informal consultations by a non-plenary organ should be made public not only to other Members of the IO but to the public at large by the normal means of (mass) communication, whereas the draft-decisions to be considered during such infor-

---

[19] *Op. cit.*, at p.51.
[20] Bailey and Daws, *op.cit.*, at 9. 394.
[21] The matter was first raised by the Syrian delegate, as reported by Bailey and Daws, *op.cit.*, at p.10.
[22] See *infra* B at page, Bailey and Daws, *op.cit.*, at 291.

mal consultations should be made available at the time when these consultations are being held.[23]

When a non-plenary organ resorts to informal consultations to regularly review its prior decisions (such as coercive measures, or the modalities and continuation of peace-keeping operations) the question was rightfully raised whether Member States should not be allowed to participate in these discussions whenever their interests are specially affected and *a fortiori* when they are a party to the dispute under consideration.[24].

Information conveyed orally by officials of the Organization's Secretariat, by its Secretary-general or Executive Head or by their Special Representatives or Special Envoys to a non-plenary organ during informal consultations, should be reflected in that organ's annual report in order to increase the accountability of both the non-plenary organ and of the officials concerned towards the overall membership.[25]

Records of discussions of subsidiary organs entrusted with the supervision of the implementation of binding decisions taken by an executive non-plenary organ should not be issued with a "limited" document distribution designation.

Attempts to make the procedures of such subsidiary organs more transparent do include the following: oral briefing by the organ's Chairman to interested members of the IO, issuing press releases after the meetings, making available the text of the decisions taken to any delegation requesting it and the preparation of an annual report to the parent non-plenary organ.[26]

These attempts are clearly falling short of the minimum standard of transparency referred to earlier and which would enable a larger degree of accountability to be achieved.

Although institutionalization of transparency-related measures e.g. by amending rules of procedures, may present itself as almost a natural way of operating in order to improve accountability, Winkelman's general *caveat* should not be forgotten: "True, transparency is hard to achieve through formal rules".[27]

---

[23] Ibid. at pp. 66-67.
[24] Ibidem at pp. 63-64.
[25] Ibid. at p. 289.
[26] UN Security Council Presidential Statements dated 29 March 1995 and 24 January 1996.
[27] Op. cit., at p. 58.

DEMOCRATIC DECISION-MAKING PROCESS

From an accountability point of view, Schermers and Blokker made it clear that rules on decision-making (partly) determine to what extent Member States can control the process by which organs employ their attributed powers to realize the functions for which they have been established.[28]

When reviewing the democratic degree of any decision-making process within an IO it is obvious that one "should look at where is the point of decision-making: the Secretary-general, a named State or States, a sanctions committee, a military commander, and so on": this observation made by Bailey and Daws in connection with coercive measures[29] undoubtedly is of general application.

Furthermore, when looking at the democratic nature of a decision-making process within an IO, one should be aware not only of closed meetings having a clear statutory existence under the constituent instrument and the relevant rules of procedure, but also of the practice of informal consultations lacking a similar statutory basis but having obtained a *de facto* official status.[30]

Under the principle of good governance, it is obvious that there is a close connection between the transparency of the decision-making process and its democratic credentials. Accordingly it is not surprising that the main area of concern about the democratic nature once again has to be situated at the level of non-plenary organs of any IO.

The following rules and recommended practices deserve careful consideration in any attempt to alleviate to some extent the democratic deficit.

Accountability towards the general membership could be greatly improved if permanent membership of a non-plenary organ possessing extensive executive powers would be subject to a periodic review clause, thus preventing such members having an irreversible status. Germany's suggestion as to the new permanent members of the UN Security Council is perfectly suitable for more general application.[31]

A fundamental distinction should be drawn, as far as the democratic degree of decision-making process is concerned, between the more preparatory stages of information, consultation and exchange of

---

[28] *Op. cit.*, para. 382.
[29] *Op. cit.*, at p. 368.
[30] *Ibid.* at p. 56.
[31] Winkelmann, *op. cit.*, at p. 86.

views which could take place in public and could be open to non-members of a non-plenary organ, whereas the actual negotiation and drafting of texts would remain open to Members only.[32]

On the other hand when interpreting objections raised by a variety of Member States or a particular group of Member States against decisions taken by non-plenary organs, if possible one should clearly distinguish dissatisfaction based upon the substance of the decisions under scrutiny from arguments linked to the procedure followed throughout the decision-making process.

Although one may be tempted to assume that the potential of accountability would be increased if any Member of an IO be given the right, under the constituent instrument, to request an urgent meeting of a non-plenary organ vested with extensive executive powers, it was rightly pointed out by Winkelman, that such an organ's "ability to decide on the main *focus* of its work" should not be jeopardized.[33]

Informal consultations may have to play a crucial role in the decision-making process especially in cases of non-plenary organs having wide-ranging executive powers. Although it has to be admitted that making such informal consultations more public could result in paralyzing them, non-members of that organ could be given the opportunity to take part in orientation debates when the organ concerned is preparing to begin consideration of a particular item.[34]

Would the increased recent use of this approach with regard to UN Security Council be suitable for general application with regard to most cases involving non-plenary organs?

It has been rightly pointed out that the danger of this proposal "is that discussion of confidential matters would be driven into more secretive and informal for a".[35] Further institutionalization of (closed) informal consultations would "reduce the scrutiny that could be placed on (Council) decision-making by the public, the media, and scholars".[36] Consequently, accountability would not be improved.

The overall conclusion with regard to this proposal seems to be that "there would a reduction in transparency. Moreover, while certain non-members may gain more information from consultations, this

---

[32] As indicated in the Presidential Statement of the UN Security Council dated 16 December 1994.
[33] *Op. cit.*, at p. 52.
[34] French proposal as discussed by Bailey and Daws, *op. cit.*, at p. 51.
[35] *Ibid.* at p. 291.
[36] *Ibid.*

information would not be public, and therefore of little use to those States who seek to increase the "accountability" of the (non-plenary organ) to the (plenary organ) through a more public airing of the arguments "which had been invoked by the members of the non-plenary organ for and against a particular decision".[37]

Perhaps one has to look for other ways to counterbalance the insufficient degree of democracy in the decision-making process within IO-s once we are entering the fora of non-plenary organs.

The democratic nature of any decision-making process by a non-plenary organ would be enhanced if, prior to the actual adoption of a decision, non-members would be invited to participate in confidential but *formal* discussions during private meetings.[38]

When direct participation in the decision-making process is impossible as a result of relevant provisions in the Organization's constituent instrument or a non-plenary organ's governing rules of procedure, briefings of non-members and other entities by the organ's Presidency could provide a useful alternative.[39]

Even here a *caveat* has to be issued as a more general question of accountability arises when "a meeting of members of a non-plenary organ" takes place rather than "a meeting of non-plenary organ all members normally attending". Indeed the ensuing statement read out by the President of the non-plenary organ would reflect the difference in its opening sentences[40] and may have to be assessed differently from an accountability point of view.

With regard to operational activities of IO-s the right for differently affected groups and entities of being consulted throughout the various stages of a particular project or operation (initiating, planning, negotiating, managing, monitoring, final review and evaluation) should be secured by appropriate and diversified steps. In this same context the department of an IO dealing with a particular category of issues may convene a briefing for members of a non-plenary organ where representatives of particular NGO-s may be given an opportunity to present their views on a particular matter or range of issues.[41]

---

[37] Ibid.
[38] Ibid. at p. 56, emphasis added.
[39] E.g. President of the UN Security Council on informal consultations, Bailey and Daws, *op. cit.*, at p. 50.
[40] Ibid. at pp. 65 and 73.
[41] Ibid. at p. 75.

Finally, every non-plenary organ's rules of procedure should provide for the possibility of it being supplied with information or being given assistance in examining matters within its competence by inviting members of the Organization's Secretariat or other persons considered competent for the purpose. Such a rule would not only increase the accountability of the officials involved but the democratic nature of the decision-making process would benefit from external expert advice e.g. by non-state entities.

ACCESS TO INFORMATION

As it has been succinctly put by Schermers and Blokker "Publicity about its achievements is important for every international organization".[42] As a result it is not surprising that since their establishment IO-s have spent time and money in developing an information strategy. As it was explained by Menon,[43] the need for such an information strategy is not only to respond to criticism of the Organization, but also to project a clear idea of what it is doing and why; in other words this goes to the heart of what accountability of IO-s is all about.

When addressing the issue of access to information held by an IO and having in mind the accountability point of view, it is relevant to be aware that internal flows of information are as important as what is directed to audiences outside.[44]

The principle of good governance seems to require the following in the area of information. There should be effective and timely information gathering. The material collected should be comprehensive and reliable in order to enable the IO to conduct an accurate analysis of that information. It goes without saying that accountability would be raised if the IO does not live up to these basic requirements as the information provided will ultimately constitute the basis for the decision-making process.

As a general standard it may be accepted that full information is a fundamental element in any attempt to improve transparency of the functioning of any organ of an IO.

---

[42] *Op. cit.*, para. 964.
[43] Bhaskar Menon, The image of the United Nations in Issues of Global Governance, *Papers written for the commission on Global Governance*, Kluwer Law International, London, The Hague, Boston, 1995, pp. 175-193, at p. 191.
[44] *Ibid.* at p. 193.

The basic rule has to be that an IO should have no secret documents.[45] If however an IO has decided to consider some (category of) documents as confidential, the organ concerned should, at least annually, decide which of these should be made public unless there are compelling reasons not to do so.

The governing rules of procedure of any deliberative or executive organ should provide that, at least for some category of important proposals, texts are being circulated in advance of the opening of a session in order not only to enable members to define their positions, but also to increase the transparency of the decision making process.[46] Making available the same texts to non-members of the organ and other entities concerned would of course benefit transparency and democratic credentials, and ultimately the *mise-en-oeuvre* of the accountability of the IO.

When used as conditions for the rendering of any kind of assistance to Member States rules adopted by an IO should always be incorporated in the governing special agreement between the IO and the beneficiary State.[47] The need for such an inclusion and the advantages as to accountability of all parties involved are obvious.

Comprehensive, reliable and disinterested information is also a prerequisite for a proper process of reporting and evaluation, which is an integral element of the principle of good governance and constitutes an important step in the *mise- en -oeuvre* of the accountability of an IO.

Another essential condition for an effective *mise-en-oeuvre* of the accountability of an IO is to be found in the recognition and preservation of the right of unimpeded access to the archives of an IO, unless the exercise of that right could endanger the life of staff members or persons who have been associated with the IO in the past.

International Organizations should annually report on the measures they have been taking to implement the rules on public access to documents and information. The report should include *inter alia* statistical data as to the origin, subject and follow-up of applications made by interested parties to obtain such access.

---

[45] Delegate from Cuba on the occasion of the drafting of the Provisional rules of Procedure of the UN Security Council as reported by Bailey and Daws, *op. cit.*, at p. 10.

[46] See also Schermers and Blokker, *op. cit.*, at para. 747.

[47] See also Schermers and Blokker, *op. cit.*, at para. 1207.

WELL-FUNCTIONING INTERNATIONAL CIVIL SERVICE.

There is no doubt that the principle of good governance requires the IO-s to ensure a well-functioning international civil service which has an indispensable role to play in the performance of the responsibilities they have been entrusted with by their Member States. In order to achieve this objective of a well-functioning international civil service, IO-s have formulated principles, recommended practices and issued guidelines and regulations, which have been confirmed, elaborated and guaranteed through the case-law of the various administrative tribunals.

Schermers and Blokker have listed a number of principles which could be considered as fundamental for the functioning of an IO: the principle of impartiality, the principle of loyalty to the organization, the principle of functional independence and the principle of discretion[48] Zacklin and Tarassenko consider only the former three to constitute a fundamental basis for the proper functioning of an international administration.[49]
Delicate issues are bound to arise when the daily operation of these principles through regulations, guidelines and practices is being confronted with the (overriding) concern of accountability of the IO. It should be noted indeed that the principle of loyalty and discretion, if upheld in an absolute, unrestricted way under all circumstances, could in some cases lead to serious difficulties when the accountability of the IO and/or either the civil servant are likely to be raised. The Secretariat's dual function i.e. to serve the Member States and having an independent responsibility in the pursuance of the objectives of the Organization could only exacerbate this potential conflict.[50]
Once more a delicate balance will have to be found as the application of functional imperatives of the civil service's well-functioning inevitably is going to be qualified by the legitimate demands of accountability.

Given the lack of permanent control comparable to that of a national Council of Ministers or Parliament, the responsibility of individual international civil servants may be more extensive than those of their national counterparts as pointed out by Schermers and Blokker.[51]

---

[48] *Ibid.* at paras. 516 and 524.
[49] R. Zacklin and S. Tarassenko, Independence of International Civil Servants. Privileges and Immunities, in C. De Cooker, (Ed.), *International Administration. Law and Management in International Organizations*, Kluwer Law International, loose-leaf publication, p.13.
[50] Schermers and Blokker, *op. cit.*, at para. 555.
[51] *Op. cit.*, at para. 435.

It has to be acknowledged that administrative control rather than political supervision is a major concern for supervisory bodies of the Secretariat of an IO, usually the board and the plenary organ.[52]

Another leading authority has observed that although an administrative nexus between the Secretariat and the Organization has to exist, there has been a trend towards avoiding the situation where the independence of Secretariats may be compromised by undue influence being exerted by administrations through control over administrative oversight.[53]

The considerable power of the Secretariat of an IO is largely based on it being best informed on all documentation and practices of the Organization.[54]

On the other hand the Secretariat operates to safeguard the interests of the Organization and may accordingly be less influenced by political factors than policy-making organs.[55] As pointed out by the same authors[56] it has also to be recognized that not merely factual information provided by the staff of an IO undoubtedly influences delegations' positions and may be coloured by the staff's own opinions on the matters at hand. It goes without saying that the degree of accountability of the Secretariat and of its staff members should be determined accordingly.

There is an obvious correlation between the degree of active policy displayed by the Secretariat of an IO – e.g. in proposing new activities to delegations when preparing the Organization's budget or on other occasions, by influencing the well-functioning or malfunctioning of the organs of the IO, in transferring funds within sections of the budget (thus favouring some activities to the detriment of others)[57] – and their share in the accountability of the IO they serve. From an accountability point of view supervision by another organ, plenary or non-plenary or a combination of both depending upon the institutional balance within the IO, is absolutely essential.

---

[52] *Ibid.* at paras. 435 and 441.
[53] C.F. Amerasinghe, The Future of International Administrative Law, *I.C.L.Q.*, 1996, pp.773-795, at p. 784.
[54] C.F.Amerasinghe, *Principles of the Institutional Law of International Organizations*, Cambridge university Press, 1996, 519 pp., at p. 156.
[55] Schermers and Blokker, *op. cit.*, at para. 1412.
[56] *Ibid.* at para. 444.
[57] *Ibid.* at paras. 461, 462, 465, 714, 1097.

The maintenance of the authority of the Secretary-general or Executive Head of an IO to deal effectively and decisively with the work and operation of the Secretariat in conditions of flexibility and adaptability depends, in its exercise, in large measure upon the observance of procedural safeguards.[58] Substantive safeguards include the duty to act reasonably in carrying out functions vis-a-vis staff members.[59]

SOUND FINANCIAL MANAGEMENT.

Since financing is at the heart of the functioning of an IO,[60] the requirement of sound financial management constitutes an important aspect of the principle of good governance and thus of the overall accountability of IO-s.
Although is has to be admitted that there are no general principles as such that apply to the preparation of the budget,[61] a standardized budgetary presentation is one of the essential conditions for the efficiency of an IO.[62] More importantly, such a presentation will greatly contribute to more transparency which in turn is an essential prerequisite for enhanced accountability of IO-s. Accordingly IO-s should refrain from altering the structure of their budget too frequently.[63]

The proposal to adopt a result-based budget system also remains under review according to the UN Secretary-general who added that the initiative is of the utmost importance as no single measure would do more to increase accountability and efficiency in the work of the Organization.[64] This statement obviously maintains its validity across the different categories of IO-s. From the point of view of supervision of the budget of an IO, and thus of its accountability, the classification of budget items according to both the instrument and the field of activity are necessary.[65]

The role of the Secretariat in the field of sound financial management is vital. In preparing the budget the Secretariat can take some

---

[58] As pointed out by UNAT, Amerasinghe, *op. cit.*,(note 54), at p. 358.
[59] C.F. Amerasinghe, *Developments in the Jurisprudence of the World Bank Tribunal since 1987*, in C. De Cooker, (Ed.), *op. cit.*,(note 49), V.8, at p. 7.
[60] C.F.Amerasinghe, *op. cit.*, (note 54), at p. 291.
[61] Ibid. at p. 294.
[62] Schermers and Blokker, *op. cit.*, at para. 933.
[63] Ibid., at para. 1099.
[64] A/53/1, Report of the Secretary-general on the Work of the Organization, para. 9.
[65] Schermers and Blokker, *op. cit.*, at paras. 931-933.

initiatives by proposing the allocation of funds for new activities, while it is again the Secretariat which controls the spending of the funds.[66]

As part of sound financial management no resolution involving expenditures should be recommended by a Committee for approval by a plenary organ unless it is accompanied by an estimate of expenditure prepared by the Secretariat. The vote on the draft resolution should only follow an assessment by the Organization's Administrative and Budgetary Committee of the effect of the proposal on the budget estimates of the Organization.[67]

The principle of institutional balance implies that the organ adopting the budget of an Organization may not refuse to allocate finances for activities initiated by another principal organ which is exclusively competent to decide upon such activities.[68] In the last resort the Organization's plenary organ would be free to overrule such an interference.[69] The organ vested with the powers of approval of the budget has a duty to consider in good faith, bearing in mind particularly the need to fulfil the functions and purposes of the Organization, the requests for finances submitted by other organs.[70] On the other hand, the same organ has a legal right not to approve appropriations which in its judgement, exercised in good faith, and after taking into account the need to fulfil the functions and purposes of the Organization, it considers unnecessary or excessive.[71] From an accountability point of view that organ should be under an obligation to act in this way. It is also important to stress that plenary organs should use the budgetary procedure to discuss and review the policy of the IO.

The budget serves as an essential yardstick for the auditing agency to compare expenditures with appropriations.[72]

Sound financial management requires the review of the regularity of all transactions, the conformity of obligations and expenditures with the appropriations and the economic use of the resources of the Organization; this function is carried out in the process of internal auditing.[73]

---

[66] Ibid., at para. 443.
[67] Schermers and Blokker, op. cit., at para.769.
[68] Ibid., at para.23.
[69] Amerasinghe, op. cit., (note 54), at p. 295.
[70] Ibid., at p. 321.
[71] Ibid.
[72] Schermers and Blokker, op. cit., at para. 1091.
[73] Amerasinghe, op. cit., (note 54), at p. 296.

Sound financial management also requires the review whether funds appropriated in the budget have been spent in accordance with the provisions of the budget and of the financial regulations of the Organization; this is done by external auditing.[74]

It goes without saying that within the context of sound financial management, one "of the primary tasks of financial authorities is to examine whether expenditures can be cut by increasing the efficiency of the instruments through which the organization operates".[75]

From an accountability perspective it is worth noting that the budgetary control apparently is less specific than for staff members when an Organization is hiring outside experts.[76] Furthermore it should not be forgotten that administrative expenditures of an IO are subject to a different system of approval and control because of the assumption that the Organization is competent to enter into these financial obligations, whereas in the case of operational expenditures the procedure for approval and control is different and generally more extensive[77] and this is irrespective of whether the Organization's competence to engage in such activities has to be demonstrated or is commonly understood as being inherent to every IO.

In order to maximise the chances for accountability it may be reasonable to demand separate budgeting for operational expenditures and to put some limitations on the inherent power of IO-s to undertake operational activities, either by not pursuing the activity in case of strong objections from the largest contributors or by keeping transfers of funds within narrow limits.[78]

Issues of accountability may become more complicated when an activity is financed by voluntary contributions from only a group of the Organization's Members or even outsiders: Schermers and Blokker rightly pointed out that "it is no longer the organization which acts ...and (there) is no longer a common responsibility for all activities."[79]

Sound financial management of IO-s may further be hampered as ordinary management approaches will not work satisfactorily when the unique factors such as the special characteristics and problems of IO-s

---

[74] Ibid. at p. 297.
[75] Schermers and Blokker, op. cit., at para. 1118.
[76] Ibid., at para. 467.
[77] Ibid., at paras. 939-940.
[78] Ibid., at para. 1211.
[79] Ibid. at para. 1024.

are insufficiently taken into account.[80] May be that is why management audits have become a highly effective oversight mechanism.[81]

REPORTING AND EVALUATION

Reporting and evaluation are inherently intertwined as any exercise of evaluation is impossible without due reporting.

The processes of reporting and evaluation are situated at a crucial juncture of the principle of good governance and the *mise- en- oeuvre* of accountability of an IO in a dual sense: they constitute at the same time the vital preconditions for and integral parts of the whole process of its mise- en -oeuvre.

The point of departure as to reporting is undoubtedly the acknowledgement that plenary organs of an IO possess the inherent powers to require other organs to submit reports on their activities.[82] The debate by a plenary organ over the reports submitted to it by other principal or subsidiary organs should be of a substantial nature in order to increase the potential impact of its supervisory function. The consideration of annual reports should become a major and important method for the *mise- en -oeuvre* of the accountability of IO-s towards its Member States.

As to the more *procedural* requirements of reporting, transparency would demand that the discussion by a non-plenary organ of its draft report to be submitted to a plenary organ for its consideration, should take place during a public meeting.[83] It is self-evident that reports should be submitted in a timely fashion.[84] The presentation of an organ's report for consideration should as a general rule be made by the reporting organ's President or Chairman. Assessments of the work done by an organ of an IO and which are made by the organ's President or Chairman, preceded by the disclaimer that the assessment should not necessarily be considered as reflecting the views of the organ concerned, may raise additional issues of the President's or Chairman's functional accountability.

---

[80] Dijkzeul, *op. cit.*, at p. 21.
[81] A/53/1, Report of the UN Secretary-general on the Work of the Organization.
[82] Amerasinghe, *op. cit.*, (note 54), at p. 137.
[83] As is the case e.g. with the draft report of the UN Security Council since 1993, Bailey and Daws, *op. cit.*, at p. 57.
[84] E. Suy, The role of the United Nations General Assembly, in Hazel Fox, (Ed.), *The changing Constitution of the United Nations*, British Institute of International and Comparative Law, London, 1997, 120 pp., pp.53-69, at p. 68.

With regard to *substantive* requirements, Bailey and Daws pointed out that the format and content of the report should be such as to "provide the means for Member States (of an IO) to assess (the reporting organ's) actions and, when necessary, to respond or make appropriate recommendations,"[85] although the way of functioning of a non-plenary organ inevitably has a bearing upon the descriptive rather than analytical nature of its reporting,

Suy is right to stress the need to have "a qualitative report rather than a documentary compendium".[86] His remark made in connection with the report by the UN Security Council to the General Assembly is generally applicable. Accordingly the reports by an organ of an IO should contain explanations of its decisions, and a genuine substantial account of the actions or inaction during the relevant period to such an extent as to allow the supervisory organ to fulfil its role in an efficient and appropriate way.

From the point of view of shared, joint or concurrent accountability it is of the utmost importance that IO-s should establish and utilise reporting techniques incumbent upon Member States to ensure the proper exercise by Member States of any authorisation granted to them and e.g. allowing them to take all the necessary measures to achieve the aims set by a particular decision.

When program partners become dissatisfied with program progress and results, they have three basic options: redefining the policy problem, reformulating the program design, or revising program implementation.[87] This aspect is connected with the larger issue of remedies which will be dealt with in a later publication.

---

[85] Bailey and Daws, *op. cit.*, at p. 289.
[86] Suy, *op. cit.*, at p. 68.
[87] Dijkzeul, *op. cit.*, at p. 149.

PART TWO: OBJECTIVES, PRINCIPLES AND CONCEPTS COMMON TO ALL IO-S.

From the outset the general *caveat* issued by Amerasinghe should not be forgotten: there is a difference between similarity of texts and practices which reflect only a pattern towards both uniformity and diversity, on the one hand, and a consistency of practice which may create general principles on the other hand.[88] In the following pages an attempt is made to identify, apart from objectives and concepts, general principles common to all IO-s. These general principles have either already developed or are in (different stages of) development; as a result we will cover general principles both of a *lege lata* and of a *lege ferenda* character.[89]

The category of practices merely reflecting a pattern will deserve further study.

THE GENERAL PRINCIPLE OF GOOD FAITH IN INTERNATIONAL LAW

The fundamental principle of good faith is governing all acts, activities and conduct of IO-s, irrespective of their individual or particular category features, and this to the same extent, also from an accountability point of view, as it operates vis-a-vis States and other actors on the international scene. The principle's fundamental character has given rise to other important principles such as the principle of protection of legitimate expectations[90] which will be reviewed later, and compelling standards of honesty, fairness and reasonableness. These standards permeate acts and activities of IO-s, both of an institutional and operational nature, and their interpretation and application is dependent upon prevailing views in the international community at any given time.[91]

---

[88] Amerasinghe, *op. cit.*, (note 54), at pp. 17-18.

[89] A number of the principles listed here are the result of an extremely cautious extrapolation from general principles of EC law as reflected in the ECJ and CFI's jurisprudence, and only to the extent that their applicability could be removed from the special features of the EC as an IO. The following pages owe much credit to the brilliant study by john Usher, *General Principles of EC Law*, Longman, London, New York, 1998, 167 pages.

[90] ECJ as referred to by Usher, *op. cit.*, at p. 7.

[91] J.F. O'Connor, *Good Faith in International Law*, Dartmouth Publishing Company, Aldershot, 1991, 148 pages, at p. 124.

From an accountability perspective, the principle of good faith means that the conduct of an IO should be evaluated and assessed in the light of information available to it at the relevant time.[92] This could be particularly relevant when activities such as peacekeeping-operations are being scrutinized: for instance the justification for not having taken protective measures in a particular situation should not be reviewed with the benefit of hindsight. One should immediately add that lessons drawn from previous experiences in peacekeeping could come and qualify this mitigating approach.

Although the principle of good faith because of its fundamental nature is clearly underlying the other principles reviewed in the following pages, one could add, at this stage, another example of its impact: the principle does not seem to tolerate the imposition by an Organization in cases of humanitarian or development assistance of terms of reference which are unrealistic in the context of a beneficiary State's economic situation .

THE PRINCIPLE OF CONSTITUTIONALITY

The European Court of Justice has made it perfectly clear that as a premise it should be accepted that IO-s are based on the rule of law, and that as a consequence their Member States nor their organs can avoid a review of the question whether the decisions and measures adopted by them are in conformity with the basic constituent instrument.[93] The application of this premise and of the ensuing principle of constitutionality does provide a crucial yardstick for the *mise-en-oeuvre* of the accountability of IO-s; this is irrespective, at this stage, of the serious problems linked to the availability and modalities of a constitutionality review and which will be analysed in a further publication dealing with the remedies.

Schermers and Blokker have rightly pointed out that the "functional finality" of any IO entails three normative aspects: the authorization given to the Organization by its constituent members, the limits to this authorization flowing from the Organization's objectives, and the obligation to perform the functions they have been entrusted with by the members.[94] It is clear that issues of accountability of IO-s may arise under each of these separate headings.

---

[92] Usher, *op. cit.*, at p. 102.
[93] ECJ as referred to by Usher, *op. cit.*, at p. 86.
[94] *Op. cit.*, at para. 17.

Given the predominant role of an Organization's constituent instrument in the application of the principle of constitutionality, and which is subject of course to overriding peremptory norms of international law, several points which are relevant to accountability may be indicated here.

First of all, IO-s are not free to decide whether or not to carry out their functions; they have a legal obligation to do so as pointed out by Paul Reuter.[95] In this context it should be noted that plenary organs of an IO have not only the right but also the duty of establishing the policy of the Organization.[96]

Secondly, powers derived externally from general international law have to be exercised by an organ of an IO receiving them in parallel to the constitutionally conferred powers of the organs.[97] This parallelism is bound to influence the *mise- en oeuvre* of the accountability.

Thirdly, the principle of constitutionality also imposes constitutional limits upon the exercise of the inherent competence of an IO to engage in operational activities as recalled by Schermers and Blokker[98] who also pointed to further limits flowing from the general rules of equity and fairness.[99]

Fourthly, Amerasinghe rightfully recalled that the interpretation of constitutional and associated texts should be fair in its application to all Members of an IO.[100] This aspect of the principle of constitutionality is obviously also linked to other principles such that of objectivity and impartiality, the obligation to motivate decisions, the requirements of due process, and the principle of proportionality. The importance of this linkage in terms of accountability does not require further elaboration at this stage.

Finally, the principle of constitutionality requires that all organs of an IO should function effectively according to the powers and functions conferred upon it.[101] The association with both the principle of good

---

[95] As cited by P. Bekker, The Legal Position of Intergovernmental Organizations. A Functional analysis of Their Legal Status and Immunities, Martinus Nijhoff Publishers, Dordrecht, Boston, London, 1994, 265 pp., at p. 50, note 218.
[96] Amerasinghe, *op. cit.*, (note 54), at p. 137.
[97] Hugh Thirlway, The Law and Procedure of the International Court of Justice 1960-1989, Part Eight, B.Y.I.L., 1996, pp. 1-73, at p. 33.
[98] *Op. cit.*, at para. 1215.
[99] *Ibid.*
[100] Amerasinghe, *op. cit.*, (note 54), at p. 34.
[101] Thirlway, *op. cit.*, at p. 27.

governance and the principle of institutional balance which will be reviewed next is clear.

THE PRINCIPLE OF INSTITUTIONAL BALANCE

The essence of the principle of institutional balance has been aptly described by Sarooshi[102] when he wrote hat it entails that organs of an IO cannot step over "the institutional restraints laid down in the constituent instrument" and in determining how they exercise their powers cannot "perform a function which is antithetical to the processes of decision-making with which they have been invested...".

Schermers and Blokker have formulated the principle in a more positive way by saying that it requires each organ of an IO in exercising its competencies to respect other organs' competencies.[103]

The principle of institutional balance has been duly recognized upheld and elaborated in the case-law of international and regional courts and by international administrative tribunals.[104]

From an accountability perspective the principle of institutional balance does not prevent IO-s to be bound by binding decisions taken by a competent organ of that IO and addressed to the Member States.[105]

As to lower organs the principle of institutional balance requires them because of their hierarchical subordination to apply rules contained in recommendations issued by principal organs and addressed to Member States; in case the recommendation originates from another lower organ, each organ of the same level should at least be under an obligation to take the other's position into account.[106]

It may be added that the implications of the principle on the accountability of the IO and/or of the organs concerned, will be further determined by the corollary principle of subsidiarity and the principle of supervision and control .

---

[102] D. Sarooshi, the Legal Framework governing United Nations Subsidiary Organs, B.Y.I.L., 1996, pp. 413-478, at p. 464.
[103] Schermers and Blokker, *op. cit.*, at paras. 220 and 222.
[104] Certain Expenses Case ICJ, ECJ and UNAT body of jurisprudence.
[105] *Ibid.* at para. 1327.
[106] Schermers and Blokker, *op. cit.*, at paras. 1241 and 1243.

THE PRINCIPLE OF SUBSIDIARITY

In general term the organizational principle of subsidiarity as it is commonly understood requires that "a central authority should have subsidiary functions, performing only those tasks which cannot be performed effectively at more immediate or local level".[107] In other words the principle consists in "conferring or recognizing to each level those attributions which it is best able to make use of".[108]

From an accountability perspective the two faces and the two functions of subsidiarity as they have been identified by Constantinesco[109] are particularly relevant.

On the one hand, subsidiarity includes a protective prohibition under which anything that can be achieved by own efforts at a particular level should not be taken away and dealt with by some other level.

On the other hand, subsidiarity operates as a positive incentive when the ability at one level turns out to be inadequate: first appropriate measures should be taken to build up that ability at the lower level, before a transfer to a higher level.

Procedures for implementing the principle of subsidiarity should be put in place to govern the manner in which the powers assigned to organs of the IO are being exercised. Under such internal procedures, principal organs of an IO, -exception made for those of a judicial nature- shall regularly check that action envisaged complies with the provisions concerning subsidiarity as regards both the choice of legal instruments and the content of a proposal.

From the accountability perspective the question could be raised whether the principle of subsidiarity has a direct bearing not only on the extent to which supervision and control has to exercised over these organs, but may be even on their very establishment by principal organs. The latter aspect will be briefly dealt with now, while the principle of supervision and control will be addressed in the next subparagraph.

In passing it may be observed that if it would be accepted that the principle of subsidiarity was to allow action by an IO only "if resources permit"[110] then additional problems of accountability could certainly

---

[107] S. Peu, The subsidiarity model of global governance in the UN/ASEAN context, *Global Governance*, 1998, at p. 431.
[108] V. Constantinesco, Who's afraid of subsidiarity?, *Yearbook of European Law*, 1991, pp. 33-55, at p. 34.
[109] *Ibid.* at p. 35.
[110] *Ibidem*, at p. 52, note 65.

arise, also in combination with the sound financial management part of the principle of good governance.

As to the establishment of subsidiary organs, concerns of accountability do not seem to require the principle of subsidiarity to restrain or limit the inherent power of principal organs to establish them so that they can be of assistance in the exercise of their own express and implied powers under the constituent instrument.[111] This argument would apply *a fortiori* in cases where the establishment is aimed at performance by subsidiary organs of functions which the plenary organ cannot itself perform.[112] Indeed, as pointed out by Schermers and Blokker[113] an organ of an IO delegating some of its powers to other, inferior organs remains accountable for the actions of that subsidiary organ. And this will also provide the basis for the obligation of supervision and control. Under the same conditions the principle of subsidiarity certainly empowers primary principle organs to bring matters to the attention of secondary organs.

As to the accountability of the IO as such, it should not be forgotten that subsidiary organs once they have been lawfully established become subsidiary organs of the IO as a whole and not just subsidiary organs of their parent organs.[114]

The Principle of Supervision and Control

The principle of supervision and control through periodic evaluation of the activities of an IO and of its constituent organs may be considered to be in the process of developing into a general principle of contemporary international institutional law.

Suffices it to stress that the yardstick for the evaluation of *operational* activities should have been clearly conceptualized and articulated before its very start, in consultation between the IO and all beneficiary entities. As to *institutional* activities the principle of good governance provides the necessary guidance.

It goes without saying that the application of the principle of supervision and control occupies a prominent place in the overall context of accountability of IO-s, and this is irrespective of what kind of actors are exercising supervision and control: be it Member States and non-

---

[111] See Sarooshi, *op. cit.*, at pp. 422-431.
[112] *Ibid*.
[113] Schermers and Blokker, *op. cit.*, at paras. 225 and 230.
[114] Sarooshi, *op. cit.*, at p. 414.

state entities monitoring the conduct of IO-s, from both within and outside the IO, or principal organs vis-a-vis a variety of subordinate organs within the IO. We are only concerned here with this last modality.

Principal organs of an IO are under an obligation to exercise supervision and control over subordinate organs, whether they are auxiliary organs or subsidiary organs they themselves have established. It should be recalled that the rights which Member States or other entities possess with regard to a principal organ of an IO, they also possess in respect of its subsidiary organs.[115]

In order to qualify as "subsidiary" an organ, according to Sarooshi[116] necessarily needs a certain degree of independence from its parent organ in exercising its powers and functions, but as Thirlway has pointed out[117] this independence should not be unlimited if the organ is to remain subsidiary. The independence of a subsidiary organ from its parent organ may relate to administrative, political or legal matters, thus entailing a corresponding form of the subsidiary organ's own accountability. In spite of the importance of *budgetary control* remaining with the parent organ, the inter-linkage of the different forms of accountability (administrative, political, financial and legal) is undeniable both in terms of principle and as a matter of fact.

That a principal organ may be unable to exercise *operational control* over its subsidiary organ is not necessarily important in terms of characterizing an entity as a subsidiary organ[118], but it will certainly have a decisive impact on the accountability for whatever kind of operational activities might have been undertaken. In this same regard it is worth noting that Amerasinghe pointed out that subsidiary organs are under the functional control of the principal organ which has established them, whereas this functional control is lacking in the case of subordinate organs.[119]

In general it may be argued that an insufficient degree of supervision and control by the parent organ may result in a state of *de facto* independence with ensuing consequences in the field of accountability.

A few observations could be made with regard to the scope and extent of the supervision and control envisaged here.

---

[115] *Ibid.* at p. 447, note 145.
[116] *Ibid.* at p. 416.
[117] Thirlway, *op. cit.*, at p. 56.
[118] Sarooshi, *op. cit.*, at p. 440, note 116.
[119] Amerasinghe, *op. cit.*, (note 54) at p. 143.

Given the basic fact that IO-s are subject to the rule of law, the supervisory function of their primary organs implies that they should use their supervisory and controlling power to overrule any decisions by a subordinate organ if that decision is -even on a *prima facie* basis - contrary to any of the applicable legal layers mentioned in the Committee's First Report.[120]

Having regard to the juxtaposition of principal organs within most of the IO-s, the right of a principal organ to receive reports submitted by other principal organs for its consideration, does not include the right to issue directives to other principal organs unless this is expressly provided for in the constituent instrument.[121] From an accountability perspective the proper consideration of such a report, which has been submitted in conformity with appropriate requirements as to its format and content, should arguably imply the right of the principal organ to question the way in which the reporting organ has exercised its competence, and to voice its opinion on that, without however undermining the respect for the principle of institutional balance. An exception should be made of course for the exercise of its judicial competencies by any judicial organ; consideration of its report has to be limited to administrative and financial aspects of supervision, without however producing a negative impact on the performance of the judicial function proper.

The situation is different of course in the relationship between a principal organ and a subsidiary organ except once more if the latter has been established to carry out functions of a judicial nature. In the latter case, the parent organ cannot change individual decisions of the subsidiary organ which are an exercise of those unique powers and functions, which the parent organ could not itself perform, thus placing limitations on the exercise of supervision and control.[122]

In the other more common situation i.e. when the subsidiary organ has been established to assist the principal organ in the performance of its express or implied powers, the parent organ in exercising its supervision and control may and in some instances has to review and to change the decisions of its subsidiary organ.[123]

---

[120] *Op.cit.*, (note 3), at p. 591.
[121] B. Simma as cited by Sarooshi, *op. cit.*, at p. 474, note 277.
[122] Sarooshi, *op. cit.*, at pp. 452-453 and at p. 455.
[123] *Ibid.* at p. 457.

The Principle of Stating the Reasons for Decisions or a Particular Course of Action

The interconnection between the principles reviewed here and to which reference has already been made several times, also applies with regard to the principle of stating the reasons for decisions or particular courses of action.

The obligation to motivate its decisions and course of action (or inaction as the case may be) serves multiple purposes with regard to a particular organ. Compliance with this obligation will contribute to greater transparency, it will have an impact on the kind of procedure for the decision-making process, it will alleviate the democratic deficit, and it will undoubtedly enhance the chances for mechanisms of accountability to operate properly, e.g. through the exercise of supervision and control as indicated in the previous subparagraph.

The extent of the obligation to state reasons depends on the nature of the decision in question and on the context in which it was adopted.[124] Accordingly a distinction has to be drawn between decisions of a general nature and those having an individual character.

As to the first category the duty may be "confined to indicating the general situation which led to its adoption...the general objectives which it is intended to achieve".[125]

In order to give the parties (potentially) affected by a decision of an individual nature an opportunity to defend their rights and to enable Member States and all other interested entities to ascertain the circumstances in which the organ of an IO has applied the constituent instrument, the principal issues of law and fact upon which the decision is based should be set out in a concise but clear and relevant manner, so as to render understandable the reasoning.[126]

The vital place occupied by this principle in the accountability framework has to be duly recognized, even with regard to the majority of IO-s where no mechanisms of judicial review have been put into operation.

The case law of international administrative tribunals has demonstrated the way the principle has to be interpreted and applied in the field of employment relations within an IO. Suffices it here to indicate that the requirement of reasoning with respect to an internal measure

---

[124] ECJ as referred to by Usher, *op. cit.*, at p. 114.
[125] ECJ as cited by Usher, *ibid.*
[126] ECJ as referred to by Usher, *op. cit.*, at p. 115.

appears to be less strict according to whether it adversely affects merely the personal position of an international civil servant as compared with measures adversely affecting the staff member's statutory position.[127]

The Principle of the Protection of Legitimate Expectations.

Compliance with the principle of stating reasons for decisions or for a course of action also plays a role in connection with the principle of protection of legitimate expectations. Application of the former principle may indeed contribute to the creation of these legitimate expectations, while there will be an obligation to explain how and why an organ of an IO has acted, particularly when an affected party is treated otherwise than it might normally expect to be treated under applicable rules.[128]

The principle of the protection of legitimate expectations is underlying the requirement that IO-s should behave in a consistent manner,[129] and clearly contributes to optimizing the conditions in which issues of accountability may be raised. Indeed, it is clear that the "exercise of legislative and administrative discretion (by an organ of an IO) may be subject to severe constraints in situations where a legitimate expectation has been created".[130]

Although the principle of the protection of legitimate expectations appears to lend itself more to application to individual decisions, it could also relate, when appropriate, to the exercise of more general powers.[131]

Generally it has to be acknowledged that legitimate expectations may be based on an assurance given in precise terms but not on a statement made by an organ of an IO in general terms.[132] In this same line of thought one should add that the non-approval of a proposal by an organ of an IO does not necessarily carry with it the inference that a collective pronouncement is made in a sense opposite to that proposed.[133]

---

[127] ECJ as referred to by Usher, *op. cit.*, at p.117.
[128] ECJ as referred to by Usher, *op. cit.*, at pp. 112-113.
[129] *Ibid.* at p. 103.
[130] *Ibid.* at p. 57.
[131] ECJ as referred to by Usher, *op. cit.*, at p. 57.
[132] *Ibid.*
[133] ICJ in the Namibia Advisory opinion as referred to by Thirlway, *op. cit.*, at p. 30.

The application of the principle considered here obviously varies according to the identity of interested parties and the kind of decisions or course of conduct implicated in its invocation. At least one thing is clear: the principle does not mean that interested parties may always rely on it that the particular way in which certain problems have been treated by an IO in the past will remain similar in the future.[134] The following examples may help to demonstrate that.

Liability may arise for harm caused by an act of an organ of an IO infringing the principle of protection of legitimate expectations by failing to allow a transitional period before abolishing a system of a compensatory nature e.g. in staff employment regulations.[135] Affected *third parties* however are not allowed to assert vested rights when confronted with internal rules of an IO being amended.[136]

With regard to IO-s operating in the areas of economic, financial and commodity transactions, economic operators may not have a legitimate expectation -which could claim protection- that a situation which may be modified at the discretion of an organ of the IO will be maintained.[137]

The ordering or authorizing of coercive measures by an executive organ of an IO may or is bound to override the protection of legitimate expectations of the traders in question, be it alone because their adoption may have been a matter of urgency.[138]

The principle of the protection of legitimate expectations does not imply that Member States and other interested entities may rely on previous lawful conduct of an organ of an IO with regard to coercive measures which may be imposed for breaches of applicable law,[139] but on the other hand the principle would seem to imply that a target State may rely on coercive measures against it being relaxed, suspended or withdrawn once it has fulfilled the conditions set forth in the enabling resolutions. Conversely an organ of an IO cannot be forced by virtue of the principle of the protection of legitimate expectations to apply governing rules *contra legem*.[140]

---

[134] Schermers and Blokker, *op. cit.*, at para. 1339.
[135] ECJ as referred to by Usher, *op. cit.*, at p. 56.
[136] Schermers and Blokker, *op. cit.* at para.1200.
[137] ECJ as referred to by Usher, *op. cit.*, at p. 58.
[138] See further Usher, *op. cit.* at p. 53.
[139] *Ibid.* at p. 107.
[140] CFI as referred to by Usher, *op. cit.*, at p. 61.

The principle also implies a prohibition for an organ of an IO to provide misleading information, which could have caused an error in the mind of a prudent third party.[141]

THE PRINCIPLE OF PROPORTIONALITY

Each IO should ensure compliance with the principle of proportionality according to which any action of an IO shall not go beyond what is necessary to achieve the objectives of the constituent instrument.[142] This principle which embodies a basic concept of fairness[143] clearly has to be interpreted and applied in relationship with other relevant principles such as good governance, the principle of constitutionality and the concept of functional necessity still to be reviewed later.

The potential scope of application of this principle as it was indicated by Usher[144] can claim general validity to all IO-s. The proportionality may be tested in the context of determining the competence of an IO and of its organs, it may operate in relation to the burdens imposed on Member States and other entities coming within an Organization's functional jurisdiction and in assessing the conduct of Member States.

Th principle of proportionality requires that measures taken by the organs of an IO should be appropriate to achieve the objectives pursued without going beyond what is necessary to that end.[145] In order to establish consistency with the principle of proportionality, "it is necessary to establish, in the first place, whether the means it employs to achieve the aims corresponds to the importance of the aim and, in the second place, whether they are necessary for its achievement".[146] Relevant questions of accountability may arise in connection with the mandate and further terms of reference of peacekeeping-operations or with regard to the imposition and continued application of coercive measures by executive organs of an IO. In this last respect, still a further question concerns the accountability of the IO in the process of monitoring the implementation of coercive measures at the national level by Member States.

---

[141] ECJ as referred to by Usher, *op. cit.* at p. 112.
[142] *Ibid.* at p. 7. Article 1 of the Treaty of Amsterdam.
[143] *Ibid.* at p. 37.
[144] *Ibid.*
[145] *Ibid.* at p. 38.
[146] ECJ as referred to by Usher, *op. cit.*, at p. 39.

Further elaboration of the principle brings to the fore that when there is a choice between several measures, recourse must be had to the least onerous, and the disadvantages caused must not be disproportionate to the aims pursued.[147]

The principle of proportionality would be breached if Member States or another party were to be penalized by an IO for its failure to comply with a secondary obligation as severely as in cases where a primary obligation is at stake.[148] Examples of this may be found not only in the area of staff employment relations but also with regard to private law contracts with providers of goods and services for the daily or emergency operations of an IO.

Technical requirements and considerations of cost-effectiveness may however in practice limit the principle of proportionality. Furthermore, the test of reasonableness comes in relating to both the burden imposed on e.g. the trader or the staff member, and on the competent organ of the IO.[149]

THE PRINCIPLE OF PROCEDURAL REGULARITY

Because general principles of law, such as objectivity and good faith are providing insufficient guarantee for the protection of minorities and individual Members of an IO the constituent instrument should provide for the elaboration of rules of procedure. This justification given by Schermers and Blokker[150] also applies to the protection of international civil servants, and to a lesser degree, to that of interested or affected third parties.

Analyzing the "mature body of substantive law" which has been elaborated by international administrative tribunals, Amerasinghe drew a distinction which is of a more general application, between substantive and procedural irregularities.[151] Abuse of discretion, error of law or fact leading to mistaken conclusions would come within the first category, with arbitrariness operating as a residual concept; a broad concept of due process is at the heart of procedural regularity, with the residual

---

[147] Ibid..
[148] ECJ as referred to by Usher, *op. cit.*, at p. 43.
[149] Ibid. at p. 50.
[150] Op. cit., at para. 1205.
[151] Amerasinghe, *op. cit.*, (note 53), at p. 788.

idea of fair treatment, with its reference to the general, legal notions of procedural justice and fair play.[152]

From an accountability point of view, the right to a fair procedure when discretionary decisions are being taken is particularly important when mechanisms of judicial review are not available or are not open to affected parties.

The right to a fair hearing and the right to be heard must be guaranteed in all proceedings before an organ of an IO initiated against a Member State or a non-State entity or an individual and which are liable to culminate in a measure adversely affecting that Member State, non-state entity or individual.[153] For instance, except in cases of urgency, an express requirement of prior notice to an offending member of an IO, with the possibility of due process, should be an essential part of the procedure to be followed by any organ vested with executive powers when it is considering the imposition of coercive measures.[154]

It should be added that with regard to operational activities of IO-s in the areas of humanitarian and development assistance, the general rule applies that a person whose interests are perceptibly affected by a decision taken by a public authority must be given the opportunity to make his point of view known.[155]

THE PRINCIPLE OF OBJECTIVITY AND IMPARTIALITY

From both the spirit of a constituent instrument of an IO and from the express provision of a competence to adopt internal rules of procedure, a general principle may be drawn of objectivity and impartiality in the conduct of the work of its organs.[156] The principle of objectivity and impartiality is of a fundamental nature for a proper functioning of an IO both in its institutional and operational activities. Even wrongful perceptions that an IO is not fully complying with the principle are likely to undermine the Organization's credibility.

Compliance with the different aspects of the principle of good governance, such as transparency, access to information, and good reporting and evaluation will create the necessary conditions for any

---

[152] See also Yehuda Z. Blum, Eroding the United Nations Charter, Martinus Nijhoff Publishers, Dordrecht, Boston, London, 1993, 285 pp., at pp. 9-10.
[153] ECJ as referred to by Usher, *op. cit.*, at p. 73.
[154] Based on Amerasinghe, *op. cit.*, (note 54), at p. 117.
[155] ECJ as referred to by Usher, *op. cit.*, at p. 76.
[156] Conforti as cited by Blum, *op. cit.*, at pp. 9-10.

assessment as to conformity by the IO with the principle of objectivity and impartiality.

The principle of objectivity and impartiality has been described as the heart and the soul of the office of the Secretary-general of an IO by former Secretary-general Javier Perez de Cuellar.[157] The Secretary-general's personal accountability may be raised in cases where serious doubts exist as to his full compliance with the principle.

Presiding officers of an organ of an IO and Chairmen of Committees have to perform their functions on behalf of the entire membership of that organ or Committee in a fair and impartial way and to ensure a balanced debate.[158]

From an accountability perspective operational activities of an IO are particularly vulnerable to charges and allegations that the principle of objectivity and impartiality is being violated e.g. in the areas of humanitarian and development assistance, or peacekeeping-operations.

THE PRINCIPLE OF DUE DILIGENCE

The principle of due diligence entails a number of basic obligations for the Member States as members of organs of an IO, for organs of an IO as such, and for officials, staff members and experts. Some of these obligations mirror aspects of other principles mentioned before.

From an accountability perspective the following obligations could be mentioned: to secure the lawfulness of actions and decisions of the IO; to secure the financial efficiency of these actions; to secure the administrative efficiency of these actions; to prevent harm caused by decisions and actions; and to redress or remove damages.

In certain areas of the functioning of IO-s where sovereignty of Member States is being exercised collectively e.g. through a non-plenary organ vested with executive powers or otherwise, it could be argued that even the principle of *utmost care* is applicable.

The principle of due diligence covers *inter alia* the duty to reply to requests and to act in due time and the duty not to delay rectifying wrongful information.[159]

---

[157] Cited by Schermers and Blokker, *op. cit.*, para. 462.
[158] Blum, *op. cit.*, at p. 163.
[159] Usher, *op. cit.*, at pp. 107 and 111.

The Principle of Promoting Justice.

Every IO should in general take all the appropriate steps available to it to promote the interests of justice.[160] The scope of application of this principle covers both the internal and external functioning of an IO.

As it is the accepted purpose and function of an IO to employ staff and to conduct smooth and effective personnel relations, it has an inherent power to set up an administrative tribunal.[161] The principle of promoting justice seems also to require that statutes of administrative tribunals should not exclude from the scope of their jurisdiction certain kinds of employment disputes arising from the application of resolutions of the highest legislative bodies of the IO if they are "effectively to discharge their function of giving staff adequate protection".[162] It would also not be in the best interest of international administrative justice that IAT-s "unnecessarily interpret their jurisdiction narrowly".[163]

In the external sphere of its functioning an IO should be bound by a duty to secure co-operation with both international and national judicial authorities who may contact it in order to obtain information which organs of an IO can supply to it.[164] Issues of potential accountability of the organs of an IO, of the IO as such or of its officials may very well be at the roots of difficulties arising in respect of this duty to supply information to national or international judicial authorities. The ongoing debate about testimony before the Ad Hoc International Criminal Tribunals and about potential limits to be imposed upon the claims to immunities before domestic courts bear witness of this dilemma.

The principle of promoting justice clearly is also underpinning the need for IO-s to provide remedies to all interested parties who want to raise the accountability of a particular IO for not having complied with any of the yardsticks which the Committee has been referring to in its First Report.[165] The complex question of the establishment and operation of these mechanisms for redress will be dealt with separately in a later publication.

---

[160] Council of Europe Report 1969 as referred to by Bekker, *op. cit.*, at p. 185.
[161] Amerasinghe, *op. cit.*, (note 54), at p. 451.
[162] Amerasinghe, *op. cit.*, (note 53), at pp. 785-786.
[163] *Ibid*.
[164] ECJ as referred to by Usher, *op. cit.*, at p. 66.
[165] *Op. cit.*, (note 3) at pp. 601-602.

THE CONCEPT OF FUNCTIONAL NECESSITY.

At this stage it is worth recalling that the Committee has recognized from the start of its activities that the envisaged model rules will have to keep the balance between preserving the necessary autonomy in decision-making of IO-s and guaranteeing that they will not be able to avoid accountability.[166] It is at this juncture that the concept of functional necessity becomes instrumental.

The political and financial independence of IO-s is of a functional nature i.e. it is limited to what is necessary and nothing more "to enable an organization to exercise its functions in the fulfilment of the purposes for which it was created".[167]

Although the concept of functional necessity has mainly or exclusively been used in connection with issues of privileges and immunities of IO-s it seems to have a more general scope of application as a restraining factor on the arguments and mechanisms an IO may invoke or turn to in order to limit, to render difficult – or impossible even – the *mise-en-oeuvre* of its accountability or to create a maze in the net of accountability for decisions or acts or omissions which allegedly were not in conformity with the multiple, applicable yardsticks.

The concept of functional necessity ranges in its application from a maximum standard in order to determine whether an IO has a justified need for protection, to the minimum requirement that exclusion of a particular treatment does not result in preventing the IO from effectively exercising its functions.[168]

It is important to note that the inherent right of an IO to unilaterally qualify its activities is not unlimited: independent review of that qualification, using *inter alia*, the concept of functional necessity, may constitute an important element in the *mise-en-oeuvre* of the Organization's accountability.

PROPOSITIONS ON FINANCIAL ACCOUNTABILITY

After a thorough analysis of the relevant jurisprudence of the International Court of Justice Amerasinghe has formulated a number of propositions on financial accountability which may be transposed to IO-s in general and which are reproduced here without any changes.

---

[166] *Ibidem*, at p. 602.
[167] Bekker, op.cit., at p. 109.
[168] *Ibid.* at pp. 115-116.

"Administrative expenses" (those in the regular budget) are not the only expenditures for which an organization is responsible.

Expenses of an organization include expenditures resulting from the functional operations of an organization authorized by its constitution.

Expenses incurred in accordance with resolutions of organs of an organization which are made in conformity with its constitution and are, therefore, not *ultra vires* are expenses of the organization.

Expenditures incurred pursuant to resolutions of organs which are within the scope of functions of an organization, but are not in conformity with its constitution in a "non-essential" particular are expenses of the organization.

Expenditures incurred pursuant to resolutions of organs which are not within the scope of functions of an organization or are within the scope of functions of an organization but do not conform to the provisions of its constitution in an essential particular and are, therefore, *ultra vires* are not expenses of the organization.

Expenditures incurred by the executive organ of an organization pursuant to decisions of other organs, which are not *ultra vires*, or incurred directly pursuant to provisions of the constitution are not expenses of the organization, if the act of the executive organ is outside the "scope of its apparent authority", while they are such expenses if the act is within the "scope of its apparent authority".

The same principles apply to organizations in general as reflected above in regard to tortuous acts of servants and agents, breaches of contract, judicial and arbitral awards and extra-judicial settlements. It may be concluded that all expenses incurred as a result of the responsibility of an organization are expenses of the organization."[169]

The further issues relating to the *mise-en-oeuvre* of the financial accountability of IO-s, including the problem of the distribution of the financial burden between the IO-s and their Member States will be reviewed in a later publication.

CONCLUSION

The codification of the principles reviewed in this paper would constitute a first but crucial step in establishing a comprehensive account-

---

[169] Amerasinghe, *op. cit.*, 9 (note 54), at pp. 313-314.

ability framework for the decisions, conduct and omissions of international organizations.

VIEWS FROM PRACTICE

Larry D. Johnson[*]

Before I comment on the topic before us, I should stress that what follows are my own personal observations and do not in any way reflect any official views on the part of the organization with which I am affiliated. Having said that, I was intrigued by the subject matter since I have difficulty understanding precisely what is at issue or what the purpose of the question is. I am not sure what is meant by "proliferation of accountability" or "rules on accountability of international organizations".

A few basic points of departure, at least from my own perspective which is that of a practitioner, not an academic:

- What is accountability? From my own perspective, it simply means responsibility of one actor for conduct (acts or omissions) owed to another actor.
- Accountability of whom and to whom? For an international organization as a whole, accountability can be to its Member States (the creators and "owners" of the organization) and/or to the public or other outsiders. Within an organization, organs are usually accountable to each other, all depending on the division of functions as set out in the constituent instrument and rules of the organization.
- Are there control mechanisms to ensure accountability (sanctions, etc.)?

With the above framework in mind, I have attempted to gather what at least I consider to be examples from UN practice of accountability. To begin, I will consider accountability within the internal regime of an international organization. I have done so from the standpoint of four "actors" within that regime:

- Member States
- Organs or bodies of the organization
- The Chief administrative officer
- The staff

---

[*] Legal Advisor, IAEA

As will be seen, there is obviously a good deal of overlapping and whether or not it is possible or particularly helpful to draw conclusions from the limited examples is an open question, at least in my view.

ACCOUNTABILITY WITHIN THE INTERNAL REGIME OF AN INTERNATIONAL ORGANIZATION

ACCOUNTABILITY OF MEMBER STATES

To other Member States

Obviously basic contractual and treaty obligations are owed by the Member States of an organization to each other: they are bound to fulfill the obligations of the constituent instrument which they have freely accepted. Article 2(2) of the UN Charter provides that all Members shall fulfil in good faith the obligations assumed by them in accordance with the Charter. They may also be bound to fulfill obligations to other Member States set out in other instruments, such as those detailing the privileges and immunities to be accorded to representatives of Member States to the organization (see Article 105(2) of the Charter). Such other agreements may be a "general" convention on privileges and immunities or an ad hoc host country agreement (either for the headquarters of an organization or for the holding of a particular conference or meeting).

As to fulfilling the general obligations under the treaty establishing the organization, each treaty may contain its own "control" or sanctions provisions in case a Member does not fulfill its obligations. In the UN Charter, for example, Article 6 provides for expulsion from the Organization of a Member "which has persistently violated the Principles" of the Charter and Article 5 provides for suspension of the exercise of the rights and privileges of membership of a Member "against which preventive or enforcement action has been taken by the Security Council". In the Statute of the International Atomic Energy Agency, there is a similar provision regarding suspension from the exercise of the privileges and rights of membership (article XIX.B) and a further provision that if a Member is found to be in non-compliance with its obligations under the Agency's safeguards regime, the Agency shall report the non-compliance to the UN Security Council and the General Assembly (article XII.C).

To organs or bodies of the organization

Within the UN, Members are responsible for paying their apportioned share of the expenses of the Organization (Article 17) and if a Member's arrears in payments equals or exceeds the amount due for the preceding two full years, it shall have no vote in the General Assembly (Article 19). However, should the General Assembly be satisfied that the failure of the Member to pay "is due to conditions beyond its control", it may nevertheless permit that Member to vote. The Assembly has established a procedure to examine claims by such members that failure to pay was due to conditions beyond their control (the Committee on Contributions examines the claim and makes a recommendation to the Assembly).

Another example is that Members of the UN are obliged under Article 2 (5) to give the Organization "every assistance in any action" it takes in accordance with the Charter. Under Article 25, Members agree to accept and carry out the decisions of the Security Council and to that end, the Security Council has established "Sanctions Committees" to oversee the implementation and application of sanctions imposed under Chapter VII and to which Members are to submit reports, requests for interpretation, etc. In the legal field, Members undertake to comply with decisions of the International Court of Justice in cases to which they are party (Article 94(1)). Moreover, if any party to a case fails to perform the obligations incumbent upon it under a judgment rendered by the Court, the other party may have recourse to the Security Council which may, if it deems necessary, make recommendations or decide upon measures to be taken to give effect to the judgment (Article 94(2)).

There are countless other examples where agreements are made between an organization and a Member which engage the responsibility of a Member vis-à-vis an organ or body of the organization. For example, contracts, technical assistance/UNDP agreements and host agreements for meetings often contain clauses by which a Member agrees to "hold harmless" the organization in the event of claims, liability, etc. In those cases, the Member is firstly accountable to the Secretariat with whom the agreement was concluded, but may eventually be accountable to the intergovernmental body which has mandated or approved the particular activity or which is responsible for administrative and financial matters.

To the Chief Administrative Officer; and to the staff

The most obvious example here is Article 100(2) of the Charter by which Members undertake to respect the exclusively international character of the responsibilities of the Secretary-General and the staff and undertake not to seek to influence them in the discharge of their responsibilities. Similar provisions appear in the constituent instruments of other international organizations (e.g., IAEA Statute, article VII.F). Article 105 of the Charter of the UN provides for privileges and immunities for the Organization as a whole as well as for officials of the Organization and, as was noted above with regard to privileges and immunities of representatives of Members, additional agreements to which Members are bound may also cover this subject matter. Intergovernmental organs of an organization may focus attention on particular obligations owed to the staff, such as providing the safety and security necessary for the staff to exercise their functions.

In the programme and budget field, Member States are responsible for establishing/eliminating programmes (without prejudice of course to legally mandated programmes under the constituent instrument or international agreements) and for setting priorities among them; chief administrative officers often attempt to hold them accountable for this responsibility.

ACCOUNTABILITY OF ORGANS OR BODIES OF THE ORGANIZATION

To Member States

In this area one finds the usual important questions of principle; after all, the Member States have established the organization, given the organs various mandates to perform and in the final analysis the organs are responsible to the mandate-givers for that performance. For example, in Article 2 of the Charter setting out its Principles, it provides that the Organization, as well as its Members, shall act in accordance with those Principles, including the famous para. 7 which states that nothing in the Charter shall authorize the UN to intervene in matters which are essentially within the domestic jurisdiction of any State or shall require the Members to submit such matters to settlement under the Charter (without prejudice to the application of enforcement measures under Chapter VII).

Policing of organs to ensure compliance with mandates or that organs act within the confines of constitutional provisions, has not normally been assigned by constituent instruments to any particular organ, nor, at least in the UN system, to any court or tribunal (the EU or treaty-based systems are not covered here). Although according authority to the International Court of Justice to act as a sort of "constitutional court" was suggested at San Francisco, it was not accepted. In some sense, the advisory opinion facility in the Statute might be seen as one way to deal with such questions, albeit only if an authorized organ requests an opinion and that the Court's conclusion is advisory. Otherwise, organs police themselves and deal with challenges of lack of mandate, ultra vires actions, competence, etc. within the context of their own rules and procedures. In the first instance, subsidiary organs have to determine any such challenges and questions, and if they have determined incorrectly or have questions, it is for the parent organ to resolve the matter.

What happens if a Member State believes that an organ has acted ultra vires, but is not in a position to challenge the action or has not succeeded in persuading the requisite majority of the correctness of its view? From a practical point of view, there are few options:

- withdrawal from membership. In the Charter there are no provisions for withdrawal, but Indonesia in the 1960s purported to withdraw, but upon its change of mind, simply resumed its participation more or less as if nothing had happened. In other organizations, withdrawal is envisaged as a possibility, e.g. article XVII.D of the IAEA Statute provides that at any time after 5 years from the entry into force of the Statute (1957) or whenever a Member is unwilling to accept an amendment to the Statute, it may withdraw from the Agency by notice in writing to that effect given to the depositary (US Government), which shall promptly inform the Agency's Board of Governors and all members. The Democratic People's Republic of Korea is an example of a State having withdrawn from Agency membership.

- unilateral measures. Some States boycott meetings or conferences or activities, although this may be of limited, and perhaps counterproductive, value given what happened in 1950 when the Security Council took decisions calling for assistance to the Republic of Korea at a time when the USSR was boycotting the Council over the seating of the Republic of China. Other measures may entail withdrawal of funding for voluntary programmes or failure to follow what are sometimes referred to as "moral or political" – but not legal – commitments. Illegal measures may also be taken, such as not paying assessed contributions.

To other organs or bodies of the organization

Accountability between co-equal organs is not readily apparent, other than each organ performing its statutory functions. In the Charter, there are several instances where the Security Council makes recommendations to the Assembly which takes the final decision (see e.g., membership, suspension, expulsion, appointment of Secretary-General); each organ must act within its own sphere and not purport to assume the role of the other. With regard the subsidiary organs, the situation is clear: they are responsible to the organs which established them.

Article 12 of the Charter is of interest since it provides that the while the Security Council is exercising in respect of any dispute or situation the functions assigned to it in the Charter, the General Assembly shall not make any recommendations with regard to that dispute or situation unless the Council so requests. That provision has not been easy to apply, given the obvious factual/political questions of what constitutes a dispute/situation, when is the Council "exercising" its functions with regard to such a dispute/situation, and does the bar to making recommendations prevent the Assembly from inscribing an agenda item on the matter and holding a debate thereon. In practice, the Assembly has "policed itself" by debating and adopting resolutions on various questions which were also on the agenda of the Council, without the Council indicating formally any difficulty with the Assembly having done so. The clearest case with which the Council might indeed have difficulty would be both organs meeting at exactly the same time on the same dispute/situation.

Another example of the inter-play between these two organs is with respect to the maintenance of international peace and security. As a result of the veto, the Assembly has devised a procedure (the 1950 "Uniting for Peace" resolution) whereby if the Council fails to exercise its primary responsibility for the maintenance of international peace and security because of "lack of unanimity" (i.e. a veto was cast), the Council by a procedural vote or a majority of the members of the Assembly may call for an "emergency special session" of the Assembly to consider the matter. The legality of the Assembly establishing peace-keeping missions and approving expenses as "expenses of the Organization" was considered by the ICJ in its landmark 1962 "Certain Expenses of the United Nations" advisory opinion.

To the Chief Administrative Officer

Again, the main responsibility is for the organs to perform their statutory functions while allowing the Chief administrative officer to perform his/hers. Experience has shown a great deal of Member State interest in how a Chief administrative officer acts in the areas as budget and personnel, sometimes, in the view of the Chief administrative officer, interfering with the exercise of his/her statutory or mandated authority. In other cases the Secretary-General is left a degree of latitude, such as in the day-to-day running of peacekeeping operations, but while maintaining constant informal consultations with the Council and its members. In some cases, areas of responsibility are more clearly delineated between States Members, organs and the Chief administrative officer, such as in financial rules and regulations.

It may be noted here that the Secretary-General does not have the facility to request an advisory opinion of the ICJ which could be used to challenge what he/she perceives to be ultra vires actions on the part of an organ or body of an organization. While several Secretaries-General have requested authorization to do so under Article 96(2), the Assembly has not acted on those requests.

To the staff

A few basic obligations obtain, again to fulfill statutory functions such as establishing staff regulations (e.g., Article 101 of the Charter) and upholding decisions and procedures concerning staff representation and grievances, such as providing some form of in-house labour grievance machinery involving third-party dispute settlement (e.g., various Administrative Tribunals). Organs are required to follow the judgments of such Tribunals and appropriate any funds due to implement monetary awards granted in judgments, as per a 1954 ICJ opinion on "Effects of awards of compensation" made be the UN Administrative Tribunal.

There are no procedures as such for "controlling" organs vis-a-vis responsibilities owed to the staff. Although staff unions exist, the "right to strike" is controversial and has not to my knowledge been formally accepted by a UN intergovernmental body (the ILO may be a different matter). There are staff rules and regulations prohibiting individual staff members or groups thereof from lobbying or making representations to Member States, other than through authorized staff representatives or by the Chief administrative officer on their behalf.

Accountability of the Chief administrative officer

To Member States

The Chief administrative officer, as well as the staff, are accountable to Member States to ensure compliance with the obligation not to seek or receive instructions from any Government or from any other authority external to the Organization and to refrain from any action which might reflect on their position as international officials responsible only to the Organization (Article 100(1) of the Charter and Article VII.F of the IAEA Statute).

In addition, in the recruitment and employment of staff and in the determination of conditions of service, the paramount consideration to be given by the Chief administrative officer is the necessity of securing the highest conditions of efficiency, competence, and integrity, due regard being paid to the importance of recruiting the staff on as wide a geographical basis as possible (Article 101 (3)). In may be of interest to note that other criteria may be listed, e.g. in the Statute of the IAEA, in addition to the foregoing, the Director General shall also pay due regard to "the contributions of members of the Agency" (article VII.D).

Particular obligations may be assumed by Chief administrative officers vis-a-vis certain Member States, such as the host country of the organization or of ad hoc meetings or conferences, principally in the privileges and immunities field. For example, such officers normally have the right and duty to waive the immunity of any official in any case where, in his/her opinion, the immunity would impede the course of justice. In addition, Chief administrative officers agree to cooperate at all times with the appropriate authorities of Member States to facilitate the proper administration of justice, secure the observance of police regulations and prevent the occurrence of any abuse in connection with privileges, immunities and facilities granted to officials (see sections 20 and 21 of the Convention on the Privileges and Immunities of the UN).

To organs or bodies of the organization

Besides being responsible to the various organs and bodies for the implementation of statutory functions and mandates, the Chief administrative officer may be "under the authority and subject to the control" of an organ (e.g. article VII.B of the IAEA Statute).

As indicated above, complying with mandated functions and tasks and the consequential oversight thereof by organs may lead to situations of perceived "micro-management" or, at best, a high degree of organ interest in the actions of the Chief administrative officer. This might well be understandable in areas of the budget and personnel, where Member States' funds are being expended by the Chief administrative officer. One example is a resolution adopted by the General Assembly in April 1999 on "Procurement-related arbitration" by which the latter expressed "deep concern" about the increase of such arbitration claims instituted against the UN and requested the Secretary-General to submit a report covering, inter alia: the roles/mandates of negotiating teams in arbitration and settlement processes; the selection of outside legal counsels and provisions to preclude conflict of interest; disciplinary action taken against staff members responsible for wrongdoing that resulted in arbitration; measures taken to prevent/reduce contract disputes leading to arbitration in future (resolution 53/217 of 7 April 1999).

If the Chief administrative officer finds it is impossible to perform a particular mandate for any number of reasons, ranging from changed factual situation to lack of resources, such non-compliance and reasons therefor should be reported back to the relevant organ. At least in the UN and the IAEA, there is no statutory provision for removal from office of the Chief administrative officer.

To the staff

As Chief administrative officer, he/she is responsible for applying and implementing staff rules and regulations, as well as the judgments of the relevant Administrative Tribunal.

This appears to be the one case where the question of "proliferation" of accountability has arisen. Within the UN system of organizations, at least 3 Administrative Tribunals exist (UN, ILO and World Bank Administrative Tribunals) each with its own judges and jurisprudence. The argument can be made that at least for the organizations members of the "common system" (those subject to ICSC decisions re terms and conditions of staff employment), a common administrative tribunal makes sense. On the other hand, even with a "common system" each organization maintains its own staff rules and regulations and decisions of any tribunal would by definition have to be based on the rules and practices of the organization in question. Although a proposal was put forward in the UN for a single administrative tribunal for the "common system" organizations, it was not pursued by Member States.

Accountability of staff

To Member States

The accountability of staff is identical to that mentioned above with regard to that of the Chief administrative officer.

To organs or bodies of the organization

Accountability of staff is maintained through accountability of the Chief administrative officer. Just as staff are not to individually lobby or attempt to influence Member States or organs, so to Member States and organs should address all requests, complaints, questions to the Chief administrative officer or his/her duly appointed representative, not to individual staff members.

To the Chief Administrative Officer

This section would be too over-burdened if it were to go into any great detail on this issue, since obviously this relates to a contractual employer-employee situation, involving the interpretation and application of staff rules, regulations and practices of each organization. As indicated above, even with the "common system" each organization has its own rules, regulations and practices to be followed.

As to "control", in this area it takes the form of disciplinary measures for misconduct, or of reimbursement to the organization for financial loss suffered by the organization as a result of negligence or violations of any regulation, rule or administrative instruction (e.g., IAEA Staff Rule 13.03.4). Recently, organizations have begun to turn cases of alleged criminal conduct over to local jurisdictions for investigation and/or prosecution, even though such action might involve waiver, at least to a limited extent, of the immunities of certain officials who might have to file the complaint and/or appear as witnesses in domestic court proceedings.

ACCOUNTABILITY OF AN ORGANIZATION AND ITS STAFF TO OUTSIDERS

To Third-Parties

Normally, international organizations maintain immunity of their property, including assets, from attachment or execution, as well as immunity of their staff for official functions (the latter being waivable as indicated above). Third parties must, however, be offered some form of alternative peaceful settlement of disputes, normally arbitration.

Liability of the organization

Some organizations, such as the UN, are self-insured against liability claims and have their own claims boards, etc. (sometimes with a liability limit set by an intergovernmental body). Others maintain liability insurance.

Peacekeeping/peace enforcement situations

Recent questions have arisen with regard to the liability of the organization to third parties arising out of peacekeeping operations. The General Assembly has adopted decisions regulating this matter (i.e. resolution 52/247 of 17 July 1998).

On the question of the observance of United Nations forces of international humanitarian law, the Secretary-General has recently issued a bulletin setting out the fundamental principles and rules of international law applicable to UN forces conducting operations under United Nations command and control (ST/SGB/1999/13).

On UN officials appearing before international criminal tribunals established by the Security Council as enforcement measures under Chapter VII of the Charter, arrangements have had to be worked out between senior officials of certain programmes (e.g. UNHCR) and officials of tribunals, to ensure responsiveness to questions from the tribunal while at the same time preserving those aspects of the programme's work which require confidentiality in order to maintain the credibility of the programme.

Indebtedness of staff members to outsiders

Staff members are expected to meet their legally established personal financial obligations and conduct themselves in a manner befitting that of international civil servants (including personal integrity). Yet it is not possible for the court of a local jurisdiction to order the attachment of the salary of a staff member as a result of his/her indebtedness to third parties. However, in 1999, the Secretary-General issued a new bulletin concerning the family and child support obligations of staff members in which he set out the conditions under which the Organization would authorize deductions from a staff member's salary to meet third party indebtedness obligations in the case of final court orders for family or child support (ST/SGB/1999/4).

ACCOUNTABILITY TO THE "OUTSIDE" WORLD AT LARGE

It is sometimes said that organizations should be held accountable to the public at large or to "civil society" for their actions since it is the general public through taxes which funds the organizations and which ultimately must show support for the organizations. Transparency and involving as many actors from civil society as possible warrant increased out-reach by organizations, it is said. This view may well be a valid policy position, but does not involve the kind of accountability previously discussed which focused more on accountabilities generated by legal texts, rules and procedures.

THE QUESTION

Returning to the question posed, from my perspective of what is meant by accountability, I do not believe it is readily apparent that there is a need for general rules of accountability of international organizations, nor do I believe it would be desirable or possible in some areas to do so. With the possible exception of a single administrative tribunal, I see no need, from a practitioner's point of view, to pursue the question. Although no doubt an examination of the different varieties of accountability/responsibility may prove interesting and perhaps useful from an academic point of view, I remain to be convinced that from the practical point of view, it would serve any particularly useful purpose to develop "general rules on accountability of international organizations".

THE WORLD BANK INSPECTION PANEL: A MODEL FOR OTHER INTERNATIONAL ORGANIZATIONS?[*]

By Sabine Schlemmer-Schulte[**]

INTRODUCTION

The session of the conference for which this paper was solicited dealt with "The Proliferation of Accountability: Separate Rules for Individual Organizations or General Rules on Accountability of International Organizations?" In view of this topic, two observations of a more general nature should be made before entering into a discussion of the specific issue of the extent to which the World Bank Inspection Panel can serve as a model for other international inter-governmental organizations.

---

[*] Paper presented at the conference on "Proliferation of International Organizations: Legal Issues" held from November 18 to 20, 1999 in Leiden, the Netherlands. This paper reflects the personal views of the author and should not be attributed to the institutions she works for or is affiliated with. The paper is intended to contribute to the discussion on possible inspection functions in international organizations other than the World Bank rather than to prescribe the Inspection Panel as a model for these organizations with which the author of this paper is less familiar than with the World Bank both from an academic's as well as a practitioner's point of view.

[**] Dr. jur., LL.M. (International Business Law), LL.M. (European Banking Law), LL.M. (European Union Law), LL.B., L.E.D., Attorney at Law; Senior Counsel, Office of the Vice President and General Counsel, World Bank; Adjunct Professor, Washington College of Law of American University, School of Advanced International Services of Johns Hopkins University, both Washington, D.C., and John Marshall School of Law, Chicago, Illinois; and Member of the Committee on Accountability of International Organizations of the International Law Association (ILA). The author is grateful to Dr. Ibrahim F.I. Shihata, Secretary-General, ICSID, former Senior Vice President and General Counsel, World Bank, and legal architect of the Inspection Panel, for sharing his insights in Panel matters with her since she started working with him in 1995. She would also like to thank Dr. Andrés Rigo Sureda, then Acting Vice President and General Counsel, World Bank, for supporting her participation in the conference. Finally, she thanks Mr. Ko-Yung Tung, Vice President and General Counsel, World Bank, for his encouragement in the finalization of the paper after the conference.

The first observation relates to the discussion of the accountability of international organizations in general. In this respect, it may be noted that the issue of accountability of international organizations is, in principle, not new. Accountability of organizations *vis-à-vis* their members, or the organizations' internal accountability (e.g. the accountability of staff to their superiors, of the lower organs to the higher ones in the organizations' governance structure, or of the organizations as a whole to their members) have long been an integral part of international institutional law. Accountability of international organizations *vis-à-vis* third party non-State actors (or an organization's external accountability) is, however, a notion that emerged only recently, primarily in discussions on international development law. The notion has been introduced in particular in connection with calls for transparent, participatory, and evaluatory systems of monitoring progress towards sustainable development.[1] According to scholars and advocates of development theory and strategy, the purpose of accountability of international development agencies towards third party non-State actors is to ensure that the poor and vulnerable would be able to voice their concerns about developmental activities and trigger redress or remedial actions when they are adversely affected by developmental activities of international bodies.

Partially in response to this debate as well as in response to increasing internal concerns about the performance of the projects and programs it finances, the World Bank[2] decided in September 1993 to establish the Inspection Panel[3] which became operational in August 1994. The Inspection Panel is the first accountability mechanism ever set up by an international organization allowing third party non-State

---

[1] See, e.g., Peter Slinn, Law, Accountability and Development, Third World Legal Studies vii-xx (1993) (noting the emergence of the notion of accountability in connection with debates on the role of law in the development process). See more recently, The Struggle for Accountability – The World Bank, NGOs, and Grass Roots Movements (Jonathan A. Fox & L. David Brown eds., 1998).

[2] Reference is made here to the International Bank for Reconstruction and Development (IBRD) and the International Development Association (IDA).

[3] See Resolution No. 93-10 IBRD, Resolution No. 93-6 IDA, The World Bank Inspection Panel, dated September 22, 1993 [hereinafter Resolution establishing the Panel]. The text of the Resolution was published in 34 ILM 520 (1995). It is also available on the Bank's website at *http://www.worldbank.org.html/ins-panel*. For a detailed account on the developments that led to the creation of the Inspection Panel, see Ibrahim F.I. Shihata, The World Bank Inspection Panel 5-13 (1994) [hereinafter The World Bank Inspection Panel], and *ibid.*, The World Bank Inspection Panel: In Practice 1-27 (2nd ed. 2000) [hereinafter The World Bank Inspection Panel: In Practice].

actors to hold the organization accountable for its own failures in respect of its operational activities.

Here the second observation of more general nature may be made. Since the World Bank established the Inspection Panel, only two other international organizations have followed suit and also established accountability mechanisms allowing third party non-State actors to hold the respective organization accountable for the failure to comply with its own standards in carrying out its operations. In August 1994, the Inter-American Development Bank (IDB) approved the establishment of an independent investigation mechanism to hear complaints from people adversely affected by IDB's non-compliance with its own policies in connection with the projects it finances. Similarly, in December 1995, the Asian Development Bank (ADB) approved the establishment of an inspection function to hear the views of project affected groups.[4] Compared to the hundreds of international organizations that exist, the current total of three inspection mechanisms formed within six years after the creation of the first such mechanism shows that this type of accountability mechanism is still a novelty.

While all other sessions of the conference discussed the phenomenon of proliferation of international organizations in light of inflationary multiplication of international organizations or expansion of their functions with potentially negative side effects (e.g. the "mushrooming" of specialized agencies and programmes within the United Nations (UN) system,[5] or the creation of several affiliated organizations within the World Bank Group (WBG) and the multiplication of special funds administered by the World Bank[6]), it cannot be said that we face a similar problem of proliferation of accountability mechanisms of the type of the World Bank Inspection Panel. To the contrary, few such mechanisms exist and hence the question which this paper attempts to answer deals with the opposite problem. The paper calls for a moderate increase in the number of accountability mechanisms such as the World Bank Inspection Panel and a transfer of the Panel's model to other

---

[4] The IDB's and ADB's inspection mechanisms have been patterned after the World Bank Inspection Panel. They differ, however, in one important aspect. They do not consist of a standing panel with its separate secretariat. Rather, each has a roster of names from which in an actual case members of the panel will be chosen to investigate the matter once a complaint is lodged. The IDB's and the ADB's panels investigating requests are thus of an *ad hoc* rather than permanent nature.

[5] See the contribution by Blokker to this book.

[6] See the contribution by Shihata to this book.

international organizations on the basis of its possible positive effects on the work of an international organization. The paper also tries to prepare for the realization of such an increase in the number of accountability mechanisms similar to the Panel by a theoretical feasibility study.

The question of whether the World Bank Inspection Panel can serve as a model for other international organizations will be approached in several steps. Before discussing this question, it is relevant to describe the Panel's mechanism as laid down in the Resolution establishing it and as reflected in real practice. Thereafter, the potential of the Inspection Panel to be a model for other organizations will be analyzed by drawing from the wisdom of the subtitle which the organizers of this conference gave their well-known treatise on international institutional law, i.e. "Unity within Diversity."[7] As *Henry Schermers* and *Niels Blokker* emphasized, international organizations vary greatly, but have also much in common. Presuming, like *Schermers* and *Blokker*, that there are common denominators and distinguishing factors in international organizations, this paper will describe the particularities of the setting in which the Panel functions and of the Panel's own features. These particularities should allow for an inference of a possible application of the Panel model to other international organizations as well as for a determination of the limitations to such application.

THE WORLD BANK INSPECTION PANEL

The Inspection Panel was created to provide the Bank's Board of Executive Directors with an independent review of controversial Bank-financed projects through an investigation and assessment of the extent to which the Bank actually lives up to the standards it has set for itself in its operations. The independent review is triggered by complaints of groups of individuals in the territory of a borrower whose rights or interests are adversely affected by the Bank's failure to comply with its policies and procedures in the design, appraisal, and/or implementation of Bank-financed projects.

The Panel complements the function of the Bank's Operations Evaluation Department (OED) which carries out *ex post* evaluations of

---

[7] See Henry G. Schermers & Niels M. Blokker, International Institutional Law – Unity Within Diversity (3rd ed. 1995).

projects after project completion but does not assess projects during the design and implementation phase.[8] OED has only an indirect impact on the performance of the Bank's portfolio through the lessons the Bank may draw from its *ex post* evaluations and apply to future operations, while the performance of ongoing projects may be directly influenced and improved through the Panel mechanism.

COMPOSITION OF THE INSPECTION PANEL

As an independent body within the Bank's structure, the Inspection Panel is composed of three members, each of different nationalities from Bank member countries.[9] These three members are nominated by the Bank's President and appointed by its Board of Executive Directors.[10] The Panel members are selected on the basis of their ability, integrity, independence from Bank Management,[11] and exposure to developmental issues and living conditions in developing countries.[12] It is desirable, but not necessary, that they have knowledge of and exposure to the Bank's operations.[13] Nevertheless, to avoid conflicts of interest, a Panel member's prior affiliation with the Bank must date back two years before he/she becomes eligible for appointment to the Panel.[14] Panel Members are appointed for a 5-year non-renewable

---

[8] It may be noted that OED is an in-house evaluation function which, unlike the Inspection Panel, does not undertake evaluations when triggered by outsiders' requests but exercises its functions on the basis of internal guidelines as its regular business. OED exercises its performance assessment functions from a point in time from which on the Panel can no longer entertain a request, i.e. after the Closing Date of the loan financing the project.

[9] See Para. 2 of the Resolution establishing the Panel. The first three Panel members were Ernst-Günther Bröder, a German national, Alvaro Umaña Quesada, a Costa Rican national, and Richard E. Bissell, a US national. In August 1997, Richard Bissell was replaced by James MacNeill a Canadian national. In August 1998, Edward S. Ayensu, a national of Ghana, replaced Alvaro Umaña Quesada, and, in October 1999, Martje van Putten, a Dutch national, replaced Ernst-Günther Bröder.

[10] *Ibid.*

[11] The term "Management" refers to the Bank's President or the staff he has designated to perform the respective business of the Bank. See Article V (especially Section 5) of the IBRD Articles of Agreement and Article VI (especially Section 5) of the IDA Articles of Agreement.

[12] See Para. 4 of the Resolution establishing the Panel.

[13] *Ibid.*

[14] See Para. 5 of the Resolution establishing the Panel.

term.[15] After their service on the Panel, they are prohibited from returning to or joining the Bank.[16] Removal of Panel members from their office is only possible for cause and by a decision of the Board of Executive Directors.[17] The Panel members select among themselves the Panel's chairman who works full-time on Panel matters. [18] The other two members work on a part-time basis unless their work-load would require their full-time engagement.[19] The Panel has its own secretariat, led by an Executive Secretary and also including an Assistant Executive Secretary.[20]

FUNCTIONING OF THE INSPECTION PANEL MECHANISM

Under the Resolution, the Panel's role is in principle to be performed in two stages.[21] In the first stage, the Panel registers the request for inspection.[22] Management is then asked to respond to the concerns expressed in the request.[23] Thereafter, the Panel has to assess whether the request meets the eligibility requirements of the Resolution.[24] The

---

[15] See Para. 3 of the Resolution establishing the Panel. It may be noted that the first three Panel members had staggered terms of three, four, and five years length.

[16] See Para. 10 of the Resolution establishing the Panel.

[17] See Para. 8 of the Resolution establishing the Panel.

[18] See Paras. 7 and 9 of the Resolution establishing the Panel.

[19] See Para. 9 of the Resolution establishing the Panel.

[20] See Para. 11 of the Resolution establishing the Panel. The Panel's Executive Secretary is Eduardo G. Abbott, a Chilean national. Its Assistant Executive Secretary is Antonia Macedo from New Zealand.

[21] For a more detailed overview of the process for requests before the Inspection Panel, see Annex I to this paper, at 528.

[22] See Para. 17 of the Resolution establishing the Panel (implying registration of the received request by the Panel).

[23] See Paras. 12 and 13 of the Resolution establishing the Panel. It may be noted that one or more Executive Directors may also ask the Panel for an investigation. In addition, the Executive Directors, acting together as the Board, may, at any time, instruct the Panel to conduct an investigation.

[24] Ibid. and Para. 14 of the Resolution establishing the Panel. In the exercise of the first stage of its function, the Panel has to establish four elements of jurisdiction, the first of which does not apply in the exceptional case where a request is made by a member or members of the Bank's Board: (i) the Panel's competence relating to the person of the complainant (*ratione personae*); (ii) its competence regarding the subject matter of the complaint (*ratione materiae*); (iii) its competence relating to the timing of the complaint (*ratione temporis*); and (iv) the admissibility of the complaint in the absence of other grounds excluding it under the Resolution (e.g., when Management has already dealt with the subject matter or is taking adequate steps in that direction). For a comprehensive description of the Panel's role in the first stage, see Ibrahim F.I. Shihata, Legal Opinion of the Senior Vice President

Panel assesses in particular (a) whether the request was brought by a grouping of individuals with common interests or concerns, and (b) whether *prima facie* a serious violation by the Bank of its operational policies and procedures resulting or likely to result in material and adverse harm to the requesters is present to which Management has failed to respond adequately. On the basis of this assessment, the Panel recommends to the Executive Directors whether or not to authorize an investigation.[25]

In the second stage, which takes place only after the Board of Executive Directors authorizes an investigation, the Panel carries out its investigation on the merits of the request.[26] As a result of the investigation, the Panel reaches its findings on whether the Bank has been in serious violation of its operational policies and procedures with respect to the design, appraisal, and/or implementation of the project involved having a material adverse effect on the requester.[27] Thereafter, Management has the opportunity to respond to the Panel's findings and make recommendations for corrective actions to be taken in their light.[28] The Board of Executive Directors considers the Panel's report on the investigation together with Management's recommendations in response to the Panel's findings and makes the ultimate decision concerning the request.[29]

THE INSTITUTIONAL SCOPE OF THE INSPECTION PANEL'S MANDATE

The institutional scope of the Panel's mandate covers non-compliance with policies and procedures regarding projects financed by IBRD and IDA. Activities by other institutions of the World Bank Group (WBG)

---

and General Counsel of January 3, 1995, The Role of the Inspection Panel in the Preliminary Assessment of Whether to Recommend Inspection, published in Ibrahim F.I. Shihata, The World Bank in a Changing World, Vol. 2, Annex III (D) (1995), and also published in 34 ILM 525 (1995) [hereinafter Role of the Inspection Panel in the Preliminary Assessment of Whether to Recommend Inspection].

[25] See Para. 19 of the Resolution establishing the Panel.
[26] See Paras. 20 and 21 of the Resolution establishing the Panel.
[27] See Paras. 12, 13, and 20-22 of the Resolution establishing the Panel. The Panel conducts the investigation by checking the pertinent Bank records, interviewing Bank staff and other persons and, if needed, carrying out an investigation in the territory of the borrowing country with the borrowing country's consent.
[28] See Para. 23 of the Resolution establishing the Panel.
[29] *Ibid.* The Board may either agree or disagree with the Panel's findings and Management's recommendations. In connection with its decision, it may instruct Management to take corrective actions.

[30] such as IFC and MIGA are not subject to investigation by the Panel. While not explicitly mentioned, Bank actions as trustee of the Global Environment Facility (GEF) and the other trust funds are implicitly covered by the Panel's "jurisdiction."[31]

THE INSPECTION PANEL'S CASE RECORD

The Panel's case record to date is impressive.[32] The Panel started operating in 1994. By December 31, 1999, it had received twenty-one requests for inspection.[33] Three of these requests fell clearly outside its mandate and were therefore not registered. Of the other eighteen requests, sixteen concerned various infrastructure, environmental and land reform projects, while two related to adjustment operations. In most requests concerning infrastructure projects, the requesters alleged non-compliance by the Bank with Bank policies and procedures cover-

---

[30] The World Bank Group consists of five legally separate institutions. These include the International Bank for Reconstruction and Development (IBRD) and the International Development Association (IDA), both making and guaranteeing loans to developing countries but with IDA lending to the poorest of them; the International Finance Corporation (IFC), making loans and equity investments in private enterprises in developing countries; the Multilateral Investment Guarantee Agency (MIGA), providing guarantees to foreign investors in developing countries against losses caused by non-commercial risks; and the International Centre for Settlement of Investment Disputes (ICSID) providing facilities and procedures for arbitration and conciliation of investment disputes between foreign investors and host country governments. Within the World Bank Group, the International Bank for Reconstruction and Development (IBRD) is the oldest in the Group. It was established in 1945 after the Bretton Woods Conference.

[31] See Ibrahim F.I. Shihata, The World Bank Inspection Panel, *supra* note 3, at 39-41. This view has been confirmed by the Board's tacit agreement to the Panel's acceptance of dealing with a request regarding a project that was partially financed from GEF sources.

[32] For a more detailed account of the Panel's case work, see Sabine Schlemmer-Schulte, The World Bank's Experience with its Inspection Panel, 58 Zeitschrift für ausländisches öffentliches Recht und Völkerrecht (ZaöRV) (Heidelberg Journal of International Law) 353 (1998) [hereinafter The World Bank's Experience with Its Inspection Panel], and Ibrahim F.I. Shihata, The World Bank Inspection Panel: In Practice, *supra* note 3, at 99-154. See also Richard E. Bissell, Recent Practice of the Inspection Panel of the World Bank, 91 American Journal of International Law 741 (1997), and, from the perspective of the Inspection Panel, The Inspection Panel: The First Four Years (Alvaro Umaña Quesada ed., 1998). See further Lori Udall, The World Bank Inspection Panel: A Three Year Review (1997).

[33] For an overview of the requests received by the Panel to date, see the chart "Chronology of Requests before the World Bank Inspection Panel" in Annex II of this paper, at 541.

ing primarily environmental issues and the social interests of affected people.

Fourteen of the eighteen registered requests have been disposed of, four cases are currently pending. Altogether, the Panel recommended investigation in seven cases. The Board of Executive Directors formally authorized an investigation in two cases (in these cases following the Panel's recommendation), and asked the Panel to make assessments *de facto* amounting to an investigation in a third case. In a fourth case in which the Panel had recommended an investigation, the Executive Directors, acting as a Board, instructed the Panel to conduct an investigation regardless of the Panel's recommendation.[34] In four more cases, the Board requested the Panel to follow up on the progress of remedial action plans agreed upon by the borrowers or other bodies responsible for project execution and project improvement. These investigations and other fact-finding activities of the Panel in a total of eight cases are testimony of the active and useful role the Panel plays in the enhancement of the performance of the Bank's operational functions. From a legal point of view, it may be noted that the decisions made by the Board in connection with cases before the Panel started creating a body of "case law" consisting of interpretations of and practices developed under the Resolution.[35]

The Panel has also been subject to two general reviews by the Bank's Board of Executive Directors.

THE FIRST INSPECTION PANEL REVIEW AND THE 1996 CLARIFICATIONS

The first review was required by the Resolution establishing the Panel and took place in 1996.[36] This review resulted in the issuance by the Board of Executive Directors of Clarifications of Certain Aspects of the

---

[34] In the case referred to, the Board decided to bypass the Panel's recommendation, i.e. not to act on its basis and thus neither agree with that recommendation and authorize an inspection nor disagree and not authorize an inspection. Instead, the Board decided to make use of its power to ask the Panel to undertake an investigation at any time notwithstanding a request for inspection from outsiders and the Panel recommendation related to that request. See for this power of the Board, Para. 12 of the Resolution Establishing the Panel.

[35] For a more detailed discussion of the "case law" that is building up under the Resolution, see Sabine Schlemmer-Schulte, The World Bank's Experience with Its Inspection Panel, *supra* note 32, at 379.

[36] See Para. 27 of the Resolution establishing the Panel.

Resolution establishing the Panel.[37] The 1996 Clarifications may, from a legal point of view, be regarded as an authoritative "commentary" on the Resolution, including general interpretations of notions in the Resolution and flexible practices developed under it approved of by the Board of Executive Directors, i.e. the organ that created the Panel and is vested with the authority to interpret the Panel's constituent instrument.[38] In terms of substance, the 1996 Clarifications explain and determine a number of aspects of the Panel's function and procedures. These include, *inter alia*, issues of the Panel's function such as the two-stage procedure (with the addition of a "preliminary assessment" in the first stage), issues of access and eligibility, outreach, composition of the Panel, disclosure of documents in the Panel process, etc.

THE SECOND INSPECTION PANEL REVIEW AND THE 1999 CONCLUSIONS

Controversies in connection with some requests over the decision on whether to authorize investigations in these cases led the Board of Executive Directors in September 1997 to initiate a second review of the Panel which resulted in April 1999 in the issuance of another set of clarifications of the Resolution, i.e. the 1999 Conclusions of the Second Review of the Panel's Experience. Legally, these Conclusions constitute additions to and revisions of the 1996 Clarifications to the Resolution (or the authoritative "commentary" on it).[39]

Substantively, the 1999 Conclusions consolidated the concept of the Inspection Panel as an accountability mechanism by which the

---

[37] For a comprehensive analysis of the 1996 Clarifications, see Ibrahim F.I. Shihata, The World Bank Inspection Panel: In Practice, *supra* note 3, at 156-172. See also Clarifications of Certain Aspects of the Resolution Establishing the Inspection Panel of September 30, 1996 which were approved by the Bank's Board of Executive Directors on October 17, 1996 [hereinafter Clarification or 1996 Clarifications]. These Clarifications have been made publicly available and can be accessed through the Bank's website.

[38] For a more detailed discussion of the 1996 Clarifications as an authoritative "commentary," see Sabine Schlemmer-Schulte, The World Bank's Experience with Its Inspection , *supra* note 32, at 380-386.

[39] For a detailed account of the discussion on the occasion of the second review of the Inspection Panel and a detailed analysis of the 1999 Conclusions, see Ibrahim F.I. Shihata, The World Bank Inspection Panel: In Practice, *supra* note 3, at 173-203. See also Daniel D. Bradlow, Precedent Setting NGO Campaign Saves the World Bank Inspection Panel, Vol. 6, Issue 3, Human Rights Brief of the Washington College of Law of American University 7 (1999).

ultimate beneficiaries of the projects the Bank finances can hold it accountable.[40]

In particular, the 1999 Conclusions reversed a trend in the Panel's practice that had resulted in an overemphasis on assessing harm to the requesters in the first stage of the Panel process rather than concentrating on the assessment of the Bank's non-compliance with its policies and procedures in its operational activities.[41] This trend had contributed to misperceptions of the Panel mechanism as a whole by creating the wrong impression that remedial action in response to harm was at the heart of the process, as opposed to accountability of the Bank for its failures. The 1999 Conclusions brought an end to this focus on the harm done to requesters. They require the Panel to pay equal attention to the question of the Bank's compliance with its policies and procedures and the harm done to requesters resulting from that non-compliance.[42]

The 1999 Conclusions also reversed the trend of Management submitting borrowers' remedial action plans after the Panel issued its recommendation on whether to investigate but before the Board met to decide on that recommendation.[43] While the Resolution referred to the submission of remedial action plans by Management in the first stage only at the time Management responds to the request, i.e. before the

---

[40] For an overview of the significance of the 1999 Conclusions of the Second Review of the Inspection Panel, see Sabine Schlemmer-Schulte, Conclusions of the Second Review of the Inspection Panel's Experience—Introductory Note, in 39 ILM 243 (2000) [Conclusions of the Second Review]. See also Conclusions of the Second Review of the World Bank Inspection Panel approved by the Bank's Board of Executive Directors on April 20, 1999 [hereinafter Conclusions or 1999 Conclusions]. These conclusions have been made publicly available and can be accessed through the Bank's website or found in 39 ILM 249 (2000).

[41] See also Ibrahim F.I. Shihata, The World Bank Inspection Panel: In Practice, *supra* note 3, at 213 (noting that the Panel process was, until the second Board review addressed that issue, focusing on ascertaining the harm inflicted on affected parties while "downplaying" the Panel's main function of verifying the Bank's compliance or failure with respect to its policies).

[42] In the first stage of the Panel process, the Panel has to concentrate in particular on the assertion (rather than a true finding) that a "serious violation by the Bank of its operational policies and procedures has or is likely to have a material adverse effect on the requester," or, in other words, on *prima facie* evidence of (i) a non-compliance by the Bank with its policies and procedures, and (ii) resulting potential or material harm in the requester caused by the Bank's failure. See 1999 Conclusions of the Board's Second Review of the Inspection Panel, at Para. 9(b).

[43] See also Ibrahim F.I. Shihata, The World Bank Inspection Panel: In Practice, *supra* note 3, at 220-225 (identifying the trend of Management submitting borrowers' remedial action plans and discussing the trend's distorting effects compared to the original intention of the Panel process under the Resolution).

Panel issues its recommendation, (and in the second stage when Management responds to the Panel's findings), Management had actually forwarded to the Board remedial action plans in three cases after the Panel had issued its recommendation but before the Board's meeting on the latter.[44] This practice had the effect of reducing the Board's inclination to authorize investigations. The 1999 Conclusions no longer allow for an impediment to authorizations of investigation in the form of remedial action plans agreed upon with the borrower and submitted by Management shortly before Board consideration of the Panel's recommendation. The Conclusions expressly prohibit Management from bringing forward a remedial action plan at this time.[45]

Finally, the 1999 Conclusions made it clear that the Panel process relates to the Bank's failures, not the borrowers' failures. Management's responses and remedial action plans submitted by it had not clearly distinguished between the Bank's and borrowers' failures (and corresponding remedial actions) so that the impression had been created that the Panel process would be addressing borrowers' failures instead of Bank failures, although it was meant to address only the latter's failures.[46] The 1999 Conclusions now require Management, in its response to the request, to distinguish, where failures of compliance with policies and procedures in connection with Bank-financed projects exist, between (i) failures exclusively attributable to the Bank, (ii) those exclusively attributable to the borrower (or other external factors), and (iii) those that are attributable to both the Bank and the borrower (or other

---

[44] In another case, the plan was introduced and explained in the Board meeting considering the Panel's recommendation on the request. In two further cases such action plans were submitted together with Management's response to the request. In one further case, such plan was submitted after investigation was authorized by the Board but before the Panel had completed its investigation.

[45] It may be noted that Management was fully authorized under its general business powers under the Bank's Articles of Agreement and in the absence of a provision to the contrary in the Resolution to submit remedial action plans at this time. The 1999 Conclusions commit Management now to refrain from using its general business powers in conjunction with the Panel process by prohibiting it to submit remedial action plans at a time not expressly identified for such action in the Resolution.

[46] See also Ibrahim F.I. Shihata, The World Bank Inspection Panel: In Practice, *supra* note 3, at 176-181, and 220-225 (identifying the lack of distinction between Bank failures and borrower failures in Management's response and the Panel's recommendation and discussing a solution to the problem which the author of the book referred to in this footnote proposed in the Bank as the Bank's then General Counsel and which was later to a great part accepted by the Board as reflected in the 1999 Conclusions).

external factors).[47] Any measures taken by Management and referred to in its response should only address Bank failures. The Panel, while free to adopt its own assessment, must also distinguish between the three categories of failures and ultimately in its recommendation only focus on the Bank's failures (exclusive or partial).[48]

THE INSPECTION PANEL AS A MODEL FOR OTHER INTERNATIONAL ORGANIZATIONS

In order to assess whether the Bank's Inspection Panel may be a model for the creation of similar accountability mechanisms in other international organizations, the Panel's mechanism will first be subjected to a more abstract structural and functional analysis. Thereafter, four hypothetical cases of an application of the Panel model to other international organizations will be discussed.

STRUCTURAL – FUNCTIONAL ANALYSIS OF THE CHARACTERISTICS OF THE INSPECTION PANEL MECHANISM

In the abstract, three major components determine the unique concept of the Inspection Panel mechanism. These components are: (i) the profile of its users, (ii) the characteristics of the target of the Panel's investigation, and (iii) the overall character of the Panel mechanism as an accountability body as opposed to remedies bodies.

The Panel's Users

The Panel mechanism is triggered by non-State actors. The latter have standing before the Panel, as an "affected party" under the Resolution establishing the Panel, if they fulfill the following three requirements.

---

[47] Both Bank and borrowers' failures may especially exist in the case where the borrower fails to implement the project and the Bank fails to follow up on the borrower's non- or misimplementation required by it as the supervisor of project execution.

[48] It may be noted that action plans agreed between the borrower and the Bank including remedial efforts by the borrower for borrower failures will be communicated to the Board but separate from documents required by the Panel process. They will eventually be considered in conjunction with Management's response to the findings of the Panel after an investigation was carried out. The Panel's involvement in a review of these action plans shall be limited to an assessment of the consultation with affected parties on the action plans.

Community of Persons

First, they must form a "community of persons, such as an organization, association, society or other grouping of individuals."[49] A single individual does not qualify. As was further explained in a legal opinion by the Bank's General Counsel which was endorsed by the Bank's Board, the explicit language of the Resolution suggests that requests submitted individually by a number of persons, each acting in his/her own single capacity, without any common bond between them, would not meet the requirement of a community of persons. While the group of individuals need not have the juridical personality of an association, corporation, etc., it has to be a group which represents a commonality of interests.[50] The 1996 Clarifications repeated that requests must be from "any two or more individuals with common interests or concerns."[51]

---

[49] See Para. 12 of the Resolution establishing the Panel.

[50] For a detailed explanation of the first stage of the Panel's function, see Ibrahim F.I. Shihata, Role of the Inspection Panel in the Preliminary Assessment of Whether to Recommend Inspection, *supra* note 24.

[51] See 1996 Clarifications, *supra* note 37, on the term "affected party" in the section on eligibility and access. It may be noted in this respect that the Panel Resolution's requirement clearly exceeds the requirement as formulated in the Panel's own Operating Procedures which state that an affected party could be "any group of two or more people." See Para. 4(a) of the Operating Procedures as adopted by the Inspection Panel on August 19, 1994. It also goes beyond the description that the notion "affected party" had found in some writings which referred to "any two or more persons." See Daniel D. Bradlow, International Organizations and Private Complaints: The Case of the World Bank Inspection Panel, 34 Virginia Journal of International Law 553, 583 (1994) (stating implicitly that any two or more persons may lodge a request with the Panel by noting that "any 'affected party' except a single individual" is allowed to bring a complaint under the Resolution and omitting a reference to any interests that complainants must share); Kathigamar V.S.K. Nathan, The World Bank Inspection Panel - Court or Quango, 12 Journal of International Arbitration 135, 141 (1995) (stating that "[t]he 'jurisdiction' of the Panel extends to an affected party which should consist of at least two persons in the territory of the borrower country," but also not referring to any common interest that the requesters must share); and Daniel D. Bradlow, A Test Case for the World Bank, 11 American University Journal of International Law and Policy 247, 261 (1996) (arguing against an interpretation of the term "affected party" as requiring a commonality of interests from complainants by making the case that such a requirement would unduly restrict access to the Panel and, for example, exclude individuals who are affected by the same Bank-financed project, but on different grounds).

No Actiones Popularis (or Requirement of Direct and Individual Concern of Requester)

The second requirement for standing of requesters regards their allegation that "[their] rights or interests have been or are likely to be directly affected by an action or omission of the Bank."[52] This requirement is designed to exclude complaints on behalf of the public at large (or *actiones popularis*). In general, rights mean special powers, privileges, faculties or demands, inherent in one person and incident upon another.[53] Interests denote claims, titles, or legal shares in something.[54] The contents of rights or interests of individuals that need to have been or are likely to be affected to give an affected party standing before the Inspection Panel may in the first place be determined by recourse to the domestic laws of the borrowing country in which the project is financed.[55] The contents of such rights or interests may, in addition, especially in cases where the borrowing country's domestic law lacks respective rights or interests, also be determined by reference to provisions of Bank policies and procedures, as they have become part of the borrower's obligations under the loan agreement financing the project.[56]

---

[52] See Para. 12 of the Resolution establishing the Panel.
[53] See Black's Law Dictionary 1324 (6th ed. 1990).
[54] *Ibid.* at 812.
[55] See Ibrahim F. I. Shihata, The World Bank Inspection Panel: In Practice, *supra* note 3, at 35-55.
[56] In the view of the author of this paper, recourse to Bank policies and procedures for the determination of a requester's rights or interests for standing purposes should be allowed in order to avoid that requesters are subject to different standing standards depending on in which borrowing country the project is located. In other words, the reference to Bank policies and procedures serves guaranteeing a more uniform standard of standing before the Inspection Panel. It especially avoids extreme results of discrimination among requesters such as in a case of resettlement of people, who in a country that does not know property or lease rights may be removed from their land without any rights/interests being violated or threatened and therefore without having standing before the Panel, while people in the same situation in another country that knows property or lease rights would have standing. A reference to the Bank's policies on resettlement would, on the basis of detailed provisions on resettlement and compensation, also give people to be resettled from the country without property and lease rights standing to bring a complaint before the Panel. It may be noted that guidance for the determination of rights and interests of individuals through recourse to Bank policies may be received from the concepts of "direct effect" and "State responsibility" developed by the European Court of Justice (ECJ). For more details, see note 125, *infra*, and accompanying text.

The possibility of a violation of or threat to rights or interests of individuals may be easily assessed in connection with the Bank's financing of a specific project. The adverse effects of a specific project resulting from non-compliance by the Bank with its own policies and procedures become visible upon project execution and are usually limited in terms of the territorial reach of the project as well as its reach to individuals. Analogous (as to the factual although not the legal side of the situation) to the circumstances in a domestic law context in which a State's administrative decision or action addresses the concrete case of specific individuals, the project's adverse effects reach a limited number of specific, identifiable individuals in a concrete territorially and otherwise determinable situation, different from the situation of others.

By contrast, this cannot be said of the potential adverse effects through non-compliance with policies of the Bank's adjustment operations. Adjustment operations are those Bank operations which do no finance specific projects but finance broad macro-economic policy, structural or sectoral adjustment measures.[57] Because of the broader design of these measures, any adverse effects that may result from them cover broader circles of the population and situations than are reached by the effects of specific projects. For example, large segments of a country's population may be potentially affected by reforms of certain industry sectors such as privatization programs or civil service reforms in the form of job loss etc. Compared with a State's action in the domestic law context, the situation created by Bank-financed adjustment operations is similar to a State's legislative/regulatory measures with their abstract-general character, covering a rather unlimited number of situations as well as an unlimited number of individuals. Such measures in themselves, because of both their sector orientation and their abstract-general character, hardly violate rights and/or interests of indi-

---

[57] Under the Bank's charter, financing of specific projects is the rule while non-project financing is the exception permitted only under "special circumstances." See Article III, Section 4(vii) of the IBRD Articles of Agreement and Article V, Section 1(b) of the IDA Articles of Agreement. It may be noted that the implementation of policy measures at the core of adjustment operations is legally not a borrower's obligation under the loan agreement the borrower concludes with the Bank. It is only a condition set by the Bank which, if met by the borrower, leads to disbursement of adjustment loan tranche(s), but, if not met, does not result in a violation by the borrower of its obligations under the loan agreement. For details of the distinction between project and adjustment operations, see Ibrahim F.I. Shihata, The World Bank Inspection Panel: In Practice, *supra* note 3, at 37-41.

viduals in a direct and immediate way.[58] They do so only when, in a second step, more specific measures singling out the individuals subjected to them are taken on the basis and in application of the abstract-general measures.[59] An immediate and individual concern of identifiable individuals would emerge only at this second step of policy implementation.

This is why, among others,[60] the question whether rights or interests giving standing to requesters can arise in the mere belonging to a sector that is being addressed by a structural adjustment operation, while substantive or procedural rights or interests of more individualized nature are not yet visibly at stake is not yet satisfactorily answered. The Bank's Board of Executive Directors has yet to discuss this question. The two requests before the Inspection Panel which raised this issue did not lend themselves to an open discussion in the Board since the Panel, for reasons other than the issue of standing, did not recommend an investigation in these two cases. The Board agreed to both recommendations on a no-objection basis, i.e. without meeting for a discussion.[61]

The risk of accepting complaints by the public at large given the effects of adjustment operations on large segments of the population in a borrowing country may be overcome to a great extent by reducing such acceptance to cases in which adverse effects have already been felt

---

[58] See Sabine Schlemmer-Schulte, The World Bank's Experience with Its Inspection Panel, *supra* note 32, at 369-70 (questioning whether the requirement of a violation of or threat to rights and interests of affected parties would be met in connection with adjustment operations).

[59] The situation may be compared to one in which a country has adopted a law expropriating a certain industry. Normally under most domestic laws, an owner of a company from the industry targeted by the expropriation law would only have standing in court to go against the contemplated expropriation if he or his firm would have been specifically addressed by the administration in charge to realize the expropriation planned by law, i.e. to announce to this owner/firm that in his individual case an expropriation will take place.

[60] Another argument against adjustment operations as subject-matter of Inspection Panel investigations relates to the required "project" quality of subject-matters before the Panel according to Paragraph 13 of the Resolution establishing the Panel. Under Bank terminology, the meaning of "project" does not include adjustment operations. See Ibrahim F.I. Shihata, The World Bank Inspection Panel: In Practice, *supra* note 3, at 37 *et seq.*

[61] See Ibrahim F.I. Shihata, The World Bank Inspection Panel: In Practice, *supra* note 3, at 37 *et seq.* and 154 (in the first place discussing the legal question of the requester's standing in connection with adjustment operations generally and in the second describing the request concerning the Argentina Special Structural Adjustment Program).

by an individual or are about to being felt shortly, i.e. where an execution measure taken by the State has produced or is about to produce immediate effects on individuals. Only then, i.e. at the stage of the second step of the implementation of an adjustment program, is it possible to assess the material violation of or immediate threat to rights or interests of the complainant as a result of the adjustment operation.[62] (Nevertheless, even then the number of potential claimants may exceed greatly the average number of potential claimants in the project-lending context simply because adjustment operations reach out to greater parts of the population.)

In addition to the formal legal concern that the Inspection Panel was not designed to entertain complaints by the public at large, other considerations may, however, need to be taken into account in the debate of the eligibility of requests brought before the Inspection Panel in connection with adjustment operations. Such considerations include the risk that an acceptance of Panel requests in conjunction with adjustment operations would eventually also reopen debates over the efficiency of macro-economic policy changes required by the borrowers as a condition for adjustment lending in the Board on the occasion of the discussion of the Panel case, while the debate over such matters should have been in principle closed upon approval of the operations.

Geographical Connection of Requester

Last, but not least, the affected party must be "in the territory of the borrowers."[63] The latter requirement must be distinguished from the possibility of representation before the Panel.[64] The affected party need not act in his/her own name. He/she can bring the request through a local representative, or, in exceptional cases when local representation is not available and foreign representation is approved by the Bank's Board of Executive Directors at the time it authorizes inspection, the

---

[62] The solution sought here parallels the parameters developed in most domestic legal systems for the standing of individuals. For details, see Albert Bleckmann, The Aim of Judicial Protection: Protection of the Individual or Objective Control of the Executive Power? The Role of *locus standi*, in Judicial Protection against the Executive Power, Vol. 3, 19 (Hermann Mosler ed., 1985) (stressing that in all domestic laws a special relation of the plaintiff to the matter in controversy must exist).

[63] See Para. 12 of the Resolution establishing the Panel.

[64] *Ibid.*

affected party can use a foreign representative, e.g., an international non-governmental organization (NGO).[65]

The Panel's User Profile in a Nutshell

Altogether, the Inspection Panel user profile may be briefly summarized as relating to non-State actors in the Bank's borrowing countries who have common concerns regarding a Bank operation and who are directly and individually affected by such an operation.

The Target of Panel Investigations

The major subject-matter of the Panel's investigations is "the Bank's failure to follow its operational policies and procedures with respect to the design, appraisal, and/or implementation of a project financed by the Bank (including situations where the Bank is alleged to have failed in its follow-up on the borrower's obligations under loan agreements with respect to such policies and procedures) provided [...] that such failure has had, or threatens to have a material adverse effect [on requesters]."[66] In other words, the object of Panel investigations is non-compliance by the Bank with the standards it has set for itself in the financing of development projects and programs as long as these failures result in harm suffered by the requester.

For the purposes of transferring the Panel model to other organizations, it is necessary to analyze the legal setting in which the potential breach of the Bank's own rules in connection with its operational activities takes place.[67] It is also necessary to determine the legal status of the ultimate beneficiaries affected by such Bank breaches. The legal setting of the Bank's operations rests on its Articles of Agreement, i.e. the charter creating it and the practice that developed over the years under that charter. The status of project beneficiaries can be inferred from the legal setting of the Bank's operations.

---

[65] Ibid.
[66] See Para. 12 of the Resolution establishing the Panel. While Para. 12 explicitly spells out eligibility criteria of a request that need to be met *"prima facie"* before an investigation would be authorized, it implicitly also spells out the focus of an investigation of the merits of a complaint. An assessment of the merits concentrates on (1) a serious violation of the Bank's operational policies, and (2) resulting material harm to requesters.
[67] For a brief overview of the setting in which the Inspection Panel functions, see also Sabine Schlemmer-Schulte, The World Bank, Its Operations, and Its Inspection Panel, 45 Recht der Internationalen Wirtschaft 175-81 (1999) [hereinafter The World Bank, Its Operations, and Its Inspection Panel].

The World Bank's Mandate

The World Bank[68] was created in 1944 to assist its members in the reconstruction and economic development of their territories by facilitating and financing investment for productive purposes.[69] Under its Articles of Agreement, the Bank is explicitly prohibited from taking non-economic considerations into account in its decisions.[70] The provisions of its Articles of Agreement make the Bank an international economic and finance development institution. They have served the Bank well and enabled it to establish an outstanding record of financing and promoting economic development.[71] Under them, the Bank has been able to meet new challenges and, based on purposive interpretation of its mandate, to move into new areas beyond the narrow literal meaning of its charter provisions, while, at the same time, respecting its charter's express limitations. Today, the Bank's financial assistance covers thus a broad range of areas from the traditional areas of infrastructure, industry and agriculture, to the social sector,[72] a country's

---

[68] Reference is made here to the International Bank for Reconstruction and Development (IBRD) only. IBRD's soft-loan window IDA, which is lending to the poorest countries, was created 12 years later.

[69] In the words of its charter, i.e. the Articles of Agreement, the Bank's express purposes are to "facilitate the investment of capital for productive purposes," to "promote private foreign investment... for productive purposes," and to "encourage international investment for the development of the productive resources of members, thereby assisting in raising productivity, the standard of living and conditions of labor in their territories." See Article I (i–iii) of IBRD's Articles of Agreement. Compare also Article I of IDA's Articles of Agreement, which, to a certain degree, uses similar language.

[70] The relevant provisions here read that "the Bank and its officers shall not interfere in the political affairs of any member, nor shall they be influenced by the political character of the member or members concerned" and that "only economic considerations shall be relevant to [the Bank's] decisions." See Article IV, Section 10 of IBRD's Articles of Agreement and Article V, Section 6 of IDA's Articles of Agreement.

[71] For details about the Bank's character as an international economic and finance development institution and, by extrapolation, its non-political character, see Ibrahim F.I. Shihata, The World Bank in a Changing World, Vol. 1, 97 (1991), Chapter 3 (The World Bank and Human Rights) [hereinafter The World Bank in a Changing World, Vol. 1]; *id.* The World Bank in a Changing World, Vol. 2, 553 and 567 (1995), Chapter 18 (Human Rights, Development, and International Financial Institutions) and Chapter 19 (The World Bank and Human Rights); and *id.* Democracy and Development, 46 International and Comparative Law Quarterly 635 (1997).

macroeconomic and structural framework,[73] environmental concerns,[74] "governance" issues,[75] legal and judicial reform,[76] and gender issues. To use the formula of the Bank's "Mission Statement," a broad range of aspects must be addressed "to fight for poverty reduction."

The World Bank's Lending Operations

To effectively carry out its development assistance function in this described broad range of areas, the Bank is authorized to make loans and guarantees for the financing of specific programs and projects.[77] In special circumstances, the Bank is also allowed to engage in non-project financing.[78] According to its Articles of Agreement, the Bank enters into loan and guarantee agreements with the governments (or any political sub-division thereof) of its member countries.[79] The Bank can also make loans and guarantees to borrowers other than the government of a member country (e.g. private investors), if the member country in whose territory the project is located or its central bank fully guarantees the repayment of the loan and all charges connected with

---

[72] For a description of the Bank's experience in development assistance over the decades since its inception, see World Development Report – Poverty (World Bank 1990).

[73] See generally, World Development Report (World Bank 1980) and World Development Report – From Plan to Market (World Bank 1996).

[74] See World Development Report - Development and the Environment (World Bank 1992).

[75] Under the rubric of "governance," the Bank is assisting developing countries in a number of areas with clear relevance to their economic development such as their efforts to improve public sector management, address weakness in the civil service, strengthen legal regulatory and judicial frameworks, and combat corruption. For a definition of the term "governance" in the Bank's work and the legal rationale of extending the Bank's work to governance issues on the basis of the charter, see Shihata, The World Bank in a Changing World, Vol. 1, *supra* note 71, at 53, Chapter 2 (The World Bank and "Governance" Issues in Its Borrowing Members). See also Governance: The World Bank's Experience (World Bank 1994).

[76] For a comprehensive description and analysis of the Bank's reform work, see Ibrahim F.I. Shihata, Complementary Reform – Essay on Legal, Judicial and Other Institutional Reforms Supported by the World Bank (1997).

[77] See Article III, Section 4 of IBRD's Articles of Agreement. Compare Article V, Section 2 of IDA's Articles of Agreement (limiting the Association's form of financing in general to loans).

[78] See Article III, Section 4 (vii) of the IBRD Articles of Agreement and Article V, Section 1(b) of the IDA Articles of Agreement.

[79] See Article III, Section 4 of IBRD's Articles of Agreement and Article V, Section 2(c) of IDA's Articles of Agreement.

it.[80] In the overwhelming number of cases in practice, the borrower is a member country.

The Project Cycle

Technically, the Bank's development assistance is organized as a "project cycle," as the unique structure of the Bank's lending operations for specific development projects is called.[81] The project cycle consists of the following stages: (1) selection of the project to be financed; (2) design and preparation of the selected project; (3) thorough appraisal of the proposed project and approval of the loan financing it; (4) implementation of the approved project; (5) supervision of the project's implementation; and (6) systematical overall evaluation of each project financed by the Bank.

The Bank and the borrower each have their specific roles in the project cycle. The selection of the project is both the Bank's and the borrower's task. Design and preparation of the project is the borrower's responsibility. Appraisal of the project is done by the Bank as well as approval of the loan financing the project. Implementation of the project is the borrower's responsibility (which often sub-contracts private business for the purpose of execution of the project), while the supervision of the implementation rests with the Bank as well as project evaluation.

Policies and Procedures

The Bank is required to follow a great number of policies and procedures throughout the various stages of the "project cycle." Legally, these policies and procedures are originally binding only on Bank staff.[82] However, once they have been incorporated into the loan agreements, they become binding on the borrower at those stages of the project cycle which fall into the responsibility of the borrower. Bank policies and procedures have no binding effect on project beneficiaries.

---

[80] See Article III, Section 4 (i) of IBRD's Articles of Agreement. Compare Article V, Section 2(d) of IDA's Articles of Agreement (leaving the requirement of a government guarantee up to the discretion of IDA).

[81] For a comprehensive description of the project cycle, see Warren C. Baum, The Project Cycle (World Bank 1982).

[82] See Ibrahim F.I. Shihata, The World Bank Inspection Panel, *supra* note 3, at 42-47 (discussing the legal nature and function of Bank policies and procedures in detail).

The Bank's policies and procedures have been streamlined and simplified within the last eight years in a process called conversion. They are contained in the Operational Manual which consists of two volumes.[83] Volume I of the Manual includes all policies and procedures regarding strategies and financial products. It covers the thematic areas of country focus, sector strategies, financial products and instruments and partnership arrangements (in particular co-financing and trust funds). Volume II contains those policies and procedures that relate to project requirements. It includes safeguard policies (e.g. environmental aspects, indigenous peoples, involuntary resettlement and international waterways), economic project analysis, fiduciary aspects of Bank operations (e.g. procurement guidelines), financial aspects and "management" of operations (i.e. project supervision, monitoring and evaluation), and contractual aspects of the financial agreements.

Status of Non-State Actors in the Context of the Bank's Operations

Individuals who are potentially affected by the Bank-financed projects are neither the contractual partners of the Bank, nor the addressees of an administrative decision or subjects of a factual action (e.g. an action that constitutes a tort) taken by the Bank *vis-à-vis* them, at any stage of the project cycle. Legally, these individuals (or ultimate project beneficiaries) have thus the status of third parties *vis-à-vis* the Bank as the latter entertains a legally significant relationship only with the borrower (i.e. in most cases in practice the borrowing member's government).

Nevertheless, participation of individuals in the Bank's development assistance process of a nature other than a contractual, administrative, or factual relationship with the Bank exists. The inclusion of a diversity of stakeholders other than the borrowing member's government including project affected parties is, according to Bank policies, made an obligation at particularly two stages of the project cycle, i.e. the preparation and implementation of the project. As these stages fall into the responsibility of the borrower, the Bank requires the borrower to ensure participation of ultimate beneficiaries of the projects it finances.

For example, during the design and preparation of a hydro-electric dam, Bank policies and procedures may require the undertaking by the

---

[83] The Operational Manual can be accessed through the World Bank's website, at http://wbln0018.worldbank.org/institutional/manuals/opmanual.nsf/.

borrower of environmental studies,[84] the elaboration of resettlement plans,[85] and the identification of indigenous people.[86] Participation of project affected people in the context of such studies and plans will involve consultation by the borrower with the people living in the area proposed as the construction site of the dam as well as with local NGOs representing those people, to determine the environmentally most sustainable framework for the project, elaborate appropriate resettlement measures, and work out protection measures for indigenous people.[87]

During the execution of the project, the borrower will need to ensure that a resettlement plan is followed and that people moved from one location to the other are compensated for any losses, according to obligations in the loan documents that originate in the standards of Bank policies and procedures. The Bank is supervising the execution of the project by the borrower, including the borrower's observation of participation requirements. Where the Bank finds the borrower has defaulted on its contractual obligations under the loan agreement, including observance of provisions that in their substance originate in

---

[84] See, e.g., Operational Policy (OP) 4.01 Environmental Assessment (1999), replacing Operational Directive (OD) 4.01 (1991), (standardizing a process in which projects to be financed by the Bank undergo a specific assessment to ensure that the environmental effects of Bank-financed projects are discovered as early as possible in the project cycle and that measures are incorporated to minimize, mitigate or compensate for adverse impacts of the projects or to enhance their environmental benefits).

[85] See Operational Directive (OD) 4.30 Involuntary Resettlement (1990), now being converted into Operational Policy (OP) 4.12 (establishing procedures to ensure that the population displaced by a project receives benefits from it by compensating them for their losses, assisting them with the move and their efforts to improve their former living standards, income earning capacity, and production levels, or at least to restore them).

[86] See Operational Directive (OD) 4.20 Indigenous People (1991) (describing Bank policies and processing procedures for projects that affect indigenous people to ensure that the latter do not suffer adverse effects during the development process).

[87] In addition to the Bank policies referred to *supra* in notes 84-86 including participation procedures for affected people, see also Good Practices (GP) 14.70 Involving Non-governmental Organizations in Bank-Supported Activities (2000), replacing Operational Directive (OD) 14.70 (1989), (describing the ways of involving NGOs in Bank-supported activities, *e.g.* information exchange, while, at the same time, emphasizing that the Bank does not lend directly to NGOs when it finances a project).

Bank policies and procedures, it may impose sanctions on the borrower for the borrower's failure to observe contractual obligations.[88]

In spite of the absence of a legally significant relationship by the Bank with project beneficiaries, the Bank's non-compliance with its own policies and procedures may result in material harm to the beneficiaries as such non-compliance reflects on the project the design and implementation of which the Bank influences through its adherence or non-adherence to policies and procedures. In this sense, the Bank's influence (positive or negative) on the situation of project beneficiaries goes beyond that usually exercised by a lender.

The Two-Part Target of the Inspection Panel

In terms of the constellation of operations to which the Inspection Panel applies, it is important to keep two points in mind. First, the Panel checks the Bank's compliance with the standards it has set for itself and which have *a priori* no legally binding effect on project beneficiaries or borrowers (the latter are bound by the policies only upon their incorporation into the financial agreements the Bank concludes with the borrowers). The Panel does not check the borrower's compliance with obligations under the financial arrangements unless the borrower's compliance needs to be looked at as a prerequisite for the finding of Bank failures in supervising the project's execution.

---

[88] According to General Conditions Applicable to Bank Loan and Guarantee Agreements, the Bank may in such situations suspend the right of the borrower to make withdrawals from the loan account, and, in the case that non-observance of contractual obligations persists, the Bank may ultimately cancel the borrower's right to make withdrawals from the loan account. See, e.g., Article VI (Cancellation and Suspension) of the IBRD's General Conditions Applicable to Loan and Guarantee Agreements and Article VI (Cancellation and Suspension) of the IDA's General Conditions Applicable to Development Credit Agreements. In addition, it may be noted that (under Article VI, Section 2 of the IBRD Articles of Agreement and Article VII, Section 2 of the IDA's Articles of Agreement) the Bank may even suspend a member's membership if "a member fails to fulfill *any* of its obligations" to the Bank. (Emphasis added.) Such suspension power reflects yet another opportunity of the Bank to influence a borrowing member's fulfillment of obligations as well as a possibility of failures on the Bank's side if it does not even consider the application of sanctions where a member's failure exists. As was mentioned earlier, see note 57 *supra*, non-implementation of policy measures asked for by the borrower in connection with adjustment lending may not be qualified as a violation by the borrower of a contractual obligation but as a mere non-fulfillment of a condition for disbursement. Bank failures in this context would, for example, exist in overlooking that a condition was not fulfilled and disbursement followed without that disbursement being justified. Such Bank failures would eventually contribute to the perpetuation of harm to requesters.

Second, the Bank's non-compliance must have a direct material external impact on the project beneficiaries through Bank influence on the project's design and implementation with whom, as mentioned earlier, the Bank has, however, neither a contractual nor an administrative or factual relationship (e.g. arising through tortuous behavior). In other words, the Panel assesses Bank behavior which might have a negative effect on non-State actors although the Bank does not conclude contracts with them, does not take any decisions directly addressed to them, nor exercises any factual activity that could constitute direct tortuous behavior *vis-à-vis* them.

The Panel Mechanism's Overall Character

While no contracts concluded by the Bank with project beneficiaries, no Bank decisions addressed to them, or Bank actions taken *vis-à-vis* them exist, which the beneficiaries, when adversely affected by Bank-financed projects, could challenge in a court with jurisdiction over the case and in respect of which they could ask for redress from such court, there exists the possibility of people adversely affected by Bank-financed projects raising concerns regarding Bank failures in connection with the design, appraisal, and/or implementation of projects before the Bank's Inspection Panel.

In recognition that Bank behaviors can nevertheless harm third party non-State actors, the Panel was established to serve as a competent complaint mechanism filling what progressive advocates of international development law had long perceived as a gap in terms of legal protection of project-affected people against activities of international organizations.[89] As the Inspection Panel is thus a novel complaint mechanism, its peculiar nature must be stressed in order to be able to assess its potential applicability in the context of other international organizations.

Accountability versus Remedies Concepts

The Inspection Panel's mechanism stands for the concept of accountability.[90] This concept must be distinguished from the concepts of legal

---

[89] It must be stressed that, by the standards of traditional international law, the absence of a complaint mechanism to third parties non-State actors looking at an international organization's failures cannot be identified as a gap but must be taken as normal state-of-art in international law.

[90] Accountability originally denotes answerability for the performance of an office, a charge, or a duty. It is not an entirely legal concept, but it refers to standards of conduct of ethical, institutional, and also legal nature within an organization. See

liability and international responsibility.[91] The general distinctions existing between all three concepts relate to the different fora, the different criteria of standing before these fora, different applicable standards, and differences regarding the nature of remedial measures under each concept.[92] From a legal point of view, one particular difference between the accountability concept and the two other concepts must be primarily emphasized. Both legal liability under domestic law and international responsibility can be clearly characterized as traditional legal remedies concepts. They are based on the philosophy of legal action and remedies. This means that their essence under the old maxim of *"ubi jus, ibi remedium"* is that, under them, someone who has been wronged by another has a right to be remedied and will receive an enforceable court judgment if he/she brings an action before the court requiring the wrong-doer to correct the wrong, compensate the wronged, or put him/her in the position he/she was before the wrong-doing occurred. By contrast, the accountability concept, for which the Inspection Panel stands, is essentially not a remedy concept. It does not give a right to remedial measures and it also does not provide for a corresponding enforceable judgment.[93]

Avery Leiserson, Responsibility, in A Dictionary of the Social Sciences 599, 600 (Julius Gould & William L. Kolb eds., 1964) (discussing the distinction between accountability and legal responsibility and, in this context, pointing out that legal responsibility includes the elements of an obligation, the breach of that obligation, harm caused to third parties by the breach, and the duty to remedy the harm, while accountability does not include the element of liability for harm caused to third parties).

[91] For a detailed analysis between the Inspection Panel's accountability concept and the concept of legal liability, see Ibrahim F.I. Shihata, The World Bank Inspection Panel, *supra* note 3, at 106-115, and *id.* The World Bank Inspection Panel: In Practice, *supra* note 3, at Chapter 5. See also Sabine Schlemmer-Schulte, The World Bank Inspection Panel: Accountability to Non-State Actors, Translex, Vol. 2, No. 1 (April 1999) (discussing the distinction between the concepts of accountability, liability and international responsibility in connection with the activities of international organizations in general and the Bank's work and its Inspection Panel mechanism in particular).

[92] For an overview of all three concepts and the distinctions between them, see the chart " 'Actions' by Non-State Actors against the World Bank under Three Different Concepts" in Annex III to this paper, at 545.

[93] The enforcement of legal rules is not the concern of the accountability concept of the Panel. Consequently, the accountability concept, with the Inspection Panel as its prototype, is not entirely about law, of which one essential element is its enforcement.

The Prototype of an International Organization's External Accountability Mechanism: The World Bank Inspection Panel

The accountability mechanism of the Inspection Panel shows the following features in terms of the criteria of standing, applicable standards, remedial measures, and type of forum. It gives groupings of individuals the right to bring complaints before it. The applicable standards before the Panel to measure Bank failures are the Bank's internal policies and procedures. The Panel does not provide for a right to remedial measures or any other corrective measures. If the latter are taken in connection with a request before the Panel, they are vested in the discretionary power of Management or the Board of Executive Directors to perform their functions assigned to them under the Bank's charter. The Panel is not a court before which an adversarial proceeding is brought but a special independent, and investigatory body. The result of the Panel process is not an enforceable judgment but findings by the Panel on the basis of investigations which are submitted to the Bank's Board of Executive Directors. The Board's decisions, while binding on the Bank's Management, the organ the Board supervises under the Bank's charter, are not judicial decisions in favor of, or against affected parties.

Legal Liability and International Responsibility: Remedies Concepts Unavailable for Project-affected People to Reach Out against the Bank

Actions brought against the Bank in a domestic court by individuals adversely affected by Bank-financed projects under the concept of legal liability on the basis of applicable domestic law (e.g. contracts, torts, or lender liability) would be inadmissible because the Bank benefits for its operations from immunity.[94] Notwithstanding the Bank's immunity, such actions would also fail on their merits because a substantive basis for the claim would be lacking in the applicable domestic laws. No contracts claim can be established as the affected people do not have any contractual relationship with the Bank. No basis for an action in tort exists either since the Bank is only supervising the project's implementation but not involved in any on-site execution of the project so

---

[94] As a general matter, the Bank is under its Articles of Agreement and its Headquarters and Establishment Agreements it entered into with the countries where its headquarters or resident missions are located, immune from suit in domestic courts with respect to its operational activities, unless it waives its immunity. For a more detailed analysis of the concept of legal liability in connection with Bank operations, see Ibrahim F.I. Shihata, The World Bank Inspection Panel, *supra* note 3, at 106-113.

that it cannot cause the harm required for a tort law claim. Legal liability of the Bank based on the concept of lender liability may not be established either as this concept is not commonly acknowledged in the world's main domestic legal systems.[95]

Actions intended to be brought against the Bank in an international court by individuals adversely affected by Bank-financed projects under the concept of international responsibility, i.e. responsibility for breaches by the Bank of its international obligations, may in practice never be launched.[96] There is no international judicial forum before which individuals could bring claims against the Bank for violation of international legal standards even if a country would espouse such a claim against the Bank.[97] The merits of such claims for violation of international legal standards could hardly be established. A finding of a violation of Bank policies and procedures in the design, appraisal,

---

[95] Even in the United States, where it has been introduced as statutory law with the 1980 Comprehensive Environmental Response, Compensation and Liability Act (CERCLA), lender liability is a relatively new concept. See the US Comprehensive Environmental Response, Compensation, and Liability Act (CERCLA or Superfund) set forth at 42 U.S.C. §9601 *et seq.*, under which lenders may be held strictly liable for their debtor's environmental liability as "owners and operators" of polluting facilities. According to the 1996 Asset Conservation Lender Liability and Deposit Insurance Act, which circumscribed CERCLA, secured lenders, i.e. any lender who "without participating in the management of a vessel or facility, holds indicia of ownership primarily to protect his security interest in the vessel or facility," are, however, excluded from this liability. See Public Law No. 104-208, 1996 U.S.C.C.A.N. (110 Stat. 30009), at 1166. For details on lender liability under US law, see Tracy K. Evans, Lender Liability, 16 Annual Review of Banking Law 40 (1997). For a first reference to the issue of lender liability in the context of the Inspection Panel, see Sabine Schlemmer-Schulte, The World Bank, Its Operations, and Its Inspection Panel, *supra* note 67, at 181, and for a comprehensive overview of the issue of lender liability in the context of the Inspection Panel, see Ibrahim F.I. Shihata, The World Bank Inspection Panel: In Practice, *supra* note 3, Chapter 5.

[96] For a discussion of the World Bank's potential international responsibility and the Inspection Panel's role in clarifying some of this notion's complex aspects, see Daniel D. Bradlow & Sabine Schlemmer-Schulte, The World Bank's New Inspection Panel: A Constructive Step in the Transformation of the International Legal Order, 54 Zeitschrift für ausländisches öffentliches Recht und Völkerrecht (ZaöRV) (Heidelberg Journal of International Law) 392, 409-411 (1994) [hereinafter The World Bank's New Inspection Panel].

[97] Fora for violations of international obligations by the Bank exist only for disputes between the Bank and borrowing countries and non-borrowing countries. See, *e.g.*, Jerzy Sztucki, International Organizations as Parties to Contentious Proceedings before the International Court of Justice (ICJ) 141 (A.S. Muller et al eds., 1997) (noting that the ICJ is not a forum for claims brought by individuals and discussing the various proposals advanced during the second half of the 20th century to change this).

and/or implementation of a Bank-financed project in the Panel process does in principle not reflect a violation of international legal standards.[98] It would finally be difficult to show causality between Bank actions and the harm potentially suffered by individuals in light of the division of roles between the Bank and the borrowing country in the project cycle, with the latter and not the former being responsible for the execution of the project.

The Inspection Panel: An External Accountability Mechanism

To summarize the features making up the Inspection Panel's overall character, it may be noted that the Panel represents an accountability mechanism of a character distinct from traditional remedies mechanisms. While the Panel users' rights or interests must be violated or threatened through Bank failures in order for these users to have standing before the Panel, it is not the enforcement of the respective rights which is the objective of an investigation of a case before the Panel. Violation of or threat to these rights give the harmed individuals the procedural right of standing before the Panel to trigger an investigation into Bank behavior without the possible consequence of a judgment enforcing the requesters' violated rights.

This accountability nature of the Inspection Panel may reduce its potential value as a model for other international organizations from the point of view of the inspection function's users in cases where remedies mechanisms exist which would offer better legal protection.

HYPOTHETICAL CASES OF APPLICATION OF THE INSPECTION PANEL MECHANISM TO OTHER INTERNATIONAL ORGANIZATIONS

In view of the particularities of the Inspection Panel mechanism, i.e. its user profile, the target of its investigation, and its nature as an accountability mechanism, it may be argued that the Inspection Panel mechanism may be transferred to other international organizations engaged in operational activities which could potentially have an adverse effect on non-State actors. To use the terms which *Ibrahim Shihata* employed in

---

[98] It must be emphasized here that the standards embodied in the Bank's policies (e.g. on resettlement, indigenous people, environmental assessment, and participation) go usually beyond the ones in binding international instruments. Non-compliance with Bank policies therefore does not result in a violation of general international law. Another test under the applicable international legal standards must be undertaken to find a violation of international law.

an intervention during this conference to point out a generally important distinction between international organizations such as the World Bank and others, it may make sense to apply the World Bank's Inspection Panel mechanism to other "activities-oriented" international organizations,[99] while it may not make sense to apply it to "debate-oriented" organizations.[100] Possible candidates for an application of the Inspection Panel in the category of "activities-oriented" organizations include:

(1) other international financial institutions (IFIs);
(2) other developmental and operational programmes; and
(3) organizations engaged in non-developmental activities (e.g. peace-keeping activities).

The possibility of extending the Inspection Panel mechanism to non-operational or "debate-oriented" international organizations should also be discussed in more detail. In all and especially the latter contexts, it will be worthwhile to think about the application of a modified Inspection Panel to other organizations, adjusted to these organizations' different tasks and resulting different needs, a task that can only to a very limited extent be accomplished by this paper.

Other International Financial Institutions

Inter-American Development Bank and Asian Development Bank

As mentioned earlier, two other multilateral development banks (MDBs), i.e. IDB and ADB, have established inspection functions. These do not differ much from the World Bank's Inspection Panel with respect to the functions' user profile, the targets of their investigations, and their overall nature. They differ, however, in terms of general institutional and procedural aspects.[101] Contrary to the World Bank's

---

[99] "Activities-oriented" international organizations are those which engage in operational activities such as financing projects and rendering technical assistance.

[100] "Debate-oriented" international organizations are those which primarily offer their members a forum for discussion of issues of worldwide or regional relevance and possible negotiation of new treaties on these matters.

[101] For a more detailed overview of the inspection functions of the World Bank, IDB, and ADB, see the comparative chart in Annex III of Ibrahim F.I. Shihata, The World Bank Inspection Panel: In Practice, *supra* note 3, at 491-500. This chart reveals a difference regarding the scope of the mandate of the inspection functions. While the World Bank's and IDB's inspection functions also cover these institutions' private sector operations, the ADB's inspection function extends explicitly only to public sector operations, thus excluding ADB's private sector operations. It may be noted that IFC and MIGA, the WBG's private sector arms, are discussing the establishment of their own inspection function. IFC and MIGA are analyzing

permanent body of an Inspection Panel, IDB and ADB maintain a roster of independent investigators/experts from which inspection panels are drawn on an *ad hoc* basis upon the respective Board decision that an investigation is warranted. Because the IDB and ADB panels are only activated at the time the Boards make the decision to go forward with an inspection, the IDB and ADB panels are not involved in a preliminary assessment of eligibility or admissibility of complaints. In the case of IDB, it is the President who undertakes to make this assessment and recommends to the Board whether to investigate. In the case of ADB, a newly created standing committee of the Board of Directors, the Board Inspection Committee (BIC), initially reviews inspection requests and then recommends an inspection to the Board.

Other Multilateral Development Banks

Other MDBs engaged in the same business as the World Bank, IDB, and ADB, such as other regional MDBs (e.g. the European Bank for Reconstruction and Development (EBRD), the European Investment Bank (EIB), the Nordic Investment Bank) could theoretically also establish an Inspection Panel. Their development finance business also requires compliance with internal policies and procedures. Failures in this respect may result in harm to an identifiable narrower circle of people who are the ultimate beneficiaries of the projects these MDBs finance. The performance in and supervision of their operational activities may benefit from the establishment of an accountability mechanism of the nature of an Inspection Panel with similar users and similar targets of inspection as the World Bank's Panel. Any broader adjustment operations these MDBs may finance, would before their investigation by an inspection function, be subject to the considerations laid out in connection with the discussion of World Bank adjustment operations in the Inspection Panel context.[102] The MDB's decision-making organs could perform the function of the World Bank's Board of Executive Directors, i.e. authorizing the inspection function's investigations.

---

the IDB and ADB models. For details, see Ibrahim F.I. Shihata, The World Bank Inspection Panel: In Practice, *supra* note 3, at 157 *et seq.*

[102] See *supra*, at 495 *et seq*. Special considerations regarding private sector business may be taken into account through exclusion of that business from the inspection function, an amended function, or a separate one. See, in this respect, the discussions on a separate inspection function for IFC and MIGA as summarized in Ibrahim F.I. Shihata, The World Bank Inspection Panel: In Practice, *supra* note 3, at 157-162.

International Monetary Fund

The application of the Inspection Panel to the International Monetary Fund (IMF) encounters more difficulties. The IMF's core business differs fundamentally from the World Bank's business so that the Inspection Panel's functional trio of user profile, target of inspection, and accountability nature of the Panel's mechanism may not easily find their concrete counterparts in connection with IMF activities.

The IMF's principal business consists of assisting its member countries to deal with their balance of payments difficulties.[103] To this end, the IMF makes its resources available to members to correct balance of payments imbalances and to thereby lessen the degree of disequilibrium in the international balances of payments of members. Legally, the transaction between the IMF and a member involving IMF's resources constitutes a sale by the IMF of the currency (or currencies of other members or of Special Drawing Rights (SDR))[104] in return for an equivalent amount, in terms of the SDR, of the purchasing member's currency.[105] Most of the transactions by which the IMF makes its resources available to members take place under standby or extended arrangements. Standby arrangements are decisions by the IMF giving members for whose benefit they are approved the assurance that they would be able to engage in transactions in accordance with the terms of the decision during a specified period and up to a specified

---

[103] Under its charter, the IMF's purposes include the promotion of international monetary cooperation, the facilitation of balanced growth of international trade, the promotion of exchange rate stability, the assistance in the establishment of a multilateral system of payments and in the elimination of foreign exchange restrictions that hamper the growth of world trade, the making available of its resources to its members to correct balance of payments imbalances without resorting to trade and payments restrictions, and the provision of a forum for consultation and collaboration on international monetary problems. See Article I (i – vi) of the IMF's Articles of Agreement. For general information on the IMF, see also Financial Organization and Operations of the IMF – Pamphlet Series No. 45 (IMF 5th ed. 1998) [hereinafter IMF Pamphlet]; and David D. Driscoll, What Is the International Monetary Fund (IMF 1998).

[104] The SDR is an international reserve asset created by the IMF following the First Amendment of the IMF's Articles of Agreement in 1969. Its value as a reserve asset derives from the commitments of participants to hold and accept SDRs and to honor various obligations connected with its proper functioning as a reserve asset. The SDR is essentially a basket of currencies determining its value and linking the rate of return on the SDR to market yields.

[105] For further details on the legal aspects of the transactions between the IMF and its members, see Joseph Gold, Balance of Payments Transactions of the International Monetary Fund, in International Financial Law, Vol. 2, 65 (Robert S. Rendell ed., 1983). See also IMF Pamphlet, *supra* note 103, at 8 – 10 and 58 *et seq*.

amount. Fewer transactions take place outside an envelope such as a standby arrangement. As balance of payments problems are generally regarded to be of a short-term nature, a member is supposed to make use of the resources only for a short period of time. As a general rule under the IMF's Articles of Agreement, the member is obliged to repurchase the currency it had transferred to the Fund no later than five years after a purchase,[106] or even earlier under the specific terms of the arrangement. All transactions include a letter of intent in which the member's authorities set forth the macro-economic and financial program they intend to follow during the period of the transaction. These letters of intent reflect what is otherwise known as conditionality of the IMF's financial activities. Conditionality refers to the policies that the IMF expects a member to follow to enable it to use the IMF's resources.[107] These policies should help the member to overcome its balance of payments problem without necessarily resorting to measures detrimental to its general welfare, and help it to achieve and maintain a sustainable balance of payments position over a reasonable period of time.

The transactions from the IMF's general resources account as well as the connected monetary and macro-economic policy measures undertaken by a member country in fulfillment of IMF conditionalities have a more generalized impact on the member country's economy as compared with the individualized impact of MDBs' project-centered activities. The activities of the latter may eventually, upon project implementation, harm a clearly identifiable group of people, who may be distinguished from other, unaffected people, and who, upon that qualification, may become the users of the Panel mechanism. By contrast, the IMF sponsored activities (financial resource input and policy measures tied to the resource transaction) generate an impact on the whole economy of a member country likely to affect several sectors and larger segments of the country's population. Establishing an Inspection Panel in connection with the IMF's core business would thus not mean creating a complaint mechanism for a group of individuals which is especially and differently affected by the international organization's activities but would mean opening a complaint mechanism for the

---

[106] See Article V, Section 7(c) of the IMF's Articles of Agreement. It may be noted that in the cases of IMF assistance through the Extended Fund Facility or under extended arrangements the period of time for the repurchase of the currency by the member is 10 years.

[107] For details see, e.g., Erik Denters, Law and Policy of IMF Conditionality (1996).

public at large. Legally, the risk of complaints by the public at large before a contemplated inspection function may be eliminated on the basis of the same techniques referred to in connection with the discussion of adjustment operations financed by the World Bank. The techniques in the latter context consisted of allowing complaints only at the stage of the implementation of the macro-economic policies through the application of respective laws, regulations, decrees etc. to concrete cases and individual market participants. At that stage, the adverse material impact through a tangible action by the State receiving development assistance (through administrative decision or factual action) would manifest itself so that the initial requirement for the standing of people before the Inspection Panel would be met.[108]

The IMF's activities concerning the general resources account would allow for targeting harm incurred by the requesters as singled out above and potentially resulting from the IMF's allegedly inadequate design of conditionality policies or its alleged failures in following up on the member's implementation of such policies. While, like in the case of World Bank adjustment operations, the member purchasing IMF resources is not legally obliged to implement the IMF recommended policies, as they constitute only a condition for the transaction but not an obligation the breach of which can be sanctioned, any inadequate recommendation by the IMF, inappropriate or complete lack of follow-up of policy implementation (and improper making available of IMF resources instead of withholding them) could nevertheless cause harm and thus, as a failure on the part of IMF, be a target of inspection. The IMF's Executive Board would be the natural organ authorizing inspections.

Whether or not the introduction of an external accountability mechanism such as an inspection function would make sense in the context of IMF's general resources account activities requires, however, further reflection. The desirability of an IMF inspection function may need to be discussed under aspects beyond the legal problem of standing. Thus, the risk of the mechanism entering into a debate over macro-economic policies which are in principle a matter for national

---

[108] The determination of individuals' rights or interests in the context of IMF operations may take place by recourse to domestic laws including those implementing IMF recommended policy changes as well as the IMF policies themselves. As was mentioned in connection with World Bank operations, see note 56 *supra*, two concepts developed by the ECJ, see, note 125 *infra*, may be useful in determining individuals' rights or interests for the purposes of standing before an IMF inspection function.

governments to discuss with the IMF and decide on when these governments request IMF support may need to be considered.

In addition to its general resources, the IMF has generated other resources to provide low-income developing countries with relatively long-term assistance on concessional terms. Such assistance was first made available to eligible members through the Trust Fund (established in 1976), and later through the Structural Adjustment Facility (SAF) (established in 1986), and respectively its successor, the Enhanced Structural Adjustment Facility (ESAF) (established in 1987).[109] The Trust Fund was terminated in 1981 and SAF phased out by the end of 1995, while ESAF continues to support the strong and comprehensive adjustment programs that the poorest countries need in the IMF's view to undertake to restore and maintain balance of payments viability in addition to achieving high and sustainable rates of economic growth. ESAF structural adjustment programs are financed by loans and do, in their structure, resemble World Bank adjustment operations.

Thus, similar arguments as in the context of World Bank adjustment lending may be made in favor of and against the transfer of the Inspection Panel model to the activities the IMF has engaged in through separate facilities such as ESAF. The legal, policy, and institutional concerns referred to above in connection with the Bank's adjustment operations (and the IMF conditionalities for IMF's core operations) may be recalled here.

Other Developmental and Operational Programmes

The United Nations Development Programme

Besides MDBs, a number of other organizations are engaged in development assistance on the international level. Most prominent, among those other organizations, is the United Nations Development Programme (UNDP). Because of the operational nature of UNDP's business, the potential application of an Inspection Panel mechanism to this programme may be considered.

UNDP was created in 1965 through a merger of two predecessor programmes for UN technical cooperation.[110] Today, UNDP is the

---

[109] For further details, see IMF Pamphlet, *supra* note 103, at 74 *et seq*. For the legal aspects in establishing trust funds under the auspices of an international organization, see Joseph Gold, Trust Funds in International Law: The Contribution of the IMF to a Code of Principles, 72 American Journal of International Law, No. 4, 856 (1978).

[110] See UNGA Resolution No. 2029 (XX), November 22, 1965.

UN's largest source of assistance and the main body for coordinating its development work. Technically, it may be noted that UNDP is not itself an international organization. It is an organ of the UN, linked to the UN General Assembly through the UN Economic and Social Council. UNDP's mandate was reshaped in 1995, focusing UNDP's mission on the most important development needs and potentials of today, including poverty eradication and creation of livelihoods for the poor, good governance, public resource management for sustainable human development, and environmental resources and food security.[111]

UNDP provides assistance through various means, mainly by giving concessional loans to governments of developing countries for a variety of programmes in the areas of UNDP's mandate. Like the Bank, UNDP stresses that the recipient government of its aid is in principle responsible for the execution of a programme,[112] while UNDP is overseeing that execution (monitoring and evaluating it). Identification and design of a programme, which are carried out prior to the execution of the programme, apparently constitute responsibilities shared by both UNDP and the government. The identification, design, and execution of programmes, all follow a number of principles or guidelines established by UNDP.[113]

Users of an inspection function, similar to those who use the Bank's Inspection Panel, would be present in the context of UNDP-financed programmes. In case the programme supports specific purposes, those who may be potentially harmed by it may be identified and could, similar to an affected party before the Bank's Inspection Panel, benefit from the availability of an accountability mechanism at UNDP.

A target for investigations by an inspection mechanism would also exist in the UNDP context. Failure of UNDP to follow the relevant principles at all stages of the programme realization can affect the implementation of the programmes and potentially result in harm to non-State actors.

---

[111] See UNDP Today – Introducing the Organization 3, 5-7 (September 1998).

[112] See Standard Basic Assistance Agreement between the Recipient Government and the UNDP (in Article III stating that the government "remain[s] responsible for its UNDP-assisted development projects and the realization of their objectives as described in the relevant Project Documents, and shall carry out such parts of such projects as may be stipulated in the provisions of this Agreement and such Project Documents" while "UNDP undertakes to complement and supplement the government's participation in such projects through assistance to the government").

[113] See UNDP Today – Introducing the Organization 4 (September 1998).

An inspection mechanism could complement UNDP's existing monitoring and evaluation functions. Such a function, while it may need to be adjusted to the institutional and operational environment of UNDP, especially regarding the identification of a suitable body to take on the task of authorizing inspections, could strengthen, through its being set in motion by outsiders, UNDP's overall efficiency and accountability.

Other international programmes which function like UNDP, may also consider the establishment of an inspection function.[114]

Organizations Engaged in Non-Developmental Activities

The UN Peace-Keeping Operations

The most well-known activities other than development assistance in which an international organization is engaged are the peace-keeping operations carried out under the UN framework for the maintenance of international peace and security. As is commonly known, the peace-keeping operations by coercion, as explicitly envisaged in Articles 41 and 42 of the UN Charter, failed long in practice because of a lack of consensus among the major military powers in their capacity as members of the UN Security Council to directly undertake non-military coercive measures or use military force.[115] Instead, a multilateral practice of conflict containment and resolution through peace-keeping operations by cooperation and consensus evolved under the UN framework which was not exactly prescribed by the UN Charter. This practice consisted of establishing two different kinds of military units. On the one hand, military observer groups, and, on the other hand, the so-called peace-keeping forces in the strict sense which were engaged in real activities to contain a conflict, in particular facilitating cease-fires and preventing a resurgence of hostilities through actions on the ground.[116] Recently, the system of collective security has been moving closer to the original concept of the UN Charter with the Security

---

[114] Among such other international programmes which may consider establishing an inspection function would be the Food and Agricultural Organization (FAO), the United Nations Conference on Trade and Development (UNCTAD), the United Nations Children's Fund (UNICEF), and the United Nations Educational Scientific and Cultural Organization (UNESCO).

[115] For a detailed account on the history of the UN peace-keeping by coercion, see Michael Bothe, Peace-Keeping, in The Charter of the United Nations – A Commentary 572 (Bruno Simma ed., 1994).

[116] For further details, see *ibid.* at 573.

Council playing a greater role in the Kuwait and Kosovo crises than over decades. However, it still falls short of the fully-fledged role envisaged for the Council by the UN Charter in managing the collective security system.[117]

Regarding the formation and functions of the UN peace-keeping forces as they evolved in practice since the 1940s, it may be noted that the forces' features follow a uniform pattern to some degree, while in some other degree their features vary. The unit of peace-keeping forces is formally created by the resolution of a UN organ, as a general rule the Security Council but sometimes also the General Assembly.[118] The resolutions support reports submitted by the Secretary-General which establish the mandate of these units as well as the details of their functioning. In addition, there is an agreement between the parties concerned either in the form of a direct agreement between the parties to a conflict[119] or in the form of an acceptance of a resolution by those parties individually expressed by each of them. Finally, there is usually an agreement between the UN and the State on whose territory the unit is to function, i.e. the host State, regulating the details of the relationship between the UN and the host State.[120] The latter determines the status of the forces in the territory in which they perform their functions.

The forces' functions include observation and verification of ceasefire, disengagement, or withdrawal agreements along demarcation or boundary lines, interposition (i.e. serving as a buffer between parties), maintenance of law and order, humanitarian assistance, and, as *ultima ratio*, the use of force (in self-defense as well as, if necessary, to fulfill the forces' other functions). The performance of these functions follows general guidelines developed internally at the UN.[121] To some extent,

---

[117] For further details see, e.g., Alan James, Action by the Security Council: Evolving Practice Beyond Traditional Peace-Keeping, in Contemporary International Law Issues: Conflicts and Convergence 281 (Wybo P. Heere ed., 1996).

[118] For a more detailed discussion of the legal basis in the UN Charter for peace-keeping forces, see Bothe, *supra* note 115, at 590-92. See further D.W. Bowett, United Nations Forces – A Legal Study (1964).

[119] For details, see Draft Model Agreement with Participating States, UN Doc. A/46/185, June 3, 1991.

[120] See Draft Model Status of Forces Agreement, UN Doc. A/45/594, October 9, 1990.

[121] See Draft Requirements for Peace-keeping Operations, UN Doc. A/45/217, May 8, 1990; Draft Training Manuals for Peace-keeping Operations, Doc. A/45/572, October 5, 1990; and Draft Standard Operating Procedures for Peace-keeping Operations, UN Doc. A/45/602, October 10, 1990.

these guidelines are also reflected in the status-of-forces agreement which the UN concludes with the State in which the forces will be stationed, i.e. the forces' host State.

The status-of-forces agreement outlines the legal status of the forces, in particular the privileges and immunities they enjoy in the host State. In connection with these privileges and immunities, the status-of-forces agreement delimits the spheres of jurisdiction of the host State and the UN. Generally, the territorial sovereignty of the host State has to be respected. That means that all members of the UN forces have to respect the law of the host State. But the host State recognizes the jurisdiction of the UN over its own forces. Consequently, the relations between the UN and the members of the force are, in principle, not subject to the law of the host State. Even where the law of the host State remains applicable that State waives its right to enforce its laws and exempts members of the force to a certain extent from the criminal and civil jurisdiction of the host State.

It is evident that the UN itself is not subject to the jurisdiction of the host State. As the UN itself enjoys full immunity and members of the forces enjoy immunity from the criminal and the civil jurisdiction as far as their official acts are concerned, the host State's nationals and residents may not sue the UN or the members of the forces before the host State's courts in case they have suffered damages as a result of the forces' actions performed in the exercise of official duties. Most status-of-forces agreements thus include a reference to either mixed commissions set up between the host State and the UN or claims commissions set up by the UN to deal with damages caused by the forces or its members in the exercise of their official duties.[122] While not a court but special dispute settlement mechanisms, these claims commissions' rulings on the compensation owed by the UN to host State inhabitants having suffered damages from the forces' activities are binding on the UN. The rulings thus offer a great degree of legal protection to the host State's inhabitants against the forces, reaching in some way the degree of legal protection given by court systems.

Theoretically, it would be possible to establish an inspection function similar to the World Bank Inspection Panel in the context of the UN peace-keeping forces. The inhabitants of a host State fit the Panel's user profile. Those, whose property or physical integrity (as guaranteed under domestic laws and referred to in the status-of-forces agreement)

---

[122] See, e.g., Draft Model of Status of Forces Agreement, *supra* note 120, at paras. 51-3.

is affected by the forces' activities, could be identified and distinguished from those inhabitants who would not be affected and not have suffered damage.

One would also be able to determine whether the harm to the host State's inhabitants would have resulted from the forces' non-compliance with UN guidelines or the applicable host State law. It may be noted that, in this respect, the UN's peace-keeping role is even greater regarding the potential real impact of UN action on host State inhabitants and closer to those potentially affected by the peace-keeping forces than the World Bank's smaller and more distant role as a lender for development projects *vis-à-vis* project beneficiaries. The UN (through the UN troops) engages directly in the potentially harmful activity, while the World Bank does not execute nor manage the project from which potentially adverse effects result to people. In this sense, the UN's contribution to any harm to the host State's inhabitants can in terms of causality be assessed more easily than the World Bank's contribution to harm to people adversely affected by Bank-financed projects.

The question, however, which needs to be asked in the context of the UN peace-keeping forces is whether it would make sense to consider the establishment of an accountability mechanism such as an Inspection Panel in light of existing dispute settlement mechanisms such as the claims commissions. If the claims commissions offer protection for host State inhabitants superior to an inspection function, especially because the commissions have the competence to issue decisions regarding compensation binding on those who caused the harm, i.e. the UN through the troops acting under UN helmets, there may be no need for an inspection function of the type of the World Bank's Inspection Panel. The Panel, as may be recalled, only engages in fact-finding regarding Bank failures. Based on the Panel's report (and Management's response), the Bank's Board makes a decision confirming the finding or disagreeing with it. Unlike the claims commissions which have been established for the purposes of compensating host State inhabitants for harm suffered as a result of the forces' activities, the Panel was not established for the purposes of compensating affected parties. Corrective measures for the benefit of requesters before the Panel, even though they may be taken, are not the primary objective of the Panel process. They lie entirely within the discretion of the Board of Executive Directors.[123]

Consequently, an inspection function may in theory be a model for the UN peace-keeping activities. Its practical usefulness requires, however, further analysis as existing mechanisms compensating for harm to people caused by the forces appear to protect people better than an inspection function would because these mechanisms operate more as remedies mechanisms than accountability mechanisms such as the Inspection Panel. It may be finally noted here that, were a Panel mechanism to be found desirable in the UN peace-keeping forces context, an appropriate body authorizing inspections may also need to be identified.

Extension of the Inspection Panel Model to Non-operational (or "Debate-oriented") International Organizations

Most international organizations engage in discussions in the respective areas of international cooperation for which they have been set up. Through these discussions, they often either prepare legally non-binding recommendations to their members or draft legally binding conventions/treaties for the members' (and potentially further States') signature and ratification and for States' cooperative actions and implementation of the instruments upon their entry into force.

For example, the UN General Assembly debates a broad range of political, economic, and social issues in the interest of global peace and security, and human rights. Its resolutions on the various matters constitute legally non-binding recommendations to UN member States. Under the auspices of the UN, numerous treaties on a similarly broad range of issues have been prepared which, after their ratification and entry into force, became binding on the States parties to them. Similarly, regional organizations, such as the Organization of American States (OAS) or the Council of Europe are engaged in discussions of interest to the respective regions, or prepare treaties, e.g. on human rights matters (Inter-American Convention on Human Rights and European Convention of Human Rights), to which their members may become parties.

---

[123] It may be noted that the supervision of the Bank's Management as the Panel's primary objective may eventually even bypass the interest of the Board in looking into the issue of corrective measures unless Management volunteers itself, on the basis of its own business judgment, to undertake such measures, to which the affected people have no right.

In the context of these "debate-oriented" organizations, the user profile, target for investigations, and need for accountability in the sense of the Inspection Panel model may in principle hardly be found.

The "products" of these "debate-oriented" organizations have generally no external effect on individuals. Where the organizations' debates result in legally non-binding recommendations, such an external effect on individuals is *per se* impossible. Where their debates revert into treaty commitments by which their member States (and potentially further States) will be later bound, it will be the States' actions implementing, not implementing, or improperly implementing the treaties which could eventually harm individuals but not the international organizations' actions. In the absence of actions undertaken by "debate-oriented" international organizations and external effects on individuals resulting from such actions, i.e. in the absence of targets of investigations and potential users, there is no room for application of the Inspection Panel model to these organizations.

Targets of Panel investigations and Panel users may, however, be found in the situation where international organizations exercise supervisory tasks over the States' implementation of treaties.

A link between external adverse effects on individuals arising in the course of a State's failure to implement treaties, or a State's mistakes in the implementation, and an international organization's behavior may be established where the task of the international organization would consist in the supervision of the State's implementation of treaty commitments provided this supervisory task would go beyond recording and reporting failures of or mistakes in treaty implementation and include the organization's powers to impose sanctions on the non-compliant member State so that failures by the international organization in the supervision could constitute the cause of adverse effects on individuals. The situation here would parallel the one in which the World Bank supervises the implementation of a project by a borrower according to the Bank's policies and procedures as incorporated in the loan documentation. Where, in the latter scenario, the borrower fails to implement the project, and the Bank fails to identify the borrower's failure and, through the pressures at its hand, i.e. possible suspension or cancellation of the loan (or disbursement of a tranche of an adjustment loan instead of withholding such disbursement), prevent the harm to people (or contribute to the harm's perpetuation), the Bank would be found partially responsible for the harm.

As may be recalled, Panel users had to be individually affected people, not the public at large. In principle, a failure of or mistake in the implementation of a treaty brought about by an international organization's failure to supervise the treaty implementation properly has potentially a negative effect on a great number of people in the non- or misimplementing State assuming that the treaty includes State obligations which would need to be translated into abstract-general provisions of national legislation.[124] Non- or misimplementation of a treaty thus creates potentially a situation in which an unlimited number of cases exists with all people whose rights were not implemented potentially demanding standing before an accountability function within the organization supervising the States' implementation of the treaty. Like in the case of non-compliance with World Bank policies in connection with adjustment operations or with IMF conditionality, the situation of an *actio popularis* may here be avoided by awaiting the moment of application of a misimplemented treaty to a specific individual (or individuals) in a concrete case by the agency of a State party to the respective treaty rather than focusing on the pending threat of an adverse effect on an unlimited number of people before such application. In the case of non-implementation of a treaty including a provision according benefits to an individual, such a moment may realize when the country's administration addresses the individual based on earlier law including provisions that are more detrimental to the individual instead based on provisions in the new treaty that are more favorable from the individual's point of view. Where the country's administration in the case of non-implementation of a treaty remains simply passive and does not apply the beneficial treaty provision, it may be more difficult to identify a person who is directly or individually concerned by the absence of treaty implementation. In the absence of a visible action by the country's administration, a person's direct and individual concern may, however, be found where, in theory, based on the assumption of treaty implementation, that person would be better off than he/she is in reality.

Before the immediate effect of treaty non- or misimplementation through supervisory mistakes on the rights or interests of potential complainants is assessed, logically the contents of the potential complainants' rights or interests must be determined. Local law which is supposed to be changed and improved through the international treaty

---

[124] It may be noted that the case of a "self-executing" treaty is not discussed here as few countries in the world integrate international treaties into their domestic legal system without implementation measure by automatic internalization instruction regarding such treaties in their constitution.

to be implemented may not lend itself to determine the potentially affected rights or interests. Mostly, these may be found in the treaty to be implemented itself to which recourse may need to be taken, therefore, for the determination of standing purposes. Examples of the criteria that would need to be developed to identify the contents of rights or interests of individuals in the treaty to be implemented to handle the standing problem before a contemplated inspection function could be found in the criteria developed by the European Court of Justice (ECJ) for its concepts of "direct effect" and "State responsibility" in connection with Member States' non- or misimplementation of European Union (EU) Directives resulting in a violation of rights of individuals and in damages incurred by them.[125]

---

[125] According to the concept of "direct effect" as developed by the ECJ, a provision of the EU-treaties or a non-implemented Directive would produce direct effects and thus create individual rights where they described beneficial positions of individuals in a "clear, positive or negative way [i.e. describing either the individual's right to something or giving an instruction to the State to act or not act in a certain way vis-à-vis individuals], unconditionally, and containing no reservation on the part of the [EU-] Member State." See Case 26/62, N.V. Algemene Transport en Expeditie
Onderneming van Gend & Loos v. Nederlandse Administratie der Belastingen (1963) ECR 1. "Direct effect" in other words would be given to an EU-norm which determines clearly in an abstract general way the right holder, the content of the right, and the obligor whose duty it is to ensure that the right is given to his/her beneficiary. Where a "direct effect" of an EU-treaty or legislative norm could not be established because the obligor of the individual's right in question was not sufficiently defined, the ECJ introduced the concept of "State responsibility" for States' non-implementation of Directives. It is important to emphasize that both concepts were ultimately established to ensure justiciability of individuals' rights on the basis of EU-norms. It was also because of that very purpose of the two concepts in the EU legal order that the ECJ drew a line for application of the concepts by accepting the concept of "direct effect" of a Directive only in "vertical" contexts, i.e. where an individual would seek the enforcement of rights against a Member State or its agencies, while not allowing for the concept's application in "horizontal" contexts, i.e. where an individual would seek the enforcement of rights against another private individual. For the ECJ, private individuals, who were made subjects of obligations under Directives, were not to be sanctioned for a failure (i.e. non-implementation of a Directive) that was the Member State's but not their own fault. As the concept of "direct effect" as well as the concept of "State liability" would in connection with contemplated inspection functions in other international organizations not be used for the purposes of justiciability of individuals' rights but only for the purposes of determining the individuals' standing before the new accountability mechanisms, the distinction between "vertical" and "horizontal" situations may not be necessary in the inspection function context. It may be finally noted that the "direct effect" doctrine may even be helpful in connection with recourse to Bank policies and procedures to determine the rights and interests of requesters for standing purposes before the Panel although the Bank's policies and procedures are generally formulated with a view

In practice, supervisory bodies in international organizations which may be the cause of adverse effects on people when they fail to supervise the States' implementation of international treaties would not include the UN human rights (HR) supervisory bodies.[126] The activities of neither the charter-based UN-HR supervisory bodies[127] nor the treaty-based UN-HR supervisory bodies go beyond reporting, reviewing, and commenting on functions to allow the supervisory bodies, based on the recommendation of another organ within the organization, to take sanctions against the member State failing to implement a treaty.[128]

---

to address Management. For more details on the ECJ's jurisprudence in connection with EU-Member States' non- or misimplementation of EU-Directives, see, in terms of the concept of the "direct effect" of Directives, Paul Craig & Gráinne de Burca, EC Law 151-198 (1995), and, in terms of the concept of "State responsibility" for such EU-Member State failures, see Sabine Schlemmer-Schulte & Jörg Ukrow, Haftung der Mitgliedstaaten für Nichtumsetzung von EG-Richtlinien, Europarecht 82-95 (1992), and J. Steiner, From Direct Effects to Francovich: Shifting Means of Enforcement of Community Law, 18 European Law Revue 3-22 (1993).

[126] See generally on the normative and institutional framework of international human rights, especially in the UN context, Henry J. Steiner & Philip Alston, International Human Rights in Context-Law, Politics, Morals: Text and Materials (1996).

[127] It may be noted that the notion of charter-based UN-HR supervisory bodies is used in the narrow sense, i.e. excluding charter-based organs that may perform a role in the supervision of human rights treaties observance by UN members such as the UN Secretary-General, the ICJ, or the UN Security Council etc. but which have, for various reasons, not always done so in practice as their primary functions required them to focus on issues other than the supervision of implementation of or compliance with human rights treaties. Reference here goes in the first place to the Commission on Human Rights, the Commission on the Status of Women and similar commissions. For an overview of both the charter-based UN-HR supervisory bodies and the treaty-based UN-HR supervisory bodies, see Figure on "UN Organs with Responsibilities in the Human Rights Area," in Philip Alston, Critical Appraisal of the UN Human Rights Regime, in The United Nations and Human Rights 1, at 6-7 (Philip Alston ed., 1992).

[128] For details of the UN-HR supervisory system, see The United Nations and Human Rights: A Critical Appraisal (Philip Alston ed., 1992). It may be noted that the public "blacklisting" of States in non-compliance with HR-treaties which some UN-HR supervisory bodies may employ on the basis of their findings does, in the view of the author of this paper, not constitute a method having sufficient teeth to be able to exert the type of influence on a non-compliant State which, if not used, could be generally qualified as a direct cause for the harm suffered by individuals through the State's non-compliance. Similarly, the existence or absence of special rapporteurs is of such uncertain influence on a country's observance of HR-treaties as that the failure of a UN-HR supervisory body to appoint rapporteurs could be qualified as a cause (even only contributory) of HR-violations.

By contrast, the ILO's machinery supervising the implementation of ILO Conventions includes a range of sanctions beyond mere monitoring and reporting.[129] After "blacklisting" a member failing to implement an ILO Convention, the ILO machinery allows for suspension, and, as *ultima ratio*, also termination of membership.[130] Here, the establishment of an inspection function watching over the performance of the ILO supervisory machinery regarding implementation of ILO Conventions could be considered, strengthening the general system of treaty implementation through holding the ILO accountable for weaknesses in the exercise of its supervisory function regarding implementation of ILO Conventions by ILO member States. An adjustment of the inspection function to the institutional ILO environment would, however, be needed.

It is obvious that a discussion on a transfer of the Inspection Panel to treaty systems which include commissions or courts before which individuals adversely affected by a State party's non-compliance with the treaty can directly complain (such as the regional HR-treaty systems under the European Convention of Human Rights or the Inter-American Convention on Human Rights) is superfluous as these treaty systems offer legal protection of a value superior to the advantages of an inspection function from the perspective of the complainants.[131]

---

[129] For a detailed discussion of the ILO's system of supervision, see Nicolas Valticos, Once More About the ILO System of Supervision: In What Respect is it still a Model?, in Towards More Effective Supervision by International Organizations – Essays in Honour of Henry G. Schermers 99 (Niels Blokker & Sam Muller eds., 1994), and Lee Swepston, Human Rights Law and Freedom of Association: Development through ILO Supervision, 137 International Labour Review, Issue 2, 169 (1998).

[130] According to the ILO Constitution, ILO members, which are believed to have failed to observe an ILO convention which they have ratified, may be brought before a Commission of Inquiry. See Article 26 of the ILO Constitution. The Commission investigates the member's alleged non-observance and may, if it finds the allegations to be true, issue recommendations as to the proper steps to remedy the situation. In the case, a member fails to carry out the recommended steps within the time specified in the recommendations by the Commission, the ILO's governing body may recommend to the ILO's (member) conference "such action as it may deem wise and expedient to secure compliance therewith." See Article 33 of the ILO Constitution. While not explicitly mentioned, suspension and termination of membership may be among the sanctions the ILO may threaten to a member in an attempt to secure that member's compliance with ratified ILO Conventions.

[131] An inspection function within these systems could only be useful in the cases where States parties to the systems have not accepted the jurisdiction of the courts of the systems. A similar argument could be made for the supervision of treaty compliance in the system of the World Trade Organisation (WTO) in case indi-

CONCLUSION

The creation of a formal accountability mechanism such as the World Bank's Inspection Panel whereby non-State actors can hold the organization accountable for non-compliance with its own standards was unprecedented in the work of international organizations.[132] The Bank pioneered with the establishment of the Inspection Panel, the prototype of a mechanism which realizes, for the first time, the concept of accountability of an international organization towards non-State actors with whom the Bank has neither a contractual nor an administrative or direct factual relationship but who are, nevertheless, the ultimate beneficiaries of the projects it finances.[133]

The Inspection Panel mechanism (or external accountability concept) has proven valuable in practice. The mandatory first review of the Panel mechanism at the end of two years after its inception resulted in the decision by the Bank's Board of Executive Directors to continue the Panel's operation. A second review has further clarified the Panel mechanism's processes and confirmed its increasing value to the Bank's work. Similarly, most outsiders view the Panel as a positive development.

Is the Inspection Panel a Model for Other International Organizations: "Yes, but ...!"

In light of the general consensus on the Panel mechanism's success, an examination of a potential transfer of the Panel model to other international organizations seems sensible. The examination undertaken in this paper answers the question of a potential transfer of the Panel model

---

vidual traders would in the future be allowed to bring complaints before the WTO panels and Appelate Body.

[132] The earlier case of the jurisdiction of the European Court of Justice (ECJ) over decisions of the European Communities should not be counted here because of the distinct supranational nature of the latter.

[133] For a more detailed discussion of the contribution to the development of international law in terms of accountability of an international organization for its own acts and omissions as well as procedural rights for non-State actors to trigger such accountability mechanism, see Ibrahim F.I. Shihata, The World Bank Inspection Panel, *supra* note 3, at 118-124, and *id.* The World Bank Inspection Panel: In Practice, *supra* note 3, at 261-267. See also Daniel D. Bradlow & Sabine Schlemmer-Schulte, The World Bank's New Inspection Panel, *supra* note 96, at 392 *et seq.*, and Sabine Schlemmer-Schulte, The World Bank's Experience with its Inspection Panel, *supra* note 32, at 379-386.

with a qualified "yes." The details of this qualified "yes" are the following.

Theoretically, the model of the World Bank Inspection Panel may be transferred to other "activities-oriented" international organizations as these organizations' actions, similar to the Bank's project-related activities of project design and supervision of project implementation, may generate external negative effects on individuals. Identifiable users of an inspection function and targets for inspections exist thus in the context of "activities-oriented" international organizations. An extension of the Inspection Panel model may even be considered to "debate-oriented" international organizations provided these exercise supervisory functions over member States' treaty implementation and their improper supervision impacts negatively on individuals.

This theoretical finding of other areas for an application of the Panel mechanism on the basis of an analysis of the Panel's meaning in the abstract as well as the theoretical limits to such application confirms the wisdom that the organizers of this conference have followed in their book to describe international organizations. The paradigm "Unity within Diversity" is in principle valid for another micro-aspect of international organizations, i.e. their accountability *vis-à-vis* non-State actors.

In practice, the extension of an Inspection Panel may, however, be more limited than at first glance evident in theory. Often, there may be simply no need for the introduction of an accountability mechanism where existing mechanisms offer better protection for individuals against harm caused by international organizations than an inspection function would. Other practical considerations revolve around the suitability of an accountability function either on the grounds of its desirability as a matter of policy and/or in light of the risks of the confusion which such a function may create in practice.[134]

Legally, the structure of an inspection function receiving complaints by non-State actors who are individually and directly affected by the actions or omissions of "activities-oriented" international organizations and those of "debate-oriented" organizations exercising supervisory tasks *vis-à-vis* States which may be the cause of adverse effects on individuals may be set up in a sound and unequivocal way.

---

[134] It may be noted that some of the confusion that may result from new inspection functions may not be new. It may be similar to the confusion that arose in connection with the World Bank Inspection Panel.

Techniques well known in domestic laws and EU-law may be used to determine when standing criteria for such an inspection function for the purpose of exclusion of complaints by the public at large would have been met. Thus, in the context of World Bank (and other IFIs') adjustment lending, IMF's general resources business, other development programmes' policy-oriented development assistance as well as in the context of certain supervisory functions regarding treaty implementation exercised by international organizations, standing criteria before the new inspection function would be met by analogy from the situation found in domestic administrative law (i.e. including, as preconditions for standing, steps that would be taken by the States receiving assistance and implementing policy changes or implementing treaty obligations) to determine when the potential users of the Panel would be individually and directly concerned.

The contents of standing criteria (i.e. the determination of the right-holders – and thus potential requesters – and what their rights would be) could be determined beforehand in the abstract-general way on the basis of an analysis of the applicable domestic laws, the organizations' policies which are relevant in the respective activity (as referred to in the transaction/contract etc. relating to the activity that is subject to inspection), or in the treaty the implementation of which is to be supervised. While it may, however, be possible to establish useful standing criteria using concepts developed under domestic laws and EU-law (such as the theory of "self-executing" treaties and "direct effect" of EU-Directives), this method may create confusion, even among lawyers. It may be difficult to clarify that all concepts that would lend their idea to the establishment of criteria of standing before the inspection function would be used for standing purposes only, i.e. only for the purposes of checking the admissibility of requests before the accountability mechanism, while these concepts, in the environment in which they had been originally developed, are primarily used for the purposes of assessing the merits of a claim with a view of the claim's later enforcement. Especially the concept of "direct effect" of EU-Directives[135] enables individuals to enforce the procedural and/or substantive rights granted to them by the Directive in the case of the Di-

---

[135] This concept finds its parallel in general international treaty law in the concept of "self-executing" treaty norms developed under the US Constitution's provision of automatic incorporation of international treaties into US domestic law whereby such incorporation was reduced to those treaty norms which could be applied without a need for further implementation measures, e.g. those norms that contained clear and unconditional rights of individuals.

rective's non-implementation (or misimplementation) although, under the general rule, a Directive's provisions can only be enforced on the basis of an EU-Member State's implementation measure. It may be difficult in practice to prevent that those establishing a new inspection function in another organization, those who will use it, and those who observe that function's work would not subconsciously associate with the use of standing criteria drawn up along the lines of the "direct effect" doctrine the purpose of enforcement/justiciability which the "direct effect" concept has but which is alien to the accountability concept of the World Bank Inspection Panel. By the use of the "direct effect" doctrine even only for purposes of determining a requester's standing, confusion may thus abound about the nature of the new inspection function.[136] Such confusion may not be legally justified because "complete rights" that may be enforced[137] (i.e. a clear and unconditional description of right-holders, the contents of their rights, and the obligor of these rights) may rarely be found in the provisions of World Bank policies, IMF conditionalities, and other developmental agencies' policies. These instruments were not intended to create "law" in the sense of enforceable rules but were rather designated from the beginning to constitute "incomplete legal norms" to intermediate and impact in spheres far away from and among players other than non-State actors who are, in the domestic law sphere, the primary addressee of the law. In this light, the use of the concept of "direct effect" developed in connection with non-implementation of EU-Directives may clearly not serve as an analogy but as an inspiration only. Standing rights by recourse to World Bank policies, IMF conditionalities and guidelines of other international developmental agencies may only be

---

[136] It may be noted that such confusion did even occur in the history of the World Bank Inspection Panel in connection with which never ever a reference was made to the ECJ's "direct effect" doctrine.

[137] With the notion of "complete rights," reference is made to a phenomenon described in domestic law as making up the essence of a complete legal norm, i.e. consisting of an abstract-general description of players acting in a certain way under certain circumstances and, by law, attributing to such behavior a certain legal consequence, i.e. making actions and omissions or players in a legal order subject to enforcement possibilities. See, e.g., Karl Larenz, Methodenlehre der Rechtswissenschaft 240 *et seq*. (5th ed. 1983) (noting that the logical structure of a complete legal norm contains an abstract-general description of the facts of and the players in a certain situation as well as the legal consequence attached to that situation which may be enforced in court). In the words of Karl Larenz, "die Bestandteile des vollständigen Rechtssatzes ... ordnen dem generell umschriebenen Sachverhalt, dem 'Tatbestand,' eine ... generelle umschriebene 'Rechtsfolge' zu."

found in an aggregate view of the entire development package rather than in a single provision.

The confusion risks inherent in the use of "direct effect" and other concepts in connection with an analysis of World Bank policies, IMF conditionalities and guidelines of other international developmental agencies may for some even turn into a misperception of the legal nature of the instruments to which recourse is taken for the purposes of determining the standing of a requester before a new inspection function. Such misperception could lie in the wrong belief in a legally binding nature of some of the recourse instruments, e.g. the international organization's policies, similar to the theory of "subjektive öffentliche Rechte" (or individual rights being inferred from internal administrative provisions under certain circumstances).[138] While an international organization's policies and procedures such as the World Bank's are internal instructions issued by the organization's management for the purpose of staff guidance, i.e. binding on staff and not intended to develop external effects (unless e.g. turned into obligations of the borrower through insertion into World Bank loan agreements), the search for rights of individuals in these policies for the purpose of determining individuals' standing before an inspection function may lead to the assumption that the rights described in such policies might become externally binding through their use in connection with an inspection function, like administrative norms under the "subjektive öffentliche Rechte" theory of German law. Under that theory, an administrative norm with initially internally binding force only, i.e. only binding on the civil servants applying it, with the consequence that an individual may in principle not base a legal claim on it, may, as an exception from the general rule, become externally binding if otherwise a fundamental constitutional right of the individual would be violated.[139] Presuming a similar external effect in the context of an international organization's internal policies would, however, be going too far. It must be emphasized here that the context in which an international organization's policies such as the Bank's policies are applied is not the context of a domestic legal order. It is especially not the context in which a separation of legislative, executive, and judicial powers with

---

[138] On the ill suited analogy with "subjektive öffentliche Rechte" in connection with World Bank policies and procedures, see already Sabine Schlemmer-Schulte, The World Bank, Its Operations and Its Inspection Panel, *supra* note 67, at 178.

[139] See Eberhard Schmidt-Aßmann, Kommentar zu Artikel 19, Absatz IV, Rz. 132, in Maunz/Dürig – Kommentar zum Grundgesetz (1991) (loose-leaf commentary).

refined checks and balances exist and in which theories such as the "subjektive öffentliche Rechte" theory were developed to ensure constitutionally guaranteed safeguards for individuals *vis-à-vis* the executive. Also, unlike the administration in the German law context, the international organization's organs such as the World Bank's Management do not take decisions or actions *vis-à-vis* individuals on the basis of their policies, as noted above in the discussion of hypothetical cases of a transfer of the Panel mechanism to other international organizations (except for the case of the UN peace-keeping forces for which a Panel mechanism would however not be needed on other grounds).

An even more fatal possible confusion in the use of the "direct effect" concept of the ECJ could abound where the concept is employed for the determination of individuals' standing before a new inspection function established for the investigation of an international organization's supervision of States' implementation of HR treaties. In the latter context, the use of the "direct effect" concept may be particularly dangerous because the HR treaties, the implementation of which is to be supervised, are likely to include complete legal norms susceptible of "direct effect" or "self-executing" effect in the sense of their justiciability in court. Therefore, the fact that the concept is only used as an instrument for the sole purpose of determining the Panel users' standing may not be understood and a misunderstanding of the Panel mechanism to be a remedies mechanism altogether, although it is only an accountability mechanism, may result.

In addition to the practical dangers of confusion related to the employment of legal concepts and techniques borrowed from legal environments other than the ones of the international organizations which may consider the establishment of an Inspection Panel (although these concepts and techniques could be employed in a legally sound way), it may not be wise either as a policy matter to extend the Inspection Panel function to the work of international organizations in the area of macro-economic policy changes (i.e. to World Bank adjustment lending, IMF conditionalities both regarding the general resources as well as the ESAF activities, and similar activities of other development programmes). The financing of macro-economic policy changes involves difficult choices for both the country receiving the financing and the financier as such changes inevitably result in both positive and negative economic and social effects although their overall effect is supposed to generate improvements in a country's econeomy. The risk of reopening the debate on these choices were such financing subject to an Inspection Panel is realistic. As such discussion may not be avoided on the occasion of discussions of matters brought before the Panel, international institutions may find the establishment of a Panel, although theoretically possible, not advisable in this context.

Another great potential for confusion in connection with an extension of the Inspection Panel relates to a possible lack of clarity in terms of the target of the Panel. While the Panel is an accountability mechanism empowered to look only at the failure of the international organization which created it, the Panel may increasingly be seen as mechanism to investigate both actors' actions in situations where State actions constitute a logical prerequisite for a finding of the organization's failure (or even where they don't but the Panel may need to check whether they do).[140] The risk of such a distorted view of the Panel as an accountability mechanism assessing not only the international organization's failures but also the failures of the States in which it secures peace, the development of which the organization finances, or which the organization supervises when these States implement international treaties, increases with the decreasing degree of activity exhibited by the organization itself and the increasing degree of activity shown by the State. The smaller and more marginal the role of the international organization in the context of the activity to be looked at by the Panel becomes (and the smaller the chances of the organization to have caused harm to the requesters), the greater, of course, the risk of misperceiving the Panel's role. In addition, even if there may be still some accountability shared by the organization in the cases where it has a marginal role, it will be the States whose breach of their legal obligations is primarily at stake. It therefore may seem odd to create an Inspection Panel for the oversight of an international organization's behavior in these cases. The temptation to see the Panel in these cases as a watch-dog of States' behavior may be too great.

As great may be the temptation among requesters and critics of the activity concerned, who are frustrated with a State's behavior as well as that State's domestic policies and governance system, to abuse the Panel

---

[140] As can be seen from the experience of the World Bank Inspection Panel and the discussion on the lack of distinguishing between the Panel's assessment of Bank or borrowers' failures during the second review of the Panel's experience, the risk of confusion in terms of the target of an inspection function is quite great. It took great time and efforts, especially by the Bank's then General Counsel, Ibrahim F.I. Shihata, and the Board of Executive Directors' Working Group on the Inspection Panel to come to a conclusion on the issue and end the debate on it. For details, see Ibrahim F.I. Shihata, The World Bank Inspection Panel: In Practice, *supra* note 3, at 173 *et seq.* For a summary of the second review's discussion, see Sabine Schlemmer-Schulte, Conclusions of the Second Review, *supra* note 40, at 246.

mechanism, where the lines between the organization's and a State's failures become blurred. Such an abuse could occur where the Panel would be turned into an indirect "enforcement" mechanism of rights against a State, e.g. through the pressures that may be felt by States merely because of their behavior being discussed more prominently in practice and from the wrong angle than contemplated in theory on the occasion of a request before a new Inspection Panel. Instead of facing this risk of a diversion of attention from the international organization's failures to the States' failures in the cases where the organization plays a marginal role but the States are non-compliant with obligations undertaken at the international level, it may make more sense to invest in capacity-building in those non-compliant States to facilitate these States' compliance with international obligations. In the long run, assistance for such capacity-building in countries may be preferable over the creation of accountability mechanisms for a negligible mass of actions by an international organization.

Last but not least, it may be noted that the debate over a proliferation of accountability mechanisms of the type of the World Bank Inspection Panel has only begun recently, as had the debate over the external accountability of international organizations generally with the Bank's Panel being the first response to the debate in practice. The discussion of the potential model character of the World Bank's Inspection Panel for other international organizations in this paper hopes to have modestly contributed to the ongoing debate without suggesting any premature solutions to the issues at stake on which each international organization will have to decide on its own as it sees best fit for its work, as did the World Bank when it decided to create the Inspection Panel in 1993.

ANNEX I

The Process of Requests Before the World Bank's Inspection Panel

FIRST STAGE

I. *Receipt of Request by Inspection Panel*

II. *Registration of Request from Affected Party by Inspection Panel*

III. *First Management Response*

- Informing whether Management has already dealt with request and whether it has in this respect followed or is taking adequate steps to follow Bank policies and procedures
- Management opinion on eligibility of request, especially on question of failure (exclusive failure of Bank; exclusive failure of borrower; or partial failure on both sides)

IV. *Eligibility of the Request* (Ascertained by the Panel)

1. The Panel's Competence Relating to the Person of the Complainant (*ratione personae*)

    - affected party = community of persons
    - in the territory of the borrower
    - rights or interests of the affected party must have been or are likely to be directly affected by an action or omission of the Bank
    - representation (on his/her own; through a local representative; through international NGO in exceptional cases)

2. Competence Regarding the Subject-Matter of the Complaint (*ratione materiae*)

    - alleged failure of the Bank (exclusive or partial) to follow its operational policies and procedures with respect to the design, appraisal and/or implementation of a project financed by the Bank (including failure to follow-up on the bor-

rower's obligations under loan agreements with respect to such policies and procedures)
- alleged violation of Bank policies and procedures must be of a serious character
- material adverse effect of violation on the affected party, i.e. material harm

3. Competence Relating to the Timing of the Complaint in Terms of the Project Cycle (*ratione temporis*)

- exclusion of requests filed after the closing date of the loan financing the project or after the loan financing the project has been substantially (i.e. at least 95%) disbursed

4. Admissibility of the Complaint in the Absence of Other Grounds Excluding It Under the Resolution

- Management's compliance or intention to comply with the Bank's relevant policies and procedures so that the subject-matter of the request is dealt with and the need for an inspection is obviated
- complaint must not relate to actions which are the responsibility of parties other than the Bank, such as the borrower
- no complaints regarding a matter or matters on which the Panel has already made its recommendation

V. *Recommendation of Panel on Eligibility of Request*

- Recommendation to authorize or not to authorize investigation

VI. *Board Decision on Panel Recommendation regarding Eligibility of Request*

- Authorization or Non-authorization of recommended investigation, or
- Notice of recommendation to not investigate, or
- Instruction to investigate despite Panel recommendation to not investigate

SECOND STAGE

VII. *Panel Findings on the Merits of the Complaint upon Investigation*

- serious failure of the Bank (exclusive or partial) to comply with its policies and procedures with respect to the design, appraisal and/or implementation of a project
- having a material adverse effect on the affected party

VIII. *Second Management Response*

- Response to material elements of merits of complaint
- Proposal of remedial actions

VII. *Board Decision on Panel Findings and Management Response*

- Approval or Non-approval of Panel Findings
- Discretionary power to instruct Management to take corrective measures

ANNEX II

Chronology of Requests before the World Bank Inspection Panel *

Requests	1st Management Response	Panel Recommendation	Board Decision	Panel Findings	2nd Management Response	Final Board Decision
1. Planned Arun III Hydroelectric Project/Nepal (received Oct. 1994); IDA	Reported compliance	Investigation recommended	Investigation authorized	Bank failures found	Failures accepted and adoption of remedial action plan agreed upon with borrower by Management even before Panel completed its report on investigation	None because of the President's decision no longer to proceed with the project
2. Papassinos/- Ethiopia (received March 1995 but not registered); IDA	N/A	N/A	N/A	N/A	N/A	N/A
3. Emergency Power Project/Tanzania (received March 1995); IDA	Reported compliance	Investigation not recommended	Investigation not authorized on the basis of Panel recommendation	N/A	N/A	N/A

* This chart gives an overview of the course of requests brought before the Inspection Panel by December 31, 1999. N/A stands for "Not Applicable."

Requests	1st Management Response	Panel Recommendation	Board Decision	Panel Findings	2nd Management Response	Final Board Decision
4. Rondonia Natural Resources Management Project/Brazil (received June 1995); IBRD	Acknowledged partial non-compliance and announced efforts to take care of failures	After additional review upon Board request, investigation recommended	Because of adoption of remedial action plan agreed upon with borrower and submitted by Management before Board consideration of Panel recommendation, investigation formally not authorized but Panel was asked to follow-up on progress in implementation of remedial action plan	N/A	N/A	N/A
5. Pangue/Ralco Hydroelectric Complex/Chile (received November 1995 but not registered); IFC	N/A	N/A	N/A	N/A	N/A	N/A

Requests	1ST Management Response	Panel Recommendation	Board Decision	Panel Findings	2nd Management Response	Final Board Decision
6. Jamuna Bridge Project/Bangladesh (received August 1996); IDA	Reported compliance referring to an action plan adopted at the time of the response	Investigation not recommended	Investigation formally not authorized on the basis of Panel recommendation but Panel was asked to follow-up on the progress in implementation of the remedial action plan	N/A	N/A	N/A
7. Yacyretá Hydroelectric Project / Argentina / Paraguay (received September 1996); IBRD	Disputed eligibility of request and reported compliance	Investigation recommended	Because of adoption of a remedial action plan agreed upon with borrower and submitted by Management before Board consideration of Panel recommendation, investigation formally not authorized but Panel was asked to follow-up on progress in implementation of remedial action plan and to review compliance with policies and procedures	N/A	N/A	N/A

Requests	1ST Management Response	Panel Recommendation	Board Decision	Panel Findings	2nd Management Response	Final Board Decision
8. June Sector Adjustment Credit/ Bangladesh (received August 1996); IDA	Reported compliance	Investigation not recommended	Investigation not authorized on the basis of Panel recommendation	N/A	N/A	N/A
9. Itaparica Resettlement and Irrigation Project / Brazil (received March 1997); IBRD	Disputed eligibility of request and reported compliance	Investigation recommended	Because of adoption of remedial action plan agreed upon with borrower and submitted by Management before Board consideration of Panel recommendation, investigation formally not authorized but Panel was asked to follow-up on progress in implementation of remedial action plan	N/A	N/A	N/A

Requests	1ST Management Response	Panel Recommendation	Board Decision	Panel Findings	2nd Management Response	Final Board Decision
10. NTPC Power Generation Project/India (received May 1997); IBRD	Acknowledged partial failure and submitted remedial action plan	Investigation recommended	Investigation authorized in form of desk-study	Bank failures found	Basic acknowledgement of failures	Follow-up on the progress of the implementation of the remedial action plan took place
11. Ecodevelopment Project / India (received March 1998); IDA/GEF	Reported compliance	Investigation recommended	Investigation formally not authorized but Management offered in Board meeting on Panel recommendation to address Panel's concerns by strengthening supervision of implementation of project and agreeing on measures with State Government of Karnataka, especially regarding microplanning. Panel was asked to be involved in follow-up progress on implementation of remedial actions.	N/A	N/A	N/A

Requests	1st Management Response	Panel Recommendation	Board Decision	Panel Findings	2nd Management Response	Final Board Decision
12. Lesotho Highlands Water Project / South Africa (received May 1998); IBRD	Reported compliance and emphasized ineligibility of request	Investigation not recommended	Investigation not authorized on the basis of Panel recommendation	N/A	N/A	N/A
13. Drainage and Sanitation Project/Nigeria/ Lagos (received June 1998); IDA	Reported compliance	Investigation not recommended	Investigation not authorized on the basis of the Panel recommendation	N/A	N/A	N/A
14. Land Reform Poverty Alleviation Pilot Project/Brazil (received December 1998); IBRD	Disputed eligibility and reported compliance	Investigation not recommended	Investigation not authorized on the basis of Panel recommendation	N/A	N/A	N/A
15.Swissbourgh Diamond Mines (Pty) Ltds. & Others Regarding Highlands water Project/Lesotho/south Africa (received May 1999); IBRD	Disputed eligibility of request and Reported compliance	Investigation not recommended	Investigation not authorized on the basis of Panel recommendation	N/A	N/A	N/A
16. Western Poverty Reduction Project/China (received June 1999); IBRD/IDA	Reported compliance	Investigation recommended	Investigation authorized, however, not on the basis of the Panel's recommendation but based on the Executive Directors' own power, acting as the Board, to instruct the Panel to conduct an investigation	Pending		

Requests	1st Management Response	Panel Recommendation	Board Decision	Panel Findings	2nd Management Response	Final Board Decision
17. Argentina Special Structural Adjustment Loan/Argentina (received August 1999)	Reported compliance	Investigation not recommended	Investigation not authorized on the basis of Panel recommendation	N/A	N/A	N/A
18. Land Reform and Poverty Alleviation Pilot Project (2nd filing regarding project)/ Brazil (received September 1999; IBRD	Reported compliance	Investigation not recommended as request was found ineligible for lack of having brought the matter to the attention of Management	Pending			
19. Lake Victoria Environmental Management Project/ Kenya (November 1999); IDA/GEF	Reported compliance	Pending				
20. Mining Development and Environmental Control Technical Assistance Project/ Ecuador (received December 1999); IBRD	Pending	Pending				
21. NTPC Power Generation Projet/ India (received November 1999 but not registered); IBRD	N/A	N/A	N/A	N/A	N/A	V/A

ANNEX III

"ACTIONS" by Non-State Actors against the World Bank under Three Different Concepts*

	ACCOUNTABILITY	LEGAL LIABILITY	INTERNATIONAL RESPONSIBILITY
FORUM	Inspection Panel (IP)	domestic courts (preliminary question: immunity)	no international judicial forum; if at all, international arbitration
STANDING	grouping of individuals (whose rights/interests have been or are likely to be adversely affected)	any individual (with close connection to the matter at stake)	State acting on behalf of individuals (with close connection to the matter at stake)
STANDARDS	the Bank's internal policies and procedures	domestic law (contracts, torts, lender's liability)	International law applicable to the Bank (loan agreement does not include any commitment vis-à-vis individuals; if at all, customary international law)
REMEDIAL MEASURES	not required but possible under IP-Resolution or policies and procedures; any corrective measures within discretionary power of Management and Board	prescribed by law (damages or restitution)	prescribed by principles on international responsibility (restitution)

* While this chart outlines the distinction between the three different concepts, it should be noted that there exist also parallels and/or connections between the different concepts which, however, for lack of space could not be integrated in the chart.

FINAL REMARKS

Henry G. Schermers [*]

CONCLUSION

Conclusions were not drawn, resolutions not adopted. The conference was an exchange of ideas based on reports by scholars with great practical experience. After the conference the authors could adapt their reports and incorporate parts of the discussion in them. In some cases new reports were added. My final remarks are a subjective impression of ideas I obtained from the conference.[1]

PROLIFERATION

Proliferation has a pejorative connotation. Proliferation of international organizations suggests a wish to reduce their number, or at least not to increase that number any further. However, notwithstanding opposition the number of international organizations increases continuously, because there is a continuous need of supra- national rules and as they are needed in widely divergent fields specialized organizations are created. One large, strong hierarchically structured organization might be more effective but, apparently, governments do not want that kind of threat to their sovereign powers. Too large a number of international organizations lead to a waste of infrastructure, each organization having staff in bodies like administrative organs, financial departments, and staff tribunals which are too small to be fully effective and to build up experience.

---

[*] Van Asbeck Professor of European Human Rights Leiden University, former member of the European Commission of Human Rights, member of the Institut de Droit International.

[1] These final remarks are only partly my own. Most of them stem from the discussion during the conference. The best remarks are quotes from statements made by experts in the discussions. Because of the informal and confidential nature of the conference I do not quote names. Credit is to be given to the collective body.

The main purpose of international organizations is to establish rules binding for communities larger than states. For a consistent system of international rules one big organization may be more effective than many small organizations. To fill the need of supra-national rules by many different organizations leads to gaps and overlappings. Overlaps cause conflicts of competence and duplications.

In the field of human rights, e.g., there are six different committees supervising the different obligations states have undertaken in different treaties. Is that too many? Is it better to have a large number of separate independent organizations or fewer large comprehensive organizations? There is no single answer. Six supervising organs over different human rights conventions may be too many. One organization to supervise all human rights may have too little expertise in individual fields.

Proliferation of international organizations is not necessarily bad. In all sorts of fields the need increases for regional or universal rules. Separate organizations can collect expertise and focus on their specific tasks. In one large organization important political aims may overrule specific technical duties or may draw away attention and budgetary provisions from these technical aims. Heavy political weight of large organizations leads to more interstate competition for influence in the organization, e.g. by weighted voting or by high administrative posts for their own nationals. Such tensions may be detrimental to a good administration. Separate organizations also offer the possibility for diversions in structure. Some international organizations have been created as separate entities because the founding states wanted a different method of decision-making, such as weighted voting or a greater possibility of binding decision-making, possibilities which might exist for a particular specialised organization, but not for a large general one. For some tasks co-operation with NGO's may be more desirable than for other tasks, in the ILO representatives of workers and employers participate, the need for privileges and immunities may be greater in political organizations than in technical ones. Separate organizations offer more possibilities for variety.

When structures have advantages and disadvantages one tries to find compromises. Is it possible to combine the advantages of many separate organizations with the advantages of unity? Several middle courses have been taken. The three European Communities share the same institutions. This brings them so closely together that one may speak of one organization, even though there are three legal personalities. The International Finance Corporation has its own Board of Governors which, however, consists of the same persons as the Board of the World Bank. Several organizations in the Bank Group share the same Secretariat, many organizations share administrative tribunals. Many trust funds are almost separate international organizations even if they operate under the authority of the World Bank.

Recently, governments are rather reluctant to create new international organizations. This has the effect that several tasks, such as the protection of the environment and the protection of human rights have been attributed to different existing international organizations. This leads to problems of co-ordination, to overlapping and to gaps. Creation of separate organizations might have been more effective. Once different organs perform the same or similar tasks merger becomes difficult. Practice showed how difficult it is to merge for example the administrative tribunals of ILO and UN or those of the Bretton Woods institutions.

One large international organization, hierarchically supervising and co-ordinating all activities of other organizations may become so powerful that a sophisticated system of democratic legitimacy would be required. No really strong power centre can be accepted without some kind of democratic control. The great difficulty of creating such control pleads against the forming of a powerful international governmental centre.

Perhaps, part of the advantages of having one large organization can be obtained by creating a kind of "holdings" as umbrella organizations for special clusters of international organizations with similar business. To some extent such umbrella organs already exist.

Proliferation of organizations and especially proliferation of courts may also promote specialisation. Legal issues come to be more complex and can be solved better by specialised courts such as the International Tribunal for the Law of the Sea or the Appellate Body of the World Trade Organization than by a general court. Specialised organizations have shorter lines of command than large general organizations. The long lines of command make large organizations ineffective and bureaucratic. The report of the United Nations on Bosnia, published 15 November 1999[2] offers a clear example. There were not enough troops for protecting the population. On 6 July 1995 150 solders of the Dutch contingent of the UN Force in Bosnia, protecting the town of Srebrenica were attacked by some 2000 Serbian troops with artillery and tanks. Several times the Dutch commander begged for support by the

---

[2] UN document A/54/549.

air force.[3] This request had to go to the commander in Tuzla, who needed authority from UNPROFOR headquarters in Sarajevo, who needed to contact his superiors in Zagreb. The final line of command went even further, through the Secretary-General of the UN to the Security Council in New York. A green light had to go back along the same lines. Some of the requests never led to a decision. In other cases the decision came with too long delay.[4]

A small organization aiming at the defence of the people of Bosnia might have been more effective.

Not only because of the time it takes, but also for the sake of the content, long lines of command are undesirable. Pressing, urgent requests may end up as weak wishes, data may be deleted, it will all be hearsay from hearsay.

CO-ORDINATION

For many reasons it may be desirable to have specialised organizations and specialised courts. But every organization and every court also meets general problems, therefore we need co-ordination to keep some unity in the wide diversity. The more institutions there are the greater the need for co-ordination will be. Probably informal co-ordination is more fruitful than strict rules or superior organs imposing co-ordination. It would be helpful if, e.g. the members of the six different bodies, who supervise human rights treaties, would occasionally meet together to discuss experiences. In practice, the chair persons of these six committees already meet annually. This must be of some help in their mutual co-ordination.

The Administrative Committee on Co-ordination in which the heads of the many organizations in the UN system meet under chairmanship of the Secretary-General of the UN has a long tradition of informal talks. Common meetings of members of different organizations, such as common meetings of the independent experts who supervise the different human rights treaties, also seem desirable. But often these independent experts do not find the time to keep themselves informed about development in other expert committees. Often, they do not even find the time to properly serve the organs to which they

---

[3] *Idem*, paras 243, 252, 284.
[4] *Idem*, para 295-304.

have been appointed. Perhaps, more critical rules must be adopted for the appointment and performance of experts in many bodies.

The main responsibility for co-ordination remains with the member states themselves. In particular the smaller states that have insufficient staff to send different representatives to different organizations, have a role to play. When the same national representative is sent to many different organizations he may have insufficient time and expertise to perform an important role in the substantive task of the organization, but better than anyone else he may be able to handle problems of co-ordination with other organizations in which he also represents his own country.

Some co-ordination stems from the aims for which organizations have been established. According tot the International Court of Justice this applies in particular to the organizations linked to the United Nations. Whatever one's opinion on the WHO case of the ICJ[5] may be, the case indicated that some division of tasks must be based on the purposes of the different organizations.

The main task of the United Nations Development Programme is to co-ordinate the activities of all parts of the UN family within developing countries. In a way it is to supervise the other organizations of the UN system. However, the organizations of the World Bank Group do not accept any hierarchical supervision. The different voting system makes the organizations of the Bank Group substantially different from the other organizations in the UN family. The centre of power is amongst the Western states who provide the financing. These states cannot accept supervision by an organ dominated by other states. For any form of hierarchical structure not only the same member states should be involved, but also a similar power structure.

Overlaps and gaps can be prevented or diminished by a clear delimitation of competences. However, too sharp a delimitation in the constitutional documents of international organizations is difficult to reconcile with the necessary dynamics that an organization needs in a changing world. An obligation to consult and co-operate may be more effective than a sharp delimitation of competence.

The reluctance to create new organizations has led to an increasing number of joint programmes of different organizations, such as the Joint United Nations Programme on HIV/AIDS, the Global Environmental Facility and the Arctic Council.

---

[5] WHO opinion, ICJ Reports, 1996, 66.

With respect to the co-ordination of international courts and administrative tribunals it might be considered to make the ICJ competent to decide on the competence of each court or tribunal in case of dispute. A mutual possibility to request preliminary rulings of other courts on their field of specialisation may also be helpful.

TREATY LAW

The treaty is the traditional instrument through which new rules of international law are made. It was an effective means in the time when few rules above the national level were needed. In our modern society law making through treaties is deficient. Treaty making is slow, legal binding requires ratification of the states concerned. There are always states who ratify late or who do not ratify at all. It is the rule rather than the exception that treaties to which all participating states agreed enter into force only after many years. Our modern dynamic world meets with frequent changes of circumstances which require adaptation of existing rules. The amendment of a treaty is as difficult and as slow as treaty making itself.

In the ILO amending of conventions was found so difficult that the ILO made entirely new conventions when they wanted to overrule a former one. The effect was that some states remained bound by the unamended text and others by the amended one.

Uniformity of treaty law is also hampered by the possibility of states to make reservations. The effect of a reservation is that the obligations of states are not the same which makes later amendment of the rules more difficult. Further conventions building on a former one are also hampered if the former one is not fully applicable to all participating states. Under international law other parties to a treaty may object against reservations. The tradition of the UN to require such objections within a period of 90 days may be wrong. 90 days is too short a period for states that want to co-ordinate their objection with other states or that want to lobby for concerted action. In many cases a more active role of the Secretariat could also be desirable.

It is understandable, that in modern international law it is tried to avoid treaty making as much as possible.

For the establishment of new international organizations treaties are still the most appropriate instruments. They define the aim and the competence of the organization, they attribute powers to the different institutions of the organization and they create the legal personality necessary for recruiting a staff and for undertaking financial and other obligations. However, in recent years there are many examples of new organizations that had to be established quickly and therefore could not use the treaty as a foundation.

A new organization can be formed as a joined programme of several existing organizations or as an independent institution of one particular organization. Several new international organizations, such as **UNDP, UNICEF, UNCTAD, UNAIDS** and **WFP** have been created as organs of the UN, others, such as the Trust Funds as organs of the World Bank. In fact these organizations can operate almost in the same way as organizations established by treaty. By the creation of independent organs the definition of "international organization" was blurred. Next to organs operating as independent organizations there came also organs almost independently operating and all sort of semi-independent agencies, what is called by Von Bogdandy "The Underworld of Committees". At the other side of the spectrum it is unclear whether the European Union is an international organization or not. It is composed of three European Communities which each have separate legal personality, but nowhere it is officially stated that the Union has a personality of its own. Because of its position under international law it is most likely that it should be accepted as an international organization.

Most international organizations have the power to draft treaties which become binding law after ratification by the Member States. In this kind of law making the drawbacks of treaties are still stronger. For establishing a new international organization certain delays may not be too harmful, but for needed legislation a greater speed is usually required and a possibility for amendment is usually needed. We noticed, therefore, that the use of treaties for international law making is declining. Increasingly, international organizations are empowered to take binding decisions or to make recommendations which are so urgently needed that all states will apply them even when they lack formal legal force such as safety rules in air navigation or technical rules in telecommunication. Amendment of treaty rules can be circumvented by wide interpretation of existing rules. Through the principle of implied powers competences of international organizations can be expanded. The problem of long delays in ratification are sometimes overcome by stating in a treaty that it enters into force on a particular date or that it will be applied provisionally from that particular date irrespective of the number of ratifications received. As long as states actually apply these rules there will be no problem but legally they can not be held liable if they do not.

DECISIONS

To cope with the problems attached to law making through treaties an increasing number of international organizations is empowered to take decisions which may be applied as universal rules even if they are not ratified and often even if the constitution does not attach legal force to them. The advantage of rule making by decision are that it is much faster than treaty making and that the rules can be amended by subsequent decisions.

A problem of decision making in an international organization stems from the voting system. The normal rule in most international organizations is that each Member State has one vote. In a community of states this seems a good democratic rule. In a community of peoples it seems utterly unfair that the representative of 100 million people has the same vote as the representative of 300 thousand people. In a community of economic activity it seems unfair that the representative of a large economic unit has the same voting power as the representative of a small isolated commercially inactive group of people. In an organization established to regulate the financial market or the banking systems in the world it seems unfair that the representatives of the rich communities with great financial interests have the same voting power as the representatives of poor ones.

The tensions created by the one state one vote system has caused an increasing tendency to take international decisions by consensus. Only rules that have found general support are sufficiently legitimate to claim universal applicability. However, the requirement of consensus has a freezing effect. Every state can block a decision; law making becomes difficult. Some organizations rejected the one state one vote system. This has been possible only in more integrated societies such as the European Union or in organizations with a strictly restricted task. In an organization with the sole purpose of increasing safe air navigation one can imagine a voting system in relation to the number of aircrafts a country has, in organizations like the IMF and the International Bank one could relate the voting to the financial contribution of the state concerned.

Because of the different voting system the rich countries have a majority in the IMF, the World Bank and the organizations related thereto whilst they are a minority in the other organizations of the UN system. Because of this the rich countries are more willing to provide funds in the financial organizations and therefore permit them to undertake activities which the other organizations of the UN system could not finance. This demonstrates that the organizations which have a more realistic voting system have also better opportunities to make universal regulations. Law making possibilities depend on the way law can be made.

THE ILC AS A LAW MAKER

The International Law Commission (ILC) is the most appropriate body for the codification of existing rules of public international law. In this field, the ILC has performed an important role in the past with respect to the preparation of many treaties, such as the 1958 Conventions on the Law of the Sea, the Vienna Conventions on the Law of Treaties and on Diplomatic and Consular Relations. With respect to progressive development of the law the ILC has been less successful. Politically sensitive questions are less suitable for treatment by the ILC.

The authority of the ILC is of the greatest importance. As long as it is generally recognised as a most competent body of expert lawyers its reports will be taken seriously. Even if it is not followed by a convention a report of the ILC can be seen as a restatement of the law. As long as the governments do not openly disagree with such restatements interested parties will follow them and they will have strong persuasive force in court proceedings. The draft articles on state responsibility are a good example of this. On several occasions the International Court of Justice referred to this draft. Of course, not all forms of law can be developed through a restatement by the ILC, which includes progressive development as well as codification. Direct obligations of states, such as the obligation to report periodically can only be imposed by treaties.

In a committee of individual experts political bargaining is difficult as the experts cannot know whether their government will subsequently support the bargains. A committee of government representatives can reach compromises more easily. Special advantages can be granted to reluctant governments. Finally this may lead to less uniformity in the law but to wider acceptance. Convention N° 1 of the ILO on the hours of work (industry) of 1919 which excludes some states from the obligation of accepting a 40 hours work week and which sets different standards for some other countries, offers a good example of compromises which were reached in order to get wide acceptance for the Convention.

It may be questioned whether a body of independent experts is the most appropriate institution for creating new law. Independent experts may take positions which subsequently are not followed by their governments. A preparatory committee of government representatives offers more probability that compromises reached will subsequently be supported by the respective governments, for two reasons, (1) Government representatives operate under instruction of their Governments. As long as they can stick to these instructions, they can be reasonably sure that their position will subsequently obtain Government support. (2) Government representatives normally have the support of many government agencies and are therefore better able to take positions which subsequently will be adhered to by the governments themselves.

Perhaps the ILC could perform a useful role in advising other law making bodies on the way legal rules should be drafted and on the general provisions which should appear in all legislative documents.

OTHER LAW MAKERS

Binding rules of international law have to be laid down in treaties. Treaty making has always been the prerogative of states. Even when important drafts have been made by the ILC the final text of the treaty was established in an intergovernmental conference. When international organizations have powers to make rules which are either legally or in practice binding upon states, then also the drafting will be attributed to an organ in which the interested states are officially represented.

Apart from drafting rules by governmental bodies new rules of law can also be developed in universal organs with sufficient authority. Racial discrimination and a policy of *Apartheid* were not illegal in 1945. They were made illegal, partly through the texts of conventions, but also, and even for states which did not adhere to such conventions, through a long series of resolutions of the General Assembly which finally made the prohibition part of the law, possibly even of *jus cogens*.

The need for rules may be an important additional source of law. When no binding rules exist in a field which badly need regulation, the most interested parties will invoke drafts of the ILC, non-binding resolutions of international organizations and similar authoritative statements as if they were binding law. When no alternatives are offered the statements may become customary international law.

The influence of governments and the influence of political bargaining can be reduced by privatising or partly privatising international organizations. In the International Telecommunications Union (ITU) private companies have always played an important role. Also in the World Tourist Organization representatives of private tourist agencies participate in decision making. Recently the International Maritime Satellite Organization (INMARSAT) has transformed itself from an intergovernmental organization into a private company under Dutch law. By doing so the shareholders got full control over the organization in proportion to their financial interest.

HUMAN RIGHTS

Since the Second World War human rights law is developing as a separate branch of public international law. Rights are attributed to individuals, not to states, obligations are attributed to states, not to individuals. State sovereignty is largely set aside. The special role of human rights law means that special expertise is required of those who make and supervise the rules. The often-existing tradition of appointing ambassadors with widely different interests as experts in drafting committees and in supervisory organs is wrong for this branch of international law. Also the traditional rules on reservations to treaties should be approached differently. Liability and accountability require special attention. The development of international criminal law is an important branch of human rights law and the creation of an international criminal court is an essential element thereof.

As the protection of human rights is fundamentally a protection against governments it is of the greatest importance that those who monitor the different conventions are independent from their governments and are well prepared experts. In several UN supervisory bodies it still happens that members come to meetings unprepared because they are occupied by a great variety of very different tasks. This weakens the supervisory organs and it underlines the need for expert secretarial support which can coach the weaker members of the supervisory body. In several UN supervisory organs the Secretariats are too weak to sufficiently prepare sessions of the supervisory organs. In this respect the further developed European system may serve as an example. There the expert secretariat to the human rights organs plays a much stronger role. Once when a country had proposed too weak a candidate as a member of the European Commission of Human Rights a high official of the Secretariat went down to the government and persuaded them to nominate a higher qualified person. In cases where states made reservations to the European Convention on Human Rights the Secretariat also played an important role in persuading other governments to protest. For the time being such an active role of the Secretariat is inconceivable in UN bodies. When these bodies are supported by strong and expert Secretariats it may be desirable to allow these Secretariats to be better heard.

Governments should be criticised when they establish supervisory committees but do not provide the Resources necessary to enable those committees to function effectively. The absence of adequate secretariat support and often the failure to nominate experts of the calibre that would be desirable, often also the failure to facilitate the operation of the accountability seriously weaken the systems of human rights protection. Still the effect of supervisory organs can be significant if extensive reports are published. On the basis of such reports follow-up can then be given by NGOs and by national parliaments and national pressure groups. In many respects the Supervisory Committees, as well as the conventions themselves act as catalysts for national campaigns to change law, practice and budgetary allocations.

For national changes the South-African Constitutional Court offers us a welcome standard by citing the jurisprudence of other national and international bodies in the field of human rights protection.

ACCOUNTABILITY

The last subject of the conference, *accountability* was the victim of lack of time. Many international organizations need a possibility to keep information confidential. The World Bank, for example, would not receive needed information of governments without the condition of confidentiality. A proper balance between accountability and confidentiality can be difficult.

Of course staff-members of international organizations are accountable to their chief, secretaries-general are accountable to executive boards and boards to general conferences. General conferences are composed of representatives of states. These representatives should be accountable to their parliaments and the parliaments to the people. This does not mean, however, that staff-members, secretaries-general or even executive boards can be held accountable to the public at large or to NGO's representing interests of the people.

Who is accountable to whom? Inspection panels may offer a useful tool, strengthening the accountability of international organizations as units for acts committed. To go further down and hold those states who voted for the particular activity individually accountable would endanger the functioning of the organization, as it may move states to abstain from supporting action which they would consider useful.

FINAL REMARKS

The conference presentations and discussions raised a number of questions. They also demonstrated that there is an increasing awareness of the legal and practical problems of the co-existence of a large number of international organizations. There is a reluctance to create new organizations. Attempts are made to streamline and co-ordinate the activities of existing organizations.

At the same time however, there is a development in the opposite direction. Often there is no alternative for the creation of a new organization, as the cases of the World Trade Organization and the Organization for the Prohibition of Chemical Weapons have shown. In addition, the independent status that is usually given to international organizations to make it possible to perform their functions may in practice have disadvantages. It may hinder cooperation with other organizations, and it may make it more difficult to dissolve an organization when its purposes have been fulfilled or when its tasks have been taken over by others.

INDEX

A

ACC *see* Administrative Committee on Co-ordination
Access to information 434, **443-444**, 465
Accountability 100, **433-470**, **471-482**, 508-512, 557, **558-559**
    Democratic 215
    Financial **468-469**
    Functional 450
    Internal regime **472-478**
    Political 179, **196-199**, 208
    Third parties **481-482**, 484
Acquis communautaire 189, 386, 398, 401, 402
Acquis conventionnel 419
Ad Hoc Committee on the Indian Ocean 137
ADB *see* Asian Development Bank
Administrative Committee on Co-ordination 160, 245, 359, 554
Administrative tribunals **241-249**; *see also* International Labour Organization; International Monetary Fund; League of Nations; World Bank
Advisory opinion *see* ICJ
Agenda 21 127, 159
Agenda for peace 76
Amsterdam Treaty 23, 46, 194, 201, 203, 204, 205, 209, 211, 382, 399
Arbitration 117, 132, 266, 272, 281, 293, 294, 479, 481
Arctic Council 9
Asian Development Bank 485, 513, 514

Attribution of competences 101, 386

B

Baltic Council 13
Basel Convention 162, 173
Belilos judgment 57
Benelux 44
Binding precedent 337
Biodiversity Convention 125, 127
Biodiversity Secretariat 166
Biological Weapons Convention 136, 142
Black Sea Economic Co-operation 13
Bretton Woods institutions 37, 40, 42, 107, 111, 244, 248
Bruce Committee 35, 36
Brussels Treaty Organisation 22, 26, 27

C

Cartagena Protocol 162, 173
CDF *see* World Bank Comprehensive Development Framework
Central American Court of Justice 281
Central authority 91
Centralisation 92, 177, 203
CFSP *see* Common Foreign and Security Policy
Chicago Convention 274
Citizenship *see* EU
CJEC *see* European Court of Justice
Clearing-house mechanisms 170

Climate Change Convention 126-127
Climate Change Secretariat 162, 165
'Closed circles' 402
Closer co-operation *see* Flexibility
Collective security 90, 92
Combination of ACOs **139-141**
Commission on Sustainable Development 152, 154, **155-156**, 156, 157, 175, 352
Committee for the Progressive Development of International Law 219, 221
Committee on Security and Co-operation in Europe *see* Organisation on Security and Co-operation in Europe
Common defence policy 24
Common Foreign and Security Policy 391, 392, 407
Common goals 96
Commonwealth of Independent States 13
Competence
    Exclusive 91, 268, 409; *see also*: International Court of Justice
Compliance procedures 170
Comprehensive Development Framework 17-18, 123
Comprehensive Test-Ban Treaty Organisation 135, 140, 142
Compulsory jurisdiction 111, 117, 354; *see also* WTO; Council of Europe
Conciliation 117
Conference on Disarmament 137
Confidentiality 444, 481
Conflict
    Of decision 271, 277, 284, 286

Of jurisdiction 259, 262, 270, 271, 358
    negative 268
Consensus 231, 556
Consent 277, 290, 353
Consequential rules 396, **397**, 399, 401
Consistency 383, 386, 400, 408
Constitution 97, 189
Constitutive rules 396, **397**, 399
Constructive abstention 391
Content rules 396, **398**, 399, 402, 408
Contradictory decisions 270
Convention on Biological Diversity 162, 163, 165
Convention on Jurisdiction and Enforcement of Judgments in Civil and Commercial Matters 203
Convention on the Privileges and Immunities of the UN 478
Co-operation 238, 384
    Institutional limitations **399-403**
    Flexible co-operation **403-407**
Co-ordination **42-44, 59-60, 65-84**, 89, 160, 186, 202, 208, 238, **552-554**
    Procedures 73-74
Council of Europe 25, 26, 160, 230, 244, 254, 362, 416, 524
    Compulsory jurisdiction 419
    Expulsion 418
    Lowering of standards 416, 420, **421-422**
    Margin of appreciation **424-425**, 431
    Standards 416, 420, **421-422**, 431

Suspension 418, 420
Country Assistance Strategy (CAS) 123
Court of Justice of the European Communities 60
Covered agreements *see* WTO
Creditworthiness 115, 122
CSCE see Organisation on Security and Co-operation in Europe
CSD *see* Commission on Sustainable Development
CTBTO *see* Comprehensive Test-Ban Treaty Organisation
Customary international law 30-31, 228, 283, 326, 558

D
Debt relief 128
Debt sustainability analysis 128
Decentralisation 92, 194
Declaration of Philadelphia 377
Deduction from staff member's salary 482
Delegation (authorisation to use force) 80
Delimitation of competences 15, **16-48**, 49, 553
  Decentralized approach 33-44
  Centralized approach 44-48
Democracy 434, 437, **440-443**, 553; *see also* European Union
  Democratic deficit 99, 214
  Democratisation 182
Development 91
Direct applicability 200
Direct effect 201, 527-526, 532-536
Disarmament Commission 137
Disciplinary measures 480
Discretionary powers 99
Discrimination 403
Dissenting opinion 266
Draft Articles on the Most-Favoured Nation Clauses 232
Draft Code of Offences against the Peace and Security of Mankind 224, 236
Due diligence 434, **466**

E
Earth Summit +5 157, 159
ECB *see* European Central Bank
ECE Convention on Long-range Transboundary Air Pollution 152
ECHR *see* European Court of Human Rights
Economic and Social Council 6-8, 36-40, 54, 92, 98-99, 154, 155, 156, 157, 160, 519
Economic Community of West African States 81
Economical and Monetary Union 382, 389, 409
ECOSOC *see* Economic and Social Council
ECOWAS *see* Economic Community of West African States
ECSC *see* European Coal and Steel Community
EDC *see* European Defence Community
Effective control test 31
Emission reduction 132
EMU *see* Economical and Monetary Union
Enabling clauses 384
Enforcement action 78-83
ENMOD *see* Environmental Modification Convention
Enumerated powers 101

Environment 90, 122, 151, 159
Environmental Modification Convention 137, 142
EPU *see* European Patent Union
Equality 423-424
ESA *see* European Space Agency
Espoo Convention on Environmental Impact Assessment in Transboundary Context 163
Euratom 138
Euro zone 56
EUROCONTROL *see* European Organisation for the Safety of Air Navigation
European Bank for Reconstruction and Development 5, 514
European Central Bank 396
European citizenship 204, 206
European Coal and Steel Community 27, 253
European Commission of Human Rights
    Complaint 415, 425
European Communities 25, 26, 72-73
European Conference of Postal and Telecommunications Administrations 47
European Convention on Human Rights 524, 529
European Court of Human Rights 26, 32, 56, 202, 254, 265, 281, 361-364
European Defence Community 22, 27
European Family of Nations 422
European Investment Bank 514
European Organisation for the Safety of Air Navigation 12, **20-22**, 47, 60

European Patent Union 55
European Space Agency 25, 47, 244
European Union 44-48, 10, **177-217**, 230, **381-410**
    Agencies 212
    Central Bank **209-210**
    Committee of the Regions 209
    Competences 185, 186, 194, 196, 199, 203, 205, 208, 211
    Constitutional legitimacy 190
    Council of the European Union 185, 193-195
    Council of Ministers 188
    Court of Auditors 193-195
    Court of Justice 186-188, 193-195, 197-198, 200, 210, 213, 289
    Democratic legitimisation 190
    European Commission 188, 193-195
    External relations 409
    Ombudsman 186
    Parliament 186, 188, 193-195
    Sociological perspective/approach 191, 194
    Citizenship 387, 402
Europol 10
Exclusive competence *see* Competence
Expenses Case 97, 102
Express limitations 103
Expressed powers 102, 103

F
Fact-finding 319, 322, 324, 491
Fair procedure 465
FAO *see* Food and Agriculture Organisation

Final Act of Helsinki 51, 52
Financial management 447
Flexibility **55-57**, 206, 216, 217
    Closer co-operation 382, 384, **385-389**, 396, 403, 406
    Council of Europe **417-418**
    European Union **381-410**
    International Labour Organisation **366-372, 374-378**
    Specific forms **389-391**
Food and Agriculture Organisation 9, 73, 160, 166
Force of *res judicata* 266, 273, 277
Forum shopping 246, 259, 270
Fragmentation of international law 177, 206, 207, 262, **262-267**, 358
Framework approach 152
Freedom of association 376, 377
Freedom of expression 426
Freedom of political debate 429
Functional decentralisation 36, 40, 41, 48
Functional finality 453
Functional necessity 434, **468**
Functional specialized agencies 92
Fundamental conventions *see* ILO

G
G-8 (G-7) 6, 10
GATT *see* World Trade Organisation
GEF Trust Fund *see* Global Environmental Facility Trust Fund
General Assembly *see* United Nations
General principles of law 243
Geneva Conventions on the Law of the Sea 220, 557
Geneva Protocol 142
Genocide Convention 264, 269

Global Environmental Facility 9, 122, **125-127**, 166, 170, 490
Global Environmental Facility Trust Fund 122, **125-127**, 166, 170
Global governance 91
Global Navigation Satellite System 20
Global warming 125
Globalisation 12
Good administration *see* Good governance
Good faith 367, 376, 386, 387, 397, 401, 434, **452-453**, 472
Good governance 434, 435, **436-451**
Good neighbourliness **25-33**, 49, 60, 240
Greenhouse Gas 130
Guidelines on Reservations to Treaties 236

H
Helsinki Act 51, 254
Helsinki Convention 163
Hierarchy
    Between universal and regional organisation 71-72
    Of courts 262
    Of norms 408
HIPC Trust Fund 123, 125, **127-129**
Human rights 56, 81, 90, 94, 98, 108, 202, 220, 229, 236, 238, 239, 279, 280, 362, 375, 376, 402, 436, 522, 528, 550, **559-560**
    Universality 416, 422
Humanitarian emergency 81-82

I
IAEA *see* International Atomic Energy Agency
ICAO *see* International Civil Aviation Organisation
ICC *see* International Criminal Court
ICJ *see* International Court of Justice
ICRC *see* International Committee for the Red Cross
ICSC *see* International Civil Service Commission
ICSID *see* International Centre for the Settlement of Investment Disputes
ICTR *see* International Criminal Tribunal for Rwanda
ICTY *see* International Criminal Tribunal for the former Yugoslavia
IDA *see* International Development Association
IDB *see* Inter-American Development Bank
IFAD *see* International Fund for Agricultural Development
IFC *see* International Finance Corporation
ILC *see* International Law Commission
ILO *see* International Labour Organization
ILOAT *see* International Labour Organisation Administrative Tribunal
IMF *see* International Monetary Fund
Immunity 481, 520
    State 235
    Jurisdictional 238, 241
    Waiver of 480
Impartiality 434, 445, **465-466**
Implied powers 29, 101, 103, 555
Inconsistency
    of decision 259, 260
    of *obiter dicta* 263
Independence
    Financial 468
    Functional 445
Individual responsibility 280
Informal consultations 439, 441
Information sharing 170
Information strategy 443
Inherent powers 29
Inhumane Weapons Convention 142
Institutional balance 32-33, 434, 448, **455**, 459
Institutive rules 396, **397**, 399, 400, 405, 408
INTELSAT 61, 119
Intent 103
Inter-American Convention for Illicit Trafficking in Firearms 136
Inter-American Convention on Human Rights 522, 524, 529
Inter-American Court of Human Rights 281, 284
Inter-American Development Bank 118, 485, 513, 514
Interfet 12
Intergovernmental Panel on Climate Change 9
Internal society 92
International Atomic Energy Agency 136, 138, 139, 142, 233, 472
International Bank for Reconstruction and Development 111-134, 489

Affiliated institutions 113, 114, 121
International Centre for Public Enterprises 5
International Centre for Settlement of Investment Disputes 33, **116-117**, 242
International Centre for the Promotion of Enterprises 5
International Centre for the Settlement of Investment Disputes 33, 242, 280
International Civil Service **445-447**
    International Civil Service Commission 244
International Civil Aviation Organisation 98, 245
International Committee for the Red Cross 30
International Convention against the Taking of Hostages 229, 235
International co-operation 11, 12
International Court of Justice 54, 57, 58, **85-109**, 93, 228, 241, 252, 253, **279-295**
    Ad hoc chamber 281
    Advisory opinion 19, 272, **274-277**, **288-293**, 299, 356, 357, 475, 477
    Contentious jurisdiction 100, 272, 274, 288
    Exclusive competence 268
    Position and status 261
    Supervisory role 272, 294, 295
International Criminal Court 252, 276, 280, 290, 352
International Criminal Tribunal for Rwanda 252, 269, 276, 280, 289, 290, 352

International Criminal Tribunal for the former Yugoslavia 30, 252, 264, 266, 269, 276, 280, 284, 289, 290, 352
International Development Association 33, 71, **115-116**, 118, 126, 242, 489
International Development Strategy 40
International Finance Corporation 33, 71, **113-115**, 118, 242, 490
    Articles of Agreement 113-115, 118, 120, 121, 124, 133
International Fund for Agricultural Development 40
International Labour Conference 366, 368, 375, 376
International Labour Organization 34, 41, 62, 71, 74, 90, 106, 233, 254, 293, **365**-379, 479, 529
    Administrative Tribunal 58, **241-249**, 293
    Complaint 375-377
    Convention 366
        abolition of the worst forms of child labour convention 372, 376
        discrimination convention 370
        employment policy convention 370
        fundamental conventions 368
        hours of work convention 367
        minimum age convention 370-372, 376
        night work convention 367

night work of young persons convention 367-368
ratification 373
revision 373
social security conventions 371
workers' claims convention 371
Global Report 377
Governing Body 366, 368, 374, 377
Recommendation 366, 374
Representation 375, 376
Sanction 375
Tripartite consultation 372
International Law Commission 58, 96, **219-240, 557-558**
International law status 185
International Maritime Organisation 159, 245
International Monetary Fund 13, 39, 111, 124, 249, 515-518
    Administrative Tribunal 244, 249
    Conditionality of activities 516, 517, 525, 535
International Monetary Trust Fund 124
International Office of Epizootics 26
International Olympic Committee 166
International organisation
    Closed 69
    Commodity- 5
    Constitution 12, 13
    Disguised 9,10
    Dissolution of 63-64
    Establishment 51
    General 65, 69

Sectorial 65, 66, 68, 69
Subdivisions 3, 4, **66-70**
Subordination of 66-67
Unidentified 9
Universal 74
International personality *see* Legal personality
International Refugee Organisation 55
International Satellite Monitoring Agency 141
International Seabed Authority 254
International Telecommunication Union 1, 71, 74, 98
International Tribunal for the Law of the Sea 252, 254, 256, 257, 260, 266, 270, 276, 282, 285, 299, 351-360
    Seabed Disputes Chamber 355
International trust funds 124
International waters 126
Interpretation 385, 434
    Customary rules of 316
    Teleological 29, 106, 120, 133
Invalidating rules 396, **398**
IOC *see* International Olympic Committee
ISMA *see* International Satellite Monitoring Agency
ITU *see* International Telecommunication Union
IUCN *see* World Conservation Union
Ius cogens 82

J
JHA *see* PJCC

Joint United Nations Programme on HIV/AIDS *see* United Nations Joint Programme on HIV/AIDS
Joint Vienna Institute 5
Judicial economy 321
Judicial review 100, 437
Juridical personality *see* legal personality
Jurisdiction
    Advisory 277
    Conflict of 259, 262, 270, 271, 358
    Contentious 100, 288
    Exclusive 268
    Negative conflict of 268
    Optional clause 269, 270, 272, 286, 293
    Ratione materiae 280
    Ratione personae 280
Jus cogens 224, 558
Justice 434, **467**

K
Kosovo crisis 1, 6, 81
Kyoto Protocol 129, 130, 152

L
Labour conditions 90
Landmines Convention 142
Law of the Sea Convention 254
League of Arab States 34, 69
League of Nations 34-36, 253, 366
    Administrative Tribunal 242
Legal basis 437
Legal institutions **394-398**
Legal personality 9, 10, 52, 53, 71, 103, 113, 164, 166-168, **181-185**, 187, 194, **196-199**, 210
Legal principles 180

Legal responsibility 164-168, 179, 197, 198, 208
Legal review 99
Legal unity (EU) 391-394
Legally binding decisions 159
Legitimate expectations 434, **461-463**
Liability 183, 197-198, 210, 462, 481, 559; *see also* World Bank Inspection Panel
of co-sponsors 9
LNAT *see* League of Nations Administrative Tribunal
Lockerbie Case 100
Loizidou case 265, 286
Lowering of standards *see* ILO; Council of Europe
Loyalty 400, 445

M
Maastricht Treaty *see* Treaty on the European Union
Margin of appreciation *see* Council of Europe
Marrakesh Agreement 13
Membership
    Expulsion 476
    Growing 415-432
    Suspension 526
    Termination of 529; *see also* Termination
    Withdrawal from 475
Merger Treaty 188, 192
MIGA *see* Multilateral Investment Guarantee Agency
Mixed agreement 409
Model Rules on Arbitral Procedures 236
Montego Bay Convention 255

Montreal Protocol on Substances that Deplete the Ozone Layer 162
Motivation 434, **460-461**,
Multilateral Investment Guarantee Agency 33, 71, **117-118**, 242, 490
Multiplication (of international organisations) 65

N
Nairobi Declaration 157
Nationalisation 116
NATO *see* North Atlantic Treaty Organisation
Negligence 480
NGO *see* Non-Governmental Organisation
Nicaragua test *see* Effective control test
Non-compliance *see* World Bank Inspection Panel
Non-discrimination 238, 386
Non-Governmental Organisation 7, 57, 62
Non-military enforcement action 82
Non-Proliferation Treaty 136, 138 ,142, 229
Nordic Investment Bank 514
North Atlantic Treaty Organisation 22, 24, 69, 81, 160, 244, 362
NPT *see* Non-Proliferation Treaty
Nuclear weapons 54, 94; *see also* WHO Opinion on the Use of Nuclear Weapons
Nürnberg Tribunal 224

O
OAS *see* Organisation of American States
OAU *see* Organisation of African Unity
Objectivity 434, **465-466**
Observer status 74
OECD *see* Organisation for Economic Co-operation and Development
OEEC *see* Organisation for European Economic Co-operation
OPANAL *see* Organisation for the Prohibition of Nuclear Weapons in Latin America
OPBTW *see* Organisation for the Prohibition of Bacteriological (Biological) and Toxin Weapons
OPCW *see* Organisation for the Prohibition of Chemical Weapons
Opinio juris 228
Opting-in 390, 406, 409
Optional clause 269, 270, 272, 286, 293
Organisation for Economic Co-operation and Development 28, 44, 63, 160, 244
Organisation for European Economic Co-operation 60, 63
Organisation for the Prohibition of Bacteriological (Biological) and Toxin Weapons 135, 139, 229
Organisation for the Prohibition of Chemical Weapons 135, 139, 142
Organisation for the Prohibition of Nuclear Weapons in Latin America 136, 138
Organisation of African Unity 8, 14, 26, 69, 230
Organisation of American States 69, 136, 137, 230, 524

Organisation on Security and Co-operation in Europe 51, 52, 69, 136, 137, 160, 230, 241, 254, 362
   Court of Conciliation and Arbitration 282
Organisational unity 199
OSCE *see* Organisation on Security and Co-operation in Europe
Oslo/Ottawa Landmines Convention 136, 233
Ozone layer issues 125

P
Partial Test Ban Treaty 137
Participation (of regional organisations in universal organisations) 72-73
PCIJ *see* Permanent Court of International Justice
Peace and security 70, **75-84**, 95, 98, 101, 106, 524
Peaceful coexistence 32
Peace-keeping operations 102, 103, 453, 466, 477, 481, 513, 520-524
Permanent Court of Arbitration 252, 267, 284
Permanent Court of International Justice 253-255, 267, 284, 285
Permanent relations **70-75**
Personality *see* legal personality
Petersberg tasks 23
Pillar structure (EU) 46
PJCC *see* Police and Justice Co-operation in Criminal Matters
Police and Justice Co-operation in Criminal Matters 391, 392, 407
Political review 99
Political system 92
Politicisation **105-108**, 222

Poly-centrism 92
Poverty reduction 113, 503
Practices 29, 433, 446, 480
Preliminary ruling 407
Principles of international law 288
Privatisation 4-5, 61-63, 121
Privileges and immunities 468, 474, 478, 522
Procedural regularity 434, **464-465**
Progressive development 224, 226, 237, 240, 290
Proliferation 2-11, 53-55, 351, 549-552
   Advantages 14, 255-259, 259-262, 279-283
   Disadvantages 14, 259-262
   Of administrative tribunals 241-250
   Of arms control organisations 135-150
   Of international judicial organs 251-278
   Of law making organs 219-240
   Of standards 365, 372-374
   Organisational 177-217
   Role of the International Court of Justice 279-295
   Techniques to avoid 111-134
Proportionality 454, **463-464**
Prototype Carbon Fund 125, **129-133**
PTBT *see* Partial Test Ban Treaty
Public authority 189, 191, 201, 465

Q
Qualified majority 388

R

Rationalisation 39, 66
Recours en nullité 294
Referral (of cases) 270
Regional organisations 69-70, 77, 80-83
Register
  of Conventional Arms Transfers 136, 142
  of Military Expenditures 136
Reimbursement 480
Relationship agreements 36, **37-38**
Removal from office 487
Reparation Case 101, 102
Replenishment 116, 123
Reporting and evaluation 450, 459, 465
Reservations 239, 265, 269, 272, 418, 554
Responsibility *see* State responsibility; World Bank Inspection Panel
Right of initiative 401
Rio Declaration 151-152, 154, 155, 159
Rome Statute on the International Criminal Court 233
Rotterdam Convention 162, 163, 173
Rule of law 418, 453

S

Safeguards functions 138, 139
Sanctions 471, 472
Schengen (agreements) 10, 56, 217, 382
Schengen acquis 202-204, 390
Seabed Placement Treaty 137, 142
Seabed Tribunal 58
Secretary-General 156
Sectorial powers 86
Self-contained regime 262
Self-inspection 138
Self-interest 89, 90, 437
Separate opinion *see* Dissenting opinion
Separation
  Organisational 194, 197, 200
  Of powers 99, 195
Settlement of disputes 73, 170
Simic case 30
Single European Act 382
Sixth Committee 221, 223, 238
Social Charter 417
Social Protocol 389
Soft law 52, 57
South West Africa case 255
Sovereign guarantee 114
Special Rapporteur 225, 228, 233
Speciality 65, 101, 104
Specialisation 57-58
Standards *see* Council of Europe; International Labour Organisation
Stare decisis 337
State responsibility 225, 226, 228, 236, 286, 527, 559
State succession 232
Stockholm Conference 153, 254
Subsidiarity 386, 434, **456-457**
Subsidiary powers 101
Sugar Council 73
Supervision and control 446, 450, 455, **457-459**
Suspension 476
Sustainable development 122, 151, 152, 159, 161, 172, 174, 175, 484
Synergy 175

T

Tadic case 31, 252, 286, 359

Teleological interpretation *see* Interpretation
Terminative rules 396, **398**
Termination 61-64
Third Committee 229
Third parties 464; *see also* World Bank; World Trade Organisation
Trans European Networks Programme 20
Transparency 386, 434, **436-439**, 465, 482
    Collective 438
    General 438
    Individual 438
Treaty law **554-555**
Treaty of Amsterdam 23, 389
Treaty of Versailles 367
Treaty on European Union 22, **177-217**, 399
Treaty on Principles Governing the Activities of States in the Exploration and Use of Outer Space 230

U
United Nations
    Administrative Tribunal 58, **241-249**, 276, 289, 292, 477
    Charter 36-37, 78-79, 82, 94, 97, 98, 126, 219, 224, 244, 255, 256, 258, 276, 287, 289, 352, 472, 476
    Children's Fund 6, 55
    Commission on International Trade Law 229, 233
    Conference on a Human Environment 151
    Conference on Environment and Development 127, 151, 172
    Conference on the Law of the Sea 230, 232, 270
    Conference on Trade and Development 55, 63, 156
    Convention to Combat Desertification 162, 163, 166
    Development Assistance Framework 17-18
    Development Programme 6, 7, **16-20**, 42, 126, 141, 156, 165, 518-520, 555
    Economic Commission for Europe 160, 164
    Educational, Scientific and Cultural Organisation 6, 37, 40, 60, 106, 111, 242, 293
    Environmental Programme 9, 59, 141, 152, **154-157**, 165, 166, 171, 175, 229, 233
    Framework Convention on Climate Change 129, 130, 152, 161, 163, 164, 230
    General Assembly 26, 58, 59, 98, 99, 102, 126, 136, 137, 141, 142, 154, 156, 160, 171, 219, 222, 225, 235, 246-247, 254, 275, 277, 289, 290, 292, 358, 473
    High Commissioner for Refugees 9, 55, 141, 481
    Human Rights Committee 239
    Industrial Development Organisation 40, 55, 63
    Institute for Disarmament Research 137
    Institute for Training and Research 233
    International Drug Control Programme 7

Joint Programme on HIV/AIDS **6-9**, 10, 42
Joint Staff Pension Fund 245
Registers of Military Budgets 142
Security Council 76, 77, 79-81, 92, 99, 102, 141, 216, 270, 276, 437, 473
Sudano-Sahelian Office 157
System 90, 93
Umbrella 88
Unanimity 45, 186, 388
UNAIDS *see* United Nations Joint Programme on HIV/AIDS
UNCITRAL *see* United Nations Commission on International Trade Law
UNCTAD *see* United Nations Conference on Trade and Development
UNCLOS *see* United Nations Conference on the Law of the Sea
UNDCP *see* United Nations International Drug Control Programme
UNDP *see* United Nations Development Programme
UNECE *see* United Nations Economic Commission for Europe
UNEP *see* United Nations Environmental Programme
UNESCO *see* United Nations Educational, Scientific and Cultural Organisation
UNFCCC *see* United Nations Framework Convention on Climate Change
UNHCR *see* United Nations High Commissioner for Refugees

UNICEF *see* United Nations Children's Fund
UNIDIR *see* United Nations Institute for Disarmament Research
UNIDO *see* United Nations Industrial Development Organisation
Uniformity 381-383, 406, 417, 425
Unilateral measures 475
Unique competence *see* Competence
UNITAR *see* United Nations Institute for Training and Research
United States/Iran Claims Tribunal 252
Unity of administration 187, 188
Unity theory/thesis **177-217**
Unity-building 177
Universal Postal Union 1, 12, 13, 34, 63, 98
Universal Verification Organisation 141
UNPROFOR 80
UPU *see* Universal Postal Union
Uruguay Round 301
Utilisation of regional arrangements 79

V

Vienna Convention
 for the Protection of the Ozone Layer 162
 on the Law of the Treaties 220, 224, 239, 316, 557
 on Diplomatic and Consular Relations 220, 557
Volonté distincte 10, 11
Voluntarism 65

Voluntary contributions 449
Voting system 556; *see also* Consensus; Qualified Majority; Unanimity; Weighted Voting

W
WACA *see* World Arms Control Organisation
Wassenaar Secretariat 136
WBAT *see* World Bank Administrative Tribunal
Weighted voting 111, 550
Western European Union **22-25**, 47, 64, 81, 244
WEU *see* Western European Union
WHO Opinion on the use of nuclear weapons 37-38, **85-109**, 555
WHO *see* World Health Organisation
WIPO *see* World Intellectual Property Organisation
WMO *see* World Meteorological Organisation
World Arms Control Organisation 137, 142, 143
World Bank 6, 13, **16**-20, 34, 39, 62, 71, 112, 113, 160, 210, 242, 248
    Administrative Tribunal 242, 244, 248, 479
    Advisory services 121
    Comprehensive Development Framework 17-18
    Inspection Panel 280, **483-548**
  case record 490-491
  composition 487-488
  mandate 489-490

Inspection Panel Mechanism
  actio popularis 496
  affected party 495
  clarifications 491-492
  community of persons 496
  corrective measures 521
  functioning 488
  geographical connection 500-501
  individual concern 499
  interest 497-500
  investigations 494, 499
  liability 509-511
  non-compliance 493-495, 498, 501, 506, 508, 525, 529
  recommendation 489, 494, 499
  responsibility 509-511
  review 491-495
Mandate 501-502
Lending operations 503-504
Non-state actors *see* Third parties
Operations Evaluation Department **486-487**
Policies and procedures 504
Project Cycle 504
Third parties 505-507
World Conservation Union 165
World Court 285
'World Environment Organisation' 172-175
World Health Organisation 6, 8, 9, 38, 54, 59, 71, 90, 93, 159, 242
World Intellectual Property Organisation 40
World Meteorological Organisation 9, 26, 59, 159

World Tourism Organisation 61, 63
World Trade Organisation 40, 41, 63, 72-73, 107, 172, 174, 233, 253, **297-344**
  Appeal 336
  Appellate Body 252, 284, 298, 302, 306, **313-315**
    appellee's submission division 314, 332, 334
    implementation 337
    mandate **315-317**
    members 313
    oral hearing 333-334
    proceedings **331-337**
    report 335
    rules of conduct 314, 335
    secretariat 314
    working procedures 332
    written submission 332, 335
  Arbitration 305, 307, 338-341
  Complaint 300, **307-308**
    legal basis 318
  Compensation 305, 339
  Compliance 339, 343
  Compulsory jurisdiction 302
  Conciliation 305
  Confidentiality 325, 335-336
  Consensus 304, 315, 336
    reverse consensus 309
  Consultation 298, 300, 306, 310, 325
  Covered agreements 302, 304, 306, 315
  Dispute settlement **297-344**, 352, 353
  Dispute Settlement Panel 284, 304, 308
    ad hoc working procedures 324
    burden of proof 329, 330
    composition 311
    deliberations 330
    establishment 317, 318
    evidence 324, 329
    experts 327
    interim review 330
    jurisdiction 317
    mandate **317-321**
    nomination 311
    'objective assessment' 319, 322, 327
    panellists 311-312
    proceedings **324-331**
    recommendations 320, 337
    report 298
    rules of conduct 312
    suggestions 320
    'substantial interest' 325
    terms of reference 317
  Dispute Settlement Body **309-310**
  Dispute Settlement Understanding 252, 269, 284, 301, 303
  GATT 172, 174, 253, 301
  Good offices 305
  Legal interest 308
  Mediation 305
  Nullification or impairment 303, 307, 340
  Object and purpose **305-307**
  Panel *see* Dispute Settlement Panel
  Period 323-324

Review
    scope **321-323**
Suspension of concessions 305, 309, 340-342
Third party 308, 321, 332, 334
WTO *see* World Trade Organisation